THE ROMANTIC PERIOD
IN MUSIC

Sonata, Op.31, No.3, first movement

Beethoven

THE ROMANTIC PERIOD
IN MUSIC

KENNETH B. KLAUS

Alumni Professor of Music,
Louisiana State University

ALLYN AND BACON, Inc.   BOSTON

TABLE OF CONTENTS

v

PREFACE

THE ROMANTIC MOVEMENT IN MUSIC, as in the other arts, was a very complex one—a movement which defies description in a simple, singular manner, since it developed neither simply nor in a single direction. Even with the perspective of time, the Romantic Period cannot be viewed as a period of unified style; rather, it was a broad period of transition which was unified only in the sense that it moved ultimately toward the modification of the traditional tonal system and of the old rules for musical composition. Music, of course, has always been an art in transition, but the nineteenth century was especially preoccupied with change in both the vertical (harmonic) and horizontal (melodic and rhythmic) dimensions of composition.

Romanticism existed long before the nineteenth century and has continued, to a degree, even to the present day. This book discusses the romantic tendency from the works of Beethoven through the music of the "postromantic" composers of the early twentieth century. It discusses primarily the music which forms *today's* repertoire of nineteenth-century works (and which undoubtedly will furnish part of the standard repertoire for many years to come), although lesser-known composers and works are given appropriate coverage. Much of this music is now over a century old, and its appeal has been recognized by several generations. It is the purpose of this book to uncover its lasting values for the serious music student, and to this end the discussion has been supplemented by selected musical examples.

The organization of the book is a practical one through which the reader can follow developments in melody, harmony, counterpoint, form, orchestration and other topics. In addition, separate chapters concentrate on nationalism, keyboard and solo music, chamber music, vocal music and orchestral music. The text includes historical information, develops concepts of romanticism, analyzes outstanding works and presents some of the interesting controversies surrounding the subject. Thus, the broad range of romantic music is treated comprehensively: there are facts, there are speculations and there are some opinions. Above all, there are fascinating paradoxes!

Acknowledgements

Many people have been helpful in developing this book, but I especially wish to thank Nelson Jansky, Allyn and Bacon, Inc., for his kind encouragement and sage advice; my wife, sons and relatives for typing and "coolie labor"; Beth Rudd for typing the manuscript and her husband, Dr. Michael Rudd, for reading it; and also Dr. Wallace McKenzie for reading it. I wish also to acknowledge Dr. Everett Timm, Dean of the Louisiana State University School of Music, for his encouragement and expert knowledge of wind instruments. I appreciate the professional personnel of many libraries for their assistance: among them, Louisiana State University Library, Emory University Library, University of Maryland Library, New York Public Library for the Performing Arts at Lincoln Center, Columbia University Library, Boston Public Library and Boston Museum of Fine Arts. I wish to thank Dr. Otto Bettmann of The Bettmann Archive, Inc., for his help in supplying the photographs used in the book. I acknowledge with great appreciation the publishers who have granted me permission to quote from their publications or books, as indicated in the footnotes. And finally, my thanks to Russell Mead, editor, for his help in editing, proofreading and designing this book.

THE ROMANTIC PERIOD
IN MUSIC

Romanticism is beauty without bounds—the beautiful infinite, just as there is an exalted infinite. (1804)

Jean Paul

Music is the Most Romantic of all the arts—one might almost say, the only genuinely romantic one—for its sole subject is the infinite. (1814)

E. T. A. Hoffmann

The artist may pursue the beautiful outside the rules of the school without fear that, as a result of this, it will elude him. (1855)

Franz Liszt

Romanticism encounters what looks like irreducible contradictions because it starts from man and accepts the contradiction which exists in him. (1950)

Jacques Barzun[1]

[1] Jacques Barzun, *Berlioz and the Romantic Century* (Copyright 1949, 1950 by Jacques Barzun. By permission of Atlantic-Little, Brown and Company, Boston.), p. 379.

INTRODUCTION:
SOME PHILOSOPHIES

THERE LIES BEHIND US the great musical legacy of the nineteenth
century. Eventually it will be old enough to invite the interest of more
scholars and some hard and fast principles will be discovered. The computer will be of great assistance in establishing honest rules of actual
musical practice *as it has been left in its notation.* But will a knowledge
that a certain facet occurred X per cent of the time really prove anything other than an ontology of that facet? Even if the computer studies
can be made on a higher level,[1] the fact will still remain that in art, as
Karl Jaspers might say, it is the *unique* which is important; or, if you
will, originality which remains originality. It is just possible that the
minority percentage speaks more eloquently than the majority. After all,
a man may go to church every week, but the visits which are for his
christening, his marriage and his funeral are in the minority percentage.

This book ponders the problems inherent in the above paragraph.
True, the majority percentage must be *learned first* in order to understand the true import and uniqueness of the minority percentage. To go
back to church: christening, marriage and Christian burial have little
meaning without the context of the *other* visits to the church. In the
romantic century these are important considerations, since the cult of
the individual was so important. There was a conscious effort to write

1

music in a different way; the rules were willfully stretched, expanded and downright broken.

But presenting the unknown is frightening to many. Nicolas Slonimsky's *Lexicon of Musical Invective*[2] is a collection of frightened and angry responses from the press and elsewhere to music which is now standard fare. He precedes the quotations with a brilliant and witty essay on the whole question.

One can amass an imposing stack of favorable comment about the same works and the works of hundreds of lesser composers who were fortunate enough to be performed. It is also a fact that some new works, when first performed, were given impossible performances and the critics were probably right. We know that there were low performance standards almost everywhere, but the works which the selfsame critics enjoyed might have been given the same bad performances. Judgments regarding the best music are not to be made after only one hearing; if a piece is a true work of art, there must be exposure to it over a long period of time. Immediate appeal is not necessarily a vice or a virtue.

This introductory chapter serves as an overview of the age, including: 1) some delving into the myriad voices "explaining" romanticism; 2) a concept of romanticism which ties together what seems to be of common opinion, but allows different ideas propounded on the subject to collide in order for the student to understand that honest differences of opinion do exist; 3) a purely musical definition of romanticism, a technical one— that romanticism is that collection of factors which changed the course of music from "pure" tonality (the "common practice") to the post-tertian[3] period in which we find ourselves today. This was not the *intention* of any composers—each one used tonality in his own way; indeed, they probably had no idea that the ultimate result would be such a bending of the tonal system that one can barely hear it in much of the best music of the late part of the era in question; any real adherence to the "common practice" principles of the eighteenth century is found only in textbooks which stem, in almost every case, from the aftermath of the famous *Traité du Harmonie* of Jean Philippe Rameau. As Cecil Gray says: "Rameau in one word was the father of modern textbook harmony and all the vices and heresies to which it gives rise."[4]

Kitson saw this early in our century, when he wrote:

The history of the evolution of harmonic resource is of course the history of the infraction of rules. Thus the innovation of one period becomes the commonplace of the next so that in such matters it is absurd to attempt to give absolute rules.[5]

I am also indebted to Westrup and Harrison for the concept presented in their excellent *The New College Encyclopedia of Music*, where they say:

The Romantic era in music may be dated c. 1820 (Weber's *Der Freischütz* was produced in 1821, Schubert scored the *Unfinished Symphony* in 1822 and wrote *Die schöne Müllerin* in 1823) to c. 1920 (Schönberg arrived at the principles of "twelve-tone composition" in 1921; Stravinsky composed *l'Histoire du soldat* in 1918).[6]

I am indebted to Donald Grout for a slightly different statement of the same principle in his very important book, *A History of Western Music*, where he says:

To a large extent the task of composers in the twentieth century has been to work out new concepts of, or find an adequate substitute for, tonality and to reconcile with new harmonic idioms the other musical elements of instrumentation, counterpoint, rhythm, and form.[7]

For better or worse, the romantic composer changed the theoretical basis of music from "pure tonality" to something else. A large part of the story is the resistance to these changes; each age has its share of artists who attempt to maintain the *status quo*. The nineteenth century had its classicism too; and there were those who were convinced that revolutions might be desirable for countries, but leave music alone.

All of this by no means implies that all change was for the good or that due to the nascent adolescence of the period no works of maturity were produced—nothing could be further from the truth! We must be cognizant, as T. S. Eliot said, ". . . of the obvious fact that art never improves, but that the material of art is never quite the same."[8]

The nineteenth century is treated neither as a regrettable episode, nor as a Golden Age. There is no attempt to speculate as to what it should have been, nor is there any attempt to "prove" that it and no other period had all of the answers. There is reason, however, to point out areas where "pop" art existed because the nineteenth century for the first time attempted to make an art for all men—a noble sentiment, but one that should, in my opinion, never be a criterion, only a fond hope. *Great* art can never be for the common man since it is created by *un*common men. If our "common man" begins to comprehend great art, he then ceases to be a "common man." This is why we have "pop" art, and have always had "pop" art.

Berlioz had a similar opinion. Strunk points this out:

"Music is not made for everyone, nor everyone for music"—this is perhaps the central article of Berlioz's critical creed, and in the essay (Rossini's *William Tell*) it recurs again and again with the persistence of an *idée fixe*. But in writing on *William Tell*, Berlioz also reveals many of the other facets of his critical personality—his preoccupation with the poetic and the picturesque, his capacity for enthusiasm and for indignation, his horror of the mediocre and his impatience with all that fails to measure up to the very highest standards, his contempt for everything academic, his intense dissatisfaction with the commercial and official aspects of musical life.[9]

This all involves many opinions, but opinions shared by many, as the course of the book will show. What is of importance here is the perpetual dichotomy: art vs. "pop" art. It is also important to point out that some music seems to serve only its own time (Kalkbrenner and Herz) and other music is destined for the ages, while still other music may be in and out of favor according to current fashion. All of this is still in the general category of "serious" music. There is also an enormous body of sociologically important music which was popular in the taverns and like institutions all over the world—the music to which the common man relates. There are also imperishable tunes which seem to spring from the people as real folk art—this is just as important as the most admired art music of any time or place. But even here there is a great deal of "cashing in" on style, not content. Even Mendelssohn was moved to say:

But please, no national music! To the devil with all this "folksiness"! Here I am in Wales . . . and a harper sits in the vestibule of every inn and never stops playing so-called folk-melodies, that is, infamous, common faked stuff . . . If, like me, you can't stand Beethoven's national songs, then come here and listen to these tunes growled out by harsh nasal voices, accompanied by awkward bungling singers—and don't complain! [In the letter follows a music example with nothing but parallel fifths, possibly a remnant of medieval organum.][10]

But the moneychangers will always be in the temple!

Mendelssohn's comments seem to be very much alive today. Do not confuse this with nationalistic art music, a vital force in the last decades of the century. One should also not confuse *authentic* folk music with commercial pseudo-folk music. The motivation is obviously at odds here: singing about how you really feel vs. selling records. Some commercial "folksy" music may have authenticity. It is already authentic as an index of public taste, as indeed were Biedermeierisms or the old minstrel shows.

The mention of Biedermeier is of utmost importance. The "sweetness of life" mentioned by Talleyrand (see quote at head of Chapter I) was, and is, greatly desired by most people. The middle class in the early nineteenth century embraced the kind of life as depicted by Biedermeier as security and stability. Biedermeier was a fictional character created by Ludwig Eichrodt (1827-1892). Gottlieb Biedermeier was a Philistine poet who soon became a household symbol of conservative German middle-class life. The name soon spread to a style of furniture which was similar to French Empire as well as being the "inspiration" for reams and reams of unproblematic, Pollyanna, pseudo-artistic literary and musical trivia.

Plate I

Music making in a typical Biedermeier home in Basel, Switzerland.
Painting by Seb. Gutzwillwe (*Courtesy The Bettmann Archive, N.Y.*).

It was one manifestation of a return to order after and during vital
revolutions which were taking place during the time.

Paul Henry Lang states:

> Romanticism undoubtedly grew from subjectivism, which it increased to over-
> flowing. But romanticism was also bound with many ties to the Revolution.
> The Revolution emancipated the middle classes and in so doing yielded cul-
> tural leadership to the petty bourgeois spirit, with its eyes set on the practical,
> and with its urge for a continuation of the movement of the Enlightenment
> according to its own precepts. . . .
>
> Gottlieb Biedermeier, the humorous Philistine character and imaginary author
> whose verses appeared in the *fliegende Blätter,* the favorite family magazine of
> the small bourgeoisie, gave the name to a whole period of culture, a period
> which left indelible marks on romanticism. The psychological foundation of the
> Biedermeier era is a smplification of classic forms and a retreat from romantic
> pathos, a tired flight into bourgeois quietude, modesty and simplicity. . . .

And further:

> ROMANTICISM bequeathed to Europe, together with subjectivism, the notion
> of the genius, a notion unknown to the Biedermeier period.[11]

While there are some who feel that the word *romantic* should never
be applied to music, I feel it must; simply because the romantic composer
often called himself just that. It does not necessarily follow that this
should be a limiting definition, *i.e.*, calling "romantic" only the ones

who called themselves romantic; not all composers had the gift for the prose pen as did Berlioz or Schumann.

Here are the words of Schumann and a comment by Strunk:

"The present is characterized by its parties," Schumann writes in another connection (1836). "Like the political present, one can divide the musical into liberals, middlemen, and reactionaries, or into romanticists, moderns, and classicists. On the right sit the elderly—the contrapuntists, the antichromaticists; on the left the youthful—the revolutionaries in their Phrygian caps, the antiformalists, the genially impudent, among whom the Beethovenians stand out as a special class; in the *Juste Milieu* young and old mingle irresolutely—here are included most of the creations of the day, the offspring which the moment brings forth and then destroys."

In his day, Schumann stood at the very center of the romantic movement in German music, yet he makes little effort to define its aims and aspirations for us. To him, clearly, these were self-evident: "It is scarcely credible that a distinct romantic school could be formed in music, which is in itself romantic." But in his review of Stephen Heller's Opus 7 (1837) Schumann comes as close as he ever does to a definition and in so doing defines for us also his own personal style. "I am heartily sick of the word 'romanticist,'" he says; "I have not pronounced it ten times in my whole life; and yet—if I wished to confer a brief designation upon our young seer, I should call him one, and what a one! Of that vague, nihilistic disorder behind which some search for romanticism, and of that crass, scribbling materialism which the French neoromanticists affect, our composer—thank Heaven!—knows nothing; on the contrary, he perceives things naturally, for the most part, and expresses himself clearly and judiciously."[12]

Virtually every descriptive term used in the history of music has undergone great change from its inception. Even the words "music" and "history"—to say nothing of "music history"—mean something quite different today than they did in the past. One needs only to recall the remark made at the premiere of Franck's Symphony in D Minor:

"That a symphony?" he replied in contemptuous tones. "But, my dear sir, who ever heard of writing for the English horn in a symphony? Just mention a single symphony by Haydn or Beethoven introducing the English horn. There, you see—your Franck's music may be whatever you please, but it will certainly never be a symphony."

And further:

. . . when Franck turned to that form about 1886-1888 and composed a serious, tightly constructed symphony in D minor, he was writing an unwanted work. At its first performance in 1889 the symphony was ridiculed for its chromatic harmony, its free modulations, and its part for English horn. One wonders whether the critics had forgotten that Berlioz had used that instrument and whether they knew that Haydn had employed two English horns in his "Philosopher" Symphony of about 1765. But Franck's composition has outlived its critics and remains one of the dozen most popular symphonies of all time.[13]

Or, further, the decree of Pope John XXII issued from Avignon in 1324, which allows ". . . some concords such as the octave, fifth, and fourth . . ." (No mention of thirds or sixths!) Andreas Werckmeister (1645-1706), in his preface to *Der Edlen Music-Kunst, Wurde, Gerbrauch und Missbrauch*, says that music is a gift of God and should be used only in his honor. Dr. Charles Burney (1726-1814), in his *General History of Music* (1776), defines music as a luxury, unnecessary to our existence. Rousseau maintained that to sing more than one melody at a time was to make two speeches at once to be more forceful; while Donald Grout says that Mozart's contrapuntal influence from Bach was ". . . deep and lasting; it is manifested in the increasing use of contrapuntal texture throughout Mozart's later works."[14]

A *symphony* was once just an instrumental passage in a vocal work, a *concerto* was a piece which explored contrasts among voices and instruments, a *sonata* was a piece played by instruments while a *cantata* was one which was sung . . . and so it goes. The study of the history of music should be, in large part, studying the history of change in meaning of these words. We should be interested in all phases of music, not just a list of who wrote what when. We need to know the philosophical climate, the social backgrounds, the effects of political change and the sum total of man himself as he leaves behind a trace of how he felt, thought about and performed his music. It is also important *how* he wrote it, and how he put it together.

This view of the nineteenth century is of great importance, since for the first time in music history the composer seeks to express himself; he strays far from uniform dogmas, tries very hard to be different—even strange and unfettered. Yet, this very individuality, in the final analysis, unites all romanticists: they are alike in that they are all different—hence, *romanticisms*, not just *romanticism*.

But rigid definitions or boundaries of romanticism are often laid out by diverse critics in all arts without realizing that to define romanticism is almost to destroy it. As is the case with many terms used in art criticism, "romanticism" was once used in an uncomplimentary way as in the seventeenth and eighteenth centuries, when it was applied to works which were "unreasonable" or impossible, unreal or fantastic. Such words were compliments for many in the nineteenth century, but in the twentieth century there are many composers who would be unhappy indeed if they were called "romantic artists." The word "romantic," then, is a loaded one which must be used with caution, since it means something different in almost every application.

A philosophy which seeks freedom rather than any kind of a closed system will of necessity be paradoxical, although it must be remembered that pursuit of freedom *per se* is a kind of bondage; if one avoids any manifestation of a set of rules, he is motivated by the avoidance rather than a true freedom which might involve some use of the code rather than a blanket negation. Perhaps the most blinding dogma is one which doubts *everything*.

In his *Journals*, Kierkegaard states:

It is a positive starting point for philosophy when Aristotle says that philosophy begins with wonder, not as in our day with doubt. Moreover the world will learn that the thing is not to begin with the negative, and the reason why it has succeeded up to the present is that it has never really given itself over to the negative, and so has never seriously done what it said. Its doubt is mere child's play.[15]

For examples, the Impressionists trying very hard to be anti-romantic end up as another vital romanticism; an atheist who *disbelieves* the Bible literally; a twentieth-century composer who avoids "atonality," one who pursues "atonality"; all are strongly influenced in a *negative* way. We shall see, however, that the romantic problem as far as music is concerned did resolve itself into a dichotomy or actual bifurcation of music in a manner that does not imply total antithesis as much as the members of each camp would lead one to believe in their prose writings. We are speaking of the Liszt-Berlioz-Wagner vs. Hanslick-Schumann-Brahms, a real solidification of apparently antipodal views which are in reality more like two sides of the same coin, or a contemporary misunderstanding of the principle of changing definition of romanticism, a realization that romanticism is almost like a living organism which constantly changes but remains the *same* organism. This principle was not realized by the people who were living it at the time, but it is quite apparent to us today.

This, then, is our task: to see how the romantics are alike and how they are different. This is, of course, the real problem of any day and age, but it is intensified in the nineteenth century, since the pursuit of individual differences leads to dramatic individual differences. There are differences among the lesser classical composers (such as Hoffmeister and Cimarosa), but it takes a real expert to detect them; even the truly great (such as Haydn and Mozart) seem to be very much alike to the student and the average concert audience. The differences between Wagner and Tchaikovsky are such that only the most insensitive fail to hear them. For the student's more complete understanding we *must* first study the similarities and *then* the differences, and at no time merely memorize a list of "romantic traits" which then must fit all romantic composers; some traits do, some don't. To do this, we shall allow these paradoxes and antipodal ideas to collide to get a feeling for the great issues of the age.

There are also *other* romanticisms in the other arts, and a rigorous application of general principles is difficult—if not impossible *and* downright misleading. I must take exception with some writers who classify some nineteenth-century artists as anti-romantic simply because they are of the here and now and the element of yearning is not there. Quoting Werner:

He (Mendelssohn) admits to being an opponent of the Middle Ages, thus differentiating himself from the dyed-in-the-wool "Romanticists": "Thank God that these highly-praised Middle Ages are past and can never return. Don't show this to any Hegelian, but it is so. . . ."
    . . . This opinion is also in contradiction to the then popular synesthesia of the literary Romanticists who tried to blend colors, scents, words, and tones into a total work of art (Gesamtkunstwerk)—from Novalis and E. T. A. Hoffmann to Richard Wagner to Scriabin and beyond.[16]

Honest differences of opinion exist about most important matters. One needs only to look at religion, philosophy, even astronomy and the other sciences and the arts, to see almost bewildering alignments of diversified opinion with regard to origins, belief, relative importance of data, meaning of life, death, forms of governments, etc. While we can be sure of some things such as gravity, sunlight, darkness and the like, man is the most differentiated about ultimate questions such as, "What is absolute truth?"

But the historian must find common tendencies that really exist and not conjure them up just for purposes of neat classification or as a teaching device. The one great unity of the nineteenth century was its disunity and its love of individualism which leads to disunity.

An age is unified by the questions it asks as much as by the answers it provides.

The history of ideas presents a see-saw battle between the objective and subjective aspects of all intellectual activity and the art of music is especially sensitive to this, since it is at once both objective (in performance) and subjective (in the effect). The nineteenth century was one which showed (in various degrees of violence) a decided reaction to the rationale of the Age of Reason. The objective aspects of art are the "reasonable" ones and we find a condition called "classical" as far as music is concerned. The forms have become rather standardized, there is a common practice of harmony and counterpoint, there is great attention to balance, to "ethos" and the intellect, and a general clarity of line, a decided distinction between melody and accompaniment, regular phrase structure, and an apparent norm from which all musical practice seems to stem. There is a common misconception that there was little or no attention paid to sentiment or feelings in Classical Period music—nothing could be further from the truth; there is also the misconception that the music we now call "romantic" was all feeling and no form. The great artist is one who defies pigeon-holing. He has the remarkable balance of form and content which makes him a real master of *both*, even though his personality may favor a balance not quite 50-50. Great art is firm but not rigid, flexible but not amorphous.

The nineteenth century was not all romantic. Classic and romantic traits co-existed in different schools of thought and even in the careers of the same men. (Mendelssohn is a good example.) The Classical Period wasn't all classical either: some composers anticipated romanticism, while others were still content to live in a past further back, to whom the music of Mozart seemed to be that of a depraved ear.[17]

The nineteenth century was a period of great change, changes greater even than those of the eighteenth and earlier. The great confidence in all things explained by reason began to be shaken by the very discoveries that had been brought about by the tools of discovery of reason itself. How ironic that reason does not always stand to reason! One of the greatest breakthroughs was in the area of anti-Aristotelian reasoning. Too many events in the laboratory and in man's own mind showed that the great Aristotle was not infallible. Men demanded rigorous proof; quoting the old authorities was not enough. Even the church had been questioned. Kierkegaard asked embarrassing questions, questions which men had perhaps thought about but had not dared to ask. The big question was, "Who am *I*?" Men no longer accepted their accident of birth in a certain time, place or position, noble or not. Man was thought to have his *own* dignity whether poet or peasant. We now read Kierkegaard as a real spokesman of his age. He despised closed systems and greatly emphasized *subjective* elements. One of his favorite words was "passion." While he was tortured with the burning question, "What does it mean for me to be a Christian?" artists of the age were asking what it meant to be an artist. It matters not if Kierkegaard was or was not read by composers all over the western world, these matters were "in the air." It is important for the understanding of common tendencies to trace this questioning, for a man questions when he wants to know or if he clearly sees that what he has been told is either not true or does not tell the whole story. How does one know when the whole story has been told? Quoting from Werner's *Mendelssohn*:

Of his contemporaries, probably Kierkegaard alone understood the dilemma with which Mendelssohn was confronted consciously or unconsciously. The following words of the Danish thinker seem intended for Mendelssohn, the scorner of the "estheticians, without all of whom he could do very well:

"So, then, one either has to live esthetically or one has to live ethically. In this alternative . . . there is not yet in the strictest sense any question of a choice; for he who lives esthetically does not choose, and he who after the ethical has manifested itself to him chooses the esthetical is not living esthetically, for he is sinning and is subject to ethical determinants even though his life may be described as unethical. Lo, there is, as it were, a *character indelebilis* impressed upon the ethical, that though it modestly places itself on a level with the esthetical, it is nevertheless that which makes the choice a choice. . . . By the absolute choice the ethical is always posited, but from this it does not follow by any means that the esthetical is excluded. In the ethical the personality is concentrated in itself, so the esthetical is absolutely excluded or is excluded as the absolute, but relatively it is still left."[18]

Goethe, in *Faust*, has Faust in his study state point blank that he has not found the end in philosophy or in theology or in any "ology."[19]

His ensuing pact with the devil was an important influence on art in the nineteenth century, and the Faust concept was directly responsible for over 100 musical works on the Faust story and many more on the Faust idea.

To be transcendent! This was the passionate cry of so many artists; and if they could not find an answer, they created one. Some (Dostoyevsky, for example) accepted the impasse and were racked by despair and heavy pessimism. The great objective optimism of the Age of Reason now became the great subjective pessimism of stark reality. The artist did not try to escape through his dreams but suffered in his all-too-immediate misery. Some say that this tendency is anti-romantic, that romanticism can be only optimistic idealism, but this overlooks a very important fact: while it may be real it certainly is felt, and this passion of the moment was captured and preserved for posterity. It is probably romantic to us, since to us it is a remote time—can't the faraway place be painful as well as delightful? Art, then, begins to act as the recorder of the passions of an age as never before. Art was the diary of the age, noting the commonplace as well as the sublime.

Or in Wordsworth's famous *Preface to the Lyrical Ballads*:

To this knowledge which all men carry about with them, and to these sympathies in which, without any other discipline than that of our daily life, we are fitted to take delight the Poet principally directs his attention. He considers man and nature as essentially adapted to each other, and the mind of man as naturally the mirror of the fairest and most interesting properties of nature.[20]

Just as repeated readings of any literature give different impressions, the same music is different upon different hearings; and, therefore, what is still more important is the impact of any art on *our* time or on *any* time. This means, of course, that a work of art—especially music—is not, cannot be a static thing, since music to exist must have: 1) a composer, 2) a performer and 3) a listener; obviously (for most music, at least), only the composer is a constant. Even a recording may vary from phonograph to phonograph and varies even on the same machine, since one can't possibly hear the work in precisely the same way each time.

Now the same principle holds from generation to generation. We must be aware that an important factor of change is in the work itself; it says different things to different people in different situations. While the study of *Aufführungspraxis* (performance practice) is of great importance, it would be of little value to play a work *exactly* as done in the past even if we could. To prove this statement, listen to some of the older recordings, discounting, of course, recording quality. The music was recorded in the taste of the day, something not as constant as we might think. The same artists recording the same work at a later time show a different factor: the deepening or ripening of an interpretation, or the inverse, getting stale.

Again, compare early recordings of, say, *Le Sacre du printemps* with later ones and it is very apparent that Stravinsky's masterpiece is now a classic, almost enough of a classic to be played with some devotion. Alban Berg made a legendary remark replete with great wisdom: "One should play contemporary music as if it were classical and classical music as if it were contemporary."

The foregoing is of utmost importance in the study of nineteenth-century music, since for the first time in music history almost all composers wrote for the future and the possibility of introspective interpretation becomes a factor. The performer not only learns a piece, but he thinks about it, mulls it over in his mind, improves it here and there in a *subjective* way, as well as develops a more perfect objective technical mastery.

Music, then, is the most subjective art and yet is one of the most objective. It is subjective in its effect on the listener, although there have been objective results as well: changes in the galvanic skin response, heart beat, respiration and other purely physiological responses which, of course, show great individual differences from person to person. The deepest meaning of music is as yet intangible and will probably remain so; music communicates a subjective meaning through the performer from the composer to the listener—it cannot be stated in any way other than music. The *optimum* success requires a performer who understands the composer, interprets the music and adds something of himself without distorting the wishes of the composer; *and* it also requires a listener who is capable of responding.

A new audience appeared for the artist. The common man discovered he had an insatiable appetite for music and for the first time in history *his* pleasure, rather than the pleasure of a patron, became the concern of the composer and the performer. Ideally, the common man's taste should have been improved through this contact with music and art, but, unfortunately, the artist and the masses met halfway in order to please the masses (and to sell tickets for performances and copies of the latest hit!). The masses have always had music in almost every culture, but never before had prominent composers ever become involved with common man's music except for church music, and the music heard there was not for sheer sensual pleasure. Times had changed.

Times always change, even though there have been periods in history where the cultivation of the *status quo* was of the utmost importance. The nineteenth century saw the possibilities of progress. There was a great summation of new ideas which had been inherited from the Age of Reason and now combined in ways to make new products for a society which could buy them. People built factories to make their products and employed people who would in turn buy more products. The nineteenth century, then, was a time when the old established order was challenged; *when it was found wanting*, it was replaced by something which to them was better, or at least different.

The concept of change is never uniform, even within a restricted area such as music. The nineteenth century teaches us that more than one idea of change can be of significance. This fact leads some to speak of "Romanticisms," or of one type of romanticism to fit the philosophy of the individual artist; this concept became of great importance to the nineteenth-century artist.

It is apparent, then, that a closed definition of romanticism is not very romantic. Many will reject some artists of the nineteenth century as being even anti-romantic, since they have some quirk which sets them apart, such as Dostoyevsky's preoccupation with the here and now. Others have come around to the idea that romanticism exists when the artist emphasizes subjectivity, even the subjectivity of reality, as it affects the individual. Herein lies another paradox: the more individual art becomes, the more romantic it becomes; at the same time, it becomes less romantic in the way the early romantics talked about themselves, since there are involved personal tragedy and personal love affairs—not a dream world at all. As the century advances the dream becomes a nightmare, and the twentieth-century movement we call "expressionism" seems to be the old romanticism stood on its head. Expressionism was a direct reaction to impressionism, which in turn was supposed to have been a reaction to colossal romanticism. While we cannot say that things reacting to the same thing are equal to each other, we can say that romanticism had either changed into something else, or had disappeared. Therefore, if feeling or subjectivity is the chief criterion, then expressionism is indeed *deeply* romantic—so deep that it involves the subconscious and owes a great deal to the work of Freud and others in the field of depth psychology. It is also influenced by the "problem" literature of the late part of the century.

The early twentieth century, then, is more properly the outgrowth of romanticism; and if one important aspect of romanticism is the spirit of rebellion, then rebelling against romanticism could also be romantic. The apparent discontinuity was in many ways more technical than philosophical or aesthetic. Tonality in the old sense was breaking up, and perhaps too much attention was attracted to the theory of this and not enough to how this "new" music actually sounded. The reign of tonality as a "divine right of tonics" had been threatened throughout the century, but it never abdicated nor was it purposely deposed until after about 1928. Instead, it was discovered that tonality was a much wider and deeper tool than had been thought before. Attempts to make it a closed system had all failed, since music is written by men and man's collective mind is not a closed system. *One* man's mind often is, however.

The revolutions in France and America, and the rise of a more affluent middle class, caused the utter collapse of the small duchies and the like. Many cities had maintained orchestras, opera houses, chamber groups, choirs and organists, and this led to a situation which freed the musician as he had never been free before—he was out of a job! But the world needed music, and the new affluency of the industrial classes rose to the occasion and in a very real sense took over the patronage of the arts—but not without a struggle. Many musicians did suffer in garrets and did get tuberculosis, but this is not prerequisite for musical success, as romantic as it may sound.

The newly found freedom from the wants of the nobility had a great impact on music. People began to find interesting things about other "common" people; they also had deep passion, fear and all the other traits. The "person of consequence" in a tragedy need not necessarily be a Prince of Denmark or a Greek god, nor did he have to live in a castle—a cottage could do just as nicely as a stage setting for an opera. The "hero" could be a clown, a cobbler or even an artist.

This book explores musical freedom, departures from accepted principles, by tracing some of the most important developments of a great transition period: ca. 1789 to ca. 1925. There is no attempt to call this a uniform style period. It was instead a time of fascinating paradoxes.

Notes

1. Computers can be programmed to make very sophisticated analyses. The human element, however, must eventually be considered. The computer is a

memory bank and can scan data in a way that the human mind cannot. It is obvious that important musical studies can be made for all periods, and that important factors of composition will come to light. At present, most studies reflect the analyst who programs the composer.

2. Nicolas Slonimsky, *Lexicon of Musical Invective* (New York: Coleman-Ross Company, Inc., 1965).

3. There seems to be no logical name as yet which identifies the present other than "post-tertian," which has been used with some frequency. "Tertian" refers to the practice of building chords in thirds. Music prior to 1600 A.D. is sometimes called "pre-tertian." Peter Yates implies an interesting concept in the title of his book: *Twentieth Century Music, Its Evolution from the End of the Harmonic Era into the Present Era of Sound* (New York: Pantheon Books, 1967).

4. Cecil Gray, *The History of Music* (London: Kegan, Paul, Trench, Trubner and Company, Ltd., 1945), p. 161.

5. C. H. Kitson, *The Evolution of Harmony* (London: Oxford University Press, 1945), p. vi.

6. J. A. Westrup and F. L. Harrison, *The New College Encyclopedia of Music* (New York: W. W. Norton & Company, Inc., 1960), p. 555.

7. Donald Jay Grout, *A History of Western Music* (New York: W. W. Norton & Company, Inc., 1960), p. 609.

8. T. S. Eliot, "Tradition and Individual Talent," from *Selected Essays, 1917-1932* (New York: Harcourt, Brace & World, Inc., 1960).

9. Oliver Strunk, ed., *Source Readings in Music History: The Romantic Era*, Vol. V (New York: W. W. Norton & Company, Inc., 1965), p. 68.

10. Reprinted with permission of the Macmillan Company from Eric Werner, *Mendelssohn*, trans. D. Newlin. Copyright © by the Free Press of Glencoe, a Division of The Macmillan Company, 1963, p. 152.

11. Paul Henry Lang, *Music in Western Civilization* (New York: W. W. Norton & Company, Inc., 1941), pp. 805, 806, 1014. Copyright renewed 1968 by Paul Henry Lang. By permission of J. M. Dent & Sons, Ltd.

12. Strunk, ed., *op. cit.*, pp. 87-88.

13. Homer Ulrich, *Symphonic Music* (New York: Columbia University Press, 1952), p. 230.

14. Grout, *op. cit.*, p. 463.

15. Ralph B. Winn, *A Concise Dictionary of Existentialism* (New York: Philosophical Library, 1960), p. 77.

16. Werner, *op. cit.*, pp. 169-170.

17. The source for these amazing opinions of Mozart is A. Hyatt King's *Mozart in Retrospect* (London: Oxford University Press, 1955). See especially page 5, but the entire first chapter is of interest. The entire book is a valuable contribution to Mozart scholarship.

18. Werner, *op. cit.*, p. 500.

19. Goethe's *Faust*, Act I, Scene 1.

20. Wordsworth, *Preface to the Lyrical Ballads*. My immediate source is *The Complete Poetical Works of Wordsworth* (Boston: Houghton Mifflin Company, 1932), p. 795.

CHAPTER I

ROMANTICISM: A FASCINATING SET OF PARADOXES

TALLEYRAND USED TO SAY that only those who lived before 1789 knew the sweetness of life. What he meant was that the French Revolution first unleashed the forces that would ultimately engulf the individual's life to subordinate it to the *res publica*, to the masses. And the masses, their weight, their importance, their desires, and their power, were responsible, even if indirectly, for the helpless foundering of culture at the beginning of the twentieth century; for the culture of the century of romanticism was not designed for them, they acceded to it only in the expectation of assimilating it or replacing it by their own.[1]

Paul Henry Lang

At the stroke of midnight on the thirty-first of December, 1799, the music world did not stop being classical, nor did it start to be romantic. January 1, 1800, was not too different from the previous day, and music composed on that day was not necessarily "romantic" even though it had been written in the nineteenth century. As Stephenson says,

"Historical works on the romantic composers will continue to be in a bad way as long as there is no agreement on the range of this concept, which can no longer be just considered to be equivalent to the 19th century as the easy way out."[2]

The French and American Revolutions and others were dramatic, related, world-shaking affairs which, although long festering or gestating (depending on the point of view), "unleashed forces that would ultimately engulf the individual's life to subordinate it to the *res publica*, to the masses."[3]

Revolution was in the air in the arts, too, and music was more in the vanguard than anyone realized at the time. The masses became the concern of the artist, so a great paradox emerges at once: the greatest composers, in quest of originality, looked to the feelings, the heart, the mind of the masses and then poured out their own hearts in empathy or at least in sympathy; the masses, however, did not recognize this at first and could not identify. The "revolution" in music was subjectively an approach to subjectivity and objectively a rebellion against "classical" norms. As Harman, Milner and Mellers state:

. . . for if Haydn and Mozart were incipiently revolutionary composers, Beethoven is overtly so. The Fifth Symphony revolutionizes the then accepted notion of symphonic form, and its technical revolution is inseparable from the fact that it conveys in musical terms a message—a new approach to human experience. If we ignore that message we cannot claim to understand Beethoven; but we must be sure that the message we discover is Beethoven's, and not our own or someone else's. It must be a deduction from the nature of the musical technique, not something tacked on to the music fortuitously.[4]

Carl Bamberger says this so well:

Although Haydn, Mozart, and Beethoven are usually considered the triumvirate of Classical music, Beethoven actually speaks to us from an entirely new sphere: Romanticism. Where heretofore music was marked by firmness of form, a veiled spirituality, a purity of color close to the black and white of preceding times, tempo changes mostly limited to different movements, and a disciplined freedom into which the creator's subjective emotions did not intrude, with Beethoven the drama of the ego and of a personalized humanity was admitted. During the nineteenth century there was an ever-growing intensity of subjective utterance—Romanticism in full flower. The Romantic composer wanted his work to reflect the fate of the world as well as his own fate; the form he used, dealing with human tensions, joys, and pains, became fluid, with freer execution, rubatos, ritards. It tried to amalgamate abstract music and concrete ideas, to explain transcendental concepts with the thinking mind. But one of the most striking characteristics of Romanticism is consciousness; in contrast with Romantic trends in earlier music, the nineteenth-century composer brought Romanticism into the musical concept by willful planning, in the sense of Schiller's statement: "Purposeful Romanticism is different from inadvertent Romanticism."[5]

This "purposeful Romanticism" is the point of departure—the breakthrough, as it were, for the composers who were to come in such profusion after Beethoven. 1789 is an important date for romanticism, since the masses as a force in music begin to rise. To restate the great paradox: there is the will of the masses and yet the individuality of the artist— there is less and less of the aristocratic patron who "consumed" music as a part of high society, but there is a public who doesn't know anything about music, but knows what it likes and buys what it likes. The past had not seen anything like this and music (all art for that matter) was put on a different basis. This, of course, leads to a strange kind of double standard: what the composer writes for public consumption and what he writes to satisfy his own creative urge—art for art's sake. As Werner states:

They all faced the same dilemma: should they serve the highest aims of art, or strive to become as popular as possible? The problem had become acute because of the uncritical worship of all folklike art by romantic poets; however, real folksongs and popular (folklike) imitations were often confused. Schiller had already recognized the growing conflict and dealt with it in unforgettable words. He wrote: "At present there is a very great gap perceptible between the elite of a nation and its masses. . . . As a result, it would be in vain arbitrarily to lump under one heading what has long been differentiated. Therefore, a popular poet for our times would have a choice between the simplest and the most difficult of tasks: either to accommodate himself exclusively to the powers of comprehension of the great masses and to do without the applause of the cultivated class—or to bridge the tremendous gap between the two groups by means of the greatness of his art and to pursue both aims at once. What an undertaking—to satisfy the hypersensitive taste of the connoisseur without thereby becoming unpalatable to the great masses—to adapt oneself to the childish powers of comprehension of the people without throwing away any of the dignity of art!"[6]

As one result, since 1789 (the French Revolution) music has been in a more rapid state of flux. We search in vain for neat, nailed-down principles which last for any length of time to be significant, even in the works of one composer. The composer seeks individuality and originality or else tries to catch the current taste, or both. There are many who maintain that there is a uniform common practice, and in many instances prior to the Romantic Period (and since) there was a common practice, a kind of *ars combinatoria*: artistic creation consisting of different combinations of art materials with little or no new materials admitted from work to work. But new materials coming in bit by bit over the years will cause new sets of accepted principles, something like the change in the appearance and totality of a human being which daily is slight but over the years becomes greatly different. In western music, at least, there are always some changes and we search for the times when there were more nearly uniform practices, list these, name the period and admit that one period is different from the other. The problems arise when we look closely at the troubled times in between, when, for a variety of reasons, changes are occurring more rapidly—the period around 1600, for example.

We often create uniformity for our own convenience, where historically not too much really ever existed. Is it really more important to find out what a composer does all or most of the time and neglect what he does but once? Yes, we must know what happens most of the time, but not end there. If an artist does something significant and does it but once it is important, perhaps even more important than what he does most of the time. (The day a man dies is more significant than the day he puts on his shoes.) One must know what the composer does most of the time, however, in order to determine if a certain chord, form, orchestration, texture, harmonic progression or any other musical dimension is a significant departure from his usual practice.

This brings us right back to the problem of trying to find some unifying threads for musical development in the period 1789-1925. We must recognize the great importance of the date 1789 as at least the beginning of a more rapid transition from musical classicism to romanticism, which as a set of tendencies did not conveniently end at 1900 but still remains to a certain extent. Even now some principles of romanticism are applied dogmatically, the same principles which once were held to be the epitome of *un*music since they were *un*classic. This is part of what Lang is saying:[7] *we* are living the culture of the nineteenth century in a way that they could not, and we tend often to react according to nineteenth-century traditions. The most significant artists of our own time have pointed this out to us, but apparently "free" principles of our most advanced art will be "dogmas" at a later time. Although writing about religious thought, Reardon applies it well for all uses:

If the eighteenth century can be summarily characterized as the Age of Reason its successor is less amenable to facile generalization: the tendencies and developments of which the historian has to take note are more numerous, diverse and complex. In particular the nineteenth century, far more obviously than its predecessor, was an era of change. Again, a large measure of the appeal which the latter has for the modern mind lies not only in its comparative simplicity of aspect but in its remoteness: to study it is to encounter, as it were, a prepossessing stranger. With the nineteenth century, however, we are aware of a closer affinity, so that it has for us the sometimes tiresome familiarity of a kinsman. Yet the student of religion is likelier to find it of much greater interest. Its forerunner represents a time when the religious spirit blew but fitfully; convention, decorum and prudence were the usually accepted marks of a right-thinking man, and faith itself admitted reason as its better part. By contrast the century which began with revolution and general war, and whose early temper was displayed in the emotional and imaginative vagaries of the Romantic movement, turned to religion with a new concern, as to something holding the key, it might be, to the interpretation of man's historic life itself, a belief fostered and stimulated by a growing knowledge and appreciation of the phases through which that life had actually passed. If man has in his hands the means of shaping his own terrestrial destiny—as in this century it was increasingly realized that he had—it was because, nevertheless, he himself was the product of an historical evolution no part of which was irrelevant to the self-comprehension to which he aspired. His life might be many-sided, intricate and devious —far more so than the rationalists of an earlier day had supposed—but it might also be possible to detect a purpose within it which gave confident hope—and as the century advanced this expectation swelled—of a richer, ampler future. If, then, one does venture to epitomize the epoch in a phrase one might call it the Age of Progress. It is not surprising that religion itself should have both reflected and promoted the current forward-looking idealism.[8]

Of particular interest to us in this lengthy quotation is the realization that the world became greatly different in the nineteenth century. Certainly the romantic composer was convinced that the age was one of progress, although one might doubt the validity of many value judgments which were made. One need only consult the prose works of composers such as Schumann, Berlioz, Liszt, Wagner and our own Edward MacDowell to find this great feeling of optimism. Somehow the romantic appeared to have a grasp of eternal verities in a way which the Age of Reason could not have comprehended. In a word, then, it was a "brave new world."[9]

What happened to music that was so different? This book will discuss this from several points of view. The period is replete with paradoxes which will now be recognized rather than reconciled. There is a paradox at the outset: in order to understand romanticism one must first understand classicism:[10]

1. Classicism sets and maintains standards. In the hands of a great composer great musical meaning transcends the standard; for lesser talents the standard is only filled out. The great artist *makes his own outline*, and while it may resemble that of another, it is different in the most important aspects, *i.e.*, form and content are so inexorably woven together that one is a part of the other. The student can get valuable lessons from this by comparing first-movement forms of various composers and the form as used by the same composer in different works. The lesser composer will almost always have a high predictability, while the great composer will have the significant unexpected. Mozart's *Ein musikalischer Spass* (Musical Joke), K. 522, shows this to a remarkable degree—indeed, that is one of the jokes:[11] predictability.

2. Classicism has more uniformity, a cultivated uniformity in the actual musical practice of the time. The Age of Reason certainly had its counterpart in music; and it is easy to draw parallels between the "naturalness" of tonality and the ability of reason to solve all problems. However, actual events since 1789 have shown that tonality as exemplified

by some treatises was at best a hopeful abstraction, and the thinkers of the nineteenth century, time and time again, recognize that there is much more to man than his sense of reason.

The nineteenth century's progressive composer cultivated differences, tried to express something of himself to other people. He looked upon this great audience as "humanity" with personal feelings not stereotyped. This idea prevails among us yet today, since we are still conditioned by the great romantic artists.

Langer, in her essay "On Significance in Music," raises some pertinent questions regarding the emotional content of music: whose emotions are they? Does the performer have these emotions as he performs? If he has emotional content in his playing, how can he announce the program in advance since he does not know how he will feel at the performance? Does the work evoke the proper emotional content just by performance or hearing, or do we feel what we have been told we ought to feel?[12]

We tend to recreate the past in our own image. It is difficult to be phenomenological and report *exactly* what happened. A writer who admires neat classifications will find some, a writer who loves great freedom will find freedom and there are many positions in between. The nineteenth century, then, is one in which change was of the utmost importance: an evolutionary change, a cultivation of change. Therefore, our task will be to trace the evolution of the various musical elements from the classical standard which, it must be remembered, had evolved from something else and was cultivated to a certain extent, but for different reasons. As Brandt asserts so well:

Generally, the Classic composer works well within a tradition, seeking no surprises or innovations for their own sakes. He may, by the constant practice of his art, broaden and gradually expand the tradition in which he began, bringing it to new heights hitherto unsuspected and unappreciated by his contemporaries. But this, we must remember, represents the evolution developed during a lifetime of music.[13]

There is no reality in western music of a permanent or static condition. The interesting factor is that the rate of change is almost never a constant, and that rapid acceleration can be observed at the end of an old period and at the beginning of a new one. Old formulae become worn-out and are either evolved into a different set of concepts or are completely discarded to be replaced by others. New formulae now appear, are absorbed, become dogmas. (How often a heresy of one age becomes the credo of another!) These new principles are frequently the result of a natural reaction, especially at the times of the greatest upheavals in music history: *Ars nova* vs. *Ars antiqua,* ca. 1300[14] or *Stile antico* vs. *Stile moderno,* ca. 1600.[15] New principles are also the result of a breakthrough in knowledge. Good examples are:

1. The great advances in efficient notation such as Franco of Cologne's *Ars cantus mensurabilis* (ca. 1280), which for the first time presented a nearly foolproof notation of durations.
2. The improvement of musical instruments as more complete, chromatic, flexible tools.
3. The discovery of past history: the utilization of older forms and styles given new life through new combinations of ideas.
4. Extra-musical changes which are the result of external affairs and have a decided impact on music: world events, politics, religions, the other arts, philosophies, etc.
5. Printing as an accurate method for the proliferation of many copies, such as the impact of *Musica Transalpina* in 1588 on English music.[16]

We can truthfully say, then, that the nineteenth century poses special problems since, historically speaking, we are still very much a part of it and it is still difficult to view it with complete objectivity. We are also faced with the strange problem of having almost too much data, since nineteenth-century composers *preserved* their works and libraries, publishers and the musicians themselves saw to it that there was a great proliferation of copies. How different are the earlier periods, which must be reconstructed from smaller sets of data! We are so guilty of judging the whole from a part,[17] but what else can we do?

Interesting questions now arise. Are these great individual differences of the nineteenth century so apparent because of the prolixity of data? Or, because we are so close to it and can discriminate? Or, *only* because the composers themselves cultivate differences as a trait of the age? One can support affirmative answers for all three questions, and still others could be posed. Of the greatest importance is the fact that interest in older music barely exists until the nineteenth century, except as theoretical speculation; some early histories delineate the earliest period of music history as extending from the Garden of Eden to the Great Flood.[18] But these pre-1850 histories have little to do with the music itself: the specific works of musical art studied in their historical environment for the purpose of a more meaningful performance and/or understanding of the works. Instead, they have to do with theoretical speculation of origins, the use of music and the like. The "Great Man" theory of music history comes to the fore in the nineteenth century, bringing about the adulation of the composer as a real creative artist entitled to honor, no longer a part of the nobleman's livery but his equal or even his superior. As a legendary king has been quoted: "There are many kings, but only one Beethoven." Concert programs contain more old music than new, and composers realize that at some time in the future *their* music will be old and will be played; hence, greater care in notating and editing was exercised by romantics, so that we are the heirs of a very fecund century: ream upon ream of music was written. As Adam Carse says:

The records of the past show clearly enough that composers have always been as plentiful as flies in summer-time. It is a mistake to suppose that the ability to compose music is a rare gift, one which when discovered should be carefully nurtured, treasured, and be given every possible encouragement. It is a very common gift, and can be found in abundance in every civilised community. At any given time, hundreds of musicians can always be found who can compose, and who appear to be doing their job quite well; but, unfortunately, there seems to be no reliable method of finding out at the time which are, so to speak, worth keeping, and which should be thrown away. If we destroy the lot, we may be destroying just the one we ought to have kept. So we have to put up with a lot of dross, and must leave it to Time to make the selection which will eventually give us the few prizes in the lottery.[19]

But the music alone is not the whole story. Composers, smitten by the posterity complex, wrote diaries, letters, articles and books, which in turn were printed in great numbers and also have had a good survival rate. Result: still more data, perhaps not as reliable, but data nevertheless. One can *say* almost anything about music, but a score always speaks the truth about it, providing the music receives a good performance. People other than composers also do a great deal of writing about music, which can give us further data—good, bad and misleading. In our day we have the added advantage of rapid communication media, especially the phonograph and radio, which add to the efficiency and the din, as well as the profusion of data.

Why this preoccupation with what should be a computer's dream—lots of data? Just this: it is all so conflicting and there seems to be today (although subsiding somewhat) a strident chorus of, "I hate romanticism!" Gertrude Stein even said, "Kill the nineteenth century dead!"[20] The experts and some artists speak this way, but not the public. The bulk of our concert and opera programming, most recordings of serious music and most music sold for study is from the nineteenth century. As a result, "Historical works on the romantic composers will continue to be in a bad way as long as there is no agreement on the range of this concept, which can no longer be just considered to be equivalent to the nineteenth century, as the easy way out."[21]

Music is not alone in this muddle. Barzun, in discussing the romantic period in general, asserts:

In those two decades before the second world war, the nineteenth century was considered a regrettable interlude with but a few isolated figures to redeem it. The early, or Romantic part of that century was held in particular detestation and contempt: it was naive, silly, wrongheaded, stupidly passionate, criminally hopeful, and intolerably rhetorical. The word "romantic" in fact stood for these defects wherever they might be found, as well as for anything else suggestive of that remote generation which had either not lived in the world we knew, or lived in it with all its senses stopped, including its common sense.[22]

And in a different work Barzun says:

Romanticism was a constructive effort after a great revolution which had leveled off old institutions and old notions—including the mechanical materialism of the eighteenth century. Romanticism, as we all know, valued individual freedom, subjective feeling, human reason, social purpose, and above all, art. Granted that it failed to win the world, it was the right kind of failure; and the replacement of this productive Romanticism by the neo-materialism of the mid-century was in fact a regression we are now paying for in the form of private neuroses and public massacres.[23]

But the opposite view is often found: that the teachings of the nineteenth century are to be accepted without question. Any other way of thinking *seems* wrong since it *seems* to destroy a valuable criterion. Quoting from Oscar Thompson's *How to Understand Music*:

Much of the mistaken judgment that has plagued musical criticism in the past undoubtedly was due to mistaking recipes for laws. Good music had been made in certain ways. Time proved that those ways could be altered and good music still comes out of the making; unless one is to accept the laments of those few and scattered individuals who believe that music stopped short with Palestrina, or Mozart, or Brahms or Debussy.[24]

In daily life this is probably true: we *must* breathe, we *must* eat, we *must* sleep. In art a new practice in no way destroys the art of the past, it only changes the *modus operandi* or adds something new. Schoenberg's discoveries have in no way destroyed the beauty of the Beethoven string quartets any more than Beethoven's discoveries destroyed the beauty of the Masses of Palestrina. How fortunate is the man who is responsive to the beauty of all ages!

Karl Jaspers, in his essay "On My Philosophy," gives one an important set of insights into the study of philosophical history which can certainly apply to the study of music history:

Our questions and answers are in part determined by the historical tradition in which we find ourselves.[25]

The following comment on the history of philosophy is especially relevant:

In what way the history of philosophy exists for us is a fundamental problem of our philosophizing which demands a concrete solution in each age. Philosophy is tested and characterized by the way in which it appropriates its history. It might seem to us that the truth of present-day philosophy manifests itself less in the formation of new fundamental concepts . . . than in the new sound it makes audible for us in old thoughts.[26]

Jaspers's listing of the characteristics of a history of philosophy are also significant and worthy of pursuit by the serious student of music:

1. The real import of history is the Great, the Unique, the Irreplaceable. . . .
2. Understanding of the ideas demands a thorough study of texts. . . .
3. Understanding of philosophy demands a universal historical view. . . .
4. The philosopher's invisible realm of the spirit. . . . Any objectivication, whether it be the formation of schools or sects, is the ruin of philosophy. For the freedom that can be handed down in philosophizing cannot be handed down by the doctrine of an institution. Only as an individual can man become a philosopher. . . .
5. The universal-historical view is a condition for the most decisive consciousness of one's own age.[27]

Jaspers would admit, I am sure, that such a list is probably possible only in the twentieth century; he would not be true to what is being said if this were not so. One can trace back through history and find the various ages during which these great concepts were added, hence one can only wistfully speculate what additions (or deletions) might be made in the future.

Jaspers's first characteristic (*the Great, Unique, Irreplaceable* apropos music) is obvious: the great man—performer or composer, critic, theorist or musical historian. The Unique is applicable to any true work of art, and the Irreplaceable are all of these plus our musical instruments and other tools which stay around because we want or need them. The pianoforte did not really replace the violin, nor did the first caveman who beat a drum cause any sudden cessation of vocal music—let us ponder this before deciding that electronic music will somehow do away with string quartets or girls' glee clubs, to say nothing of the *Society for the Preservation and Encouragement of Barbershop Quartet Singing in America*. True, the serpent, sackbut, ophicleide and others are gone, but they *were* replaceable and their best features still live on in instruments that seem to be irreplaceable; only time will tell. New instruments or ways of making music do not entirely replace or destroy those already in existence any more than new techniques of composition replace old ones.

Jaspers's characteristic number two should be underlined in the minds of all music students: "*a thorough study of the texts!*" Not just the textbooks, but the *music itself*. How often immature students "shoot down" a piece of great music with devastatingly succinct criticism: "I don't like it!" And after one hearing, too! As Haydon says:

Even if we listen closely, our attention is psychologically limited to a half dozen items at one time; awareness flits from one aspect of the composition to another. And whether it is the tone of the oboe, the swing of the rhythm, or the contour of the melody, the particular aspect is always something less than the whole. In listening to a string quartet, for example, we can follow the various motives or themes as they pass from instrument to instrument, and leave the harmonic and other details more or less in the background of consciousness. We can pay attention to the cello especially, and, although we may be vaguely aware of what the other instruments are doing, the cello part will stand out in our experience; or we may derive great pleasure from concentrating upon almost any aspect of the composition. But, certainly, we do not hear all the details of the composition at once; we cannot make one all-inclusive synthesis of the experience.

Because great works of art have some complexity either of detail or of implication, we do not grow tired of them after a few hearings. We hear a great symphony again and again, and constantly find new interest. Why? Partly, at least, because of this analytic nature of intelligent listening.28

A study of the texts for a thorough understanding requires Jaspers's characteristic number three: *a universal historical view*. A more profound, introspective interpretation of music *requires* this—not a dull, deadly, academic approach, but a deep, significant one. To quote Jaspers again:

. . . the manner in which history is to be studied is entailed: a theoretical attitude toward it becomes real only in the living appropriation of its contents from the texts. . . . *To apprehend thought with indifference prevents its appropriation* [Italics mine].29

And now we come to Jaspers's characteristic number four: *the realm of the spirit*. Since this is the most elusive it is the most talked about in each age. The "philosophers ask the questions, the theologians answer them"—how can such a list of subjective questions have any kind of objective answers? It is similar to measuring a man's height by the gallon. The nineteenth century really worried about things of the spirit; most people knew that the Age of Reason had only *said* that it had all of the answers, but they tried to escape even the inner spirit. Some say that the only true romanticism is this desire for release to another place or time. "Romanticism is flight from the present, whether into the past, the future, or another world, dreams, or, most often a vague fog."30 But one escapes not his own spirit—not even when he sleeps, since he dreams. Therefore the romantic often realizes this and accepts his lot: his own spirit in his own time. "True romantic art . . . does not refuse the most pedestrian realism. *Robinson Crusoe* is as realistic as it is romantic:

both qualities are pushed to an extreme, and neither suffers."[31] This statement by Robert Louis Stevenson also applies to Jaspers's last point, a consciousness of one's own age through the universal-historical view: any time can be romantic, any place can be romantic, or it cannot. Thomas Hardy sees this: "Romanticism will exist in human nature as long as human nature itself exists. The point is . . . to adopt that form of romanticism which is the mood of the age."[32]

By now it should be apparent that romanticism is replete with paradoxes and contradictions—not the art works themselves as much as the works *about* them. Kurt Stephenson concludes his valuable essay on musical romanticism by again voicing Einstein's lament that there is *still* no such thing as an "unequivocal definition of musical romanticism."[33] This author would like to *attempt* a technical definition, based on several principles:

1. The notion suggested in Westrup and Harrison's *The New College Encyclopedia of Music*, in the article "Romantic Music," that "romanticism in music as a period ends c. 1920 (Schönberg arrived at the principles of twelve-note composition)."[34]
2. Music romanticism is almost never discussed in terms of its own vocabulary, even in technical works.
3. The recognition of a series of historical events which actually happened, uncolored by wishful thinking that they did not (I am only too aware of the fact that one can also wish the opposite).
4. The concept that a word may have more than one meaning: such as the word "miscellaneous," which *in toto* has one meaning but item by item always represents a different summation; or the German word "Strauss," which can mean a man's name, a nosegay, a fight or an ostrich; or the English sound of "to," "too" and "two."
5. The concept, so congruent with what has happened in music history, that the exact meaning of a word changes. If the meaning can change, the resultant work of music will be different in many details.

To summarize: romanticism in music seems to be an attack on the accepted, standard practice—"to go out of bounds," as it were. Since the great binding force in the classical period was the major-minor key system of tonality, and since the Baroque had developed and had come to full flower *as a system* by and through factors discussed in the treatise of Rameau (1722) and other important theoretical works,[35] and, more important, in the *actual musical practice* of the best composers, then it follows that the romantic tendency slowly but surely tore down this great edifice and replaced it with something else, just as tonality itself had done *exactly the same thing* (under somewhat similar musical circumstances) to modality in the sixteenth and seventeenth centuries—tearing it down and replacing it with something more congruent with the mood of the times: a reasonable system, neatly following well-regulated progressions and principles. Remember that the modes were also a neat system, but a *different* one from keys. I am not saying that keys and tonality or even the modes are dead or that they should be, but it is quite apparent at this time that treatises like Rameau's have little to do with the common practice of composers as actually found in the greatest art music since the time of J. S. Bach! As Goldman says:

The fundamental syntax of Western music in its traditional period is that of the harmonic language that reached its highest expressiveness from the time of Bach to the time of Wagner and Brahms. This language represents one of the greatest intellectual accomplishments of Western man. In the words of Sir Donald Tovey: "Our Western art of music stands in the unique position that its language has been wholly created by art. . . . When we trace the slow and difficult evolution of our harmonic system, we cease to wonder that it was not evolved sooner and elsewhere, and we learn to revere the miracle that it was evolved at all." One of the central facts about our harmonic system or language is, as Tovey points out, that it is invented. Although certain basic elements are taken from the natural overtone series, the developed relationships that form the language are, in a sense, arbitrary. The basic or fundamental tonal relationship, that of dominant and tonic, on which all further development rests, corresponds to no acoustical law, and has no "scientific" basis. The musical relationship is wholly invented, or "created by art."[36]

This book will show in greater detail, from time to time, how this is apparent. This is not to say that composers had in their mind that "we must kill the key principle!" To them tonality was a way of life—but how can one reconcile tonality in Wagner and tonality in Cimarosa as the same thing? There is such a thing as evolution of an idea, but the end is usually quite different from the beginning. Are we the same now as when we were infants? We are the same human beings, but our roles and functions have changed with time; we are the result of what time has done to us, and are certainly different from what we would be in a different time or place. The same principle applies with music since, after all, music comes from men. In short, romanticism as a summation of ideas and forces changed the key system to such an extent that it no longer existed. It had been replaced by something else, for better or for worse. Philip Friedheim says:

Anyone attempting to analyze 19th-century music is confronted with the fact that the final shape of many compositions is frequently conditioned by extra-musical influences. How much can a harmonic analysis of a Schubert Lied explain the full effect of the text-music relations? What is the "form" of a symphonic movement by Berlioz based on a Shakespearean narrative? What, in short, constitutes a sound basis for a structural analysis of 19th-century music? Certainly this basis must be rooted in the nature of tonality and its historical evolution through the century. One point of view reveals the central European music of this period moving between Beethoven on one hand and Schoenberg on the other. Rephrasing this in purely analytical terms, one can say that the music moves from the height of Viennese Classicism and the perfection of tonal structures to atonality and the elimination of a functioning tonic. It is thus possible to view the harmonic style of the 19th century as part of a historical tradition that explores the areas leading to the dissolution of tonality. Such an approach, limited only to purely musical (*i.e.*, harmonic and structural) material, can be legitimately revealing even when applied to compositions supporting the heaviest programmatic content.[37]

Another dimension of the meaning of musical romanticism is the act of seeking something new, reacting to and not accepting past practice *carte blanche*. Hence, we are faced with the concept that ROMANTIC is a constant, since it is always happening in varying degrees from the Garden of Eden until now, and that ROMANTIC is a variable, since the separate and distinct works of romantic music are very different from each other. It is obvious that two words are needed: *romantic* for the variable, and perhaps the French *romanesque* for the constant (and indeed it is sometimes used this way), but there is danger in confusing this with a vital period in the history of architecture.

Romanticism by its very nature is paradoxical, even antithetical. Einstein's great book on the Romantic Period speaks of this in Chapter V, "The Contradictions."[38]

We shall look further into this, which will enhance our understanding of the century, since perhaps the greatest paradox of all is the historical fact that not all that happened in the century was romantic. It cannot be stressed too much that more than one set of values and/or tendencies can exist at a time, even in the works of one man.

One cry which was sung was, "Let us be free!" Some even dared to say, "*I* shall be free!" Robert Haven Schauffler wrote a book called "Beethoven, the Man Who Freed Music."[39] The final chorus of Rossini's *William Tell* states:

> About us all changes and grows.
> Fresh the air!

Georg Büchner often said, "Something that lives!"[40] Most people were so concerned about freedom to live as they wished (the great concept of the political rebellions), that it now became a battle cry for the artists.

But freedom from what? Do they mean musical anarchy? Certainly not; anarchy becomes a reality in art music[41] only in the second half of the twentieth century. Freedom is a strange concept. It is basic that in most human affairs my freedom ends where yours begins; in art there are no such boundaries *except* the boundaries of man's own mind. If one is completely free as a composer, he tends to be the prisoner of his own mind, limited by the experiences and scope thereof. Hence, one who has experienced much, and who has learned much, knows more possibilities than one who has done less. The great philosophers have pondered long and hard on this problem but as yet seem to have found no real solution. The fact remains that some minds grow and the "cell" of the "prison" becomes ever larger. Consider the dog who works and works to free himself from a leash, only to find that he is in a room 9′ × 12′; he escapes, only to find that he is still in the house, from which he escapes only to find that the house is surrounded by a fence, etc. Other dogs are content to stay on the leash, so they never go too far. A child who is allowed to do exactly as he wishes is indeed an unhappy child—it is no fun to rebel if there is no resistance!

This is perhaps one of the greatest paradoxes: there is no concept of freedom without a concept of bondage. Until the interesting attempts at a completely free, aleatory music of our times, composers were quite content to confine themselves to certain ground rules—just which ones were in operation depended on the age. One is reminded of Dumas' *Count of Monte Cristo*, who, as Edmund Dantes, was an ordinary fellow, but after being wrongly imprisoned was forced to use the best of his mental faculties with the help of the old priest who was in the next cell. Dantes escaped his mental and physical prison by going outside his own mind through the mind of the priest. A good composer must force himself to do something like this, but his is a prison of his own choice from which he learns by stretching his mind. Real freedom for the artist, then, is not anarchy. The law of the great artist is the law of his own making, *but* it is the result of learning from other minds. One cannot know what to do until he knows what has been done. A truly great composer is one who leaves music in a different and better state than the way he found it, but he must have freedom.

Romanticism, then, is a multi-paradox. As we have said, to define it is in a way to destroy it or to make it classical. Can romanticism be codified? Should it be codified? What is the reality of an age of illusions? What is illusion in an age of reality?

There are many explanations, and almost all are different.

Often too much attention was paid to what was said and written, rather than to the real sound of the music. Games are played on the field, music is studied and played; no amount of journalism wins pennants or explains a mediocre symphony into a great one, or deprecates a great one into the horror one is led to believe it is. Composers are often forced into making statements which haunt them forever, no matter how often their actual work denies what they may have said. We have become an age that prefers a one-sentence or one-word classification to a thorough study. How can a problem which takes volumes to state be solved in a sentence? We dote upon what has been said and written about something (especially music), rather than look (or listen) directly at the source. We search for a "typical" example; in art this is impossible, for no real work of art typifies anything but itself.

When we search for common tendencies we have again arrived at the greatest paradox of all: are the common tendencies of romanticism representative of the age, or are the individual differences?

Music became larger and larger, longer and longer, louder and louder. There was expansion and inflation. The sonata-allegro principle, already gigantic in much of Beethoven's music, became a long succession of closed forms which in summation became a large sonata. Wagner searched for and found continuous melody for the entire act of an opera—the "aria" became a whole act, as it were. Length was certainly a factor in the colossal Baroque, but the composer rarely if ever called for the huge instrumental forces with many entirely different parts common in the colossal Romantic. Size, therefore, was huge in length, huge in numbers and huge in sound.

But music also became smaller—in length, in intensity of sound and in the importance of solo music (not the concerto or sonata, but short pieces for *Hausmusik*). Here is part of the explanation—places for public concerts were getting larger and larger, while "echoes" of these concerts and operas were played at home as never before throughout most of the nineteenth century. Available were the inevitable piano duet versions of symphonies and shorter orchestral works and solo piano transcriptions. Variations on opera airs, at almost every taste and difficulty level, were heard from homes in almost every block, and provided the most popular type of music played by the great piano virtuosi. We remember and study Chopin, not Kalkbrenner; Schumann, not Sterndale Bennett.

Music's size was also reflected by the size of the room in which it was performed. In the nineteenth century halls got larger, opera houses got larger. But the drawing room, salon or ballroom, the "chamber" of Baroque and Classical fame, remained an important hearing place. It was here that Liszt, Chopin, Gottschalk, Thalberg, Clara Schumann, *et al.* were at their best. The string quartet, long a great vehicle for *Hausmusik*, turned professional following the lead of Beethoven's intimate, Schuppanzigh, who as early as 1804 was giving *public* chamber music concerts. How now! The most intimate music, chamber music, in public! The halls became larger and larger, demanding bigger sounds from the players and bigger works for the quartet. At the same time, *Hausmusik* continued, but now in the more humble homes, in smaller and smaller "family rooms" across the land. It became fashionable for young ladies to play the piano, and this versatile instrument replaced all others as the instrument of the home. With the rise of mass production techniques the price of a piano, especially the upright, became low enough to be readily available; this, in turn, created a mammoth market the world over for music of all kinds. Many wagonmasters on the American frontier cursed the precious piano as it loaded down the wagons on steep hills and treacherous fords. It is not inconceivable that lonely campfires in the wilderness were considerably brightened by the piano and other instruments. One wonders if a Beethoven sonata or Chopin waltz ever shared a program with the *Dill Pickle Rag* or the *Old Arm Chair*!

The pianoforte itself was called upon for bigger sounds as the concert halls in the big cities got larger and the beer halls got noisier. One wonders sometimes why it is called "piano" rather than "forte!" The other instruments followed suit, including use of the human voice, although one could certainly not do much to "improve" upon the material of the voice as had been done in the wind instruments: the flute became metal toward the end of the century, louder, more brilliant, but less mellow and intimate. Violin strings and techniques were designed for more brilliance and bigger sounds. And so it went—hardly an instrument escaped modification in the direction of bigger, more brilliant sound. These modifications were the result of three important factors: the composers demanded it, the great virtuosi demanded it, and the instrument makers provided it, made possible by scientific and industrial discoveries in acoustical knowledge, ability to make and duplicate delicate measurements and mass produce these on rods, springs, drills and the like. There were great strides in metallurgy, making possible the great improvements on the brasses (mainly the valves). Only the stringed instruments were not basically changed, although great strides were made in more efficient gadgetry, more durable strings and the great improvements in the bow made by Tourte and Dodd during Beethoven's lifetime.

But these "improvements" were not all good, in that a certain refinement of tone is often sacrificed in order to make the mechanism of an instrument more facile or better in tune. In large halls, however, this refinement is all but lost and we prefer the clarity and better intonation of the instruments as the Romantic Period helped improve them.

The new concepts of a bigger sound were also heard in ever larger orchestras in the concert hall and in the opera house. In 1795 the Salomon orchestra in London had about 40 strings and probably about 12 winds. In 1841 the Berlin opera had 54 strings, 28 winds, 2 harps and 2 or 3 percussionists. (The increase in the strings was mostly in violas, cellos and basses, showing greater demands on inner and lower voices.) The Wagnerian orchestra at Bayreuth in 1876 had 64 strings and 4 each of the woodwinds, 8 horns, 4 trumpets, bass trumpet, 3 trombones and bass trombone, contra-bass tuba, and extra harps and percussionists.

Wagner, Verdi and others needed these large forces to tell their great tales on the operatic stage. One needs these huge orchestras for the heavy storms which begin *Die Walküre* and *Otello*, but what justifies the huge forces called for by the non-programmatic scores of Bruckner, Mahler or early Schoenberg? The answer is that people just liked the sound of large orchestras, and they still do. The Romantic Period saw the publication of several important textbooks on the art of orchestration; these exerted a great influence on all orchestral composers, great and small. Composers were fascinated by the new sounds; and, as the nineteenth century moved on, the texts and the new conservatories springing up in the major cities produced better trained orchestral players and composers. The most important text was certainly the one by Berlioz, first published in 1844 and still used today in a revision by Richard Strauss. There were similar works from as early as 1792 (Francoeur's *Diapason général de tous les instruments à vent*), and they are still being written today. The Berlioz treatise is unusual on several counts, but mainly for its comments on the art of combining instruments and because, of all the early writers on orchestration, Berlioz is the only one who was a major composer. The earlier ones tended to be manuals for instrumentation, content only to give ranges of the instruments, transpositions and the like.

Large orchestras call for large pieces and the composers obliged, producing the longest symphonies since the Beethoven *Ninth*, as if trying to break his record. There was often a confusion of bigness for greatness. Many of these monstrosities were not organic unities at all but were short pieces strung together, attempting a mastery of form by trying too hard to follow the dictates of classical form, understanding its letter but not its spirit. One does not make a mighty symphony by stringing together one little piece after another.

But excellent little pieces were written, just a page or so—exquisite miniatures. Most of these were for piano but some were for violin or other instrument and piano, or voice and piano. Most painted little pictures or captured the mood of the moment, although some were teaching pieces loosely called "Sonatinas" or simply "studies" or "études." An overview of these show an interest in both the subjective and objective aspects of music. A Chopin can create drama with the piano which exceeds the dramatic symphonic gesturing of a Raff; a Mahler with a huge orchestra can show greater delicacy than a Heller in a tiny character piece for piano.

There are other paradoxes inherent within the context of the foregoing. Among these are theatricality vs. intimacy, self-expression vs. expression of popular taste, self-expression vs. universal expression (perhaps *Weltschmerz*), and the oldest artistic problem of all: form vs. content.

Being theatrical in and of itself is not necessarily an artistic crime, but there is such a thing as bombast, cliché and the expected obvious. Many successful "hits" of the Romantic Period were almost the exact opposites of artistic ideal, even the most free romantic ideal. There are tons and tons of this chaff, most of it designed for immediate sale. I am not speaking of music written by serious composers, but rather that of the charlatan, always with us. There is no greater hypocrite than the pseudo-artistic carpetbagger peddling pap to people who truly want and genuinely need *real* culture, only to be "handed a stone when they asked for bread." Gilbert Chase, in his fascinating book *America's Music*, describes this in the chapter entitled "The Genteel Tradition," where, after describing one such horror by Henry Russell ("The Ship on Fire"), he says: "This is the genteel tradition's equivalent of purging the spirit through pity and terror, running the gamut from bombast to bathos."[42]

The key words are "bombast" and "bathos." How different are the songs of Stephen Foster! Yet, the musical style is superficially the same as Russell's. Somehow, Foster still touches the heart today and is true gold. The Russell songs are all "bombast" and "bathos," while almost all Foster songs have a genuine and intimate pathos—they are as big as they are, and this seems to be a cardinal principle of art. It must be remembered that this "genteel" music was held to be "serious," or, if you will, "art" music. It is important to study this music as a sociological phenomenon, for here is a real example of "typical" non-art. It was the only contact with concert music which many people had, not only in America but in Europe as well. They consumed it, paid for it and loved it, right along with their statues of Venus de Milo with a clock in her stomach.

The truly great art songs, especially German Lieder by the masters, had a more difficult time and didn't figure prominently on concert programs until late in the Romantic Period, although they were widely sung at private soirees throughout that era. It is significant that performers and audiences preferred theatrical settings for songs like Russell's as well as serious Lieder concerts. The "Singing Hutchinsons" were among the vocal groups famous for their histrionics, especially the heart-rending renditions of "The Maniac." The serious concert, on the other hand, while still trying to create the proper atmosphere, isolated the singer and pianist in various ways, giving the audience the ever-present potted palms, lavender twilights and other romantic visual effects. The artists were hidden so as not to distract the audience!

A quotation from an article by Wilhelm Mauke, writing in the *Frankfurter Zeitung*, August 10, 1899, shows an extreme case:

The auditorium, whose seats are arranged in the shape of an amphitheatre, affords only enough light to permit the audience to read the text of the lieder. Neither the piano nor the pianist is visible. The singer is not dressed in taste-less attire, but in the symbolic broad, white robe of an Apollonian priest, or is clad in the attire of a singer of Bacchus—costumes which he changes according to the mood of each song. His voice touches our hearts as being heard through a sea-green web of liana plants. An aroma of Heliotrope passes through the hall when sensuous sultry love songs are sung. Serious lieder are heard with incense that comes from rows of columns that are embraced by holy groves of cypress. The hymns of summer night rock one to sleep in the midst of large umbellated buds, violet-colored clouds, stars that glitter gently—everything is in mystical darkness. The passionate cries of erotic songs speak to the imagination and to the intimate emotions of the audience, which is thrilled with perplexity and pain.[43]

But enough of the mawkish Herr Mauke! He is a nadir example of non-musical explanation.

This book approaches romanticism as an unfixed tendency. We shall now dig deeper and deal with specifics, first with the dense but fascinating underbrush in the remarkable forest of the nineteenth century. Some trails are blazed, some are even interstate highways, but many, I fear, only encircle the forest. The question of, "What is romanticism?" must be pursued further in order for the student to appreciate the great dif-ference of opinion—not to confuse, but to clarify. We shall view the subject from many different angles, restating some themes as *idées fixes*, others as variations and others as recapitulations. Part of the book is devoted to analyses of specific works of music as the "Great, Unique, Irreplaceable" musical art of the nineteenth century—not only as art works, but as examples of techniques which enriched a very noble and remarkable time in our musical history.

Notes

1. Paul Henry Lang, *Music in Western Civilization* (New York: W. W. Nor-ton & Company, Inc., 1941), p. 1027. Copyright renewed 1968 by Paul Henry Lang. By permission of J. M. Dent & Sons Ltd.

2. Kurt Stephenson, *Romanticism in Music* (Cologne: Arno Volk Verlag, 1961), p. 5.

3. Lang, *ibid.*

4. Alec Harman with Anthony Milner and Wilfred Mellers, *Man and His Music* (New York: Oxford University Press, 1962), p. 631.

5. Carl Bamberger, ed., *The Conductor's Art* (New York: McGraw-Hill Book Company, Inc., 1965), pp. 8-9.

6. Reprinted with permission of The Macmillan Company from Eric Werner, *Mendelssohn*, trans. D. Newlin. Copyright © by The Free Press of Glencoe, a Division of The Macmillan Company, 1963, pp. 131-132.

7. Lang, *ibid.*

8. Bernard M. G. Reardon, *Religious Thought in the Nineteenth Century* (Cambridge, England: University Press, 1966), p. 1.

9. See *The American Composer Speaks,* Gilbert Chase, ed., article by Mac-Dowell, "Suggestion in Music" (Baton Rouge: Louisiana State University Press, 1966), p. 77.

10. This is not the proper place to discuss classicism thoroughly. Good summaries are to be found in the standard histories listed in the bibliography in the back of this book. There are many books and articles about specific facets of the Classical Period, but few in English which deal with the period in general. A recent book is Reinhard Pauly's *Music in the Classical Period* (Englewood Cliffs: Prentice-Hall, 1965). The student is urged to read the defining articles in the standard dictionaries and encyclopedias of music and is admonished not to attempt a simple, one-sentence catch-all definition.

11. Mozart's *Divertimento,* K. 522, *Ein musikalischer Spass,* is an amazing work which, although trying to be funny, anticipates some twentieth-century musical practices and is an example of a great artist writing something so bad that it is good. He makes every mistake that lesser composers make: awkward phrasing, too many themes and motives, wrong transpositions. He writes into the music mistakes that a performer might make, *viz.,* a horn player with a wrong crook, or the concertmaster "getting lost" in the high positions and making a modulation by mistake. In spite of all this, the work *as a whole* makes a complete arch, and perhaps that is the biggest joke of all—was he really joking?

12. Paraphrased by permission of the publishers from Susanne K. Langer, *Philosophy in a New Key* (Cambridge, Mass.: Harvard University Press, Copyright, 1942, 1951, 1957, by the President and Fellows of Harvard College), p. 215.

13. William E. Brandt, *The Way of Music,* 2nd Ed. (Boston: Allyn and Bacon, Inc., 1968), p. 202.

14. Donald Jay Grout, *A History of Western Music* (New York: W. W. Norton & Company, Inc., 1960), p. 106, states it so well, "Comparatively speaking, the thirteenth century was an era of stability and unity, the fourteenth one of change and diversity."

15. See Grout, *op. cit.,* p. 269.

16. The *Musica Transalpina* was printed in 1588 and was the first appearance in England of Italian madrigals with English words. The effect on English madrigal compositions was quite pronounced. Curt Sachs, in his *Our Musical Heritage* (Englewood Cliffs: Prentice-Hall, 1948), on p. 190 says apropos *Musica Transalpina:* "The public response was extra-ordinary."

17. Although speaking of Karl Jaspers's philosophical concepts, David E. Roberts, in *Existentialism and Religious Belief* (New York: Oxford University Press [Galaxy Books], 1959), on p. 230 says: "Whenever we try to reach Being itself by generalizing on the basis of one aspect of reality—either matter or mind, either the world or the self—we make the mistake of attempting to explain the whole by means of a part." The application of this principle to music history is obvious, the application to any historical study is not only obvious but absolutely necessary. Suppose we were to judge Beethoven only by *Wellington's Victory?*

18. See Bourdelot-Bonnet, *Histoire de la musique, et de ses effets depuis son origine, les progrès successifs de cet art jusqu'à présent* (Paris: Cochart, 1715). The divisions are according to the great events of Biblical and ancient Greek

history such as the time of Socrates. Padre G. B. Martini's *Storia della musica*
1757-1781 is organized along similar lines. The best English source discussing
the history of music history is Warren D. Allen's *Philosophies of Music History*
(New York: American Book Company, 1939).

19. Adam Carse, *The Orchestra from Beethoven to Berlioz* (Cambridge, England: W. Heffer & Sons, Ltd., 1948), pp. 3-4.

20. Peter S. Hansen, *An Introduction to Twentieth Century Music*, 2nd Ed.
(Boston: Allyn and Bacon, Inc., 1967), p. 93.

21. Stephenson, *ibid.*

22. From *Classic, Romantic and Modern*, by Jacques Barzun, by permission
of Little, Brown and Co., Boston, copyright © 1943, 1961 by Jacques Barzun,
pp. xv-xvi, Anchor Books.

23. From *Darwin, Marx, Wagner*, by Jacques Barzun, by permission of Atlantic-Little, Brown and Co., Boston, copyright © 1941 by Jacques Barzun, p. 17,
Anchor Books.

24. Oscar Thompson, *How to Understand Music* (New York: Premier Books,
Fawcett Publications, Inc., 1962), p. 15.

25. Karl Jaspers (1883-   ), author of many important books on psycho-
pathology and philosophy, has taught philosophy and psychology at several
universities, notably Heidelberg and Basel. He is considered one of the most
important theistic existentialist philosophers as well as an authority on the history of philosophy. My immediate source is Felix Kaufmann's translation of
Jaspers's essay "On My Philosophy," which appears in Walter Kaufmann's
excellent book *Existentialism from Dostoevsky to Sartre* (New York: Meridian
Books, The World Publishing Co., 1956), p. 133. The original publisher of
Jaspers's books is R. Piper & Co., Verlag, Munich, Germany, and permission
was granted by them.

26. Kaufmann, *op. cit.*, p. 134.

27. Kaufmann, *op. cit.*, p. 135 *et seq.*

28. Glen Haydon, *Introduction to Musicology* (Prentice-Hall, Inc., copyright
1941), p. 117. Reprinted by permission of Prentice-Hall, Inc., Englewood Cliffs,
N.J.

29. Kaufmann, *op. cit.*, p. 134.

30. Kaufmann, *op. cit.*, p. 13.

31. From *Classic, Romantic and Modern*, by Jacques Barzun, by permission
of Little, Brown and Co., Boston, copyright © 1943, 1961 by Jacques Barzun,
p. 160, Anchor Books.

32. Barzun, *op. cit.*, p. 167.

33. Stephenson, *op. cit.*, p. 16.

34. J. A. Westrup and F. L. Harrison, *The New College Encyclopedia of
Music* (New York: W. W. Norton & Company, Inc., 1960), p. 555.

35. Rameau's works on music theory were not immediately accepted and are
once again in some disrepute. (See the article on "Harmony" in Grove's.) It is
amazing that it came out the same year as Bach's *Well-Tempered Clavier*, Book
I, 1722. The fact remains, however, that Rameau's theories are still the basis
of most harmony books and courses from his time to our own, whether or not
the author knows or acknowledges it. Rameau believed that there must be a
mathematical and physical basis for music, and he seeks this rather successfully
in his treatise. It is the first important treatise which attempts to codify what
we know as tonality. The music students of the nineteenth century in most
cases did not work directly with Rameau's treatise, even though it was widely

read. Far more popular were counterpoint manuals and harmony exercise books by more practical men. Rameau, it must be remembered, was also a great composer, perhaps the greatest of the French Baroque. Counterpoint books which were slaved over by the nineteenth-century music students were Fux's *Gradus ad Parnassum* (1725) and treatises by Marpurg and Kirnberger, to name but a few. Harmony books began to be written for the specific use of the conservatory students of the times, and those of Richter, Jadassohn and many others were studied. In addition there were complete composition courses such as Reicha's or d'Indy's. Cherubini is mentioned several times in the text as an author of important theoretical but still pragmatic works for use in classes, rather than the speculative kind of treatise such as Kepler which one finds earlier. One dangerous game, it seems to me, is the attempt to distill for teaching purposes the harmonic or contrapuntal practice of a composer or a period into one volume. Even if Jeppeson's great works on the Palestrina style are valid for Palestrina, are they necessarily valid for Lassus? An even worse situation exists in the attempts to reduce all tonal harmony to the Bach chorales. Granted, it is a good point for a take-off, but too many small planes never leave the runway.

36. Richard Franko Goldman, *Harmony in Western Music* (New York: W. W. Norton & Company, Inc., 1965), p. 4.

37. Philip Friedheim, "The Approach to the Tonic: A Problem in Nineteenth-Century Musical Analysis" (Paper at National Meeting of American Musicological Society in New Orleans, La., Dec. 28, 1966), p. 1.

38. Alfred Einstein, *Music in the Romantic Era* (New York: W. W. Norton & Company, Inc., 1947), p. 37.

39. Robert Haven Schauffler, *Beethoven, the Man Who Freed Music* (New York: Tudor Publishing Company, 1946).

40. Georg Büchner (1813-1837) is best remembered for his psychological drama *Wozzeck*, which was made into one of the best twentieth-century operas by Alban Berg (1885-1935). Büchner must be considered an important German romantic writer, since he treated psychotic characters with such astonishing skill for a man so young. He was also a university lecturer in anatomy, and sometimes carries the atmosphere of the dissecting room into his dramas (all of them have been set as operas) and could perhaps be called one of the first expressionists. It has been said that expressionism is "Super-charged romanticism."

41. While some would deny that aleatory or chance music is anarchy, some aleatory procedures are "happenings." Some of the best aleatory music, however, has boundaries for the performers and during performance certain elements are controlled. The student is referred to a large and growing list of articles in the current literature on the subject, *e.g.,* the article by Earle Brown in Gilbert Chase's *The American Composer Speaks* (Baton Rouge: Louisiana State University Press, 1966). Any article by John Cage will at least allude to the subject. Aleatory music is not all anarchy, but often approaches it.

42. Gilbert Chase, *America's Music* (New York: McGraw-Hill Book Company, Inc., 1955), p. 169.

43. Quoted in the excellent article by Edward F. Kravitt, "The Lied in 19th Century Concert Life," *Journal of the American Musicological Society*, XVIII, No. 2 (Summer 1965), p. 218.

CHAPTER II

MELODY IN THE
NINETEENTH CENTURY

IN THE NINETEENTH CENTURY melodic concepts changed considerably from the classical ideals of clarity, balance and periodicity. The more passionate passages from the truly great of the late Baroque (J. S. Bach, Handel, Rameau and others) and those of the Classical (Haydn, Mozart, C. P. E. and J. C. Bach and some others) were exceptional and were initially misunderstood by publishers, performers and public. Since it was the tendency of the romantic to "go out of bounds," it follows that the classical ideal, although never a dead issue, had to be expanded, extended and changed in many other ways. The old order was passing. Schumann was moved to say, "You must invent daring new melodies."

The most important musical elements which affected melody, and which will now be discussed, were:

1. Differentiations among terms used in discussing melody.
2. The importance of unifying devices in writing.
3. The added importance of tone color, and changes in it.
4. Sources of melodic contours.
5. Importance of instrumental vs. vocal concepts in writing.
6. Importance of harmony on melodic effectiveness.

7. Importance of articulations, dynamics and nuances.

8. Uses of silence.

9. Phrase structure and the relationships of melody and poetry, both positive and negative.

10. Length of melodies.

11. Texture.

12. Melodic formulae.

13. Variation, development and non-literal restatement.

14. Melody induced by harmony, and vice versa.

15. New approaches to cadence.

16. Importance of range, register and tessitura.

17. Specific examples from the most important composers.

18. New approaches to tonality, modality and artificial scales.

19. Programmatic motivation for new approaches to melody.

Obviously, most of these facets are functions of the others and the true impact of all music is the integrated summation of all facets. Isolation of one facet can be dangerous, especially in nineteenth-century music. Melodic writing is not only enhanced by the total atmosphere at any given moment, but the melody by itself would probably be quite meaningless out of context. Many of the most beloved melodies can be arranged for anything capable of producing musical sounds, but many of them defy representation in other ways and some have been brutally excised. In short, then, *melody in the context of the best nineteenth-century music means much more than TUNE.*

Of all the elements of music, melody is undoubtedly the most beloved by most people. Melody is a word we all know but cannot define in a rigorous way. While we may say that a melody is any meaningful series of pitches presented in a meaningful series of durations, we might as well say that a pretty girl is a meaningful glob of chemicals!

"Melodies" were also known as "themes" or "motives," or even "figures." Hard-and-fast differentiations among these terms are difficult, if not impossible. A "melody" *per se* is usually intended to be sung, or could be sung, while a "figure" *per se* tends to be an instrumental device, often of programmatic significance, used as accompaniment or as part of a contrapuntal texture. "Motives," on the other hand, are either "generating" or, as in the case of Wagner's "leading motives," can be either sung or played. A *generating motive* is a short statement of a few notes from which the music grows—the famous four notes which begin Beethoven's *Fifth Symphony* may be the most familiar example.

Many melodies prior to the nineteenth century were not necessarily associated with any given timbre. The association of a melody with a particular instrument, so important in the twentieth century, began to be important in the late eighteenth and earlier: such as J. S. Bach's solo winds in vocal works or in the *Brandenburg Concerti*. The appropriateness of fanfares by brasses is, of course, obvious; but a more subtle instrumentation of melody is apparent in Mozart and Haydn. Mozart's use of the clarinets in the trio of the minuet from *Symphony No. 39* (K. 543) and Haydn's doubling of the celli at the octave above in the oboe in the slow movement from *Symphony No. 88* are good examples.

Beethoven's use of the contrabassoon in the dungeon scene in *Fidelio*, Berlioz' use of the E-flat clarinet in the finale of the *Fantastic Symphony* or of the solo viola in *Harold in Italy* are early and middle romantic examples. While these are certainly aspects of orchestration, they are also a part of the art of melody writing—*many important nineteenth-century melodies were written with a specific timbre in mind.*[1]

Berlioz's use of natural horns crooked in four different keys in the dramatic symphony *Romeo and Juliet* shows the extreme to which a composer would go to preserve just the right timbre for a melody. There is no doubt that Berlioz was chafing at the limitations imposed by the natural horns, but one horn in each of four keys was a good solution for such a chromatic melody.

It is apparent, then, that the boundaries separating musical elements are not sharp and distinct. Melody is not just pitch and rhythm, but color as well; and certainly the effect of a melody is greatly enhanced by how it is harmonized, as we shall see presently.

Melodic contours also changed during the Romantic Period. The classical composer would often use the outlines of triads for the initial statement of "principal themes" in sonata movements—first movements of symphonies, string quartets, concerti, etc. These were of such common occurrence during the heyday of the Mannheim school that this type of theme is called the "Mannheim rocket" by many scholars.

The "singing" melodies in almost all music of the Classical Period and much of the early Romantic were diatonic or scale-like in contour, with only a few skips. Most of the notes were found in the scale in which the composer was writing his piece. Some composers introduced altered tones in the melodies, particularly in the minor keys.

Composers were also discovering that one could get beautiful melodies by outlining chords which were more complicated than the simple tonic or dominant triad. Mozart made an interesting use of the dominant major ninth in the *Fantasia in C minor*, K. 475. Note its use in measure two of the example. The chromatic passing tone is the augmented eleventh.

Figure 2-1

Tchaikovsky, in the famous song "None but the Lonely Heart," uses notes from the dominant ninth chord and achieves a marvelous pathétique effect with a melodic minor seventh descending, resolved by a major sixth.

These illustrate another important tendency in melodic writing during the nineteenth century: angularity, resulting from moving about in the more complicated sonorities which often became a matter of course in the Wagnerian welter. These seem to be of two main types: first, the use of more complicated chords within the key (sevenths, ninths, elevenths and thirteenths) and, second, tones from altered chords, tones not in the key signature and the moving from one altered chord to another or to different alterations of the same chord before resolution. Melodies were not just harmonized, they often resulted by inducing lines from a complex of sonorities and scoring them with extra edge or weight.

These were not really new ideas; they had appeared in music before. The point is that what had been a rare thing became the practice of almost everyone.

The tonality of a melody is of utmost importance for several reasons: 1) the key can cause the voice or instrument to use tones which are brighter or darker, according to the acoustics of that instrument—some songs are transposed to accommodate voices of different ranges, but the piano part (as well as the "color") is thereby changed considerably, mainly where black-white keys fall; 2) the composer may modulate within the melody, with surprising changes of key at times; 3) keys may be used which do not have any real signature, but are logically an outgrowth of the context; 4) some composers, performers and listeners associate different colors with different keys—this is an individual matter and, although much more research is needed in this area, there appears to be a great difference of opinion, even among famous musicians; 5) many composers use well-known "favorite" keys for a certain kind of expression —Mozart and E-flat, Beethoven and C minor, Brahms and D (or B♭) major, etc.; 6) near the end of the century composers all but lost key in the normal sense, either through the freer use of chromatic harmony or a revival of interest in the modes. Modes are an extremely important aspect of music which many musicians do not appreciate, since they have not been exposed to them in their training, but they have had to play modal works from time to time.

The renewed interest in modality in the late nineteenth and early twentieth centuries can be ascribed to the following: 1) melodies and harmonies with a "different" sound, a truly romantic desire for faraway places in time and space; 2) the nationalistic interest in folk modes; and 3) a new interest in traditional music of the Roman Catholic Church by composers and musicologists.

Harmony is also of great importance. *Any melody can be harmonized in many different ways.* A study of several harmonizations of the same Lutheran chorale tune will show this, or a comparison of the many arrangements of some "standard" popular songs such as "Star Dust." A given melody need not be harmonized according to the "implied" harmony. It would be criminal, however, to change the harmony of a masterpiece in any way, since the choice of progression, voicing, complexity, etc., is an integral part of the work. One fine sublety of great art music is the differentiation of harmonies associated with a given theme as it appears at different times in the work. A fascinating example of this is found in the Schubert *Quartet in G*, D. 887. Note how the triad color changes, and how other harmonic uses vary; Schubert is no mere copyist:

(a) Exposition

(b) RECAPITULATION

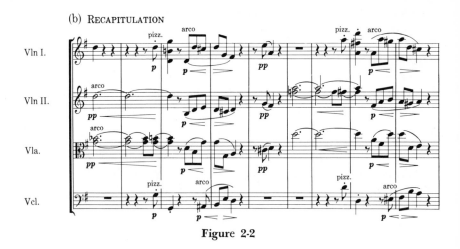

Figure 2-2

Also in Beethoven's *Piano Sonata No. 26 in E-flat,* Op. 81a (The Farewell):

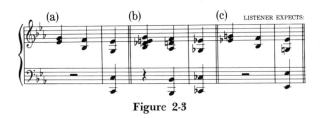

Figure 2-3

This factor of changing harmonies is an important feature of variation technique.

Another facet of melodic writing which became very important during the nineteenth century was the use of subtle markings for dynamics, nuances, articulations and qualifying terms scattered throughout the printed page. The Baroque and earlier periods either did not see fit to include them, or else did not even think about them. Some of the first attempts to tell the performer something other than what was "obvious" by context were probably done by Giovanni Gabrielli in the late sixteenth century. The idea did take, and many composers were at least including the markings *piano* or *forte* during the Baroque. The Mannheimers were among the very first to attempt a gradation of dynamics through a sign or expression to the player. This factor of changing dynamics had been handled through orchestration, adding or taking out the number of players, by organ registration, by division of the chorus, by the use of keyboards constructed for contrast (as in the organ and harpsichord) and in the natural crescendo of the voice and most wind instruments as the melody rose in pitch. (With the double reed family the effect is opposite, the tone growing weaker as the pitch rises.) These methods of changing the loudness, however, were mostly sudden changes—or "terrace" dynamics, as they are often called. Any gradual change in loudness must have been in the sensitive playing or singing of the performers, and was done at the player's own fancy. This is another of the many paradoxes of the Romantic composer: as he strove for freedom of expression he tended to allow the performer *less* freedom.

The following example, from the prelude to Wagner's *Tristan und Isolde*, will show how much more editing was done by the middle and late nineteenth-century composer, and how it went to the extreme of telling the performer exactly how to play almost every note. Note the many directions to the players.

Figure 2-4

This sort of editing was done on new editions of older music, and often resulted in nineteenth-century versions of music even as old as Palestrina. The editions of J. S. Bach and Handel printed in the nineteenth century were especially strange in this regard. While each age tends to re-create the past in its own image, one should not be too surprised to find this at the time in music history when the percentage of older music being performed was increasing; hence, it was necessary to bring this music "up to date" and put it into a form which the performers could understand. We are actually just as bad today in our attempts to be purists, in trying to reconstruct a performance practice which has been lost forever.[2]

The performers, then, had a more difficult problem: they had to play what was printed! This required a musician of considerable technical control. The ability of a performer in the past was judged by how well he could improvise, as well as his tone and technique. The work itself became the important consideration, although there was—as there should be—room for the interpretation of the individual artist.

Another factor important in melodic writing is phrase structure. The romantic in his striving for the unusual often came up with irregular phrases, longer or shorter than the standard four-bar phrase which seemed to be the norm much of the time in the Classical Period, especially in the music of the less inspired composers. There were many reasons for this desire for irregularity other than just novelty. A few of these were: less dependence on the rhythms of poetry, even in vocal music, but especially in instrumental music; less regular poetry, since poetry also was affected by the romantic age; less dependence on stock harmonic progressions in which the four-bar phrase is almost a requirement; many elisions;[3] and the element of surprise, especially in story-telling music.

Most elementary theory texts present rules and principles regarding melodic writing and many point out that the best melodies have certain intangible characteristics. This, of course, is at the root of what *art* is in the first place: the communication of a subjective idea in a manner comprehensible to a sensitive other person through the medium of the art in question, which can be expressed *exactly* in no other way. An inspired melody certainly is this! Great music, to be truly great, requires a great composer, a great performer *and* a great listener.

As Leonard Bernstein says:

"Meaning" in music has preoccupied aestheticians, musicians, and philosophers for centuries. The treatises pile up, and usually succeed only in adding more words to an already obscure business. In all this mass of material we can discern four levels of meaning in music:

1. Narrative-literary meanings (*Till Eulenspiegel, The Sorcerer's Apprentice,* etc.).
2. Atmospheric pictorial meanings (*La Mer, Pictures at an Exhibition,* etc.).

3. Affective-reactive meanings such as triumph, pain, wistfulness, regret, cheerfulness, melancholy, apprehension—most typical of nineteenth-century romanticism.

4. Purely musical meanings.

Of these, the last is the only one worthy of *musical* analysis. The first three may involve associations which are good to know (if the composer intended them); otherwise they are concerned only with arbitrary justification, or prettifying for the commercial reasons mentioned before. If we are to try to "explain" music, we must explain the *music*, not the whole array of appreciators' extramusical notions which have grown like parasites around it.[4]

Aaron Copland expresses similar ideas in his *What to Listen for in Music*, where he delineates three listening planes: the sensuous, the expressive and the sheerly musical.[5]

The length of melodies is an interesting aspect of melodic studies. In classical music one often finds beautifully balanced phrases which become beautifully balanced periods, in total becoming a completely balanced movement. The composer sometimes would unify through a rhythmic figure, a melodic inflection and, often to a fault, the use of sequence. Many of the best melodies can be found in the operas of the period, and instrumental music often reflected this aspect in quasi-vocal linear writing for a solo instrument, or perhaps a section of violins. Composers do use certain formulas, even Mozart; and we are again aware of the *ars combinatoria* in operation. Szabolsci's *A History of Melody* discusses this in some detail (pp. 135-139). Later on in the nineteenth century one finds very long melodies which, although maintaining a kind of periodicity, seem to soar. In the opening theme of Bruckner's *Seventh Symphony*, note the extreme length, pitch gamut and great expressive nature.

Figure 2-5

The success of such melodic writing depends to a large degree on the richness of harmony, which is somehow more than just accompaniment. Bruckner often presents themes in pairs or even threes; one would be complete without the other(s). This is the exposition of the second theme from the first movement of the *Fourth Symphony*; note that there are four different melodies.

Figure 2-6

The use of melodic formulas was not confined to pre-nineteenth century. Luigi Dallapiccola's article "Words and Music in Nineteenth Century Italian Opera," is an interesting discussion of such a theory: that the melodic "lie" of an aria reflects the emotional rise to a climax in the typical quatrain or logical expansions thereof. While the arias of Verdi are specifically cited, Bellini, Donizetti and Rossini, and even Mozart, are shown to follow the same principle. Some paragraphs from the article are especially important:

About thirty years ago, when I was asked by Edward J. Dent whether I knew any Italian treatise describing the principles of the composition of arias in Italian opera, I had to answer in the negative. Now, however, I believe that there existed at least a tradition for composing arias, one perpetuated orally and by example.

I should like to consider here what the poetic quatrain offered to the composer of the Italian melodrama as a basis for the construction of operatic forms, with specific reference to arias, ariosi, and cavatinas.[6]

. . . Regardless of whether there existed a literary tradition that, consciously or unconsciously, determined the aria-form in Italian melodrama, there are certainly an immense number of *closed quatrains* in poetry (*i.e.*, quatrains ending with a full stop)—an immense number of rhymed quatrains in Italian and French, from Dante to Baudelaire—in which the second line merely continues the first, increasing the emotional level but little. The climax appears in the third line; and in the last, the conclusion brings diminishing intensity.[7]

It is indeed astonishing that there is both a great variety of actual melody and yet great similarity from aria to aria. Perhaps this is one reason the audience could go home whistling tunes from new operas: they had so much in common with the old tunes! The conclusion of the argument states the matter so well:

But the composer's genius, the "genius of the dramatic accent," according to Busoni's beautiful characterization, has surmounted the incredible situation, the absurd language, the lame syntax, the pathos of the formalistic style of the Italian melodrama.[8]

Unlike the Bruckner examples, the length of these melodies depends on the poetic structure of the text. It can be seen, then, that there is a divergence which parallels to a certain extent the "double mainstream" idea of nineteenth-century music. Some music still uses poetic structure even when purely instrumental, while other music has more and more the characteristics of prose: such as the use of unequal, asymmetrical segments of a through-composed nature even though the smallest elements could be related. In the case of Wagner and many other composers since, there is a tendency away from regular periodicity toward a more nearly continuous melody, perhaps achieved only in works such as Schoenberg's *Erwartung*.

The principal theme of the finale of Brahms's *Double Concerto* is a good example. It seems to be continuously generated, even where actual cadences occur.

Without a text or a simulation of poetic structures the composer often does something similar by building themes according to well-established chord progressions, Many different melodies have identical chord progressions, which is a kind of converse to the principle that a melody can be harmonized in different ways (the same harmony used to accompany many different melodies).

Another form of melody is that derived from a melody heard earlier or to be heard later: *i.e.*, the outlines which come from variation, development, enlargement, reduction or other manipulations of melodic material—pitch, duration, tempo, timbre or articulation. A good term often used is *thematic transformation*. In an important book on the subject Reti calls it "thematic process." Music throughout its history has seldom been free from these devices, and each age adds its own ideas. Two separate types emerge, the same two quasi-extremes which seem to be present in almost every discussion: 1) exact, literal; or 2) those similar in "spirit." Contrapuntal treatments demand a more accurate imitation, while developments in homophonic forms are far less literal although often suggested by a contrapuntal device. In the contrapuntal form the composer wants the listener to notice the imitation, while in the homophonic form it is necessary only to show a feeling of belonging to the whole—musical unity. In discussing Schumann's *Kinderscenen*, Op. 15, Reti states:

Schumann at this period of his production especially cultivated a compositional type in which small pieces are accumulated to form a great whole. *Carnaval, Davidsbündler, Kreisleriana,* are other examples in this direction. In one instance, in his *opus 13*, the *Études symphoniques*, he even termed the pieces "variations." However, the *Études symphoniques* can hardly be regarded as much closer to the outspoken variation form than the *Kinderscenen*. Actually, all these works lie somewhere between mere suites on the one hand and genuine variations on the other.[9]

Another converse is now apparent: one can write melody which outlines certain harmony, but one can also stand a theme "on its head" and derive a chord from the tones of the melody which may not necessarily be a common chord. We have stated earlier (see the Introduction), and will state from time to time, that one active aspect of Romanticism was to go out of bounds and attempt to "beat" the rules of strict harmony and thereby create sonorities not known before. From about 1859 on, this was especially in evidence.

In the latter half of the nineteenth century the avoidance of poetry-like periodicity in musical utterance was evidenced in cadence evasion, and even in the avoidance of elision. The music seems to float, as it were, or even drift, as if not moored to the pier of tonality and the hitching posts of regular cadences. Not until the twentieth century do we find a composer writing an *entire* work in this way; the Romantic composer used drifting harmony only at times; and sometimes these cadenceless passages lasted for some time, but there was almost always an allusion eventually to some kind of a final cadence—if not of the movement, then at least of the section.

At the beginning of Chapter I the lack of acceptance of music by the masses was mentioned. The common man missed the regular cadence; some musicians did too, and at first this kind of music was called "Romantic" in a snide way. Robert Schumann was even moved to say, "the philistine, to be sure, mixes everything together and calls that which he doesn't understand 'romantic.' "[10] Much new music of any period, even today, suffers from this—the composer is simply ahead of the public (and he should be, or we would all still be doing war dances or rain songs in stone-age surroundings). How normal Wagner sounds to us now! While his music contains harmonic and rhythmic problems as well as melodic, I must point out again that music at any moment is a summation, or better still, an integration of all musical and psychological elements—a summation which, so often, is greater than the sum of all its parts. A composer's real sound world, then, is the summation of the actual sounds at any given moment, tempered by what was just heard and what comes next. It obviously makes a difference if you *know* what comes next instead of being surprised. We have in music the delicious possibility of the unexpected expected and the expected unexpected.

The *actual* sounds emanating from the sound source are of great interest to the professional musical artist. It is a serious oversimplification to say that a C is a C or a major chord is a major chord, for instance. The exact octave, the exact tone color, the exact voicing, the exact tessitura (remember that a listener can have a tessitura too: he can become too accustomed to a sound; we all have had the experience of "hearing" a sound only when it ceases), and variables such as intensity and changes in intensity are all important. A "simple" major triad can be represented in thousands of different ways. In addition to the well-known inversions, remember that there are $3 \times 2 \times 1$ possibilities for voicing in all. The six basic voicings of any triad are shown in Figure 2-7. One can derive many other possibilities through doublings and

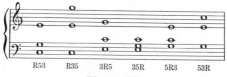

R53   R35   3R5   35R   5R3   53R

Figure 2-7

spacings. The important point is that the *actual sound* is determined as much by the placement of the chord tones above the bass as by the inversions.

The above example is abstract, and would have entirely different results in differing contexts of timbre and progression.

As I have said from time to time, our habit of naming something and thinking that we have therefore analyzed it is not very satisfactory! There are so many passages which would have exactly the same chord analysis, but are obviously different.

In the next chapters specific melodic practices of most of the most important composers will be discussed in some detail. Melody was supremely important in the nineteenth century, so an understanding of various applications of the principles already delineated and others to be discussed when applicable are of utmost importance. Do not feel that you will no longer love a melody if you know how it was built; chances are you will think even better of it. Since melody will be the first facet to be discussed in connection with specific composers, it is essential that some introductory and other comments be kept in mind as one studies other aspects of a composer's work later in the book.

Notes

1. Timbre, or quality, has probably always been important. A good musician obviously would favor the sound of one lute or violin over others, or the singing quality of one person's voice over someone else's. There was also a consideration of timbre in the choice of instruments in orchestration prior to the nineteenth century. The important point is that many melodies and instrumental passages were conceived directly for the instruments indicated in the score. Arrangements are seldom satisfactory; the original conception, in the case of the great masterpieces, is almost always better. The orchestrator after Berlioz had a guide, and the *actual sound* (the *color* of the sound) assumed great importance. The student is referred to Alfred Einstein's *Music in the Romantic Era*, p. 7 *et seq.*, for an interesting discussion of this question. Timbre is the summation of overtones, and is physically comparable to color.

2. Even with recordings, performance practices of times as recent as fifty years ago are difficult to reconstruct exactly. It is obvious that in the centuries before recordings accuracy becomes all but impossible—important treatises such as the Johann J. Quantz's *Versuch einer Anweisung die Flöte traversiere zu spielen*, 1752; Leopold Mozart's *Versuch einer grundlichen Violinschule*, 1756; C. P. E. Bach's *Versuch über die wahre Art das Klavier zu spielen*, 1753 and 1762 notwithstanding. These are important treatises which are not only method books for the instrument in the title but are important source books for performance practices of the period. Even with these, the actual sounds are lost forever, especially that intangible quality which is provided by the personality of the player. Schoenberg, in a famous letter to Fritz Stiedry July 31, 1930, pointed

out that what the Bach organ was like and how it was played we know not at all. That statement is a little too strong in view of modern research, but there is a sizable grain of truth: we really do not know *exactly* the level of subtlety befitting the greatest artists. We must always remember that our audiences are alive *today!*

This is not to be construed to mean that ignorance of excellent research should prevail, and that we should perform all old music "the way we feel." Quite to the contrary, faithfulness to the spirit of the times is essential; faithfulness to the letter can be ludicrous. If we were to be literal, we should play Beethoven's symphonies with out-of-tune and cumbersome woodwinds, all viola players should be people who for some reason or other can't play the violin, the brasses should still be crooked, the conductor (as did Habeneck) should conduct from a first violin part, the hall should not be air-conditioned nor electric lights used, and above all, the orchestra should not have been rehearsed. This is in all seriousness a very real problem when performing music of the past; what we are actually doing is throwing back upon history our insistence upon faithfulness to the text, even to the days when the printed text was but a guide for the performer. The student would enjoy reading Gerald Abraham's *One Hundred Years of Music*, where in the opening pages the low state of performance is discussed. As in all matters, the important thing is to know where to draw the line. One mark of an educated musician is to know what the very best musicians feel is important.

3. In general, elision means cutting. Its specific usage in music refers most often to a melody note or a chord which not only ends one phrase but also begins the next. This obviously keeps the music moving. Here is a good example from Schubert's *Impromptu*, Op. 142, No. 3, D. 935.

Figure 2-8

Note that the D downbeat of the third bar is the resolution of the E-flat of the previous bar and still starts the consequent of the phrase, and the device is used at the end of the phrase. Classical music has many such devices also, but the nineteenth century used them with greater frequency.

This theme, by the way, is from Schubert's *Rosamunde* (third entr'acte), and appears in C major in the *String Quartet in A minor*, Op. 29, No. 1, D. 804, which is historically his most important use of it.

4. Leonard Bernstein, *The Joy of Music*. Copyright © 1959 by Leonard Bernstein. Reprinted by permission of Simon & Schuster, Inc., p. 16.

5. Aaron Copland, *What to Listen for in Music* (New York: McGraw-Hill Book Company, Revised Ed., 1957), p. 9.

6. Luigi Dallapiccola, "Words and Music in Nineteenth Century Italian Opera," *Perspectives of New Music*, 5:1, Fall-Winter 1966, p. 121.

7. *Op. cit.*, p. 126.

8. *Op. cit.*, p. 133.

9. Rudolph Reti, *The Thematic Process in Music* (New York: The Macmillan Company, 1951), pp. 31-32.

10. There are many allusions to this statement of Schumann in the literature. The original source is *Neue Zeitschrift für Musik*, XVI, 1842, 142, GSK II, 72. My immediate source is Plantinga's article "Schumann's View of Romantic," *Musical Quarterly*, April 1966, Vol. LII, No. 2, p. 224.

CHAPTER III

MELODY IN BEETHOVEN, SCHUBERT AND SCHUMANN

Beethoven

IT IS IMPOSSIBLE TO derive a set of rigorous conditions which would tell us all about Beethoven's thematic material. Beethoven did work according to certain principles but these varied, even in one work.

Therefore, several important Beethoven works will be cited which illustrate non-classical aspects in particular, and which can be applied to most composers. I shudder at the thought of classifying any master's melodic practice, since there is the danger of one's assuming that this is what the composer always did.

1. Beethoven almost always shaped and reshaped his themes until they were finalized to his satisfaction. While not all of Beethoven's great melodies have come down to us in these steps of metamorphosis, his best works frequently came into being in this way, even though we do not have all of the sketches. His less durable works seem to be those written in haste without much revision. Beethoven probably knew deep down which works were of lasting value, and which ones would be suddenly very popular and then fade.

2. Many of Beethoven's themes are "hymnic" (chordal) in style, not unlike a chorale but usually more massive and conceived for the particular timbre which was to perform it.

3. Many begin with a texture like a hymn, and the melody is accompanied by imaginative figurations of the harmony.

4. Some are shaped by the limitations of certain instruments, such as this theme from the *Fifth Piano Concerto* ("Emperor"), first movement. The intervallic relationships of this melody are often found in orchestral music—the so-called "horn fifths."

Hn.

Figure 3-1

This theme is treated differently by the rest of the orchestra, but is very characteristic of music playable on natural horns.

5. Fragments of melody are often tossed about the orchestra antiphonally. The first movement of the *Fifth Symphony* is almost entirely structured on the idea of antiphony, almost to the point of hocket, but with new power and sweep.

6. Beethoven sometimes borrowed a melody or a melody type. Some of the melodies taken for variation are almost ridiculous in their musical paucity (*Diabelli Variations,* Op. 120). Others are among the most sublime ever penned: for example, his variations on Mozart's theme from *Don Giovanni* for two oboes and English horn, "Là ci darem la mano." The Razumovsky quartets use folk material, as do his settings of Irish and Scotch songs, to say nothing of at least two uses of the tune we now know as "God Save the Queen (King)" or "America" which he used for a charming set of variations for the piano and as the basis for the most interesting section of the *Battle Symphony (Wellington's Victory).* Beethoven in a sense borrowed from himself, in the remarkable history of the common thematic material used in the ballet *Prometheus,* the so-called *Prometheus* or *Eroica Variations,* Op. 35, and the *Eroica Symphony.*

The use of *semplice* melodies in the *Violin Concerto* and in the *Ninth Symphony* recall tunes from Dutch hymnody. Lest the student wrongly think that Beethoven always used lesser tunes for variations, let him note at least two occasions when the theme was a high point even for Beethoven. (See the slow movement of Opp. 12, No. 1 or 57.)

7. Beethoven could be very ornate and expressive at the same time. (Adagio of *Ninth Symphony,* first violin part.)

8. Certain themes can only be called declamatory. (Slow movement of *Fourth Piano Concerto.*)

9. Frequently themes have characteristic rhythmic mottoes.

In conclusion, one of Beethoven's greatest attributes as a composer was the great variety of his utterances. Beethoven wrote almost every kind of melody possible. Melody alone is not enough, however. One of the most important aspects of any musical work is the way in which the melody is worked out, developed, varied, harmonized or changed in any number of ways. Beethoven was one of the first composers to realize the great musical value of development sections in extended works. His orchestral and chamber works reveal a great mastery of melodic writing for specific instruments which is idiomatic and interesting, and, in many works, displays advances in the technique of the instrument and certainly in the treatment of the human voice. Beethoven's deafness is a puzzling factor since he obviously heard his most advanced works only in his mind. One wonders, if he had heard the miserable orchestras in most cities, if he would have written as he did![1] William McNaught[2] asserts that Beethoven was the first great composer to emotionalize instrumental melody in such a way that it still keeps an intensity for us today. One aspect was Beethoven's habit of fragmenting a theme and tossing it about in the orchestra, not merely for fun, but to show the fragment in new lights and colors. Many of Beethoven's melodies will stand alone, but most of them are a part of a much larger whole, a truly integrated summation. Other composers may have written prettier tunes, but few ever built such mighty structures of tone.

Schubert

Schubert's great gift for melodic writing is well known, but it would be a mistake for one to assume that all of his melodies are vocal and that they have no instrumental effectiveness. Many of Schubert's songs did find their way into important instrumental works—*Die Forelle* (the song and the quintet) and *Der Tod und das Mädchen* (the song and the string quartet); also see the *Wanderer Fantasy*, and the lovely theme from *Rosamunde*, which Schubert cast at least twice in other forms (as a small piano piece and as a theme for some variations in the *Quartet in A Minor*, Op. 24, No. 1 (D. 804).[3] These are among Schubert's most important works, especially the string quartet which has the movement based on *Der Tod und das Mädchen*. These great melodies have the marvelous quality of being able to be sung and played with equal effectiveness and, as the *Forellen* quintet shows, they can be played well at the keyboard along with a sustaining instrument.

We unfortunately do not have with Schubert voluminous sketchbooks (as with Beethoven), but we can assume from a practical standpoint that Schubert must have written his melodies spontaneously and with little revision, since he wrote so much music in his all-too-short life (1797-1828). One is awestruck when standing in the library before the volumes of the Schubert or Mozart *Gesellschaft*, wondering how one man could do so much and have so much of it be of the highest quality! The mental prowess of these young giants must have been as prodigious as their inspiration was divine.

Schubert wrote his share of hymnic melodies; *Der Tod und das Mädchen* is a good example, as are many of his simple strophic songs.

Schubert's figurated accompaniments are extremely fascinating. While they are always well within the scope of tonal harmony, they use those principles with great imagination. Often the figurations in the songs provide the harmony, double the singer heterophonically and at the same time create a marvelous atmosphere for the song. *Gretchen am Spinnrade* is one of the best; the piano part certainly suggests the whirring of the spinning-wheel and also provides the harmony. The figure in *Die Forelle* is suggestive of an active fish in a clear brook, or it could be just an abstract figure. The student would gain much from studying the other songs of Schubert, to see and hear how these principles are applied again and again.

The opening statement of the *Great C Major Symphony*, D. 944, is not only a great theme, but it is an example of how an imaginative composer was able to get more notes from the natural, non-valved French horn by using notes which can be produced only through altering the pitch, by inserting the hand in the bell. In the *Unfinished Symphony*, D. 759, the repeated sixteenth-note figure in the violins is an effective background for the almost fragmented woodwind statements. Only strings can play this kind of figuration in a way which would be appropriate for the woodwind melodies. While this is not formal counterpoint, it is nevertheless a good example of three separate and distinct musical elements occurring at the same time.

Schubert rarely borrowed melodies from other sources—he didn't need to! He borrowed from himself, as we have noted above, and wrote variations on *Die Freunde von Salamanka* (1815) (a duet from a Singspiel), and a theme from *Rosamunde* for the *Quartet in A Minor*; this same theme is also used for the piano *Impromptu*, Op. 142, No. 3, D. 935. The minuet of the quartet also starts with a quotation from an earlier song. Schubert would occasionally borrow a *style*, such as the Overtures in the Italian style and many melodies which seem to resemble German folk songs.

In Schubert there is not the great differentiation of style that we find in Beethoven—he didn't really have time. There is still a great variety, with perhaps the greatest being in the songs. Schubert's songs encompassed his entire career; and although the growth of a great artist was apparent, he was capable of producing masterpieces at a very tender age. Although *Gretchen am Spinnrade* dates from 1814, that was still his 118th work!

Melody in Schubert is very much influenced by the harmony, especially his shift from minor to major and vice versa. He also loved to use the

Plate II

An evening of Schubert. Painting by Moritz von Schwind (*Courtesy The Bettmann Archive, N.Y.*).

mediant relationship (keys up or down a third) and the Neapolitan triad. This latter device is the altered supertonic in first inversion, a major triad originally formed by lowering the second scale degree in minor— in C tonalities, Db F Ab, which moves to the dominant or dominant seventh. Schubert was fond of this progression, and it affected the melodic writing at cadence points.

Schubert's music was quite new, considering when it was written, but it was little known to the general public until after the 1860's; therefore, it had little or no influence—as Einstein says, ". . . he left no successors." His music was published bit by bit, but was known by only a small circle. Very important was Schumann's discovery of the *Great C Major Symphony* and the performance of it for the first time in Leipzig by Mendelssohn's Gewandhaus orchestra (in 1839). It met great enthusiasm, quite unlike the first attempts at a performance in Vienna during the composer's lifetime, when the work was dismissed as being "too difficult and too long," among other uncomplimentary remarks. Other conductors and officials in other cities said the same, but posterity has proved Schubert right and the smaller men wrong! Schumann's famous remark about Schubert's "heavenly length" was made in connection with this symphony, but he did not mean that the piece was too long, as some have said.[4] Too long for *whom?* Schubert's mark on musical history is indelible, and he is remembered more for the sheer musical value of his compositions than for being a strong force changing the course of history—as was Beethoven. The Schubert cause was given great impetus through the splendid though lengthy article by Sir George Grove in the earlier editions of his famous Dictionary—this was the longest article in the entire work!

With a tragic figure such as Schubert, one can find many touching incidents. Goethe, whose poetry was set by Schubert in over eighty songs, did not understand Schubert's music and was quite vocal in his praise for the far less talented Zelter. Schubert even had the misfortune of having the only copy of his opera *Claudine von Villa Bella* (to a text by Goethe) used for kindling a fire! This happened in 1848, long after Schubert's death (in 1828). In Einstein's opinion this work was Schubert's operatic masterpiece.[5] The first act still survives for study. How unfortunate that tragedy can still happen after the man himself is gone!

Some of Schubert's songs show characterizations by means of register. One of the best examples is *Der Erlkönig*: note the lines for the child, the father and the Erlking. Each character is suggested by the "lie" of the voice when that character is speaking.

Schubert's melodic writing is more direct than Beethoven's, and therefore does not have the ornate qualities we often find in adagios, but there are some in the slow variations. Themes resembling chants are often used in his songs as well.

In conclusion, Schubert's melodies are unique as they stand, not as dependent on treatment as those by Beethoven or by some other composer. They are, however, more greatly enhanced by their harmonic subtlety than by subtlety of orchestration—as compared to Berlioz, Liszt, Wagner or even Mendelssohn. We can see Schubert's great worth by comparing his settings of poems with those of other composers, in addition to different settings he made himself. He apparently was very well taught by Salieri, and in addition was a somewhat experienced orchestra player, but he was never a strong force in the professional music world, as were men such as Spohr. That his music is so highly regarded today is a real testimony to the old saw that "talent will out."

Schumann

Schumann's melodies are extremely engaging. They have great expressive qualities and ingenious technical structure. Schumann makes use of the *soggetto cavato*: a "carved out" melody making use of implied musical letters in a name, poem or inscription. Such a device is as old as the solmization syllables of the Guidonian hexachord (Guido d'Arezzo, ca. 990-ca. 1050); it was frequently used by composers in the Netherlands schools (Josquin's mass *Hercules Dux Ferrarie*, for example), and had a strong renewal of interest through the use by J. S. Bach in the unfinished portion of *The Art of Fugue*—where he used the spelling of the name BACH as a musical subject (in German, B-flat, A, C, B; B natural in German is H). The Bach motive was used time and time again throughout the nineteenth century, and is still in use today.

Schumann's *soggetti cavati* are found in *Theme on the Name Abegg with Variations*, Op. 1, 1830-1832, and in the *Carnaval*, Op. 9, of 1834-

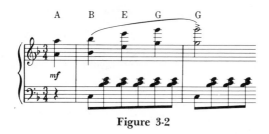

Figure 3-2

1835, which he subtitled in French: *Carnaval, Scènes migonnes sur 4 Notes*. He discovers that the home town of a girlfriend, Ernestine von Fricker, and the musical letters in his own name have something in common. In German S could stand for Es, which is E-flat, and similarly As is A-flat. This leaves SCHumAnn, and ASCH or AsCH. These are

Figure 3-3

readily seen other than in the "Sphinxes" in the midst of the suite, and they are cleverly used in permutation, transposition and other musical manipulations. Note that, in Figure 3-4a, the first four notes spell ASCH.

Figure 3-4a

In Figure 3-4b, note the uses of the "Dancing Letters."

Presto ♩ = 84   SCHUMANN: *Carnaval*, Op. 9; "Lettres Dansantes"

Figure 3-4b

Schumann also pays homage to Bach in the *Six Fugues on the Name of BACH* for pedal piano or organ, 1845, Op. 60. Schumann's friend, the Danish composer Niels Gade (1817-1890), was honored at least three times (the *Northern Song* for piano is the most famous example). Schumann also wrote an article for the *New Magazine* (*Neue Zeitschrift für Musik*) where he not only pointed out that GADE are the open strings of the violin, but also that the letters could be expressed as a puzzle. (See Schauffler's *Florestan, the Life and Work of Schumann*, p. 291.)

Schumann also made considerable use of a descending-fifths motive which Schauffler[6] called the "Haydn source motive," almost always referring to Clara.[7] Schumann, however, did not need such given melodies—most of his are heaven-sent.

Schumann did not stoop to the current practice of fantastic variations on the latest opera hit, as did many of his contemporaries. Schumann did, however, make etudes from Paganini caprices which were technically eclipsed by those of Liszt.

In the works of Schumann we find beautiful melody after melody, truly inspired through their whole treatment: the rhythm, harmony, phrase structure and a definite psychological state—exemplified by the split-personality inherent in Schumann's own indications of "Florestan,"

Plate III

Clara Schumann, nee Wieck (1819-1896), wife of Robert Schumann
and famed pianist and interpreter of her husband's works (*Courtesy
The Bettmann Archive, N.Y.*).

the heroic romantic; "Eusebius," the dreamy romantic; and sometimes
"Raro," the philosophical romantic. However, Schumann did not always
admire the appellation "romantic," but his literary orientation, the influence of Jean Paul Richter and the subjective qualities in his music
make him one of the *true* romantics. Schumann also disliked the Philistine,[8] and created the "Society of David" to fight against the commonplace
sameness of so much music of the period (music we rarely, if ever, hear
now). Also, as Schauffler quotes:

. . . to express contrasting points of view about art, it seemed not unfitting to
invent antithetical artistic characters, of which Florestan and Eusebius were the
most important, with Master Raro as intermediary. This "Davidsbündler" idea
runs like a red thread through the paper (the N. Mag. for M.), humorously
combining *"Warheit"* and *"Dichtung."*[9]

Riemann (see Schauffler, p. 80) made the discovery that if you join
together the Schumanns' names you get: claRARObert. All of this could
be interesting coincidence, but it makes sense in view of the propensity
of Schumann to give his favorite (and not-so-favorite) people nicknames.
Clara was "Chiarina," Mendelssohn was "Felix Meritas" and G. W. Fink
was "Knif," among others.

Leon Plantinga's paper in the *Musical Quarterly* for April 1966, Vol. LII, No. 2, entitled "Schumann's View of Romantic" points out the important place of Schumann's writings in the *Neue Zeitschrift* as a source of the concepts of "romanticism" and "classicism" as they appeared to some of the best musicians of the 1830's. There was a rival pen and paper, G. W. Fink and the *Allegemeine musikalische Zeitung*, where the works of Chopin, Liszt, Hiller, Schumann and others were referred to with contempt as a "romantic movement." Schumann later, however, was not even mentioned—the epitome of adverse criticism. The earliest battles were fought in the field of piano music, and the idea of any kind of "romantic revolt" was not in Schumann's mind at all. He was convinced (and so am I) that the best music of the period was a continuation of the great tradition in German music which had actually begun with J. S. Bach (not the culmination, as some would like to believe), and continued with Mozart, Beethoven and, of course, himself. The veneration of Bach in the nineteenth century would, in itself, be an influence in many ways. It is true, of course, that J. S. Bach was the last of the great contrapuntists, but this is not the whole story by any means. Equal temperament (in which all semitones are the same size) was firmly established, and a harmonic language which in Bach took Baroque forms and in the Classical Period took on the newer classical forms—especially the sonata-allegro. It is significant that Mozart and Beethoven both knew the *Well-Tempered Clavier* and could not help being influenced by it. The influence of Bach on Mendelssohn is well-known.

Schumann was one of the first successful composers of exquisite small pieces. He could be child-like, but he was never childish. The short piano pieces for and about children are found mostly in the *Scenes from Childhood*, Op. 15, of 1838 and the *Album for the Young*, Op. 68, of 1848. Some of the titles were placed at the time of composition, and were the result of a literary impetus which was important in much of Schumann's music. This was always of importance in the songs, which are sometimes short and folklike, sometimes long. Many are among the best examples of the German through-composed Lied. Schumann could also produce themes and melodies of many kinds which are appropriate to large instrumental works—themes which lend themselves to development or cyclic treatment, as in the piano concerto.

As an example of a great melody in a small work note the contour of *Träumerei*, one of the world's best-loved melodies.

It soars slowly through the compass of an eleventh and then takes its time about coming down to earth again, only to soar once again in slow motion. It is sadly happy, wistful, pensive, full of just plain music. Schumann makes the most of non-harmonic tones; each one is expressive, each sound is voiced with richness and there are just enough notes. Not

SCHUMANN: *Scenes from Childhood,* Op. 15; "Träumerei"

SCHUMANN: *Album for the Young,* Op. 68; "Romanze"

Figure 3-5a, b

too many artists have been able to capture these universal delights. The effectiveness is, of course, dependent on all musical elements, but the melodic aspects of these pieces are worthy of study, since one can find here an abundance of melodic freshness missing in reams of music by lesser men who criticized Schumann. Later composers have tried to attain Schumann's level in music for the young pianist, but, aside from Bartók and a few others, few have succeeded.

In some of his larger works Schumann can be tiresome, not in the melodic writing but in the connective tissue. This is especially true in his symphonies, which are not well orchestrated (mainly because of too much unison doubling), but they contain some of the finest music ever penned—another paradox! The adagio from the *C Major Symphony* is beautiful; note the expressive descending sevenths. This theme is given

Figure 3-6

its most touching setting when doubled at the octave. This device is used by many composers, not always with effectiveness; Schumann's passage work in some of his orchestral music would have been better without the doubling.

His small piano pieces even show the value of octave doubling: such as the *Little Romance*, No. 19 from the *Album for the Young* (see Fig. 3-5b). The difficult octave fluttering in *Papillons* is very effective. In chamber works Schumann obtains a powerful effect from this kind of octave doubling.

Schumann's songs are special, as are Schubert's. Since harmony is of utmost importance in Schumann's *Lieder*, they will be discussed in greater detail in the chapter on harmony and in the one on the song. Suffice it to say here that Schumann was a man of letters; no other songwriter has ever had a greater feeling for the poet's pen than he.

Many of Schumann's songs employ expressive leaps which became common *after* his time. Note this line from the second song of *Frauenliebe und Leben*:

Figure 3-7

It has been pointed out elsewhere in this book that the nineteenth century attached importance to the downward leap of the minor seventh as an expressive device. From Wagner's *Ring* (*Die Götterdämmerung, Act III*):

Figure 3-8

The next excerpt, from the last part of Tchaikovsky's *None But the Lonely Heart*, shows the main theme in the piano and a countermelody in the vocal line, a common device of the period.

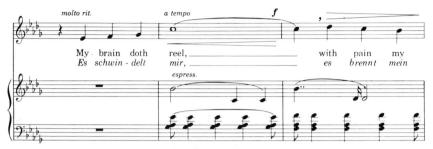

Figure 3-9

From the same composer's *Manfred Symphony*:

Figure 3-10

From Liszt's *Faust Symphony*:

Figure 3-11

Schumann likes to leap within the same chord and use the more expressive leap if the chord is a seventh. Sometimes an expressive leap occurs on a tone from the previous harmony, but he changes the chord in a surprising way. The great *Piano Quintet*, Op. 44, begins with bold leaps.

The harmony is also worthy of mention, since it dictates the voice-leading. The D-flat is a seventh, making the tonic chord a V_7—dangerous this early, since it can make a modulation to the key of the subdominant. However, Schumann comes right back to a diminished seventh, which resolves well to the original tonic.

Figure 3-12

Many have pointed out that Schumann often used the interval of a descending fifth. We see this in the following lovely theme from the same work. The theme is actually two bars in the cello, answered by two bars in the viola.

Figure 3-13

Note that the second half of this theme is an inversion of the first half.

Schumann's melodies, even in the most idiomatic instrumental passages, often move as if they could speak, as if they *could* have a text. In the case of Schubert, as we have seen, songs were used as the bases for abstract instrumental works. Schumann, however, may have had some words in mind as he wrote his instrumental works. We can only speculate, but his themes are very much like vocal themes, although they are in many instances difficult to arrange for singing. (To my mind, it is a travesty to do so in the first place—if Schumann or any other composer had wanted words, there would have been words; or, as with Schubert, they would have been left out.) Szabolcsi[10] points out repeatedly that the romantic composer had a kind of *maqam*, a melodic type which often falls in the *ambitus* (range) of the $^6_4$ chord—another example of the use of the larger intervals, especially the downward sixth one would get in the tonic six-four from scale-degree three down to scale-degree five. Perhaps *maqam* is too Arabian in flavor to use as a term. I prefer to consider it a facet of melodic *ars combinatoria*, and similar in principle to Dallapiccola's findings apropos nineteenth-century opera aria melodies quoted earlier. Brahms also uses similar patterns; the horn theme in the finale of his *First Symphony* shows this very well. Brahms borrowed this theme from an Alpine horn-signal, "hoch auf'm Berg."

Many romantic melodies fall in the range of dominant to dominant, while many classical melodies fall tonic to tonic. It would be a mistake, however, to consider this as a rule; it is, rather, a tendency which can be observed in some important works.

Look now at a lovely little song, "Mondnacht," from Schumann's famous song cycle *Liederkreis*, Op. 39. This song illustrates many of the Schumannesque melodic principles discussed above.

Note that the singer must sing only one eight-bar melody a total of four times, with no change. A final statement of the same eight bars follows a related eight-bar period which does change the vocal line; this is a magical touch, in view of the shift in emphasis in Eichendorff's poem from the beauty of the moonlight night to the flight of the soul. The principle of the *maqam* or six-four *ars combinatoria* is much in evidence in the tessitura of the entire melodic line, resolved only when the last note of the song rests on the tonic pitch.

The first bar in the piano part starts with an implied dominant ninth which is outlined in the atmospheric piano melody.

The first vocal note brings an interesting change of harmony before it moves to the scale line leading to the high F-sharp. The E-sharp in the vocal part is a beautiful cross-relation to the E in the piano, and shows that the romantic composer has no qualms about raising the tonic pitch to form a chromatic passing tone. The rising line certainly suggests the word *Himmel*, and the descending fifth on the second syllable illustrates the pathétique quality of the melodic leap downward, occurring here from the fifth to the root of dominant harmony over a dominant six-five. This downward interval of the fifth occurs often in the music of Schumann.

die Ah - ren wog - ten sacht. es rausch - ten

leis___ die Wal - der, so stern - klar war___ die Nacht.

ritard

Und mei - ne See - le spann - te

ritard

weit ih - re Flü - gel aus,___ flog durch die stil - len

Lan - de, als flö - ge sie nach Haus.___

Figure 3-14

The final phrase of the oft-repeated eight-bar melody illustrates the importance of tonality. The final upward fifth is significant in the chord change to the dominant, even when the tone itself is a member of the tonic triad.

The student can readily observe the great difference in melodic effect by noting how the piano part changes for each statement of the repeated melody: this is how Schumann creates variety and yet unity.

The approach to chromaticism is also important: the E-sharp to F-sharp already pointed out and, perhaps even more interesting, B-sharp to C-sharp on the text, *"Flügel aus."* This shows how tones which might have had a more common harmonic function are harmonized differently —a principle of the utmost importance in melodic writing, since it changes the entire harmonic coloring.

Finally, rhythmic subtlety is important, not in the direct leading of any line, but in the differentiation from one line to another.

Schumann shows how a great creative genius can find the greatest profundity in imaginative applications of well-known principles. He was criticized in his time, however, for not following formulas *exactly*. This was a major concept in early romanticism: some new music was created simply by tilting the old principles just a little bit, but little by little soon becomes much.

Men like Ludwig Rellstab failed to understand the changes which must take place. He was the editor and one of the most important contributors to *Iris im Gebiete der Tonkunst,* an important magazine in Berlin and an important voice of musical conservatism. This caused Schumann and others to engage in journalistic work, which is of great help to scholars seeking polemics from all sides. The paper which Schumann helped to found was the *Neue Zeitschrift für Musik,* which first appeared in 1834 and continues today as a valuable German-language periodical under the title *Zeitschrift für Musik.* Pantheon Books has published a book entitled *Schumann on Music and Musicians* (edited by Konrad Wolff and translated into lively English by Paul Rosenfeld), which is valuable reading on Schumann's opinions and times. Rellstab's paper had an American counterpart in John Sullivan Dwight's *Journal of Music,* published 1852-1881.

Notes

1. Gerald Abraham, *One Hundred Years of Music* (Chicago: Aldine Publishing Company, 1964). The student should read this entire book. Chapter I begins with a discussion of orchestral conditions.

2. William McNaught, "Beethoven" article in *Grove's Dictionary of Music and Musicians,* ed. by Eric Blom (New York: St. Martin's Press, 1966), Vol. I, p. 560.

3. The D. refers to the chronological numbering of Schubert's complete works by Otto Deutsch. See Otto Deutsch in coll. with Donald R. Wakeling, *Schubert, Thematic Catalogue of All His Works in Chronological Order* (London: J. M. Dent & Sons, Ltd., 1951).

4. See Einstein, Alfred, *Schubert, a Musical Portrait* (New York: Oxford University Press, 1951), p. 292 *et seq.*

5. *Ibid.,* pp. 74-75.

6. Robert Haven Schauffler, *Florestan, the Life and Work of Robert Schumann* (New York: Henry Holt and Company, 1945), p. 285.

7. Clara Wieck (1819-1896) was Schumann's wife and the daughter of a famous piano pedagogue, Friedrich Wieck (1785-1873), who had a unique system of piano teaching. It must have been successful, since both Robert and Clara were fine pianists, as was Hans von Bülow (1830-1894)—also a Wagnerian conductor of some brilliance who kept on championing him, even after Wagner literally stole his wife, Cosima, who was the daughter of Liszt. Cosima was Wagner's second wife, and the lovely *Siegfried Idyll* was written for her by Wagner.

Clara Wieck was in the first rank of pianists, and did much to dignify the possibility that a lady could be a touring concert pianist. It is eternally to her credit that she knew the true worth of Robert's work and did much to promote international interest in it.

8. A "Philistine" is one who is generally indifferent to or ignorant of art. In Schumann's time the term was broadened to include people who were reactionary in their conservatism. The Davidsbündler (Society of David) was formed to combat this artistically and journalistically.

9. Schauffler, *op. cit.,* p. 78.

10. Bence Szabolcsi, *A History of Melody* (New York: St. Martin's Press, 1965). See especially pp. 170-174 and 205-215, where he develops a strong case for his theory.

CHAPTER IV

MELODY IN CHOPIN, MENDELSSOHN AND BRAHMS VS. BERLIOZ, LISZT AND WAGNER

Chopin

CHOPIN, THE PASSIONATE POLE, wrote some of the most expressive and most original melodies up to his time. He was one of the first truly great specialists, and his fame rests almost entirely on piano music which is among the finest ever written. There is more than a streak of melancholy; it is almost all sad and mournful, even when fast and bravura. One is hard pressed to find what one could call a happy phrase in his music, happiness such as the rustic contentment of Schumann's *Happy Farmer*. Not even the lilt of a dance rhythm will remove the sadness. We come close to happiness in the Waltzes and in some of the Mazurkas, where there is sometimes a wry smile, but never a real sense of humor.

Chopin's melodies are well suited for cantabile playing at the piano; they truly sing. Other composers present problems for melodies on the keyboard, especially in chamber works where a theme is to be played by strings and at another time on the piano. In Chopin the melodies always fit and resonate with the well-shaped chords and figurations which comprise the rest of the texture—sonorities which are the fruitful results of much experimentation at the keyboard. Few composers have had the tonal imagination of Chopin, and no composer, not even Liszt, influenced keyboard writing more until the time of Debussy. Chopin himself was influenced by Field and some others and was known to have studied Bach on his own, although little influence of Bach is seen.

Some of Chopin's most interesting melodies resulted from chromatic extensions of diatonic harmony, such as the following from the *G Minor Ballade*:

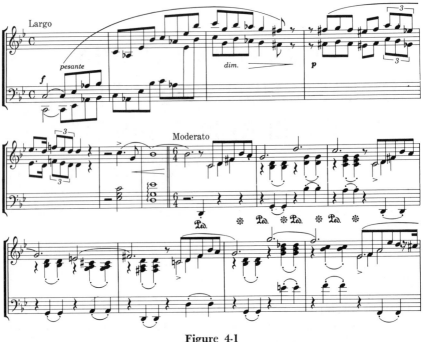

Figure 4-1

This melody is replete with originality and invites interesting variation. One could not have found many melodies like this in the Classical Period;

Figure 4-2

the principal theme of Mozart's *C Minor Fantasy* is of similar structure but the treatment is very different. (See Fig. 4-2.)

There are epic themes such as the *Revolutionary Etude*, sweet-scented themes from the nocturnes, nocturne-like passages in larger works and hair-raising themes which illustrate the highest level of instrumental-technical writing in the concerti, etudes, sonatas, ballades and scherzi. Few composers employ such a great variety, and yet almost all his themes are melancholy.

Chopin's themes are often the result of his original approaches to tonal harmony. There are some influences of Polish and Slavonic folk music, but these are rhythmic aspects rather than melodic; hence, intense nationalism is implied in the music but is explicit in titles such as "Mazurka" or "Polonaise." Chopin belonged to the mainstream of the west and, as a displaced Pole in France (mostly Paris), he was exposed to most of the significant new music being played there. He even heard the great American, Louis Moreau Gottschalk.[1] (Perhaps the reader will permit me to say that Chopin was more polish than Polish.)

Chopin often writes beautiful hidden counterpoint. In the *Prelude in A Minor* the left hand plays a hidden yet distinct statement of the *Dies Irae*:

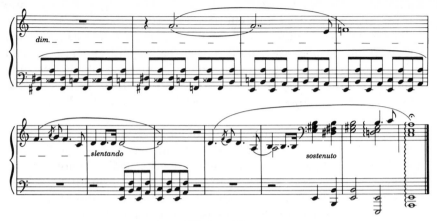

Figure 4-3

This is quite apparent in the accompaniment most of the time. Also funereal is the very end, which quotes his own "Funeral March" from the *Sonata in B Minor,* and also the "Winter Wind" Etude.

I have quoted the entire prelude so the student might see not only these things, but also that the dirge melody adheres to the principle of following the ambitus of dominant to dominant. Note further the very important chromaticism which is apparent mostly in the accompaniment; the melody uses both F and F-sharp in prominent places, and the piquant C-sharp in measure ten.

The critic Rellstab and others lavished vitriol on every work of Chopin as it appeared. How the Rellstabs appear in each generation, and are remembered mainly for telling the public that the best composers should have written differently! What a shame that Rellstab could not have taught Chopin how to compose properly! In Herbert Weinstock's admirable and thorough study of Chopin there is an interesting quote from Rellstab in his opinions of the *Five Mazurkas,* Op. 7, especially the chromatic melody and harmony in the second one which Weinstock quotes.[2]

This same Ludwig Rellstab (1799-1860) has been given credit for naming Beethoven's *Sonata quasi une fantasia,* Op. 27, No. 2 the "Moonlight."[3] In all fairness it should be said that the writings of Rellstab are a valuable source of information and opinion for that period. He was a champion of Beethoven and a gifted writer.. His journalistic wars with Spontini and Schumann were especially colorful.

It is possible to have diatonic melody and diatonic harmony, diatonic melody and chromatic harmony, chromatic melody and diatonic harmony or chromatic melody and chromatic harmony. The conservatives reacted unfavorably mostly to the total chromatic situation, as Rellstab did apropos Chopin's *Mazurka*, Op. 7, No. 2.

In conclusion, it should be pointed out that Chopin did not use borrowed melody as often as did many of his contemporaries. The variations are by and large from good melodic sources, and although there are some on popular opera melodies, they are a far cry from some by his contemporaries, which were only salon pieces of the worst kind. Those of Liszt are extremely varied in quality, and probably represent something of a cross-section of that kind of work which was so popular with audiences and which are perused only with curiosity today. Chopin was above these.

Chopin did not have the feeling for cyclic treatment as did many of the other masters of his time. His large works are not as unified as those of Schumann or Liszt. Even Schumann had mild objections to Chopin's sonatas being called sonatas. All of this illustrates further the fact that the great romantic composers were very different one from another in esthetics, approach, sheer sound and in almost every detail. It is absurd to assume that there is no unity in Chopin's work simply because there are no obvious generating motives; some of the world's worst music is the best organized. The highest unity is that which is internal and inherent in the music itself. Most works of Chopin have this in the highest degree. In all considerations of musical form the question of repeating something previously heard is of the most importance. Chopin is very rewarding to study from this point of view: to observe just how parallel passages are derived. Examination will show Chopin's great art of internal variation: as in the restatements of the theme in the *Ballade in G Minor,* starting in the eighth bar. Note how this theme grows from the eight notes in the introduction, and also how the outline is supercharged on the last page.

Mendelssohn

Mendelssohn would have been a success in any of several fields he might have entered. Many, for example, have expressed wonder at his apparent great gifts for watercolors, and his letters show that he inherited at least some of the literary gifts of his grandfather, Moses Mendelssohn.[4]

There is a classical gracefulness to most of Mendelssohn's melodies which belies the genuine romantic traits he displays from time to time. As a cultured gentleman he favored a cultured kind of musical utterance which reflected the social amenities of the times. His keyboard music, although effective, was perhaps a little too polite. The small pieces, *The Songs Without Words*, border on sentimentality and are almost bathos;

Plate IV

The St. Thomas Church in Leipzig, where J. S. Bach was choral
director. A drawing made by Felix Mendelssohn (*Courtesy The
Bettmann Archive, N.Y.*).

he was unable to control the small piece with genuine charm as was
Schumann. Mendelssohn's masterpiece from his teens, the incidental
music to *A Midsummer Night's Dream*, somehow permeates much of his
other music. There is not the great variety in his fast movements that we
find in those of Beethoven. The finale of the violin concerto, great as
it is, is still a kind of delightful fairyland. In *Elijah* and *St. Paul*, and in
some of his other large works, he was able to find a deeper kind of
expression more in tune with the underlying misery of the times; these
show how he probably felt himself as a Jew at a difficult time in Germany.

Some Mendelssohn themes have a great sweep, such as those from the
incomparable *String Octet*, Op. 20. Note how much one of them resembles the first theme in Strauss's *Ein Heldenleben*; of course, the total
effect is entirely different, but there is a resemblance.

Mendelssohn wrote effective hymns; the beloved "Hark the Herald
Angels Sing" is musically from a *Festgesang* for male chorus and orchestra, and is only one of many sacred works in hymn style. There is
some influence here of J. S. Bach, but there is not the vital interplay
of inner voices that we find in Bach.

As with many tonal composers, Mendelssohn uses outlines of the tonic
triads in interesting ways: such as the first movements of the *Italian
Symphony* and the *Violin Concerto*. Through the use of non-harmonic
tones the tonic triad is extended to form a striking programmatic theme
for the *Fingal's Cave Overture*.

There are many beautifully arched themes, such as in the slow movement of the *Violin Concerto*, the aria "If With All Your Hearts" from *Elijah* or "It is Enough" from *Elijah*.

All three of these are examples of entirely different kinds of expression, from sweet angelic vision to entreaty to the depths of despair. Mendelssohn is a clear-cut case of a composer who looks back to the peaceful melodic lines of the classical period and then looks forward to almost Tristanesque lines, such as in the motet *O lux Beata*. The overture to *Elijah*[5] is a remarkable study in fugue which is chromatic and yet Baroque; it is richly expressive, and uses such devices as melodic inversion. In this part of the exposition, note the use of large intervals in the subject.

Figure 4-4

The influence of Bach on Mendelssohn is often mentioned; although it was indeed a great influence, at the same time it poses a complicated problem. When one hears a sacred choral work of Bach and then one of Mendelssohn, one is impressed by the great *difference* of approach. Mendelssohn is much more like Handel in the treatment of the chorus and like Haydn in the orchestration. The influence of Bach is most noticeable in the use of more vital counterpoint, an interest in the Lutheran chorale and, at times, a richer chromaticism. All of these factors come to the fore, expectedly, in the *Reformation Symphony*. There is evidence that the chorale was of importance *before* the discovery of the *St. Matthew Passion*. Werner (see Werner's *Mendelssohn*, p. 209) even suggests that Mendelssohn stayed closer to original chorale tunes than did Bach.

In conclusion, Mendelssohn's star has been somewhat on the wane, but it will certainly never disappear. His music is put together too well, and it has too much to say to neglect. His chamber music is once again .attracting attention. His music is attractive and even "pretty" at a first hearing; in his best works this attractiveness wears well, while in his lesser ones it soon cloys or becomes tiresome. The chief strength or weakness most often lies in the melodic material and its repetition. While this is a problem in all music, it is especially true in Mendelssohn. Where the melodic material is well orchestrated or handled in a variety of harmonizations and/or textures, there is a lasting strength. For two examples, let us consider two of his most famous melodies which are technically similar, but different in expression. The *Violin Concerto* and the *Italian Symphony* both begin after a short introduction. A smooth, yet somewhat ruffled statement of the tonic triad starts the concerto:

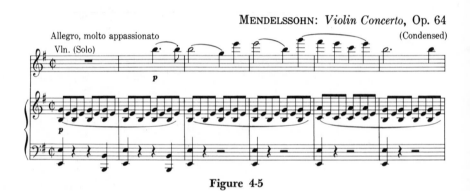

MENDELSSOHN: *Violin Concerto*, Op. 64

(Condensed)

Figure 4-5

The *Italian Symphony* has an excited staccato statement of the tonic triad in the woodwind as accompaniment (see Fig. 4-6). In each work the theme is a doubled-back statement of the tonic triad, a marvelous variation on the old idea of the principal theme outlining the tonic triad.

For dullness, let the reader doze through works such as the "War March of the Priests" from his score for Racine's *Athalie*. Some of the *Songs Without Words*, in spite of their alleged formal correctness, contain too much literal repetition and lack of chord color, or a too sentimental expression of an age long gone. There are many passages in his keyboard works which are rather empty figurations on common chords. His music was very influential in England and in the rest of Europe. He was held by some to be the last bastion of classicism against the onslaught of the Wagnerian horrors. In many thematic respects Mendelssohn was well ahead of his time, and he worked newer ideas into the fabric so well and so smoothly that his contemporary critics could not detect in his music

MENDELSSOHN: *Symphony No. 4* ("Italian"), Op. 90

Figure 4-6

the very devices which inspired adverse criticism in the music of other composers. One of the most striking is his use of cyclic treatment, which was by no means new in music but was not found in conscious use by many composers of the first half of the century. The cyclic device seems to have been well exposed in the works of Berlioz, Liszt and Wagner, but hidden or at least not given programmatic connotation in the music of Schubert, Schumann or Brahms; but is often there, nevertheless.

For brilliance in cyclic treatment the student would do well to study the *Reformation Symphony*, noticing the "Dresden Amen" as a source motive. The use of "Ein feste Burg," however, is not so brilliant. Other works are well-knit as well: the *G Minor Piano Concerto*, even *A Midsummer Night's Dream* (see Werner's *Mendelssohn*, pp. 408-412).

Finally, one should note the influence of Mendelssohn on Wagner: such as the use of the "Dresden Amen" in *Parsifal,* or the obvious seascapes which could be called "The Flying Dutchman in Fingal's Cave." There is always the problem of deciding if an earlier composer anticipates a later one or if the later one is influenced by the earlier. In the case of Mendelssohn and Wagner the latter is certainly the case. They knew each other from their first acquaintance in 1835 to Mendelssohn's death in 1847, and Wagner undoubtedly learned more from Mendelssohn than vice versa. In Wagner, even in *Die Meistersinger*, there is never the scherzo quality often found in Mendelssohn. Perhaps one could say that Mendelssohn's greatest gift of melody was the elfin scherzo.

Brahms

Elsewhere in this book Brahms's distaste for the newer German school is discussed. Yet, Brahms was perhaps even newer than Wagner. Most great composers look both backward and forward, and the forward looking of Brahms is not noticed as much by the public today as it was by our grandparents. We tend to call him a "classical-romanticist," or vice versa, and find it hard to realize that at one time his music was considered unintelligible and "scientific."

Oscar Thompson states:

If as recently as, let us say, 1900, when Johannes Brahms had been dead for three years, the statement had been made that the four Brahms symphonies were in danger of being overplayed, or that they stood next to Beethoven's nine in popularity, there would have been a raising of eyebrows. Tchaikovsky was then at his zenith; staid Boston Symphony audiences wept over the lamentations of the 'Pathétique.'

The music of Brahms, the songs excepted, was exclusively for the 'high-brows'; it was abstruse and difficult; there were those who understood and those who pretended to understand, as there were those who didn't understand and made no pretense at understanding—the last-named comforted and, in a sense, encouraged by otherwise discerning critics like the late Henry T. Finck, long of the New York *Evening Post*; and by a famous conductor, afterward something of a Brahms specialist, Felix Weingartner.

Nothing could be more unfair to the Felix Weingartner of later days than to go on quoting the depreciation mixed with the praise in his book of more than thirty years ago; it is enough to recall the singular fact that for the Weingartner of that day, already established as one of the world's eminent inter-

Plate V

Johann Strauss and Johannes Brahms (*Courtesy The Bettmann Archive, N.Y.*).

preters of symphony and as a leader of great orchestras, the music of Brahms was 'scientific music, composed of sonorous forms and phrases' and 'not the music of humanity, mysterious but still infinitely expressive and comprehensible'; it was 'not the language which the great masters knew how to speak, and did; the language, in fact, which moves and stirs us to the depths of our being, because we recognize in it our own joys and sorrows, our struggles and our victories.' For this representative musician of his age, 'the music of our great masters is artistic; that of Brahms is artificial'—and more that would be beside the point if re-stated here, since this same conductor long since made handsome amends to Brahms, not only by what he wrote and said, but by the character of the performances of Brahms's music given under his eloquent baton.[6]

Brahms was at his worst in orchestration, and at his best in all of the other aspects. I seriously doubt that his music would be played at all today if it did not have such a profound content, since, by and large, it is difficult music to perform. Orchestral players note that Mendelssohn always writes passages which lie well for the instruments, but Brahms has a knack for writing music which is awkward. The *Violin Concerto*, for example, was called a concerto "against the violin, not for it!" His late works do not improve in this regard.

But it is worth it. If I may be personal for a moment, let me say that I have found the works of Brahms to be among the most rewarding to perform, and that repeated performances of works as popular as the *Second Symphony* do not dim the brilliance nor cool the warmth. As a child I recall vividly the impression of Brahms as music which continuously unfolds, music which does not stop and start as much music often does. While it is true that many of Brahms's melodies are quite short in length (Tchaikovsky complained about this), it is also true that the connective tissue is so vital that one is often not really sure where the theme *per se* ends and the transition begins. One can test this with almost any of his symphonic themes, even where he has borrowed tunes, as in the *Academic Festival Overture*; old German university tunes are used, but they are so beautifully integrated into the totality of Brahms's musical fabric that he has made the themes truly his own.

In spite of the typical Brahms complexity, there is often a simple, almost folk song quality which reminds one somewhat of Schubert. Some of these themes are actually folk songs, while others are "im Volkweise" (in "folk song style"), without actually being true grassroots melody. Brahms works them in so well that the seams do not show.

The folk element is not always German. In finales particularly, there is an Hungarian quality which one often finds in other Germans, such as in Schubert finales. This is a German's idea of Hungarian, however. How odd that even Franz Liszt's Hungarian music is more Gypsy than the true Magyar ethnic stock, as Bartók so carefully annotated in his great work on the folk music of the Hungarians and their neighbors!

It is often said that Brahms was a classical composer with romantic things to say. He was content to push the boundaries rather than to go too far outside—evolutionary rather than revolutionary. The second theme of the first movement from the *Third Symphony* is a case in point.

FIRST MOVEMENT, SECOND THEME

Figure 4-7

This is a beautiful example of instrumental lyricism; one could not really sing this. As you see the theme there is not much to wonder over, but now observe the first theme. While this is also of importance in formal considerations, it is also important for the expression of the second theme. Note that in a "correct" sonata-allegro form the tonality of the second theme should be in the key of C major if the first theme is in F major, the meter and key signatures should be the same, and the tempo

FIRST MOVEMENT, FIRST THEME

f passionato

Figure 4-8

should be the same. In this example the tonality is A major, the major mediant key, the meter has changed from duple to triple, and many conductors play the theme a little more slowly. The theme also keeps coming back to the starting note—a habit with Brahms and, as we shall see, also with Franck. (Beethoven's *Waldstein Sonata*, Op. 53, has the same upper mediant, second theme, first movement: C major to E major.)

Many of Brahms's themes start on the third of the tonic triad, rise to the fifth and then fall an octave. These three notes are often sounded together in orchestration and in his piano works.

Brahms wrote magnificent sets of variations on his own themes and on themes by Schumann, Haydn, Handel and Paganini. He was capable of finding in these themes some very remarkable music. The theme by Paganini is especially fascinating, since variations on that theme are to be found by many composers. In the sets by Brahms one is impressed by the ability to pass from one variation to the next and retain something of the previous variation, as if that were the theme for the next. In this way, of course, the music continues to grow and grow, but in a different manner from the additive variation technique which one finds in, for example, the keyboard variations of Handel. Brahms also finds new life in the older chaconne-passacaglia-ground bass variations, as in his *Fourth Symphony* (last movement) and the final variation of the *Haydn Variations*.

There is probably more difference in style evident in the vocal themes than in the instrumental themes. Yet Brahms is not really what one would call an idiomatic composer, in the sense that Chopin and Liszt are idiomatic keyboard composers, or Mendelssohn, who usually wrote in a facile manner for all instruments and voices. The songs of Brahms are among the greatest in that rare category of great art songs, the German *Lieder* of the nineteenth and twentieth centuries. Those of Brahms, however, are quite distinct from those of his forerunners, but they show strong influences on the composers who follow. If there is any earlier influence, it is his friend, Schumann, and, of course, Schubert. The Brahms songs show a remarkable rhythmic structure, which is really a characteristic of almost all of his music: irregular phrases, syncopations and, on occasions, somewhat awkward setting of the syllables. It has been stated by many that Brahms had a strange taste in poetry and did not have the great feeling for good literature which Schumann had by learning and Schubert seemed to have by instinct. In the chapter on vocal music this factor is discussed in more detail, but it should be mentioned here that perhaps a lesser poem needs music while the truly great one does not. This may or may not have been Brahms's motivation in setting some of the poems that he did, but many lesser German poems would be all but forgotten were it not for Brahms's settings.

Brahms, like Mendelssohn, Schubert and Schumann, was an unsuccessful suitor of that fickle lady, opera. Beethoven's *Fidelio* has even been called the "worst great opera ever written." Perhaps in all of these composers the sense of drama is latent or is better left unspecified. None of these composers needed the program or extramusical idea in the same way as did some of their contemporaries, but when the program was provided, as in a song, they were able to rise to the occasion and suggest in many works far greater drama than all the theatrical trappings of the current stage and/or diminished seventh-laden blood-and-thunder tone poems. Keats, in the "Ode on a Grecian Urn," said that "Heard melodies are sweet, but those unheard/Are sweeter. . . ." In great abstract music there is a similar concept: that dramas which are imagined are far more dramatic, but the stimulus must be present.

Economy of means is typical of Brahms, and is one of his most widely admired characteristics. While his symphonies abound in this kind of construction, one finds it in his other works as well. Not all of these are immediately obvious, and I am convinced that computer studies to be made in the future will show up even more of them. The student would do well to study the essay by Schoenberg which is in the anthology *Style and Idea*,[7] where Brahms is brilliantly discussed as a *progressive* composer. Some of these ideas in connection with specific works will be pointed out later. The technique of Brahms is related to similar approaches by other composers, but Brahms has his own way of working which varies from work to work, or from movement to movement within the same work. For a quick example, note that the melodic characteristic of the first subject in the first movement of the *Third Symphony* is a downward motion of three notes diatonically.

FIRST MOVEMENT, FIRST THEME

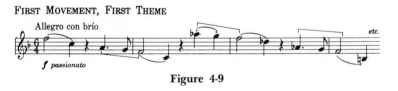

Figure 4-9

FIRST MOVEMENT, SECOND THEME

Figure 4-10

The second subject, in addition to the *differences* pointed out above, links itself motivically with the first through a predominance of the same three notes—but now upward.

The second movement changes the position of the first two notes—a device called "interversion."[8] The second subject is a mildly decorated quasi-inversion, with the three-note motive still very obvious. The third movement brings back the motive simply and is answered by beautiful non-harmonic tones which most theorists would call appogiaturas. The appogiaturas show intervallic expansion between the second and third notes, while the first two remind one of the downward moving motive.

THIRD MOVEMENT, FIRST THEME

Figure 4-11

The second subject of the third movement has similar treatment and is modified rhythmically for contrast, but is still based on the three-note scale up in the antecedent and balanced by expanded intervals in the consequent—the same general approach to the construction of the principal theme in this movement, one of Brahms's loveliest. The finale shows a similar design.

FOURTH MOVEMENT, FIRST THEME A

Figure 4-12

In conclusion, Brahms's melodies are perhaps best described as rich. They often occur in middle registers and are set against rich harmonies which can become thick if poorly performed. The phrase structure, duration series, over-all rhythmic scheme and ingenious use of syncopations are all still refreshing and place Brahms among the very greatest of masters. There is much inner strength, and the lovely countermelodies and figurations become apparent to the listener only after familiarity—certainly a factor in the durability of his music. There is almost never any virtuoso passage work just for the display of technical brilliance, hence there are not drab stretches where the listener hears how well an artist can play this or that arpeggio. In Brahms, somewhere, someone is presenting an important musical idea—quite the opposite of Fauré's advice, "Don't try to be a genius in every bar!" Brahms, in his best music, *is* a genius in almost every bar, and the great ability to use melody to get from one place to another is one of the most important factors in this high quality.

Berlioz

Barzun[9] has repeatedly shown that Berlioz is not as programmatic as one would make him out to be (perhaps he did bring it upon himself after all!); therefore, we tend to make *a priori* judgments about his music, and our minds put more wildness into it than there really is. In his best known music, the *Fantastic Symphony,* we hear the program in the summation of the musical elements, which is as it should be. The *themes,* however, are quite another matter. The *idée fixe* theme is as follows:

BERLIOZ: *Symphonie Fantastique*; IDÉE FIXE THEME

Figure 4-13

(From William E. Brandt, *The Way of Music,* 2nd. Ed., p. 349. © Copyright 1968 by Allyn and Bacon, Inc., Boston.)

This theme could have been given classical treatment, and Berlioz himself comes close to this in some of the statements in this symphony. There are no notes as yet not in the original key. If we now hear the *entire* theme as it occurs conveniently as the first theme in a pretty good approximation of a classical sonata-allegro, we can see, as the theme unfolds, that it becomes more and more chromatic and, where the triplets first occur, it becomes more angular—two important characteristics of romantic melody:

FIRST MOVEMENT: IDÉE FIXE THEME; ALLEGRO

Figure 4-14

(From William E. Brandt, *The Way of Music*, 2nd. Ed., p. 349. © Copyright 1968 by Allyn and Bacon, Inc., Boston.)

While it may or may not be important, note that the theme and its harmony soon spend all twelve tones; this is in an exposition where the classical composer was more concerned about keeping the original key firmly established. In this theme other factors can be observed which point out the romantic aspects: 1) The phrase and periodic structure begin quite normally, but as the music becomes more agitated, the irregularities begin to appear. 2) The accompaniment is almost awkward, but perfect for the poetic idea—reticent at first, becoming more and more insistent; and yet, at the point where it almost takes command, the rhythm of the theme changes to the triplet and the accompaniment is almost embarrassed as if it had committed itself too soon, and the melody again leads the proceedings. 3) The over-all construction is marvelous; the second portion is a sequence which starts to modulate but doesn't, an act which introduces the chromatic byplay of the F-sharp and then the F natural. Berlioz seizes upon this and carries it still one step higher, and is now content to sequence just the consequent, which is a descending scale. The chromatic byplay is now on A-flat and then A natural, and then is done still one more time, finally reaching the high C which, although being the tonic, is not the real goal of the melody until the very end. The goal is now E, especially E as a resolution of a dissonant F. The leaps form a beautiful balancing and actually serve to bring the melody down to earth again to the final cadence in the 40th bar of the theme. The entire theme, therefore, is 40 bars long. 4) The length is much beyond the typical classical theme; in this case the length is brought about by real symphonic structuring, not just by sequence and repetition. 5) The older devices of dissonance such as the suspension are now done in an exaggerated, but still effective way.

In the rest of the symphony Berlioz states the theme only once more *in toto*, but uses the first portion as the theme of obsession which carries forth the idea of the story (see the chapter on orchestral music). The rest of the theme is used as a source for thematic and figuration ideas. Berlioz and others achieve a certain amount of unity this way with varying degrees of success; Berlioz certainly was successful in this composition, one of the best of the poematic symphonies. The work appeals to us today more for its music than for its rather odd story, which might have authenticity with some young artists today; but most people are more interested in the way Berlioz uses his thematic fragments and how he orchestrates them than in his extracurricular posturing.

Berlioz is, however, mostly remembered today as a great master of orchestration; and we must admit that without his brilliant scoring we just would not sit through many of his passages. Still, these melodic ideas are so right in Berlioz's best works! It is not really fair for us to take the themes from their settings, since they lose so much this way. After all, a composer intends his work to be done as a whole, not to be picked to pieces and isolated. Berlioz was certainly one of the first to use sheer sound as an important aspect of music, and it has been important ever since.

Liszt

Liszt is also tolerated through brilliant scoring, although we find in Liszt's music a greater variety of colors, since he used more media than Berlioz. Berlioz wrote little significant piano music, while Liszt wrote much, and Liszt was more outstanding in the field of the art song—the lovely *Nuits d'Été* of Berlioz notwithstanding. It is significant that neither man wrote any significant chamber music, although there are many passages in their

Plate VI

Franz Liszt and his friends, Musset, Victor Hugo, George Sand, Berlioz, Rossini and Countess D'Agoult. Painting by Danhauser (*Courtesy The Bettmann Archive, N.Y.*).

orchestral music where the soloistic nature of woodwinds and horns are like chamber music in concept—a factor which is important in much orchestral music since 1850. The actual themes in Liszt are extremely striking and, by and large, are far more chromatic than those in Berlioz.

The cyclic treatment used by Liszt in *Les Préludes* is well known. He developed in his other works a sophisticated melodic development which is usually called "melodic transformation." The *Sonata in B Minor* is also outstanding for its cyclic treatment. The use by Liszt falls between the *idée fixe* of Berlioz and the *Leitmotiv* of Wagner. In Berlioz most of the time the exact part of the story can be known: in the *Fantastic Symphony* the program can be followed in "blow-by-blow" detail. Berlioz himself said that the program should be like the libretto of an opera. In some works of Liszt one can find a literal program too, but his abstract works show a brilliant use of thematic transformation.

Wagner

One of Wagner's best known characteristics is the attempt to achieve a
continuous melody where repetition would occur according to the sense
of the music drama, and not according to the dictates of a previously set
musical form which might develop in the wrong psychological direction.
Older operas had had libretti written with the musical forms in mind,
and this, of course, would affect the whole sense of the drama. Wagner
and the other romantics did not go along with the old idea—why should
art be one formula after another? Wagner's answer was in great measure
a melodic one, since the whole fabric was woven through restatement,
variation and development of the *Leitmotiv*: a short, graphic bit of music
which suggested a person, place, thing or concept. Since the sense of the
drama is thereby told in the orchestra as well as on the stage, it follows
that the old ideas would not work. Wagner knew about them, since his
early works reflect the older opera conventions; it can even be shown
that his earliest works were studies in the various national opera conventions and that he knew perfectly well what he was doing when he
killed them.

The *Leitmotiv* had to be open at both ends: *i.e.*, one must be able to
get into or out of the motive easily, since it can occur at any time in any
key and at different registers. Some of these motives have a periodic
structure, and require an incisive rhythm. Others are sometimes described
as "oozing," and do have a kind of opulent amorphic quality with
blurred outlines. *Tristan* is the best example, 'and the famous beginning
will illustrate this.

Figure 4-15

Wagner employs a great deal of repetition, as we have pointed out
above; and as he developed, learned how to repeat motives without bore-
dom and without the artificial demands of square poetry. Wagner does
this through a complex technique of melodic transformation which involves harmonies and contrapuntal textures. This technique is similar
to that of Liszt and Berlioz but is far more subtle. It is not enough to say

that Wagner uses a "calling card" for each character. It is far more accurate to say that the motive is important as it is presented, and that it will change as the situation changes. Wagner is also very careful to present a certain ambiguity, and it is impossible at times to tell which motive is being developed. Note how the *Erda* motive resembles that of the *Rhine*, and how the *gold* motive resembles the *sword* motive:

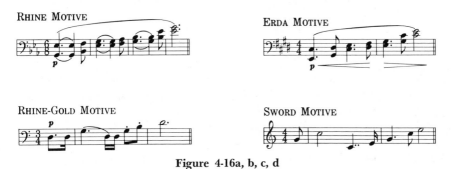

Figure 4-16a, b, c, d

Analysts have had a field day with these motives, and there is no difficulty in philosophizing about why the motive of Erda would be like the Rhine, since each is a concept of a source. Nor is it difficult to trace the musical development of most of the other motives. Wagner's peculiar harmonic style has much to do with the melodic effectiveness, and much more will be said on that subject in the chapter on harmony. While it is true that Wagnerian harmony opens the way for the dissolution of the key system, it is equally true that Wagner *did* know the rules of harmony, and therefore knew how to stretch them. We know that Wagner had a great feeling for tertian harmony, since so many of his motives are actually broken triads. He also tends to destroy tertian feeling through the use of many chords, such as the augmented sixth, which are formed through a purposeful distortion of the tertian sonority. The so-called "German sixth" is enharmonically a dominant seventh, but Wagner uses more complicated ones which are very difficult to explain as tertian sonorities, since many of them do not resolve in a "correct" way. We can get some insight into this purposeful ambiguity by comparing the many different attempts to analyze the *Tristan* Prelude or almost any other famous chromatic passage. (The analysts cannot even agree on what key it is in, if any! The only point of agreement is that it is beautiful music, and it sounds so right that it *must* be right!)

The harmony and its complication affects the melodic writing and leads to countermelodic chromatic complexity, much of the time much more complex than the principal voice at the time. (Almost any page of the *Ring* will illustrate this.)

Wagner did not invent the *Leitmotiv* idea, nor was he the last to use it. The *Leitmotiv* idea is as old as opera itself, and has been used by composers in varying ways. Wagner was the first to weave the entire fabric so that the most important melodic material was composed of these themes. Since Wagner, others have worked in a similar way, and music history's course was radically changed by this strange man who has inspired voluminous biographical and analytical literature.

Conclusions: Berlioz-Liszt-Wagner

The fate of the melody is more important than the melody itself. Cyclic treatment becomes a more important factor than ever before. The audience is expected to follow the musical design, since there is almost always an extramusical consideration. The melodies of Liszt and Wagner use chromaticism to a great extent, although this is also found in Berlioz. In the works of all three composers the atmosphere provided by the "coloration" of the music is of utmost importance, whether the "coloring" be through harmony, orchestration or both.

Notes

1. See Vernon Loggins, *Where the Word Ends (The Life of Louis Moreau Gottschalk)* (Baton Rouge: Louisiana State University Press, 1958), p. 57 *et seq.* for an interesting account of their meeting.
2. Herbert Weinstock, *Chopin, the Man and His Music* (New York: A. A. Knopf, 1959), p. 185.
3. Robert Haven Schauffler, *Beethoven, The Man Who Freed Music* (New York: Tudor Publishing Co., 1946), p. 443.
4. Moses Mendelssohn (1729-1786) was an outstanding man. He was a good friend of Lessing (they met over a game of chess); Lessing's *Nathan the Wise* personifies him and is dedicated to him. Moses Mendelssohn's writings on religion, especially on the Jewish faith, are outstanding examples of religion and reason from the point of view of a Jewish scholar. Well-versed in philosophy and science, he even wrote a little treatise on the physical and mathematical nature of music. His masterpiece, *Jerusalem*, teaches tolerance and is considered a major work in the field of reform Judaism. He also translated some of the Hebrew scriptures into German. Eric Werner's *Mendelssohn*, tr. by Dika Newlin (London: Free Press of Glencoe, Collier-Macmillan Ltd., 1963), is a good source of information about the entire Mendelssohn family—especially their religious convictions, which present complicated problems, and Werner clears them up very well.
5. The overture to *Elijah* is not the first number. It follows a recitative by Elijah which speaks of the great drought. This is something of a rarity, although Offenbach's *M. Choufleuri restera chez lui le . . .* begins with spoken dialogue as if it were to be a play. The characters, for comic effect, suddenly remember

that it is an operetta and that it should begin with an overture, whereupon the orchestra obliges and plays the overture!

6. Oscar Thompson, *How to Understand Music* (New York: Premier Books, Fawcett Publications, Inc., 1962), p. 111.

7. Arnold Schoenberg, *Style and Idea* (New York: Philosophical Library, 1950), pp. 52-101.

8. Interversion is discussed in Alan Walker's provocative book *A Study in Musical Analysis* (New York: The Free Press of Glencoe, 1962). The word was probably coined by Rudolph Reti, in his book *The Thematic Process in Music* (New York: The Macmillan Co., 1951); and it is a handy word to use to describe what one might call "slight" permutations of the melody notes, or any other factor or parameter, for that matter. Interversion refers to one or two or a few of the possible permutations of a series of notes. If the melody has, say, 5 notes—1 2 3 4 5—and the composer chose to write the melody with notes 2 1 3 4 5, we would have one of the 120 possible permutations of those notes $(5!=5\times4\times3\times2\times1=120)$. What I have pointed out by numbers is exactly what Brahms did with the three-note motto: three tones either up or down diatonically, followed by a leap in the same direction of either a fourth or a third. In the context of the key of the second movement, the motto would read: DCBG. Brahms chose to write CDBCG, with the second C as an insertion. It could be, of course, that Brahms had nothing like this in mind, but if the reader will analyse the symphony with this motto in mind he will find remarkable uses of this motto, or *Urkeim*, or *Grundgestalt*, or the cyclic motive—all terms apply.

9. Jacques Barzun, *Berlioz and the Romantic Century*. Copyright 1949, 1950 by Jacques Barzun. By permission of Atlantic-Little, Brown and Company, Boston.

CHAPTER V

NATIONALISTIC MELODIES

IT WOULD BE SO easy to say that the nationalistic composers wrote music based on folk songs! The fact is that most of the great composers used folk material for their own purposes and made the themes a part of their work in such a manner that it is almost impossible to tell the folk themes from those which are not. What one finds more often is a certain style which has become associated with a certain ethnic music. There is, for example, a "Spanish" style of music which we find in Sarasate's violin music or Granados' piano music. Many French composers have written "Spanish" music: Bizet's *Carmen*, Debussy's *Ibéria* and Ravel's *Bolero*, among others. As with other melodic styles, there is a set of harmonic formulae which goes with the tunes. There is often a characteristic rhythm, frequently a dance rhythm from a given region. It is significant that the nationalistic "schools" of music which produced the most important nationalistic music were from countries which did not have long and important histories of art music. Most advanced countries imported musicians, many from Italy. There has always been the fascination for someone else's music, although there have been times when nationalism became chauvinism. There is this paradox, then: composers look to far-off lands and try to evoke what is to them an exotic atmosphere, and at the same time look to their own country's folk mores for ideas.

The important nationalistic movement in music is found rather late in the period, and is a complex problem. It is not enough to say that the "composers were interested in folk music." Why were they *then*, and less at earlier times? Was it only a result of political nationalism, a pride in homeland as democracies arose? Was it a part of the cult of the individual, an individual nation in this case? In the nineteenth century there was progressively less and less a universal style as the composers themselves cultivated individual differences. This is not the place to do more than ask these questions, nor is it the place to discuss folk music *per se*. We are interested here in the use of folk materials in art music which actually resulted in a fusion of concert music and folk styles. Forms in folk music are not always simple, and they are certainly not sonata-allegro when they are complicated. We find one changing the other: for instance, folk tunes used for first themes of epic symphonies, and composers searching folk songs and dances for new forms or at least newer applications of older forms.

Dvořák and Smetana are interesting to compare, in order to illustrate some of the concepts delineated above. Dvořák even tried to point out to American composers, when he came to the United States, how we might find the great truths from the grassroots; but few American attempts were successful. America is an alloy, heterogeneous, eclectic, syncretic—a paradoxical melting pot which has produced a highly striated culture. This was true even in 1892-1895, the years of Dvořák's sojourn to the United States. Dvořák could not have felt the true spirit of either New York or the rolling hills of fertile farmland in northeastern Iowa, but he could still feel his own homeland. The American works—*New World Symphony, Cello Concerto, American Quartet* and the famous *Humoresque*—are among Dvořák's best and do have themes which sound "American," but the treatment is certainly Bohemian and belongs to the mainstream of symphonic musical development in Europe. This was *cultivated* by Dvořák and Smetana.

It was in Russia that the *Five* and others tried to avoid the mainstream, as it were, and find a pure Russian music. Because of this, Russian nationalistic music often sounds far more exotic to our ears than that of the Bohemians or Scandinavians. The "American" melodies are not authentic in Dvořák's work, nor did he want them to be! He was after only the flavor, and was insulted at the allegation that he had "arranged" Indian or Negro tunes in his American works. He was too concerned about the symphonic tradition of Mozart and Beethoven. We must remember that he was a great music educator[1] as well; and it is to his credit that he was only slightly academic at times. Dvořák had been accused of having too much "Teutonism" in his music, and it does display *good* influences from Wagner and Liszt. Dvořák was a Czech through and through, and had a genuine feeling for the Slavonic soul. Smetana, on the other hand, was more intense in his desire for a kind of music which was also Czech through and through, but with little or no influence from either east or west. Smetana lived most of his life under Austrian rule and spoke the Czech language, but not as well as did Dvořák. It must be remembered that most educated Bohemians were at least bilingual: German and their local dialect.

In spite of Smetana's inability to speak Czech to perfection, he still dreamed of a national musical theater where the Czech tongue would be sung. (It seems that all countries but Italy have had difficulty presenting opera in the local tongue!) His dreams were only partially fulfilled.

Smetana's best contribution to this kind of theater is the delightful opera *The Bartered Bride,* an unfortunate "English" title from the German *Braut,* which means "bride" in most cases where *Braut* is a prefix—as in *Brautnacht* (wedding night). The word usually means "betrothed," and certainly in the story-line of the opera this is the meaning— "fiancée" or "intended." There are other examples where strange English titles have resulted.[2] The opera has been called *The Bartered Bride* for so long, however, that it has become habitual.

The Bartered Bride has been extremely popular from its premiere to the present time. Its tunefulness is probably the reason, as is the case with most successful operas which are loved generation after generation by the general public. The melodies have a marvelous lilt, in part through the application of polka, furiant and other folk dance rhythms throughout. The overture, although gay and fit for a comedy, has always seemed to me to have an underlying seriousness and epic flavor, especially the theme at the very opening.

Smetana's best known string quartet, *From My Life* (1876), was his first and is a masterpiece. The opening theme of the first movement is a marvel of fateful declamation. (See Fig. 5-1, the viola part.) How violists love to play this theme! The motive of the falling fifth is of utmost importance in the work, and the very working out of the theme itself is an interesting application of quasi-Lisztian thematic transformation. Note that the anacrusis is the same pitch as the upper note of

FIRST MOVEMENT, FIRST THEME

Figure 5-1

the first falling interval. The second falling interval expands the fifth to a sixth, and the anacrusis is a semitone lower. The third interval sequences the idea and the fourth one returns to the falling fifth, but uses an anacrusis from a whole tone lower. Up to this point Smetana has given us an imaginative outline of the tonic triad with lower neighbors to the chord tones. The rest of the theme is intensified by more rapid notes and the addition of more chromatic tones, but it still has been all tonic for the first twelve bars! Later in the work he (as Dvořák also does) incorporates a polka which is delightful, but without the gay qualities of those from *The Bartered Bride*.

Smetana's works which he considered mature do not make a long list. His fame rested on this opera, although it was but the second of eight finished operas covering a variety of story types, all nationalistic in some manner; the quartet, although there is a second one which is also autobiographical; a cycle of symphonic tone poems *My Country (The Moldau* is the best known); and some piano music which deserves to be better known. His piano music is Lisztian in concept, with Slavonic and Slavonic-like melodies. They are of the utmost technical difficulty, which may be one reason why we do not hear them more. Smetana was not interested in church music, nor did he write the wealth of symphonic and chamber music as did his younger compatriot, Dvořák.

Dvořák was a complete composer. A perusal of his complete works[3] creates a profound impression on the browser. Here is a composer of first rank whose masterpieces suffer neglect because other of his works have become too popular! In my opinion, the *Symphony in D Minor*, Op. 70, is a greater work than the *New World*, but it receives few performances. *The G Major Symphony*, Op. 88, is also a delight, a romp through Slavonic folk idioms cast in fascinating applications of academic large forms. The contrast to the tragic *D Minor Symphony* is astonishing, and it is nothing like the *New World* either. A chief cause of this differentiation is the thematic material and the way it is treated.

For inherent differentiation in the Slavonic temperament, one needs only hear one Slavonic Dance of Dvořák after another to find a great wealth of expression. These dances were originally for piano duet, and were orchestrated by Dvořák, Szell and others. Perhaps this is the best place to explain the nationalistic adjectives "Bohemian," "Slavonic" and "Czech," which have been used interchangeably. The Slavs are a group of peoples who speak a related language: Poles, Czechs, Russians, etc. Bohemia was the largest province of Czechoslovakia, a country created precariously by the Treaty of Versailles. In the aftermath of World War II the whole country became a Soviet satellite and the province of Bohemia was abolished. This beautiful corner of the world has had a long and colorful history, full of events which lend themselves well to epic treatment.

We shall meet Dvořák frequently in this book; suffice it to say here that he was a great master of musical economy and used techniques for musical unity which are original, vital and important in the development of the craft of musical composition. The *New World Symphony* is a good work to study to find the *Grundgestalt*, the basic musical shape which underlies the work. The famous melody played by the English horn in the adagio, called "Goin' Home," is the full-blown manifestation of the basic melodic material. Here again is a great paradox of the nineteenth century: the great, emotion-charged works are almost without exception put together in the most careful manner by the best composers.

This economy of means is the source of Dvořák's anger at the suggestion that he had borrowed *any* tunes. He knew that even if he had, 99 per cent of the work was yet to be done! These quasi-folk songs actually came *after* the symphony, especially "Goin' Home." The same is true of the *Cello Concerto*, which contains themes faintly like tunes of Stephen Foster (second theme, first movement), and of the *Quartet in F*, unfortunately called the "Nigger Quartet" in much of the literature. It is now most often called the "American"—which is far better, not only for obvious reasons, but for the fact that there are as many American Indian "influences" as Negro ones and the transplanted Bohemian polkas which he heard in the Bohemian colony at Spillville, Iowa. Much of the Negro folk song flavor in Dvořák's American works is achieved through a use of the pentatonic scale, characteristic of much of the world's folk music. Unlike many folk songs, however, Dvořák often spins out long melodies which have charming periodicity. He is able to do this in part through his ability to build and build from generating motives, and to throw new light on the material in surprising ways through the use of the furiant, polka, dumka or some other dance rhythm. Note the beginning of the finale of the *American Quartet*:

FOURTH MOVEMENT, INTRODUCTION

Figure 5-2

The hopes of a continued major nationalistic school might have been realized in Joseph Suk (1874-1935), Dvořák's son-in-law. Suk was Dvořák's pupil, and there was every promise that Suk would develop into a major composer, but tragedy struck: his wife died a year after her father, and this double blow was more than Suk could bear. After a nervous breakdown, he returned to composition and did write some fine music; but the atmosphere which was present from 1898-1905, the years of his marriage, was gone and, apparently with it, Suk's gift.

The realized career was that of Leoš Janáček (1854-1928). His music has only recently been heard to any extent in this country, and recordings have greatly helped. In Europe he was not too well known until the sensation produced by his opera *Jenufa*, in 1918. Another important premiere was *The House of the Dead* (1928), a twentieth-century masterpiece. Janáček was born in Hukvaldy, where a peculiar kind of folk music has flourished. It is modal and the language is, as is sometimes the case in border areas, a mixture of Czech and Polish. Janáček's music uses but few melodic formulas; but with his technique of continuous variation, there is never any lagging of interest. His harmonies are extremely vivid and constantly throw the thematic material into new lights. While it would be easy to say that Janáček is another romantic who lived well into our century, the truth is that he is a figure comparable to Bartók, and may some day be held in as much esteem. The student is referred to William Austin's *Music in the Twentieth Century*,[4] pages 77-83, for an interesting and informative discussion of Janáček. I must quote part of it, since it includes comments by Janáček himself:

Janáček's peculiar treatment of motifs is regarded by Racek and other students of his whole work as the chief characteristic of his style. According to Racek, motifs throughout his music are mostly derived from speech, and their repetition in phrases is freely derived from folksong. Janáček's own testimony tends to confirm this. His intensive study of folksong, especially Moravian and Slavonic, was partly guided by the philologist Frantisek Bartoš (1837-1906). Janáček provided an essay for the collection of songs edited by Bartoš in 1901, in which he argues that "folksongs originated from words." In 1905, he wrote in the magazine *Hlidka*:
"The melodic curves of speech are an expression of the complete organism and of all phases of its spiritual activities. They demonstrate whether a man is stupid or intelligent, sleepy or awake, tired or alert. They tell us whether he is a child or an old man, whether it is morning or evening, light or darkness, heat or frost, and disclose whether a person is alone or in company. The art of dramatic writing is to compose a melodic curve which will, as if by magic, reveal immediately a human being in one definite phase of his existence."
He repeated and amplified this theory many times. In 1926 he stated it again, concisely and forcefully, in a letter to Jan Mikota:
"After having studied the musical side of the language, I am certain that all melodic and rhythmical mysteries of music in general are to be explained solely from rhythmical and melodic points of view on the basis of the melodic curves

of speech. No one can become an opera composer who has not studied living speech. I wish that this could be understood once and for all."
Janáček thus pushed to an extreme a notion that had been important for Mussorgsky and to some extent for many other composers. Janáček seems not to have borrowed the idea from anyone else, but to have arrived at it in this extreme form by himself.[5]

The modal flavor, which is found with some frequency in the Bohemian masters, is a very important factor in Russian nationalistic music. Russia is an extremely wealthy musical country. They had imported important musicians from Europe (especially Italy) from as early as the eighteenth century. They had a rich heritage of liturgical music which is different from the Roman Catholic and Protestant heritages of the West. There was also a rich and varied background of indigenous music, music which was frowned upon by the snobs as "coachman" or "peasant" music. As conditions developed in Russia during the nineteenth century, more and more attention was paid to the "soul of Russia" by all of her artists. In literature especially, there was a kind of "golden age," with writers such as Pushkin,[6] Gogol, Dostoyevsky, Turgenev, Tolstoy and others.

In music the way was pointed out by Mikhail Glinka (1804-1857), one of the first of an important group of amateurs who were extremely gifted men of real genius. Glinka conceived the idea of a national opera as the result of several influences: a genuine love of his homeland, the beauties of the countryside and the kind of music it evoked in the folk songs of the Caucasus and Poland, and as a kind of mild reaction to the dry studies he had made in musical theory. The first work to make a great mark was his *A Life for the Tsar*, which was produced with much success in 1836.

Glinka's music is often, however, not too different from music produced in Italy or Germany during the same time. The Overture to *Russlan and Ludmilla*, probably Glinka's best known work to concert audiences, is stylistically not too far removed from Nicolai or Weber, but the opera itself is more original as a complete opera than the earlier *A Life for the Tsar*. Grout, in his excellent *A Short History of Opera*, quotes the "Bridal Chorus" in Act III of *A Life for the Tsar* as a mild example of Glinka's use of the Russian folk song idiom, and points out that one would expect more in view of the subject matter of the opera. Grout goes on to delineate some important characteristics of Russian music.[7]

The *Russlan and Ludmilla* Overture is not representative of the opera; it is cosmopolitan—as sunny as Italian opera comedy overtures, as well orchestrated as the French and as full of lasting substance as the better of the German operas of the period. Glinka's piano music is charming, as are his several songs. Some of the melodies use whole-tone scales, exotic quasi-Oriental modes or mode-like melodies, but most show that he was a clever eclectic who nevertheless did establish an important nationalistic school of composition. Many of his other works are as pleasant as the *Russlan and Ludmilla* Overture, and deserve to be heard.

Glinka's direct heirs were mainly Dargomyzhsky and the "Mighty Five." Dargomyzhsky will be discussed later, as will the Five. The only comment here is to point out that, of the Five (Balakirev, Cui, Rimsky-Korsakov, Borodin and Mussorgsky), Mussorgsky is the real giant and Rimsky-Korsakov is the kind, well-trained professional musician who often helped his compatriots in technical matters and, as we shall see in appropriate places in the future, often misunderstood the nature of the original work—*Boris Godunov*, especially.

The Five had certain ideological differences with their contemporaries; even Tchaikovsky was not immune. He was considered to be tainted by musical ideas from the West: ballet and opera from France, and symphonic treatment from Germany. In spite of this Stravinsky was moved to say, "Tchaikovsky was the most Russian of us all."

Tchaikovsky, although getting a late start as a musician (as did Glinka and some of the others), mixed technical skill with a strong feeling for the Russian soul and soil. The Five felt that the greatest art came from the heart and passions of the people, and that technical skill would stand in the way of expressing what needed to be expressed. It is astounding what greatness resulted from the sheer genius of these men! What if they *had* studied? Speculation is useless; their attitude is a testimonial to the sad state of affairs in the conservatories regarding the study of composition and theory. Naturally, there could be no lively interest for them in the dull classroom where exercises were worked over with little bearing on any musical situation, past or present. I wonder (as did Donald Tovey) where Cherubini and the others got their rules for fugue or anything else.[8] There were some good teachers; but, by and large, the best composers taught themselves. In many cases they had encouragement and advice from great colleagues, and they learned as they conducted and rehearsed in the theater and concert hall. I do not believe it to be axiomatic that music theory must move behind practice, although there is certainly one branch of theory that should: thorough analysis. But there should also be a study of theory which keeps pace or goes ahead of practice, and this is what the Five were actually doing in philosophizing if not in actual technical practice. Vladimir Stasov, the critic, was such a theoretician.[9]

Mussorgsky expressed as part of his general education a great interest in Vissarion Belinsky, who, in 1843, wrote these words which seem to be at the crux of the whole question. I quote from James Bakst's excellent book:

The sources of romanticism are in life. Where there is life, there is man; and where there is man, there is romanticism. In its essential meaning, romanticism is the inner spiritual world of man, the innermost life of his heart. The secret source of romanticism is in the breast and heart of man. Feeling and love are manifestations, or actions, or romanticism. Therefore, every man is a romantic.[10]

Tchaikovsky's melodies are among the best-known of any the world over. Not a little of this popularity derives from the vulgar treatment these lovely melodies have received for the financial gain of popular musicians, who on one melody realized more financial remuneration than Tchaikovsky ever received. But the very melodies which have been smeared by silly words have assumed an erotic content which was foreign to Tchaikovsky. Sexual overtones are but partial testimony to the slice of life which was becoming a part of all art, and which was soon to become pungent indeed. Consider what happened in the twentieth century in art. When all of life is brought in, ugliness cannot stay out.

But an ancient function of art has been to transcend man's misery and to create a dream world which can be more beautiful; or, as in the case of Tchaikovsky, sometimes reach the plane of sheer musicality. In his best passages he is very good indeed, and his best features involve melodic and thematic treatment. In his worst passages there is trouble with form, especially with regard to connective tissue. He has difficulty getting from one part of the form to another.

Tchaikovsky and other late-nineteenth–century composers often resort to an unimaginative, wandering kind of recitative in the baritone register (usually celli or bassoons) in order to get to another key or to another place in the form.

Since Tchaikovsky and his fellow Russians were colorful orchestrators and so concerned with the common man, it follows that there would be a popular following of some magnitude, helped at the present time through the hi-fidelity spectacular recordings of their orchestral works. Tchaikovsky and Rimsky-Korsakov especially were brilliant orchestrators, and the latter wrote a good pragmatic text on orchestration which exists in an excellent English translation.

Tchaikovsky's themes, then, are always well scored and usually lie well for the instruments. The famous horn theme from the *Fifth Symphony* is a good example; it couldn't have a better tessitura. (Consult the score and trace the theme through the entire movement.) This theme is stated in different ways by the orchestra, and each one has its own special beauty. The repetition of themes in new garbs is a strong point with Tchaikovsky, and can be seen in almost all of his major works.

The structure of the themes and the development of them are also admirable features of his three last symphonies. He was a master of the generating motive, and was among the first of several Russian composers for whom this kind of motive structuring was especially important. His pupil Taniev became a great teacher of many fine Russian musicians. Taniev's own works display a remarkable structure, and his textbook *Convertible Counterpoint* is one of the great theoretical treatises of the times.[11] Medtner, Rachmaninoff, Glazunov, Liadov, Scriabin and others form a list which would take us to the present time, since there is a clear line of development—although, as can be implied from the foregoing discussion, there is also an inherent divergence regarding the natural, inspirational ideals of the Five, which was shared by Tchaikovsky, and the resurgence of a more esoteric musical theory which was to become almost mathematical by Taniev and mystical by Scriabin.

Tchaikovsky, then, is important historically as a kind of crossroads of East and West—or, if you will, a rather clear case of fusion of these not necessarily disparate ideas. His music is opulent testimony to the balance which one can achieve.

Tchaikovsky was a complete composer, mastering almost every medium of expression. His least successful works, in my opinion, are those for piano, an instrument he did not play very well. The great *Piano Concerto in B-flat Minor* is a notable exception, but he had the orchestra to lean on. As with the other masters of his time, the passage work is done imaginatively and does not have the empty padding which one finds in works such as the *Concerto in D Minor* of Rubinstein—a composer who wrote some pleasant trifles, including the *Melody in F*, which has had the dubious distinction of having been arranged for just about everything but a quartet of two koto, a crwth and a serpent! Anton Rubinstein was a versatile musician: pianist, composer, conductor and teacher, and was somewhat out of step with the mainstream of Russian music; he was much too conservative and "classical" in his viewpoint. He, as with others of his time, just could not pile up one little idea after another and end up with a successful large form. (One does not build a great cathedral by simply piling up dozens of small chapels.)

Building the large, successful musical edifice, as Tchaikovsky often did, requires the great grasp of musical architecture which the truly great always seem to have. There were many composers with more technical skill than Tchaikovsky, among them the late Rachmaninoff (who musically was still in Tchaikovsky's generation), but few composers made up for soft spots in skill with such splendid heights of sublime music.

The inner parts in Tchaikovsky are usually striking, and add contrapuntal interest to the texture. The voice leading often results in extremely fascinating artificial scales, especially in the more rapid, exciting passages. These are brought about through a command of chromatic harmony which is still tonal, but utilizes the remote relationships which by the 1890's are almost commonplace and to our ears are beautiful only when done in the best way: well scored, well voiced and when accompanying beautiful melodies.

Tchaikovsky was influenced by Liszt to a certain extent, especially with regard to thematic transformation and a certain bombast when all else fails—even though he disliked Liszt's music. Tchaikovsky, however, did not always seem to need the extramusical impetus, although his program music is often very good—the *Romeo and Juliet* wears especially well. He drew from a variety of sources for his subject matter, and was well-versed enough to fully understand Shakespeare's *Romeo and Juliet*. One weakness which Tchaikovsky shares with Liszt is too much repetition *within* periods, although I admit this shows up at its worst in some of his ballet music, where he must fill in to allow enough steps or beats for the dancers, and sometimes where he repeats to "fill in" a classical form; the "Waltz of the Flowers" fades quickly.

One of his most striking themes is in the $\frac{5}{4}$ movement from the *Sixth Symphony*, which really is in that meter: it is not forced, and is a delight. The trio portion returns to the dark tones of the symphony, however. Darkness is common with Tchaikovsky, and maybe his brilliance is that much more brilliant because of this. Few composers (except possibly Mahler) have ever written music so gloomy in aspect; note the beginning of the *Manfred Symphony*.

Tchaikovsky borrowed some folk songs for his works, but almost always made them like his own. His own themes are almost classical, in that they use tones from the common major and minor keys and on some occasions have a modal flavor. He tends to save chromaticism for developments. He develops themes in a manner similar to Liszt, but also is related enough to Wagner for his treatment of cyclic material to be called a *Leitmotiv*.

The beginning of the last movement of the *Pathétique Symphony* has a unique bit of melodic writing. Note that the melody is not played by any one instrument, but the pitches are passed back and forth in hocket; the melody is given a very special strained quality in this way. Some conductors have even ruined the effect by rewriting the whole thing so that the theme is played by the first violins and the harmony by the seconds. The newer seating of the violins (beside each other) is not as effective as the older seating (opposite).

TCHAIKOVSKY: *Symphony No. 6*
(*"Pathetique"*), Op. 74

Figure 5-3

Let us consider one final aspect of Tchaikovsky's melodic writing: the great contrast between the first and second themes in almost every large movement, be it in sonata form or not. He goes to great lengths to make the second theme as different as possible from the first, and yet we know it still belongs to the same work.

Other Russian composers did not attempt such affinities with classical forms. When one of the Five set out to write an abstract work there was an avoidance of these forms, in part on purpose and in part in ignorance. There was almost a monothematic movement, a spinning out of themes from logical outgrowths of the motto (the *Urkeim,* as Liszt called it) heard at or near the beginning. The first movement of Borodin's *Second Symphony* or the first movement of Balakirev's *First Symphony* are good examples. While these are formal considerations, they are mentioned here since the ideal in tonal Western musical form has been the theme itself and its relationship to the whole. It is an important aspect of melodic writing too, contrasted either by being completely foreign or by using differing aspects of the same material. Key relationships are often remote, and there is the possibility of going from a key to a key or from a key to a mode, or vice versa. Also of importance is the melodic doubling used by the composer—not for power, but for color. The accompaniment is also colorfully orchestrated.

The actual use of folk material in Russian music is more often than not stylistic, in true romantic fashion—the spirit rather than the letter of the law. The student should not assume that the use of a folk song consists only of a quotation or a new harmonization, or only variations or developments; one can find all of these possibilities. After all, the composers in the latter half of the nineteenth century did not really know too much about folk music. Using music played by tavern bands is not necessarily folk music, since there is a complicated mixture of oral tradition and sheer musical panhandling. ("If they like what I play, they will throw me a coin; therefore, I will play what causes the most coins to be thrown.") Much of what passes as "folk music" is the product of crass commercialism, no matter what kind of interior decorating has been done in the place where the "folk song" has been heard. When Julius Melgunov (1846-1893) asserted that Russian folk music was indeed polyphonic and brought forth printed collections in 1879-1885, he was not thanked by the composers; Rimsky-Korsakov even viewed them with contempt.[12] The contrapuntal parts were perhaps not taken down with the utmost accuracy. These parts were often harmonically crude but were straight from the people. The Five and the others refused to recognize the *whole* musical substance; they took only the tune and then harmonized it in colorful ways, thereby creating what they ostensibly abhorred: sophisticated music, but not folk music. Melgunov's work was substantiated in subsequent research by Evgenia Linev and many others, where the actual music was recorded, so that the performances could be heard again and again to detect all of the peculiarities. Bruno Nettl, in his *Folk and Traditional Music of the Western Continents*,[13] discusses the polyphonic nature of this music and, on page 96, asserts, "Polyphony is one element of music that characterizes all of Eastern Europe."

The greatest authority of all on this question was Béla Bartók (1881-1945), one of our greatest contemporary composers; but we must include him as continuing the nationalistic tradition. He is one of the high points or perhaps the culmination of this kind of music. In *Béla Bartók, a Memorial Review of His Life and Works*[14] there is an article by Bartók himself, "The Influence of Peasant Music on Modern Music," in which he discusses two extremes: 1) setting the melody as if it were a precious stone, its beauty *enhanced* by what the composer has done; and 2) considering the melody as a motto and that which is built around it as important—the melody or a shape from it being the nucleus from which the rest has grown, as in all living things. Of course, the final maturation can be a monster or a beauty, in life or in composition. This article by Bartók was originally published in 1931 and was translated into English by Eva Hajnal-Konyi. Bartók was probably thinking of the Russians as well as others, when he said:

At this point I have to mention a strange notion wide-spread some thirty or forty years ago. Most trained and good musicians then believed that only simple harmonizations were well suited to folk-tunes. And even worse, by simple harmonies they meant a succession of triads of tonic, dominant and possibly subdominant.

How can we account for this strange belief? What kind of folk-songs did these musicians know? Mostly new German and Western songs and so-called folk-songs made up by popular composers. The melody of such songs usually moves along the triad of tonic and dominant; the main melody consists of a breaking up of these chords into single notes ("Oh Du Lieber Augustin"). It is obvious that melodies of this description do not go well with a more complex harmonization.

But our musicians wanted to apply the theory derived from this type of songs to an entirely different type of Hungarian songs built up on "pentatonic" scales.

It may sound odd, but I do not hesitate to say: the simpler the melody the more complex and strange may be the harmonization and accompaniment that go well with it. Let us for instance take a melody that moves on two successive notes only (there are many such melodies in Arab peasant music). It is obvious that we are much freer in the invention of an accompaniment than in the case of a melody of a more complex character. These primitive melodies moreover, show no trace of the stereotyped joining of triads. That again means greater freedom for us in the treatment of the melody. It allows us to bring out the melody most clearly by building round it harmonies of the widest range varying along different keynotes. I might almost say that the traces of polytonality in modern Hungarian music and in Strawinsky's music are to be explained by this possibility.

Similarly, the strange turnings of melodies in our eastern European peasant music showed us new ways of harmonization. For instance the new chord of the seventh which we use as a concord may be traced back to the fact that in our folk melodies of a pentatonic character the seventh appears as an interval of equal importance with the third and the fifth. We so often heard these intervals as of equal value in the succession, that what was more natural than that we should try to make them sound of equal importance when used simultaneously. We sounded the four notes together in a setting which made us feel it not necessary to break them up. In other words: the four notes were made to form a concord.

The frequent use of quart* intervals in our old melodies suggested to us the use of quart chords. Here again what we heard in succession we tried to build up in a simultaneous chord.

Another method by which peasant music becomes transmuted into modern music is the following: The composer does not make use of a real peasant melody but invents his own imitation of such melodies. There is no true difference between this method and the one described above.[15]

These are the words of a great authority on the matter!

There are too many instances where a simple folk tune was forced into the square patterns of conservatory exercise, and not always with happy results. Folk music is not simple just because simple people sing and play it. Since much of it is improvised, there are possibilities for

* Bartók means the interval of a fourth.

many different versions. Since it is learned by ear as speech is learned, the parts which seem frightfully complex to the outsider are not so to the player or singer, since he is producing them "naturally" in the same way one speaks his native tongue. We tend to worry about being "correct" when speaking a learned language more than the mother tongue.

The theories of musical learning recently advanced by Shinichi Suzuki are based on similar theories, and there are many fine violinists to prove the validity of the theory. There have been many folk virtuosi of various instruments; their performances not only have fascinated composers, but technical devices found therein have been used in various ways by the composers. Many passages of local color, when either the program or the subject matter of a stage work called for it, were based on special figurations—those used by shepherd pipers, gypsy and other folk violinists, horn signals from mountain hornists, keening of sorrowing women, calls of peddlers selling their wares, chanting done in remote village churches, wedding music and all kinds of dances and festival music.

The use of whole-tone melodic materials in Russian music has often been discussed,[16] as well as the artificial scale invented by Rimsky-Korsakov.[17] Also of importance is the discovery by Melgunov that much Russian folk music is based on descending modes which have the same orientation of tones and semitones as an ascending major scale, but which are taken for the descending scale: such as a semitone between 3 and 4, or 7 and 8. We can find this on the piano by playing a C major scale from e down to e an octave below. The result is a descending Phrygian mode, which was used as a natural minor, while the regular major was used for major.

To summarize: the late nineteenth-century Russian composers utilized certain aspects of folkishness but were not ready to go all the way; as a result, they created a vital school of musical composition which combined the tonal tradition and a quasi-folkish flavor.

The influence of Liszt has been mentioned above, and should now be elaborated upon. He, too, used only a quasi- or even pseudo-folk idiom in his "Hungarian" compositions, mostly as a vehicle for brilliant elaboration. Liszt's music is an amalgam of many influences. In Russia his two works which exerted great influence were the musical numbers for Nicholas Lenau's *Faust* (*Zwei Episoden aus Lenau's "Faust"*), especially the "Mephisto Waltz"; and the *Totentanz* for piano and orchestra, which is a symphonic, fantastic set of variations on the Gregorian *Dies Irae* (the sequence from the Proper of the Gregorian *Missa pro defuncta*, the *Requiem*). The tune of the *Dies Irae* is attributed to Thomas a Celano (d. 1256), and is one of the most famous melodies in Western music. It was especially attractive to romantic composers, who, we must admit, were almost necrophiles. Berlioz's uses of this theme in the *Fantastic Symphony* and in his *Requiem* were so successful that he influenced other composers to use at least the opening phrase of it as a tune source suggestive of death. The list of composers using it is quite long, and the resulting works are greatly different in value. Of the better works using it, there are several by Rachmaninoff (1873-1943)—such as *Isle of the Dead* and *Rhapsody on a Theme by Paganini* (also containing another famous theme)—and it can be expected to crop up almost anywhere in his music, since he had a morbid fascination for this melody. Rachmaninoff's music is almost always melancholy; sadly, the man's music suffers from his having been born too late. Had he been born in the same generation as Tchaikovsky or the Five, he would have been more at home. Of the colossal romantics, he had one of the best techniques as a composer. Since several of his works are still enormously popular because of their melodic appeal, it is worthwhile to quote two of his melodies in order to see some important features.

The *Rhapsody on a Theme by Paganini* is actually a set of variations for piano and orchestra on Paganini's *Caprice No. 24*, originally a set of variations for unaccompanied violin. Rachmaninoff's work is justly popular and its date of composition (1934) is hard to believe. The melody which Rachmaninoff derives as the basic material for variation No. 18 is a beautiful example of Russian melody.

VARIATION XVIII

Figure 5-4
(Reprinted by permission of Charles Foley, Inc., New York)

Let us now take the first five notes and transpose them to start on A:

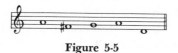

Figure 5-5

If these are in turn inverted, we have the first five notes of Paganini's *Caprice*!

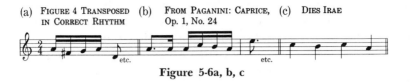

Figure 5-6a, b, c

Note further: if we change the first note from A to C and invert, we have the motto of the *Dies Irae*. This theme from the *Second Symphony* is also very beautiful:

Figure 5-7

One aspect of its beauty is the melodic use of seventh chords which are sequenced so that the listener hears a major seventh chord, a diminished minor seventh chord and a minor seventh chord, all coming very naturally from the scale of A major. Another expressive feature is the downward leap of a minor seventh to start each new sequence. The special pathétique quality of a downward minor seventh has been mentioned several times before.

Rachmaninoff was also influenced by Liszt as a pianist. One of his teachers was Alexander Siloti, who had studied with Liszt and Nicholas Rubinstein. His composition teachers were Taniev (which explains his mastery of compositional techniques) and Arensky. His music "sounds Russian," although he seldom used actual folk materials. His music draws heavily from Tchaikovsky and, although it rarely if ever reaches the heights of Tchaikovsky's best, it never contains the musical wasteland that we sometimes encounter in Tchaikovsky. Rachmaninoff learned from Taniev about connective tissue. Taniev, by the way, was often consulted by Tchaikovsky on theoretical matters—another case of a teacher learning from a pupil.

But it was all a little too late. What was once a lively issue, when the writings of Vladimir Stasov[18] were exciting to groups of intellectuals and artists of all kinds, was now a question almost of dogma at the conservatory. The battle had been won, but the fun was in the fighting, not the aftermath of winning. There is, however, something attractive about all of this music; and even though the *Prelude in C-sharp Minor* has probably been laid to rest, Rachmaninoff's music is put together too well to neglect.

Some of these same tendencies can be observed in Prokofiev and Shostakovitch and in the early works of Stravinsky, but newer political pressures, a newer society, war and revolution have somehow artificially retained elements of a world which no longer exists. A discussion of the impact of communism on music belongs properly in a study of twentieth-century music. The Soviet government has agencies which try to keep alive a true folk tradition and which sponsor research into the vast subject of the folk and ethnic music of all the Soviet peoples.

A contemporary and onetime friend of Rachmaninoff was Alexander Scriabin (1871-1915; some sources give 1872 due to a calendar change), who was not really a nationalistic composer, but did belong to the same group of musicians who studied with Taniev and Arensky. He was once considered the bright and shining light of early twentieth-century music, but others have since eclipsed him. His melodic practice derived much from Chopin, Liszt and Wagner, until he began to ascribe certain mystical qualities to music and found tonal combinations from unusual theories of harmony—these we will discuss in greater detail in the chapter dealing with harmony.

The Scandinavian countries produced composers who were primarily important in composing miniatures, some of them still delightful. Edvard Grieg (1843-1907) was one of the most important of these, a Norwegian who studied in Leipzig, but was able to flavor his music with local color from applications of folk idioms. These in turn he spiced with his own harmonic treatment, and it is this combination which is basic to his melodic style. Grieg's most famous major work, *Piano Concerto in A Minor*, is a good example. It obviously derives from Liszt in its approach to piano fireworks and orchestration, from Schumann and Brahms in themes and harmonies, and from Norway in the folk flavor of the second movement and the finale. The *Peer Gynt* music is also well-known, but is a stringing together of small pieces which pleasantly combine a mood with a kind of melody which one does not forget. This music has little to do with the great play of Ibsen! The student probably has heard the *Peer Gynt Suite* by now, since it is "common knowledge music" and is one of the first pieces played for elementary school children in an attempt at "music appreciation." One should now read the play, if he has not— he will soon see that Grieg's pleasant music has very little to do with the essentials of the play.

An appealing Swedish composer who has been played more of late is Franz Berwald (1796-1868), who, unlike most Scandinavian composers, wrote few songs or piano pieces, but was a symphonist and a composer of significant chamber music. John Horton characterized his melody thus: "His melodic patterns are extremely varied in construction, sometimes keeping mainly to stepwise motion, at others springing and soaring through wide diatonic intervals. . . ."[19] Berwald also wrote some operas and nationalistic cantatas in response to the intense national feelings aroused by historical events around 1848. His music is very well written and his handling of the orchestra is especially good; the inner parts are not musical sawdust, but add color and harmonic spice while still keeping the sonorities crystal-clear.

Musical affairs in the Scandinavian countries were not unlike those in the United States at the same time with respect to advanced musical study. American composers went to Germany, especially to Leipzig, but to other centers as well, to study with men such as Raff, Richter or Jadassohn. Liszt was often around to lend encouragement, as he did to MacDowell. One great difference existed, however. The Scandinavian composer at least knew which folk music was his, even if he did not really know too much about it. The American, to this day, is not really sure what constitutes American folk music—a music with which *he* can identify. One of America's greatest composers was Charles Ives, who took his Americanisms from real slices of American life: the revival meeting, Fourth of July, Decoration Day, etc., in much the same way as nationalistic composers had done in Europe, especially in the Slavonic regions. Ives is held in high esteem now all over the world, especially for his symphonies. The Americans will be discussed in more detail later.

Another Scandinavian who was well-known in Germany was Niels Gade (1817-1890). Gade's friendship with Schumann has already been pointed out. He was perhaps even closer to Mendelssohn, and he took over the Gewandhaus concerts upon Mendelssohn's death. When Gade returned home to Copenhagen to conduct the Musikforeningen, he introduced Danish audiences to the great German classics from J. S. Bach to his contemporaries on both sides of the mainstream: Liszt, Wagner and Brahms. The music of Berlioz was often programmed, exerting a profound impression on all who heard it. Gade himself as a conductor learned much from studying scores, and he advanced well in his own technique as a composer. His works are not performed much today, even in Denmark, but at one time they were quite popular.

Grieg was profoundly influenced by Gade and was led to try his hand at a similar kind of musical utterance, which mixed German and Scandinavian romanticism. Grieg, however, was most successful in his songs and in his lyrical piano pieces. The masters of the large forms came a little later: Carl Nielsen (1865-1931), who studied at the conservatory in Copenhagen when Gade was still the director; and Jean Sibelius (1865-1957), the voice of Finland. Appreciation of Nielsen's work was late in arriving in England and the United States, while Sibelius was extremely popular in those countries due in part to the constant programming by Sir Thomas Beecham. Interest in the too-popular works of Sibelius is now waning, but interest in his lesser-known works continues. Although both men lived well into the twentieth century and were often very original, they continued a romantic tradition and did not, as Bartók, become strong voices for "new music."

In the same generation must be included the great Englishman Ralph Vaughan Williams (1872-1958), since he was also a great symphonist. He studied on the continent with Bruch and Ravel, two diverse figures, and yet was able to establish a style of his own which is definitely English and twentieth century. His nationalism is two-fold: the study of English folk music and the study of older English art music, especially that of the Tudor Period. This opens the door to still newer possibilities: new applications of old ideas and textures. Of the many who have attempted this, Vaughan Williams is one of the most successful. His music has a great melodic charm, which combines modal tunes and textures with more complicated harmony.

A parallel development in Spain is seen in Manuel de Falla (1876-1946), who combined a French atmosphere with Spanish tunes—especially Andulsian. He studied carefully the folk music of Iberia, and was very meticulous in classifying it. A closer look at his music, however, belongs in the study of twentieth-century music.

In conclusion, most of the nationalistic composers combined a solid technique with some aspect of folk tunes and rhythms. In the most successful works there is a vivid new style of music which must be likened to an efficient hybrid. The intrusion of folk and Gregorian modes, exotic artificial scales and colorful harmonizations thereof, as romantic as they all were, actually contributed much to the ultimate downfall of textbook harmony and counterpoint (textbook orchestration was not as yet old enough). Here, then, is another fascinating paradox: the free, untutored music of the people, especially the peasants, finds its way into the most sophisticated of musical forms. There is even some feedback as city music shows an impact on the music of the hinterland, which in turn comes back to the city for the learned composer, and so on. This cycle of folk art is often discussed and is the basis of many different theories and ideas about the nature of what folk music is and what it ought to be. In subsequent chapters many of these concepts will be discussed as they relate to harmony, form, orchestration or other musical elements.

Notes

1. After receiving an honorary doctorate at Cambridge and another from a Czech university, Dvořák began a teaching career in 1891, after some private teaching and triumphant performances in England and on the continent. He taught composition, orchestration and form at the Prague Conservatory. From 1892 to 1895 he taught at the National Conservatory in New York, and after returning home resumed his duties at the conservatory. He was appointed direc-

tor in 1901, and held that post until his death. Otakar Sourek's article on Dvořák in *Grove's Dictionary* speaks in glowing terms of Dvořák as a teacher.

2. One of the most famous and misleading is the common *Well-Tempered Clavichord*, when it should read *Clavier*: i.e., any keyboard. The clavichord is quite incapable of sounding much of Bach's great work. In Bach's time the word referred to the harpsichord as well. The first English version of *Musikalisches Opfer* was "Musical Sacrifice."

3. Antonin Dvořák, *Critical Edition Based on the Composer's Manuscripts* (Prague: Artia, 1960).

4. William W. Austin, *Music in the Twentieth Century* (New York: W. W. Norton & Company, Inc., 1966). Reprinted by permission of J. M. Dent & Sons Ltd.

5. Austin, *loc. cit.*, p. 80.

6. The musical compositions based on literary works of Pushkin are impressive. In a footnote on page 38 of Richard Leonard's admirable book *A History of Russian Music* (New York: The Macmillan Co., 1957), a list of only the larger works appears. Major works by Glinka, Dargomyzhsky, Mussorgsky, Tchaikovsky, Stravinsky and others show that Pushkin was a major force in the development of a Russian national school.

7. Donald J. Grout, *A Short History of Opera* (New York: Columbia University Press, 1947).

8. See Donald Tovey's *The Mainstream of Music* (New York: Oxford University Press, 1949), p. 45. This passage is quoted in the present book, in the chapter on counterpoint.

9. Vladimir Stasov (1824-1906) was a major force in all intellectual Russian life during the time of the nationalistic artists. His book, *Twenty-five Years of Russian Art*, points out that abstract or pure art does not really represent the Russian people. He recognized the importance of men such as Glinka and Mussorgsky, and coined the name "Kuchka" (group) for the Mighty Five. The discussions which he had with these artists and the free exchange of ideas must have been very stimulating. Stasov's theories were quite in line with the symphonic literary programs of Berlioz and Liszt; he was the antithesis of critics such as Hanslick, who held that music should express only itself. Hanslick is discussed elsewhere in this book.

10. James Bakst, *A History of Russian Soviet Music* (New York: Dodd, Mead & Co., 1966), p. 136.

11. Sergei Taneev [note spelling], *Convertible Counterpoint in the Strict Style*, trans. and ed. by G. Ackley Brower (Boston: B. Humphries, 1962).

12. Folk music was collected in Russia by order of the government. Some of the most famous composers, such as Rimsky-Korsakov, were involved in compiling this music which was long a part of the Russian life. Melgunov was not an important composer, but an illustrious scholar who believed in preserving the music as it really was. Rimsky-Korsakov did not understand the importance of folk polyphony, which he thought was barbarous. He preferred to have these melodies harmonized in the style of Glinka. Melgunov was apparently one of the first to realize the dichotomy which exists between the unspoiled entire corpus of authentic folk music and the professionally trained *idea* of what the music is. The student is referred to specialized histories of Russian music such as Gerald Abraham's *On Russian Music*, Leonard's *A History of Russian Music*, Bakst's *A History of Russian-Soviet Music* and the article in *Grove's* on Melgunov written by Rosa Newmarch.

13. Bruno Nettl, *Folk and Traditional Music of the Western Continents* (Englewood Cliffs, N.J.: Prentice-Hall, Inc., © 1965), p. 96.

14. Boosey and Hawkes (eds.), *Béla Bartók, a Memorial Review of His Life and Works* (New York: Boosey and Hawkes, Inc., 1950), p. 72.

15. *Ibid.*, pp. 72-73.

16. Many authors discuss the use of the whole-tone scale or whole-tone fragments in Russian music. For some reason, composers associated evil characters with it: Chernomor in Glinka's *Russlan and Ludmilla*, the statue in Dargomyzhsky's *The Stone Guest*, the Headsman in Rimsky-Korsakov's *May Night*. See also Chapter V, "The Whole-tone Scale in Russian Music," in Gerald Abraham's *On Russian Music* (New York: Charles Scribner's, 1939), pp. 62-72. It is possible that an influence of the Lydian mode (C D E F# G A B) in the lower tetrachord would suggest whole-tone treatments. The Lydian mode was found quite often in Slovakian folk music. Another possibility is that all fourths are augmented in the whole-tone scale—the devil in music.

17. See note 9 above.

18. See note 9 above.

19. John Horton, *Scandinavian Music, a Short History* (London: Faber and Faber, 1963), p. 113.

MELODY IN ITALY, FRANCE, POSTROMANTIC GERMANY, ENGLAND AND THE UNITED STATES

Italy

ITALY WAS IN THE forefront of musical development from the six-teenth century to the late eighteenth, and had composers of the first rank as early as the fourteenth. It is no accident that Italian is the universal language for tempo, agogic and dynamic markings. In the late eighteenth century, however, Italian musicians began to specialize in opera at the expense of other forms of music, and the most important internal developments shifted to the German-speaking world. Italy, how-ever, had exported many important musicians, and other composers of the greatest fame (Handel and Mozart) had been strongly influenced through visiting Italy.

Melody has always been an important aspect of Italian music, and with the rise of a popular opera and an entertainment kind of instru-mental music melody of a "catchy" nature became much in vogue; it was a mark of success if a composer's tune was sung or whistled on the streets the day after the premiere. There are even intriguing stories about a composer keeping his "hit" tunes a secret until the public premiere.

Such a milieu leads to formula, and, sorry to say, a cheapening to a certain extent of the noble art of music; but, as has been said earlier, each man is entitled to his own kind of music. There were some composers, however, who were able to transcend this problem and with sheer genius put into their music a lasting quality which is still admired and which was important in the development of dramatic music. Paganini (1782-1840) was supremely important in the development of violin technique and was an important influence as a virtuoso on Liszt and, in somewhat peculiar ways, on Berlioz.[1] Opera, then, was not the whole story.

Above all, there was the personality of Verdi (1813-1901), who did the impossible and actually developed public tastes for the better as he grew in his own command of musical theater. Few composers display such a steady rise from his earliest works to the sublime operatic heights of *Otello* and *Falstaff*, the great beauty of the *Requiem* or the contrapuntal skill of the *String Quartet in E Minor*.

Melody in Italy is almost synonymous with opera, and will be discussed in detail in the chapter on vocal music, along with other aspects of opera. Italian melody in most cases was "enclosed"[2]—it was of regular design and periodicity, as one would expect when accompanying a poetic text. Aria texts particularly followed specific designs. Because of this and their inherent tunefulness, based on common chords and scale lines, the public displayed an immediate liking for them; structures which were "open," as in Wagner, were less easy to follow. There was not much vital chromaticism until late in the century, except in passages where dramatic intensity was needed. The diminished seventh really got a workout! There were some refreshing modulations made possible through imaginative uses of the Neapolitan sixth, which was probably named for its common occurrence in that kind of opera. Operatic recitatives were freer in design, but still tended to be formula-ridden. The function of the recitative is to inform the audience, and in a way the beauty of the set numbers is enhanced by the dry qualities of the recitative. As set numbers left opera and the musical line became more continuous, the vocal melody approached a mean in many instances: the arias became more like recitatives, and the recitatives became more like arias. Accompanied recitative also became important, and proved more interesting musically. Toward the end of the century there was a tendency toward angularity, as had been observed in the other countries.

Italian instrumental music developed mostly along the lines of a higher, more brilliant instrumental technique, led by Paganini. The melodies of these instrumental works were almost operatic in conception, and the music was distinguished by complex technical passage work and fantastic exploitation of borrowed melodies—such as the famed *Moses Fantasy* from Rossini's *Mosè in Egitto*.

A great triumvirate in the early part of the century consisted of Rossini (1792-1868), Donizetti (1797-1848) and Bellini (1801-1835). All three of these composers still displayed classical traits in their melodic writing, but tinges of romanticism began to appear, especially in passages calling for greater emotional intensity. The subject matter was romantic, but opera had many conventions to be overcome.

Verdi was the great man who overrode these conventions to become one of Italy's most illustrious composers. Other masters who still hold the stage today are Ponchielli (1834-1886), Boito (1842-1918; he was also Verdi's best librettist), Leoncavallo (1858-1919), Mascagni (1863-1945) and some others. The best composer after Verdi was Puccini (1858-1924), who had a melodic style all his own which, with deft touches, could characterize a young Japanese girl or a flippant Musetta. Like Verdi, he used the orchestra well; he employed a "recall system" of motives which is effective but is not responsible for the whole texture, as is the case with Wagner and his heirs.

While there was never a real reaction against romantic opera, Italian composers since the late nineteenth century have joined the mainstream, and once again there is significant abstract music being written by Italians. One Italian who is somewhat comparable to the more brilliant French impressionists was Respighi (1879-1936), who has to be included as a true romantic—at least in his Roman tone poems,[3] which are inspiring to hear if well played. Although written in the twentieth century, they utilize romantic notions of large orchestral music and yet have certain impressionistic qualities. Respighi sometimes used Gregorian chant as a melodic source.

France

In France there were several different styles: some coming from the Paris Conservatory, some from the stimulating new sounds from renegades such as Berlioz, some from the great instrumental virtuosity heard in the salons from artists all over the world, and the impact of music by Wagner, Chopin, Liszt and other foreigners. In a sense, Paris was a crossroads where the talented young composer could be exposed to a fair representation of the world's music. There was French opera (Grand and Comique), and such diverse figures as Auber (1782-1871) and Meyerbeer (1791-1864), a German who wrote mainly Italian and French opera, Hérold (1791-1833), Halévy (1799-1862) and Offenbach (1819-1880), to name a few of the important ones. In addition to the transplanted Meyerbeer there was also Cherubini (1760-1842), an Italian who became almost another Lully[4] in France. Cherubini was a very skillful composer and an enormous influence in the development of French music, his misunderstandings with Berlioz notwithstanding.

Cherubini, as one of the transition composers from classicism to romanticism and as director of the conservatory, felt that he was a keeper of the true canons of the art. He could be classical (see the beginning of his second keyboard sonata). He could also be quite romantic (see parts of his *Requiem in C Minor*).

A contemporary at the conservatory who taught Berlioz was Lesueur[5] (1760-1837), who was very strong in his positive feelings about pictorial music. He was also a teacher of Gounod, and undoubtedly had much more in common with the new movements in music than Cherubini.

With Franck (1822-1890), Saint-Saëns (1835-1921), Fauré (1845-1924) and d'Indy (1851-1931), there was a solid group of men who were interested in classical forms and abstract music and, in a way, did more for the cause of classical reverence than men such as Cherubini and Meyerbeer, who succumbed to the public taste for gigantic opera scenes (conflagrations, floods and avalanches) but whose music did not advance in significant inner details as did that of their contemporaries. Berlioz was right when he contended that his music for a big fire scene from one of his works could not possibly be reduced for the piano, since it depended on the actual sound of the orchestra for the right effect.[6]

The role of Anton Reicha (1770-1836), an extraordinary musician, cannot be overlooked. He taught at the Paris Conservatory from 1818 and counted among his pupils Berlioz, Liszt, Gounod and Franck. Reicha was the same age as Beethoven and the two were friends. They even played in the same orchestra in Bonn: Beethoven played the viola and Reicha played second flute. A cosmopolitan, Reicha worked in Cologne before Bonn and then in Hamburg, Paris, Vienna (where he saw Beethoven again) and then back to Paris. He learned much about music from the intimacy one can gain only from performing it (he also played violin and piano in addition to the flute). His theoretical studies were the works of Kirnberger[7] and Marpurg.[8] In Paris his music was considered a little strange by the conservatives (he is even mentioned in that light in Balzac's *Les Employés*), but he was fascinating to people like Berlioz. Reicha wrote didactic works which attempted to cover the entire art of music, and in which some novel theories were advanced; some of them are discussed in the chapter on counterpoint. Of especial interest were his prophetic discussions of polytonality, polymodality, quarter tones and the use of unusual meter signatures such as $\frac{5}{8}$. Franck and other pupils learned about the internal structure of J. S. Bach and Handel.

Reicha was deeply concerned about music having a discipline *based* on the past but *not* an imitation of it. Also to his credit is his study of old French music which no one else at that time thought to be of any importance. Later, Saint-Saëns and others shared his enthusiasm. Needless to say, in the intrigues of Paris Conservatory faculty politics Reicha and Cherubini were on opposite sides. Norman Demuth[9] comments on the discipline Reicha expected from his pupils and the clarity of his corrections. The exercise books of Franck under Reicha still survive, and can be studied. Franck also learned much about teaching composition and had a remarkable group of students himself to attest to this. Franck's studies with Reicha were done privately; his student days at the conservatory were after Reicha's death.

Plate VII

César Franck at the organ. Tableau by Mlle. J. Ronjier *(Courtesy The Bettmann Archive, N.Y.)*.

César Franck was actually Belgian by birth and almost German by taste. (He admitted that the three-note figure which generates his *Symphony in D Minor* was suggested by the motive of fate from Wagner's *Ring*.) Franck's melody fits his own particular kind of chromatic harmony. In the beautiful *Violin Sonata*, the first entrance of the violin is an outline of a diminished minor-seventh chord[10] which is actually a part of the dominant of A major—the root is in the bass of the piano part and the violin is then outlining like a "Mannheim rocket," but here the chord is a whole ninth chord, not just a triad:

Figure 6-1

In the same work note the angularity and at letter H the frequency of the pitch C-sharp and one statement of the famous canon:

Figure 6-2a, b

This sonata is well constructed with cyclic treatment, as are most of Franck's works. Another feature of Franck's melodic treatment is the tendency of a theme to gravitate around one pitch.

The unjustly neglected *String Quartet* cycles about this theme:

Figure 6-3a, b

This theme undergoes many striking transformations, including the beautiful slow fugue.

D'Indy was a pupil and disciple of Franck. He set up the *Schola Cantorum* in opposition to the Paris Conservatory and its sometimes rather deaf conservatism. Franck had been a professor at the Paris Conservatory, but was officially assigned to teach organ. It was an unkept secret that he taught composition in the organ loft. D'Indy's music is unified in much the same way as Franck's, but is more diffuse, less direct and somehow does not wear as well. The *Second Symphony* of d'Indy is a good example of cyclic treatment. It also has an expressive fugato in which the germinal motive is used as a subject. For Americans the theme of the finale of d'Indy's *Symphony on a French Mountain Air* somehow reminds us of "This is the Army, Mr. Jones!" Another appealing work is the set of orchestral variations, *Istar*: fascinating melodically, since the variations are "unwrapped" and the more simple variations occur last.

Also in this group of Franckians were Chausson (1855-1899), Lekeu (1870-1894), Alexis de Castillon (1838-1873) and Henri Duparc (1848-1933). These men are worthy of a separate study. Through some strange set of circumstances, they all met with violence or personal tragedy, as did Franck himself. (He died from injuries suffered from being struck by an omnibus; he did not seek immediate medical attention, and worked for a short time after the accident. Some say he might have survived had he not tried to work.) Castillon was wounded in the Franco-Prussian War, and died later from his wounds. Lekeu died at the age of twenty-four of typhoid fever. Chausson was killed in a bicycle accident, while Duparc came down with an incurable nervous disorder in 1885 which prevented any further work. All of these men were extraordinarily gifted. Duparc is well-known in this country through his exquisite songs, while Chausson is played with some frequency (*Poème* for violin and orchestra, *Symphony in B-Flat, Concerto* for violin, piano and string quartet, and some songs). Lekeu is known by some violinists for a beautiful violin sonata, but Castillon is not often played. It is idle to speculate about what these men would have been able to do had they lived out normal lives.

D'Indy was also a good teacher of composition, and his treatise is still read. As was the case with many disciples, he tended to apply Franck's principles with rigidity rather than keen imagination.

Bizet (1838-1875), Gounod (1818-1893), Massenet (1842-1912) and Gustave Charpentier (1860-1956) were the most important of a group of composers known for the extreme popularity of a few works.

Bizet's masterpiece is *Carmen*, an opera which still lives on largely due to the beauty and/or atmosphere of the melodies. One motive permeates the opera, and is often called the "fate" or "knife" motive:

Figure 6-4

The augmented second helps to give the music a Spanish flavor. There are several transformations of this theme.

Bizet was a brilliant orchestrator, admired even by Rimsky-Korsakov, and the effectiveness of his melodic writing is in large measure a result of the scoring. In *Carmen* and other works of Bizet we also find a facile kind of clean and clear counterpoint. *Carmen* has been called one of the most successful realistic operas. Operatic realism was a romantic development observed in Italy as well as France. Bizet was a product of the Paris Conservatory, having studied there with Zimmerman (a pupil of Cherubini) and Gounod.

Gounod is a bit of a puzzle, since some of his recorded comments about music (contra Franck, for example) seem to be at odds with the music he wrote. Perhaps he was an example of the principle often heard to the effect that a composer should keep his mouth shut and his pen busy on score paper. Some composers, however, write and speak so well that this cannot be a universal principle. Gounod's *Faust* is too popular: we are a little numb to its beauties, and we neglect his other works. Unlike Bizet, Gounod wrote quantities of sacred music—a by-product, no doubt, of his studies for the priesthood. Gounod overused the device of sequence; here is one of the best-loved melodies from *Faust* which illustrates this:

Figure 6-5

Along with most of the other major French composers, Gounod was a recipient of the *Prix de Rome* in 1839.[11] He too studied at the Paris Conservatory, mainly with Halévy in counterpoint and Lesueur in composition. It was from the latter that he probably learned about atmosphere, which is very effective, especially in *Faust* (study the prelude and the *Walpurgisnacht* music). A melody which in a way is a travesty, but still has some merit, is the "Ave Maria" written to be accompanied by the "Prelude in C Major" from Volume I of Bach's *Well-Tempered Clavier*. The conservatory assigned this project to all students of composition, and many dozens were written; but only the Gounod setting is famous. In concept the melody is not too unlike the French opera aria of the period.

Massenet is best known for his *Manon*. (The same story was set by Puccini, and a comparative study is rewarding for the student.) His best work, however, is held by many to be *Werther*, based on Goethe's famous novel. Massenet was also a successful teacher at the Paris Conservatory, where he had many famous pupils. He had studied at the conservatory himself under Ambroise Thomas (1811-1896), the composer of the still-popular *Mignon*. Massenet had a remarkable gift for melody, and used the *Leitmotiv* in a quasi-Wagnerian way which was by no means an imitation of Wagner.

Massenet often uses the fourth with the third inside—B, A-sharp, F-sharp, as in the line in *Manon* sung by Lescaut in the fourth act (the Chansonette, *"C'est ici que celle . . ."*). This is permuted very often, such as E, B, D in Des Grieux's *"Manon, sphinx étonant"* (also Act IV).

Figure 6-6a, b, c, d

These are the result of motivic treatment, but his other works also show the same formula.

The student will notice that, in 6-6a, the motive is found: G, F, D; D, C, A; and varied in the last measure with an anacrusis. Note the imaginative expansion and permutation in the other examples. Remember that the motive also can go upward; note especially 6-6b and 6-6d.

Massenet also used ascending large intervals to good effect, then descending slowly, as in the famous "Elegie" (originally a song, but now arranged for everything possible). The famous "Meditation" from *Thais* has suffered perhaps even more, but is a beautifully arched melody using notes from the tonic triad. *Thais* abounds in lovely melodies, and it is a shame that *Thais* or *Werther* are not performed more, to give poor *Manon* a rest (lovely as it is).

Charpentier is remembered today mostly for the opera *Louise*, which is another example of French operatic realism. An entrance line such as, "Is the soup ready?" is quite realistic, as is the scene where Louise and other girls are working at sewing machines. Charpentier's melodic gift is well-shown in the melodic line of the justly popular "Depuis le jour." The first two bars of the vocal line represent a kind of *Leitmotiv* used psychologically; this one refers to the happiness of Louise as she here and later recalls specifically her first kiss from Julian and in general her happiness over Julian's love for her. Other motives are also prominent. The motive of Julian is more than Julian. It is a symbol of the feelings aroused in a young girl by the man she loves. Charpentier studied with Massenet at the Paris Conservatory and also won the *Prix de Rome.*

Opera in general occupied much attention, but there were also some outstanding composers of virtuoso instrumental music who, like Chopin, were successes in Paris. Some of this music is still played today, at least by students, while most of it has all but sunk into oblivion until it is old enough to interest musicology students. An important violinist-composer was Henri Vieuxtemps (1820-1881), a Belgian child prodigy who studied in Paris with de Beriot. Vieuxtemps' *Concerto in D Minor* for violin and orchestra, and some shorter pieces, are distinguished more by handling of themes rather than by any innate distinguishing characteristics. Alkan (1813-1888) was a pianist-composer who is once again beginning to attract attention after many years of unjust neglect. Some feel that he was the "Berlioz of the piano." His music is of remarkable brilliance and is fiendishly difficult. He was a strange man, and did not seek public acclaim as most of his contemporaries. His music, like Chopin's has a somber cast, even when brilliant. He was well-read; one day, when reaching in the library for a book on Hebrew philosophy, he was killed when the bookcase fell on him—another case of the tragic death of an outstanding French musician. His real name was Charles Morhange.

The Paris Conservatory has been given unfair treatment in many sources, primarily due to the way in which the more progressive composers were misunderstood and the often bad political situations which prevailed there. Many of France's finest talents studied and taught there, and still do. Massenet (1842-1912) contributed much, as did Gabriel Fauré (1845-1924). One problem was the age-old one of *status quo* versus change. Some of the directors were pedantic and single-minded, while others saw the need for a free forum of ideas. Other problems existed from time to time in the dialogues of students and faculty. The case of Berlioz is widely publicized, but Debussy and other great talents also had difficulty. There was some justification for d'Indy and other French musicians to expand the *Schola Cantorum* in opposition in 1894, to teach the whole art of music rather than liturgical music and chanting, which had been the original purpose.

The cyclic method of composition, which meant so much to Franck and his coterie, is a factor which was of utmost importance in melodic construction. The Chausson *Concerto* builds much from this motto; note how it is used.

CHAUSSON: *Concerto for Piano, Violin and String Quartet*, Op. 21

Figure 6-7

Many chromatic melody lines are induced from the harmony and, vice versa, cliché-like lines are given new life by the way they are harmonized. We can see a propensity for triads with a major third and diminished fifth—often called the "French triad," such as:

Figure 6-8

This is often used as a part of somewhat more complex harmony, such as a minor triad with added major sixth—A C E F#—or a diminished minor-seventh chord—F# A C E—or a complete ninth chord (as in the Franck example above). Harmony is so much a part of melodic writing that one can often conclude that the entire texture was conceived as a whole rather than as a "soprano line with harmonization." Almost any song of Duparc will illustrate this.

In *Chanson triste* the first phrase has a melodic line one could find in thousands of songs. The effectiveness of this one, however, derives from two kinds of harmonic complication: 1) the pedal point, the overtones of which color the outline of the dominant seventh in the piano, and 2) the interest of the little countermelody E-flat–D, which Duparc clearly marks with double stems.

DUPARC: *Extase*

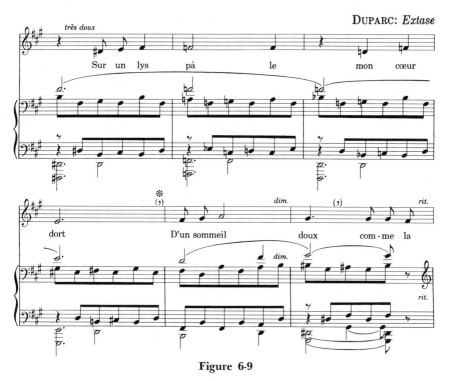

Figure 6-9

From "Extasse," by Henri Duparc (by permission of the International Music Company, New York).

The E-flat is also in the pedal point, but in the upper part there is the sound of the 4-3 resolution as the E-flat (the eleventh) resolves to D, the chord tone, the third of the dominant seventh.

In the second bar of the example the effect of the E-flat in the voice part is greatly enhanced by the chord change and change of bass. Here

DUPARC: *Chanson Triste*

Figure 6-10

From "Chanson triste," by Henri Duparc (by permission of the
International Music Company, New York).

there is in effect a major triad with added sixth, but the notes could
also form a minor-minor seventh chord—although I feel the intent is
for the ear to hear subdominant harmony with the added F and the
use of the "French triad." This illustrates the mixing of two chords
(A-flat major and F minor), and is at least the beginning of the concept
that two chords may sound together. In this case, however, there is a
logical explanation through considering the F as a non-harmonic tone.
Note the next phrase of this song:

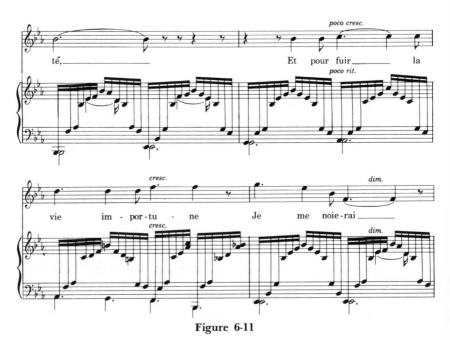

Figure 6-11

From "Chanson triste," by Henri Duparc (by permission of the
International Music Company, New York).

It has a beautiful arched, somewhat unusual melodic line which settles back in an interesting manner on the words "Je me noierai," which are notes taken from the harmony. In the second bar of the example there is some unusual harmony. On the second beat is the dominant seventh of C, which often resolves deceptively to the major triad on the lowered sixth degree as in minor—here an A-flat major chord which is in the upper part of the harmony. The bass, however, is F, and we must assume that Duparc (if he ever bothered to analyse his own music) considers the F to be the supertonic, in view of the continuation of the harmony through the dominant seventh to the tonic. This supertonic then, would be a minor-minor seventh chord as it appears naturally in major. The G major-minor seventh chord (dominant seventh in quality) pulls the ear one way, and the effect of the third beat is quite surprising. The melody here presents only chord tones.

Some space has been taken to discuss these few bars (much more could still be said), since it is my belief that a good singer and a good pianist would look into these matters for a better understanding of the song. Often the voice student does not sing the right pitch, since he is simply not hearing the harmony correctly. In the songs of Duparc, and in most good art songs, the piano does not just accompany; the mood and atmosphere cannot be created without it. Try singing Duparc's *Chanson triste* without the piano, and chances are you will imagine quite a different harmony from the one which is there! For this same reason, audiences find this music hard to understand at first hearing. The whole work is important, not just the solo vocal part. Note further how careful Duparc is to help the pianist and the singer capture the right mood: "slow, with tenderness and intimacy," and for the pianist, "always with much smoothness." I have heard this song performed where the pianist apparently thought that "strisciando" meant "in an irritated manner"; when, in reality, it is the word we should probably use instead of "glissando," which is a bad corruption of French and Italian.

Franck and his school exerted a strong influence on other French composers, in addition to some composers from other countries. Camille Saint-Saëns (1835-1921) was a pupil of Halévy at the conservatory, but was strongly influenced by the cyclic treatment of Liszt (the two had met in 1852) and, in a way, was also influenced by Franck. Saint-Saëns' treatment of Franck was often shabby,[12] but Franck apparently bore no rancor and even dedicated works to him. The music of Saint-Saëns is often shallow and glib, displaying great technique but little profoundity. His best opera, *Samson et Dalila*, was not performed in Paris until 1892, even though Liszt had done it at Weimar with some success in 1877. The melodies of Saint-Saëns often have an immediate appeal ("The Swan"), but his best ones are those used with some care in the works employing cyclic treatment. The *Third Symphony* (for organ and orchestra) is all based on one fragment. In the slow part of the first movement he spins out this lovely theme:

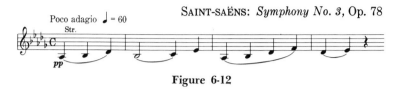

Figure 6-12

Another important cyclic· work is his *Concerto in B Minor* for violin and orchestra.

Saint-Saëns had a fine sense of humor; he wrote the delightful *Carnival of the Animals,* which borrows Rameau's "La poule" to suggest the poultry, but uses fine musical imagination to suggest the other parts of the zoo. We shall discuss his symphonic poems and the concerti below.

Fauré was a pupil of Saint-Saëns, and was himself a great teacher of composers. His tenure as director of the Paris Conservatory (1905-1920) remains a high point in the history of that august school. Among his pupils were Florent Schmitt, Enesco, Koechlin and, most important, Ravel. Another pupil who became a great teacher herself was Nadia Boulanger, who contributed mightily to the development of American music through teaching many important American composers. Fauré was plagued by deafness near the end of his life; this was especially tragic, since he had an unusually sensitive ear and was one of the first composers to thin out the often-rank growth of too many notes which characterizes much music of the colossal romantic. This thinning-out and refinement does not really represent a looking back, since his harmonies are still very much up-to-date for the times. His best works are probably the songs, which show a remarkable line of development. Unlike other great French composers, Fauré's orchestral works were scored by others.

The *Violin Sonata,* Op. 13 (the songs will be studied below), is a work which is often compared to the Franck *Violin Sonata;* indeed, Fauré was accused of copying from it. However, the Fauré is a youthful work dating from 1876, while the Franck dates from ten years later—1886. (The student is urged to compare the two sonatas.) The melodies in both works obviously draw from the harmony, a melodic characteristic which they retain—a line which sets harmony well, rather than the opposite. There is a story about Ravel in which he is reputed to have said in effect, not too long before the premiere, that all of *Daphnis and Chloe* was composed but the themes. And why not? Composers work this way, even though music students usually harmonize a soprano—a composer is always a student but a student is not always a composer.

French composers wrote their share of program music, and, along with their contemporaries in other countries, were concerned about the meaning of music, pictorial and otherwise. Claude Debussy (1862-1918) is usually discussed as a twentieth-century composer, but in many respects was the most romantic of them all, since he actually accomplished in his music the basic freedoms which other composers either talked about or displayed in their works as expansions of classical principles. Debussy wrote music which one might call frankly programmatic; at least they have that kind of title, and one can find suggestions of the title in the music. Debussy's music has much in common with the symbolists,[13] and is called "impressionistic."[14]

Debussy is one of the greatest composers France ever produced. He is great both in the intrinsic value of his music and as a strong influence for the good on twentieth-century music. His work is admired by most schools of thought—rare indeed in our times! He was a colorist, and therefore needed unusual harmony. As with Fauré, we find here the need to recognize that melody is but one adjunct of music and not necessarily the most important. Note the great variety of his melodies. It is an oversimplification to say that he used the whole-tone scale. The opening flute melody from *The Afternoon of a Faun* is chromatic. The *Violes* does show whole tone, however. He also used pentatonic (*Pagodes* is a good example) and other exotic scales. One of his most important works, albeit early, is the *String Quartet* (1893), which uses some modality, another source of color. In the middle part of the "Sarabande" from his *Suite pour le piano* there is another factor which is of extreme importance for Debussy, Ravel and many other composers: *parallelism*. This is a result of melodic doubling at various intervals, which not only creates new colors through the doubling but higher-order dissonance as well—dissonance which does not resolve and is used as an integral part of the texture. Since Debussy is quite consistent in this, we can see that his role in the dissolution of tonality cannot be underestimated; he should perhaps be looked upon as the one who, while reacting to the excesses of the colossal romantics, was himself not only closing out the Romantic Period, but was paving the way for many important developments in the twentieth century.

There were many significant talents at the turn of the century in addition to Ravel. There was Roussel (1869-1937), a pupil of d'Indy at the Schola Cantorum who started late as a composer and then passed quite quickly from a Franckian texture through impressionism to a style quite his own which has some traces of neo-classicism. He used exotic materials in his music (*Padmavati* is an opera based on Indian Ragas) and still followed the cyclic ideal, as in the *Third Symphony*. A Fauré pupil was Koechlin (1867-1950), who would be better known if Koechlin himself had not been so horrified at publicity. He taught several important twentieth-century French composers. Koechlin is bound to survive, however; his music is too good and is quite voluminous. He orchestrated some of Fauré's music, including the incidental music for Maeterlinck's *Pelléas et Mélisande*. He was a good musical scholar and wrote well about music (as did Debussy). He is well-known to some American musicians, since he taught for some time in the United States.

The most unique composer of the time was Satie (1866-1925), one of the great musical satirists, friend of many early twentieth-century giants such as Picasso, Cocteau and Diaghilev. His teachers had been both d'Indy and Roussel, but his best-known music is like neither. Satie's esthetic belongs more to the modern period than to the romantic. He is mentioned here in view of his birth date and as another example of reaction *against* romanticism, the dogmatic romanticism which prevailed and was actually taught in the schools. Romanticism, as has been said time and time again in this book, can be neither taught nor codified for the creation of new romantic works; it can be taught and codified *after* the work of art, not before. At the time of writing there can be no such thing as "correct" romanticism.

Postromantic Germany

By German, it is meant that the composer speaks German as his mother tongue. Mahler and Bruckner were actually Austrian, but are usually considered in the broad Germanic stream of musical development. The late nineteenth-century German-speaking composers pose several problems. They are the colossal romantics, and therefore call for huge forces in their orchestral or operatic music, and for many of them their best work is found there. There is some divergence of opinion among musicians and music-lovers regarding the worth of this music. It is either loved or hated; few are neutral, even today. It is transition music, the last dying gasp of a movement which started with Berlioz, Liszt and Wagner and ends with Schoenberg—although, as you know, Schoenberg discovered an important new way to compose music which is nevertheless based on tradition, not a little of it the tradition of his immediate predecessors. There can be and will be questioning volumes written about the traces of classicism which can be found even in a symphony by Bruckner—should a symphonic movement as long as a Bruckner first movement be allowed to use sonata form? We will look into some of these details from time to time.

The most important composers seem to be Bruckner (1824-1896), Mahler (1860-1911), Hugo Wolf (1860-1903), Humperdinck (1854-1921),

Richard Strauss (1864-1949), Max Reger (1873-1916), Arnold Schoenberg (1874-1951), Alban Berg (1885-1935) and Anton Webern (1883-1945). There are others, of course, but those listed are still programmed and studied to a great extent. I am including the "Big Three" of dodecaphonic serial music (Schoenberg, Berg and Webern), since they rightfully belong to the "Götterdämmerung" of colossal romanticism in much the same way that (at the other end) Beethoven is still somewhat classical.

The German music world had been split quite badly by the journalistic skirmishes between the "new German" school (Wagner and company) and the composers of whom Brahms and Hanslick approved (the anti-Wagnerians). Brahms was one of the greatest composers of all time and Hanslick was one of the greatest music critics of all time. We in our day sometimes wonder what all the fuss was about, but it was very real in Germany and elsewhere at the time the issues were red-hot.

Little did Bruckner know that, for all practical purposes, he represents a kind of fusion of these disparate elements. His orchestra is Wagnerian, his themes are Wagnerian but abstract and he is Wagnerian in orchestration; but his formal symphonic approach is often so similar to Brahms! Poor Bruckner could not really understand why it was considered impossible to admire both Brahms and Wagner.

Bruckner's melodies depend on the supporting harmony, a harmony which is often the result of other melodies being sounded at the same time. Bruckner rarely has to resort to stock patterns of accompaniment. He also derives simultaneous melody from the harmony. Few of the later Germans used "noodles and boom chinks," and in some cases a certain thickness results. Bruckner, however, writes rather clean textures when they are well played. The instrumental parts are often fussy-appearing in their "lie," and have unusual chromatic twists. The first violin and other upper parts often illustrate this, and Bruckner requires unusually good orchestral players. He also has the habit of jumping a pattern through octaves as one would do on the organ. This gives the string player great difficulty (other Germans have also been guilty of this, notably Schumann and Brahms). Here is an example from the *Fourth Symphony*:

BRUCKNER: *Symphony No. 4*

Figure 6-13

Bruckner's music is tied in with organ concepts, since he was for years organist at St. Florian's (and is buried beneath the organ there). This is not to say that his orchestral music suffers from this, or that it even attempts to sound like an organ (except the woodwind scoring at times). However, Bruckner attempts to transfer manual or stop changes and other aspects of organ technique to the orchestra; some of these are effective, others are not.

Some Bruckner themes have been quoted in Chapter II. Here is another excerpt, included since it illustrates his predilection for the rhythmic pattern: ♩♩♩♩♩ and the use of quasi-inversion.[15] Note the "quasi-inversion" answer in the violins of the theme in cello and bass. This is an ancient device, certainly not new in Bruckner.

Figure 6-14

Bruckner was a specialist, having written mostly symphonies and large sacred works. He wrote some of the largest sonata movements in existence. Large movements need large themes, and Bruckner usually succeeded in providing those themes and was very capable in developing them. There is sometimes a problem in developing the material between the themes, a common difficulty with other colossal romantics. One of his loveliest is the theme from the second movement of the *Fourth Symphony*.

In *Time Magazine*, June 23, 1967, appeared this article about Mahler which is so eloquent and to the point that it must be quoted *in toto!*

COMPOSERS

The Man Who Speaks
    To a High-Strung Generation
        After the première of Gustav Mahler's *Third Symphony* at the 1902 Krefeld Festival in Germany, one reviewer concluded that "the composer should be

shot." The first Vienna performance of Mahler's *Fourth* drove the audience to such fury that fistfights broke out all over the concert hall. Conductor Hans von Bülow refused to perform Mahler's works because they were "much too strange." In the face of such hostility, Mahler remained stoic. "My time will come," he predicted.

Today, 56 years after his death, it has. His nine symphonies and the unfinished *Tenth*, several symphonic song cycles and numerous lieder came out of eclipse after World War II, nudged into the periphery of standard works in the early '60s, and now—played and appreciated as never before—are sparking a full-scale Mahler boom.

In the U.S., the number of recordings of Mahler works has leaped from ten in 1952 to 81 this year—three of which are currently among the 40 best-selling classical LP's. At least four record companies are issuing complete sets of the symphonies under a single conductor. The Pittsburgh Symphony's William Steinberg is planning an unprecedented series of seven Mahler concerts for the orchestra next season, three of them in New York. In Paris, no fewer than ten concerts since January have featured Mahler compositions. And in Austria last week, the Vienna Festival wound up a month-long, twelve-concert survey of nearly all of the composer's major works. Appropriately, leading Mahlerite Leonard Bernstein climaxed the festival by conducting the Vienna Philharmonic and a 100-voice Vienna Opera choir in an incisive, wrenchingly emotional performance of the *Second Symphony* ("The Resurrection"), which ends with the choral prophecy: "Thou shalt surely rise again."

Mahler's own musical resurrection is all the more impressive in view of the practical and esthetic difficulties that bristle throughout his work. Most of his symphonies are so long that they take up an entire concert, often require more than 100 instrumentalists and at least that many singers (his *Eighth Symphony* is scored for as many as 1,000 musicians). Folk tunes, military marches and café ditties jostle each other in the symphonies—sometimes with deliberately sarcastic effect—against rich, romantic textures and harsher lines that range out boldly to the limits of traditional tonality. Mahler plunges the listener from surging eddies of counterpoint into brooding, tragic depths, or lifts him with sudden paroxysms of melody into the heights of metaphysical yearning.

Naked Nerves. Why does this appeal so powerfully to modern audiences? U.S. Critic Jack Diether points to the "existentialist" strain in Mahler: "He is the only composer who looked into our whole civilization, who questioned the whole basis of our existence." Says Rafael Kubelik, who conducted Mahler's *Eighth* at Vienna last week: "He's a sufferer who forces man to look into a mirror. He exposes naked nerves." The *Angst*, as well as the questing spirit of Mahler's music, no doubt explains its special meaning for today's college-age youth, who are among the biggest buyers of Mahler recordings, and who made up about 40% of the Vienna Festival audience. As Conductor Steinberg puts it: "Mahler was a high-strung genius who speaks today to a high-strung generation."

Mahler, born in 1860, was one of the last great Romantics. Because of the way he transformed the symphonic tradition extending from Mozart to Anton Bruckner, he was also, in Steinberg's words, "the father of contemporary music —the forerunner of Schoenberg, Berg and Webern." Yet no composer was ever less interested in the objective development of musical form as such. For Mahler, composing was a highly subjective process of grappling with the deepest, most painful questions of life. "The creative act and actual experience," he said, are "one and the same."

Shadow Plays. In his struggle to maintain that fusion, he very nearly realized the wish that he once expressed as a little boy—to grow up to be "a martyr."

He was accepted at the Vienna Conservatory at 15, later supported himself by conducting, and at 37 became director of the Vienna Opera. He swept out has-been singers and dusty traditions, and turned out the polished, provocative productions that made him one of Europe's major musical forces. He was also a fanatical-looking figure—5 ft. 6 in. tall, thin, gazing fiercely from behind rimless spectacles—yet, as his protégé Bruno Walter wrote, "his spirit never knew escape from the torturing question: 'For what?' " Demon-driven, he sought the answer in the music he wrote in spare moments, making each piece a gigantic shadow play of the dark forces that struggled in his soul.

Shortly before leaving the Vienna Opera in 1907, Mahler learned that he had a serious heart ailment. He said his farewell to earthly joys and confronted death in the hauntingly bittersweet song cycle *Das Lied von der Erde* (The Song of the Earth) and the coolly spiritual *Ninth Symphony*. Weakened by overwork, he caught a streptococcus infection while struggling feverishly with his *Tenth Symphony* ("The devil is dancing with me!" he scrawled in the margin), and died at 50 in 1911. His life was incomplete but, as he once expressed it, "I am a musician; that says everything."[16]

Mahler and Bruckner are almost always mentioned with one breath, since admiration for one usually means admiration for the other. There is a Mahler-Bruckner Society which promotes interest in their music and has a forum in the organization's journal, *Chord and Discord*— a good source of information, although there is a certain amount of hero-worship.

Mahler is known mostly for his mammoth symphonies and some exquisite songs. The songwriter is often evident in the symphonies, and the symphonist is often evident in the songs. Mahler was a man of the music world at the highest levels. He was one of the great symphonic and opera conductors of his time. He conducted in the United States as well as in Vienna and elsewhere on the Continent. Bruckner's life was far more simple; one is often reminded of Schubert. In spite of this, Mahler's music is full of nature and folklike themes. He is often accused of using too many themes, as if there were a play with too many characters. While many of Mahler's themes are longish, some are shorter, built of seemingly unrelated fragments when not successful, but very expressive when done well—as in *Das Lied von der Erde* (The Song of the Earth), which is a large symphony-song cycle. The thematic material is drawn from the motto AGE, which forms a kind of *Urkeim*. These pitches are from a gapped pentatonic scale,[17] which helps impart a quasi-Oriental flavor well in keeping with the Chinese origins of the texts.

It has been pointed out above that sometimes a composer will have a melodic formula which he uses or even overuses. In the case of Mahler this is a striking factor, since he repeats formulas and entire themes in symphonies which he has also used in songs. Grieg did this, too. The *Cello Sonata*, for example, draws material from the *Piano*

Concerto, and the results are not happy. In Mahler, however, there is usually successful integration.

Mahler was very taken by the anthology *Des Knaben Wunderhorn,*[18] as were other famous composers. From the collection he borrowed atmosphere and texts and worked them into his gigantic scores, notably symphonies 2, 3 and 4 and many Lieder. Many Mahlerites call this his first period. The second period produced the symphonies 5, 6 and 7, which are purely instrumental, less programmatic, but as intense and powerful as the others. In all of his orchestral music there are many passages which are soloistic or chamber-like in concept, and his middle-period works are exceptionally important in this development. The third period marked a return to using the human voice with the orchestra but there is a mystical approach, not only in the texts but in the purely instrumental ninth and unfinished tenth symphonies. There are still the Mahlerian volcanic eruptions and contrasts, which can be called only wild and violent. In fact, violent contrast characterizes much of his music from the very beginning, whether programmatic or not.

These sudden changes of mood and a very unhappy childhood have given musicopsychoanalysts a field day. It is often said that Mahler was demon-possessed. The unfinished *Tenth* (recently finished by Cooke, and recorded by Ormandy) is frankly quite autobiographical; along with the *Eighth* (which uses the "Veni Creator spiritus" and the same choral finale text from *Faust* used by Liszt in his *Faust Symphony*) it reflects his conversion to Roman Catholicism. The third movement of the *Tenth* was to have been "Purgatorio," while the fourth movement, a scherzo, bears some strange marginal comments and an unfinished inscription on the title page of the scherzo—did he intend for these to be included if the score had been finished and published? I rather think not; it is too personal to appear and Mahler asked his wife to destroy the sketches; fortunately she saved them. Here is what he wrote to his wife, Alma. I will quote it in German, commenting only on the word "Saitenspiel" which is not to be taken literally. It was a pet name for Alma, his wife, and perhaps a clue to a possible hidden meaning in his string writing—or perhaps he meant that she was his lyre, or lute.

Du allein weisst, was es bedeutet. Ach! Ach! Ach! Leb' wohl, mein Saitenspiel!
Leb wohl, leb wohl, leb wohl. Ach wohl, Ach, Ach.
Für dich leben! für dich sterben!
("You only know what it means . . . Oh farewell . . .
To live for you, to die for you")

The fourth movement ends with a single stroke on the bass drum, which is described in Alma Mahler's[19] moving biography of Mahler. Dika Newlin tells the whole story in her remarkable book *Bruckner, Mahler,*

Schoenberg.[20] While in New York, the couple had witnessed a funeral procession and a brief ceremony to honor a fireman who had died a hero's death. The proceedings ended with a muffled drum stroke. Mahler was moved to tears, and planned to end the fourth movement in the same manner.

On one of the title pages (for this same fourth movement) Mahler wrote:

The devil dances with me. Madness seizes me, accursed that I am, annihilates me, so that I forget that I exist, so that I cease to be, so that I. . . .

Mahler himself breaks off the writing—was he finished, or couldn't he continue?

This lengthy digression has been necessary in order to help in understanding a very complex man. If he got an idea from a fireman's funeral and immortalized it in music, is it not probable that other such incidents had similar effects? The drum stroke cannot be a theme *per se*; other places in Mahler's work display a cryptic use of what some would call "non-music," since there is no melody and no harmony, but there is sound.

Mahler's melodic characteristics are carefully studied in Neville Cardus' thorough study of *Gustav Mahler: His Mind and His Music*, Volume I, pp. 26-33. Cardus points out Mahler's use of the appogiatura as an intense expressive device. Many times Mahler will notate very carefully an exaggerated string portamento[21] to the dissonant note, notating it by a straight line before the note:

MAHLER: *Symphony No. 4*

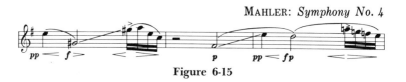

Figure 6-15

Mahler apparently anticipates the "liberation" of pitch in this device, since the gliding tone obviously uses microtones and, further, each player executes it differently.

This presents a problem to modern string players, since the portamento as an expressive device is used sparingly—even in romantic works.

Some other notable Mahler traits include a rather odd use of the ornamental turn. This expressive device has been used in much Baroque music, finally dying out in the *First Chamber Symphony* of Schoenberg. It often precedes a dissonance, as in the "Prayer" from *Rienzi* which

Wagner quotes in the overture. For another, Mahler takes an old tune and changes it to suit his own purposes, such as the "Frère Jacques" in the *First Symphony* (putting it into the minor).

The magnificent horn call which begins the *Third Symphony* has a decided resemblance to the principal theme of the finale of Brahms's *First Symphony*, which Brahms himself was accused of stealing from Beethoven's *Ninth* (see Cardus, p. 85).

Mahler also uses trills in an unusual way.

Detractors have said that Mahler wrote one symphony ten times, and maybe there is some truth in the remark!

Another romantic paradox is the ability of Mahler and other colossal romantics to compose exquisitely small *Lieder*. They could be quiet and delicate in the largest symphony, and intense and powerful in a small song.

Since Mahler is a master of the orchestra, one would expect passages to prove easy for the players, but they do not; yet, they are very effective when well played. His orchestration calls upon the entire orchestra for solo display at some time or another. There is hardly ever any filler; hence, an interesting contrapuntal texture is almost always there. Some of the melodic lines played by the instruments are almost *concertato*, and many are derived from a rich, chromatic harmonic fabric. Harmony controls much of the later romantic melody. One unique carry-over from the Baroque is the string of suspensions, which the romanticists use for enrichment and smoothing out. Another folksy quality in Mahler is the frequent occurrence of Ländler-like themes, which are usually diatonic.

The melodic characteristics listed below are discussed by Cardus and are delineated here, not only for completeness, but to show Mahler's great importance as a real bridge from the Wagnerians to the Schoenbergians. Quoting Cardus:

The music of Mahler is permeated by symbols conveying broadly the emotional and mental states in which Mahler found himself as he composed.[22]

He goes on to point out that Mahler uses recurring motives as identifiable as any Wagnerian *Lietmotiv*. Of one such "source motive" Cardus says, "The most recurrent theme in Mahler clearly denotes his state of lost-ness in the world."[23] The motive consists of a rising line scalewise of three or four notes, followed by an appogiatura which is then resolved. Variety is achieved through such means as changes in rhythm, placement in the phrase, and sharpness and type of dissonance at the point of the appogiatura. Perhaps the most beautiful theme of all occurs in the "Adagietto" of the *Fifth Symphony*. Cardus goes on to say:

I know of no other instance in symphonic (or any other) music where throughout a composer's corpus a single personally-flavoured motif is constantly coming in. . . .[24]

Cardus next points out the use of bare intervals, a feature of Bruckner also. Then he cites a "throbbing" interval suggestive of anything that throbs, but used as effective transition or accompaniment figures. We have already noted above that Mahler, knowing the orchestra well, has a habit of almost overediting. Cardus even declares that the only expression omitted is *Rauchen verboten* (no smoking)!

Much space has been devoted to Mahler, since he has been such an important influence on later composers as diverse as Schoenberg and Shostakovitch.

From time to time I have pointed out the paradoxical nature of the nineteenth century, and the whole Bruckner-Mahler question is replete with contradictions in addition to those implied and stated above. One of the most striking is the character of Mahler himself. He was certainly an individual and yet was a typical artist of his time, in that he was complex emotionally and in many ways had strange parallels to his contemporaries and even to some earlier men of the century. Berlioz comes to mind, as do all sorts of Dostoyevskian-like characters such as August Strindberg or almost any of the Russians. He anticipated Klee, Wedekind, Brecht and others. It has now been confirmed that Mahler saw Freud at least once,[25] which does not necessarily indicate any psychosis—although in Redlich[26] and other sources there are references to Mahler's "mother-fixation." Some artists of the times feigned all sorts of mental aberration, but Mahler was probably honest. How anyone could compose as much as he did and still keep up such a back-breaking conducting schedule is a remarkable achievement. It is, I think, typical of a romantic composer that much of himself goes into his music. Mahler is an extreme case: *each* work is "Aus meinem Leben," even "Ein Heldenleben" —Straussian, but not Strauss-like.

In passing through real life we constantly meet with violent contrast— one thing after another; jarring interruptions. When we are accidentally burned by something hot that we did not know was hot, there is no modulation, no preparation. For security we try to prepare ourselves for almost every possibility; with some people it is almost a fetish. We try to maintain security, perhaps with a favorite personal object-symbol (Linus and his blanket),[27] but life will not allow us to be so ordered. So it is with many romantic composers and their works, Mahler especially. If we let life enter art then we must expect art to be more like life; few lives are lived classically, even when the individual tries. Cherubini tried. He wore his clothing in a certain order, and even on his deathbed chided a servant for mopping his brow free of death's perspiration with a handkerchief used out of order!

Plate VIII

Bronze statue of Mahler by Rodin *(Courtesy The Bettmann Archive, N.Y.).*

Mahler is an example of a composer who repeats himself, and yet his material is somehow new in each new setting. Some composers display a unique existence in each major work, while others, like Mahler, seem to elaborate on a certain idea which grows from work to work—almost as if the whole output is a theme and variations.

Hugo Wolf is known today mostly for his beautiful Lieder, which rank with the very best. He also wrote music in other forms, but he is at his best in the short, graphic statement. He left many works unfinished which were on the grand proportions of his late-nineteenth–century contemporaries. (Since his songs are so important, they will be discussed in the chapter on vocal music.) He had a mental breakdown in 1897 and could work no more, hence his creative life was all in the nineteenth century. Wolf belongs to the group of composers who were expert at creating the great *small* piece. Greatness is inherent in his music; let us not mistake bigness for greatness. He would have been a colossal romantic if he could have continued writing.

Most of Wolf's songs are through-composed; when they are strophic, they display clever changes in repeated material to fit the changing mood or idea of the poem.

Wolf was a Wagnerian, hence was in the anti-Brahms group; but, like Brahms, his songs often show the influence of Schumann. Wolf's setting of syllables derives from Wagner: few melismas and a surprising lack of many neumatic syllable settings. Syllabic settings such as these can be choppy, but both Wagner and Wolf handle them with consummate skill. The musical rhythms fit the poetic meter without imitating it. Polysyllabic words are almost always set so as to reflect the way the word is pronounced. Long notes—so important for the singer in producing the utmost in vocal beauty—occur on syllables which do not obstruct the understanding of the text or the movement of the poetry. In short, Wolf has written vocal lines which project the text with utmost clarity.

Wolf admired Brahms as a young man, but was summarily snubbed by Brahms in 1879 when he tried to get him to look at some of his songs. Brahms rather pointedly suggested that Wolf would do well to study some counterpoint with Nottebohm.[28] This incident undoubtedly had much to do with his later hatred of Brahms, and especially with Brahms's announced position *contra* the "new German school" of ardent Wagnerians (Bruckner, Mahler, *et al.*). Wolf wrote plenty of anti-Brahms prose himself,[29] much of which today does harm to Wolf; how often personal injury affects and damages one's judgment!

Another Wagnerian, Liszt, knew and encouraged Wolf; but Liszt thought that he should compose big tone poems, and the symphonic tone poem *Penthesilea* was the result.

But Wolf was destined to be a "specialist." His songs contain his best music—a fantastic variety. He had failed at opera, but his songs are filled with drama. They are subtle essays in poetry and music, and are examples of chamber music at the highest level. The chamber-music concept is important in Wolf's case, since there is great importance attached to the role of the piano; very often the song will have a piano postlude which is an integral part of the work. Many fine musicians have been righteously incensed at some audiences' insistence on applauding when the singer is finished, leaving the pianist accompanying applause. (One would expect some of the bad manners of opera audiences to be checked at the door with the hatcheck girl when one attends a song recital.) This all too well illustrates the basic misunderstanding of what music really is. In Chapter II it was pointed out that there is much more to nineteenth-century music than tune; the complete atmosphere is important, and *every note* is meant to be heard. Performances of art songs must have this fidelity in the same way that string quartets have it. (Some singers have even cut the final postludes of Wolf songs!)

Here are some of these postludes. In "Anakreons Grab" the musical idea of the whole song is resolved only in the postlude. The student is urged to study Wolf's harmonies in this example and in the song in Fig. 6-17. Note how many principles discussed in Chapter VII are in operation.

WOLF: *Anakreons Grab*

Figure 6-16

"Gleich und gleich" is truly an *Albumblatt*, a one-page song, but notice how much of the song remains after the singer has ended!

Quite extended is the postlude to "Epiphanias" which, however, was a Christmas present for Melanie Köchert; the first performance was by the three Köchert children dressed as the three kings. The postlude, then,

Figure 6-17

with its note from the composer directing the performers to leave the stage one at a time in the character of the king in question, is one which poses problems on the concert stage even today! In the main body of the song Wolf has given admirable characterizations of each king. The postlude reviews this: each one has a different four-bar phrase, a different

key and a different character. This is followed by the march tune for
the three kings marching together, as they disappear over the horizon.
This is typical of the romantic composer—write a masterpiece just because you want to!

"Erschaffen und beleben" has a curious postlude to a curious setting
of a curious poem about God's creation and Noah. There is humor,
but piety too.

The above-quoted postludes are from the *Goethe-Lieder*, but a perusal
of the *Spanisches Liederbuch* reveals that the postlude is again important
—as in song XXIV, "Komm, o Tod," based on the first melodic inflection
of the song; how the F-flat sets *Tod*, the word for death! It is part of a
beautifully voiced diminished seventh (in the third bar), but becomes a
clear F-flat–major chord in the next bar. In the postlude, however, the
F-flat and the whole motive is handled in a new light with quiet, hopeful
resignation.

Wolf wrote beautiful countermelodies in the piano, such as the beginning of "Bedeckt mich mit Blumen."

If the student will now look again at Wolf, he will observe that most
of his songs are indeed chromatic but still tied to key. Often the voice
pitch is not duplicated in the piano, but is integral in the harmony.
Wolf requires careful study by any who would perform his music; there
are beautiful modulations which come from the imagination and not
from the textbook. (Textbooks should be made by studying music such
as Wolf's, not the other way around!)

Wolf's melodic lines use chromatic tones in essential places as chromatic non-harmonic tones, and, as we have said, tones which are part
of chords which are chromatic themselves, a common late-nineteenth–
century practice.

Some of Wolf's most imaginative Lieder are to be found in the *Mörike
Lieder*. Mörike often wrote strange verses. "Das verlassene Mägdlein"
is an early morning song with the atmosphere that only early morning
can have. Augmented triads help create the mood:

WOLF: *Das verlassene Mägdlein*

Figure 6-18

In bars nine and ten there are some dissonances which do not really resolve:

Figure 6-19

In the late nineteenth century almost all of the progressive composers had extended the idea of what a chord is to include sevenths, ninths and even chords which are non-tertian. This obviously affects the melodic writing, since these chords are outlined in the voice or the composer will move from one chord to another. In bars nine and ten of the song last quoted the vocal line is a simple falling fifth and yet the harmonic function changes. The C is the fifth of the F major-major seventh chord (or is it an A-minor triad with added sixth?), while the F is clearly the third of a D minor-minor seventh chord. Is the harmony tonic with added note to subdominant, or submediant $^6_5$ to root-position subdominant? The voice-leading of the bass would lean one toward the former. Note the contour of the bass through the whole passage leading to the augmented triad. Recall the point first stated in discussing Duparc above: the vocal line taken by itself is not too far out as A minor, but how it is enhanced by the piano part!

The pleasant ennui of the early morning is suggested by the constancy of the rhythm: ♩ ♫ ♩ , which could be tiresome but for Wolf's harmony in all its aspects: chord choice, progression, voice-leading, voicing and role of the voice line in either doubling harmony notes or not.

Wolf wrote some moderately successful chamber music such as the famous *Italian Serenade*, which was originally cast for string quartet and then later for small orchestra (some think Reger may have scored it; at least he edited it).[30] The original plan was apparently to compose an extremely long work in several movements: a classical serenade in the eighteenth-century style of Mozart; but the other movements never appeared. The main melodic material poses a problem: did Wolf intend for the solo part to be played by the English horn, the viola or both alternately? Frank Walker seems to have solved the problem. He points out that to save mere copy work Wolf wrote in longhand in the score for the viola to play throughout (see page 310 of Walker's definitive biography). Einstein speaks so well of this work when he says it has "merry, profound grace. . . ."

Wolf knew and was known by most of the important composers of his time, and profited from conversation, advice and professional admiration of men such as Bruckner, Mahler and Humperdinck. Engelbert Humperdinck (1854-1921) was one of the Wagnerians who was able to add a touch of delicacy to the Wagnerian mechanism. The opera *Hansel and Gretel* is by no means as popular as it once was, but it is still a delight. Almost all school children have sung the famous prayer. There are many Leitmotives used in the Wagnerian fashion, and there is no real feeling of imitation as there is in a work such as Reyer's *Sigurd*,[31] or the many other "ersatz *Rings*" which are still being written.

Note how many of the tunes from *Hansel and Gretel* have a lilt and are in the style of German folk songs; yet the music is put together with a fine technique. A fine passage comes after the wicked witch has been killed. Note the facile counterpoint. The student is urged to consult the full score and to hear this passage for its full effect. Each line in the music has had melodic importance earlier. This is somewhat reminiscent of the merry counterpoint in Wagner's *Die Meistersinger*. Humperdinck was closely associated with Wagner for a number of years, especially during the *Parsifal* years. Other works of Humperdinck have merit, and do not deserve the neglect they have always suffered; *Hansel and Gretel* is almost too popular, and audiences expect his other works to be in the same vein. (Richard Strauss conducted the world premiere in 1893.)

Humperdinck was also a professor of some reputation, but teaching did not stimulate him to further important works. He apparently gave his all for the students or else lost interest, since he did not compose in the last ten years of his life.

Aside from the true musical value of *Hansel and Gretel*, it was used in England and elsewhere as competition for the current Italian hits, the "verismo" operas of Mascagni, *et al.* These were a little too much like life for some people, and the childlike innocence of *Hansel and Gretel* was a proper kind of theater where "one could take the whole family."

Its success was short-lived, however, since the great operas of Puccini literally "took over" and still command attention wherever opera is sung.

It is apparent, then, that there were at least two camps, each armed with pens. An important performer-composer who exerted a profound influence on a host of composers, violinists and conductors from Mendelssohn to Brahms was Joseph Joachim (1831-1907). Joachim had been a desk-partner of Ferdinand David at the Gewandhaus under Mendelssohn; he associated for a short time with Liszt at Weimar, moving thence to Hanover, and finally (in 1868) becoming the first head of the Royal Academy of Arts in Berlin. Joachim had much to do with the composition and performance of new violin concerti, and was a close friend of Brahms, Clara and Robert Schumann and many other famous musicians. Joachim was especially admired in England, where he introduced the string works of Brahms and other composers in the Brahms faction of the German mainstream—the anti-Wagner ones. Joachim's works are not often performed today, except for excellent cadenzas to violin concerti of Mozart and the Beethoven concerto. Of even greater importance is his devotion to the works of Bach, the solo sonatas and partitas particularly. His great success with Bach was of importance to many German composers of the period, who did not want to write *Ring Cycles*. In short, he was a prime-mover in the "back-to-Bach" movement which is still evident in Germany and elsewhere. The veneration of Bach took many directions, as we have said. Reger and some others tried to bring back the spirit of Bachian counterpoint in the frameworks of late-nineteenth–century harmony.

Max Reger (1873-1916) was one of the Germans who could see that there was good in both Wagner and Brahms, and his studies reflect well both schools of thought. He met great opposition, therefore, from both sides. He was a piano virtuoso and achieved public acclaim as a concert artist, specializing in Bach and Mozart. He is reputed to have had one of the best pianissimos in the history of piano playing. (Perhaps some of the difficulty Reger has had with audience acceptance is lack of delicacy by the performer!) His music looks dense, and often it is, but the performer should thereby take greater pains.

To this day Reger is not always given a fair shake in the literature and is usually dismissed as a composer who wrote Bach with too many voices— an uninspired, tireless worker who mechanically filled ream after ream of music paper with dull contrapuntal exercises. I seriously doubt that many of these authors have ever heard or played, or even looked at scores by Reger. The list of Reger's complete works is long and impressive—perhaps too long; perhaps he *should* have revised more. It is significant that Reger's complete works are now available in a matched set[32] and that more of his work is available on phonograph records.

Aside from texture (which is usually the first comment made about his music), one should mention his extreme skill and imagination in modulation. His only literary work is, significantly, *Beiträge zur Modulationslehre* (1903). These modulations affect the melodic writing, not only of the leading voice(s) but the rest of the texture, since Reger was a great master of counterpoint and seldom wrote mere "accompaniments," even in his concerti. The *Violin Concerto* even outdoes Brahms in the importance of the orchestral parts.

Plate IX

Max Reger writing *(Courtesy The Bettmann Archive, N.Y.).*

Reger took one of Mozart's best-known melodies and wrote the beautiful *Variations and Fugue on a Theme by Mozart*, Op. 132. The theme is from Mozart's *Piano Sonata in A Major*, K. 331, on which Mozart also wrote variations. Reger, however, does not pattern his set after Mozart, but there is a remarkable resemblance in treatment to Brahms's *Variations on a Theme by Haydn*. Like the Brahms, these orchestral variations also exist in a version for two pianos.

The beginning of Variation I will be quoted to show several important points: 1) the score looks complicated; 2) great delicacy in execution is required; 3) the moving parts are clearly outlines of the harmony, with a few non-harmonic tones; 4) the harmony is also sustained in the horns and first violas; 5) the harmony is outlined with delicate pizzicati in part of the string section; 6) the melody is doubled by oboe and clarinet, a device often used by the later Germans, perhaps to give a sound more like the oboe stop on the organ (Reger was an important composer of organ music); 7) the melody itself is changed but little; 8) the string section is divided: half muted, half not, a delightful effect often used by Reger (again showing his wish for delicacy).

Variation II carries over some ideas from Variation I (the sixteenth notes), but is essentially the theme inverted (oboe and unmuted first violins) accompanied by a lovely countermelody in the muted violins and second flute; note that *other* countermelodies occur in both viola sections and in the bass instruments. Reger has also used the mediant relationship between this and the first variation.

Each successive variation gets farther and farther away from the theme. Reger builds upon himself, as do other late Germans. Brahms's variations almost always are additive in this manner. Variations are even cleverly combined; for example, Variation VI combines the rapid figuration from Variation I with the rhythmic alteration of the theme in Variation III.

Mozart's rhythm is not too far removed from a siciliano—and Reger's Variation VII takes advantage of this, as did Brahms in his *Haydn Variations.*

Variation VIII is the most intense, the most romantic and one of the best examples of chromatic, expressive lines induced by complex chromatic harmony and complex chromatic harmony induced by interesting melodic lines interwoven by the composer. (A good performance of this variation is an unforgettable experience!) Reger's music must be well-rehearsed and his many remarks to the players scrupulously followed. After such emotional intensity the fugue is indeed welcome. Note again the delicacy! The fugue is not only good music, it is a summation of the whole work. At the climax Reger quotes the original theme as a chorale. This spot usually brings a smile to the face of the listener, although I am sure this was not Reger's intention.

The treatment of the theme as a chorale is characteristic of Reger's music. He manifested his "back-to-Bach" ideals through actually using chorale tunes in some lovely cantatas which evoke the spirit and the techniques of the Baroque church cantatas of northern Germany. Reger enriched the organ literature with some chorale preludes—an approach to counterpoint which is still taught in composition classes in Germany, England and the United States. The "easy" chorale preludes of Op. 67 are fifty-two lovely settings of some of the most famous of the Bach chorale harmonizations. (If organists are ever at a loss for quiet meditation music in church, let them look to these!)

The reflection of Bach is well seen in his works for unaccompanied stringed instruments. Some moments are dull, but other passages are great. All are worthy of study by young composers, since Reger cannot depend on a wealth of lines even though he, as did Bach, wrote com-

Figure 6-20

plete fugues for unaccompanied instruments. He also wrote magnificent chaconnes for unaccompanied violin.

We shall meet Reger again later in this book. He was caught between two worlds—almost too modern to be romantic and too romantic to be modern.

The same could be said for Richard Strauss (1864-1949), although in most books he is considered a twentieth-century composer. He was a remarkable heir to the great German traditions from both sides of the mainstream, but his fame today rests on his graphic symphonic tone poems, perhaps the last great works in the genre of Liszt; several colorful operas which continue the music-drama ideals of Wagner; and Lieder which approach the best of Brahms, Wolf and the others. Strauss was one of the best orchestrators who ever lived, and his orchestral music is well-known through many brilliant recordings. He was one of the great conductors of his time and knew well what worked in the orchestra and on the stage. Some of his music was well-received from the very beginning, but some—especially two operas, *Salome* and *Elektra*—were severely criticized for their modernity. Many today regard these as his finest works, since they are more original. Strauss is one of the few major composers who began as a conservative and became avant-garde after "conversion" through the influence of Alexander Ritter,[33] only to be outstripped in "modernity" by the giants of our time who went beyond romanticism— which Strauss never really did.

Strauss's best-known works today are not from the period of his earliest works, nor was he at his best in his declining years. There are many theories about this, but no one will ever really know. Some of the works originally held by critics and audiences to be inept, lifeless, senile and uninteresting, however, were re-heard after World War II and new or revised opinions were voiced—especially about *Arabella, Ariadne auf Naxos* and *Die Frau ohne Schatten* (which Strauss considered his masterpiece). Some very late songs called *Four Last Songs*, which were about his last works (1948), are considered to be among his very best. Perhaps if he had not written mostly for the stage, but had continued a more universal approach, his later works could have been stronger.

Strauss was a Wagnerian, but he used Wagnerian ideas and ideals to his own ends. The *Leitmotiv* was in Wagner either objective or subjective or both, or the connotation was contextual. Strauss seemed to objectify his motives in each work and followed a philosophy of musical representation which few composers have ever surpassed. There are bleating sheep in *Don Quixote* (why not use a section of sheep!); Till Eulenspiegel thumbing his nose; the heroic Don Juan; the heroic Strauss himself in *Ein Heldenleben*; the sparkle of the silver rose in *Der Rosenkavalier*. The list could go on and on; Strauss's characterizations are very apt—perhaps the very best program music *per se* the world has yet seen. In a sense he is closer to the Baroque in his philosophy, such as the Biblical sonatas of Kuhnau or the bucolic onomatopoetics of Vivaldi's *Seasons*. One can, however, derive musical satisfaction without knowing the program, as is the case with all good program music. Some authors comment about his subject matter becoming less and less poetic until it becomes as mundane as possible in the *Domestic Symphony* (which has a sequel, by the way, called *Parergon to the Domestic Symphony*, an even more prosaic piece for piano solo left-hand and orchestra written for the famed Wittgenstein, for whom Ravel and others had written important left-hand works).

Strauss's themes are characterized by their extreme wide range, side-slipping tonality, non-raucous dissonance (unless the program calls for it) and almost always a certain sweetness which is enhanced by rich and colorful harmony. His lines often form a fabulous *atmospheric* texture, but he could also write excellent fugues. Although to a certain extent the culmination of the programmatic school which began with Liszt, Strauss often used unique applications of the old forms. Some of his tone poems are actually poematic symphonies not unlike those of Berlioz in concept. Some of his loveliest themes, however, occur in the Lieder.

Strauss still figures so often on our symphony and opera programs that we will meet him again later in this book. He is included in this book since, like Rachmaninoff, he never ceased to be a romanticist, even though a considerably different one from the earlier composers.

England and the United States

Another composer who lived well into our century was Sir Edward Elgar (1857-1934), who was one of England's greatest of the period. He was a complete composer and a veritable master of all forms, although he wrote no operas. Still widely performed in England, he is best-known here for the oratorio *The Dream of Gerontius*, his *Cello Concerto*, his *Violin Concerto* and the orchestral variations called *Enigma*, which are all masterpieces. He is too well-known at commencement time for one of the "Pomp and Circumstance" marches, which is just worn out, and a tid-bit called "Salut d'amour," which at one time was in the repertoire of every hotel dining room's string ensemble. As with Strauss and a few others, Elgar left behind some recordings in which he was the conductor. One of the best is Menuhin's recording of the *Violin Concerto*, which was conducted by Elgar near the end of his career and near the beginning of Menuhin's.

Elgar and many other Englishmen were profoundly impressed by Brahms and Wagner; even the music of the great English scholar Sir Donald Tovey sounds very Brahmsian. Brahms was not the only German who influenced England: Handel, Haydn and Mendelssohn had made great personal impressions on their trips to London, and most nineteenth-century composers got "oratorio fever" and wrote many themselves. England abounded in very fine musicians, composers, teachers, scholars and performers, and it could boast some of the best performing companies in the world. There were no *truly* great composers, however, between Purcell (ca. 1659-1695) and some of the possible current ones. Much fine music was written by Boyce, Arne and others in the eighteenth century and by men such as Parry and Stanford in the nineteenth, but it reflected activity on the continent, just as music in America did. (MacDowell's music could have been written in Germany by a German; Ives's music could have been written only by an American.) Elgar was not nationalistic at all, but was very English in an intangible way. His themes are handled in a manner similar to those of Brahms and/or Wagner, but Elgar still has a style of his own. Some of Elgar's loveliest melodies are from his *Violin Concerto*.

English musical nationalism was important at the same time. In addition to Ralph Vaughan Williams there were folk song collections made by Cecil Sharp and folk songs used in an unusual way by Gustav Holst (1874-1934)—whose best work, in my opinion, is a poematic suite called *The Planets*. This outstanding orchestral work calls for an enormous orchestra (it was a "dream piece" which he apparently never intended to be performed).

In America the important composers studied mostly in Europe and continued to write German romantic music back home. They did establish music schools at colleges and universities, and this influence is still felt. Aside from Ives a true original spirit was the great pianist Gottschalk (1829-1869), who wrote trash as well as some of the finest nationalistic music ever produced by an American composer.

Dvořák exerted a strong influence, and his coming to the United States was like a shot in the arm for some of our native composers. Arthur Farwell (1872-1952) and Henry Gilbert (1868-1928) were important Americanists, but as Grout[34] says, we lacked a "Mighty Five."

Some composers deserve special mention, since they occupied an unusual category and yet were so different in their careers: the American Stephen Foster (1826-1864), whose melodies need no quoting; or the Englishman Sir Arthur Sullivan, who might have ended up as a Parry or a Stanford with an impressive list of sedative oratorios, but (with the lively libretti of Gilbert) produced some of the most delightfully funny musical theater in existence. In France there was Offenbach (1819-1880), and in Vienna the other Strausses, Lehar, *et al.* All are theatrical types very much alive today on Broadway and elsewhere.

The melodies of most of the men discussed in this chapter represent a dying movement. Late romanticism carried the seeds of its own destruction and became decadent; there had to be an infusion of new ideas. The change in direction was clearly pointed out by men such as Debussy, Bartók and Schoenberg. Schoenberg, as a wag once said, "Pushed Wagner to the brink and pushed Strauss over!" Schoenberg's earliest works should be enormously popular, and the sextette *Verklärte Nacht* is. The magnificent *Gurrelieder*, the tone poem *Pelleas and Melisande*, the early songs and chamber music are very much like the other colossal romantics; if they were as well-known as those of Strauss or Mahler, they would probably be fully as popular. The melodic construction exemplifies principles we have listed time and time again: diatonic with chromatic accompaniment, chromatic melodies based on notes from complicated chords, melodies spun out through motive structuring, angularity and many different pitches.

The early works of Alban Berg (1885-1935) are ardently romantic, especially the *Seven Early Songs.*

Anton Webern (1883-1945) also wrote some intensely romantic works in his early years. Schoenberg, Berg, Webern and others of their group actually intensified romanticism, to produce one of the most vital movements in twentieth-century music. (Future historians may place the ending of the Romantic Period as late as 1945!) True, there were new approaches in the early part of the century, but many composers were actually putting into practice what other romanticists had only talked about or thought they had put into their music.

On a different plane are some of the unique melodies which have appeared mostly in England and America, such as hymns. Musicians once scorned these as "cheap" music, but now consider them an authentic voice of the people. Many excellent studies have been made.[35] Ives and other American composers have used these tunes in a manner vaguely similar to the use by other composers of German chorale tunes, Gregorian chants or folk songs.

Some of these tunes were traditional English airs, while others grew out of separate religious movements: the Shakers, Moravians, the Presbyterian and Methodist revivalists, Baptist revivalists, the Mormons and a remarkable proliferation of Protestant and quasi-Protestant sects and cults. The musical value of these tunes is very uneven, but as pragmatic music they served their purpose; many souls "went forward" after hearing "fire-and-brimstone" preaching and singing.

A few musicians tried to civilize this music, and came up with uneven and debatable results. The most famous was Lowell Mason (1792-1872), who was also prominent in the early stages of public school music in America. Mason published many songbooks which were very popular, and some of his songs and hymns are still sung: "My Faith Looks Up to Thee," "Nearer My God to Thee" and many others. He also added "codas" to other people's hymns and made arrangements of "good" music as hymns—such as "Joy to the World," which comes from Handel. Such use of music from famous works may or may not be valuable; this problem is discussed thoroughly by Gilbert Chase in his excellent *America's Music*.[36]

The Mason family produced several important musicians. One of the best was Daniel Gregory Mason (1873-1953), grandson of Lowell who was an important writer on music and a good composer. He was an eclectic, taking what suited him from the Germans or the French (especially d'Indy, one of his teachers), or drawing from American lore. He did not self-consciously pursue an "American" idiom *per se*, but realized that the future of American art music was probably best realized in a cosmopolitan approach. He drew on American life, however, for some works: *A Lincoln Symphony, String Quartet on Negro Themes* and the overture *Chanticleer* (based on a quotation from Thoreau).

America's aboriginals, the Indians, have a rich and varied musical culture which still awaits an American Bartók. There have been several important scholarly studies of their music,[37] but the usage of Indian music so far has been anything but authentic—MacDowell's beautiful *Indian Suites* notwithstanding. He made the same mistake as some of his European contemporaries: he forced the themes into "correct" patterns learned at the conservatory. Ives did not do this. Had Ives been more interested in Indian music, he might have been our Bartók; as it is, his treatment of American tunes and melodies of his own is quite remarkable. In many instances he anticipates techniques which were later used by the greats of our century.

There is no point in listing America's other nineteenth-century composers in this chapter which is most concerned with melody. Original American melodies were cropping out in popular music—not the melodies themselves, but melodies to fit particular rhythms, harmonic progressions and/or social conditions.

In this chapter we have reviewed specific composers in Italy, where the opera reigned supreme and produced some unforgettable melodies which became more and more subtle throughout the century. In France there were diverse tendencies; near the end of the century, composers took the lead from Berlioz and refined his ideas of the *idée fixe*, combining it with a slightly different application of the *Urkeim* principle of Liszt or the *Leitmotiv* of Wagner. The Germans were divided—Wagnerites vs. Brahmsians—along with a few brave souls who saw good in both schools. The glorification of the motive became important as orchestras became larger and larger. In England there was a decided influence of Brahms, added to the already considerable influence of Handel, Haydn and Mendelssohn. Nationalism also began to influence English composers. The Americans—almost to a man—were a branch of German symphonism, but with Ives and some others and the rise of a lively popular music, the stage was set for important musical activity in the twentieth century.

The late Romantic Period must include Impressionism, even as the early Modern Period must include it. The music of Debussy and Ravel had a remarkable influence in almost every major musical country: Delius in England, Schrecker in Germany, Scriabin in Russia, Respighi in Italy, Griffes and Loeffler in the United States; and it crops up in passages in Schoenberg, Vaughan Williams and other modern composers.

In the next chapter we will study more closely factors which have been mentioned earlier: mainly, romantic harmony, which in most cases makes romantic melody "romantic."

Notes

1. Paganini's playing undoubtedly gave Berlioz ideas for string writing in his orchestral works, although the two works for solo strings and orchestra (*Harold in Italy* and the little-known *Reverie and Caprice* for violin and orchestra) are remarkably free of Paganini influences. The *Romeo and Juliet* of Berlioz is dedicated to Paganini. There was the famous emotion-charged incident in which Paganini publicly bowed in homage to Berlioz, called him a true follower of the path of Beethoven and actually presented him a purse of 20,000 francs—and Paganini was a miser! See also Chapter XIV.

2. One of the best discussions of "enclosed" melody is found in Szabolcsi's *A History of Melody* (New York: St. Martin's Press, 1965). Most textbooks on form merely say that there is such a thing as *closed* form or *open* form or both; for example, a rondo has a refrain which is a closed melody and episodes which are open. In Italian opera the enclosed nature is certainly a factor in the ability of the audience to remember melodies so well. The phrase, it must be remembered, is in reality an integration of melody, rhythm and harmonic cadence. See also the discussion in Chapter II.

3. The Roman tone poems are still very popular. The use of the recording of a nightingale in *The Pines of Rome* is a kind of breakthrough, since it is the first time in history that a composer of any repute uses a mixture of recorded and live music; in a sense, this is aleatory music.

4. Jean-Baptiste Lully (1632-1687) was born in Italy but was taken to France as a lad. In France he worked up from scouring pots and pans to become a virtual dictator of musical affairs in Paris. He was an important composer, and

wrote works of great influence on later composers and often of great intrinsic value.

5. Lesueur's theories were actually realized in the music of Berlioz. His own works, although they enjoyed a certain popularity in his lifetime, were old-fashioned and did not really match his colorful imagination in theatrical matters.

6. Many works since then present the same problem. After all, why should a good orchestra score *necessarily* be reducible to a piano score? This is a problem in the rehearsal of operas and the like, but in my mind there is no question but that opera is the better for this problem, earlier masterpieces notwithstanding. This is not to say that it cannot or should not be done, but the twentieth-century concept of voice and orchestra is the child of the nineteenth century. While we can put up with black and white reproductions of paintings, a picture of Mona Lisa with flaming red hair would be unthinkable. By the same token, no work intended for orchestra should be judged by how well it sounds on the piano!

7. Johann Kirnberger (1721-1783) was a pupil of J. S. Bach. A composer of some distinction, he is best remembered today for his important two-volume treatise *Die Kunst des reinen Satzes* (1771-1776) and many other theoretical works. His fugues are known for their "correctness." He also developed some amazing theories on the mathematical composition of music, both analytical and creative. The earliest manuscript of Bach's *St. Matthew Passion* is a copy made by Kirnberger. Another high point was his public disagreement and criticism of Marpurg, and vice versa.

8. Friedrich Marpurg (1718-1795) wrote a significant handbook on figured bass which was frankly based on the theories of Rameau. He knew Rameau personally and was a prolific writer on theory, criticism and music. Lieberman sums it up so well:

Throughout the history of polyphony, theorists maintained divergent views about melody appropriate to the style, the treatment of discord, the relevance of harmonic influence and the structure of various types of polyphonic music. Theory generally lagged behind practice, so it is not surprising that shortly after Bach's time, such theorists as Albrechtsberger, Cherubini and Marpurg considered Bach's music too radical a model for student imitation. J. J. Fux, a minor composer and contemporary of Bach, sought to check the current harmonic counterpoint, to reverse the trend toward instrumental melodic style and to counteract the freedom or 'licences' in the music of the time by upholding sixteenth century polyphony as a standard of perfection. In his *Gradus ad Parnassum* he reverts to vocal diatonic melody in the modes, insists on strict handling of discords and employs a series of artificial rhythm schemes with canti firmi which presumably would eventuate in Palestrina-style counterpoint.

Paradoxically, Fux's outlook and the species technique which was intended to countervail the influence of music such as Bach's, was adopted by eighteenth and nineteenth century pedagogues in teaching tonal harmonic counterpoint. Treatises multiplied, with mechanical repetition of arbitrary rules and prohibitions which often had no relevance to the practices of Bach, Handel, Purcell and other eminent contrapuntists. No other musical discipline has been so resistant to the need for a realistic approach or been shackled for so long to outmoded rules and a technique so ill suited to its objective. While Bach was acquainted with the species approach, he evidently found the methods of earlier and a few contemporary German masters to be more practical. According to Kirnberger, his disciple and ardent admirer, Bach urged his students to absorb his style by playing his music before mastering thorough-bass. Non-harmonic tones were employed in chorale harmonizations. Contrapuntal instruction began with the four lines of figurated harmony and then moved on to the composition of inventions, canons and fugues. Maurice Lierberman, *Creative Counterpoint* (Boston: Allyn and Bacon, Inc., 1966), pp. v-vi.

9. Norman Demuth, *César Franck* (London: Dennis Dobson, Ltd., 1949), pp. 15-18.

10. This terminology is widely used. The first term refers to the color of the triad, and the second refers to the size of the seventh. In this case: G-sharp, B, D is a diminished triad and G-sharp up to F-sharp is a minor seventh, hence the whole thing is a diminished minor-seventh chord. This terminology is used throughout this book.

11. The Prix de Rome is discussed in some detail in Grove's Vol. VI, p. 935, where a complete list of winners is given. While the roll call contains some important names, most are strangers. It is a highly coveted award from the *Institute de France*. The winner is paid by the government for a year's stint in Rome for creative work and further study. The other arts also have awards.

12. Demuth, *ibid.*, p. 36; also see Chapter XII.

13. The symbolists were in the main anti-realistic writers who used objects as symbols of the idea: the idea is not the object, nor is the object the idea. Maeterlinck and Mallarmé were two of the most important, since both were artistic influences on Debussy.

14. "Impressionism" was once applied in derision by critics, first to painting and then to music and poetry or other literature which had similar qualities. An impression of reality is created but not really stated. Musical works are not programmatic in the same sense as Liszt, since they consist of ideas suggested rather than expressed.

15. *Quasi-inversion* means that the composer inverts all or part of the melody, but not strictly, using modifications far beyond the possibilities of tonal inversion. Such a process is one of the many freedoms which romanticism admitted into musical technique. This is not the place to argue about the musicality of inversion; it is enough to point out that almost every age has used it in some way or another since its discovery.

16. Courtesy *Time*, The Weekly Newsmagazine; Vol. 89, No. 25, pp. 54-55. Copyright Time Inc., 1967.

17. A *gapped scale* is one which includes an interval larger than some kind of a second.

18. The Second Symphony uses texts from *Des Knaben Wunderhorn* and verses by Klopstock (the lovely "Auferstehung"). The Third also uses the great folk anthology and some text from Nietzsche, while the Fourth is all drawn from the anthology. There are nine early songs, twelve middle-period songs and at least two from his very last years.

19. Alma Mahler, *Gustav Mahler, Memories and Letters*, translated by Basil Creighton (New York: The Viking Press, 1946). This fascinating book gives one the insight into a famous man that only his wife would possess. It is strange that "Saitenspiel" is translated as "lyre," when she tells of finding the sketches of the Tenth after Mahler's death. Alma Mahler was later married to other celebrities, including the architect Gropius and the writer Franz Werfel.

20. Dika Newlin, *Bruchner, Mahler, Schoenberg* (New York: King's Crown Press, 1947), p. 202.

21. The *portamento* is a gliding from one note to another; it is used also by singers and, if the pitches lie well, can be done on wind instruments. Its usage is a matter of taste; romantics were very fond of the effect.

22. Neville Cardus, *Gustav Mahler: His Mind and His Music* (New York: St. Martin's Press, 1965), p. 26.

23. *Ibid.*, p. 26.

24. *Ibid.*, p. 26.

25. H. F. Redlich, *Bruckner and Mahler* (London: J. M. Dent and Sons, Ltd., 1955). See note 1, p. 112.

26. *Ibid.*, p. 112.

27. The insecure but often wise friend of Charlie Brown in Charles M. Schultz's comic strip which is much more than a comic strip: "Peanuts."

28. Grove's, Vol. IX, p. 332. Martin Gustav Nottebohm (1817-1882) was primarily a music historian who edited Beethoven's sketchbooks and was one of the first to make a catalogue of the complete works of both Beethoven and Schubert, including a thematic index.

29. Hugo Wolf was a critic for the *Wiener Salonblatt*. By and large his articles are completely acceptable today, but for his blind spot about Brahms. See Frank Walker's *Hugo Wolf*, Chapter VIII, for a good discussion of Wolf as a critic.

30. See *Grove's*, Vol. IV, p. 558.

31. *Sigurd* and *Salammbo* enjoyed some popularity, and used Wagnerisms in an original way. No works, however, retain to this day the genuine charm of Humperdinck's *Hansel and Gretel*.

32. These are being issued by the Max Reger Institute, Wiesbaden, having started in 1954.

33. Alexander Ritter (1833-1896) was a conductor and composer who was an ardent Wagnerite, having been associated with the Weimar Liszt circle and with Hans von Bülow in Meiningen.

34. Donald Grout, *A History of Western Music* (New York: W. W. Norton & Company, Inc., 1960), p. 591.

35. There is an excellent bibliography in Chase's *America's Music*, p. 696-697.

36. Gilbert Chase, *America's Music*, Rev. Ed. (New York: McGraw-Hill, 1966). Chase discusses this in the main in Chapter VIII, but other chapters in the book also allude to the problem.

37. *Ibid.*, p. 717.

CHAPTER VII

HARMONY IN THE NINETEENTH CENTURY

THE NINETEENTH CENTURY SAW the beginning of the end of a glorious period of musical practice: the "tonal" or "tertian" period, which began about 1600. There was a steady increase in importance of tonality, or major and minor keys, over the modes which had prevailed in most Western art and folk music in the previous era. The modes were so well entrenched that there was much opposition to the newer ideas which came in with the Baroque Period, ideas which changed the course of music history. The modes, however, were doomed, at least as the *sole* theoretical basis. There is a tendency for some to think that tonality is also sacred and should not be changed or discarded. But tonality did run its course, at least the so-called "pure" tonality which is abstracted in most theory books. Just what it has become is not as yet completely clear, but it will never be the same. Tonality served its purpose and was the theoretical basis of some of the greatest music the world will ever know, but the world in which it was created no longer exists. Our present age is the offspring of the nineteenth century, and we have carried on with the tendencies which were very much in evidence throughout the entire century and even before.

The break probably begins with *equal temperament,* a system of tuning which, by leveling out differences in tuning, greatly simplifies the enormous problem of tuning a keyboard instrument so that it can play in all of the possible keys, not just a few.[1] Without this compromise it would not be possible to play the enharmonic equivalents with the same key; that is, C-sharp and D-flat are played by the same key on a piano, organ or harpsichord (or what have you) and the frequency of the pitch is precisely the same, even though theoretically D-flat is almost always somewhat lower than C-sharp, an amount which many musicians can actually hear.

J. S. Bach was the first truly great composer to use equal temperament and believe in it; in fact, he was so enthusiastic about it that he wrote many works which require the keyboard to be tuned in equal temperament. The most famous of these works are the two volumes of *The Well-tempered Clavier* (1722, 1744), each containing twenty-four preludes and fugues, one in each of the theoretical keys or tonalities, but equal-tempered tonalities. What is even more significant is that *within* one prelude or one fugue Bach also uses enharmonic functions. If the student will examine these—even the "simple" C-Major Prelude from Volume One—he will see that Bach *does* use all twelve tones, some with more than one harmonic function! What this means, of course, is that all keys are available during the composition for the purpose of modulation or that the pitches can be used for chromatic ornamental tones, as Bach certainly does in much of his most significant music. This is a major factor contributing to the greatest tonal music from J. S. Bach and his talented sons, J. C. Bach and C. P. E. Bach; Handel; Haydn; Mozart; Beethoven and so on throughout the nineteenth century.

The arguments regarding the merits of equal temperament are still raging to a certain extent, but it is doubtful if theory and practice would have developed as it did without it, since equal temperament made possible enharmonic practices which were unthinkable in the older theoretical systems. In 1914 A. Eaglefield Hull wrote the following:

Is music, then, condemned to be suspended ever between the two opposing temperaments, or will the "duodecuple" scale decide once for all in favour of the equal division of the octave in theory as well as in practice?[2]

The last half of the tertian or tonal period, then, was governed to a large extent by the availability of these chromatic tones. The story of romantic harmony is the story of how these tones were used in new and unusual ways, and how new relationships were discovered and older practices discarded or expanded. This was a direct result of composers in the Romantic Period trying to express themselves; each developed to a certain extent his own harmonic language within the context of tonality.

Just how was this done? This is a difficult question, which can be answered only partially. There is also a certain intangible element in harmonic treatment which eludes a rational explanation, and this is probably as it should be. Indeed, the deepest aspects of art *are* irrational, and can't be completely rationalized.

As Ross Lee Finney says:

I came to feel that the 19th century had misunderstood tonal function and that many works were really very bad. I began to listen all over again. The conviction that one must understand by listening—must accept nothing except as it is confirmed by the ear—strongly influenced me and still remains the basis of my teaching. This concern for function does not preclude a mathematical logic (certainly not in electronic music), for it is obvious that everything in music can be explained mathematically *except the psychological experience*. To control this experience, the composer must work with functions—at least I call them that for lack of a better word.[3]

What we *can* say is this: composers used more dissonance, more complex chords, more altered chords, more chromatic modulation, distant key relationships, free resolutions, faster harmonic rhythms, more keys with many flats or sharps, even "artificial" keys, orchestration-enhanced coloristic harmonies and more color chords, exotic scales and harmonies, folk modes, and so on.

Let us now discuss these factors one at a time and see some examples.

Dissonance has always been a touchy subject, and each age has had a different notion of what it really is. It has been cursed, forbidden, philosophized about; used in spite, in vain and in a beautiful, expressive way. Dissonance and discord are not necessarily the same thing. Discord implies unpleasing sounds or relationships. Dissonance in its proper sense refers to musical tensions which are resolved to sounds which are less tense, not necessarily consonant, but less dissonant than before—its musical function depends on context, and is not necessarily absolutely dissonant. The interval of a perfect fourth, for example, sounds as a dissonance in a simple, mostly consonant texture, while it sounds as a perfect consonance in a more complex, dissonant texture. The summation tone of a fourth is, however, dissonant.[4] A chord which contains more than one dissonance usually sounds less discordant and can be made to sound mellifluous. The most discordant sound to most musicians is probably on out-of-tune minor ninth. A minor ninth in tune also sounds discordant, but in context (either melodic or harmonic) it is a very telling effect—dissonant, yes, but beautiful as it resolves, and sometimes just for itself. Both major and minor ninths can be useful. Here is an example from the late eighteenth century from Gluck's Overture to *Iphigenia in Aulis*. Note the ninths in bars two and ten, the Italian sixths prepared by a beautiful suspension in bars four and fourteen, and the marvelous use of chromaticism throughout.

Figure 7-1

From the late-nineteenth–century Franck *Symphony*:

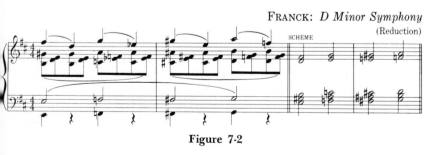

Figure 7-2

From Cherubini's *Requiem in C Minor* outlined as a theme:

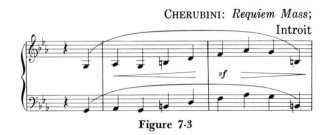

Figure 7-3

There are examples of beautiful melodic use in many composers. Often there is a compounding of dissonances which tends to soften the effect—a fact which we can observe in colors as well. Two shades of a bright color such as red-orange can be made to clash, but if we mix several shades we can get a beautiful, vibrant effect. We *can* get a beautiful effect, or if we prefer we can mix the shades to obtain a compounded clash. In music this is well illustrated at the beginning of the finale of Beethoven's *Ninth Symphony*, where all of the tones of the D-minor scale are sounded. This is for programmatic effect; he wants to create discord so he can set the text (". . . nicht diese Töne")—he wants a great contrast between concord and discord in order to establish the idea that when all mankind are brothers, there will be no more discord.

The poematic symphony and symphonic poem have many examples of arbitrary dissonance used for poetic effect. The harshness is intensified by the orchestration, as shown in the finale of the Beethoven *Ninth*. Richard Strauss's imaginative bleating of sheep in *Don Quixote* and Mozart's "wrong" notes in *Ein musikalischer Spass* (K. 522) are extreme examples. We shall see still others in later chapters.

The line between consonance and dissonance, then, is not really fixed except when the composer himself imposes the limitation. In an abstract sense we can and do draw the line, as when we teach elementary music theory; the student memorizes the names and sounds of the dissonances: major and minor seconds, sevenths and ninths; the tritone and the rather strange diminished seventh and augmented second which are enharmonically imperfect consonances. Their effect when used in actual music is the important thing, and one of the most fascinating aspects of music history is tracing the usage of these intervals. A pattern does seem to emerge, however: each age seems to be discovering another partial in the overtone series, a tendency still observable today.[5] The general principle, then, is that the lower down on the partials the more consonant the interval is with respect to the fundamental. Another relationship is the interval among the partials themselves when expressed as a mathematical ratio: for instance, 2:1 is an octave no matter how expressed (8:4, 16:8, etc.); 3:1 is a perfect twelfth, as are 6:2, 9:3, 15:5, etc.; 5:4 or 10:8, etc., are major thirds; 7:5 is a tritone, and both partials are prime factors and are out of tune in our system; the major second occurs in different sizes, as do all imperfect intervals either consonant or dissonant —one of these (for the major second) is 9:8. The semitone is 16:15. One can see that equal temperament is welcome, indeed, so that the interval is the same size no matter where it occurs or what harmonic function it has.

Apropos tuning and temperament, it should be pointed out that in practical performance today (as was probably always the case) we tend to alter the pitch we are playing in order to be in tune with the entire ensemble. If we are playing an instrument which can alter the pitch easily (all those except fixed-pitch instruments such as the piano), we tend to tune by resonance—which means that the way the overtones are sounded in any given situation will have much to do with the pitch we are actually playing. We usually think in equal-tempered terms (especially if we have had keyboard training), since it does simplify many passages. Many times we tune because we recognize specific chord progressions. When playing in a string quartet, there is a greater tendency to approach overtone tuning than when strings are playing with the piano or with woodwinds. String players are more nearly equal-tempered when playing with piano, while a still different compromise is made when playing with the winds, since wind instruments make sounds according to slightly different acoustical laws. Compromises are now built into the instruments at the factory in order for them to be played with more chromaticism; early wind instruments were quite out of tune. Greater subtlety in harmony requires more accurate tuning.[6]

A *complex chord* played well in tune can be played and/or sung in any number of ways according to voicing and orchestration, and composers in the nineteenth century made great progress in the use of chords of the seventh (other than the dominant seventh), the ninth and even beyond. They began to find that a basic theorem of Rameau[7]—which states that a chord does not lose its identity upon inversion—refers only to relatively simple chords such as triads and sevenths. More complex chords when inverted cannot escape the overtones, and tend to sound as if lower elements in the chord are acting as roots; hence many different resolutions are possible, leading to a great variety of chord progressions.

It has been stated above that equal-tempered tuning and thinking leads to more chromaticism. This happened during the latter half of the tonal period in two different but interrelated ways: chromatic nonharmonic tones (such as passing, neighboring, suspensions or appogiaturas) and chord formations themselves. These are part of the romantic harmonic vocabulary. The most important of these are:

1) Secondary dominants, also called interdominants ("Zwischendominanten"), which are dominants and dominant sevenths or even higher

dissonances on any root degree; for example, a major chord plus the other tones containing a tone or tones not in the key signature which progresses as if it were a dominant to a major or minor chord which has a root lying a perfect fourth higher (*authentic resolution*), or to a minor chord with the root lying a major second higher (*deceptive resolution* in major, quasi-dominant to submediant), or to a major chord with the root lying a minor second higher (deceptive resolution in minor, dominant to submediant). The same kinds of resolutions can also be seen when any dominant type chord is built on any tone. These are not necessarily modulations (although they can be), since the chord of resolution will have further relationships either in or out of the original key. Here are some examples:

Figure 7-4a

Schubert, "Die Forelle." The chord in question is on the word "ein," and is the most common: V^7 of V.

Figure 7-4b

This short song from Beethoven's *Gellert Lieder* abounds in secondary dominants.

Figure 7-4c

Schumann, *Piano Concerto*, cadenza in first movement.

Other names are: transient modulation, embellishing dominants and tonicization dominants.[8]

2) Chords spelled as dominant sevenths which are resolved as "German type" augmented sixth chords, and are therefore subject to all of the regular and irregular resolutions available for augmented sixth chords, or vice versa.

CHOPIN: *Mazurka,* Op. 56, No. 1

Figure 7-5

3) Diminished sevenths, which in romantic harmonic practice appear and resolve almost without restriction.

4) The enormous field of augmented sixths (long the bugaboo of music students), a family of chords described quite differently by various theorists. They are of great importance since they occur frequently, and in the final analysis are among the most successful of chords not really built on thirds.[9] They do much, then, in creating the actual sound world of much romantic music, and they also contribute to the ultimate overthrow of tertian harmony. The famous sound in Wagner's *Tristan und Isolde* is created in large measure through unusual uses of altered chords in general and augmented sixths in particular.

The augmented sixth in romantic treatment displays great expansion and freedom from the textbook treatment of flat-scale degree six to raised-scale degree four, which then resolves to an octave of the dominant as root of the dominant or as fifth of the tonic six-four.

Here are some of the romantic uses:

a) Any scale degree was preceded by its augmented sixth, not just scale degree V. (See Beethoven's *Piano Sonata*, Op. 53 ("Waldstein"), slow movement.)

b) The interval of the augmented sixth was used in nonstandard structures; almost all possible pitches can be found, in addition to the standard "Italian," "French" and "German" sixths. This usage is found as early as Mozart and others but is common in Wagner, Franck, Reger and others.

c) The resolution itself was free, and could be found in streams of chords where the *tone* of resolution is present but the whole aggregate of the sound itself is unresolved. (See the final part of Elgar's *Dream of Gerontius*.)

d) The chord of resolution itself is not really in the key—this happens as early as Beethoven. A common use is for a secondary dominant to be preceded by an augmented sixth, but many other chords can be found which are not in the key at all and not necessarily in a modulating passage. (See Brahms's *Symphony No. 1*, beginning of allegro in the first movement.)

Note the ornamentation in the Schumann *Piano Concerto*, at the beginning of the cadenza:

Figure 7-6

5) Subdominant function chords, such as the Neapolitan sixth (in root position). If a dominant or dominant seventh chord can appear anywhere, then it follows that a secondary Neapolitan can occur just before it. (Remember the formula for the resolution: $N_6I_6V_7I$.) This sequence of root movement can occur anywhere; in the formula shown the place of I can be taken by any chord of the key, or, in romantic treatment, out of the key; in other words, the secondary dominant is preceded by a secondary Neapolitan.

The role of the subdominant as a principal chord of the key was far more important to the composer in the nineteenth century than in the eighteenth. In the cadence formula: IV V I, the Classical Period composer more often than not would precede the dominant by a supertonic first inversion: ii_6 V I. The use of IV I (the Plagal cadence), however, is a very old one and is frequently found from the sixteenth century down to the triadic music of the present time. Since the tonic is the dominant of the subdominant, it is very easy to slip into the key of the subdominant. The subdominant is quite the reverse of the dominant: it turns the harmonic logic to a state of rest or completion. Frequently in the tonal period one finds modulations to the key of the subdominant near the end of extended movements (see Brahms's *Third Symphony*, finale). The dominant, however, carries the tonal logic forward. It is significant that in all of the important homophonic forms of classical music the key of the subdominant is found as an important structural device *hardly ever inside a closed form*; in the large four-movement structure it is often found as the tonality of the second movement—but not really often enough to state it as a rule.

Some theorists feel that all progression to the dominant must be counterbalanced by a comparable progression to the subdominant, but actual musical literature does not bear out this theory. It must be remembered that the subdominant's dominant is the tonic, and *that* relationship is far more significant. If this were not so, then we would have an involved theory of secondary subdominants and they would often appear in the literature. They are mentioned in some harmony books, but in almost every case other solutions making as much sense can be proposed. I must once again stress the importance of theoretical principles found in living musical literature. If a particular function is used but *once* in a masterpiece, it is important.

6) Recognition of the plurality of function of all chords, especially a major triad. Music has long employed everyday usage of common tones, common intervals or common chords. The common tone is a very customary modulation. The common interval makes possible, for example, a diminished fifth to become an augmented fourth, or vice versa—making possible the following music from Rimsky-Korsakov's *Sc9ehera-*

zade. (Remember that the trumpets are in B♭, sounding down a major second. The augmented fourth in the strings is doubled in the woodwinds; this interval, to be spelled "correctly," ought to be C-G♭ for the trumpet call, but C-F♯ for the trombone solo.)

Figure 7-7

Common chords are frequently used in modulation but until the nineteenth century were usually those of closely-related keys. Later practice allowed such unique concepts as an original dominant left as if it were a Neapolitan, or a subdominant—or anything else a major triad can be in either major or minor keys. There is in addition the use of the common chord as an enharmonic equivalent.

In the song "Widmung" of Schumann there is a striking application of this principle in the change of key at the end of the first section, where the enharmonic mediant relationship is seen; the A-flat major chord is the tonic of that key and the G-sharp is the enharmonic common tone to the new key, E major, enharmonically a major third lower. This relationship is very common in romantic music, whether enharmonic or not. But just a moment! The new key is immediately destroyed by the passing seventh (D) in the left hand and the new key becomes in reality A major, which is the real tonality of the entire middle section, although some interesting chromaticism is employed for color and expression. At the end of the section there is a cadence in A major which is left as the Neapolitan of A-flat major (enharmonically speaking, of course); the formula is followed through, except that the Neapolitan is in root position—N V₇—and, after ·roving a little bit, returns to the tonic A-flat. Here, then, is not only a case of multiple function of a major triad but also a freedom in key relationship.

As the century progressed composers used sevenths and ninths in a manner similar to Schumann's treatment of the triad.

SCHUMANN: *Widmung*

Figure 7-8a, b

A simple case in which the subdominant suddenly finds itself to be the tonic is found in the second movement of Brahms's *Symphony No. 3.* String figurations outline the harmony. Notice how Brahms uses melodic and harmonic doubling.

Figure 7-9

The subdominant which is the first beat of the fourth bar could have continued as the subdominant, but Brahms knew the value of pivoting on that chord and making it possible to introduce the B-flat major chord as the temporary subdominant of the new key. Note that Brahms goes back by the same route: the F-major triad is entered as tonic in bar five and left as subdominant of C. The article on modulation in *Grove's* fifth edition should be studied for examples of these principles.

7) Leading-tone harmony. The leading tone has traditionally moved to the tonic. The triad erected on the seventh-scale degree has caused no little difficulty in major, since it is a diminished triad. It occurs naturally in minor on the lowered seventh degree as a major chord and is, therefore, available for any major triad function. Some theorists call this the *subtonic* rather than the leading tone: in C minor the B-flat major triad—the triad of signature on the seventh degree—would be called the subtonic and could be used as the dominant of the mediant, subdominant of the subdominant, Neapolitan of the raised sixth, among other things, or a tonic in its own right. The leading-tone chord on raised seven in minor or the natural seven in major will also act as a dominant; therefore, composers used "secondary leading tones" as they did dominants, sevenths and diminished sevenths.

A different approach developed late in the century and, as with many of the new principles, came into being not by theorizing but by writing sonorities. There are other explanations possible for many harmonic successions and progressions[10] in romantic harmony. Since in the diminished seventh any tone could serve as a leading tone, some composers came up with the idea that in *any* chord *any* tone could be a leading tone, with no little amount of sideslipping in the harmony. Note this example from Reger's *Aus meinem Tagebuch*, Op. 82 (II), No. 8:

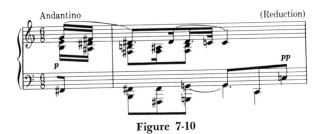

Figure 7-10

More complicated is this excerpt from Elgar's *Dream of Gerontius*:

Figure 7-11

In Elgar note the parallel fifths, which make a very good effect here. There are enharmonic spellings: the B-flat on the second chord is actually an A-sharp in a German sixth, and it is a leading tone of B just as the A in the B-major seventh chord on the first beat of the second bar is a leading tone of B-flat, the next chord. But this chord could also be called a German sixth, even though the upper B-flat is in the wrong octave. Note further that the roots move down a semitone in each chord (a chromatic bass), and that each chord is a major chord or a dominant seventh type chord.

Leading tones were moved backward, as were other chord progressions—again a sideslipping, but this time a semitone downward. In a way the augmented sixth does this *at the same time*: the augmented sixth interval (D-flat to B) classically resolves to a C octave, with the B rising up and the D-flat falling down. The use of the former is, of course, very common, but the latter can also be found. The succession of the first two chords in the Elgar example shows this, although other explanations are possible, such as a root moving down a minor second.

Perhaps this is all an attempt to justify the chromatic movement of any or all voices in parallel, oblique, similar or contrary motion. The *second* chord need not be a simple triad either; the tone which is leaned toward can be any member of the succeeding chord, and it may return the same way.

In the first bar of Beethoven's *String Quartet*, Op. 135, the lower note of an implied augmented sixth is used:

Figure 7-12

8) Parallel movements of various types become of great importance in the nineteenth century. We have already noted the numerous occasions when a composer presents parallel diminished sevenths, but other chords are also often used. Perhaps the most absorbing for the student would be delightful parallel fifths *used correctly*, since they sound beautiful; they become a standard part of nineteenth-century practice, but were *extreme rarities* in the Classical Period. Some occur in the finale of Schumann's *Faschingsschwank*, in Chopin's *Mazurka No. 21* and in Verdi's *Requiem* (in the "Confutatis," tenth bar; this is repeated, and is one of the most beautiful spots in the entire score).

Figure 7-13

The student would benefit from finding other examples and noting why they are not objectionable.

In the slow movement of the *Apassionata Sonata*, Op. 57, Beethoven disguises them through notation. The fifths occur between measures six and seven. Note that the last chord in measure six is a German sixth.

One expects parallel chords in impressionistic works, but the earlier romantics used them as well. In *Die Walküre* Wagner uses a beautiful succession which is mostly parallel major triads—one after the other. Marvelous voice-leading adds to its effectiveness. Note the contrary

Figure 7-14

motion between soprano and bass, and the root progression of upward-moving major triads:

Figure 7-15

Another kind of parallelism is found in keyboard music, where the right and left hands play the same music an octave apart.

Distant key relationships are among the logical results of the foregoing discussion. In many composers changes of key are very frequent, even in expositions—where the classical and early romantic composer is less likely to modulate except to either the key of the dominant or relative major. Franck, for example, often seems to float among keys, establishing a definite tonic; but not every phrase or so affirms it. Again: the student can find many early examples of almost every concept discussed here, but they occurred rarely in the Baroque and Classical Periods, and is a point of style with the romantics; the rare becomes the standard and even the cliché—especially the uses of the diminished seventh. Composers make fascinating uses of abrupt and gradual modulations. Tones of resolution appear in the wrong voice, often octaves away from where they would fall in a harmony exercise. Progressions move backward from where they normally would; and there develops the strange habit of ending a phrase on a dominant seventh or some other chord which usually needs resolution. The chord is either left hanging or is resolved as the first chord of the next phrase.

The best composers of the Classical and Baroque Periods often used rather fast harmonic rhythm. In the Baroque it occurred in the more complex contrapuntal works and, oddly enough, in the chorale harmonizations. In the Classical Period rapid root changes occurred quite frequently in development sections, as did rather rapid changes of key— particularly in the great works which live on well past the end of the period. A very good example is the development section of the first movement of Mozart's *Symphony No. 40* in G minor, K. 550; for Baroque usage see the *Fugue No. 24* in B minor from J. S. Bach's *Well-Tempered Clavier*. Note that these are both minor; we usually find more of this tendency in minor tonalities, partly due to the fact that more tones are available in the first place (the tones of the melodic and harmonic scale forms). It should also be remembered that minor is very difficult to explain according to the overtone series, and the attempts by some to show this leave much to be desired.

The best examples of harmonic rhythms which are fast are found in passages where the composer is moving through parallel chords which should be resolved and are not; the composers are temporarily suspending tonality, as it were. The passage in parallel diminished sevenths from Liszt's *Les Préludes* is a well-known case, as is the middle section of Chopin's *Etude in E Major*.

Liszt's *Les Préludes* is a work which deserves much study from all of these aspects, since it clearly shows almost every romantic tendency. There are moments when the harmonic rhythm is quite slow, which tends to point up even more the passages in which the harmonic rhythm is fast. Liszt keeps the excitement going through rapid passages in the strings, even though the harmony is stagnant. (We will return to this important work later.) In the *Dante Symphony* of Liszt the second movement (called "Purgatorio") illustrates an extreme case: a D-major $^6_3$ chord is figurated without change of harmony for seven pages in the full score. The composer again achieves variety through hemiola, long cantilena with non-harmonic tones and various devices of "Farbenwechseln."[11] He leaves the D-major chord in a unique way and then proceeds to continue with an E-flat $^6_3$. When the movement returns to more normal harmonic rhythms, how colorful they are!

Many passages in Beethoven continue for some time with no change. (See the finale of the *Eighth Symphony*.)

If we put together all of the foregoing, we can see that eventually the composer is going to go so far that he will stretch the relationships to the point where he must either use a key that does not really exist or else change over to the enharmonic equivalent. Mozart (whose impact on the romantics has often been overlooked) does this as early as 1785, in his *Violin Sonata*, K. 481:

Figure 7-16

If Mozart had resolved deceptively the dominant seventh and kept the original notation in flats, he would have ended up in the rather uncomfortable key of F-flat major! Being a practical man *and* a believer in equal temperament, he does the most logical thing and simply writes E major instead—much to the relief of anyone who has ever played it!

Verdi and many others actually use keys which might be called "context" keys: keys notated by accidentals in the course of the composition but which have no real key signature. Toward the end of the last act of *La Traviata* Verdi writes an extended passage in D-flat minor which carries the signature for D-flat major, the F being flatted every time it occurs. This makes a great deal of sense, since in the orchestra there is a darker sound in the key of D-flat minor than in C-sharp minor, although on the piano it would be exactly the same. If there were such a key as D-flat minor, it would be the relative minor of F-flat major—which would have eight flats, one of which would be B-double flat! One must be careful not to confuse the oddities of musical notation with *sound*—which, after all, is the true "stuff" of music! The D-flat minor *is* a different sound, however, in the orchestra—as would be the key of F-flat—which actually can be found at times in late nineteenth-century scores and is, of course, a context key, not a key of signature. Verdi also uses this device in *Il Trovatore, Falstaff* and elsewhere.

In the final analysis, the idea of using the same signature for major and minor keys *does* make sense, because we have but to flat the third scale degree to create minor from major. In the present system we have to sharp either scale degrees six and/or seven, so what difference does it make? It is common knowledge which key is the relative major, by usage of the great composers who have found a real relationship—not the phony one of the same key signature. One must remember that some of Bach's music in minor keys has one flat too few according to the "rules" of signature. They are the so-called "Dorian signatures" of the Baroque. There is also the nagging question of the modes which have the same signature and are not even considered! A real composer in the heat of creation is mainly concerned with *sound* and often uses strange notations in first drafts, which are "corrected" in subsequent versions.

The "sound" aspect of a score through orchestration and chord voicing suggests "color" chords other than the standard ones such as diminished sevenths, augmented triads, whole-tone chords and the like. The literature is replete with these, especially after about 1850. These chords seem to exist only in their original voicing and defy "arranging" in the ordinary sense; one cannot redistribute and get satisfactory results. While this has the greatest import in impressionistic scores, Wagner often employs such harmonies, as do Franck, Tchaikovsky and even Rimsky-Korsakov.

Alexander Scriabin (1872-1915) was one of the most unusual composers who ever lived. His works fall into three very marked periods: 1) imitations of Chopin; 2) great influence of Liszt and Wagner; and 3) a strange, mystical, theosophic, probably psychotic phase which mixed concepts from writers such as Turbetsky and the *Gesamtkunstwerk* ideas of Wagner. He saw colors when he heard music, but wanted to unite the senses even more to include perfumes as music is heard!

Phase three interests us here, since it is but one example of how an artist might go outside his own art and discover valid or pragmatic principles. In the "mystic chord" Scriabin intended the soul of the listener to be lifted up into higher regions, just as the tones of the mystic chord on C contain all of the tones of the partials through the thirteenth with no doubling. Scriabin then re-arranged them to form a chord which is non-tertian but has fourths of every possible size, using partials 7, 8, 9, 10, 11, 12 and 13.

Figure 7-17

Perle[12] contends that Scriabin was one of the first composers to use a *dodecaphonic set*: a conscious use of the twelve equal-tempered tones in two "hexachords" consisting, for example, of the mystic chord on C and on B, which gives us all twelve tones. Perle argues that Scriabin's *Seventh Sonata* is so constructed and presents examples to illustrate it. Scriabin is, therefore, considered a pioneer in serial music, which assumes great importance in the twentieth century.

While it would be possible in late Scriabin to name each chord as some kind of a tertian sonority, we would often be stretching a point; and it would be even more difficult finding resolutions and/or tonal progressions. Hull[13] discusses the same passage, and comes surprisingly close to Perle's conclusions (*cf.* Hull, *Modern Harmony*, 1914, pp. 72 *et seq.*). Hull, by the way, wrote an authoritative biography of Scriabin.

Scriabin was widely discussed and played from around the time of World War I through the 1930's. He was heralded as *the* modern composer who had discovered the next step music ought to take. His esoteric and extra-musical stimuli have caused some to dismiss his music as the ravings of an egomaniac (he even thought he was a kind of musical Messiah!). Perhaps it is now time to re-examine his work. We are not so disturbed nowadays by the absence of an affirmed tonic, and we can also discriminate harmonic subtleties which passed by the ears of most Scriabin contemporaries as noise or aimless wandering. (It must not be forgotten that each person hears music in terms of his own conditioning. Much music which was once considered abnormal is now considered normal, and what is "normal" is what one is used to.)

Color was of great importance to Scriabin; there was even a color organ built by Rimington for use in performances of the tone poem *Prometheus*. Perhaps the purely musical exploitation of color is his most important contribution to history.

Rimsky-Korsakov had traveled throughout the Orient in his role as an officer in the Russian Navy, and became interested in various musical ideas from the Far East. These are evidenced by many of his works in the use of fantastic story lines, Oriental and otherwise exotic scales and modes which, when harmonized, make for strange harmonies and chord progressions. He also had great command of the orchestra, which made it possible for him to orchestrate these ideas with the utmost of skill and to influence an important group of composers in Russia (the Five, or *Kutschka*: Mussorgsky, Borodin, Cui, Balakirev and himself—to say nothing of Tchaikovsky, who was not a member of the group but influenced them). Rimsky-Korsakov was also the teacher of Stravinsky.

Exoticism was also felt in a very important way by composers who did not travel so far to find ethnic and more advanced folk ideas. Musical nationalism is of the greatest importance in ridding the nineteenth century of rulebook classicism; this was doomed anyway, since the kind of world in which it had flourished as a living art no longer existed, but the rising surge of nationalism in the late nineteenth century was spreading rapidly. The composer began to look at his own folk materials, tunes, stories, dance rhythms, peasant instruments, peasant singing and even the folk dialects of languages. Carl Maria von Weber (1786-1826) had pointed the way in his operas, drawing from German language folklore. Others had from time to time used folk elements, but they were often forced into the rigid confines of textbook composition, and a fragile folk tune somehow did not always lend itself well to the rhetorical posturing of a great symphony. Toward the end of the century, at the same time as Rimsky-Korsakov, the right men came along with the right talents and techniques to make this work. The great outpourings of the Mahler symphonies draw so heavily on the idiom and feeling of folk collections such as "Des Knaben Wunderhorn"; the Wagner music dramas, with all their ego, are still among the greatest examples of epic art; the great Bohemian geniuses, Dvořák and Smetana, are able to shape symphonic form to fit their ideas, not the other way around. Last, but greatest in this area, is Béla Bartók—who must be considered as one of the romantics, especially the folkloristic ones. He was a great scientist as well, showing the correct ways folk materials ought to be studied and used in composition. He was doing this while Rimsky-Korsakov, Verdi, *et al.* were still alive, and his early works must be included in the same breath as those of Dvořák. Others who also straddle the Romantic and "Modern" Periods in this area include Kodály, Vaughan Williams, de Falla, Janáček, Villa-Lobos and Chávez.

The entire century produced a harmonic revolution. The great eruption which took place in our century was at first only a logical continuation of this. The change factor had accelerated to the extent that the public, always behind the good composer, was now left far behind. However, the best of 1910's *avant-garde* are now almost classic masters!

For all practical purposes, the tertian period ends with the discovery of the twelve-tone technique by Schoenberg and the widespread acceptance of at least the duodecuple scale (recognized as early as 1914 by A. Eaglefield Hull). As was pointed out in Chapter I, it is by no means inherent in these statements that we are necessarily speaking of atonality, although the kind of music called atonal is important. The writer is not sure that atonality *per se* can exist, although some works are obviously more atonal than others—Wagner's *Tristan und Isolde* is much more atonal than Gounod's *Faust* (written at about the same time). The worth of a work, of course, is not determined by how atonal it is or is not.[14]

H. K. Andrews, writing in *Grove's*, asserts that it is high time we stopped trying to base harmony on the theories of Rameau (ostensibly on "natural" laws), since history and practice prove his theories to be false.[15] The student would do well to study in *Grove's* the article on harmony and related articles, mainly on tonality and modulation. To believe *exactly* as Rameau is to believe that the world is flat—too much good music has been written which *disproves* the basic assumption that the perfect harmony is a vibrating string and that this produces a perfect major chord. What about minor? What about the other partials which are also sounding? This is not the place to go into this matter in great detail —is it not enough that the Fifth Edition of *Grove's* saw fit to *rewrite* the sections pertaining to harmony in view of the important data: the musical masterpieces themselves?

The problem of minor has been variously explained. It would be so simple if there were only *undertones* which were the exact intervallic inversions of overtones; thereby, one would have a nice clear minor triad (plus a lot of tones which would be ignored, since they would not fit the system). If undertones are present, they are very faint and are far more faint than the very overtones which are avoided in discussions, since they do not fit the theories; almost all partials above the seventh fit this category. Even such eminent scientists as Helmholtz, Öttingen and Riemann try to explain sound in terms of undertones, and go to great length with theories requiring intonations which would be possible only under the most accurate laboratory conditions. This is not to decry the work of these men, particularly Helmholtz. It is simply another case of trying to prove something you want to find to be true, instead of the uninvolved observation that "truth will out" no matter what. Helmholtz was a great scientist and also a good musician. As is often the case with great men, he was grossly misunderstood by scientists who were not musical and by musicians who somehow feel that science has nothing to do with music.

The tuning of the scales and the minor triad, as worked out by Helmholtz, were indeed ingenious and, needless to say, are still valid. What is not as yet explained is why so many minor works end with the *tièrce de picardie*, why large churches and halls reverberate to the sound of major; or, the most damning, the unalterable fact that the combination tone of a perfect fifth is a *major* third. This all means that a minor chord is a dissonance and can be proven through Helmholtz's own principles to be a dissonance—a much more biting dissonance than the overtones of a single tone, or of all the overtones of all the tones sounding in a major triad.

In short, we must accept the spreading out of error provided by the use of equal temperament, since it does resolve many of these problems. Music since J. S. Bach, as we have said repeatedly, developed as it did since equal temperament made possible the expansion of the tonal system until it became a very large network wherein all keys are related to all other keys. In the equal temperament system a closely-related key of a closely-related key is possible: for instance, one could start in C major, modulate to F major and then modulate to B-flat and thence to E-flat or some other key. There would be no tuning gap, as there was before. If the greatest composers accepted this idea, then we should too.

In the Fourth Edition of *Grove's* R. O. Morris, in the article on "Polyphony," summed up the whole question:

A modern composer has only to develop this method of proceeding to attain the full freedom of a twelve-note scale with no need of becoming either arbitrary or chaotic. It can thus be realized that music in 1600 did indeed stand at the crossroads, but saw only one arm. That was right at that time, but now the hour has come to go back and see where the other arm points us.[16]

In conclusion:

1) The composer in the Romantic Period did not restrict himself to the four voices of a harmony exercise and, therefore, often avoided doubling through the use of more pitch classes in a chord—hence more interesting sonorities and much better voice-leading.

2) It is dangerous for us to label every "chord" as we analyze these works. A succession of names is meaningless unless some kind of function is known: for example, the batting order of the Boston Red Sox, the first violin section of the Boston Symphony or any random names taken from the telephone book.

3) It is also dangerous to assign to notes that do not fit the system some kind of "non-essential" nomenclature—again a case of naming and then forgetting that the composer deals with a *sound* world; the best composers have no other purpose in mind than to create beautiful successions of sounds, no matter what they might be called.

4) It is even more dangerous to use the principle of point 3) to try to explain *everything* which does not seem to fit in that manner.

5) In many passages factors other than the harmonic should probably take precedence: that is, the manipulation of musical factors which are unique for the work in question. One needs only to compare several analyses of the *Tristan* Prelude to find all kinds of attempts to show that it is, indeed, related to the Bach chorales or to Schoenberg's *Erwartung*. It is far more important to find out how it is related to *itself*.

6) The whole matter of harmony comes down to:

a. How does a work derive harmonically from the past?

b. How does it point to the future?

c. What does the work possess which is unique?

Notes

1. Equal temperament and "well-tempered" tuning are not *exactly* the same thing. Equal temperament in theory uses semitones which are exactly the same size: the vibration ratios of any two tones a semitone apart will be a constant, no matter where they occur. Well-tempered tuning uses semitones which are not exactly equal but are tuned in such a way as to allow the use of all twelve keys on the keyboard within one composition. This obviously gives each tonality a different color in both melodic and harmonic treatment. (See Peter Yates, *Twentieth Century Music* (New York: Pantheon Books of Random House, 1967, p. 5.)) Many authors refer to one or the other interchangeably, but to do so is an oversimplification. *Absolute* equal temperament is almost impossible to achieve and, once achieved, will not last, since the act of playing the piano changes its tuning—to say nothing of other factors such as changes in the weather.

2. A. Eaglefield Hull, *Modern Harmony* (London: Augener, Ltd., 1914), pp. 22-23. This interesting and important work (note publication date) has been reprinted by the Kalmus Edition in paperback.

3. Quoted in Paul Cooper's "Ross Lee Finney," *The Musical Quarterly*, LIII, No. 1, January 1967, p. 4.

4. When two tones are heard—even a simple one without many partials— the ear can actually hear four: the difference of the frequencies and a weaker summation of the frequencies. By rigorous mathematics it can be shown that this combination tone is the same as the sum or difference of the ratio numbers. For a fifth the ratio is 3:2 and the combination tone is $3 + 2 = 5$, and the ratio 5:2 is a major tenth—one reason why minor chords are difficult to voice: the major third is already there! The fourth presents an extremely unique case, since the ratio is 4:3, $4 + 3 = 7$, and 7:4 is a dissonance—an out-of-tune (to our system) minor seventh. Most strict theories regard the fourth as a dissonance—and here is why. Many musicians play in such a way as to make the combination tones less obvious, at times to good effect. Some orchestrations actually voice the final chord as a six-four, but the difference tone when played well in tune at low pitches will yield a strong root: $4 - 3 = 1$, the fundamental.

5. Although our Western civilization includes some melodic styles using micro-tones (the blues, portamento, vibrato and folk modes, among others), they have not been employed extensively until recently (Carillo, Haba, Bloch, Berg, Bartók and some younger ones), and have never been used as a part of rigorous theo-retical training for the average musician. While the difference between the tuning of the seventh partial and the theoretical way it should be tuned in equal temperament is a microtone, the alignment of the partials from the 22nd through the 24th requires a microtone as a partial which is itself a microtone. For example, the 22nd partial of a B-flat is approximately an E and the 24th is an F; hence the 23rd must be a pitch lying between these two.

6. I mean here the tuning currently found in chamber groups and orchestras. Early performances on records of important twentieth-century works will show this. Compare the early version of, say, Honegger's *Pacific 231* with later ones. This has probably always been true. The beautiful chaste, transparent sounds of the *Lohengrin* Prelude were severely criticized in early performances, since these harmonies were probably *not* played in tune. In more complex harmonies

the player tries to simplify them: for instance, he hears a minor ninth and tries to make it an octave, resulting in an out-of-tune interval between the two. See Abraham's *One Hundred Years of Music*, Donald Mitchell's *The Language of Modern Music* or Peter Yates's *Twentieth Century Music* for discussions of this problem from different points of view. In the last ten years, however, performances of all music (on recordings and in live concerts) have shown far better intonation than hitherto exhibited.

7. Jean Philippe Rameau (1683-1764) has always been a controversial figure. His faction fought against the cult of Pergolesi (1710-1736) in the rather silly "War of the Buffoons"—silly, since the *music* of both men is of the highest quality. It is a common mistake, it seems to me, to require that there be a common practice, even in epochs when it appeared natural for one to exist. Common practice exists in books about music more than in music itself. These selfsame books pass off the great differences which exist among the great composers as "differences in style." A grave mistake has been made in perpetuating the figured bass far beyond its historical significance, particularly in harmony texts where Roman numerals have been used. (I have used them too!) The augmented sixth is a case in point, since one gets a concept of a fractured subdominant or supertonic *only when the numerals are used.* I have no quarrel with the figured bass Arabic figures, which are correct and have some historical precedence; but if one is to base harmony on "natural physical laws," he cannot with clear conscience call any augmented sixth a tertian sonority except the German sixth—which is still actually played with an intonation and an overtone structure not too unlike the dominant seventh.

The theoretical works of Rameau are not confined to the famous treatise of 1722; he wrote some others (see Keane, pp. 252-254; cited below), and was always expounding in his letters and elsewhere. Each generation has had its pro- and con-Rameauites, with but few of the combatants apparently ever bothering to read anything but a summary of his work. The interested student should consult *Grove's* Fifth Ed., Vol. VIII, in the article on "Theory," where Ll. S. Lloyd develops a devastating and rigorous attack on the theoretical systems of Rameau and others. In *Grove's*, Vol. IV, p. 77, in the article on harmony, H. K. Andrews states point-blank that the formation of chords from the harmonic series should be abandoned once and for all! The student is urged to study this article with care, since it is such a sensible description of the whole story of harmony—not just a faked, static "common practice" which does not and never did exist in real music by important composers.

Even in Sister Michaela Maria Keane's admirable dissertation *The Theoretical Writings of Jean Philippe Rameau*, (Washington, D.C.: Catholic University Press, 1961), where there is a little hero-worship, there is an accurate evaluation of the great worth of Rameau as a theorist—pointing out with rigor such devices as the fundamental bass, chord-building in thirds, inversions, no parallel fifths and octaves. Shirlaw's excellent work *The Theory of Harmony* (London: Novello & Co., Ltd, 1955) traces the theory of harmony from Rameau (after an introduction which discusses Zarlino and Descartes) through Tartini, Sorge, Marpurg, Kirnberger, Fetis, *et al.* Also of interest are Shirlaw's discussions of objections to Rameau by other composers and by the romantics in general. It is not Shirlaw's intent to debunk Rameau or anyone; he presents his information uncolored by opinion other than the cited opinions of others.

Many other works on the history of music theory could be cited on both sides of the controversy, which is still raging. The arguments of the pro-Rameaus and others who would base keys on some natural laws seem to me to be very poor indeed, since 1) they assume that the only harmony possible is tertian, and 2) they assume that one hears only the tones of a triad when one is sounded, when in reality one hears the overtones of each chord tone, and the combination and difference tones—which, by the way, can be shown to include all twelve tones *plus* microtones on almost all triads except those produced by sine wave generators! Since these sounds are actually present, it seems a little absurd to go to great lengths to find an acoustical basis for any scale by going out to partials far beyond *those actually heard.* It was Sir Donald Tovey who pointed out that the tonal system was *invented*; this makes it even more wonderful, since it makes sense in spite of acoustics, not because of any physical laws. Many musicians who claim to be of the Rameau school probably wouldn't be if they were to read Rameau's most basic theorem, which states that music should be reduced to mathematics. In the preface to his famous treatise—which is so seldom read but is so often used for the justification of over-simplified ideas—Rameau himself states:

Music is a science which should have definite rules. These rules should be drawn from an evident principle and this principle cannot be known to us without the help of mathematics.

May I disagree? Music is an *art* and a science. The "rules" are the rules of the human psychology of sensation and perception, not of a vibrating string or whatever—which, after all, means nothing unless a musical intelligence hears it and somehow interprets it. The most damning evidence is the unalterable fact that no other culture but the European and its spheres of influence have a tertian harmony—they have a tonality, yes; but the ragas in India, for example, are not described by Rameau at all, although they exist and have existed for centuries.

The student should study Ll. S. Lloyd and Hugh Boyle's *Intervals, Scales and Temperament* (London: Macdonald and Co., Ltd, 1963). This excellent book covers the entire subject both musically and mathematically.

8. This term is used by Roger Sessions in his *Harmonic Practice.*

9. See note 7. The so-called "German" sixth is enharmonically a dominant seventh and, therefore, tertian by itself; but the spelling and resolution make the difference. Various harmony texts disclose a variety of thought, not of usage so much as of description.

10. *Succession* means any sequence of any chords which may be completely unique in a given work. *Progression* means a standard, common practice: *ars combinatoria* harmonic sequence, such as ii₆V⁷ I.

11. *Farbenwechseln* means "exchange of color." The chord keeps the same pitches but the voices cross, which provides a "timbre progression." On the piano, of course, this is only a fiction; but in choral and instrumental ensemble music since the sixteenth century it has been used again and again. Hermann Reutter's *Die Witwe von Ephesus* is an opera of recent vintage which makes an effective use of the device. It can be seen and heard effectively in Mozart's *Serenade*, K. 361.

12. See George Perle's *Serial Composition and Atonality* (Berkeley: University of California Press, 1963), Chapter III.

13. A. E. Hull, *Modern Harmony* (London: Augener, Ltd., 1914), pp. 72ff.

14. See Hull, *op. cit.*, pp. 33-34.

15. *Grove's Dictionary of Music and Musicians*, Fifth Ed., ed. by Eric Blom (New York: St. Martin's Press, 1966), Vol. IV, p. 77.

16. *Ibid.*, Vol. VIII, p. 502. See article on polyphony by R. O. Morris.

CHAPTER VIII

COUNTERPOINT IN THE NINETEENTH CENTURY

THE ART OF COUNTERPOINT is the art of combining melodic lines. The contrapuntal essence, as an ingredient of inner vitality in music is, however, something more than a process of manipulation and combination, and it is to be found in nearly all music. That is to say, most music is to some degree contrapuntal.[1]

Walter Piston

The common opinion among too many is that counterpoint is dull, uninspired, difficult, not very beautiful, and therefore was not very important in the nineteenth century. Careful study shows that the opposite is the case.

While it is undeniable that J. S. Bach represents an apex in the art of tonal counterpoint, it is also undeniable that this art did not and should not stagnate, but must reflect other musical changes, as well as show vital growth in its own right during the nineteenth century.

All polyphonic music could be placed in one of two very large categories: 1) formal, patterned and set; 2) free and open, yet many-stranded. In the former we have such forms and processes as the fugue, canon, invertible counterpoint and the various ground bass types. In the latter we have a free movement of parts, designed only to sound well together. The precise form is determined by other factors.

The nineteenth century produced many outstanding examples of

197

each type, and one can find both categories as either complete movements or as subdivisions of movements. An added element is the programmatic one; and, strangely enough, we can find both categories in some
of the most imaginative poematic works. Double fugues abound in
strange places (the finale of Berlioz's *Fantastic Symphony*, for example).
Beethoven often turns to fugal practice in his late works, and they are
distinctly his own concept of fugue—for example, the *Grosse Fuge*,
Op. 133, for string quartet; the finale of the *Hammerklavier Sonata*, Op.
106; the *Ninth Symphony*, and many more. The overture to Mendelssohn's *Elijah* is a fugue, as are his finales to the *Quartet in A Minor*,
Op. 13, and the *Octet*, Op. 20. Even as early as Haydn one finds this
kind of thing; as Tovey says:

Enormous importance lies in these fugues. Besides achieving in themselves the
violent reconquest of the ancient kingdom of polyphony for the string quartet,
they effectively establish fugue texture from henceforth as a normal resource
of sonata style. Here and hereafter Haydn knows not only how to write a whole
fugue for instruments, but how to let a fugue passage break out in a sonata
movement and boil over quickly enough to accomplish dramatic action instead
of obstructing it. A mere revival of the old polyphony would have been as
wide of the purpose as the introduction of Greek choruses, even in Miltonic
verse, into *Hamlet* instead of the Murder of Gonzago. But, apart from its value
as a means of development, fugue texture is a most important resource as a
type of instrumentation. Obviously it solves the problem of equality in quartet-
writing by a drastic return to Nature, and puts the four instruments where
four voices were when all harmony was counterpoint. But the very nature of
contrapuntal harmony is impartially friendly to all instruments that can sing.
And all instruments try to sing as well as they can, except those whose normal
functions are thrumming and drumming. Hence, when the texture of the music
is contrapuntal, the listener's attention is no longer concentrated on the instruments in themselves; within reasonable limits good counterpoint sounds well
whatever group of instruments plays it. An endless variety of new tone-colours
becomes possible, simply because the admissible range is no longer restricted
to those effects on which the ear would dwell for their own sake. The interplay
between the polyphonically interesting and the acoustically euphonious puts
an end to monotony and to the temptation to develop luxury-scoring at the
expense of dramatic vigour. We must not be misled by the common allegation
that the fugue style lends itself to silly ingenuity; what is wrong with bad
fugue passages is what is wrong with all bad composition and bad scoring.[2]

The finale of Tchaikovsky's *Manfred Symphony* contains an exciting
fugato, Liszt's *Dante Symphony* an expressive one (marked "Lamentoso"):

Figure 8-1

Brahms uses a passacaglia-chaconne as the finale of his *Fourth Symphony*, a ground bass in the final variation of the *Variations on a Theme by Haydn*, and a fugue to end his *Variations on a Theme by Handel*. Goldmark's once-popular violin concerto has a fugato for a bridge passage in the first movement. Verdi wrote masterful fugues in many works, such as in the last act finale of *Falstaff*, in the *Requiem* (big vocal fugues are a tradition in large choral works), in the string quartet (along with some interesting canons and fugati) and a fugato in *The Masked Ball*. Wagner uses a coloristic kind of counterpoint for sound effects (the storm which begins *Die Walküre*, the "Magic Fire Music" and "Ride of the Valkyries" in the same work), and for great emotional climaxes (such as the "Immolation" in *Die Götterdämmerung*, where the most important themes of the entire *Ring* Cycle are combined in very exciting ways). Max Reger ends the *Mozart Variations* for orchestra with a very involved fugue and, in a frank Bach imitation, writes fugues for unaccompanied stringed instruments and even some gigantic chaconnes for violin alone.

And so it goes; the list is enormous. Even the chorale prelude comes back, Brahms supplying some of the most beautiful. Even the French

composers write outstanding examples—I say "even," since the French
were not as pre-occupied with counterpoint as were the Germans or the
English (except for the Franck coterie). True, Cherubini was a great
master of counterpoint, but he was a transplanted Italian. He did, however, exert a profound influence on many composers during his tenure
at the Paris Conservatory, where composers wrote fugues as exercises,
not pieces. Franck wrote a delightful canon which is the main theme of
the finale of his *Violin Sonata* (to say nothing of the last part of "Panis
Angelicus"), and his *Symphony* does a very original thing by telescoping
the song movement and the scherzo into one movement: where he presents
the song, then the scherzo, and then the two together. Vincent d'Indy,
pupil of Franck, writes a beautiful fugue in the finale of his *Second
Symphony*. Bizet wrote some of the cleanest counterpoint in the literature; *Carmen* abounds in fine examples. Berlioz writes a beautiful canon
in *Roman Carnival Overture*, and he begins *Romeo and Juliet* with a
fugue. Nor must we forget the excellent French treatises on fugue.[3]

There are many reasons for the interest in counterpoint. One is the
result of the rediscovery of Bach, Palestrina and other older masters of
the art. Another is the attempt to avoid stereotyped patterns such as the
Alberti bass. Many works possess long, expressive lines which give a
kaleidoscopic harmonic effect, yet each strand taken by itself is a pre-
sentable melody. Counterpoint assumes in some instances an adjunct
role, and is pursued for a different end—it is part of a bigger purpose,
pursued as an end in itself only as a *tour de force* (such as the overtures
to Smetana's *Bartered Bride* and *Libussa*). The rise in virtuosity of the
orchestra made possible inclusion of passages where a sweeping mastery
was required by each player. Filler parts existed less and less. Richard
Strauss, the early Schoenberg (*Gurrelieder* and *Pelleas und Melisande*)
and the somewhat romantic works of the early Stravinsky (culminating
in *Le Sacre du printemps*) all show this predilection for coloristic counterpoint, where voice-leading is not done for any closed, formal or canonic
ideas, but rather for atmosphere.

Nevertheless, formal counterpoint does become more and more important and sets the stage for our own time, which is certainly an age
of counterpoint. In the free aspects of polyphony (many-voiced but not
objectively controlled) one must also mention the use of what might be
called "counterpoint of continuity"—moving parts in secondary voices
which keep the music going in places where the music could stagnate,
such as at cadence points or at long tones in melody. Slow movements
can be especially dull if the composer has not taken care to keep melodic
or thematic interest alive. By the same token, composers in the nineteenth
century include homophonic elements within the framework of formal
counterpoint, even to the point of writing an episode in a fugue which is

largely chordal-melodic rather than a contrapuntal interplay of motives. The fugues of Beethoven often use this device—the *Grosse Fuge*, Op. 133, has extended passages of this nature. This brings up a moot point: is this a possible explanation for the finale of the Mozart *Jupiter Symphony*? (I suppose we will never stop arguing about this movement!) Some say it is a sonata with fugal episodes, others that it is a fugue with homophonic episodes, while still others say it is in a class by itself. It was greatly admired by most nineteenth-century composers, and it did influence them as it is still influencing us today to a certain extent. It is a striking juxtaposition of homophony and polyphony, and is another underrated influence of Mozart on romanticism.

The use of counterpoint in the nineteenth century points up yet another paradox—a dearth and a wealth of it! A dearth in the small lyrical forms, but a wealth in the large rhetorical works. When counterpoint was used it was often harmonically conceived, giving rise to what some theorists even call "pseudo-counterpoint"—not real contrapuntal voices, each having something melodic to say, but chord outlines arppeggiated in various ways; a complexity, but far more simple than a Bach fugue. Atmospheric scores often contain the same sort of writing, but the harmonies are more complex, and at times present a very fast harmonic rhythm, wherein lies much of the excitement of the music.

Many writers on nineteenth-century music have summarily dismissed counterpoint as a dead issue, but I feel it is a question of what one means by the term *counterpoint*. If one means only the formal, closed patterns, or the species, then indeed it is a dead issue. If one means the interweaving of voices or, if you will, a free *texture*, then it is a very lively issue. One important factor which puts the songs of Schubert into a very special category is the use of countermelodic figures in the piano, or even atmospheric touches, such as the thundering triplets in the "Erlkönig" or the swirling figure so suggestive of a lively fish in "Die Forelle." These are programmatic figures in concept not unlike those of the Baroque; but they do occur as contrast to the other "lines" in the music, the voice part and at least the bass line of the accompaniment. How this fits the romantic temper! Changing something which can be stiff and formal into a subjective, freely applied device. Unconventional? Yes, and therefore very much part and parcel of the romantic temperament.

The unconventional also takes over in the applications of formal counterpoint. Fugue, never really a closed form in the hands of a real composer, becomes even more free, especially in regard to the demands of key relationship in expositions. A subject was usually answered a fifth higher or a fourth lower (a dominant answer), but other intervals become possible, sometimes the subdominant, sometimes completely free—as we might expect in view of what had been happening to harmony. Strauss

even keeps answering at the fifth. But Mozart did too, as in the *Kyrie*
from the *Requiem*, K. 626. This, however, is in the stretto of the *Christe*
subject, where one might expect a little more freedom, but hardly to this
extent. The student is urged to study the entire *Kyrie*, which is a marvelous double fugue.

Figure 8-2

Imogene Horsley's excellent book on fugue discusses the nineteenth-century problem of the fugue in some detail. Of special interest is Anton Reicha, of whom she says:

One of the professors who fought a losing battle with the conservative Luigi Cherubini, Professor of Composition at the Conservatory from 1816 and director from 1822, was Anton Reicha (1770-1836), who was appointed Professor of Counterpoint and Fugue in 1818. A boyhood friend of Beethoven, Reicha shared with Beethoven a desire to create a new, Romantic type of fugue, and his *Trente-six fugues d'après un nouveau systême,* published in Vienna in 1805, was one of the fruits of this youthful enthusiasm. Among other innovations, he brought in answers at unusual intervals, often as real answers in keys outside the dominant. The twentieth fugue, for example, has a subject starting in A major, and the answer is an exact transposition starting in E-flat major. The harmonic style, although exceedingly chromatic, fits clearly within the prevailing tonal system. His theoretical works written for pedagogical purposes take a more traditional approach to fugue, and his later fugues tend toward the conventional subject and answer types. But even though he bowed to practicality, his approach as a teacher of composition was justified by the success of three of his students—Hector Berlioz (1803-1869), Franz Liszt (1811-1886), and César Franck (1822-1890)—whereas the names of hundreds of other graduates who distinguish themselves in composition at the Conservatory have long since been forgotten.

Reicha's treatment of conventional fugue is found in the second volume of his *Traité de haute composition musicale* (Paris, 1825). Here, he maintained that any composer who does not know how to make a correct fugal answer cannot be said to know fugue, and his discussion of the answer is thorough and reasoned, including numerous examples and showing how alternate answers can be made to certain subjects.[4]

Note this interesting application of some of his principles:

ANTON REICHA: *Traité de Haute Composition Musicale*; Fugue on theme from Mozart: *Symphony*, K. 385 ("Haffner")
(Reduction)

Figure 8-3

Reicha is responsible for many of the terms which we now use almost universally in discussing fugue, but he also encountered a great deal of opposition. A good statement of his general policies is seen in the preface to his theories:

On comparing modern music with compositions which preceded the eighteenth century a very remarkable difference is found between them. In the latter, scarcely anything more is to be perceived than complicated and artificial combinations of harmony. The musical productions of those times were rather the fruit of an abstract science than of a fine art intended to move the soul and touch the heart. Hence instruction in the art of such composition was but little favorable to taste, imagination, sentiment, or genius. That dry instruction forms the basis of the greater number of the treatises on musical composition hitherto published. It hence results that these works are found incomplete, and most frequently in contradiction with modern music; in which cold calculations are to be avoided, but, on the contrary, are to be employed only ideas, feeling, effects, melody, variety, and truth in the representations of imitative music.

It is true that some persons, of our time, passionately fond of their art, have published works, conceived in a different spirit from those which preceded them; but, notwithstanding all the good they contain, these modern works are still wanting in many necessary developments. For instance, it would be desirable to find, in the works on harmony, satisfactory explanations in regard to the following objects: first, the chief cause that renders a base faulty; second, an instructive and complete theory of modulations; third, the laws according to which nature connects the different chords together; fourth, a more extensive theory of accidental or passing notes, namely those which are not reckoned in the harmony; fifth, the method of forming harmonical progressions; sixth, the principle according to which chords may be correctly broken or divided; seventh, the harmonical resources contained in every scale; eighth, the possibility of doubling, tripling, and quadruplicating harmony in two, three, and four parts; ninth, the conditions to be observed in the exceptional connection of chords in succession; and tenth, the art of employing harmony with the orchestra.

I have endeavoured in consequence to give, in the present course, as far at least as my feeble talents allowed, the desired explanations; and I have given such, not only on the subjects before-mentioned, but also on other matters concerning practical harmony.

In order to render this work more generally useful, I have thought I should lay down rules for composing music correctly in the free style, and blend together the principles of ancient and modern music.

In a work of this nature, as the text cannot have the necessary clearness unless well supported by examples, I have given a great number; and in the impossibility of finding immediately all those I should require, I have thought that by composing them myself they would be more suitable to the text.

It has also appeared to me more advantageous for learners, to set the examples, as much as possible, on one or two staves only, and to avoid multiplying clefs without necessity.[5]

Here is almost a romantic manifesto! "Move the soul and touch the heart!"

The fugue also changed in other ways; for one thing, countersubjects became more and more chromatic, almost to a fault (see the fugati in Liszt, Tchaikovsky and others).

The fugue idea seems in many cases to be a developmental device for previously announced material, instead presenting something which needs to be developed; hence, we observe more fugati than full-blown fugues. More about fugue later.

Canon appears quite frequently, as a device or part of a parade of devices; there are many examples one might quote. Little points of imitation, antiphonal effects and other devices occur frequently; they are also used as a part of the counterpoint of continuity discussed above.

Chopin is a great master of free, almost hidden counterpoint: beautiful countermelodies which greatly enhance the effect of the work and which are often differentiated rhythmically from the rest of the texture. Since Chopin exerted a great influence, it is not surprising to find similar devices in later composers.

Quite often in the art song the composer gives the piano the melody and the voice a countermelody, usually quite simple. Songlike movements in other works are sometimes given a similar treatment. (See Tchaikovsky's "Canzona" in the *Fourth Symphony* or Wieniawski's D minor *Violin Concerto,* slow movement.)

This device, of course, adds more interest to the reprise of simple song forms than a literal repetition. It is a mark of originality, and originality is a hallmark of romanticism. In other works of different types a voice would come in as from nowhere—*Freistimmigkeit,* as it is called. One might say "pseudo-counterpoint," but there is more than one melody at a time, and a real application, admittedly simple, of contrapuntal principles. Perhaps this is another result of music for the masses. In other words: it is usually done in such a way that the layman can follow it, *if* it is pointed out to him.

Polytexture is used to great effect: instead of lines, the composer begins to deal with timbre planes. This sounds complicated, but it is a case of the explanation sounding more esoteric than the device itself. In a way the composer (in orchestral works mostly, but elsewhere also) replaces the old soprano, alto, tenor, bass alignment with woodwinds-brass-strings-percussion bands or stripes of "wide" sound rather than a single voice, writing in planes, as it were, or mixing choirs.

Patterns of mixed color are often used and a new kind of counterpoint results, which comes about through the discovery of orchestration as a vital art, rather than just a *medium* of expression. This aspect is discussed here as an adjunct of counterpoint rather than an orchestral effect alone, although the word counterpoint *per se* should be replaced by "counterplane," or "countertexture," or some other term. The concept is the result of a fusion of contrapuntal and coloristic ideas.

This excerpt from the prelude to the first act of Verdi's opera *La Traviata* shows this very well.

In this example there are three textures, three pitch levels and three emotional planes. The rather typical afterbeat accompaniment is the foundation, harmonically and rhythmically, and is one unit. The diatonically descending melody in the middle is another. It is as warmly expressive as the accompaniment is dry. The higher strings form the third unit, and it is contrasted in every respect; it is expressive, but gay— almost the opposite of the other melody. (One is tempted here to point out that in a sense Verdi has summarized the whole drama in this short

Figure 8-4

excerpt: the accompaniment *could* be called "La Forza del Destino" or
the footsteps of fate, the force of destiny idea which seems to permeate
many of Verdi's works; the warm melody expresses the underlying tragedy,
while the upper gaiety shows the superficial happiness of Violetta's social
world.) If we are stretching a point, let us not forget that such interpretations were expected, especially in works such as operas, where specific
actions and emotions were an obvious part of the works. Hanslick, of
course, was of a different opinion (as we shall see later).

Verdi's use is quite simple, and to be profoundly simple is very difficult
indeed. There are passages in Liszt, Berlioz and Wagner (among others)
which could also be quoted if space permitted. The twentieth century
has many examples of very complicated orchestral planes (*cf.* Ligeti's
Atmospheres). Verdi, however, was such a great opera composer that we
often overlook his great originality in purely musical matters.

The same composer's *Falstaff* abounds in this kind of thing and is
almost a treatise on this kind of counterpoint, a counterpoint of ideas
from the stage which are given musical settings in the orchestra. One
important factor in the development of this device was the mechanical
advancement of wind instruments, allowing a full chromatic range for
each one, thus making more coloristic effects possible. Once a composer

had established these planes, he could interchange the colors and achieve effects based on the same principle as invertible counterpoint. This *is* rare, but exciting.

Invertible counterpoint as a point of departure is found in other ways as well. *Stimmtausch,* or exchange of voices, is used to a great extent in chamber music. In sonatas for an instrument such as the violin or the piano one finds this in great frequency.

This device was also used to a great extent during the Classical Period, when less attention was paid to the timbre of the melody. Not all themes were conceived with instrumental timbre in mind, as we have noted above. Composers of the nineteenth century noticed that in chamber music involving the piano there was often considerable contrast in timbre when played on a stringed instrument compared to when played on the piano, or vice versa. The Schumann *Piano Quintet* points this out abundantly. Invertible counterpoint must be understood as an "inversion" of timbre; each instrument thereby has a theme or pattern which is simply traded to another instrument.

One more aspect of polyphony needs to be touched upon, and that is the thickening of the over-all sound which is so characteristic of the colossal romantic. While much of this thickness was the result of the "blanket of horns" in the orchestra, there was also much doubling, both in and out of the orchestra. In Reger, for example, one wonders if there are not simply too many voices! There are many passages where one hears a non-differentiated blend, and much of the voice-leading is either inaudible or audible only when one has the score and can see it as well! It must be remembered that this is *not* the same as the coloristic counterpoint mentioned above; these scores are not opulent and will sound lucid only when played very well indeed—if, indeed, lucidity is always to be desired!

In summary, the Romantic Period again shows a paradox, this time in its attitudes toward counterpoint. Formal counterpoint did exist in churchly works, where the style of writing was traditional and expected. Fugues, motet-style choruses and freely-written passages were almost always tied too well to the harmonic fenceposts. Program works, on the other hand, often contained brilliant fugal passages which had surprising harmonies (for effect) but were seldom fully developed. The smaller forms either had none at all or else a very simple kind of countermelody. Great ages of counterpoint displayed a fluid kind of utterance, not tied to regular periodicity (the high Baroque being an exceptional case); and the nineteenth century carried the four-measure phrase with numbing frequency (*Vierhebigkeit*). The choruses of Gounod show this, as well as a feeling for sequence which—like the four-bar phrase—is a link with poetry, the sequence being similar in effect to rhyme.

It should also be said that the rather loose use of older contrapuntal principles reflects the attitudes of the age: *the spirit not the letter*; this brings it down to where the common man can understand things—contents over "correct" form. Beethoven has no compunction about crossing the voices involved in invertible counterpoint, as in the second movement of the *Seventh Symphony*.

No, the nineteenth century was not a great polyphonic age; but some of the greatest heights were reached at the very moments when the composer once again caught the essential spirit permeating the great polyphony of the past. As the late great Sir Donald Tovey states:

Now it was not from J. S. Bach that Haydn derived his ideas of fugue. His traditions in this art were Italian, and the old text-books will not help one to understand his fugue forms; while later treatises, from Cherubini onwards, bewilder us by flying in the face of every fact in Bach's works (including his didactic last opus, *Die Kunst der Fuge*) without throwing light on any other composer. The fact is that the later text-books are trying to lay down laws of form for an art whose rules define nothing but a texture. It would be a correct use of language to speak of certain kinds of music being "written in fugue," as certain kinds of poetry are written in blank verse; and Cherubini's rules for compositions written entirely in fugue are true only in so far as they concern matters of texture. Their authority on matters of form may be gauged by the fact that though J. S. Bach's last work, *Die Kunst der Fuge*, is an explicit demonstration of all kinds of fugue in the abstract, classified in a progressive system and all written on the same subject, yet Bach shows the same shocking ignorance of the rules here as he showed in fugues written at large. Now the mystery is, where Cherubini found his rules of fugue form. Cherubini, though out of favour at present, was near enough to greatness as a composer for us to find Beethoven's enormous admiration of him not inexplicable, in the light of Beethoven's reverence for all that was austerely firm of purpose. Now, one of the formative events in Cherubini's career was the occasion when he first heard a Haydn symphony. It moved him to tears. Perhaps this fact becomes easier to reconcile with the sour martinet portrayed even by friendlier witnesses than Berlioz, when we note that the only classical fugues that faintly adumbrate Cherubini's scheme of fugue form are these quartet fugues of Haydn, and a few in Mozart's Masses, together with two in some early quartets he wrote possibly already under the influence of Haydn's op. 20. The point in which they agree with Cherubini's rules is that they tend to save up the stretto (where subject and answer are to overlap in closer and closer combination) until the end, actually separating it off by a pause on the dominant. As a fixed rule this notion is, on the face of it, unclassical. It implies that the devices of a fugue stretto are inherently surprising; whereas they were matters of course to any composer to whom fugue texture was a normal language. A more serious objection to such a rule is that it excludes all fugue subjects that are not capable of stretto, thus extinguishing some ninety per cent of Bach's fugues at large, besides thirty-five of the "forty-eight" and (as to treatment of subject) at least six of the *Kunst der Fuge*.

But if a fugue is going to be a rare and conscious essay in a form romantically or solemnly imported from an older world, it will tend to include everything that is characteristic of all the most brilliant ancient examples taken together, and will, moreover, choose old subjects markedly unlike those of more modern art-forms. Now a school of criticism may or may not like the fugues of Haydn, Mozart, and Beethoven; but whether it likes any fugues or none, it cannot dismiss those examples with facile man-of-the-world patronage as deviations into scholasticism. The aesthetics of sonata fugues are no more scholastic than the aesthetics of a play within a play, such as the Murder of Gonzago in *Hamlet*. Here are dramatic conditions in which common sense demands the use of an evidently old-world language; and it is no accident that even Haydn has, in the quartets of op. 20, a hint of the emotional and dramatic impulse which became so volcanic in Beethoven's fugues.[6]

Notes

1. Walter Piston, *Counterpoint* (New York: W. W. Norton & Company, Inc., 1947), p. 9.

2. Sir Donald Tovey, *The Mainstream of Music* (New York: Oxford University Press, 1949), pp. 45-46.

3. Some of the most important nineteenth-century treatises are:
Choron, Alexander, *Principes de composition des écoles d'Italie* (Paris: 1808).
Langlé, H. F., *Traité de la fugue* (Paris: 1808).
Fétis, Joseph François, *Traité de la fugue* (Paris: 1824).
Reicha, Anton, *Traité de haute composition musicale* (Paris: 1824-1826).
Cherubini, Luigi, *Traité de la fugue* (Paris: 1837). (Eng. trans., 1854; notes on Cherubini's course by his pupil J. F. Halévy.)
Colet, Hippolyte Raymond, *La panharmonie musicale* (Paris: 1837).
Elwart, Antoine A. E., *Le contrepoint et la fugue appliqués a la composition* (Paris: 1840).
Gedalge, Andre, *Traité de la fugue* (Paris: Enoch, 1901). (Eng. trans., 1964, by A. Levin. Mattapan, Mass.: Gamut Music Company.)

4. Reprinted with permission of the Macmillan Company from Imogene Horsley, *Fugue*. Copyright © by The Free Press of Glencoe, a Division of The Macmillan Company, 1966, pp. 104-105.

5. Anton Reicha, *Course of Musical Composition*, or *Complete and Methodical Treatise of Practical Harmony*, trans. Arnold Merrick (London: Robert Cocks & Co., 1854), frontispiece.

6. Tovey, *op. cit.*, pp. 33-34.

CHAPTER IX

FORM IN THE NINETEENTH CENTURY

THE FORMS OF MUSIC may be considered in two aspects, the texture of the music from moment to moment, and the shape of the musical design as a whole.[1]

Donald Francis Tovey

It was a romantic trait to place content above form, so few new vital forms emerged from this period. Refreshing new ideas about the old forms were advanced, and in some cases new life was given forms through a consideration of the spirit of the forms and not just the tired filling-out of the old forms.

During the Romantic Period some artists fooled themselves into believing that knowledge would stifle inspiration, and therefore rejected "learned" studies in the craft of composition. In some cases their work is naive and totally inept; but in some the genius was actually there and was not to be denied, and they literally taught themselves, producing real masterpieces. The most graphic examples are the works of the Russian nationalistic group known variously as "The Mighty Five," or "Kutschka." Rimsky-Korsakov was the only one who was a professionally trained musician, and he often generously helped the others when they needed technical assistance. Mussorgsky especially shows the power of great genius; Borodin does to a lesser degree, but is still an important voice of his time; but what of the other two? Their works, although charming and at times powerful, have few performances today. It is not claimed that training will make a genius of one who isn't, but the greatest idea in the world will be stillborn unless it can be formed into a shape that can be communicated. Here is another paradox: the best performers of the age reached great technical heights, while technical advancement filtered down to improve by far the playing ability of people of average talent. Pedagogy produced far better results than ever before. Conservatories flourished, manning orchestras and concert salons all over the western world. People practiced and practiced; those who didn't "make it" became a part of the more enlightened audience. However, there was no such excellence in formal training in theory and composition.

What is the point of bringing this up in a discussion of form? Simply this: what was happening to theoretical training? Why didn't it keep pace? Composition was studied, but it was composition of a past age; the real talents were bored to death and usually rebelled. There were a few exceptions: Schumann and Brahms, Sechter and Bruckner, Reicha and his pupils, Franck and his followers (d'Indy *et al.*); but these were rare. It was popularly believed that performers practice but composers are only inspired; of course, this is nonsense. True, those who wrote according to the textbook had a technique, but they often lacked original talent—almost as tragic as the talents who had no technique. We can see, as did earlier ages, that great art is the result of both: the great idea and the command of technique to make it speak. Berlioz states it so well:

Music is the art of producing emotion, by means of combinations of sound, upon men both intelligent and gifted with special and cultivated senses. To define music in this way is equivalent to admitting that we do not believe it to be, as some say, *made for everybody*. Whatever may, in fact, be the conditions of its existence—whatever may have been at any time its means of action, whether simple or complex, gentle or energtic—it has always appeared evident to the impartial observer that a large number of persons remained incapable of either feeling or understanding its power. *Such people were not made for it*; and it follows that it was not made for them.

Music is, at one and the same time, both a sentiment and a science. It exacts from anyone who cultivates it, whether as executant or composer, both a natural inspiration and a range of knowledge only to be acquired by long study and profound mediation. It is this union of knowledge with inspiration which constitutes the art. Outside these conditions, therefore, the musician can only be an incomplete artist; even if he merits to be called an artist at all. The grand question as to which is pre-eminent, whether a natural organisation without study, or study without natural organisation—a question, moreover, which Horace did not venture to decide positively in the case of poets—seems to be equally difficult to settle in the case of musicians.[2]

The romantic composer and writer on the subject of music in the Romantic Period often really did not know, and covered up his lack of knowledge by a lot of talk about feelings, emotions and other nonsense that really has little to do with the question at all. Of all the musical elements, form probably took the worst beating during the nineteenth century.

Clarity of form is supposed to be a classical trait and of little importance to the romantic, but the romantics were greatly influenced by attention to form—in not strictly following it (a negative influence, as it were). Still more often they tried to be free, and instead fell into somewhat stodgy ternary forms. Piece after piece fit into this category, especially the little occasional piece for home and garden. Still others followed form to the letter, with incongruous results: empty, noisy posturing first themes, saying nothing but saying it with elegance; puny, treacly sentimental second themes with hardly enough substance for beer-hall ballads; rhetorical development sections with endless sequences, diminished sevenths, literal recapitulations and brilliant codas heard a thousand times before. But these are little remembered today, and no wonder. Great forms need great ideas, and great ideas need great forms. The truly great artist recognizes the wisdom of his heritage, but is wise enough to add to that heritage and not merely repeat it. Using an old form is not necessarily to put new wine in old bottles—the idea of putting wine in bottles at all is an old idea in itself; having new wine and new bottles is still wine in bottles. Obviously, something other than wine can be put in bottles, and by the same token wine can be put in something other than bottles. Too often man has confused the container with the contents, but the important thing is that the container be appropriate to the contents. (You do not carry soup in a book, nor a novel in a bowl.)

But we are most concerned with value, and there were valuable contributions to form. The homophonic forms especially reflected the new philosophies of romanticism. The art song became an important medium with composers long before it caught on with the public. The *Lied* was of the most importance in establishing the idea of a solo singer with piano accompaniment (the *Lied* is the German language song). Many song forms are shown here: the obvious binary and ternary types were extended in various ways, depending on how the composer treated the original stanza structure of the poetry. The composer could set a stanza as a complete song form in and of itself, in a way such as this:

1. AB, *simple binary*, two melodic ideas; A modulates to a related key (dominant or relative major), B starts in that key and returns to the tonic. If a suggestion of the original comes back near the end of B

the form is called either *rounded binary* or *incipient ternary.* Simple binary was extended by repeats: AABB, or even ABAB or AAB. The romantics would often use freer key relationships.

2. ABA, *simple ternary,* similar key relationship to binary; A comes back complete and may have a short coda. This was also extended to AABA or to similar forms.

3. AAB, barform, is also popular.

The art song goes beyond this in many cases, and the over-all form is then concerned with the handling of the stanzas. If each stanza is set the same way, it is called *strophic*—a "strophe" being another name for stanza. Remember, the stanza itself can be a complete simple song form, although many strophic songs use through-composed stanzas: no principle of statement and return, the form being dictated by the sense of the poem (a common device in almost every category of romantic music, as we shall see below). Since the mood often shifts from stanza to stanza, a composer often modifies a strophic song as the poetry suggests. This type of setting is called *modified strophic.* The changes are worthwhile to study; in Brahms's "Vergebliches Ständchen," for example, the same music is used in the opposite mode.

Figure 9-1a, b

The best performers vary the interpretation of regular strophic as the poetry demands.

Schubert's "Der Kreuzzug" is also a good example; note the setting of the last stanza, where the piano takes the melody and the voice a countermelody (see the previous discussion under "Counterpoint" regarding this device)—simple, yet very telling in effect. One can find many such examples with varying degrees of modification, such as: different piano interludes to modulate either mood and/or key; change of key for change of register, perhaps higher for a female singer and lower for a male; change of harmony to include more color chords, altered chords or surprising re-harmonizations of a motive· previously heard; change of tempo and/or meter; changes in dynamics and nuances.

The most dramatic examples of this modified strophic form are the settings of ballads, a romantic kind of poetry which greatly appealed to the romantic composer. Schubert's "Der Erlkönig" is a marvelous example, and should be studied in detail by the student; notice how many of the changes listed above are actually made, and how he does it. The drama unfolds so naturally that one is unaware of a form; and yet formal perfection is there. The German *Ballade* is an important derivation of the English ballad, and is found extensively in song literature. (Carl Loewe, 1796-1869, wrote fifteen *volumes*, including another setting of Goethe's "Der Erlkönig"; these songs use adaptable formal principles from strophic through modified strophic to through-composed.) Loewe's ballade "O süsse Mutter," Op. 62, No. 3, is a clever example of strophic modification in the accompaniment. Notice the young girl's impatience at being required to run the spinning wheel when she would rather be "elsewhere." Her wheel is sticking, her thread is breaking and it is spring! His "Erlkönig" is fine, but Schubert's is great.[3]

(a)   Schnell ♩ = 152   SCHUBERT: *Der Erlkönig*, Op. 1

CARL LOEWE: *Der Erlkönig*, Op. 1, No. 3
Poem by Goethe; Eng. trans. by Theodore Baker

(b)   Geschwind. Allegro

Figure 9-2a, b

The term *Ballade* is also used for instrumental pieces, notably piano works by Brahms and Chopin. These, however, tend to be huge ternary structures (ABA), but reflect the mood and fire of the poetic ballads. Minor composers wrote *Ballade ohne Worte* (or at least in "ballad with-out words" style) in huge numbers as fanciful piano pieces, or as solo-istic pieces for violin or other instrument and piano. The colossal romantic also set *Balladen* for chorus, soloists and orchestra—which shows the propensity for inflation of small forms.

A more imaginative musical structure is found in the through-composed Lied *(durchkomponiert)*, which is a real musical representa-tion of romantic lyric poetry. In this type the composer sets the poem idea by idea, as it were, setting it against the underlying "big idea" of the poem as a whole. This is a tremendous problem for the composer, since it brings into play the possibilities of psychological form; therefore, it is not as formless (musically speaking) as one might imagine, except in unsuccessful attempts to use through-composed techniques. The form established by the poet is often captured by the composer, while at other times a certain intangible combination is found which works *for that work alone*—a dangerous game perhaps, used as an excuse by inept talents, but so right when it does communicate! Schubert's "Der Wanderer" is a marvel of this; if any romantic Lied could typify —nay, *idealize*—the romantic philosophy, this is it. The student should study this song in detail, noting the use of augmented sixth chords and other dissonances. Of even greater interest is the development of *motivic* repetition: variation and evolution, rather than complete melody repeats —a much more subtle type which achieves unity in variety and variety in unity in an integral way, not a literal way.

The chapter on vocal music will dwell on these matters in greater detail; it remains here to point out that there is a decided parallel to poematic instrumental music. The symphonic poem is often a through-composed "setting" of the program. Its parts are often presented in groups, either as a suite or as a programmatic symphony. Suites of songs are called *song cycles*, and are important contributions of the nineteenth century—beginning probably with Beethoven's *An die ferne Geliebte*. As an idea, it soon spread all over Europe, and cycles appeared in many different languages. The formal plans of these cycles are highly individualistic, ranging from through-composed throughout (from the first song to the last) to rather tightly knit. Tyndall presents a fascinating discussion of Schumann's *Frauenliebe und Leben* in his book *Musical Form*.[4] One might be surprised to learn that instrumental forms such as the rondo are used at times; but remember that the rondo itself came in principle from a Medieval French song form. Rondo structures are made to order for setting poetry, since they represent statements, digressions and restatements in various ways, a very common poetic device. Compound ternary form is also used in song literature in a manner not unlike the *da capo aria* of the past. Compound ternary differs from simple in the micro-formal elements of its larger formal divisions; therefore, the divisions are longer and more elaborate:

Big outline ABA', where
A can be ab or aabb or aaba or even abcba;
B can be cd or cdc;
A' can be literal reprise of A or can be varied; it is often shortened, and
   often has a coda or postlude.

Some songs are so complex in formal structure that they approach a sonata-allegro. Other terms are often used, such as *romanze, cavatina* and *cabaletta*—referring more to style than to form.

Just as vocal music uses certain features of instrumental form, instrumental music has always borrowed from vocal or dance music, and developed its own forms only from the Baroque Period to the present time. All of the common song forms are found in slow movements, and compound ternary forms are found in dance movements of symphonies, string quartets and trios. The Romantic Period in general accepted the classical forms, including the basic ideas of key relationship, and gradually introduced extensions, relaxations, additions and even omissions or telescoping of the older forms.

The four-movement structure, used in symphonies and chamber works, is of prime importance:

First movement: Usually fast, may or may not have a slow introduction. The faster portion of the movement is most often in extended sonata-allegro form.

Second movement: Usually slow, in a singing, lyrical style. The song forms, sonata-form, theme and variations or ground bass forms are usually employed. The movement is typically a lyrical "character piece," often in some kind of subdominant key relationship to the key of the first movement. (Sometimes the dance movement or scherzo will be the second movement, and the song movement the third.)

Third movement: Usually dance-like in character; a minuet, or *tempo di menuetto*, gradually replaced by a scherzo, almost always ternary in form, triple meter, in tonic key with contrasting key in the trio portions. Brahms's *Fourth Symphony*, third movement, is an abridged sonata (first-movement form). Although somewhat rare, it is nevertheless important, since *anything* which happens in a masterpiece is important. Perhaps Brahms uses this form here because of the rather unconventional (for a symphony) use of passacaglia-chaconne for the finale.

Fourth movement: Usually fast; was a lighter movement in Classical and early Romantic Periods. From the late Mozart and Haydn, middle and late Beethoven there is a tendency for the climax of the work as a whole to move farther and farther toward the end of the entire work, just as the climax and denouement of a drama. This is evidenced in a finale, which is not only fast and brilliant, but triumphant as well. Forms used are rondo and rondo types, sonata-allegro, sonata-rondo, theme and variations (sometimes ending with a fugue), or ground bass forms (not too common, but Brahms's use in the *Fourth Symphony* is outstanding and influenced many twentieth-century symphonies). Tchaikovsky's *Pathétique Symphony* finale is a beautiful slow movement. Key is tonic, tonic major or even relative major.

It is noteworthy how this basic four-movement structure was used with a great deal of freedom. The first movements of some works, for example, seem more like rather free preludes, and at times the finales are like free postludes. Some symphonies have more than four movements (Berlioz's *Fantastic* has five; Beethoven's *Pastoral* also has five, as does Schumann's *Rhenish*; Rubinstein's *Ocean Symphony* has seven). Some symphonies have less (Franck's *D Minor* has but three; Liszt's *Faust* has three, with a choral epilogue added later; Schubert's *Unfinished* has but two, but is, of course, a special case). Schumann's *Fourth Symphony in D Minor*, Op. 120, is actually one long movement, but contains five real subdivisions. This telescoping of movements is not really a new idea with the romantics; C. P. E. Bach's beautiful *Symphony in F Major* (No. 3) does the same thing in three connected movements, as does the early Mozart's *Symphony in E-Flat*, K. 184. Beethoven often uses a full close at the end of the first movement, but joins together the second and third movements of three-movement works (as in the *Waldstein Piano Sonata*, Op. 53, the *Triple Concerto*, the *Fourth* and *Fifth Piano Concerto*, and the *Violin Concerto*). Schumann also does this in his *Piano Concerto*. Mendelssohn, in the *Violin Concerto in E Minor*, Op. 64, links together all three movements with no real stop. Liszt uses the one-movement idea very successfully in his piano concerti and in the *Piano Sonata in B Minor*.

Let us now examine the three-movement structure as a whole. The concerto was standardized early in the Baroque as a three-movement fast-slow-fast design, and each historical period since has left its stamp on it. The classical composer established (best seen in the concerti of Mozart) a special kind of sonata-form for the concerto (discussed in detail below) to be used in the first movement; there was a contrasting key for the second movement, which more often than not was either a song form or some kind of variations. The last movement started out as a rather simple rondo type, but soon became sonata-rondo. The romantics followed suit with enlargement, relaxation, insertion of a scherzo (rare, but again done by Brahms in an important work, the *B-Flat Piano Concerto*, and Vieuxtemps' *Violin Concerto in D Minor*), or even the semblance of a program (as in *Harold in Italy*, Berlioz's concerto-symphony for viola and orchestra, or Lalo's *Symphonie Espagnole*, with five movements (the scherzo was sometimes included, but as the middle section of the slow movement (cf. Franck's *Symphony* and Tchaikovsky's *First Piano Concerto*). The concerto idea also fuses with the symphonic tone poem idea in concert pieces such as *Totentanz* (also employing variations) for piano and orchestra by Liszt, Chausson's *Poème* for violin and orchestra, Franck's *Symphonic Variations* for piano and orchestra, and Berlioz's *Reverie et Caprice* for violin and orchestra.

The chamber music of the Romantic Period followed a similar plan, but was strangely immune to programmatic viruses. Perhaps the use of chamber music as *Hausmusik,* as a romantic *musica reservata* (reserved for musicians alone) was the reason for this—how can a non-musician play chamber music? Therefore, no program was necessary for the public! The public concert of chamber music did become quite commonplace in the late nineteenth century, but chamber music has always appealed to a very special public, a public not usually attracted to story-telling music. Two outstanding chamber works were programmatic in the most romantic way, however, and that fact has not prevented these works from the repeated hearings they deserve. These are the poignantly autobiographical *Aus meinem Leben* string quartet by Smetana and the one-movement string sextet by Schoenberg, *Verklärte Nacht.*

The keyboard sonata (both piano and organ) reflects similar principles. The three-movement sonata seems to be the most common, with a movement plan similar to the concerto. The organ also has a wealth of literature in organ symphonies, which begin to be written in some profusion in the late nineteenth century. The literature for the organ reflects a profound influence of Bach—even in France, where Albert Schweitzer's influence on Charles Widor was almost as important in Bach's behalf as Mendelssohn's "rediscovery" was earlier. The organ literature was enriched by many preludes, fugues, passacaglias, variations, sonatas, concerti and even some programmatic suites. (See the chapter on keyboard music for greater detail.) The piano sonata becomes quite symphonic and very long, again the great influence of the late Beethoven. The large movements in many composers, however, are not as organic in musical architecture as are Beethoven's. Instead, they are character pieces in the same tempo alignment as a three-movement concerto. A Chopin sonata, for example, although satisfying as form, still presents a first movement which is *like* a Ballade (Chopin-style) or a Scherzo (also Chopin-style); the second movement is like a Nocturne, and the finale is like an extended etude. The variation assumes considerable importance. In the best examples by the greatest composers they are not just superficial elaborations of the latest opera hit, but are a vital re-working of the theme and its harmonies; many are not true variations in the classical sense, but are what are called "character" variations, or even developments rather than variations. Other short pieces for the piano show a bewildering variety of form and "unform"; many are like the pastiche overture, a potpourri. Most, however, are some kind of a compound ternary, or are loosely held together by a program which may or may not be inherent in the title.

The musical theater, opera, ballet and drama present a unique array of forms for the orchestra, the most important of which is the overture. The overture in the classical opera had settled down to a rather strict sonata-form not too unlike the first movement of a symphony, an important difference being that the exposition was usually not repeated in the overture. There was a carry-over from the French overture, in that opera overtures often began with stately chords and dotted rhythms, or at least a slow introduction; a fugato would often follow at the allegro (Mozart's *Magic Flute* Overture is a good example). These are different from the old French overture, in that they are very often well-developed sonata-allegro movements which may or may not have any thematic connection with tunes to be heard later in the opera. The idea of pre-hearing the hit tunes of the show in the opera overture led to what, in my opinion, is a real nadir in the history of music: the potpourri overture in particular and the potpourri idea in general. A parade of tunes is only a small part of the true appreciation of great music; it is not the tune, but what happens to the tune, that is of paramount importance in the best music of the great composers. It is only fair to state that these operas with potpourri overtures usually got the kind of overtures they deserved. A notable exception is the work of Verdi, especially such a masterpiece as the overture to *La Forza del Destino*, which somehow comes off as a great piece of instrumental music *in spite of its form*. We would rather have this than dullness in correct form; but when both are bad what can save it?

The concert overture is an important short form for the orchestra growing from specially commissioned music for a drama production, often outliving the play for which originally written. Composers soon conceived the idea of a concert overture without any play; these were very often in correct sonata-form, but in every case had a story to tell or suggest. It is obvious that the symphonic poem idea should grow from this.[5]

Other stage works, including operas, had a more or less free prelude which was to prepare the listener psychologically for the story. Wagner was outstanding in this regard, as were Verdi and Puccini. Many didn't really "end" but went right into the opera.

The forms used within the operas themselves show a great variety. The old standby pattern of recitative-aria, recitative-ensemble, etc., or the "old-numbers" opera, had to go. Even Mozart had used this idea with comic effect, and usually got down to the real business of the act in the "finale," which is often more than half of the entire act. In one way the arias became more like recitatives and the recitatives more like arias. Much of the excessive vocalism which had stood in the way of real dramatic development in many operas was now done away with, and was replaced by a different kind of vocal virtuosity—the singer had to do what was printed in order to stay with the orchestra, which by now had become in concept almost a Greek chorus, continually commenting on the action (almost the subconscious mind of the character). Different composers attacked this problem in different ways. Suffice it to say here that new formal concepts had to be introduced which were inexorably tied in with the composer's compositional technique (Wagner's *Leitmotiv*, for example). Some simple song types still prevailed, however, as did certain elements of the old *da capo* aria. Arias became character pieces, an approach we see in almost every form we discuss. The operatic ensembles also display this great variety (such as the Quintet in *Carmen*, the Quintet in *Die Meistersinger* and, one of the greatest, the fugal final ensemble of *Falstaff*). Opera choruses also assume a real character-piece style, since the chorus begins to assume a real dramatic function in the opera—especially the great choruses representing various aspects of life (such as in *Boris Godunov*, Mussorgsky's great masterpiece). Here, as elsewhere in romantic opera, we are faced with a situation similar to the art song, which is through-composed; only here the entire act is through-composed, and the librettist really has something to do with the over-all form of the act. (The student should investigate Alban Berg's significant solutions to operatic forms in the twentieth century.)[6] It is also significant that some of the best libretti were written by Boito (for Verdi's *Otello* and *Falstaff*), himself a good composer.

In the foregoing paragraphs we have seen how composers used various forms on a large scale. Let us now investigate nineteenth-century developments within these forms.

The Non-concerto Sonata-allegro Form (Single-movement sonata form)

The greatest misnomer in music is the term "sonata-allegro," since it is found in works other than sonatas and in tempi other than allegro.

The nineteenth century inherited the form in a highly developed state from the late eighteenth, sometimes called the "age of the sonata." Let us now review this form and trace the romantic development of it step by step:

First, some general comments:

1. There is a tendency for much greater length in the late nineteenth century; some movements are much longer than complete symphonies

of the Classical Period. The watchword of freedom evidences itself in many aspects. Sonata-form becomes very flexible, even in its strictest application.

2. Over-all form is still a gigantic ABA', where A is called *exposition*, B, *development* (not exactly new material, but still enough difference to seem like a digression), and A', *recapitulation*.
3. The exposition.
   a. May or may not be preceded by a slow introduction.
      1) Slow introduction loses the influence of the French overture (such as stately dotted rhythms).
      2) Slow introduction becomes in some cases a highly developed form in and of itself (Beethoven's *Seventh Symphony* and Franck's *D Minor Symphony*).
      3) Slow introduction may be motivically independent of the rest of the movement or motivically tied in with it (Tchaikovsky's *Pathétique Symphony*).
      4) Slow introduction may be in a related key, such as tonic minor or dominant (Beethoven's *Kreutzer Sonata*, Op. 47; found even in Haydn).
      5) Slow introduction may be implied by note values rather than tempo (Schubert's *Unfinished Symphony*).
      6) Material and tempi of the slow introduction may or may not be repeated as part of the recapitulation (Haydn's *Symphony No. 103*).
      7) These works have outstanding introductions, and should be studied in greater detail by the student:
         Beethoven's *Symphonies 1, 2, 4* and *7*; *Egmont* Overture; *Consecration of the House* Overture.
         Brahms's *Symphony No. One*, both first and last movements; *Tragic Overture*.
         Schubert's *Unfinished Symphony* (not set off by tempo marking); see also Gluck's *Iphigenia in Aulis* Overture and Schubert's *Great C Major Symphony*.
         Franck's *D Minor Symphony*.
         Tchaikovsky's *Symphonies 4, 5* and *6*; *Romeo and Juliet Overture*.
         Also note the first-movement beginnings of all symphonies of Mahler and Bruckner.
         Beethoven's *Pathétique Sonata*, Op. 13; *Farewell Sonata*, Op. 81a, and many others.
   b. Contents of the exposition proper.
      1) Either begins after the slow introduction or at the very beginning [such as Beethoven's *Eroica Symphony* (No. 3)].
      2) Exposition exposes the themes which will be developed later—exactly as the exposition of a novel or play (tells you who the characters are and something about them).

a) First theme section: almost always in tonic key, can contain a family of themes, can be a complete closed form in and of itself. In classical music this theme was frequently the "Mannheim rocket," outlining with telling rhythm the tonic triad.[7] In romantic music one can find many different kinds of first themes of almost any kind of expression. Most, however, are considered "masculine."

b) *Bridge* section, often called *transition,* has two primary functions: prepares the listener for the contrasting second theme group, modulates to the key region of the second theme group. Bridge can be very short or very long, can introduce new material which may or may not be used later. In some romantic works bridge is a complete closed form in and of itself. It is often scored very full and sometimes is the first tutti passage of the work (if an orchestral piece).

c) Second theme group, or *subsidiary* theme(s), or *side* theme(s) (*Seitenthema*).[8] In classical form it was almost always in the key of the dominant if tonic was major, or in relative major if tonic was minor. In many classical works the theme was merely a re-statement of the principal theme in the new key. As time went on composers became more and more conscious of contrast; in the Romantic Period we find many examples of change in tempo and meter, as well as contrast in key and expression. This is an expansion, since in the classical form these things were accomplished within the framework of the original signatures and tempo markings. The nineteenth-century composer also used more remote keys and more themes which contrasted among themselves; again, they were often highly organized into a complete closed form. In orchestral works this section was highly contrasted through softer orchestral textures—not just dynamically softer, but often a more effeminate, velvety kind of timbre.

d) Closing theme, often called *codetta*: can be quite extended, entirely contrasted to the other themes in the exposition (Mozart's *Jupiter Symphony*, K. 551); or can be very short, just enough to ensure a convincing cadence; in the key of the dominant, but the romantics were more free about key relationships in general. The closing theme is sometimes reminiscent of the principal theme, and often is accompanied by a pedal point which gives the feeling of a close. Since the exposition is still repeated in many works in the Romantic Period, the closing theme must lead well either to the repeat or to the development section. This is often accomplished through first and second endings. The repeat should always be taken in order to balance the movement properly.

3) Development sections become more and more important, taking the lead from Beethoven. The themes are literally taken apart and put back together in different ways. Counterpoint, both formal and informal, is applied. Various tricks of thematic manipulation are used: inversion, augmentation, diminution, retrograde, retrograde inversion and free combinations of any or all of these. The development is often exciting music, providing one of the great climaxes of the work. This excitement is brought about through rapid harmonic rhythms, and through rapid and frequent changes of key, causing much chromaticism (and vice versa). The student should keep in mind that development is quite different from formal variation, in that a development does not necessarily have fixed elements other than some relationship to the themes in the exposition; there are many cases where the composer introduces entirely new material in the development. In the final analysis a composer is free to add a new theme in any form—especially in the Romantic Period, when inspiration was such an important factor in artistic creation. Developments, then, *did* appeal to the romantic, even though one can often see strange manipulations in them. The composer has free reign and is limited only by his imagination, taste and the size of his composition in general.

4) The recapitulation is often called either *reprise* or *restatement*. As with other aspects, the recapitulation in the nineteenth century shows freedom and is not nearly as literal as in the eighteenth. The composer changes the orchestration or the harmony, or may even present the theme in the "wrong" key (see Schubert's *Fifth Symphony in B-Flat*).[9] Most romantic composers, though, did feel that the concept of key for the recapitulation is to show the triumphant restatement of the tonic key of the movement, so that both theme groups return in the tonic key, thus causing the bridge section to lose one of its functions: the need to modulate. Some composers saw this as a chance to show further development, either of the material from the first bridge or some previously overlooked aspect of the principal themes. Not all movements of the period were handled with such imagination, however. Many works have rather tiresome recapitulations—as if the composer had sighed, shrugged his shoulders, then did his duty and put it in. In some of the poematic symphonies this seems especially unnecessary: the *Faust Symphony* of Liszt, for example, has an over-long recapitulation, almost as if one had decided to re-read the beginning of the play! The student will be well rewarded if he makes a comparative study of recapitulations in major works of the period; look at symphonies, sonatas, string quartets, trios, overtures and what-have-you.

> *Reverse-order recapitulation* (second theme before first) gives one the effect of a "Bogen" (arch) and can be used effectively—ABCBA—but this is quite a rare device.

5) The coda assumes greater importance and does not always provide merely a brilliant ending to the movement. Since Beethoven sometimes wrote extended codas, a long coda which is actually a second development section is called a "Beethoven coda," although one can also find this type in works by Haydn, Mozart and others. Codas can also function as connective tissue, linking movements which are continuous.

Sonata-form in the Concerto

There are important differences in the form of the first movement of a classical concerto compared to that of a symphony or other uses of sonata-form. The medium of performance, of course, has something to do with it. It is natural to expect that part of the "competition" would be the exposing of the themes orchestrally and soloistically, and most classical concerti do exactly this: a double exposition written out for the orchestra first, and then for the soloist, accompanied by the orchestra with much embroidery (as befits concertato style). The opening *tutti*, as the orchestral introduction is called, does expose the principal theme(s) in much the same way as in a symphony; the difference is in the handling of the second theme group. In a concerto the orchestral exposition tends to be in the tonic key throughout, and the second theme is either abbreviated or not stated at all.

The Romantic Period, of course, did things differently. There are concerti where the first exposition is classical; others where the soloist comes in immediately (Mendelssohn's *Violin Concerto*, for example); others with a bobtailed first statement (Brahms's *Double Concerto*); still others which begin with a theme of apparently no structural importance (Tchaikovsky's *Violin Concerto* begins with a lovely theme which is never heard again), and still others which even begin with a cadenza or a cadenza-like, non-strict section (Beethoven's *Emperor Concerto* (No. 5 in E♭)). Liszt's *Concerto No. 1 in E♭* has a cadenza (actually marked *cadenza* in the fourth measure). Others still carry out an almost classical idea; in some, though, the soloist enters at the very beginning, only to drop out and rest for a lengthy tutti (as in Mozart's K. 271 and in Beethoven's *Fourth Concerto*).

In the classical concerto the cadenza came very near the end of the movement; it was usually improvised by the soloist following a fermata on a tonic six-four chord (often the final cadence, or the cadence just before the coda), with the formula I_6 V I appearing as I_6 cadenza, V— hence the name "cadenza," which means "cadence." Arias in opera were treated in a similar fashion. Some of these devices were very successful musically, while others were ludicrous and in very bad taste. It is said that at the first performance of the Beethoven *Violin Concerto* the soloist, at the point for the cadenza, played a sonata of his own invention which, to be effective, had to be played with the violinist standing on his head! If such nonsense did not always happen physically, it often was as scandalous musically. Only the Mozarts and Beethovens could improvise meaningfully on the spot. Near the end of Mozart's life he was occupied in writing cadenzas for some of his piano concerti, showing that even his faith in the art of improvisation had been shaken. Earlier he had provided complete cadenzas for his *Symphonie Concertante* for solo violin and viola, K. 364; obviously one could not expect *two* soloists to improvise simultaneously (although today such aleatory procedure would be admired). Beethoven also became disenchanted and wrote cadenzas to his and Mozart's concerti. Nevertheless, the cadenza somehow remained, either written out by the composer or else by some artist who was not satisfied with the technique of the concerto. Some absolutely ridiculous ones were written for classical concerti which were probably no better than those which had been improvised in the old days. Some of the greatest composers of the twentieth century have provided beautiful cadenzas to their concerti (such as the violin concerti of Schoenberg, Bartók and Berg); so the cadenza still does have a function, and in the hands of a real artist it can be sheer magic—a wonderful contrast to the rest of the work. There are several famous "cadenzas" for the concertmaster in standard orchestral works: Rimsky-Korsakov's *Scheherazade* and *Capriccio espagnol*, R. Strauss's *Till Eulenspiegel* and *Ein Heldenleben* (actually a veritable concerto!) and many others.

The romantic composer, in his quest for freedom, began to place the cadenza almost anywhere, and freely introduced it so that a *senza misura* passage simply emerged from the tonal mass at any time or place; no longer was there any need for the introduction or preparation through a tonic $^6_4$. Much music, in almost every period, has had two kinds of pacing: a steady tempo or a free tempo. In the Baroque one often found such conditions existing in the same work (such as J. S. Bach's *Toccata and Fugue in D Minor*). A unique aspect of music in our time is the possibility for the two conditions to co-exist. In a way, Elgar, in his beautiful *Violin Concerto in B Minor*, Op. 61, anticipates this in a cadenza in the finale which is accompanied by the orchestra in various ways; especially outstanding is the use of *pizzicato tremolando* in the strings, indeed a stunning and novel effect.

The accompanied cadenza is very much like the *recitativo accompagnato* in opera and oratorio; singers would often embellish the vocal lines, and in the pre-classical and classical concerto soloists often would play a highly embellished part, especially in slow movements. Here is another paradox of romanticism: music was played more and more as printed; composers left much less up to chance and wrote out parts almost exactly as they wanted them done, again giving less freedom to the performer, but at the same time, more freedom for the performer. The romantic composer began to have a "posterity complex," and realized that he was writing for future generations and therefore was more specific in his directions. Classical and Baroque composers often had in mind only one performance or a series of performances; therefore they would write in a context for the people they knew would play or sing their music—tailor made, as it were—and the composers knew that to do otherwise would probably be unsuccessful. This new philosophy on the part of composers (considering the new audience in the future) actually fit in very well with romantic artists' notions of a faraway Utopia, and they often wrote for Utopian musicians. One need only trace the background of Tchaikovsky's best-known concerti and Brahms's *Violin Concerto*, works which were pronounced unplayable by performers who had expected pieces in the old tradition.

These men, by the way, represent a new breed of concerto composers: those who wrote fine concerti but who were not virtuosi of the solo instruments involved. While this can lead to impossible, or at least inconvenient passages, it also can lead an imaginative composer into areas which a virtuoso might never explore: to works not "composed at the instrument," resulting in new techniques for the instrument in order to express new musical ideas. The great advances in technique on all instruments and in the voice have indeed been the combination of the virtuoso's contribution (Liszt, Chopin, Paganini, *et al.*) and that of the composer.

The student should now understand that the concerto concept is one which involves other problems interwoven with the eternal problem of form and the additional problem of the cadenza. He should study works such as the Liszt *Hungarian Fantasy* to see and hear extreme examples of the accompanied cadenza—even though in this piece a combination of folk forms and art music forms is involved. The *Lassan* portions are, by and large, lengthy cadenza-like movements, and the *Friska* tends to be in a specific tempo, since it is a dance (a czardas).

The Rondo

The rondo as a musical principle is very old and became highly developed in the Classical Period. Although loosely classifying a rondo as in ABA form, it consists basically of a simple theme which is restated; between these statements of the theme there are digressions or episodes of varying length and importance. The style of the music tends to be light and brilliant, and hence the rondo most often occurs as a finale. (Some finales are called "rondo" that are not even in rondo form!)

Of greater prominence (since usage in great works is the chief criterion) is the occurrence of a rondo-type, ABACAB'A, which combines features of rondo and sonata—especially if "B" is in the key of the dominant, "B'" in the key of the tonic and "C" is something like a development section (even though it doesn't have to be). The frequent use of the rondo by Beethoven for concerti and for the finale of the *Eighth Symphony*, and its uses by Brahms and others throughout the century point to its importance. The rondo idea often appears in twentieth-century works (as in Schoenberg's *Quintet*, Op. 26).

Rondo-forms are quite often used in interior movements by nineteenth-century composers (as in Beethoven's *Pathétique Sonata*, Op. 13 (slow movement, as well as finale), and in Schubert's great *C Major Symphony* (slow movement), and in many others). There are differences of opinion about the form: 1) a light character is retained, but vital freedoms and additions take place, and 2) with the weight climax of the work moving farther and farther to the end of the piece, it is not surprising to find rondo used in earlier movements where a lighter quality is desired by the composer, *or* it might be used in a serious slow vein (the second movement of Schubert's *Unfinished Symphony* is like a rondo). Again we are faced with the great contradictions of the nineteenth century! The composer *does* show, however, that content transcends form and that rondo can be either light, albeit a serious lightness (Beethoven's *Violin Concerto*, last movement), or slow, lyrical and serious (as in the slow movements cited above).

In classical rondo the theme came back, usually at least three times and in the same key, harking back to earlier ritornello forms and the common poetic form of verse and refrain. The romantic composer, in his quest for originality within the framework of a proven idea, found unique ways to bring back the rondo theme: 1) in a different key (Schubert's *Sonata in A Minor*, Op. 164, second movement; also Beethoven's *Violin Concerto* finale, where there is a delightful return of enough of the theme for it to be recognized, in D-flat major, the original tonality being D major); 2) in a different tone-color (Mendelssohn's *Violin Concerto*, finale); 3) in a different register—related to number 2, since a change of register results in a change of tone-color, sometimes even more than change of key (Beethoven's *Pathétique Sonata*); 4) in a different period structure—different phrase structure or different meter (simple to compound, etc.); 5) in a shortened version which merely suggests the theme; 6) in a longer version with various extensions; 7) stating only the characteristic rhythm with a different theme (the possibility of a *rhythm* theme); 8) with each appearance of the theme actually a variation (Beethoven's *String Quartet in A Minor*, Op. 132: third movement is a rondo with variations of the rondo and digression themes); 9) with the theme returned as part of a contrapuntal texture; 10) with free combinations of any or all of the above.

Many of these uses can be found in R. Strauss's *Till Eulenspiegel*, which is a far cry from rondo as found in the eighteenth century. Some even say they can't imagine *Till Eulenspiegel* even being close to a rondo—again the desire for a fixed, never-changing definition.

The setting up of the theme for restatement is of paramount importance in all good rondos. Haydn was outstanding as a musical humorist, and some of his most delicious musical levity is found in his approach to restatement.

The episodes in nineteenth-century rondos are often examples of very imaginative writing. They are sometimes little closed forms, entirely differing in character from anything else in the movement. Episodes are frequently subtle developments of elements of the rondo theme. There can also be great difference in length of these episodes; some can be amazingly long—one almost forgets what the rondo theme is by the time it is over! The exploration of remote tonalities in episodes is also a factor.

Rondos are also used for single-movement works which often explore the soloistic possibilities of an instrument. These are often of an "Introduction" and "Rondo" type, almost like the last part of a concerto (Saint-Saëns's *Introduction and Rondo Capriccioso* for violin and orchestra); or they can be piano solos (Mendelssohn's piano solo *Rondo Capriccioso*, Op. 14, which is actually an introduction and rondo). Rondo is a very handy form, in a way a set of interlocking ternary forms with a variable middle section: ABACADA . . . . . ANA (N represents the last digression—the same as the nth term in mathematics). Since many of the "free" forms in occasional pieces are large ternaries, it is not surprising to find rondo used as a logical expansion of this idea. Rondo is also used in the art song.

Variations

The art of varying musical material is one of the most vital in the entire history of music. It has been important to each generation of composers since the early fifteenth century. As is true with many forms or processes, the term "variation" is often missing in the titles of works which actually employ variation techniques. Almost every great masterpiece shows some aspect of musical variation; even something as simple as transposition is a variation. In the nineteenth century one can find a great profusion of variation techniques inside other forms and as movements in multi-movement works, in addition to the ever-popular single-movement variations which capitalized on the hit song from the latest opera success. Pianists and violinists were expected to perform these with great fire and sentiment. This is not to imply that these were *all* bad; some still have merit and say something to us today, while others are often used as technical study material for advanced students.

The student must realize that development and variation are related techniques but are not really the same by any means. The variation tends to keep the same periodic structure as the theme, while the development does not. (This does not preclude the possibility of some of the variations in the Romantic Period being actual developments, or of some areas of the development actually being variations.) In a "true" variation there are both fixed elements and variable elements, so that the listener can relate back to the original theme. The composer also will present some variations which are less complicated and sound more like a changed repetition of the theme, so that the variations themselves can add up to other forms (the Franck *Symphonic Variations* for piano and orchestra is a good example, and will be discussed later). The composer in periods prior to the nineteenth century often used figuration technique, which tends to build up faster and faster note values (Handel's so-called *Harmonious Blacksmith* is a good example). The nineteenth-century master built also, but in a more subtle way, using both figuration and harmony, amounting to variations of variations in some instances. See Brahms's *Variations on a Theme by Paganini* for very obvious use of this device, noting how some aspect of one variation is carried over into the next.

Beethoven, Mendelssohn and Brahms are outstanding examples of composers who exploit expressive aspects of variation technique—not the superficially brilliant approach for ladies who swoon in the salon in such works as the *Airs Variés* of Charles Dancla for violin and piano (good as they are for violin students), but universally meaningful master-pieces which have very great content. As Apel asserts:

With Beethoven the variation form reached its all-time peak. He replaced the more conventional methods, particularly that of ornamentation, by a wealth of individual treatments and ideas which evades all attempts at summary description. He also was the first to organize the mere succession of variations into contrasting groups, a procedure which is particularly patent in his "continuous" variations in C minor op. 32 (sometimes described as a chaconne). In his *Eroica* *Variations* op. 35 he prefaces the theme by a short group of 'negative variations,' so to speak, which are based on the bass motive only. His *Diabelli Variations* op. 120 (1823) are an incomparable treasure of ingenuity, while in the variations of his late quartets and pianoforte sonatas technical methods are sublimated into a new realm of transcendental vision, so that even the most conventional methods attain a new significance. Nowhere is this transformation more clearly patent than in the 'ornamenting' variations of the pianoforte sonatas opp. 106 and 111.

Hardly second to Beethoven is Franz Schubert in such great though little known works as his variations for four hands in B minor and in A-flat major, compositions which are quite superior to his more popular variations for two hands in B-flat major. Schumann's most remarkable contributions are the *Etudes Symphoniques* which open the field of free variations since some of them derive not more from the theme than a germinating motive. In his *Andante* and *Variations* for two pianos, on the other hand, he falls into his habit of exploiting *ad nauseam* a somewhat obtrusive figure or rhythm, as he so frequently does in his later works.

Franz Liszt made very frequent and, needless to say, effective use of a brilliant and highly virtuoso-like variation technique in many of his Rhapsodies and particularly, in his variations on the theme by Paganini (*Paganini Etudes*, no. 6) which was also used by Brahms as a theme for a series of extremely difficult and extremely interesting variations. The fame of Brahms as a master of this form rests, however, on his *Variations on a Theme by Handel* (op. 24) for pianoforte, and on his orchestral *Variations on a Theme by Haydn* op. 56 (also for two pianos).

. . . Shortly before 1900 two important examples of 'free variation' were written, Vincent d'Indy's *Istar Variations* (1896) and Richard Strauss's *Don Quixote* (1897). The former are 'variations in the reverse' in so far as the 'theme' (properly, two thematic motives) appears at the end, a procedure of 'disrobing' which is insinuated in the title, Istar being the Egyptian goddess of Sin.[10]

Since the romantic part of the nineteenth century was so interested in "freedom," it follows that the "free" variation is of great importance to us. These are, as one might predict, the very examples which live on today and are a part of the repertoire. The fixed element in this kind of variation is the motive, which makes each variation almost a development. The finale of Beethoven's *Eroica Symphony* (No. 3) is an early example, although one can find similar techniques in a work as early as J. S. Bach's *Goldberg Variations*, not so much in the variations of the bass line (after all, it is a gigantic chaconne), but in the even more fascinating and subtle outlines of the "Sarabande" theme which one can find in the non-bass parts of the work.

Richard Strauss's *Don Quixote* (1897) is a unique example of the free variation principle. Actually based on two themes, it combines many romantic features: character variations of the motive sort in order to tell Cervantes' wonderful story, *concertato* writing for the solo cello (the solo violin and viola also have much to do!), great freedoms in each musical dimension—the variation counterpart of what Strauss does with the rondo device in *Till Eulenspiegel*.

Of greater prominence in the nineteenth century is the appearance of the "double theme" variation (used quite frequently by Beethoven; also found in the famous *Variations in F Minor* for piano, by Haydn, and still important to us today). Specific examples will be examined in detail later, since this device occurs in many works of the utmost importance (Beethoven's *Symphonies 5* and *9*, for example).

This discussion applies mostly to the variation as a homophonic form. It has already been pointed out that the ground bass type of variation also appears from time to time but in rather specialized works, some of which are frank imitations of previous practice, colored by romantic touches of things such as harmony and orchestration. One must ponder from time to time: is an older composer anticipating later practice, or is the later composer showing that he knows music history—or are both factors in operation but not necessarily at the same time?

The Suite

There are inherited examples of the old Baroque dance suites which, however, are not always called "suites." There are also works called "suites" which have nothing in common with older uses of the term. These are of several types:

1) Extracts from ballets, incidental music or operas for concert use (many of these works live on chiefly in this form).

2) Multi-movement works which are unified in performance, with the composer calling the whole cycle a "suite"; today such a suite might be called "Pieces for Violin and Piano," for example.

3) Cycles of tone poems built around a common poetic idea, something like the song cycle. These are often difficult, if not impossible, to differentiate from poematic symphonies.

Examples of type 1 include the *Carmen Suite* and the *Nutcracker Suite*; most suites popular today are of this type. The composer has to change the music somewhat, so as to be effective without the stage. In some instances this amounts to a drastic rewrite, while in others certain emendations are necessary, since the stage had previously carried the action. This revision is not always done by the original composer.

Sometimes one can notice little difference in form and concept among the cycle of symphonic tone poems, the symphonic suite and the poematic symphony. The difference is apparently in the mind of the composer: if Tchaikovsky states that the *Manfred Symphony* is a symphony, then it *is* a symphony! If Franck declares that *Psyché* is a cycle of symphonic poems, or if someone else calls something or other a "symphonic suite," then we should too. Terminology is rigid only in the classroom—not always in the mind of the composer. The student need only study the works called "suite" in the Baroque and Classical Periods, and then note how many works of those periods are exactly the same which are called variously "overture," "concerto," "sonata," "serenade," "cassation," "ordres," "lezion," "partita" or "divertimento." This illustrates the variable use of terms, so it is important for the student to understand that one term *can* mean many things—he must know what terms mean and what they do not mean, and how meanings change. A composer has a reason for his title, and one can derive much insight from a composer's *changing* from one title to another.

We shall meet the term "suite" often in the nineteenth century—it was such a convenient catch-all! Among America's first internationally recognized works were MacDowell's *Indian Suites*.

The Fugue

Much has been said about fugue already in the section on counterpoint, but more should be said here, since fugue *per se* was a real problem for most composers in the nineteenth century. While it became less and less important as a strict "form" in real composition, it became more and more important in the training of the composer; a rather sterile, academic "school" fugue was taught, and fugues were written by the gross. The same thing is true even today but now almost everyone has to try, not just the composers. Although it cannot be denied that the writing of fugues is excellent training, what is deplorable is the notion that a fugue is in actual practice the so-called "school fugue." The resemblance is superficial, as are almost all textbook forms. One wonders where this school fugue came from and why we still persist in teaching it *as an end in itself.* Fugue is a great discovery, still vital today, but it too evolved—why should the evolution of the fugue stop at the death of J. S. Bach? We can only wait until more research, especially computer research, on *all* Bach fugues has been done, but will that really tell us anything? As has been said before: anything a *great artist* does only *once* is important. If he does it more than once, or as part of his habitual style, it is of course more important; but the divergence from a "norm" in art (if well done) is of more interest than the norm.

It is a real tribute to J. S. Bach that we tend to define and/or describe chaconne in terms of *his* great *Chaconne* from the *D-Minor Partita*, the passacaglia in terms of his masterpiece in C minor, and the most common model for fugue in terms of his *Well-Tempered Clavier* or the first few fugues of the *Art of Fugue*. There are many pre-Bach works of outstanding merit which have the opposite titling (chaconne and passacaglia being interchangeable pre-Bach), and there are many fugues by Bach and others which do not fit neat models. Obviously, the student should know well what a model "fugue form" is, in order to appreciate the flexibility of fugue when he encounters it in Bach and in other composers.

Perhaps we should not call fugue a "form," since in formal design one fugue differs greatly from another, even in the music of the same composer (Bach himself is a good example). Many writers prefer to use the terminology "fugue process" or "fugue procedure," but this also depends by what one means by the term "form." Are not the great sonata-forms as different one from the other as are the fugues? (Maybe all great musical forms should be called "processes"!) Stating that a fugue has an exposition, a development and a final recapitulation is to give the fugue a ternary concept which in reality it does not have (except from a tonal standpoint). The exposition is but a very short part near the beginning, and the recapitulation is a very short part near the end, while the development is a very large part in the middle. A more meaningful concept is that most fugues are similar to rondo (but with imitation), in that there are areas where the subject is present and areas where it is completely absent; the fugue idea *as a form* consists of the way in which the composer alternates. It is of utmost importance that the student realize that in the fugue the episodes are shorter than in the rondo, that they have a different periodic structure and may even be non-existent.

Probably no great composer ever "followed" any strict "form" to the letter. Part of the essential quality of composition is formal mastery, but it should never be looked upon as a mold into which a composer pours his jello. A great composer always makes *his own mold*, and no kind of musical procedure shows this better than the use of the fugue principle.

There is misunderstanding about the terms "fughetta" and "fugato." Most authors now agree, for purposes of clarity but not rigidity, that properly "fughetta" is the diminutive of "fugue," and means a more or less complete fugue but one smaller in concept, design and length—something like "sonatina" compared to "sonata." "Fugato" refers to a fugal-like texture which often consists of an exposition which is itself a development of thematic material important elsewhere in the work (as in the finale of Tchaikovsky's *Manfred Symphony* and Liszt's *Faust Symphony*).

The last point of the preceding paragraph—a fugue or fugato subject occurring as a development or variation of thematic material which is important in other ways in the work—is one of the most vital uses of the fugue device in the nineteenth century. True, this device is found earlier, but it becomes almost expected in the romantic century, either as an oath of fealty to the great Bach, or with programmatic connotation.

Apparently one criterion for calling a composer a "classic romantic" is the way he uses counterpoint in general and fugue specifically. Beethoven (once called a "romantic" by almost all authors) is one, as are Mendelssohn and Brahms. A composer does not have to use the term "fugue" as part of the title, nor does a movement need to contain a fugue throughout its course in order for fugue to be a key factor in music of the nineteenth century. Although a composer might include one canon, or part of one, just to show that he could handle it (it would have made his conservatory professors happy!), the important fact is that the important composers did use some fugue process at important points in their work, and even wrote complete fugues! One must not assume that a "school" fugue is necessarily sterile or uninteresting; one need only to play through the fugues in the appendix of the Gedalge *Treatise on Fugue* or some in the Cherubini *A Treatise on Counterpoint and Fugue* (to name just two famous texts). Many of these are quite imaginative, and some are by students who became famous (such as Florent Schmitt and Georges Enesco). In France there were highly-coveted prizes for fugue.

We find the most conservative fugues, as a rule, in large vocal works, while the most progressive ones occur in programmatic orchestral works. Some authors refuse to recognize a free fugue as a real fugue at all, since they attach great importance to key relationship, a factor which in actual practice becomes less and less important. The "freedoms" may be summarized as follows:

1. Free key relationship in all respects: key of answer, distant key relationships, no real key at all. Anton Reicha's experiments with answers at an odd interval are good examples.

2. Longer, more homophonic episodes; hybrid forms.

3. Modulating subjects which go far beyond those allowed in the school fugue (such as the use of remote keys within the subject itself).

4. Subjects which are extremely chromatic (J. S. Bach's *Fugue 24* from Vol. I of *The Well-Tempered Clavier* actually presents all twelve tones; also chromatic is his so-called "Wedge" fugue for organ, so this is not a new usage except for the fact that a greater tonal freedom is exercised in the nineteenth century).

5. Fugues with a program.

6. *Covered entries*: that is, fugue subject is not announced alone but is "covered" by the other voices and seems to "emerge" from the tonal mass. This often happens inside large works and can be canonic, not necessarily fugal. The main difference between canon and fugue is in the strictness of the imitation. To be a real canon *by definition* it must be *strict* according to the terms of the canon, while in a fugue only the subject needs to be imitated. Of course, the countersubject in a fugue, if present, is also imitated; that is what distinguishes a true countersubject from a "contrapuntal associate" in the minds of most theory teachers, although the opposite terminology is also taught. Canon *per se* is also used within the fugue as a developmental device.

The age-old devices of stretto (a subject answered at a closer time interval), pedal points, *et al.* are still to be found in the concert fugue, but are used with greater freedom, especially the pedal point found on a scale degree other than the tonic or dominant and which can be inverted (appear in any voice). Pedal points also become multiple, often becoming a complete chord which is sustained as the lowest element of the texture, the middle texture or the highest texture.

Canon, when used, seems to have been used with less mechanical "riddle" aspects such as one can find in J. S. Bach (*A Musical Offering*) and many others of his time and earlier. There does appear, however, what might be called a "spiritual" canon, in which the composer imitates only the general contour of a theme. This is dangerous ground, as is any purely subjective matter, since one can disprove its existence as well as prove it. The canon could have occurred subconsciously or deliberately—who knows? This "spiritual," or implied, or contour canon (no rigorous name has ever been given to the device) might well be part and parcel of the principle of "counterpoint of continuity" discussed in the chapter on counterpoint.

In the nineteenth century one also finds freedom in the number of voices employed in the fugue. It may begin as four voices and end up with twice that many or even more; multi-subject fugues are also found.

It is also possible for the subject to be a rhythm rather than a theme, which implies pitches and durations which are mutually exclusive. This device is used more in the twentieth century, however.

The school fugue required that the voice ranges of vocal parts be observed; crossing of parts was frowned upon, except under very special conditions. The nineteenth-century use of the fugue process applies this rule only in the composition of vocal fugues; as a result one can find many subjects which are very angular and very wide in pitch range, as benefits the instruments. Here is the Liszt "Mephisto" fugato from the *Faust Symphony*:

Figure 9-3

The episodes were either greatly enlarged (some in Beethoven are even complete closed forms), or the fugue could be intensified by one subject following another yet in non-stretto fashion (the episode equals zero). The episode could even be repeated, unheard of in pre-nineteenth–century usages. In other words, throughout the period the fugue developed along lines comparable to the rondo.

The student should remember, however, that fugue "form" was used only a small percentage of the time in the nineteenth century (except for the school fugue), but that the fugue *process* was used extensively in some of the most important masterworks of the century; therefore, fugue is important.

Graves states this matter very well:

The evolution of melody, harmony, and tonality has produced changes in fugue analogous to those in other types of music. Whether or not the tonal-structural thematic features found formerly can be assumed to exist in today's fugue depends upon interpretations under varied and sometimes highly complex conditions.[11]

And further:

As part of the main stream of twentieth century developments, fugue at present stands much closer to the stylistic spirit of the times than it did in the Romantic period. Its many new and challenging technical features are integral parts of contemporary musical style. In melody, harmony, and rhythm it speaks the musical language of our time.[12]

Graves sums up the whole question of theoretical practice so well:

The culmination of the Romantic period saw the final extensions of traditional or tertian harmonic practice. Chord relation had reached a point of ultra refinement through tenuous chromatic connection, epitomized by the late Wagner. Meanwhile the chordal structures themselves had become more complex, chiefly through chromatic alteration and extensions of the triadic principle to embrace chords of the ninth, eleventh, and so on. Some, notably Scriabin, were beginning to experiment with new principles of chord construction.

The developments subsequent to the end of Romanticism seem less concerned with harmonic connection than with new harmonic structures. New progression, if indeed possible at all, was sought in the framework of free tonal flux and with new chord structures. The dissonant contrapuntists and the later atonalists aimed at repudiating harmonic connection, at least in the sense of tonality or other predetermined pattern. These developments can be justified as a reaction to a style in which all musical events had their *raison d'être* in rich tertian harmonic pallette. In simplest terms, sovereignty of harmony was exchanged by this group for freedom of line.[13]

Good form, it seems to me, is the best possible orientation of parts. It follows, then, that we can have a qualitative proof that the whole is greater than the sum of its parts (in spite of Euclid!). We can have the parts of an automobile in a pile or the assembled car—the best form is the best assemblage of the parts. The application to art is obvious.

Notes

1. Sir Donald Francis Tovey, *Musical Articles from the Encyclopedia Britannica* (London: Oxford University Press, 1944), p. 19.

2. Hector Berlioz, *Beethoven's Nine Symphonies*, trans. Edwin Evans (London: William Reeves, 1958), pp. 1-2.

3. See Sir Donald Francis Tovey, *The Mainstream of Music* (New York: Oxford University Press, 1949), p. 109.

4. Robert Tyndall, *Musical Form* (Boston: Allyn and Bacon, Inc., 1964), pp. 95-99.

5. See William Smolden, *A History of Music* (London: Herbert Jenkins, Ltd., 1965), pp. 282-283.

6. *Wozzeck* and *Lulu*, Berg's two operatic masterpieces, have been widely discussed in the literature, especially Berg's unique use of old forms. See, for example, Donald Grout, *A Short History of Opera* (New York: Columbia University Press, 1947), pp. 532-535.

7. So-called because the device was widely used by the Mannheim school of composers in the eighteenth century.

8. The Germans sometimes call this "Gesangperiode," or "singing period."

9. Schubert's "wrong key" was almost always that of the subdominant and was perhaps an attempt to give subdominant key balance.

10. Willi Apel, *The Harvard Dictionary of Music* (Cambridge: Harvard University Press, 1947), p. 786.

11. William L. Graves, Jr., *Twentieth Century Fugue* (Washington, D.C.: Catholic University Press, 1962), p. 64.

12. *Ibid.*, p. 73.

13. *Ibid.*, p. 29.

CHAPTER X

ORCHESTRATION, CONDUCTING AND CONDUCTORS

INTIMATELY AND INSEPARABLY CONNECTED with the history of orchestration are: progress in the art and technique of musical composition; improvements in the construction of musical instruments, both of which are again associated with the growth of instrumental technique.[1]

Adam Carse

The art of orchestration is one of the latest to develop, and is one of the greatest technical contributions of the nineteenth century. Adam Carse has written important books on the history of orchestral development, and there are many good textbooks on the art and craft of orchestration.[2]

Great orchestration combines creatively the art of composition, the science of acoustics and the craft of writing parts which are idiomatic for the instruments (or at least playable, either now or in the future). It is a grave mistake for the student to assume that a composer writes a piece of music and then "arranges" it for the orchestra. We have been led to believe this, since there are so many references in letters and the like that a composer has finished his opera in every detail but the orchestration. The great composer already knows what the orchestration

241

will be, and he merely means that he has yet to make a "fair copy" of the full score.

The musical theater does have a history of arranging a short or vocal score for some sort of instrumental ensemble; one can find a fantastic differential in the quality and importance of orchestral writing—some of the very best and some of the worst. The opera well conceived in every detail dates from the very early part of the seventeenth century (the time of Monteverdi), and one can trace a steady development in opera and in orchestration from then until the present time. There seems to be a bifurcation of every kind of music: that in which quality is high in every detail, and that which is almost mass-produced in order to cash in on current taste. In order for any art to live it must have the finest of material put together in the very best way. One needs only to observe which operas, for example, seem to endure on their own merits; the rest languish either until a great singer comes along (who needs a certain work as a vehicle) or until their particular style becomes fashionable again (as with the Meyerbeer operas). Mozart's operas, of course, are among the so-called "perennial favorites." Mozart established many orchestral concepts which are still vital today. (Compare the vocal score of a Mozart opera with the full score to see and hear the difference!) There are many cases where only the full score gives one any conception of the over-all sound; the polymetric ballroom scene in *Don Giovanni* is an outstanding practical example.

In Mozart the art of combining instruments is a vital part of the score. Much of this Mozart undoubtedly learned from Haydn, but Haydn is another case of a great teacher learning from a great pupil. One often forgets that Mozart died in 1791 and Haydn lived until 1809, producing some of his best works after Mozart's death. Mozart was also greatly influenced by the Mannheim school and by the best composers elsewhere in Europe. The influences of J. C. Bach and C. P. E. Bach were also important, although to a lesser extent, for Mozart and the other composers of the early nineteenth century.

A thorough understanding of the state of affairs orchestrally in the early nineteenth century is impossible without looking back to the "Classical" Period which, after all, was the foundation of the Romantic Period as well as a source of violent reactions. Therefore, it is important to digress slightly, since the orchestral situation changed so rapidly in the decades from the late Baroque (ca. 1750) to the age of Beethoven. Haydn and Mozart are among the vanguard in these changes; since, as stated above, we are still using many concepts dating from their time, we should point out the specific details which were of such vital importance to be termed "classical."

Figure 10-1

Perhaps of prime importance is the ultimate downfall of figured bass as a procedure anywhere but in recitatives. Inherent in the figured bass is an unsettled condition regarding the middle voices—except, of course, a controlled texture such as a fugue. The Baroque (1600-1750) is perhaps best unified (if any such long span of time can be called unified at all) by the use of figured bass (keep in mind that "basso continuo," or simply "continuo," are terms also used to describe exactly the same thing). The Baroque is often called the "Figured Bass Period." While there is no doubt that the figured bass was one of the glories of the Baroque in the hands of the greatest masters, it was also something of a curse, since it was based, by and large, on mechanical principles which anyone could learn and apply and make sound great. It brought into music "automatic" progressions, as it were—progressions still to be heard in cheap music today, but which were exciting and truly original at the beginning of the period. Many works of this period survive today because of the great strength of a written-out soprano and/or alto voice, a good bass and figures which indicate good, imaginative progressions. Perhaps one of the first indicated aleatory (chance) elements can be found here, since middle voices were realized in entirely different ways depending upon who performed them. A Bach or a Handel would do a better job than the lesser musician (in both talent and training), who would do well only if he had the right chords and good voice-leading.

The old system, a formula-ridden practice of the lesser composers, makes possible the composition of a huge number of works since, after all, one of the most difficult aspects—chord progression—is all but done for you. This practice naturally results in formula types of orchestration. We tend to judge the merit of any age by the performance of the greatest; but in the late Baroque, as in each age, there are hundreds of lessers. When the age is being lived the music performed is not necessarily the best, although in the Baroque and Classical Periods contemporary music was performed most of the time and a great demand existed for music for all occasions. (One wonders how well this music was actually heard or performed!)

The breakdown of the system occurs at about the same time as the widespread use of equal-tempered tuning, and both factors represent more realistic foundations for a new approach to music, at least from a technical point of view, than some others which might be propounded.

The first point is that orchestration differed widely in concept according to the use of the orchestra. Theater scores observed one practice, church scores another, symphonic scores still another and chamber music scores yet another. These differences were in style, use of specific instruments and general attitude regarding what kind of instrument should play what kind of part. There was really far less *stylistic* uniformity than one is led to believe. Unity had more to do with harmonic progression (as guaranteed by the basso continuo) than with the actual practice in *other musical elements*—which now become of utmost importance. There seems to be a kind of false unity, induced by a bewildering array of terms, in the Classical Period. In the Baroque one can find one kind of musical form (such as large structure) called many different things and be exactly the same thing, and vice versa. A sonata can be called a suite, concerto, ordre, lezion or what-have-you. A concerto can be the same as a dance suite, or it can be a three-movement fast-slow-fast. These, however, are all in the same general category of chamber-orchestral music. This is not to say that these instrumental forms were never used in church or theater, but the orchestral concept was greatly different. In opera and oratorio there tended to be in most musical numbers a small use of real counterpoint; the middle voices often were slavish doublings of the bass line (especially viola parts) or else meaningless "noodles and boom chinks," a habit that unfortunately remained in too many opera scores throughout the nineteenth century. Adam Carse speaks so well on this matter:

As in the latter part of the eighteenth century, there continued to be a marked difference between the orchestration of works designed for the concert-room, and that of works for the theater during the greater part of the nineteenth century. The orchestration of a Rossini opera and that of a Schubert symphony, for example, seem poles asunder; yet the work of these two composers was strictly contemporary, and in their use of orchestral raw material their scores have much more in common than might appear from casual observation. Again, the musical matter and equipment of some of the above composers differ greatly; there is a yawning gap between the matter and musicianship of a Beethoven and those of a Boieldieu, yet the radii of their orchestral horizons were not really widely divergent.

. . . The close of the eighteenth century saw the last of what may be called threadbare or skeleton orchestration. Even the poorest orchestrator in the early nineteenth century provided sufficient harmonic body in the "inside" of his musical structure to ensure sonority and solidity of effect. The habitual duplication or doubling of parts, which left its traces in the scores of Italian opera composers until even late in the eighteenth century, practically disappeared during the maturity of Haydn and Mozart. Such doubling of parts as appears in nineteenth century scores is provided more in order to adjust the balance of tone, and to secure the adequate prominence of certain parts, than as the result of habit or indifference, as was undoubtedly the case during the greater part of the eighteenth century.[3]

In the Classical Period a concerto begins to mean a solo instrument with orchestra, an orchestra which includes winds, especially oboes and horns in pairs. In the Baroque the concerto concept had at first meant "contrast" or "competition" (from the Latin *concertare*, which means "to compete side by side"). This contrast was one such as vocal vs. instrumental, or loud instruments vs. soft. It was only later in the period that the concerto began to assume the characteristics we associate with it today—solo vs. orchestra *and* a standardized three-movement structure.

In a similar manner such terms as *symphony* and *overture* also begin to assume the meanings which they have had since—hence the name "classical" for this period, although there is much else (factors such as tonal harmony, Apollonian thinking and formal clarity) which caused the age to be called "classical." In short, then, what happened to orchestral forms and practice set a mode of thinking which is still valid today for much orchestral composition. The nineteenth century continued the evolution, and a real orchestral literature began to accrue. In this sense the nineteenth century was not as rebellious as it was in other aspects of music. Berlioz knew well, and accepted, the classical orchestra and built upon this foundation; he knew a good thing when he heard it! His admiration for Gluck, for example, knew no bounds.

Here is a list of important orchestral concepts which the nineteenth-century composer accepted and then evolved still further:

1. Standardized instrumentation, with but few exceptions.

2. Complete orchestration of the entire texture, with little or no substitution of parts.

3. Greater virtuosity of *all* players, although this factor gained greater importance throughout the century. The best scores of the last half of the eighteenth show a distribution of orchestral interest and activity, while others center almost all of it in the first violin part.

4. All instruments are chromatic: the strings completely, the woodwinds almost completely; only the brasses have severe gaps, but composers hit upon the idea of using horns crooked in more than one key in the same work.

5. Themes, figures and passages are conceived for the instrument which is to play it. Composers consider range, register and tessitura.

6. "Atmospheric" orchestration, although in infancy, still appears often enough to be important. Cases in point include the "Representation of Chaos" in Haydn's *Creation*, various pastorale scenes, storms and battles. The Baroque was not lacking in this, but various Baroque clichés were becoming worn out (wind instruments for underworld scenes, bird twitterings or the use of a figure by association which in another work could stand for something different). In the nineteenth century this still happens, but harmony becomes increasingly important, as do more accurate (if not as artistic) depiction of "sound effects."

7. There is no longer any figured bass, hence no clatter of harpsichords and other such instruments.

8. Music for orchestra is written to be conducted by a musician who is not playing an instrument at the same time.

9. There is recognition of unique and expressive orchestral colors through doubling, particularly at the octave, the double octave or some other interval. Colors are not used for noise, but for subtle nuances of overtone summation—sound effects based on exactly the same physical principles as mixing of colors in painting (the only real difference being the frequency range). The effect on the listener or viewer is of course different, since different receptors[4] are involved.

10. There is a greater use of heterophony, even though heterophony is most often considered a primitive polyphonic device (a melody and a decorated version of it played or sung simultaneously).

11. There is a standardization of wind instruments according to size. The "key" in which the instrument is to be played becomes less and less of a "jungle." Clarinets came mostly in b-flat and a, trumpets in b-flat and horns in f.

12. There is greater exploitation of coloristic devices on each instrument, involving such things as various manners of bowing, mutes, fluttertongue, extreme register and coloristic use of percussion.

These concepts lead to others, and are in many cases tied in with other aspects of nineteenth-century musical practice (melody, harmony, notation of nuances, even form). The student should keep these twelve points in mind as he proceeds.

In the latter half of the eighteenth century there were many mechanical improvements in the woodwinds, improvements which are still under study today. The Age of Reason contributed greatly to this, since practical science and technology had developed to the point where many of the traditional woodwind difficulties were nearly solved: 1) amount of breath required to play; 2) sensitivity of the reed and mechanism to rapid changes in pitch and register as well as tonguing; 3) intonation, scale, overblowing, relationship between where the holes were bored in order for the instrument to be played by human fingers and where they *should* be to be correct acoustically (obviously, gadgetry helps here: if keys could be placed under the fingers as they naturally fall, this key placement could open a tone hole some distance away); 4) good tone quality, not sacrificed for intonation; possibilities of alternate fingerings which facilitate passage work and trills or tremolos, giving the player a choice of intonation and tone-color; a tempering of sorts is thereby possible, increasing the flexibility of the winds; 5) addition of keys which fill the chromatic gaps which had long existed on many of these instruments.

It is my belief that one can go too far in leveling out register differences, since much great music of the past was written with color differences in register very much in mind, and many composers today still desire these coloristic features. While a nearly perfect clarinet, for example, is probably possible, one wonders if compromises on the timbre of registers are really wanted. Many composers have written very well indeed with the concept of characteristic timbres for various registers, and these works would, of course, have an entirely different effect if the differences were removed. One can only hope that intonation problems are solved, leaving something of the original instrument behind. This opinion is, no doubt, shared by many other musicians who are deeply involved with the orchestra. Far too many misconceptions about instruments in general have been perpetuated by people who really don't either know or care. One often reads that man developed musical instruments in an attempt to imitate the sound of his own singing voice— this is nonsense! (Why should man do this?) What probably did happen was that he tried to imitate sounds of nature and used these as part of his worship. There are too many legends about man hearing the music of nature (wind in the reeds, rustling of leaves, bird song, thunder or rainfall). It is doubtful, or at least argumentative, if early man looked upon *himself* as a child of nature.

Man, then, has always been looking for a different sound. Musical instruments have often been by-products of some other activity (such as the harp from the hunter's bow). Highly civilized man looks for sounds in more sophisticated ways, in new harmonic combinations. Today we are engaged in fantastic research on the possibilities of real and significant music from electronics and computers.

The nineteenth century was one which produced many composers who were concerned with this very problem: how to get new sounds? This is one of the great contributions of romanticism in music: how these new sounds were found—improvements on the instruments, new ways of playing them, new ways of combining them, new harmonies to be played by the new combinations. The strings were already at a high level of development but much remained in the development of technique. Paganini and others found new ways of bowing (the improved bow of Tourte and Dodd helped make this possible), and new ways of playing to achieve a different timbre through the use of harmonics, vibrato, double and multiple stopping, high registers on *each* string, mute, placements of the bow relative to the bridge and interesting combinations of these. While most of these devices were first used by the circus violinist and were actually forbidden by many teachers, they were eventually adopted by most soloists, then by chamber music players and then by the orchestra. Today's string player is asked to do an amazing amount of coloristic playing (consult any of Webern's scores, such as the *String Trio*, Op. 20); many scores in the early nineteenth even ask for some of these extremes—such as the use of *col legno* (using the wooden part of the bow) in the fifth movement of Berlioz's *Fantastic Symphony*.

Mutes had been used for quite some time, even as early as the seventeenth century, since Mersenne[5] mentions it and describes it as early as 1636; but as far as we know it is not called for in any music until the time of Lully. In the Classical Period there is still some confusion about the use of the string mute, since one finds the term most often used (in the *Urtext*[6]) for violins, sometimes for violins and violas, almost never for cello and bass—did these instruments not have them, or did the composer want the subtle color difference of the muted sound on top and the open sound underneath? Max Reger made use of a double string section in the latter part of the nineteenth century, where one complete section is muted and the other is open. (The effect is really quite beautiful.) The student is reminded that when an instrument is muted it is not always for the purpose of making the tone softer; the word "mute" comes from "mutation," meaning a "change of sound."

Muting also applies to the brass instruments. The mutation of sound is accomplished by altering the overtone structure which the instrument produces. The timbre of any musical sound is, of course, the direct result of the overtones (the relative strengths of those that are present and (as in the case of the clarinet family especially) some which are not present at all). Only an electronically produced "white" tone has all the overtones, just as white light contains all colors.

As early as Goethe it was known that color and sound timbre were related phenomena. The nineteenth century was the first to be fascinated by sound colors, although earlier scores sometimes give evidence of this, especially passages where the fundamental pitches do not really sound well in other timbres than the original. There are many vocal compositions of the sixteenth century, for example, which sound "right" only when sung. While this may be coincidental in some cases, the fact remains that all of these overtones were there and sounding ever since man first made music and there must have been some people here and there who were sensitive to them. It can be shown that each new age of Western music "hears" overtones which are farther out, and the youth from his earliest musical experiences becomes conditioned to the entire past in a very short time. (He hears without prejudice, it might be added!)

Musical color, then, is a new dimension in the nineteenth century. This is one aspect of Alfred Einstein's comment:

In the development of music, sheer sound has always played a role; never, to be sure, a completely negligible one—for music which does not sound is hardly music at all—but an ever-changing role, and never the significant one that it did in the Romantic Period of the 19th century. . . . In this connection it should be emphasized that new sonority is inseparable from new harmony. Haydn, Mozart, and Beethoven were themselves the great conquerors in this realm . . . with the first Romantics, sound took on a new meaning. It was a stronger factor in the body of the music than it had ever been before; it won a higher value purely in and for itself. . . . The immediate expression of this new relationship was the development of the orchestra in the 19th century.[7]

One is tempted to call it just the same as color in painting; but this is only a figure of speech, even though similar physical laws are in operation. What one *can* say is that the motivation for such interest in color is the great increase in the literary aspect of music and in the development of the musical theater.

The composer had at his disposal an orchestra of basic instruments. The profusion of instruments which must have plagued the seventeenth- and early eighteenth-century composer had all but disappeared. The composer had learned to rely on the string choir as the backbone of the ensemble, a choir of five basic sections: first and second violin, viola, cello and bass (actually *violone*). The number of players in each section varied, but at the early stages the first violins carried just about every-thing and the celli almost always doubled the bass an octave higher (frequently there was no separation of parts, and the celli played from a part called "bass," as did the violone, bassoons and archlutes). As tonal counterpoint developed, greater "democracy" developed and the string sections approached greater equality of importance. Lully, for example, often used a double viola section, as did other composers of the middle Baroque. By the time of Beethoven each section had made great prog-ress toward this ideal of equality—not to placate bored second violinists, but in order to structure a vital score in which all parts are important and in which there is a minimum of filler or "sawdust" parts. The virtuoso orchestra which developed during the nineteenth century ac-tually accomplished this; in the twentieth century the differentiation of "first" and "second" violins is only for convenience. Some composers divided the parts even more at times, so that in an eighteen-man section there might be eighteen individual parts—a far cry from the notion that all music could and should be reduced to the four voices of a hymn! The actual number of players was variable, and still is, depending on the budget and/or the taste of the conductor. What had happened in this regard was that a greater importance was attached to viola and cello for melodic, countermelodic and coloristic passages, which resulted in a steady growth in the number of players in these sections. A common distribution is: 16-18 first violins, 16-18 second violins, 12 violas, 12 celli and 10 basses.

The seating arrangements of the string choir varied according to the local situation, but a convention gradually developed in which the first and second violins were on opposite sides of the stage, with the first violins on the conductor's left (still observed in almost every orchestra in the world) and the second violins on the conductor's right. There were many beautiful effects which could be produced with this seating. Since the second violins were seated with the sound-holes of their instruments pointed *away* from the audience, the section tended to produce a veiled sound. They were in a position to answer the firsts in contrapuntal passages. There was a built-in stereophonic effect, and the audience seemed to be surrounded by violins. (One wonders if it is right to perform the great masterworks of the nineteenth century with the twentieth-century seating arrangement, which places the violins all to the con-ductor's left, with the second violins farther upstage to the first violins' left!) There are many advantages to the modern seating, or so many orchestras would not have changed. The older seating often gave the violin sections ensemble trouble, since the last desk of second violin was often nearly 90 feet from the last desk of first violin. This was particularly apparent when the orchestra was playing in a strange hall, as when on tour. The other advantage of the modern seating is the placing of the cello section on the outside where the seconds had been (they actually had only traded places). With the increased burden on the cello section for passages which must be clearly projected (such as the first bars of Wagner's *Tristan und Isolde,* or the second movement of Tchaikovsky's *Fifth Symphony*), the placement of the cello section on the outside is advantageous for live concerts. In recording sessions all sorts of seating plans are used, depending on what is being recorded and the microphone techniques available at the studio.

The string choir enjoyed its position as the most important choir for many reasons, among them:

1. Flexibility
   a. Complete pitch gamut, long range on each instrument.
   b. Ability to play same note for a very long time, or to change pitch with great rapidity—instruments do not "breathe" in the same sense as the wind choirs.
   c. Great timbre differences.
   d. Great difference from softest to loudest.
   e. Ability to change from loud to soft or soft to loud with great variation, either suddenly or very gradually.
   f. Possibility of solo, duo, trio, etc., on up to a complete section subdivided into many different parts.
2. Durability
   a. String choir can play for a very long time without resting.
   b. Audiences can tolerate and discriminate string tone for a longer time than any massed sounds other than *a cappella* choirs.
3. Availability of players
   a. Many professional and amateur players in the eighteenth and nineteenth centuries (unfortunately, this is not true today, since there is actually a shortage of good string players all over the world).
   b. Most composers played a stringed instrument in addition to a keyboard instrument.
4. Strings provided the best accompaniments for all kinds of soloists.
   a. Opera, mass, oratorio, concerto and other types.

Just as the almost exactly equal concept for each of the string sections began to be realized, composers also equalized the importance of the other choirs—in an ideal orchestra there would be no "most important" choir. (This was done for artistic and not political reasons!) The woodwinds had been used for added dashes of color here and there, mostly in a solo capacity. The works of J. S. Bach, for example, abound in beautiful solo passages for flutes (both transverse and recorder type[8]) and oboes. Rarely does one find woodwinds used for other kinds of parts until later in the eighteenth century (as in the Serenades of Mozart and the wind chamber music of Haydn). As the woodwind choir becomes more standardized, part-writing takes on new characteristics as well. This kind of writing from the beginning of Mendelssohn's *Italian Symphony* will illustrate this:

Figure 10-2

The orchestra in the early nineteenth century had one or two (sometimes three) flutes (wooden transverse), a pair of oboes, a pair of clarinets, a pair of bassoons and perhaps even a serpent (called for as late as Mendelssohn's *St. Paul*). The newcomer was, of course, the clarinet, having been used so well by Mozart in so many works that it was taken up by other composers and has remained until today one of our most durable woodwinds—the "violin" of the concert band, as some people see it.

Flutes were very soft in tone, even more so than the modern silver flute, and most composers took this into account when writing independent parts for them. At other times they were used for doubling, often playing the first violin part an octave higher—a practice not often found in Baroque writing, but perhaps actually observed in places where for some reason (garden parties and the like) the melody needed to be heard more prominently. Even the wooden flute sound carries quite well when played in the upper register. What was possibly a practical occurrence in the Baroque was actually written out in later times. This type of doubling has an antique quality to it, and is used for that purpose.

The late-nineteenth–century composer didn't use this doubling very often, except in big tutti passages. He also made frequent use of flute and violin at the unison. Lest one fear that a flute sound is lost when doubling a violin section, let him listen well to the first statement of the *idée fixe* in Berlioz's *Fantastic Symphony* or the first *Sea Interlude* from Britten's *Peter Grimes*. One can only speculate about pre-Berlioz intent, but he can be sure that Berlioz does every bit of doubling for a very good reason. Flutes are non-transposing instruments.[9]

The mechanism of the flute was greatly improved by applying principles of Boehm (1794-1881). Actually, all woodwinds in the standard orchestra benefited from Boehm's great contributions. (Details of Boehm's work are discussed below.)

While the flute came into the orchestra as a soloist, the oboe was used both for solo work and as harmonic filler. It was discovered early that a pair of oboes and a pair of horns blended very well for harmonic punctuation and often for thematic work. The oboe enjoyed the distinction of being the highest woodwind until the flute became a permanent member. J. S. Bach, Reinhard Keiser and others wrote elaborate double reed parts.[10] The oboe, although its natural scale is D (as is the flute, by the way), is also a non-transposing instrument. The student must remember that the oboe and all other double reed instruments tend to be louder in the low register and softer in the high register—just the opposite of all other wind instruments, singers and most stringed instruments. (Violins and celli project well in their highest pitches; violas are highly variable in this regard, depending on the actual instrument and the player, while the basses, except on rare occasions, do not project well in their highest registers.)

In the early part of the nineteenth century clarinets were built in the keys of A (for use generally in the sharp keys), in B-flat (for flat keys) and in C, or non-transposing. The key system of the clarinet was overhauled many times throughout the century, with systems of Albert and Boehm finally receiving the most usage. Throughout the century the C clarinet began to fall out of use. Berlioz makes an apt comment about clarinets and clarinet players in his still valuable essay "On Conducting," in which he complains that conductors do not always see to it that clarinettists are playing on the proper instruments, but that they try to play the entire piece on the B-flat model, thereby saving the trouble of changing the reed or making other adjustments. He points out that each clarinet has its own special color, and that B-flat does not have the low concert C#. One might add that a good orchestral composer knows such things as where the register breaks occur and where the best trills fall, and usually writes the clarinet part with a certain type of instrument in mind. It is obvious that even in instruments which are only a semitone apart—

such as the B-flat and the A—they would be wrongly used if a part conceived for the A clarinet were to be attempted on the B-flat.

Some composers have had some ingenious ideas to circumvent this problem. The famous passage in Tchaikovsky's *Fourth Symphony* (first movement) is a case in point: the concert key becomes B major, but the clarinets have been playing in B-flat, since the key of the symphony is F minor; there is not enough time for the player to change instruments, so instead of writing the clarinet part in C# major (a horrendous key for clarinet)—which would be the "correct" key in classical treatment, since a B-flat instrument always plays in a key a whole step *above* the concert key—the composer, believing obviously in equal-tempered thinking and tuning, writes the B-flat clarinet part in D-flat major (the enharmonic key of C#) thus creating a tolerable key climate for the clarinettist.

In the entire woodwind family the "key" of the instrument is determined in such a way that, for example, any clarinettist can play any clarinet—the notation is actually *fingering*; the actual pitches which emanate are determined by the *size* of the instrument in question. Thus any flutist knows the piccolo fingering, any oboist the English horn, any bassoonist the contra-bassoon, and any saxophonist the entire saxophone family. The composer writes the music so that the proper transposition can be made. In many scores of the twentieth century the music is written as it sounds and the parts are printed in their proper keys. The composer and conductor, then, need to know how to write and to read both types of scores.

The bassoons became the bass voice of the woodwind choir and remain so, superseding all sorts of monsters which would sound strange indeed to us today. Among these were the pommer and bombard and various attempts at a bass oboe. The bassoon has a practical design, since it achieves very low sounds by virtue of a long tube length, made possible by turning the tube back on itself so that it is double. The tone is quite uniform throughout, except for notes in the extreme high and low ranges. The bassoon is a true bass instrument and often helps support the cello and stringed bass, in addition to working well as a bass with other winds. It blends remarkably well with the horns, and is often used in scores to provide notes which are missing on the older crooked horns. The opening bars of Brahms's *Second Symphony* is a beautiful example of such a blend.

The bassoon is also useful as a solo instrument for clownish effects (as in Dukas's *L'Apprenti Sorcier*) and as a soulful singer (as in the second movement of Tchaikovsky's *Fourth Symphony*).

The bassoon tone doubles well with other instruments for good mixed color, mostly at the octave below, as well as doubling well with itself at the octave (as in the slow movement of Sibelius's *Second Symphony*).

In considering the woodwind family as a whole one must also include the horns, which are placed in the full orchestral score between the bassoons and the trumpets—instead of farther down in the brass choir, which would be the case if they were listed in exact pitch order. Horns were used mostly in pairs at first, crooked in the same key in major tonalities, but often crooked in different keys when in minor tonalities in order to provide more tones. One could also change crooks during the course of a movement. The standard procedure soon became the four-man section with four separate parts.

The woodwinds tended to be in pairs in the Classical Period, and as the nineteenth century progressed a third player was often added. The third player was also called upon to play the auxiliary instrument in the section. For the flutes this was the piccolo, for oboes the cor anglais or English horn, for clarinets the bassett horn and/or smaller piccolo clarinet and for the bassoons the double or contra-bassoon. The auxiliary instruments, almost without exception, were used at first for special theatrical effects, such as a piccolo to suggest a man whistling or an English horn to suggest shepherds. The nineteenth century also produced some instruments which either became obsolete or were used only on occasions. The saxophone is probably the most famous example: an instrument which is used commonly in twentieth-century popular music and is used only occasionally in the symphony and chamber orchestra (in works such as Webern's Quartet, Op. 22, and Berg's Violin Concerto).

The saxophone's first use in the orchestra was rather strange; consult opera scores written in Paris around 1890 (Massenet's Werther, for example). This usage was exceptional, since there was an attempt to make it a member of the woodwind section instead of a solo instrument—with results which were not always happy! Bizet's incidental music to Daudet's play L'Arlésienne is certainly one of the earliest successful uses (1872) of the saxophone in a work which is still popular with audiences.

The woodwind choir, then, was basically complete quite early in the century, aided by Boehm's principles. The Boehm system, briefly, is as follows:

Tone holes are bored as large as possible.
Tone holes stand open until closed by player's fingers or keys.
Tone holes are bored where they should be for proper sound, and not to accommodate the human hand.
Tone holes are operated by a mechanism which does fit the conformation of the hand; they are opened and closed by levers, rods and springs, often some distance from the player's fingers.

The brasses, until our own century, often came in a bewildering variety of sizes and shapes. Trumpets and horns were the first permanent members. Trombones were used in church and in the theater before they were used in concerts. The tuba was a late development.

During the nineteenth century most of the pitch limitations of horns and trumpets were solved. In the eighteenth century many clever devices were attempted, with various degrees of success: crooks were almost universally used until well into the nineteenth century, but had the disadvantage of requiring changing; side holes covered by keys were tried, and were found to be most successful on cornet-like instruments; slides such as the trombone type were used with some success on trumpets—Bach calls for this, the *tromba da tirarsi*, in some of his cantatas (some of these slides even had return springs!); *stopping* (inserting the hand in the bell) was tried, and found wanting for the trumpets, but was of common occurrence on the horn and is still used to a certain extent today. Valves were the answer, however, and by 1830 were known all over Europe. The exact history of their invention may never be known; two men claim to have invented it, around 1815.[11]

As is often the case, many performers were slow to adopt the new idea, even though it was a great improvement and actually emancipated the brasses, making them chromatic and capable of playing music which was demanding more and more chromatic pitches. Technical flexibility was also improved, since there were alternate fingerings possible. The valve added length to the sounding tube, so that the player could get the same effect as with crooks (each valve added tube length, which lowered the fundamental). With three valves the player has seven sounding lengths by using none, any one, any two or all three (valve three equals one plus two). There remains a real problem, however: since nature is not equal-tempered, notes which are supposed to be exactly the same are not exactly the same. This becomes an advantage for the artist player, since he can choose which one of the alternate fingerings is the most efficient for the function of the particular pitch desired. In general the choice of fingering determines pitch, timbre and facility of fingering for trills or other technical passages. The trombone presents a similar situation, with its slide positions. The student must remember that a brass player can play many notes, sometimes as many as sixteen, on one crook, valve or slide position. In the low register there is only one fingering or slide position possible, since the player is lowering the second partial of the whole tube length.[12]

Valves assumed different designs in attempts for greater fluency, accuracy of intonation, and the overcoming of leakage, noise and other weaknesses. The student can observe two of the most important valve designs which have survived today: the rotary valve on the modern French horn and the piston on the trumpet.

General acceptance of the valve is well discussed by Carse:

When they became known and were obtainable, valved instruments were readily adopted by military and brass bands all over Europe. As far as the orchestra was concerned, horns and trumpets were the instruments destined to be the most affected by the advent of the valve. It was not until the 'thirties that the new instruments began to find their way into orchestras, and then some twenty or more years had to pass before they came into anything like general use. Germany was the first to give the valved instruments a general welcome. Berlioz reported that in 1843 horns and trumpets with "cylinders" (rotary valves) were to be found in all the most important orchestras, as well as the valved tuba or bombardon. Schumann's symphonies (1841-1851) mark the period of transition in Germany; that composer wrote for both natural and valved instruments, using the latter rather timidly and inconsistently. Even in Wagner's early works the two types are used together, and there is some reluctance to take full advantage of the new mechanism; but after the mid-century the composer's confidence in the new instruments was firmly established, and there was no more hesitation in making use of their possibilities to the fullest extent.[13]

Carse's *The History of Orchestration* is highly recommended for more detailed study of the whole subject. The actual music written was profoundly influenced by instrumental availability and proficiency, and new instruments were invented which used the new principles. The most important was a complete family of tubas, which was a better solution for the problem of a contrabass brass instrument. (See Carse, *History of Orchestration*, pp. 216-218, for an informative and entertaining discussion.)

The tuba is the bass of the brass choir, along with the bass trombone, and is actually a complete family in and of itself. In modern usage in both band and orchestra we find the single tuba in B-flat (most common in band, where it is also called the baritone), the middle-range tubas in F and E-flat, and real contrabass instruments in CC and BB-flat. The Sousaphone and like instruments are designed for marching; although in many schools they are used as tubas, they do not match the true orchestral tuba in sound. The modern tuba is used to play many parts in early nineteenth-century scores which were originally written for ophicleide or serpent.

The Saxhorn family (named for Adolph Sax, who patented them in 1845) has been called the "mellow" brass. The characteristics of their design and tone were much emulated all over Europe, with the result that present terminology is very confusing. The cornet, which is still so important in bands and in many French scores in the period of Franck, is the most common. The modern tuba and baritone also owe much to Mr. Sax.

The Wagner tuba was still another attempt to achieve a mellow low brass sound. Wagner wished to use each instrument as part of a quartet, from flutes on down (four flutes, four oboes, etc.). The Wagner tuba does have a lovely sound due to its shape, but aside from Wagner's use in the

Ring, they have been used but little by other composers except Strauss and Bruckner. They are hard to come by, and composers tend to write for instruments which are available.

The trombone principle had been known for many years, but the instrument has had a varied existence in the orchestra. It was used much at first in the church and in the famous tower music.[14] It was brought into the theater for opera by Gluck and Mozart, but was a stranger as a regular instrument in orchestral concerts until the symphonies of Beethoven and Schubert. Around 1825 it appeared in several sizes and keys, but the smaller ones began to be called for less and less as time passed, until by the end of the century there were the common three parts: for two tenor and one bass trombone, although some variation can be found in this. There was also some confusion at times over which instrument should play the brass bass—the trombone or the tuba or both. The slide technique of the trombone led to special effects such as the *glissando*. Attempts to put a valve on the trombone have not as yet been generally accepted by serious composers or players. Trombones also used a variety of mutes—a late-nineteenth–century development, however.

The percussion instruments are among man's oldest, and in symphonic literature the kettledrums or tympani are by far the most important. The Classical Period used them mainly to support tonic and dominant harmony; the instruments were notated in C and G, regardless of the key of the music. The player was to tune the C drum to the tonic and the G drum to the dominant of whatever key was needed. The obvious use of the kettledrum to imitate thunder or artillery was discovered quite early, and still seems to be in fashion. In the middle of the nineteenth century a third kettledrum was introduced which could be tuned either to the dominant of the dominant (for modulations to the key of the dominant), to the subdominant or perhaps to the third of the tonic chord. Beethoven's tuning in octaves in the scherzo of his *Ninth Symphony* and Berlioz's imaginative treatment in work after work were exceptional for their time but prophetic, since late romantic and contemporary composers have done similar astounding things with the tympani.

For these effects the composer needed more efficient ways to tune and to change tuning quickly while the orchestra was playing. Various pedal mechanisms were invented which solved these problems and made possible rather intricate passages. Various sizes of tympani were also required, from very large ones for contrabass pitches to small ones for pitches near middle C.

It was also discovered that choice of sticks influenced the timbre, and sticks with a bewildering variety of head materials were introduced, from cork to soft felt, and from rubber to sponge. Some composers have been very careful to indicate which is desired, but most leave it up to the player and/or the conductor. The role of the tympani came to be expressive and soft as well as bombastic. The literature contains passages where two players are necessary for the performance of complete chords, where one player rolls with one stick on one drum and the other on another, or where the players use various methods of muting simultaneously.

The only other percussion instruments which can be called regular members are the bass drum, cymbals, triangle and side or snare drum. These appear with some regularity from the time of Gluck on, and are used for noise effects, storms, battles and the like. Toward the end of the nineteenth century a similar development to that of the tympani takes place, in that composers begin to explore softer effects, novel ways of playing and other color possibilities. A catalogue of these devices would be almost endless, but a few of them are: roll on the cymbals with various kinds of sticks, strike the suspended cymbal with a drumstick, strike the rim of the snare drum, roll on the bass drum with a two-headed stick or cover the snare drum with a cloth. Almost all of these instruments have been built in unusual sizes, from very large to very small. The large ones enjoyed some vogue in the massed concert extravaganzas by Jullien[15] and others. People would flock to hear the lovely sound of a monster gong-drum which was seven feet in diameter.[16]

More exotic percussion was called for from time to time for local color (such items as castanets for Spanish atmosphere, wind machines for storms, sleigh bells, and bells of many sizes and shapes). Turkish effects were very popular in concert as well as opera. The most common instruments which remained and are still found today are the glockenspiel, xylophone, castanets, tubular chimes (the closest resemblance to church bells), temple blocks, odd sized and shaped cymbals, tam-tam (gong), anvils, whips and the various Latin American devices.

The percussion are often divided into various classifications, according to pitch (definite or indefinite) or according to the material which vibrates to produce the sound. The drums are all called *membranophones*, and the metallic or wooden instruments are called *idiophones*. The modern orchestra employs a great variety of percussion instruments. They came into the orchestra throughout the Romantic Period, since they were so helpful in storytelling and in achieving unusual expression.

The harp is also one of man's oldest instruments; yet, it is one which still poses problems for the composer, since it is essentially a diatonic instrument and the demands of late romantic and modern music have called for more and more chromaticism. At the end of the Classical Period harp writing for the orchestra was indeed rudimentary and was used mostly in opera. Gluck called for a harp in *Orpheus* (1774), and for a production of Lesueur's *Les Bardes* (1804) it is said that twelve harps were used. The harp was the delight of the French, and it appeared later in other musical capitals. To this day many of the indications to the harpist are in French, although some of the earliest improvements on the instrument were made in Bavaria as far back as 1720. In 1820 Sebastien Erard produced the seven-pedal double-action model, which is basically the instrument in use today. The harp was still not completely chromatic, but with imagination the composer could devise pedal settings which would give it colorful and evocative glissandi to enhance the delicate tints of the orchestral palette. Composers would sometimes call for two harps, which were to be tuned in two different ways to supply all the chromatic tones, or which were to be doubled to give additional strength. Berlioz was one of the earliest to realize some of the potentialities of the instrument; Liszt, Wagner and others followed, leading up to the impressionists who used the harp with great effect.

The piano, toward the end of the century, was used in an orchestral capacity, leading to brilliant new uses in the early twentieth century by composers such as Stravinsky. It was used for color and also as a percussion instrument.

The organ had been used many times with the orchestra in church, and is called for many times in operatic scenes laid in church. Its combination with the orchestra is somewhat redundant, since it is similar to an ensemble of woodwinds.[17] There is also the practical problem of its relative pitch level, which does not change much during performance; but pitch level does change in the orchestra (almost all orchestras tend to go slightly sharp as the concert progresses, due to the warming of the instruments). While the same problem is present with the piano or harpsichord, ensemble works which use the organ do not use it as continually; therefore, the long-delayed first organ entrance in Saint-Saëns's *Symphony No. 3* is frequently catastrophic unless pitch levels are just right.

Beethoven's *Ninth Symphony* introduced the human voice into the symphony, and many works since have called for soloists, choruses and combinations thereof. Berlioz lost no time; his *Romeo and Juliet*, which he called a *dramatic* symphony, expanded the symphony into the dimensions of a cantata. Liszt, in his *Faust* and *Dante* symphonies, used the voice, and many great and lesser composers followed suit. Mahler, at the end of the period, made some of the greatest vocal demands in several of his symphonies. His *Eighth Symphony*, for example, has been called the "Symphony of a Thousand," since so many performers are required. The music dramas of Wagner were also influenced by Beethoven's *Ninth*, and are actually as important in the history of orchestral music as they are in the development of the music theater.

In many of the symphonic works where the human voice is used one can distinguish the vocal treatment from that in works such as masses or oratorios, mainly in the relative importance of the choral part. In a symphonic work the chorus is not necessarily "front and center" in musical importance, but is merely another choir of the orchestra; it is sometimes used for special effects, as in Debussy's *Nocturnes* or Holst's *Planets*. This is not to say that the chorus is never featured, or that it is mishandled. One need only notice the beautiful *a cappella* entrance of the chorus in Mahler's *Second Symphony*. This concept is the same as the new concept of the orchestra's role in the concerto and, indeed, even in opera. The mechanical support of the orchestra is meant as a harmonic carpet, not merely a faint kind of "oom-pah-pah"; such an interpretation would be just as wrong as the chorus drowning out the orchestra, or vice versa.

In the big oratorio choruses of Classical and Baroque works there was a division of the orchestra into two groups: those that double the chorus and those that do not. Those that did not double either accompanied or had contrapuntal parts. In the Romantic Period a similar habit was followed, but the doubling was often not as obvious and heterophony was used, as in the beginning of the Sanctus in the Verdi *Requiem*. Note that the rapid figure in the violins is really a more complex version of the fugue subject being sung by the chorus.

Beethoven's *Missa Solemnis* is surpassed only by the great *Mass in B Minor* of J. S. Bach in its use of gigantic choral-orchestral architecture. Beethoven even outdoes his own *Ninth Symphony*, and a comparison of the two works will show clearly the differences in choral concept. The chorus in the *Ninth* caps a great symphony, while in the mass it must set the words of the Holy Liturgy; the *Ninth* starts a new "tradition," while the mass continues a very old one, but in a new light (what previous mass contains anything to compare to the violin solo in the Benedictus of Beethoven's *Missa Solemnis?*).

The Brahms *Requiem* (more properly, *Ein Deutsches Requiem*) is probably somewhere in between. The words are from the Bible, not from the Liturgy. Brahms did not start a "tradition" with this piece, although he wrote almost a choral symphony.

Nineteenth-century orchestration exploited unison and octave doublings mostly for the richness and colors it could achieve. The human voice was not immune to this; beautiful effects were achieved by having the voice double almost in the same way as an instrument. Many passages in Wagner show this usage; the doubling is not meant just to give the singer his pitch and keep him on the melody! Artistic singing of all kinds, in the more elaborate orchestrations, requires that the singer be exactly in tune and rhythm with the instrument with which he is doubled.

This is another aspect of the paradoxical nature of music in the nineteenth century. As composers became more and more free with the rules of composition they require less and less freedom from the performer, except in passages *written* to be done with more freedom. Some soloists of the Golden Age would even speak instead of sing in moments of great emotion, but most passages were *written* so that they would not sound correct unless the singer performed his part *exactly* as notated. One of the best examples is in the *Agnus Dei* of the Verdi *Requiem*, where the soprano and alto soloists must sing in exact octaves. (How lovely is the sound when it is right, and how awful when the singers seem to try their hardest to be not together!)

Many of the great coloratura roles in opera are from the nineteenth century (Dinorah, Lucia, *et al.*); in addition to the vocal problems involved, there were orchestral ones as well—especially for the first flute, who had to keep up with the soloists, doubling mostly in thirds or sixths. When performed properly these passages are indeed effective, but there are many hair-raising tales told by flautists who have tried to keep pace with coloraturas who would make unrehearsed modulations or other departures from the score. Needless to say, there have been great vocal artists who did perform their parts with fidelity, especially when great conductors such as Toscanini were on the podium. (Singers can tell stories on flautists too!)

The role of the conductor during the nineteenth century changed considerably from the composer himself officiating at the keyboard—which was the case before 1800. During the first half of the nineteenth century there was a rapid development in the art of conducting the orchestra with a baton. The composer himself was still expected to be a conductor, and some of them were among the very finest: Spontini, Spohr, Weber, Mendelssohn, Berlioz, Liszt and many others. Some composers were not as effective in conducting roles, notably Beethoven and Schumann. Schubert, as far as we know, did not conduct, and he heard but few of his orchestral masterpieces actually performed.

There now grew up a new breed of men who were less talented at composition but who were very good leaders of men; they still composed, however, apparently not realizing or caring that they were not exceptional as composers. The conductor who was primarily a *virtuoso* of the baton had not yet appeared—such as some of the most glamorous musicians of our own time. Ability to play or compose is no guarantee that one can be even a fair conductor; the truly great conductor must be a man of supreme gifts, indeed—not all of them musical!

The great art of orchestration is very complicated, perhaps the most complicated aspect of musical composition. The art of conducting developed right along with orchestration, each contributing to the other. Many ideas were tried and were discarded, even ideas which apparently were successful, at least from the point of view of the audience. Other ideas were refined and remained as a part of the complete orchestral art. Among these were: seating arrangements, methods of beating time (different patterns, different kinds of batons), unusual numbers of players, unusual instruments, players offstage, players in the balcony, even players out-of-doors playing through open doors or windows, unusual combinations of instruments in the scores themselves, electric devices for keeping time (Berlioz invented one) and endless experimentation at rehearsal. It was ideal for the composer to be the conductor: he not only prepared for the next performance, he also learned for his next work.[18] Many of the men who manned orchestras became composers and/or conductors later in their careers.

Ludwig Spohr (1784-1859) was one of the most important musicians of his time; he was highly regarded as a composer, violinist and conductor. He is remembered today primarily for one violin concerto: the *Concerto in the Form of a Lyric Scene*, which still receives devoted performances by violinists, and for a very good method book entitled *Violin School*. All but forgotten are his operas (among them an interesting setting of *Faust* based on non-Goethean sources), nine symphonies, other violin concerti, clarinet concerti and many chamber works. As a conductor he was one of the first to insist on a faithful performance of the printed text. Musicians praised his great insight at rehearsals. His autobiography is an excellent source book of information regarding many aspects of nineteenth-century music and musical life.

. . . and when Spohr visited England in 1820 to direct a few concerts of the Royal Philharmonic Society, he bewildered his musicians into stupefaction at the rehearsal by pulling from out of his breast-pocket a small, heavy, stumpy stick and attempting to direct them by waving it over their heads.

He has written about the event—an all-important one in the history of conducting—in his Autobiography: "I took my stand . . . in front of the orchestra, drew my directing baton from my coat-pocket, and gave the signal to begin. Quite alarmed at such a novel proceeding some of the directors protested against it, but when I besought them to grant me at least one trial they became pacified. The symphonies and overtures that were to be rehearsed were well-known to me, and in Germany I had already directed their performances. I, therefore, could not only give the *tempi* in a very decisive manner, but indicated also to the wind instruments and horns all the entries, which ensured to them a confidence such as hitherto they had not known. . . . Incited thereby to more than attention, and conducted with certainty by the *visible* manner of giving the time, they played with a spirit and correctness such as, until then, they had never before been heard to play. Surprised and inspired by this result, the orchestra immediately after the first part of the symphony expressed aloud its united assent to the new mode of conducting, and thereby overruled all further opposition on the part of the directors. . . . The triumph of the baton as a time-giver was decisive."

The baton had now firmly asserted itself; it was henceforth to be the all-important instrument for the hand of the conductor. The first conductor to realize this fully was Felix Mendelssohn, the famous composer, who directed the Leipzig Gewandhaus Orchestra for eight years. It is probable that, according to modern standards, Mendelssohn would be accepted complacently as a third-rate conductor. Richard Wagner made many derogatory comments on the rigid formalism and straightjacket conservatism of Mendelssohn's conducting (Mendelssohn, for example, could not tolerate the use of *tempo rubato* in his performances). But his historical importance is imposing.[19]

Carl Maria von Weber (1786-1826) is best remembered today as the composer of some of the earliest romantic operas in the German language and some brilliant piano music and concert pieces for one solo instrument and orchestra (piano, clarinet and bassoon). He was much at home in the theater, and was best known as an opera conductor. From all accounts he was a severe taskmaster and a real "live wire," richly talented in all branches of music. There were many intrigues against him, especially because of his youth (he was eighteen at the time of his first appointment) and because of his great interest in the orchestra—sometimes even overlooking the singers! He apparently used a long roll of paper rather than a baton. He was also sensitive to *rubato*, and was far more flexible than Spohr. Small wonder that he should have contributed so much in his music in the way of vital orchestral colors which delightfully enhance the fairy tale atmosphere of his operas.

Gasparo Spontini (1774-1851) was a highly successful composer of French operas; *La Vestale* (1807) and *Fernand Cortez* (1809), written for the taste of the Napoleonic age, are grand productions with elaborate scenery. Like Lully and Cherubini, he was born in Italy and was a huge success in France. His work as a conductor, however, was mainly in Berlin, where his productions at the opera were famous for their excellence, especially the subtle shadings of dynamics. Even Wagner was impressed; from him we learn that Spontini used a baton of ebony with an ivory knob. It was related that he would change the sizes of his batons from long ones for choruses to rather short ones for arias. His tenure in Berlin is the envy of every conductor—he had unlimited rehearsal time! He was one of the first dictatorial conductors, and he exercised great vanity almost to the point of childishness. His music says little to us today, but there are still some who would emulate his tactics. While there is much to be said for the care and preparation he required, little room was left for the spontaneous type of performance so important to Weber and Berlioz.

Einstein discusses this factor so vividly (see his *Music in the Romantic Era*[20]).

Felix Mendelssohn (1809-1847) would have been a famous musician even if he had not been a major composer. He was a remarkable pianist and one of the first great symphonic and choral conductors. He was only twenty at the time of his famous performance of Bach's *St. Matthew Passion* in 1829. Some accounts speak of his starting a movement with the baton, after which he would stop beating time, using only a glance for an entrance or some bodily movement as the character of the music changed. It is said that he would often speed up the tempo of difficult passages so that they would not last as long! His rehearsals were outstanding, showing great insight into the music he was conducting (this is where real conducting is done—at rehearsals; at performances, it is too late!). The art of the conductor is, in the final analysis, one of preparation. Mendelssohn was not at home in the theater, but became famous for his performances of Beethoven symphonies and other concert works. His most important post was conductor of the *Gewandhaus* in Leipzig, which he assumed in 1835. He was the opposite of Spontini. Most orchestral players and singers greatly admired and genuinely loved Mendelssohn, a gentle man who in many respects never ceased to be a *Wunderkind*. Schumann and Wagner admired his work as a conductor, although Schumann was not convinced about the use of the baton and Wagner worried about Mendelssohn's fast tempi (Wagner was one to extract every bit of "juice" from a passage).

Richard Wagner (1813-1883) would have been a famous German poet had he never written a bar of music. He often regarded himself as a greater writer than composer, but history has shown the reverse to be true. Although his prose writings are extremely valuable, his libretti are slow-moving and are ennobled mainly by the great music which sets them. His essay on conducting (1869) shows great insight into the aspects of conducting above and beyond mere time-beating. Men who played under him felt that they were free and were not really being led—which is, of course, the ideal situation. Wagner found what he considered the ideal tempo in terms of a singing melody or vocalization. Wagner's work as a conductor was mostly in the theater, although he was also well-known on the concert stage. His performances of the Beethoven *Ninth Symphony* became legendary. He was a severe taskmaster, and expected the men to perform with the same devotion with which he conducted. He often rehearsed the sections individually, to ensure fine performances. He did not please lazy players and singers, nor did he please all critics. Especially trying was the 1855 season with the London Philharmonic Society, where there were difficulties with language, lack of rehearsal time and a running feud with the press. Wagner would sometimes conduct from memory, which bothered the critics more than it did the orchestra.

In Wagner we see a remarkable illustration of a composer, as conductor, learning about the orchestra, and vice versa. Wagner had remarkable gifts for subtle nuances both as a composer and a conductor. He did not really follow any set tradition in either role. Wagner's or-

Plate X

Interior of Bayreuth Festspielhaus, during a performance of *Das Rheingold*. Drawing by L. Bechstein. Note that the orchestra pit is mostly under the stage, designed for better balance between stage and orchestra *(Courtesy The Bettmann Archive, N.Y.).*

chestration draws from such composers as Weber, Meyerbeer, Berlioz and Liszt, but in the main his concept was brand new: continuous movement of the music, not broken by individual numbers (arias, recitatives, ensembles or choruses) and, therefore, kept constantly moving to sustain development of the drama. The role of the orchestra in this type of music is essential; in a sense it acts as a Greek chorus, commenting on the action, but with the great subtlety possible in the new, completely chromatic orchestra which Wagner used for his most mature works. Part of the texture is purely musical, part is color to enhance the atmosphere of the scene. This requires greater concentration on the part of the conductor, who must hold and develop this concept. Richard Strauss and many others since have continued in this line of development. Wagner's personality often alienated friends; but many, among them Liszt, recognized his great genius and helped generously with money as well as influence to build the Bayreuth Festspielhaus, which was at least a partial fulfillment of Wagner's great vision.

There were also conductors who were not such men of genius as those we have been discussing. Many of these were fine musicians who did good routine work; others brought the air of the circus to the podium (this has by no means been confined to the Romantic Period!) Perhaps the most "infamous" was Louis Jullien (1812-1860), who bragged that he had 1200 pieces of music in his repertoire. He was a dandy who cut a big swath with the ladies, a conductor people came to *see*, a show on the podium. There were many fine players in his orchestras most of the time. He did have in his repertoire great classics as well as junk, and was responsible for a certain amount of music education for the masses; but, alas, how often the public is dazzled by rhinestones, thinking they are diamonds! Jullien made a very successful tour of the United States, and was one of many European virtuosi who toured in the 1850's. According to Chase,[21] Jullien played American music on his concerts, and received mixed reviews for his works and his actions. Some classed him a "humbug" but almost all admired the excellence of his orchestra. He died a lunatic and a pauper—a pity, for he would have been so successful in Hollywood!

Many of the world's great orchestras were founded in the middle of the nineteenth century. One of the greatest was the Vienna Philharmonic, which was founded in 1842 by Otto Nicolai, the composer of the opera *The Merry Wives of Windsor*. Berlioz felt that Nicolai was one of the best conductors, and praise from Berlioz for another musician is worth noting, especially when it comes to the orchestra. The Paris *Opéra* and the Conservatoire Concerts reached a high level under François Habeneck (1781-1849), who was a fine violinist but a mediocre composer. The *Société des Concerts du Conservatoire* was founded by Habeneck in 1828, and there are many accounts by musicians of reputation that its concerts were among the best in the world.

Habeneck was a dictatorial conductor who demanded perfection from the players. Berlioz rather grudgingly admits in his writings that Habeneck knew his business (remember that all official musicians in Paris were automatically enemies of Berlioz). From Berlioz we learn that Habeneck conducted from a first violin part rather than a full score, which to Berlioz was scandalous. Be that as it may, Habeneck did introduce the Beethoven symphonies to Paris and Berlioz owed much to him for these important auditions of Beethoven. Also to Habeneck's credit were the premieres of many important operas of the period. Carse points out that the use of the first violin part by Habeneck was from force of habit, since he was also a violinist (as was so often the custom). Besides, with a violin part one is not bothered with turning so many pages; in addition, one does not or should not *read* the full score in performance— the full score is used only as a reminder (a cue card, as it were). (Performance time is a little too late to be finding new things in the score!) Habeneck was also praised for the fire and brilliance of his performances,

Plate XI

Hector Berlioz (1803-1869) conducting a "concert a mitraille." Wood-cut by Grandville (1803-1847) *(Courtesy The Bettmann Archive, N.Y.).*

even though Schindler complained that his tempi in Beethoven were too slow for his taste.

Hector Berlioz (1803-1869) was an authority on things orchestral, and it is not surprising to find that he was one of the greatest conductors of his time. In 1856 he added a chapter on conducting to his book on instrumentation. This chapter is valuable reading for us today, since it treats in great detail the exact baton technique which he had found to be the most efficient. Also discussed are seating arrangements, as well as much practical advice on how a good orchestra ought to be developed and handled. In a way this is surprising, since Berlioz is thought to be the epitome of the inspirational musician. In reality, however, one can see in Berlioz the ideal balance between inspiration and the *learning* which a musician must have in order to be able to project the subjective aspects of the music. It is significant that in the revision of the Berlioz treatise by Richard Strauss nothing was added on conducting! Strauss, it must be remembered, was also a great conductor and was as concerned as Berlioz about efficient orchestral routine.

There exist several cartoons of Berlioz before a huge orchestra, and it is not difficult to see why he was caricatured so frequently. He must have been quite a sight, with his shock of red hair and his rather fantastic histrionics on the podium—not directed at the audience, but at getting the right sounds from the men. He was never as successful in Paris as he was elsewhere, especially in Germany. His love of massed sounds might lead one to think he was another Jullien, but unlike Jullien, Berlioz was praised by the best musicians of his time. Wagner, for example, thought very highly of him as a conductor and as a composer. Berlioz, strangely enough was not a particularly good performer on any instrument; therefore, he was one of the first conductors who only played well *on* the orchestra. While all great orchestral music requires virtuoso performances, a new kind of orchestral virtuosity is needed with the music of Berlioz. His orchestral approach required different rehearsal techniques. Even the best orchestras were dumbfounded when first readings of Berlioz's works were attempted. To make matters worse, Habeneck saw in Berlioz a rival and there were many intrigues (see Barzun's *Berlioz and the Romantic Century*, Vol. I, pp. 443-445, for one such affair). Berlioz's music was often undecipherable to conductors and players of the time, since his approach to the whole question of orchestral music was that of a pioneer and an explorer. Berlioz spent most of his professional life at no regular post, and relied mostly on "free-lance" performances. Fortunately for the art of music, there were kindred spirits and the true genius of Berlioz was not to be denied.

Some of the famous conductors of the nineteenth century were singers. One of the best of these was Michael Costa (1808-1884), who was born and educated in Italy but who made his fortune in England, where he first worked as a singer in 1820. He gradually worked himself up in the rather odd orchestral situation then existing in England, and became quite famous for his masterful conducting of festival performances of large oratorios so beloved by the English. Costa's training and taste were probably more in tune with the current Italian taste, but he adapted and almost singlehandedly brought to the theater orchestra a discipline under one conductor, replacing the rather strange system of divided responsibility which had previously existed between the man at the keyboard and the concertmaster. Costa was at home in Italian opera, and soon was famous for splendid performances known for their polish and for the fine morale of the men in the orchestra. He became almost "typecast"; there were those who were sure that no other kind of music would live under his baton, especially German orchestral music. He proved, however, to be a master of German music as well, and gave polished performances which received rave notices and placed him among the world's finest conductors. He was a composer too, but none of his music has survived. He wrote some oratorios in the best "Handel wig" tradition. He apparently had control of all elements of the production in the opera theater—a situation which often caused friction, as one might imagine; in Costa's case, the drama backstage was often more interesting than the stage work which was being performed. Most English music historians tell us that Costa was just the right man at the right time to put English orchestras on a firm footing, placing them in a class with those in other continental capitals.

Franz Liszt (1811-1886) was one of the first of a long line of pianist-composer-conductor virtuosi. As a conductor Liszt's contributions while director of music at the court in Weimar (1848-1861) were enormous, not only for his own works—which were exciting new essays in orchestral composition—but also for his tireless championing of significant new music by such worthies as Wagner. Liszt was one of the greatest pianists the world has ever known, and carried over into his handling of the orchestra the same demand for brilliant playing which he made on himself. While at Weimar he took the basic programmatic idea of the concert overture, loosened the form and came up with the "symphonic tone poem" as a vital new musical art form. Liszt had learned about orchestral music by making excellent versions of many new orchestral works into piano solos. In Weimar he showed the same sensitivity as a conductor, and played what must have been exciting performances of such works as Schubert's *Alfonso and Estrella*, Schumann's *Genoveva*, Berlioz's *Benvenuto Cellini* and Wagner's *Flying Dutchman, Tannhäuser* and *Lohengrin*. Note that these works represent the two main trends among the most important composers of the time. The attention to the Schubert work so many years after his death is, in a way, ironic: Schubert tried so hard to get the officials in Vienna interested in it!

This fascinating man, Liszt, also found time to teach and advise many pianists and composers—among them Edward MacDowell (1861-1908), one of America's first composers to achieve any kind of recognition in Europe, and who also wrote some very stimulating essays on music.[22] (The student should see Strunk's *Source Readings in Music History, the Romantic Era* for an excerpt from Liszt's essay "Berlioz and His 'Harold Symphony,'" as well as Haraszti's article "Liszt—Author Despite Himself" in the *Musical Quarterly*, XXXIII, 490-516.) Liszt's music, by and large, sounds a little old-fashioned to us today, but a good performance can still be meaningful. He should be remembered for his tremendous contributions to music, and not merely for his compositions.

Space permits only this brief discussion of the development of conducting and conductors as it came to the point where the modern orchestra was clearly established. There were a host of other greats such as Nikisch and Seidl, in addition to those who were also important composers in the last half of the century (such as Mahler, R. Strauss, Tchaikovsky, Dvořák and Verdi). It remains only to point out one grave practical difficulty, which must have been very trying to musicians who were on tour. Pitch was anything but standardized until after about 1860, and then not completely. The A above middle C varied from as low as 427 to as high as 446 from city to city. Players of woodwinds who moved to new cities had to buy new instruments in order to match the local pitch. This might explain *some* of the extreme passages which we meet from time to time with respect to pitch. (Musicians with absolute pitch must have been in misery!) However, it may have been something which one became used to and lived with. Berlioz was concerned about the pitch climbing any higher; he worried that his beloved Gluck operas would be too high for singers if the trend continued.

The working conditions of the men in the orchestras were highly variable, and a study of this problem would require yet another book. Throughout the century the lot of the musician was improving, but there are still problems today in being able to pay living wages to orchestra personnel. The development of labor unions within orchestras and opera companies has helped in many countries, and government support has helped in others. Radio, motion pictures, television and the recording industries have changed conditions considerably. These media use more nineteenth-century music than any other kind, while the proportion of contemporary music played in performances of all kinds is the lowest in history!

The professional and community orchestras in the United States owe much to many conductors who came here from Europe after, in most cases, successful careers. Many of these men were also composers, but usually ones of minor importance. Many fine musicians are much better because they compose; it is not essential that all music written should be immortal. The act of composition is especially helpful to the conductor. It helps him to understand the structure of music through his own composing. By the same token, a fine composer can become better by keeping in touch with performance. Most great composers have been at least *good* performers. Some careers were very frustrating for the musician, however, since a top level was not achieved; also, some talents spread themselves too thin by trying to excel in too many different areas. (How sad that music should have produced so many self-styled "geniuses"!) Many of the successful conductors found that they were not good composers, but were expert orchestrators; many symphony programs have been padded by their arrangements. Some orchestrations, of course, were beautifully done, but many were of doubtful value. (Isn't there enough neglected music to perform?) The very best orchestrations of this type, however, have been done by important composers (such as Ravel's orchestration of Mussorgsky's *Pictures at an Exhibition*, Rimsky-Korsakov's many settings and Schoenberg's arrangements of Bach organ works). Many orchestrations were done for practical reasons: reduced orchestrations for theater and school orchestras, orchestral music for the concert band, piano and other non-orchestral music arranged for use in ballets or other theatrical pieces, expanded orchestrations of small orchestral pieces made over for larger orchestras. At worst, the "hit tunes" of a work are taken out of context and over-sentimentalized into "semi-classical" music.

Summary

The term *texture* is not a very good one to use, although it is generally used in the literature. Terms which apply more aptly to music itself would be words such as *melody, harmony* or *rhythm*. Texture is a word best used with fabrics, or perhaps even food. It is a word which requires a *tactile* appreciation and is at best only a figure of speech, an attempt to find an aural expression for a tactile sensation.

As used with music, texture refers to the number and disposition of voices, from monophonic solo chant to a dense score such as the recent *Atmospheres* by György Ligeti, which even outdoes the famous Benevoli mass in the actual number of voices used. The analogy seems to come from the interweaving of voices as the "warp and woof" of the musical fabric. This is all well and good if one is talking about only the masses and motets of the high Renaissance; it seems to be "stretching the wool" a bit when one considers the enormous possibilities of orchestral writing in composers such as Wagner, Liszt, Reger, Strauss, *et al.*!

Almost all music except for the extremes mentioned above has a mixture of polyphony and homophony, with one taking the most important interest and then the other, or one having both (*both* polyphony and homophony can be heard in many important scores from 1850 to the present).

This concept must be one of the most important contributions of the nineteenth century: a *purposeful* lack of clarity. This is important in much coloristic orchestration. Clarity was of the utmost importance in the Classical Period and throughout much of the Romantic Period; that is, there was a principal melody which was accompanied in some manner. The Baroque produced many works in two written parts: a main melodic line and a basso continuo, with the chords filled in. The concept of a melody set off against an accompaniment of lesser importance (*homophony*) is still an ideal in much music written today. The nineteenth century showed us that such an ideal is only one of many possibilities, and that factors of musical density or even "space" become important as well. Orchestration, chord voicing, kind of harmony (relation to overtones of lowest notes), loudness, rhythm, tempo and probably many other factors are all vital; lumping them all into the term *texture* simply does not seem adequate. We can find many adjectives which tell us much about cloth or dumplings or rugs, but when applied to music we ask the reader to indulge in synesthesias which he may not have! One can appreciate the roughness of a tweed by feeling it, or the smoothness of silk and satin; these are characteristics of their textures. In *music*, however, these would be articulations, not texture *per se* (see Apel, *Harvard Dictionary*, page 742). Therefore, I use the word under protest!

In the nineteenth century the melodic line itself had different textures:

I. 1. A thin line, as in an unaccompanied solo instrument such as a flute.
    2. A thin line with chordal accompaniment.
    3. A thin line with figurated accompaniment, quasi-contrapuntal.
    4. A thin line with a secondary thin-line melody (such as another flute), with the above variations.
    5. An instrument with a different tessitura to achieve various effects (the sound of a solo horn seems to be thicker than that of a solo flute but not as thick as that of a tuba).

    The low register of almost every instrument seems to be thicker, the double reeds especially. Is thickness a function of register? Is thickness an aspect of texture one hears? Octaves and fifths are "hollow," while complete triads are "full" and tone clusters are still thicker (see the very beginning of the *Alpine Symphony* of Strauss).

II. The melodic line can be a simple instrument doubled by another simple instrument at the unison, the octave, the double octave or at other intervals. This, of course, changes the thickness or texture of that particular line. In orchestration, remember that the composer has at his disposal the possibility of an instrument *A* an octave above instrument *B* or *B* an octave above *A*, etc. The solo doubling can, obviously, be accompanied by the devices listed in I. above, or it can be one strand of nearly equal voices, as in a fugue or in some coloristic writing.

III. Heavy unisons are known before the Romantic Period, but are not pursued in the way that men such as Beethoven, Liszt, Tchaikovsky and others have done. (This refers to unaccompanied quasi-recitatives with many instruments; the finale of the Beethoven *Ninth* has several for the cello and bass which have few instrumental prototypes. Later composers use baritone and bass instruments for this purpose, almost to a fault, for such things as transitions and modulations.)

    Although Alban Berg's opera *Wozzeck* is a twentieth-century work, one finds perhaps the ultimate use of this device on one note.

IV. The massed sound of a section was well-known through the use of larger and larger string sections, and composers in the Romantic orchestra experimented with many possibilities, including: any one of the string sections on the theme with various kinds of accompaniments, any section divided in octaves on the theme, any two sections at the octave or double octave or three sections at various octaves. The last movement of Tchaikovsky's *Sixth Symphony* has some very beautiful examples of this subtlety.

V. String sections can be doubled by a solo wind, with three different results possible: 1) the solo wind predominating; 2) the strings predominating; or 3) both of equal importance. The composer does not always indicate which he really wants, so it is either up to the conductor or up to chance, depending on how efficient or concerned the conductor is. It is possible, of course, for the same passage to be done differently by different conductors or players and still be beautifully done; this is one of the many contrasts in interpretation that one can hear from one performance to another. It must be emphasized that at the beginning of the nineteenth century almost all scores were composed with single dynamics in mind, but as the century progressed greater variations developed. The student can learn much through studying various scores with this in mind—compare any Beethoven symphony to any Mahler symphony.

Also of importance is the fact that this doubling can occur simultaneously at various octaves. While some composers do this for strength, others are very much aware of the subtle differences in texture which can result.

VI. The late nineteenth century saw many examples of more massive unisons, with many different instruments on the same line. Puccini used these almost to a fault, but his music is still expressive. Lesser composers obtain a massed sound which becomes a rather dirty grey, just as one would get by mixing too many colors of paint or too many ingredients in a stew. It goes without saying that these scores are sometimes performed with beauty by great orchestras, and that some scores which *seem* to be overdone when new become quite expressive upon greater familiarity by the orchestra and the audience (Brahms is the best example). Some scores, however, will forever sound like beginning band books!

VII. The student should now imagine the almost infinite possibilities of combinations of the foregoing and the additional possibilities of counterpoint scored in these ways—not only countermelodies or descants, but also formal counterpoint such as fugues, where each "voice" would be a broad band of sound. (See the chapter on counterpoint.)

There is no word for this element which is better than texture; but, as readily seen from the foregoing, this word is inadequate. While this discussion refers mainly to orchestration, similar principles apply to almost all composition in the nineteenth century. Orchestration could go only so far, and a decided reaction set in during the second decade of the twentieth century; the huge forces called for in works such as Mahler's *Eighth Symphony* and Schoenberg's *Gurrelieder* were used less and less, and the major composers became more interested in chamber music, even chamber orchestras for operas and ballets. This is not to say that the large orchestra went out of vogue—far from it. The huge virtuoso orchestra seems to be here to stay. Recent works using serial techniques have shown that the vast resources inherent in different systems of musical logic have by no means been exhausted.

Notes

1. From *The History of Orchestration* by Adam Carse, Dover Publications, Inc., New York, 1925, p. 1. Reprinted through permission of the publisher.

2. Each generation needs to update orchestration texts (for obvious reasons), yet the great books of the past still have much to say. The art of orchestration should be studied by all musicians, not for arranging a piano piece for orchestra but for acquiring a sound knowledge of this subtle art, perhaps the most neglected facet of music. Good recent texts are by Piston, McKay, Kennan and Rauscher.

3. From Carse, *op. cit.*, p. 225. Reprinted through permission of the publisher.

4. The eye as a receptor receives very high frequencies and the ear the low ones. There remains the nagging question: what happens to the frequencies which are too high to hear and too low to see?

5. For a thorough study of early violin playing see David Boyden, *The History of Violin Playing from Its Origins to 1761* (London: Oxford University Press, 1965). On page 128 Boyden states: "The theorists occasionally mention technical matters before they can be found in music. Mersenne, for instance, describes the violin mute in 1636, but no surviving music calls for it until Lully's time, some years later." There is also the possibility that musicians did many things not notated, especially in the Baroque. Boyden also points out that many advanced technical devices did not survive the player, since they were regarded as professional secrets.

6. The German word "Urtext" means an original printing made from the manuscript without any editing, a valuable source for the scholar and the performer who wishes to know such things as the composer's original slurs, articulations, dynamics and nuances.

7. Alfred Einstein, *Music in the Romantic Era* (New York: W. W. Norton & Company, Inc., 1947), pp. 7-8.

8. The recorder in Bach scores is called *Blockflöte*, while the other flute is *flauto transverso*. When *flauto* is used, it means recorder.

9. The piccolo transposes up an octave from the written notes. There is an alto flute in G which transposes down a perfect fourth. Berlioz, in his treatise on orchestration, refers to flutes in D and E-flat which are called for in some scores of his time. C flutes are almost universal now, but some symphonic bands use the E-flat model.

10. Works by J. S. Bach such as the *Christmas Oratorio, St. Matthew Passion,* several of the cantatas and the *Second Brandenburg Concerto* have prominent double reed parts. Bach used the oboe, oboe d'amore and oboe da caccia. The last two named are now obsolete, and the parts are played on the English horn.

11. For a good discussion of the invention and early use of valves see Carse, *op. cit.,* pp. 207-211.

12. The fundamental is not produced by all of the brasses. When they are used they are called *pedal tones,* and are restricted to the trombone and the horn. The trumpet fundamental is not used, so the instrument begins with the second partial, which is lowered as much as a tritone by the valves. The old crooked trumpets were twice as long as the modern valved instruments in the same key; this sometimes presents a problem in playing the older scores, since the second partial of the older instrument is the fundamental of the newer one.

13. Adam Carse, *The Orchestra from Beethoven to Berlioz* (Cambridge: W. Heffer and Sons, Ltd., 1948), pp. 415-416.

14. Also called *Turmmusik,* a type of brass music played in the towers of seventeenth-century German cities. This music was used to announce a variety of occasions or special events, such as the time of day and warnings.

15. Louis Jullien (1812-1860) was a very strange phenomenon (see p. 267 in this chapter). He established "pop" concerts and performed all sorts of histrionics on the podium, confusing noise for greatness.

16. The string bass was made so tall that a man had to stand on a box to play it! Novelty of instrument has always been more appreciated by the general public than novelty of the music itself. A one-man band playing "There's a Tavern in the Town" gets more attention than a great pianist playing Beethoven's *Sonata Op. 106*—a far more difficult feat!

17. Far more successful is combination with strings or brasses.

18. Orchestration can be learned by the composer only by actually hearing what he has done. Not all composers have had this opportunity, and some of those who have should have done better!

19. David Ewen, *The Man with the Baton* (New York: Thos. Crowell Co., 1936), pp. 78-79.

20. Einstein, *op. cit.,* p. 104.

21. Gilbert Chase, *America's Music* (New York: McGraw-Hill Book Company, Rev. 2nd Ed., 1966), pp. 327-332.

22. See, for example, Gilbert Chase, *The American Composer Speaks* (Baton Rouge: Louisiana State University Press, 1966), pp. 77-87.

KEYBOARD AND SOLO MUSIC

IN THE NINETEENTH CENTURY piano music developments paralleled developments in other kinds of music but it also had fascinating lines of its own, especially in the field of popular music (such as ragtime in the United States). The instrument we loosely call the piano was actually experiencing an important evolution during the first half of the nineteenth century; the final stage is usually held to be the principle of cross-stringing which, although invented as early as 1830 by A. Babcock, was finalized by Steinway and Sons about 1855. Changes since then have been mostly those of refinement. The pianoforte which was important to the early nineteenth century was the Broadwood (John Broadwood, 1732-1812). It was so successful that it eclipsed the harpsichord and took on the tonal characteristics we associate with true piano sound. Its construction was much heavier, allowing for greater tension and thus more sonority, as well as a somewhat heavier action than that of the pianos built on the continent (Beethoven preferred Broadwoods); it also had the pedals, which still survive. There were fantastic experiments with all kinds of pedals, including special stops for military effects and the like; many of these devices today are largely historical curiosities. Experimentation was also made in over-all design and shape for practical and acoustical reasons. The upright became the family instrument and was found in homes both great and humble. The great artists were beginning to emerge: virtuosi who changed the course of music history, who demanded the grand piano with a truly grand tone to fill the halls

Plate XII

Beethoven's piano as preserved in the Beethoven house in Bonn
(Courtesy The Bettmann Archive, N.Y.).

with sound. The big sounds which resulted were the combination of the technique of the pianist and the efficiency of the instrument. Also emerging was the amateur who played for the fun of it; his performance was humble in sound and technique. Needless to say, composers obliged with tons of music from both extremes and the countless gradations in between.

The fall from grace of the figured bass removed the necessity of realization on a harpsichord-type instrument; the most important use of the keyboard with orchestra became the solo piano in the concerto.

There is no doubt that the very best solo music for non-keyboard instruments is not to be found in the solo literature *per se,* but in the use of these instruments in a solo capacity as parts of larger works. This excludes sonatas (see the chapter on chamber music) for an instrument with piano or organ or an instrument *unaccompanied.* The concerto also falls in a separate category and is mainly discussed with other orchestal music. There are no flute solos, for example, which can compare in excellence or beauty with those of the orchestral repertoire (such as Beethoven's *Leonore* No. 3, his *Eroica* finale or any Brahms symphony) or the chamber repertoire. The initial motivation for composition is of utmost importance. Most solo music is written for the "dessert" parts of a recital, for programs in the hinterland where art music was once a rarity, for occasions such as special music in church, high society parties and the like. Much of this music is arranged for the instrument from some other work—the "nice" parts are adapted. "Nice" here usually means a beautiful melody which has a direct appeal and in most cases exists for the reason that most music exists: people like to hear it only for enjoyment, and in the nineteenth century the great touring artist would have had little or no success without the short solo piece.

But occasionally one can find a real gem, a short musical inspiration which somehow does not lend itself to development; the single, lovely blossom which would be lost in the bouquet. Sometimes it has a fanciful title, such as L. Schubert's *The Bee* or Hubay's *Le Zephyr*, both for violin and piano; others have generic titles, such as dances, folk songs, rhapsodies, fantasies and the like; others are called simply *Album Leaf*, as if suggesting that the composer really wanted to do something else with this nice musical idea, but it remained a page in an album. Another intriguing category was the solo based on an operatic aria type, such as cavatina, lyric scena or simply aria. Collections were often (and still are) of what the French call *morceau characteristique*, a piece of a certain character. The practical use of these collections by concert artists is obvious; many were written by famous soloists for their own use. Still another use today, as then, is by the student who wants something tuneful, or by the amateur who does not have the technique to play a concerto or the like.

Not all of these solo pieces, however, are simple technically, and some are among the most difficult in the repertoire. One can trace the development of technique for most instruments by studying this literature—especially solos for violin, since the most famous touring virtuosi other than pianists tended to be violinists, while cellists and performers of other instruments were less numerous. The most common concerts often featured more than one performer, each one performing a group of solos. These concerts were held in great salons in the large cities; those in Paris were especially noteworthy. There was competition for favors of all kinds from the audiences, and this certainly motivated the development of a brilliant technique and a beautiful tone. If the audience didn't weep and/or swoon, you were a failure. The soloists developed a kind of showmanship which can still be seen to a certain extent. Some of the pieces were so bad musically that the soloist must have put on a good act along with them to put them over! The stories about Paganini are probably exaggerated, but are based on the kind of behavior the public expected from such an artist. Instrumental soloists took a few pages from the books of the opera stars, and in some cases even outdid them.

The advent of the phonograph has been a sobering influence on the extra-musical aspects of performance—the record lives or dies on how it *sounds*. This, of course, has led to rather unrealistic audience expectations from the live performer, since with tape techniques it is easy to correct a "goof," and one can purchase recordings today which are almost perfect technically. The real excitement of a live concert, however, can never be captured on tape. Wondering if the player will "make" a certain passage is a legitimate part of the enjoyment at a live concert. At least performance standards are higher than ever before; and no longer is there a real hinterland. There will probably never be an end to the importance of the showmanship aspects of musical performance. Many musicians are repulsed by even considering such a thing; some concerts are more mournful than wakes, while others are utterly charming and somehow win the audience by a certain rapport which cannot be learned —it is there, or it is not. (Fritz Kreisler was a prime example.) Other soloists try too hard to win over the audience by all sorts of non-musical devices, from the hideous pasted-on smile of the pop performer to a sort of extravagantly posturing exhibitionism. One of the most common examples of bad taste is misplaced elegance.

The organ and organ music were also undergoing great changes, both technical and musical. More efficient manuals were introduced through applications of principles learned from science and technology, as with other instruments. It should be remembered that the organ key must come back up, in addition to the main problem: causing air to flow through the pipes in the desired ways. It was real physical work to play some of the early organs, since the return mechanism required heavy springs. The "tracker" action had many mechanical levers to open pipes and it was very difficult to manipulate. (In many churches where the console was hidden from the audience the organist may have dressed like a blacksmith, since he had to work as hard as one!) Various pneumatic devices have been used, but the discovery of the possibility of using electromagnets was especially important; the dates at which they were first used on organs are astonishing to the modern reader (a patent was issued as early as 1852). (How strange that organists as a group have always been interested in the latest devices to help them play, but have rarely shown the same interest in new music to play!) The names to remember in the development of the electric-pneumatic system are Albert Péschard (1836-1903) and C. S. Barker, who built successful organs with a joint patent in 1868. Improvements have been made since as more and more electrical knowledge has been amassed. There are even completely electronic organs which have had varying degrees of success.

Similar changes were being made with other age-old problems of organ building, such as the method of producing and transferring the wind pressure, and of activating stops.

Along with these blessings came some curses, in that some organists and organ composers felt that the ideal in organ music was to make the instrument sound like an orchestra. (Automation putting people out of work?) The nineteenth-century organ produced a bewildering variety of stops and couplers differing from country to country, city to city and organ to organ. This variety still disturbs some composers, since they are not really sure how their organ pieces will be "colored" by some of the people who will play them.

But imitating the orchestra did have some practical uses: transcriptions of orchestral parts of oratorios and the like for rehearsal or performance with choirs; transcriptions of orchestral music for study; and, with these varieties of stops, composers with imagination could now derive many unique musical colors, obtainable in no other way.

The greatest organ music came from J. S. Bach and before, but the nineteenth century also produced some of merit. These compositions fall into two main groups: music composed by men who distinguished themselves in other fields of musical composition, and music by those who were themselves important organists. Various countries produced different styles of organ music which, although hardly nationalistic, did reflect to a certain extent some national characteristics. Some composers, such as Liszt, fell into the common error of writing piano keyboard patterns which proved ineffectual on the organ.

Organ music will be discussed throughout this chapter in connection with each composer.

Beethoven

Beethoven's importance as a keyboard composer cannot be accurately assessed, since it is so great. The intrinsic musical value of the works themselves is only part of the story; his influence on piano writing has been "from generation to generation."

His keyboard music can be divided into formal groups:

Sonatas
Variations
Short pieces comprising dances, rondos, Bagatelles, etc.

It can also be divided into more explicit categories:

Piano solo
Piano duet
Piano and orchestra
Piano and another instrument (sonatas and variations)
Piano in a chamber music combination

The concerti are discussed in the chapter on orchestral music, and the piano with other instruments is discussed as chamber music. Beethoven's keyboard writing is quite similar, however, in each category, although there are adjustments made for the medium in question. Most of Beethoven's piano works have a *concertato* style, except for the more simple of the *Bagatelles* or the sonatinas.

Beethoven displays an amazing skill in writing for the piano at an early age (as did Mozart), which well reflects his own ability as a performer. His sonatas for piano solo are much more intimate essays than those of his greatest predecessors. Many have pointed out that these are almost an autobiography; they are at least representative of almost every phase in the development of Beethoven as a composer and as a man. The several sonatas called the "Bonn Sonatas" were written when he was only in his early teens but are prophetic of things to come. They are not included in "complete" printings.

About Beethoven's great thirty-two sonatas (dubbed by some as the pianist's "New Testament," as Bach's *W. T. C.* is the "Old Testament") there is no end of analytical literature, as befits such works of art. It is a shame, however, that most know only the *Pathéthique,* Op. 13; the *"Moonlight" Sonata guasi una Fantasia,* Op. 27, No. 2; the *Waldstein,* Op. 53; and the *Appassionata,* Op. 57; and perhaps a few others. There are perhaps practical reasons—who can really play Op. 106, *The Hammerklavier?*

These sonatas illustrate how Beethoven was a master of the single-movement sonata-form, and most of his first movements are splendid examples. They are all different and prove the principle often expounded that sonata-form is often used, since one can do so much with it. Beethoven experiments with tonalities and key relationships, non-tonic beginnings, long development sections, free recapitulations and lengthy codas. A study of these sonatas just for the purpose of learning about Beethoven's use of sonata-form is well worth the time. The great *Sonata in A-flat,* Op. 26, begins with a set of variations, then a scherzo, a funeral march, and then a very interesting sonata-allegro which is like a perpetual motion.

The second movements range from the Haydnesque ornate yet singing adagios, such as Op. 2, No. 1, to variations such as those in the *Appassionata.* It matters a great deal to the formal structure whether the sonata has two, three or four movements. Op. 111 has but two movements, the second of which is a set of highly-developed variations. Many have three movements, of which the middle movement is a closed form with a definite ending (Op. 13), or is connected to the finale with no definite final cadence (such as Opp. 53 and 57). When there are four movements, the added one is almost always a carry-over from the four-movement symphonic structure and is either a minuetto (Op. 31, No. 3) or a scherzo (Op. 106). Beethoven interchanges the dance or scherzo and the slow movement: the scherzo is the second movement, and the song is the third movement. This is often the case when the tempo of the first movement has not been brilliant (Op. 31, No. 3).

The finales consist of rondos, sonata-rondos, sonata-allegros and, as noted in Op. 111, variations. Note that there are compositional principles which occur in the keyboard sonatas much earlier than in the more highly publicized occasions in his orchestral music. The use of the scherzo is one example: the Trio, Op. 1, No. 1 has a scherzo. In his later sonatas, however, Beethoven uses the scherzo only in Op. 106.

Insight into Beethoven's late period is often discussed but really can't be explained. It is most pronounced in the late string quartets and piano works. The sonatas of Opp. 106, 109, 110 and 111 illustrate this. A few generalities might explain why these works are so different from earlier ones. They are large in length and often large in sound. Forms are stretched beyond their limits, and in some instances one feels that Beethoven has invented a new form for each particular movement. Extreme technical skill is required, not only for playing the brilliant passages, but for playing almost any passage. There are important fugues which become an integral part of the larger form. The fugue in Op. 110 shows that the *Grosse Fuge*, Op. 133, for string quartet was not just a single example of one particular kind of fugue. The fugue in Op. 106 is perhaps even bigger. Interest in Beethoven's handling of the fugue principle has attracted considerable study since World War II. John Cockshoot's *The Fugue in Beethoven's Piano Music*[1] is especially important (1959). Earlier, important analysts were also interested, Tovey and Heinrich Schenker among others. Beethoven also uses devices of fugato and canon in countless places, very often in development sections.

The greatest variations employ large fugues, the *Variations* of Op. 35 called variously *Prometheus* or *Eroica* because of the common thematic material in all these works. *Prometheus* came before Op. 35, and the *Eroica Symphony* afterwards. Beethoven's music, as is often said, depends more on treatment than on the importance of the theme *per se*. The fugue subject of Op. 35 is actually derived from the bass of the *Prometheus* theme, and the theme itself occurs as a countermelody to the subject in F minor (bar 52) followed by two other statements in different keys. In the *Eroica Symphony* finale there are actually variations on both themes, including fugal and canonic treatment. A comparative study of Op. 35 and the *Eroica* finale is rewarding.

The *Variations*, Op. 35, are Janus-like, as is much of Beethoven: they look both forward and backward at the same time. The work begins with a statement of just the unison theme. This is the way the *Eroica* finale begins also, after the mad rushing sixteenth notes. In the piano variations it serves as an introduction, which in a way is comparable to the ground bass formulas so common in the Baroque. The theme proper shows that the music of the introduction is in reality the bass line of the theme.

The variations themselves are technically arresting, in that they may use one theme or the other, or both. At the sixth variation a remarkable bit of writing shows up when the theme appears fundamentally with the same pitches as at the beginning; but the harmonies are in a different tonality, again showing the multiplicity of function which is a starting point for many devices.

The *Diabelli Variations*, Op. 120, have a curious history and have been compared to Bach's *Goldberg Variations* in treatment and design. Anton Diabelli (1781-1858) was a pupil of Haydn but was best-known as a publisher. Diabelli composed an insipid little waltz and then asked fifty composers to submit variations, which were then to be published. Beethoven was late with his set and they were not included in the published volume, but instead wrote one of the largest and most remarkable works in history. The fugue is one of Beethoven's finest; it is actually a double fugue:

VARIATION XXXII BEETHOVEN: *Diabelli Variations*, Op. 120

Figure 11-1

Compare this now to Diabelli's theme!

BEETHOVEN: *Diabelli Variations*, Op. 120: *Diabelli's Theme*

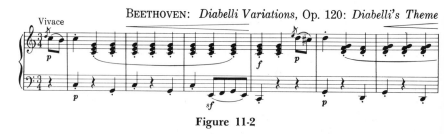

Figure 11-2

Beethoven also wrote a great set of variations sometimes given an opus number of 191. (Few now follow the continued opus numbers of Sir George Grove,[2] since they are quite meaningless.) These are usually called *Thirty-two variations in C Minor* (1806). This work is actually a chaconne with a very short ground, which makes the variations "add up" so that they complement each other. It is a real problem to perform this work, but a great performer can play it with great effect. Here are the theme and a few variations:

Variation XII

Figure 11-3

With these variations Beethoven presents an entirely different approach from that in the variations mentioned above in the Diabelli and in the variations of the *Sonata*, Op. 109. These works (and others as well) use a device called "double variation," in which the composer writes two variations for each strain instead of repeating the strain.

Beethoven wrote many other sets of variations for the piano of differing difficulty and quality. Some are based on his own themes, others on popular arias or other themes.

The short pieces are very uneven in quality. His *Bagatelles* are among the best; some of them presage the short character piece, which became a very important genre for keyboard composers.

The piano duets are not too significant, and organ music is practically non-existent.

Beethoven's keyboard works are very exploratory, introducing sonorities and technical devices not known before. In his late period he employed extreme registers, unusual trills, rhythms and meters, giving music manifold new approaches which influenced many other composers, both positively and negatively. Beethoven obviously believed in equal temperament. In his late keyboard works and in his late quartets, there is a greater subtlety of notation induced not only by his own maturity, which is unique in history, but by his deafness as well. Much has been said about his inner hearing, pro and con. His detractors have said that he wrote music for the eye and not the ear, but great performances prove that in most passages Beethoven was right—his music does sound.

Schubert

Although he was a skilled pianist, Schubert was not the great virtuoso Beethoven was until deafness forced Beethoven to halt his performances. Beethoven was a master of the much admired art of improvisation and was very much a part of concert life early in his career. Schubert, although recognized as a great talent by all who knew him, was scarcely known to the musical public; however, his reputation grew rapidly, until today he has the stature of one of the greatest composers of his time and of all history. These are not idle words; his works wear well—even those which, if less substantial, would have long since worn out (works such as the *Unfinished Symphony*).

Schubert's keyboard music can be classified exactly the same as Beethoven's, with the exception of concerti with orchestra, which he did not see fit to write. It must be remembered that in Schubert's time a virtuoso wrote his own concerti, as did Mozart, Beethoven, Weber and others. Another enormous difference is in the quality of Schubert's four-hand music. According to Einstein he is ". . . not only the most prolific but also the greatest composer of music for four hands. . . ."[3] This means, of course, that the music was intended to be played by two people: four hands at one piano. This kind of *Hausmusik* also includes his chamber music, his early church and orchestral music, his songs and his *Liedertafeln* kind of choral music; Schubert never succeeded in getting a secure position as a professional musician with large ensembles.

Some of his four-hand pieces are small and some are very large, in the dimensions of overtures (in the Italian style). Consider the "Grande Sonata" (D. 617) or "Grand Duo" (D. 812). This duo is really a sonata and is one of his best four-hand works (Joachim even orchestrated it). It is a full four-movement work, employing Schubert's "heavenly length." Some of his shorter works are variations, others include dances, rondos and marches. Most of them are marvelous and could still fill an evening with delight. Piano students would do well to learn them, and composition students might ponder the possibility of writing such ingratiating music for their friends. But how these pieces transcend all this! Perhaps the word "transcendent" is one of the best one could use to characterize Schubert's music. His early teachers often commented that his gift was from God—what else can one say?

Schubert's piano solo works range from very large to very small, from very long sonatas to short piano pieces. There are fifteen piano sonatas from his pen. These are not programmed as often as they should be; and when they are, cuts are often made. Cuts are of two kinds: excisions —which, in the case of a master's work, is inexcusable—and omissions of repeats—which today is almost standard practice, since in many works the thematic material is already known. When repeats occur in sonata-allegro movements, they usually are in the expositions. The developments and recapitulations are almost never repeated. In the other movements it is largely a question of performance time. Large binary slow movements may stand very well without repeats, but periodic variations should probably be repeated. The whole formal idea of the piece is

Plate XIII

Evening entertainment among Schubert's friends, with the composer at the left. Wash drawing by Franz Lachner *(Courtesy The Bettmann Archive, N.Y.)*.

usually lost if they are not. This is especially true in double variations, where the composer writes out a different variation some of the time and uses repeat signs for the others.

Schubert knew the music of Beethoven and admired it, but Schubert's music is almost always lyrical or brilliant; his sonatas, therefore, do not afford the great variety of expression that one finds in Beethoven's sonatas. In Schubert development sections are much less important— the theme *itself* is the important thing, not the treatment.

The first important sonata is the *Sonata in A Minor*, Op. 164, D. 537. The opening is almost Brahmsian.

Schubert's keyboard works are striking studies in the use of enharmonic relationships and extreme keys. The *Sonata in F Minor*, D. 625, is a good example, even though Schubert left this sonata incomplete. Incomplete works should never be overlooked, since they give us insights into the artist—why are they unfinished? Do we have an incomplete copy of a work which was completed but of which the final copy was lost? Did the composer lose his thread of thought? In Schubert's music especially, these are important questions.

The *Sonata in A Major*, Op. 120, D. 664, is justly popular, and is one of the smallest of the sonatas. The greatest sonata is considered his last—the *B-flat*, D. 960—but the last three form a great triumvirate. All three are very fine piano music just for playing and listening, and are rewarding to study for their excellent modulations and skilled keyboard writing.

The largest work is probably the *Wanderer Fantasy*, D. 760, so-called because the second movement is based on one line of his song *Der Wanderer* ("Die Sonne dünkt mich hier so kalt"). Here is the section from the song:

Figure 11-4

Here are some excerpts from the piano piece, which is technically important, since Kirby states that it is: ". . . the first large piano work which is completely cast in cyclic form."[4] The techniques Schubert used anticipated Liszt and Franck, and the piece was arranged faithfully for piano and orchestra by Liszt:

Figure 11-5

The contrapuntal writing in the finale is also significant.

Schubert's small pieces, like Beethoven's, led to small piano pieces in great profusion. Schubert used some generic titles, such as *Moments Musicales* or *Impromptus*. The *Impromptus* are quite important and are by no means easy to play.

For an introduction to Schubert's keyboard works the student should perhaps either hear or play through the great *B-flat Major Sonata*, which comes very near the end of his life. The slow movement is especially beautiful. Willi Apel is so right when he speaks of this movement as the "swan song," not only of a man, but of an era.[5]

Schubert's works for violin and piano are important examples of *Hausmusik*; although they are properly chamber works, the piano part is by far the more difficult and of greater importance musically. All violinists delight in playing the three sonatinas, especially the *D Major*. Violists and cellists play a curious work: an arrangement of a work Schubert dashed off for an odd instrument, the arpeggione (the sonata is named for the instrument). The themes are beautiful, but the technical passages are mechanical and contrived. There are also a large violin sonata, a rondo, a fantasy, a set of variations, some Ländler for violin and piano and some variations for flute and piano on his own song "Trockne Blumen," from *Die Schöne Müllerin*. These works are all very tuneful and deserve performance now and again; they somehow have never captured the popularity of the violin sonatinas, Op. 137, mentioned above. These sonatinas are all striking examples of Schubert's own, original approach to harmony. His uses of augmented sixth chords, enharmonic relationships and other devices are quite outstanding.

Aside from a fugue, Schubert's organ writing was confined to rather routine accompaniments for church music.

Other Keyboard Composers

There were many composers, such as Weber and a host of lesser lights, who wrote many good piano works which are well worth the study. There was the usual bifurcation: those who tended toward romanticism and those who continued a pallid classicism. Cherubini's sonatas are fine, but a little old-fashioned, even for him. There was Carl Czerny (1791-1857), pupil of Beethoven and teacher of Liszt, perhaps one of the greatest keyboard teachers, who wrote many exercises for pianists which are still studied today. Muzio Clementi (1752-1832) came somewhat earlier, but was important as one of the first keyboard composers who developed a style of writing which suited the piano and its characteristics, although he had a considerable reputation as a performer on the harpsichord. He wrote many works in various media, including many sonatas well-known to piano pupils and an interesting series of keyboard etudes called *Gradus ad Parnassum*—applying to a piano work a title well-known to musicians of his time (the counterpoint treatise of Johann Fux (1660-1741)).

The Fux treatise, written in 1725, was very important in the education of musicians in the nineteenth century. This work presents a fascinating history of master-pupil relationships: Mozart studied it with his father and with Martini (1706-1784); Haydn taught Beethoven from a summary of Fux which Haydn had made; Beethoven also learned of it from Albrechtsberger (1736-1809), who taught it to Marxsen, who taught it to Brahms—and so it went. This study of Fux is an important reminder that the nineteenth-century composer who was well-trained was not ignorant of the modes, at least as Fux taught them. Many preludes, fugues and inventions were frank Baroque imitations which were played and used for keyboard study.

There were other types of small piano pieces, of the "teaching" variety: short character pieces which might still be studies or might have fanciful titles. Many of these are minuets and other dances.

A good example of the first is "Etude" by Ludwig Berger (1777-1839), and of the second Johann Cramer's (1771-1858) "I pensieri dolente" ("Sad Thoughts").

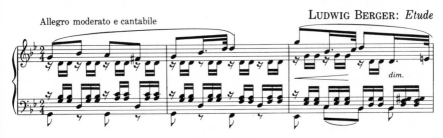

Figure 11-6

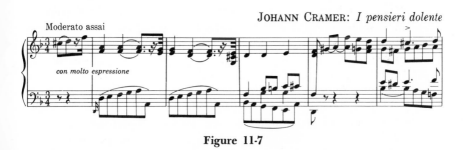

Figure 11-7

These are two brief samples from a voluminous literature.

Mendelssohn

Much more significant are the short piano pieces of Mendelssohn, Schumann, Chopin and Brahms. Mendelssohn was prolific in these, producing generic titles such as *Songs Without Words*. Some of these pieces have individual titles, and various editions use different titles, depending on the mood of the editor. People in the late nineteenth century were especially delighted by fanciful titles. The *Songs Without Words* are modest pieces, but not all are easy to play. As is often pointed out, Mendelssohn's phrase structure is frightfully predictable, and his emotional plane is more that of a genteel drawing room than that of an everyday living room.

It is significant that Mendelssohn has been given credit for being the first major composer to use the term "character piece" as a generic term (see Kirby,[6] p. 253, and Kahl,[7] *in toto*, for interesting discussions of this).

Another generic term which begins to appear is "Caprice" or "Capriccio"—which can be almost anything, as the title would imply: a "caprice" or whim of the moment. A famous work is the *Rondo capriccioso*, Op. 14, which is like any number of brilliant pieces, but has Mendelssohn's "elfinscherzo" touch.

Among the larger works are three sets of variations. The most important is the set *Variations sérieuses in D Minor*, Op. 54. This is a unique work; each variation itself could be called a "character variation." There are three sonatas which are somewhat influenced by Beethoven, but these are not as important musically as the Bach-influenced preludes and fugues. One of the most arresting is the fugue in E minor, which uses, as a quasi-chorale, *Ein feste Burg*. This fugue gathers tempo and momentum as it progresses—a custom sometimes observed in the fugal overture to Mendelssohn's *Elijah*.

Mendelssohn's Bach-influence is also found in his rather short list of organ works, which are of prime importance in the history of nineteenth-century organ music. Aside from the preludes and fugues, the six sonatas are of some importance and are well-known to most organ students. These works came into being thanks to the English admiration for Mendelssohn in general and for his organ playing in particular (he was known for remarkable pedal technique). The sonatas were first suggested to be published under the title of "Voluntaries," since it was thought the erudite term "sonata" might frighten potential purchasers. As Werner[8] points out, these works are sonatas in the loose application of the word; perhaps "suites" is a better term. The works had great teaching value from the very beginning, and were advertised as such. One can find great variety from movement to movement in these sonatas, but perhaps not often enough within one movement. Mendelssohn is not always "churchy," but his more sentimental movements have accompanied the passing of the offertory plate in many churches in England and America.

The concerted pieces with orchestra are very uneven in quality, none matching the excellence of the great *Violin Concerto*, Op. 64. The piano concerti were once very popular, especially the G Minor, but the inner parts of some movements do not maintain the great promise of the openings. The *Concerto in D Minor*, No. 2, Op. 40 (1837), has some lovely passages. The shorter works for piano and orchestra are brilliant and contain moments of great beauty; too often, however, passages are padded with etude-like writing with little musical substance.

Schumann

The most important out-and-out romantic piano composer of his time, aside from Chopin, was Schumann. His piano music was among the first music labeled "romantic" in the press—but not as a compliment. The story of his maimed hand which ruined a concert career is well-known; perhaps, as some have said, it was an "act of God" to make him turn to composition. There are some important biographical details in his career which need to be mentioned. He, unlike most composers, wrote most of his best music quite early in his career; his mental illness late in life possibly robbed the world of still greater riches.

His piano concerto is one of the best, and is discussed in the chapter on orchestral music. His sonatas are some of the best in the post-Beethoven period, although the sonata was in a state of decline. Some have laughed at Schumann for his tempo markings in the first movement of the *Sonata in G Minor*, Op. 22 ("as fast as possible," and later "still faster"). The tempo of the opening "as fast as possible" can be made still faster later, since the figuration can be played faster at the later point. The slow movement of this sonata is especially beautiful; the theme is from his song "Im Herbste."

The *Sonata in F Minor*, Op. 14, had originally been called by Schumann "Concerto without Orchestra," and the *F-sharp Minor Sonata* is an effective work. Schumann was most at home in character pieces or in collections of short pieces or suites. The other large piano work of great importance is the *Fantasia in C*, Op. 17, which he dedicated to Liszt and which was no doubt influenced by the Schubert *Wanderer Fantasy*. The "fantasy" idea would appeal to the romantic composer, since it is fantastic by definition, although as a generic title it has meant different things to different generations. This large work is often discussed in writings, since it is a virtuoso work of the highest quality. It combines the best features of Schumann's music: vitality of rhythm and harmony, singing melody, economy of means and much use of seemingly little material. One aspect often observed in Schumann is the use of the left hand in a figuration which might be an Alberti bass but often contains hidden counterfigures. The march must have been known to later composers, who have written massive chords which can't really be played without arpeggiation:

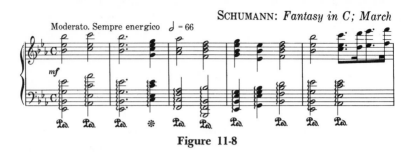

Figure 11-8

Franck, for example, uses the same device:

Figure 11-9

When approaching the small works of Schumann, one does not know where to begin. Some of them are actually summations of smaller works, which become thereby "big" works—such as the *Symphonic Etudes*, which are in reality character variations.

A chronological list is impressive, and a well-played hearing is even more impressive. Note how many of these works are cycles of character pieces (see Chapter III), where the older ideas of unity through tonality, form and symmetry are all but replaced by the careful handling of musical motives, moods and a propensity for the ABA form. Here are some of the most important pieces:

Papillons (Op. 2, 1830-1831)
Die Davidsbündler ("The Society of David") (Op. 6, 1837)
Carnaval (Op. 9, 1834-1835)
Fantasiestücke (Op. 12, 1837; contains "Aufschwung" and "Warum")
Kinderscenen (Op. 15, 1838; contains "Träumerei")
Kreisleriana (Op. 16, 1838)
Faschingsschwank aus Wien (Op. 26, 1839)

Also important are the *Abegg Variations* and variations on music written by Clara in which the variations come from both the melody line and the bass line. Some of his best variation writing occurs in the lovely *Andante and Variations* for two pianos.

A peculiar set of short pieces is the *Album für die Jugend* (Op. 68, 1848), numbering forty-three (plus eight or nine not in the original publication). They are in two main parts: the first, "Für Kleinere" ("Little Folks"), and the second, "Für Erwachsenere" ("Grown-ups"). Many of these selections are among the best-known of Schumann's compositions (such as the "Happy Farmer").

The *Waldscenen* (Op. 82) are extremely appealing. The atmosphere of No. 7, "Vogel als Prophet" ("Prophetic Bird"), is most unusual.

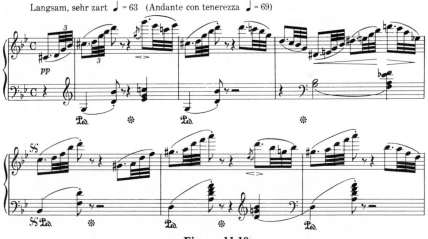

Figure 11-10

Schumann's piano writing for chamber music is considerable; he wrote effective solos for horn, clarinet, cello, viola and piano which contain some of his most beautiful music, although they are not as "showy" as solos by other composers. His violin sonatas are among the best between Beethoven and Brahms, but suffer from the difficulty of their violin passage work.

There are some clever works for "pedal-piano" (now sometimes played on the organ) and six fugues on the name of Bach for organ.

Schumann's contributions to the literature are enormous, but in a different way from those of Beethoven and Schubert. Schumann wrote some of the best short works ever written and, unlike many of his contemporaries, their musical construction has great internal subtlety even though the larger aspects of the form are often simple ternary. Schumann must be counted among the composers for whom the germ (or *Urkeim*) was important.

Chopin and Liszt

Chopin and Liszt provide an obvious contrast. Chopin's music falls mostly into generic titles: etudes, dances (such as mazurkas, waltzes, polonaises, ecossaises and tarentellas), scherzi, nocturnes, variations, sonatas, concertos, ballades, preludes (without fugues!) rondos, impromptus and others with simple tempo markings. As romantic as Chopin's music is, little of it has a romantic title except for a nickname here and there.

Much of Liszt's music has poetic titles and much of it was undoubtedly inspired by literature. Liszt also has many works which have only generic titles. How odd that Chopin, "the poet of the piano," was influenced in his music hardly at all by poetry! He wrote but seventeen Polish songs (the "Maiden's Wish" is the best-known). He knew many men of letters in the salons of Paris, but he did not share their new ideas of art, although in a way he was ahead of them. Chopin's music was influenced by his feelings about Poland (although he never returned), women (although he never married), Italian opera (although he wrote no operas) and by a study of J. S. Bach (although formal counterpoint is rarely a factor in his works). The most important factor is his own originality, which apparently was as evident in his playing as it was in his compositions. Liszt, on the other hand, was not such a "loner." For Liszt, conducting was an important activity in addition to his teaching, writing and theorizing about the "music of the future." Liszt was influential in the development of Berlioz and Wagner. It is doubtful if the music of any of these three would have developed as it did without the other two. The impact of these three men on each other is as fascinating as it is important. Berlioz concentrated on the orchestra; Liszt tried almost everything and was himself one of the greatest pianists of all time, while Wagner and his theories were concentrated almost exclusively in music dramas. Another influence which must be noted is that of other virtuosi, especially Paganini and Alkan.

With Chopin, the particular importance of Bellini must be pointed out. Chopin could make the piano sing almost like a Bellini aria: he wrote beautiful cantilenas. From another direction Chopin was influenced by the piano styles of the composers of those short pieces which we have mentioned so often. John Field (1782-1837) was certainly a major influence.

The added ingredient in Chopin's music was his unique approach to harmony, which bothered so many of his contemporaries, fellow pianists and critics. Chopin's music often employs a very fast harmonic rhythm moving very quickly from one harmony to another, touching on cadences just here and there. Some of Chopin's harmony seemed so blurred to early auditors that they "allowed" it on the grounds that it was a colorful iridescence, or a series of non-harmonic chords, an extension of the idea of non-harmonic tones, or even non-harmonic successions between the tonal pillar chords which maintain the key. These techniques, used also by others, are among those which seriously weaken the importance of the tonal cadences inside the music, approaching what has been called "the emancipation of dissonance."

The piano works of Liszt, as has been pointed out, show similar freedoms of harmony; they even go beyond, to the extent of no tonality at all in a key sense. These works do not always exploit the more acrid dissonances and never really depart from a basic tertian approach to harmony.

The student should investigate such Liszt works as "Unstern" ("Bad Luck"); "Csardas Macabre"; *Die trauerige Gondola* ("The Sorrowful Gondola," probably a funeral cortege of boats in Venice); and especially the *Malediction* for piano and string orchestra for great harmonic advances and an important adjunct of Liszt's work which even anticipates expressionism in harmonic technique and subject matter. The *Totentanz* is not a one-shot work, but represents one of several in that necrophiliac tone and mood.

Most of Liszt's music lies unplayed today, although the list of recordings is impressive. The enormous scope of his music can be appreciated only by perusing the thematic catalogue and the collected works. While it is true that Liszt is probably the only major composer who had assistance in such details as orchestration (from Raff and others), one is still amazed at the vitality of the man who not only wrote a large number of original works, but made many transcriptions of orchestral works by other composers (notably the complete symphonies of Beethoven and the *Fantastic Symphony* of Berlioz). There are also many, many songs, opera scenes and the like arranged for concert use. There is even a version of Berlioz's *Lélio* (the ill-fated sequel to the *Fantastic*) arranged for piano and orchestra, which was actually performed by Liszt with Berlioz conducting. These works all require almost the utmost in piano virtuosity; the sheer manual labor of writing so many notes in the technical passages and cadenzas is so laborious that one really wonders when he ever found the time to compose them! The technical exploitation of the piano by Liszt was inspired by the virtuosity of Paganini. Liszt realized that his music would require a different kind of piano technique and he obliged by writing *Transcendental Etudes*, which transcended the technical difficulties of any other etudes up to that time. There are two sets of these, one with completely original music. The other uses the famed Paganini *Caprices* as a point of departure. Number six uses the twenty-fourth caprice, the one which has attracted so many other composers.

The original *Transcendental Etudes* were written three times, and each new version was more difficult than the one before. In the third version titles began to appear which have remained; hence, they are extreme examples of character pieces. The Paganini set was composed first (1838, revised 1851) and was followed by a set of three *Etudes de Concert* (1849), the third of which is the well-known *Etude in D-flat*, sometimes given the title "Un sospiro." The second set of *Transcendental Etudes* was written in 1851, a second set of *Etudes de Concert* in 1862-1863 and the single Etude "Ab-Irato" in 1852. These were all written before his important orchestral works and reflect his concentration on the piano and piano technique. The titles given to the etudes reflect a variety of subjects: "Mazeppa," "Vision," "Eroica" or "Harmonies du soir." Some have only a tempo marking; No. 1 is called "Preludio."

Chopin's etudes are given nicknames, but are also "transcendental" in a subjective way, in that the meaning of the music transcends any etude or exercise. The Chopin etudes contain some of the most poetic piano music ever written. There are twenty-seven etudes in three separate sets: twelve each from Op. 10 and Op. 25 and the three "New Etudes" written for the piano method of Moscheles and Fétis which had the modest title *Méthode des méthodes* (Liszt's "Ab-Irato" was in this book, too).

The sonatas of the two men can be compared almost the same as one can compare their concerti. Chopin's first sonata is his Op. 4, and is unique only in the use of $\frac{5}{4}$ in the slow movement. The mature sonatas are the *B-flat*, Op. 35, and the *B Minor*, Op. 58, written in 1837 and 1844. These were mentioned in Chapter IV, where it was pointed out that they lack the inner cohesion of the great classical sonatas but still show Chopin's own unity. Liszt's *Sonata in B Minor* (1852-1853) uses the same kind of construction as his concerti and his symphonic tone poems: building on the *Urkeim*, or germ motive or motives, which here are heard near the beginning and permeate the entire work, which is sectional and rhapsodic. This sonata could have a program, but doesn't. It might be called a long development section. Often the works of the romantics were *called* formless simply because the classical forms were not used. It is quite apparent in the works of some composers that it might have been better if such literal attention to form had not been exercised. Two good examples are the first movements of the Chopin sonatas; these may have "too many ideas," as any number of critics have said. Weinstock[9] believes that the fault in movements such as these lies with the performers more than with Chopin.

If the Liszt *B Minor Sonata* is a sonata built like a tone poem, the *Après une lecture de Dante, Fantasia quasi Sonata* really is one. The opening tritone octaves have strong touches of brimstone. This work is also cyclic and is technically fiendish.

Liszt's *First Concerto*, the well-known *E-flat*, also begins with awesome octaves. This concerto's chromatic motto at the beginning is supposed to suggest a mocking text which has a kernel of truth, perhaps even today: "Du verstehst es alle nicht!" ("You don't understand this at all"). The work is very intriguing in many ways. It is beautifully orchestrated and the orchestra is truly symphonic in concept. There are some enharmonic touches; note this writing, where the piano and the orchestra are in different key signatures:

Figure 11-11

The use of the triangle has caused this concerto to be dubbed the "triangle" concerto, but the use is imaginative. Although this concerto has been almost *too* popular, it is important, since it represents a different direction for the piano concerto from that indicated by Beethoven. The concerti of Beethoven are very brilliant but are still firmly classical in form and treatment, even though there are some important modifications from the concerto as inherited from Mozart. The piano concerto of Schumann is closer to Beethoven than to either Liszt or Chopin.

Chopin's concerti are both unique, in that one always wonders how marvelous they would have been if Chopin had known something about the orchestra! They are reversed in numbering, as are Beethoven's first two. As a whole the *F Minor* is probably better, but both are very beautiful and the solo writing is superb. The *F Minor* particularly shows the interior Chopin unity and some rather good symphonic development. In a way each movement, as in Chopin's larger works, is a genre piece: the first movement somewhat resembles his dramatic scherzi (perhaps the Op. 31, No. 1), the slow movement is a lovely nocturne and the finale is a mazurka which is well developed. The orchestration has been tampered with from time to time, and one never seems to hear it performed the same way twice. The *E Minor Concerto* really contains poor and often impractical orchestration, such as high notes in some wind instruments without adequate preparation for the player.

This is not the place to go into the history of all the well-meaning but often ignorant and stupid editing that has been done to this concerto and to Chopin's work in general. There are many differences from one edition to another, but the complete edition clears up many problems.[10] Be that as it may, the concerto is bad as a whole, but in the hands of a great artist there are so many lovely passages that we should put up with the rest. Performing Chopin's concerti as two-piano works has merit, but the excitement of performances with orchestra cannot be overlooked. The *E Minor* is a work where you wait for the good passages, just as you must do in some other well-known works. Cutting is not a solution either. The work is still in the repertoire in spite of its shortcomings. The Chopin concerti are indeed unique.

Liszt's *A Major Concerto* contrasts well with those of Chopin and with his own *Concerto in E-flat*. The opening is adagio and expressive, and quite unsettled in its tonality. It abounds in rich effects and, as with most big works of Liszt, there is a certain amount of bombast, especially in the marches. In his day such passages were very effective, and they were so well written from a technical point of view that they have been hardly touched by the editor's pen. Almost all of the works of Chopin have a taste which has appealed to many generations. The important fact to remember is that Chopin died in 1849 and Liszt in

1886. Some of Liszt is, I fear, a product of the half century which produced much music which our generation finds to be sentimental and tasteless. When Liszt produced this music it said much to his audiences, especially when *he* performed it—it served its purpose. Hence, the student should not overlook some of the aspects of Liszt which are still important: the great advances in technique, the mastery of cyclic forms, the exploitation of colorful harmonies and new concepts in orchestration. Especially lovely are some of his works which are quiet and contemplative. Works of a diabolical or fantastic nature are also effective. The student should explore the *Sonnets of Petrarch, Totentanz* and the *Spanish Rhapsody.*

Liszt wrote only a small amount of organ music, but it is significant. These are a real tribute to Bach, using his name and some Bach themes as a point of departure. Liszt also arranged his own and other people's music for the organ.

Chopin and Liszt are at the very center of keyboard writing in the nineteenth century. Each exerted an enormous influence on the rest of the world, dominating piano style. In many cases composers using Chopin or Liszt as a point of departure would apply a national style, in a manner somewhat similar to Liszt's *Hungarian Rhapsodies.* Works by these composers are very uneven in quality. Chopin's imprint is shown in works such as the *Preludes* of Scriabin, and in the piano writing of many American and English composers. Some of the pieces of Grieg fall into the Chopin sphere of influence; his *Ballade,* Op. 24, is a good example. This is an extended piece, consisting of variations on a Norwegian folk song, and is effective when well played. Grieg's smaller pieces and his *Sonata in E Minor* are curious mixtures of Chopin, Liszt, Schumann and Grieg himself. The most original are probably the *Lyrical Pieces,* many of which have the fanciful titles so popular in the last half century.

Brahms

The Schumann influence is also felt in the works of Brahms, which are unique in the history of keyboard music. As with most of Brahms's music, they are difficult to perform, but not in a Lisztian sense. The influence of Liszt on Brahms was negative, since Brahms was morally opposed to Liszt's kind of music.

Brahms's piano music tends to fall into generic groups: sonatas, variations, ballades, capriccios, intermezzi, rhapsodies, etudes and cadenzas to concerti by Bach, Mozart and Beethoven. He also wrote significant music for piano duet, two pianos *(Variations on a Theme by Haydn)* and some important works for organ—especially the last pieces he ever wrote, eleven choral preludes. There are also the two great piano concerti.

This is an impressive list. One can see that the works vary in size considerably, which in Brahms is important, since the large works tend to come in the first part of his career (prior to about 1878) and the smaller works later, when the large works for other media occupied his attention. The sonatas are remarkable for a young composer, and contain many unusual treatments of thematic material. In the beginning of the very first one (note, Op. 1!) Brahms has already found his sound world:

Figure 11-12

These early sonatas are typical of Brahms in other ways as well. There is close attention paid to classical forms and treatment; the first movements show this very clearly, and are worth comparing one with the other and with the sonatas of Beethoven or Cherubini. In spite of their classicism the textures, expression and sheer massiveness are all romantic —made possible through the real pianoforte, which by Brahms's time was basically the instrument we know today. The slow movements are romantic, song-like or intermezzo-like (as are many of Brahms's slow movements, or even movements where a scherzo might have been written). Brahms's treatment of the song forms is very similar to what he used in later Lieder. In these sonatas Brahms wrote real scherzi; the finales are free rondos but for the F Minor, which is a sonata-allegro.

These sonatas deserve to be better known. They are beastly difficult to play and do not show off the pianist in the way that the works of Liszt and some others do. In Brahms there is always musical substance.

Brahms's variations are in a class by themselves, and most of them require consummate virtuosity. The *Paganini Variations* are especially difficult; but, more important, they are significant in the history of variation technique. Brahms was not immune to the influence of Paganini, since this work (which Brahms called "Studies") does exploit piano technique in a "transcendental" manner but without any Lisztian results. Chromaticism in Brahms is quite different from that in either Chopin or Liszt, and rarely if ever does it approach the almost impressionistic colorings of the other two masters. Brahms, rather, continues the line of development from Schumann. The beginning of the *Ballade*, Op. 10, No. 4, is a good example of Brahms's approach; so are the "Capriccio" of Op. 76 and the first intermezzo or the beginning of the first Rhapsody of Op. 79.

Few of Brahms's keyboard works have programmatic connotations; they are to be taken as pure music of the highest quality. Brahms's piano writing in the chamber music carries on the great contributions of Schumann. The *A Major Violin Sonata*, Op. 100 (1887), contains some of Brahms's loveliest music.

Important in all Brahms is the treatment of the germ motive or *Grundgestalt*. It bothers some musicians to think about which form of the shape is the *Urkeim*—or, if you will, *Urgrundgestalt*—since it does not always occur at the very beginning of a piece. (It doesn't in Bach or Beethoven either.) In many works we really have no way of knowing which idea came first. Are the subsequent ideas more complex, or are they a stripping down of the original idea? It may well be that the real musical shape that suggested the music is never stated at all in the piece itself.

Reger

Reger (1873-1916) was also important in the composition of variations in general, and especially of those for the keyboard. Nelson says that ". . . Reger is the most prolific, Brahms the most important."[11] Reger's themes are either borrowed from other composers, are original or are based on BACH. His variations run the whole gamut: the ornamented, periodic; double period (different music employed for a variation of a repeated strain); and character variations. He, like Franck, wrote Bach-derived variations ending in fugues or passacaglias and fugues. Among his best variations are those of Op. 86, *Variations and Fugue on a Theme by Beethoven.* The famous set of Mozart variations exists for two pianos, but it is more beautful in the orchestral version. There is also *Variations and Fugue on a Theme by Telemann* for piano.

Reger's organ music is voluminous; the *Introduction, Passacaglia and Fugue,* Op. 127, is one of his most important compositions. The rest of his organ music is a fascinating mixture of quasi-Baroque forms and procedures: suites, chorales, preludes, sonatas and some romantic character pieces. Reger's organ music alone would occupy a shelf of music larger than that needed for many other composers' complete works. It is important music for its time, even though much of it is thick and complicated, but it can be played beautifully and clearly. Some of the works do not deserve the limbo in which they languish simply because of the stock phrase which asserts that Reger is thick, dull and too chromatic—how many of his works do you know? Reger is surpassed only by Brahms as a late-nineteenth–century keyboard composer. His piano music is more available to most musicians, and the student will find the playing of them to be rewarding. There are some delightful character pieces, and others which make great technical demands. While there is a streak of originality in Reger, there is more than a little influence of Schumann, Chopin and Brahms. In the larger works, which come from his mature years, there are decided influences of Beethoven's large piano works and—perhaps too obviously—his admiration for the great variations of Brahms and Bach.

Aside from the concerti, Reger wrote two *Romances* for violin and orchestra which are very beautiful. There are some short pieces for violin and piano, seven sonatas for violin and piano (the *F-Sharp Minor* is particularly intriguing) and three clarinet sonatas.

Other Late Germans

Joseph Rheinberger (1839-1901) is often compared to Reger. He wrote much music for the church, some orchestral music and some chamber music, but he is best-known for some rather good organ music and some appealing piano music. There are the usual character pieces, some large works, etudes and other compositions. His organ music is far more significant. There are twenty sonatas of a planned twenty-four, one in each key. These pieces would not have been composed without the influence of Bach, but they are not always Bachian. I am particularly fond of the *Sonata in E Minor,* Op. 132, which contains one of the best passacaglias in the literature:

RHEINBERGER: *Organ Sonata in E Minor*;
Passacaglia

Figure 11-13

The sonatas of Rheinberger are striking in that they are real sonatas which use forms and styles known to the organ literature. Those of Mendelssohn are really more like suites, while many of the French sonatas are symphonic in style and, indeed, are actually called "symphonies for organ."

Siegfrid Karg-Elert (1877-1933) should at least be mentioned, since he wrote some very fine music for the organ which draws from the melos of Reger and Rheinberger and, harmonically, from some of the French composers and perhaps even Scriabin. Many of his organ works are highly regarded; they show remarkable uses of borrowed tunes (everything from "Nearer My God to Thee" to BACH). While he was not as strongly neo-Baroque as others who were to be born somewhat later, he nevertheless uses some Baroque ideas and textures. His harmonies are especially unique.

Karg-Elert exerted some influence on organ composers who exploited a different kind of chromatic harmony. He also wrote some virtuoso etudes for the flute. He was both a piano and an organ virtuoso, and toured as a virtuoso of the harmonium. This organ-like instrument should not be looked upon as an "ersatz" organ, since it is an instrument in its own right and has been called for in several important scores (including Schoenberg's "Herzgewäche"). Nevertheless, music for the harmonium is often played on the organ.

Franck

In France there was a composer who in many respects resembled Brahms, but was himself an ardent Wagnerian: Franck. Franck's keyboard textures are rich and often require very large hands, which Franck himself had. Franck also wrote some very significant piano parts in his chamber music; and, unlike Brahms, he employed a somewhat new idea in the short concert piece for piano and orchestra. There are few works comparable to Franck's *Symphonic Variations*, which are played much more often than the programmatic *Les Djinns* for piano and orchestra (based on a poem by Victor Hugo). The *Variations* are a remarkable approach to the whole art of composition. While brilliant, the essence of the work is purely musical and is a landmark in the history of variation technique, in the relationship of solo piano and orchestra and in its splendid application of cyclic principles. This work clearly shows the differences which exist between variation and development. Two themes are used. One appears in the orchestra, reminding one of the second movement of Beethoven's *Fourth Concerto*. The other theme appears in the solo piano, in the manner of a dialogue between piano and orchestra. These themes are treated in a free manner, but they must be considered as character variations or even character developments. The themes work well together, and Franck takes advantage of this fact. The first section of the work, which exposes the themes, is itself a complete piece and also shows variation.

The variations are not always separated one from the other by a double bar, and in some instances the transition is so smooth that the listener is not always aware of it. Franck himself does not mark arbitrary divisions, but textural changes often occur. The most unusual feature is probably the formal structure inside each variation, particularly the finale variation: a complete sonata-allegro.

The French heritage in keyboard literature prior to Franck was considerable, developing along lines quite different from those in other countries although there were similarities to German suites and other Baroque forms. The French clavecin composers exerted a strong influence on J. S. Bach.

Alkan

There were some notable composers living in the period when the clavecin (the French harpsichord) was dying out and the newer piano was coming in. Many sonatas and other pieces were published for either instrument, by composers such as Étienne Méhul (1763-1817) and Adrien Boieldieu (1775-1834), who are remembered more for important French operas of the period. According to Demuth,[12] Charles-Valentin Alkan (1813-1888, whose real name was Morhange) was the first of the true piano composers. Alkan is a mysterious figure, and not as much is known about him as we would like to know. His music probably reflects his own great ability as a pianist (he was a child prodigy at the Conservatory at the age of six). Alkan's works were not easy to come by until the Lewenthal Edition was published by G. Schirmer; performances of his works are not common, although they probably will be as a result of some brilliant recordings. Such pianists as Harold Bauer, Claudio Arrau, Egon Petri and, most recently, Raymond Lewenthal have included his works in their repertoire. The magnitude of these works is astonishing, so that a perusal of the list of Alkan's works (found on pp. 112-113 of Vol. I, *Grove's*) does not give one the true picture. For example, the list shows that Op. 39 (1857) is a set of twelve etudes in the minor keys. The first three are long character pieces, etudes IV-VII comprise a symphony, VIII-X a concerto *sans* orchestra, XI is an overture and XII is called "Aesop's Fables"—a fantastic set of twenty-five variations, each perhaps representing a different animal in a different fable (no indication is made of this, so the listener is free to imagine as he will). Also gigantic is the *Grande Sonata* (1847), of which the second movement is called "Quasi Faust."

Raymond Lewenthal's informative program notes to one of his recordings points out that one must keep in mind such works as the Beethoven, Op. 106, Ives and Strauss. Here is the end of the article which sums it up so well:

The chromaticism of Liszt and Chopin are nowhere in Alkan. Alkan was able to prove that the possibilities of diatonicism were by no means exhausted, and he created a highly original harmonic language of his own which will gradually become apparent to you as you attune yourself to it. If you hear Brahms at certain points in the first and last movements of the *Symphonie*, remember that it was written before Brahms knew what Brahmsian meant. The same, only more so, goes for any Bruckner or Mahler you may espy in the Funeral March. "Nice" people are not dancing Alkan's Minuet. It is full of whirring broomsticks and boiling cauldrons; and its spooks, witches and demons may make you think of Moussorgsky. The Finale is a tragic, wild ride, not *to* Hell (as in Berlioz' The Damnation of Faust) but already *in* Hell.[13]

It must be remembered that the salons of Paris were visited by all of the great pianists of the age; in a way that period resembled a gigantic composers' seminar. Liszt and Chopin had reigned there.

Saint-Saëns

Another composer who was influenced by Liszt was a Frenchman born in Algiers: Camille Saint-Saëns (1835-1921). He had the best of piano instruction from an early age, and began the study of organ (with Benoist) at the Conservatory in Paris while studying composition with Halévy (ca. 1851). It was while at the conservatory and under exposure to the musical life of Paris that he fell under the influence of Liszt, which, however, was not imitation. While he is often called the "French Mendelssohn" (the comparison has some validity), he could with some justification be called the "French Liszt." He was a great piano virtuoso and his works for piano, especially the piano concerti, exhibit his facility. He was equally noted as an organist and as an organ composer. He composed in every musical form and had success in all of them, especially in opera and in the symphonic poem. Although the latter are Lisztian, they were still quite original at the time, even though they are not often performed today. Saint-Saëns was one of the first important French musicians to become interested in older French music, and he made some practical editions. He is unique in that he came along at the right time, and was good enough at instrumental composition to excite more interest in it at a time when the Conservatory was officially not too enthused over symphonic writing. He was *avant-garde* at first but did not continue to move ahead of the other composers; the Franckians especially surpassed him in originality. Saint-Saëns used a mixture of classicism and romanticism in his writing, and had fantastic technical skill as a composer. Like Mendelssohn, there are rather dull harmonic passages in his music, but his compositions provided a welcome contrast to some of the bombast of the period and at best have a certain charm. The *G Minor Piano Concerto* (No. 2) is the best-known, but the fifth (the "Egyptian") is more advanced in its approach to harmony—it evokes the atmosphere of the Nile and the Pyramids.

Saint-Saëns should have left more piano music. What he did write is often very effective, especially the two-piano work *Variations on a Theme by Beethoven*. He also wrote very effectively for solo violin and orchestra; the *B Minor Concerto* is one of three, and the *Introduction and Rondo Capriccioso* is a piece which still delights audiences. The *A Minor Cello Concerto*, written in the single-movement Liszt tradition, is also a permanent repertoire piece. There are also many other concert works for various instruments, such as the *Tarantella* for flute and clarinet with orchestra or the *Morceau de Concert* for harp and orchestra. These works are uneven in quality, just as they are sometimes too even in their brilliant dullness. Better are some of the works for two instruments, which are soloistic and sometimes resemble real chamber music. The *Havanaise* for violin and piano is a famous piece influenced by both Paganini and the great Pablo de Sarasate (1844-1908), whose Iberian-flavored works are still studied by violinists (*Zigeunerweisen* is the best-known). In the chamber music category are a *Suite for Cello and Piano* (1866) and sonatas for violin, oboe, clarinet and bassoon (written in 1921). It has been stated that Saint-Saëns was born too soon and lived too long. He was highly honored throughout his lifetime, and in a sense established a "school" of piano playing. Although his career as a teacher was very short (at *école Niedermeyer*, 1861-1865), one of his pupils was Fauré.

Obviously Saint-Saëns knew Franck, and it is just possible that Saint-Saëns was more than a little jealous and saw in Franck something that he could not do himself. There are some famous tales told about Saint-Saëns snubbing Franck (in regard to the *Piano Quintet*)—his comments about Franck were utterly lacking in French tact.

Lesser French Composers

Among other outstanding pianists of the period who wrote effective but not really lasting piano music was Emmanuel Chabrier (1841-1894), who is reputed to have had one of the strongest techniques of the time (he broke strings and stripped off ivories). His best-known work is *España*, which is now heard on pop concerts as an orchestral piece. It is so brilliantly scored (by Camille Chevillard) that one forgets that it was originally written for the piano. Chabrier also wrote other piano music which was scored for orchestra; much of it shows a fertile imagination. He was one of the "stand-ins" in Franck's famous composition-organ classes at the Conservatory and at his house.

There were also some important violinists who held forth in the salons, played the works of the important composers and often played their own works. These works were pleasant and very important in their time, and are still being studied and played today. As with the keyboard opera paraphrases, fantasias and variations, their compositions for the violin are not often played today. What are played are some of the better concerti and some shorter pieces such as sonatas, etudes or caprices; most of these are without accompaniment, but some have had piano parts added for concert use. The violin had developed well in the Italian schools of the eighteenth century. The teacher-pupil genealogy of Viotti (1755-1824) can be traced back to Corelli (1653-1713). Viotti was the teacher of many European violinists; he traveled considerably, even going as far away as Russia. His appearance in Paris in

1782 was so successful that he stayed there for ten years. Later in his career he worked in Germany, England and elsewhere. His biography in many ways is more intriguing than Paganini's. He exerted a great influence as a player, teacher and composer. Violinists still play many of his twenty-nine concerti. Number 22, in A minor, was especially admired by Brahms and is still in the repertoire of concert artists. His complete works also list ten piano concerti and a considerable amount of chamber music for concert use, for teaching (such as the violin duos) and for the pleasures of *Hausmusik*. Viotti exerted a strong influence on his pupil Rodé (1774-1830), a composer of some standard caprices which almost all advanced violin students study, and of some concerti which are quite beautiful and deserve a better fate than that of preparation for the more virtuoso works of later vintage.

Kreutzer (1766-1831) is a name well-known to all violin students for his famous caprices and some concerti and other pieces which are perhaps too much like caprices. He is the Kreutzer for whom Beethoven's violin sonata, Op. 47, is named. Kreutzer also commanded some attention as an opera composer. He was a French composer born of German parents in Paris. The great violinist Baillot (1771-1842) was also a great admirer of Viotti. Rodé, Kreutzer and Baillot wrote a famous school of violin playing (*Art du violon*), which was adopted by the Paris Conservatory and was an important foundation work for many important nineteenth-century virtuosi. Another influence was the violin school of Spohr (1784-1859), who had been a pupil of one of the Mannheimers and thereby continued at least in part a great German tradition. Spohr, however, was an international figure and was himself influenced by Rodé as a violinist. Add to this the great performances and technical discoveries of Paganini, and the stage is set for a kind of "Golden Age" of violin playing and composition. This music is uneven in quality, as one might expect, but it did exert a strong influence on almost all nineteenth-century violin music.

Among the composer-violinists who were active in Paris were Charles de Beriot (1802-1870), Henri Vieuxtemps (1820-1881) and many others too numerous to mention. Their music abounds in striking technical devices: among them bowing styles, double and multiple stopping, harmonics and right- and left-hand pizzicato. Since the melodies are often insipid, the musical interest lies mostly in the sheer technical exploitation of the instrument, which some great violinists can play with great effect. De Beriot is played mostly by students, while Vieuxtemps receives devoted performances by both virtuosi and advanced students. His accompaniments are quite "meaty," but are hardly symphonic.

Franck and the Organists

It can be seen, then, that the music of Franck varied widely in conception, even though Franck himself had written works such as the *Variations brillantes* for piano—he was a student preparing for a concert career, and these works were expected. It was in chamber music that the new style of writing appeared, for string players and pianists, especially in the *Piano Quintet* of 1879. The French school re-discovered Bach in various ways, too. Franck was an organist, and his organ works still rank very high among organists. They showed a Bach influence and were very welcome, even though there was plenty of organ music of a brilliant nature with not too much musical substance. There were men like Lefébure-Wély (1817-1869), Batiste (1820-1876) and Lemmens (1823-1881), all of whom influenced Franck slightly. Boëly (1785-1858) was a lonely Bach player who in turn influenced Guilmant (1837-1911), Saint-Saëns (1835-1931) and, of course, Franck. Another man who should be mentioned is the great Charles Widor (1845-1937), one of the teachers of Albert Schweitzer—who actually influenced Widor's interest in Bach. Widor succeeded Franck at the conservatory. Vierne (1870-1937) also belongs to this group, having had the good forture to study with both Franck and Widor.

This is not the place to discuss the peculiarities of the organs at St. Sulpice, Madeleine, St. Clothilde, Trocadero or elsewhere in Paris. It is obvious that the men listed above wrote music which suited the instruments they had to play.

Franck's organ music is mostly of good quality and avoids the superficial brilliance which permeates so much French organ music of the period.

There are three basic groups of Franck organ music: 1) *Six Pieces* (1862); 2) *Three Pieces* (1878); and 3) *Three Chorales*. His other pieces are less significant.

In the first group the second "piece" is called *Grande pièce symphonique,* which is in reality a large sonata which anticipates his later symphony. Another outstanding piece in this same set is the *Prelude, fugue and variation,* a very famous work. It is often pointed out that this work is most unusual for Franck, in that it is not thick in texture but progresses mostly in three voices. The fifth piece, *Prière,* is long and more Franck-like in texture and presents Franck's great love of modulation. This work is more difficult to play than one would suppose.

The *Piece héroïque* is a famous piece which has been orchestrated by Stokowski and others. The "Cantabile" of this set uses Franck's famed cycle-germ technique and is a simple work for the student to analyze. Note how the ideas grow from the very beginning. Kirby states:

The unifying device of cyclic form common in nineteenth-century French music was taken by Franck, on his own admission, specifically from the later works of Beethoven.[14]

With the *Three Chorales* we have some of the greatest organ music of any time. In reality these are variations; there is no "chorale tune" *per se*. The theme of the first is a fine example of great *romantic* melody, spun out from the opening germ. This is a theme of seven distinct periods, all related, passing through *twelve* different keys. These are in reality symphonic variations, with many amazing contrapuntal devices such as invertible counterpoint. The second *Chorale* is in B Minor: a passacaglia, so that again variations are used. The third, *Chorale in A Minor*, is the best-known, since it is most readily appreciated by audiences. It is beautiful, but it does not match the other two in over-all musical quality.

Franck's mature piano works reflect the same lofty principles: a deep understanding of the true spirit of the Baroque and a fine feeling for harmonic coloring and remote relationships. In all of Franck's music there is no more question about the necessity of equal temperament. The *Prelude, Chorale et Fugue* (1884) is a great work, and clearly illustrates the principles voiced above. It uses the germ technique; therefore, the art of variation is important. The cyclic germ of the whole work is found near the beginning, in the double-stemmed notes. The "Chorale" was added later; one advantage of the cyclic form is that it is open-ended so that such an addition can be made.

The fugue (and the chorale, too) were not appreciated by Saint-Saëns, who first played the work. He complained that the chorale was not a chorale, and that the fugue was not a fugue—just as others were to say later that the symphony was not a symphony! (These detractors should have known their Beethoven better and the *spirit* of the fugue better. Small minds make large noises about small things.) The fugue subject draws from the opening germ, just as does the chorale. Note that the theme of the prelude is our old friend BACH, only transposed.

The *Prelude, Aria et Final* is also a great work, but it can suffer from an overly sentimental performance (some organists play it as if it had been written by Gounod). Even Gounod's lively fugue near the beginning of *Romeo and Juliet* cannot match the *internal* counterpoint in Franck, which is expressive, some of the most abstract music ever penned and some of the most beautiful.

Elsewhere in this book (in discussing the melodic characteristics of

Franck and his coterie) it was mentioned that Castillon, one of Franck's tragic pupils, wrote little music which is performed today. His *Piano Concerto* (1872) has merit and deserves a performance now and then— but who knows the work?

D'Indy (in 1881) wrote an important Franckian work: *Poème des Montagnes*, which he called a symphonic poem for the piano. However, this is a "heavy" piece. Although dated 1930, d'Indy's best piano solo piece is still romantic, but also well-crafted. It is called "Fantasie pour piano sur un vieil air de ronde française," and is actually a set of variations.

D'Indy wrote some first-class solo music such as the "Lied" for cello or viola and piano, which is quite lovely. There are also solos for oboe and piano and for saxophone and piano.

Brief mention should be made of Pierre de Bréville (1861-1949), who wrote some original piano works—even if a bit Franckian; Paul Dukas (1865-1935), who wrote a fine sonata for piano in 1901 and a great set of *Variations on a Theme by Rameau* in 1903. Demuth[15] ranks this work with the best keyboard variations of the century, and likens it in a way to the Beethoven variations by Reger.

Demuth makes an apt point which I would like to quote; the composer mentioned and quoted is Abel Decaux (1869-1941), who was quite obscure (*Grove's* does not even mention him):

The *cyclique* manner and its principles of thematic derivation, germination, and quotation were bound to lead somewhere further sooner or later, for the philosophy is not far removed from certain aspects of serialisation. It is a question of, in the first instance, using process as a means to an expressive end—"the making of music," in fact—and, in the second, of using it as the end in itself. In the first case the end is achieved largely in terms of tonality and tonal relations, in the second by a complete negation of them.

The resultant harmonies in Decaux' pieces were more advanced than any others written at the time:

DECAUX: *Piano Pieces*

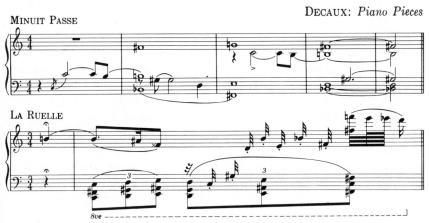

MINUIT PASSE

LA RUELLE

L e C i m e t i è r e

Figure 11-14

The titles of the pieces are: I, *Minuit passe*; II, *La Ruelle*; III, *Le Cimetière*; IV, *La Mer*. Of these, the fourth is the least venturesome but contains the most actual pianism.

It is certain that neither Matthias Hauer (1883) nor Arnold Schoenberg (1874-1951) ever heard of Decaux or his pieces and I wonder how many French dodecaphonists who worship at the shrine of Schoenberg have ever come across either this name or this music, or realise how long ago their *avant-garde* theories were forestalled—by an obscure organist. The position is analogous to that of Erik Satie.

These pieces stand in splendid isolation, anticipating the shape of things to come. Concerned as they are with sonorities proceeding out of the serialisation, they might be described as "Serial Impressionism" and said to form a natural corollary to thematic composition in the *cyclique* manner. Obscurity has caused Decaux to suffer the fate of so many pioneers in all walks of life, although his music aroused considerable interest in Germany when introduced there by Madame Gisele Brelet, the distinguished French musicologist.[16]

Fauré

Another variation in style appears in the music of Fauré: a delicate, quasi-Chopin style, very French, polished, conservative when compared to advanced works and progressive when compared to classical works— even though Fauré always displays a classical grace. In Fauré's music we find mostly a set of generic titles, such as nocturnes and barcarolles. It is not easy to play, but has real musical substance.

Fauré wrote some significant solo music. The *Ballade* for piano and orchestra (the orchestral part was added) is very beautiful. The most famous solo is perhaps the "Elegy" for cello and piano. This is one of several such short pieces (others are for violin and flute, and there are two sonatas each for violin and cello with piano). (The famous *A Major Sonata* for violin is discussed elsewhere in this book.) There is also significant chamber music involving the piano, where we find some of his best writing for the keyboard (the two piano quartets and a piano trio).

Fauré's pupils belong to the twentieth century, as does the keyboard music of Roussel, Debussy and Ravel, even though a lot of it was written at about the same time as much of the music discussed above.

Keyboard and Solo Works in the Nationalistic Schools

In Russia we must again start with Glinka, who seems to be the "Adam" of Russian music. His piano music is typical enough: there are the usual variations, character pieces and dances. His variations run from Mozart's *Don Giovanni* to a tarantella on the Russian song "In the field there stood a birch tree"—the same tune used by Tchaikovsky in the finale of his *Fourth Symphony*. There are several chamber works which are quite light and two movements of a viola sonata.

Important keyboard music was written by the "Mighty Five." There were some charming little pieces, but also some significant larger works written by Balakirev, who was himself a good pianist. Nationalistic elements are less prominent in the piano works, although his piano sonata is based on Russian folk themes. Balakirev's famous work is *Islamey* (1869), an "Oriental Fantasy" based on themes from the Caucasus and Armenia. The name comes from a dance popular in the Caucasus; the work does have rhythmic drive and uses real dance rhythms.

The greatest Russian piano work is Mussorgsky's suite *Pictures at an Exhibition*. Each main section is a musical representation of pictures by Victor Hartmann, a friend of Mussorgsky. The work opens with a "Promenade," and between some of the pictures Mussorgsky repeats this "Promenade," as he moves from one picture to another. The sections are almost like variations: each is in a different mood. There are ten pictures in all, each different in style and character; yet, as a suite, they all belong together. This composition is most famous in Ravel's marvelous orchestration, but it is equally effective in its original version. All of Mussorgsky's piano music is character music—as, indeed, is all of his music. It should be remembered that Liszt exerted an influence on Russian composers, but not through his pianistic devices. It was the music itself which influenced almost all of them—especially his *Totentanz* and the *Mephisto Waltz*.

The rest of the keyboard situation in Russia is pretty bleak until the time of Scriabin. Tchaikovsky wrote only second-rate keyboard music at best. There are plenty of character pieces. The suite called *The Seasons* contains twelve pieces, one for each month of the year, but it is not one of his happiest works. There are two sonatas, but they remain mostly unplayed. The *Concerto No. 1 in B-flat Minor*, however, is superb, as much so for the orchestra as for the pianist. It is an odd fact that two of Russia's finest instrumentalists had pronounced the two great concerti unplayable (Rubinstein the piano, and Leopold Auer the violin). Also remarkable are his *Variations on a Rococo Theme* for cello and orchestra, a brilliant and beautiful piece in the hands of a fine cellist. There are other works for solo instrument, including the *Second Piano Concerto* and the unfinished *Third*; but the best is the *Sérénade mélancolique* for violin and orchestra, which is sometimes performed with piano. There are some small pieces for violin, Op. 42 (the first of these is the discarded slow movement of the *Violin Concerto*). Before leaving Tchaikovsky, there is one more comment: there are over 100 pieces for piano, of which so few have the great Tchaikovsky touch. One set of pieces stands out, however: the *Six Pieces on a Single Theme*, Op. 21.

Scriabin and Rachmaninoff were born in the same year, and their music for piano is quite distinguished and still figures on many concert programs. Other than the "Mighty Five" and Tchaikovsky, the Rubinsteins, Liadov, Arensky and others wrote many piano pieces, large and small, which are mostly curiosities; but some (like Rubinstein's *Melody in F* and the *Romance in E-flat*) still appear in albums bearing titles such as "The World's Best Piano Music." Rachmaninoff and Scriabin were two of the best pianists in the world. Scriabin was almost forced into composition through jealousy and overpractice (he injured his wrists). Rachmaninoff's music, like most of Dohnányi's (1877-1960), belongs to the end of the nineteenth century—a marvelous extension into our time, honest, not anachronistic. It was an unforgettable experience to hear these men play, especially when performing their own works. Scriabin gazed into the future, but Bartók took us into the future. Scriabin's mysticism is discussed elsewhere in this book, but his last six sonatas are unique in the history of music. They show a strange contrast of inner spirituality with a mood of diabolic ecstacy. Here are parts of No. 7, *The White Mass*, and No. 9, *The Black Mass*:

SCRIABIN: *Sonata*, Op. 64, No. 7

Figure 11-15

No. 10 is also amazing. Just how much of this music is the product of a sick mind is debatable; it has been difficult for some people to listen to Scriabin without prejudice. (More than one composer has "gone off the deep end"!) His theories, however—once one has passed through the metaphysics—are based on sound acoustical principles. Another amazing work is the *Satanic Poem* (1904), the only time he ever used the word "Satan" in a title.

Graf[17] says that an age died with Scriabin: the age which had begun with Glinka. Scriabin and the Russian monarchy died at about the same time.

Nicolas Medtner (1880-1951) was a traditional romanticist who wrote many piano pieces which are still studied and played. The "Fairy Tales" is his best-known composition. His works do not contain the beauties of the best works of Rachmaninoff, but they will probably experience a comeback. Rachmaninoff—like Dohnányi, Paderewski, Godowsky and others—wrote much music for his own concert use, as did some of the finest violinists of the time.

Ferruccio Busoni (1866-1924) was one of the few Italian piano virtuosi who left significant music. Busoni is also remembered for his brilliant essays on the esthetics of music, which are quite original and have real foundation. He was an anti-Wagnerite; but he greatly admired Liszt. As a pianist his technical prowess perhaps even surpassed him. His parentage was mixed (German and Italian), and his lifetime, tastes and compositions point up this mixture. He was interested mainly in the large forms. His operas have some merit—especially *Dr. Faust* which, however, he did not finish. His *Piano Concerto* is a huge work, even calling for male chorus in the finale. In addition he wrote sonatas for violin and piano; pieces for cello and piano; one solo each for flute and clarinet with piano; and some character pieces for the piano. His large works for piano include preludes, fugues, "sonatinas" and a fascinating *Fantasia contrappuntistica*. This piece exists in four versions, including one for two pianos, and which "finishes" the unfinished portion of Bach's *Art of the Fugue*. Busoni had a great admiration for the music of Bizet, and wrote a once-famous fantasy on themes from *Carmen (Sonatina No. 6)*.

Busoni is a composer about whom musicians speak but whom they do not play as much as they should. Two great artists who included Busoni in their concert programs are Egon Petri and Joseph Szigeti. (I will never forget a Busoni Memorial Concert conducted by Mitropoulos, in which both gentlemen appeared.) Also of considerable interest are his cadenzas to concerti by Mozart.

Paganini

The influences of Paganini have been mentioned many times. His music still lives on today by virtue of his fantastic technical exploitation of the instrument. Best-known are the *Caprices*, which are not too far removed from the better etudes for the piano. Although each Paganini work usually presents one main technical problem, the *Twenty-fourth Caprice* is a set of variations in which each variation presents a new problem. Piano parts have been added to these pieces for concert use, with varying degrees of success.

The public knows well the *Violin Concerto in D Major*, listed as Number One. The work, however, is actually in E-flat major; Paganini tuned his violin *up* a semitone so that, when he played in *his* "D major," it would come out as E-flat major (his open D string was actually E-flat, and he played a part which was written out in D, a favorite key for violinists). This did two things: it made his part much easier to play and his violin more brilliant, and it made the orchestral violin parts sound in a different tone color, since the "color" of the string tone is a function of the tuning of the open strings. (The resonance of each instrument and of the section sounds entirely different in a different key.) This is a relative matter, but each instrument has its optimum A. The Concerto is notated entirely in D major today. Paganini's A was lower than ours, so a higher tuning would not be feasible; it is dangerous to tune our high A higher (in spite of Mahler's use of this device in his *Fourth Symphony*). This purposeful mis-tuning is called *scordatura*, and at one time it was used quite extensively (*cf.* the works of von Biber (1644-1704)). It was used by Mozart in his *Sinfonia Concertante* for solo violin and viola, K. 364 (everyone but the solo viola is in E-flat; in Mozart's day the violist played from a D major part, using scordatura). This device is also found in some twentieth-century scores, notably in Kodály's *Sonata for Unaccompanied Cello*.

Paganini's other works are once again coming into vogue, with some fine young virtuosi of our time who really can play them (such as Salvatore Accardo). Many of these works are variations on well-known tunes, such as *God Save the King* (Queen).

Among the virtuosi from other countries who wrote many character pieces, variations and concerti was Campagnoli (1751-1827), an important teacher whose etudes are still studied; his violinistic genealogy goes back through Nardini to Tartini. One of Kreutzer's pupils was Massart (1811-1892), who taught Wieniawski (1835-1880), Sarasate (1844-1908) and Fritz Kreisler (1875-1962). Kreisler was one of the most beloved artists of all time; he also contributed some remarkable character pieces for violin and piano which are still very popular. This leads to the twentieth-century artists, who in large measure still play much of the grand virtuoso literature of the Romantic Period. The Wieniawski *Violin Concerto in D Minor* has merit as a piece of important music; it is not just a vehicle for the violinist.

As usual, one finds at the end of a chapter of text a paragraph beginning: "And in America. . . ." In America there are four composers who must be singled out for having written some excellent piano music. The first is Gottschalk (1829-1869), who wrote pieces of astonishing sentimentality and equally astonishing originality. The second is Mac-Dowell (1861-1908), who wrote many small character pieces, but should be better remembered for his sonatas which, although lying somewhere between Grieg and Liszt, still have passages of greatness. The third is

Plate XIV

Louis Moreau Gottschalk (1829-1869), American pianist and composer *(Courtesy The Bettmann Archive, N.Y.).*

Ives (1874-1954), whose *Concord Sonata* and violin sonatas are among the most striking and original works ever written anywhere. Now that they have been recorded, they should become much better-known and less scorned by people who should know better—and who would know better if they really knew his music!

The other orchestral instruments do not have the rich solo literature that they deserve—not even the viola and cello, which were the only ones basically unchanged during the nineteenth century. There were many fine virtuoso cellists who played some original music, but they played mainly transcriptions of music written for other instruments. The cello has had some important concerti written for it by Schumann, Saint-Saëns, Lalo, Dvořák and Elgar; in addition there is the great *Double Concerto* (for violin and cello) by Brahms and the *Triple Concerto* (for violin, cello and piano) by Beethoven. The cello was also the recipient of some important sonatas; the best are those of Beethoven and Brahms. The cello came into its own, however, as an important instrument in chamber music groups. The cello has important parts in many of the Haydn quartets, the later Mozart quartets and the Beethoven Quartets, especially from Op. 59, 1, 2 and 3 (the "Rasumovsky") and in the other quartets of the nineteenth century. There were recital pieces written by David Popper (1843-1913). These are very tuneful, are challenging technically and are still played today. The wind instruments play their most important roles in the orchestra and in chamber music. There are some isolated examples of great works, such as Mozart's *Clarinet Concerto*, his *Bassoon Concerto* and his *Concertantes Quartette*, the woodwind solo works of Weber and Spohr, and the great sonatas for clarinet or viola and piano by Brahms (among his very last works). The Brahms works herald the beginning of a literature which begins to accrue in the very late nineteenth century to the present time.

The most voluminous solo music was obviously written for the piano. Popular demand dictated much of it, and much of it shows the composer trying to please his publisher and to write something that would sell. Other works, which were vehicles for great performers died with those performers and their disciples. The greatest solo music ranks with the best chamber and symphonic music, and is not only written well but has much to say to generation after generation.

Notes

1. John Cockshoot, *The Fugue in Beethoven's Piano Music* (London: Routledge, Kegan Paul, Ltd., 1959).

2. While Beethoven's opus numbers are not exact in their chronology, they are approximate. Grove's additional numbers do not reflect any sense of chronology. The system used by Kinsky in his *Beethoven Verzeichnis* is much better.

3. Alfred Einstein, *Schubert* (New York: Oxford University Press, 1951), p. 28.

4. F. E. Kirby, *A Short History of Keyboard Music* (New York: The Free Press, 1966), p. 108.

5. Willi Apel, *Masters of the Keyboard* (Cambridge: Harvard University Press, 1947), p. 225.

6. Kirby, *op. cit.*, p. 253.

7. Willy Kahl, *The Character Piece*, in No. 8, *Anthology of Music*, ed. K. G. Fellerer (Köln: Arno Volk Verlag, 1961).

8. Reprinted with permission of The Macmillan Company from Eric Werner, *Mendelssohn*, trans. D. Newlin. Copyright © by The Free Press of Glencoe, a Division of The Macmillan Company, 1963, pp. 424-428.

9. Herbert Weinstock, *Chopin* (New York: Alfred A. Knopf, 1949), p. 274.

10. There are several; among them are: *Fr. Chopins Werke* (Leipzig, 1878-1880) and *Chopin's Complete Works* (Warsaw-Cracow, 1948).

11. Robert Nelson, *The Technique of Variation* (Berkeley and Los Angeles: University of California Press, 1949), p. 108.

12. Norman Demuth, *French Piano Music* (London: Camelot Press, 1959), p. 30.

13. Raymond Lewenthal, program notes for the recording "The Piano Music of Alkan," RCA Victor LSC-2815 (1965).

14. Kirby, *op. cit.*, p. 359.

15. Demuth, *op. cit.*, p. 72.

16. Demuth, *Ibid.*, pp. 64-65.

17. Max Graf, *Modern Music*, trans. Beatrice Maier (New York: Philosophical Library, 1946), p. 128. This book contains an excellent summary of the Romantic Period.

CHAPTER XII

CHAMBER MUSIC

STRICTLY SPEAKING, *CHAMBER MUSIC* entails but one player
to a part, or two or more players, but not enough players to require a
conductor (just what that number is, is variable!). The term almost always refers to a small group of players who perform in a room (camera,
chambre, Kammer) and not in concert hall or church. In the nineteenth
century, however, the idea developed of using a chamber group such as
a string quartet in a hall. Touring virtuoso chamber musicians became
a permanent part of the musical scene; as you know, some of our most
outstanding performers today are members of quartets or similar organizations.

The original purpose of chamber music, however, was to serve as
pleasant music for the entertainment of nobility, or as music for playing
together with no real audience. To a certain extent both of these categories still exist today—the former, however, usually are found at universities or large libraries, while the latter are found wherever "two or
three are gathered together." There is a substantial audience for chamber
music today through the medium of the phonograph record.

The Baroque Period witnessed the development of the *solo sonata*
for an instrument and figured bass, which is the prototype of the duo
sonata. Proper performance of a solo sonata actually requires three
players, the third being a cello or other bass instrument to play the bass
line while a keyboard player realizes the figured bass and a flute, oboe
or violin plays the treble part. In the middle eighteenth century, as

323

figured bass died out, many sonatas were written for piano with a violin or other treble part as an accompaniment, the violin often merely doubling the right hand of the keyboard. The first mature violin sonatas were written by Mozart (the sonatas for violin and harpsichord by J. S. Bach are exceptional).[1] Mozart grasped an important principle: the equal status of the instruments. These sonatas are among some of Mozart's best works, especially those from K. 296 on, and anticipate romanticism.

Other *duos* were composed for two like instruments for teaching purposes and for diversion, while others were written for a treble and bass (such as violin and cello). In the nineteenth century some of these duos were quite elaborate—Charles DeBeriot's pieces for two violins are as brilliant as a double concerto, even without accompaniment. There are not too many works in this duo category, however, which one could rank in importance with the violin and piano sonatas or cello and piano sonatas of the period.

The *trio* literature is a different matter. A string trio most often consisted of violin, viola and cello; many important ones were written, the most outstanding being those of Beethoven. One can find anomalies, such as a flute rather than a violin, a clarinet rather than a viola, or a bassoon rather than a cello. The composer himself often made the alternate versions, more for practical reasons than for artistic ones. The standard piano trio was designed for violin, cello and piano, with similar anomalies (such as flute, cello and piano). Many outstanding piano trios were written in the nineteenth century. These provide convenient performance mediums, although some very bad arrangements of all kinds of music have been made for dinner music, weddings and the like.

The most important *quartet* form is the standard string quartet consisting of two violins, viola and cello. Some of the world's greatest music has been written for this combination of instruments, and much of it was written in the nineteenth century. It is significant that the greatest composers wrote some of their best music for the string quartet. Anomalies include such substitutions as a flute or oboe for one of the violins. The piano quartet is a string trio with piano added; many fine works in this genre are to be found, beginning with Mozart. Other instrumental quartets were written or music was arranged for special quartet groups, but their literature does not compare with that for the strings.

Quintets are more varied in make-up. The most successful string quintets are those which simply add an instrument to the quartet. The *Quintet in C Major*, Op. 29, of Beethoven follows the highly successful instrumentation of Mozart by adding another viola. Schubert, in his best-known string quintet (the *C Major*, Op. posth. 163, IV; D. 956) adds another cello. From the time of Mozart's great *Clarinet Quintet in A Major*, K. 481, several composers have added a clarinet to the standard string quartet (including Brahms and Reger). The quintet which would seem to be the most obvious—quartet plus an extra bass—does not exist as the instrumentation of any avowed masterpiece, except Dvořák's Op. 77 (1875). The use of the piano with string quartet has been used with varying degrees of success (the Schumann work is probably the best). One of the most unusual quintets is the *Trout* of Schubert, which uses piano and one each of the standard string instruments. There are other quintets of more heterogeneous instrumentation: Beethoven's Op. 16 is for oboe, clarinet, bassoon, horn and piano (he also arranged it for strings with piano). Late in the period composers tried adding the human voice as a fifth instrument to the string quartet (Schoenberg's *Second Quartet* is probably the most important). Composers of the twentieth century have written some good quintets (for string quartet and voice, Samuel Barber's *Dover Beach* is one which comes to mind).

With the *sextet* one approaches orchestral sonority, and there are many varieties of instrumental groups to be found. Brahms's two, Op. 18 and Op. 36, are outstanding; each one calls for two each of violin, viola and cello. Schoenberg's *Verklärte Nacht* is a romantic tone poem of the same instrumentation (1899).

The most famous *septet* is undoubtedly Beethoven's Op. 20, one of the best works of his early period. This piece employs three winds and four strings, including the string bass. Many conductors have programmed this work as a symphony, but hearing it with seven devoted virtuosi is indeed an unforgettable experience.

The most famous *octets* are Mendelssohn's works for double string quartet, Beethoven's for winds and Schubert's for a mixture of winds and strings.

These listings are of no means complete, but probably include the "cream" of the repertoire. Chamber music did not participate in the great issues of the century as did other kinds of music; there were no demonstrations or irate reviews when a new quartet was performed. Still, some of the best music of the century is to be found in the chamber music, and it also reflects the musical changes which were occurring elsewhere. Many composers did not even try to write any chamber works; many who did sometimes "forgot" that it was chamber music and turned out small "symphonies" which tried to sound big.

The nineteenth century had inherited a great chamber music tradition from Haydn and Mozart, and once again it was Beethoven and Schubert who led the transition from classicism to romanticism.

The Duo

Beethoven's sonatas for an instrument and piano consist of ten for violin and piano, five for cello and piano and one for horn and piano. These sonatas come from each of his creative periods and represent some of his finest compositions. Especially great are the late cello sonatas of Op. 102 and the violin sonatas Op. 24 ("Spring"), Op. 31, No. 2 (another great C minor work of Beethoven) and the *Kreutzer Sonata*, Op. 47.

In these sonatas one finds an amazing independence of the two instruments. In the *Violin Sonata*, Op. 12, No. 1, there is certainly independence, but one can observe the parallel period with the instruments changing roles. Note, after the initial "Mannheim rocket," that the violin has a lyrical theme while the piano plays running eighth notes. At eight measures before letter A the parts switch, the piano playing actually a variation of the violin part. At A the parts answer each other. Each instrument shares in the thematic material, but each has a life of its own.

The *Kreutzer Sonata* begins with a slow introduction which, in addition to the violin and piano dialogue, has chordal formations in which the violin plays an independent part. The key relationship is also noteworthy: from the major mode of the introduction to the minor mode of the sonata-allegro.

These sonatas also contain some of Beethoven's finest piano writing, requiring real virtuosity—perhaps a more difficult piece than a piano solo, since the keyboard part must be executed exactly with that of the violinist (who might also be having problems at the same moment). The *C Minor Sonata*, Op. 30, No. 2, is particularly demanding on both musicians, as is the *Kreutzer*.

The forms used reflect, by and large, Beethoven's usage in all his big works; no two movements in sonata-form are alike in the slightest. They not only use different themes, but different key relationships for the second theme, important development sections, free recapitulations and sometimes long codas. The slow movements are especially admirable; of particular beauty are those written in variation form, but other forms are also found. Beethoven's sonatas are almost always in three movements and the finales are often in rondo form, but not the light and airy rondo of earlier days. The finale of Op. 30, No. 1 is a delightful set of variations.

The late cello sonatas use a still different approach; the fugal finale of Op. 102, No. 2 shows amazing skill in fugal writing, and real virtuosity is required of both instrumentalists.

An unusual duo of Beethoven is the so-called "Eyeglasses Obbligato" (no opus number: WoO 32)[2] in E-flat for viola and cello, which is a delightful bit of *Hausmusik*: a concertato movement in sonata-form. Two curios are the variations of Opp. 105 and 107 for flute (or violin) and piano.

Schubert's *Sonatinas*, Op. 137, have been mentioned elsewhere but must be again here, since they are such fine examples of ensemble sonatas. In these works, although the violin part is the least demanding, it seldom merely accompanies the piano. Although they are sonatinas, they contain some of Schubert's most dramatic outbursts other than his songs. Many feel they should be called "sonatas," and I agree—they are not small works.

Schubert's other duos include the work often called the *Grand Duo*, which is really a large *Sonata in A Major* for violin and piano, Op. 162, D. 574, a work which ranks with the best of Beethoven. The second movement is a scherzo. The work makes considerable demands on both players, and employs considerable chromaticism.

The ensemble sonatas of Schumann come from unhappy times in Schumann's life (Opp. 105 and 121). They come from the Düsseldorf period (1851), as the mental illness dug deeper into his soul. These sonatas reflect his illness and are an example of works of art reflecting the times of the artist. There are moments of great beauty, but these passages do not "come off" unless great artists perform them with devotion. Better as a whole are the *Adagio and Allegro* for horn and piano and the *Fantasy Pieces* for clarinet and piano.

The three ensemble sonatas for strings and piano by Mendelssohn do not figure prominently in the repertoire. The *Violin Sonata*, Op. 14, is a youthful work and not devoid of interest, but is far less important than the two cello sonatas, which deserve more attention by cellists than they get. These works date from 1839 and 1842. The second sonata may well be one of Mendelssohn's best chamber works. Mendelssohn also wrote the *Concertantes Variations*, Op. 17, for cello and piano. This is a work which cellists should haul out again, for the piece abounds in effective technical devices and is an excellent example of his great skill at variation writing.

Brahms, as usual, provides some of the best of the ensemble sonatas for piano and another instrument:

	Publication Dates
Sonata for Cello and Piano, E Minor, Op. 38	1866
Sonata for Cello and Piano, F Major, Op. 99	1887
Sonata for Violin and Piano, G Major, Op. 78	1880
Sonata for Violin and Piano, A Major, Op. 100	1887
Sonata for Violin and Piano, D Minor, Op. 108	1889
Sonata for Clarinet or Viola and Piano, F Minor, Op. 120, No. 1	1895
Sonata for Clarinet or Viola and Piano, E-flat Major, Op. 120, No. 2	1895

These sonatas differ from each other in many details: they have either three or four movements, they express almost the whole gamut of human emotions and they employ a great variety of textures (from simple, songlike homophony to fugues); there are old-style movements such as minuets, and Brahms displays his own scherzo touch (a light heavy hand or a heavy light hand). It is often remarked that Brahms did not write any late keyboard sonatas, but these sonatas occupy the place in Brahms's career that the solo piano sonatas did in Beethoven's. Both instrumental parts are involved and difficult. Of all Brahms's great works these are among the greatest. They contain magnificent dramatic themes; beautiful lyrical, singing themes; brilliant passage work which is not empty—nor do they provide *Hausmusik* for anyone but virtuosi. They are a summation of the best of late-nineteenth–century musical tendencies which show how well a great master can keep alive classical forms and yet point to the future. These are among the most important works of this type ever written.

There were many string sonatas written at about the same time as the late Brahms pieces; among the best are those by Reger, Karg-Elert and some of the French composers: notably the violin sonatas of Franck and Fauré, which are discussed elsewhere in this book.

Chopin wrote a *Cello Sonata* and an *Introduction and Polonaise* (also for cello). The latter is a youthful work and a brilliant salon piece. The sonata, however, is a very late work and was the last work by him published in his lifetime. It is an uneven work but contains some moments of beauty.

Liszt wrote a little-known large work for violin and piano called *Grand Duo Concertant*, which has some striking passages.

The nationalistic composers wrote some ensemble sonatas, but these gentlemen were more interested in big works. (Had they known Beethoven or Brahms better, they would have known how "big" an ensemble sonata could really be.) Dvořák wrote some pieces for violin and cello, along with some pieces which are but a few cuts above the typical character piece for these instruments. The *Sonatina in G*, Op. 100, is delightful. It was written for his own children and comes from one of his "American" periods. It abounds in Dvořák "Americanisms" and contains some of his most beautiful music. The Brahmsian *Sonata*, Op. 57, is another beautiful work. (It must be remembered that Dvořák was an expert string player himself.)

Grieg also wrote some sonatas which have merit.

There are hundreds of string duos for instruction, *Hausmusik* and concert use. They are too numerous to mention; the quality depends on what one is looking for in a duo. Those of Viotti for two violins are outstanding. Works for mixtures of stringed instruments can be found, such as pieces for violin and viola or for violin and cello. Concert works— other than the great duos for violin and viola by Mozart—are found most often in the music of twentieth-century composers (such as Ravel and Kodály).

Wind duos are often arrangements of string duos. Beethoven wrote three duos for clarinet and bassoon, and there are many other pieces of less value which are used mainly for instruction.

The Trio

The obvious distinction here is between a trio with piano and one without. The professional concert world has many touring trios with piano, but few string or wind trios.

The most common trio is that for violin, cello and piano. Beethoven wrote a goodly number, including a fine trio, Op. 11, for clarinet, cello and piano. (There is somewhat of a precedent in the Mozart "Kegelstatt" trio, K. 498, for clarinet, viola and piano.) The Beethoven Op. 11 is best remembered for the variations in the finale.

Beethoven's Op. 1 consists of three standard piano trios. They are not his very first works by any means; they are only the first published. While they are youthful, their lack of maturity is more than compensated for by youthful freshness and vigor. These trios served notice on the world that here is a composer to be reckoned with—there are so many original features. One could compare these trios with those of contemporaries and find that Beethoven is really using the principle of equal temperament. He modulates in colorful ways, using the mediant relationship which Schubert was to employ so well. The very first trio begins with a common "Mannheim rocket"; the next change of harmony is to a dominant seventh, but it is a dominant seventh on the tonic root, a device Beethoven also uses at the outset in his *First Symphony* and in the Overture to *Prometheus*. Throughout this piece the violin and piano have the most fun; the cello part is not yet of equal importance.

The second trio begins almost as if he knew the Mozart K. 498. The best trio of Op. 1 is the third, in C Minor, Beethoven's favorite key. The cello has much more to say in this trio.

Figure 12-1

There are two trios in Op. 70. The first is called "The Ghost" because of mysterioso and contrast qualities in the second movement. The first movement is remarkable in its great economy. Beethoven spins out his lyrical consequent to the rush of the beginning and then builds his second theme from a fragment of the introduction. The development is remarkable in its combinations of these two ideas (in pitch essence one is the inversion of the other), and the recapitulation is quite different from the exposition. The second trio is almost Schubertian in concept.

Op. 97 is called the "Archduke," and is indeed a work of great nobility. There is concertato writing for all three instruments and a quality of "orchestration" about the whole work that gives it some novel effects. In the repertoire of all trio groups, it is one of the truly great works in its genre. The opening is marked by the size of the piano sonority and the beautiful cantilena in both stringed instruments. The scherzo is one of Beethoven's best. The slow movement is one of Beethoven's hymnlike themes with variations; its simplicity and musical honesty are a welcome respite after the virtuosity of the first two. The finale begins almost as a false start, but its speed grows and grows until the amazing presto of the hushed coda. Many trios play this coda too loud too soon. There should be a great difference between *ff* and *f*, as well as between *pp* and *p*.

One more piano trio needs to be mentioned: the curious variations "Ich bin der Schneider Kakadu." Few pieces of music have such a great contrast between the introduction and the variations themselves.

Beethoven's trios for violin, viola and cello are equally remarkable, perhaps even more remarkable than the piano trios. Little is known about them other than the fact that they are all early works probably antedating even the earliest of his quartets. It is probable that his mastery of the difficult medium of the trio strengthened his grasp of such matters as part-writing and form, so that his quartets—which are the best ever penned—are without the technical weaknesses often found in his early works. It must be remembered that Beethoven knew both Haydn and Mozart well. Do not consider his trios to be studies for the quartets, since they are high works of art in themselves—the Op. 3 is already the work of a master. Beethoven learned early to be economical in his writing and to build from mottoes. The *Trio Serenade*, Op. 8, is effective enough, but those of Op. 9 are perhaps the best in the literature, save for the Mozart E-flat, K. 563, and some from our own time (such as those of Hindemith, Schoenberg and Webern). There are three trios in Op. 9, of which the two best are the G Major and the C Minor. In the G Major the writing is so full that the work sounds like a quartet. The finale is an amazing tour de force which betrays the influence of Haydn. The C Minor is well-balanced in writing among the three instruments; it is actually designed for equal voices. Beethoven has a special affinity for C

Minor. This work is highly condensed; only the adagio is expansive. Note the key relationship.

The *Trio Serenade*, Op. 25, is for flute, violin and viola, and is a delight.

Schubert's two piano trios are in B-flat, Op. 99, D. 898 (1827), and in E-flat, Op. 100, D. 929, although there is a rather strange "Notturno," D. 897, which may be the final two movements of an unfinished trio. Many feel that the *B-flat* is an especially high point in Schubertiana. It begins with a fine verve:

SCHUBERT: *Trio*, Op. 99; First Movement

Figure 12-2

The *E-flat Trio* is also very beautiful, although the finale seems very long. The most fascinating movement is the second, which is related to the second movement of Beethoven's *Seventh Symphony* and to Schumann's great *Piano Quintet*.

Since these trios come so late in Schubert's life, it is well to point out that they represent only Opp. 99 and 100, but Deutsch lists them as 898 and 929. The highest D. number is 998, but this includes fragments and unfinished works. (Mozart's highest K. number is 626, and Einstein has shown that there are many Mozart works which Koechel did not know.) Mozart's K. 1 is a little minuet for piano written when he was only *six*. Schubert wrote his D. 1 when he was an old man: age *thirteen*! It is a three-movement fantasia for piano duet, which could even have been intended for a symphony. We cannot assume that early Schubert works such as this were his *very* first works. Schubert's career as a composer ran only from 1810 to 1827, but his output and musical growth was truly fantastic—and all with so little encouragement! Those who did encourage him were of the greatest importance, however.

There is also an unfinished (one-movement) string trio, D. 471.

Mendelssohn's trios are important. The *Trio in D Minor,* Op. 49, is still played quite frequently and is one of the best trios for violin, cello and piano. It contains a somewhat concerto-like piano part. Schumann ranked it with the great trios of Beethoven and Schubert which we have been discussing. The first movement has a main theme which—as is often the case with Mendelssohn—hovers about the notes of the tonic triad. This movement builds and builds. The scherzo is again the kind that only Mendelssohn can write. The second and fourth movements, although pleasant enough, are not up to the standards of the other two. The second trio is in C Minor, published as Op. 66. It is superior in every respect to the first trio. The opening theme again passes through the tones of the tonic triad, with the chromatic lower neighbor. In the chapter on melody it was pointed out that romantic melodies often run from dominant to dominant, as do these two trios. The slow movement is lovely. The scherzo is a real virtuoso piece; its exaggerated wittiness seems to make the finale more tragic. The finale has a theme which utilizes the interval of a ninth melodically:

MENDELSSOHN: *Trio No 2,* Op. 66; Fourth Movement

Figure 12-3

Also important are the three trios of Schumann. The third is considered by some to be the product of a sick mind, but others find it to be marvelous. I concur with those who love this work; how could a sick mind put together such a masterpiece? It contains some chromaticisms and harmonic pungencies, and has some almost impossible passages for the strings. The first trio is justly very famous; I particularly admire the opening of the first movement. The second trio is not as inspiring. Schumann also wrote a beautiful set of *Fantasy Pieces* for trio; however, as so often the case in Schumann, there is much doubling. This set of pieces was probably intended as *Hausmusik.*

The most important chamber music in the century after Beethoven was written by Brahms. The trios of Brahms are especially important. They are extensions of his ensemble sonatas, but the third instrument in each case is an integral part of the work.

Brahms's trios are:

	Publication Dates
Op. 8, for Violin, Cello and Piano	1859; rev. 1891
Op. 40, for Horn, Violin and Piano	1868
Op. 87, for Violin, Cello and Piano	1883
Op. 101, for Violin, Cello and Piano	1887
Op. 114, for Clarinet, Cello and Piano	1892

It is not really correct to look upon the later version of Op. 8 as a revision, since it is really a new work based on *some* of the themes of the old one. A comparative study of the two works proves very rewarding. The later work begins with an expansive, yet expressive theme:

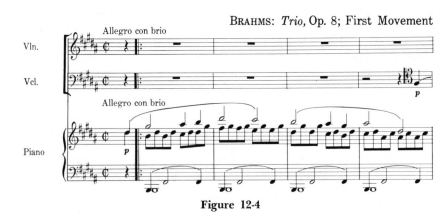

BRAHMS: *Trio*, Op. 8; First Movement

Figure 12-4

The horn trio and the clarinet trio were given alternate versions, where in each case the wind instrument was replaced by the viola. However, Brahms did not like the results: the wind parts were too well-conceived for the instruments in question. The horn for which Brahms wrote is actually the Waldhorn (a natural horn without valves). Space does not permit detailed study of these works here. Each trio is remarkable in its use of instruments pitted one against the others. The doublings are well-done, not like the overdoubling which plagues the Schumann trios. As was stated in discussing Brahms's songs, the doubling occurs at points requiring greater power and expression. In Schumann one sometimes feels that the strings in octave dialogue with the piano should be answered by the piano; nevertheless the musical content is so great that we would rather put up with problems like these than play the dull or "pretty" salon trios written by others (such as the piano trios of Godard).

In all piano chamber music there is the decided problem of effective string themes being equally effective on the piano, and vice versa. Brahms almost always comes up with themes which do work well in both media, and knows how to modify them when needed.

Brahms knew how to take a long theme and spin it out to cover long stretches. His motive structuring is very important internally, but we must not lose sight of the fact that for Brahms the theme *per se* is of extreme importance; his forms grow from the classical considerations of thematic contrast, and his development sections are drawn from techniques learned from the extensive counterparts used by Beethoven. Brahms is also progressive, mostly in matters of key relationships of main themes and in movements and modulations *within* the themes themselves (a feature often seen in Schubert as well).

The *C Major,* Op. 87, is particularly fascinating to study, to discover how Brahms derives new themes from the first one.

Reger's chamber music should be better-known than it is. (Perhaps there will be a movement to his music from that of Mahler and Bruckner.) There is one standard piano trio, Op. 102, and an early trio for violin, viola and piano, Op. 2. The most famous works (aside from the great clarinet quintet) are the two *Serenades* for flute, violin and viola, Opp. 77a and 141a, of which there are alternate versions for violin in place of flute. These works undoubtedly draw from Beethoven's Op. 25, but they have many touches of their own, such as the flute playing a bass part against the other instruments.

REGER: *Serenade,* Op. 77a
First Movement

Figure 12-5

As with all Reger, his use of counterpoint is very striking. More serious works are his two standard string trios, Opp. 77b and 141b.

Aside from salon trios and interminable arrangements, France produced its best chamber music in Franck and his coterie. Most of Saint-Saëns's chamber music is more fun to play than to hear.

Like Beethoven, Franck's Op. 1 consists of three piano trios (remember that the expression "piano trio" *always* means violin, cello and piano, never three pianos!). Franck called his Op. 1 *Trios concertants,* and they are studied for insight into the young Franck as a serious composer (1841).

The trios show some aspects of the Franck to come, and it is possible that he raided his own early works as many composers do. The *Fourth Trio*, Op. 2, was originally planned as the finale for Op. 1, No. 3, which, on the advice of Liszt, became a separate one-movement work. This work is historically important, since it is one of the first truly cyclic works of Franck; the germ itself presages the much later violin sonata. When musicians speak of "the Franck trio" the fourth is the one they mean, but the first also has much merit.

In all fairness, it must be mentioned that chamber music in France was not dead. Performers played the classics, such as Haydn and Mozart. As early as 1814 Baillot, the great violinist, was giving such concerts. The public found his own music too modern and preferred the quartets of such men as Onslow. The Gymnase Musical was formed about 1835, and was devoted to chamber music as well as solos. Most of the composers represented at these concerts are practically unknown today: such men as Gouvy, Bertini and Reber. Reicha was also played, and it is certain that Franck and other important composers were more than a little impressed with him. While his quartets and quintets are more important musically, Reicha also wrote some good violin sonatas, a flute sonata and twelve piano trios of uneven quality.

D'Indy is a Franckian who is currently somewhat out of vogue but who is historically very important through his teaching and his didactic works. His works are somewhat remarkable in their use of the cyclic principle, which he carries almost to the point of *isomelos*.[3] The *Trio for Piano, Clarinet and Cello* (1887) is of some importance, and can be studied for its striking applications of the cyclic principle. It is sometimes played with a violin substituting for the clarinet. Other trios were written by Saint-Saëns, Chausson and—most important—Ravel (a twentieth-century work). The Chopin trio contains some pleasant music, but remains today a curiosity; this work contains Chopin's only violin writing.

The nationalistic works for chamber groups are not numerous but are often very important. Smetana's *Trio*, Op. 15, of 1855 is somewhat auto-biographical, as is his great *E Minor Quartet*. It was written in memory of his eldest child, the daughter Fredericka, who died at the age of four-and-a-half after displaying talents as a child prodigy. The opening is a poignant melody for the violin; note the expression: *sul G*, which gives high pitches a special, strained quality. This work is an unjustly neglected masterpiece.

Dvořák wrote four piano trios and the *Terzetto* for two violins and viola. Dvořák's chamber works are surpassed only by his symphonies, and one could argue about that. He wrote a grateful kind of string chamber music which, however, does not always lie violinistically; there are times when sheer musical consideration takes precedence over instrumental consideration. In this regard he is unlike Brahms and Schumann, who give the string players figurations which lie well on the piano. The cello part in the opening of Brahms's Op. 111 is a nightmare, as is the cello statement of the main theme in the finale of Schumann's last trio. Dvořák's *Terzetto* is a piece which is fun to play and a delight to hear. Only Kodály's *Serenade* uses this unusual combination of instruments (two violins and viola)—a cello would be helpful at times, though. It is significant that few composers have ever written significant works for a group consisting of the same instruments. The Dubensky *Fugue for 18 Violins*, Klengel's *Hymnus* for cello choir and Villa-Lobos's *Bachianas Brasileiras* (Nos. 1, 2, 5, 7 and 9) are exceptional.[4]

Dvořák's piano trios are greatly different one from the other. The *G Minor* of Op. 26, like the *Stabat Mater* and like the Smetana trio, was the result of grief over the death of an infant daughter, Josefa. The *Trio in F Minor*, Op. 65, also comes from a difficult period in his life (see Clapham, pp. 10-11). This work is a personal favorite of this writer and there is a temptation to dwell long upon it. It begins with a theme in octaves in the strings, which is doubled for its *expressive* value. The work is important in its development of the cyclic principle, especially its melodic germs, but its rhythmic germs as well. Although an intimate work, it belongs on the concert stage, and is one of the most important essays in the trio form. The "Dumky" Trio, Op. 90, has six movements and is in reality a suite of Slavonic laments; as in much other folk music and concert music, this piece is full of abrupt changes in mood. The entire work is unified internally by a common spirit, as are the Mazurkas, Op. 7, of Chopin. Works such as these in no way attempt any allegiance to classical forms and are, therefore, real folk-inspired works. The cello plays an unusually important role in these works.

In Russia there were many examples of light salon music (no country really escaped it). Tchaikovsky wrote an important piano trio, Op. 50 (1882), in memory of Nicholas Rubinstein, one of Tchaikovsky's teachers and a great pianist. There is much of the great Tchaikovsky in this work, and some pages are perhaps his very best. Someone once said, "It is too long for its length." (Even with cuts, most performances last at least forty-five minutes.) The best movement is probably the variations on this theme:

Figure 12-6

Variation VIII is an arresting fugue:

Figure 12-7

Note that the subject again goes from dominant to dominant (*cf.* Szabolcsi, pp. 168-174).

There were many trios written in England, but none of first rank until our century. In America there were also several. Among the best are Daniel Gregory Mason's (1873-1953) *Sentimental Sketches* for piano trio; some exotically beautiful trios by Charles Martin Loeffler for piano, oboe and viola called *L'Etang* and *La Cornemuse* (both from 1905) and *Four Poems* for voice, viola and piano; in these the viola part is by no means "just an obbligato" but is an integral part of the score, as are the viola songs of Brahms. The American masterpiece of the period is the *Piano Trio* of Ives *(ca.* 1898). This great work may some day be regarded as highly as his quartets. The opening of the first movement is particularly good. Ives also manages to work in some well-known tunes. In America we are somehow embarrassed when we hear a familiar tune used in a serious work, and damn the work as cheap. When comparable tunes from other countries are used, people are entranced at the use of "nice folk songs." (Why are we so embarrassed by our own?) Ives will one day be regarded for his true worth; indeed, his esteem increases with each new book on the subject and with each new recording.

Yates[5] devotes a long chapter to him, Salzman[6] several pages in a rather thin book, and both Austin[7] and Hansen[8] discuss his curious music with some thoroughness.

There are many splendid examples of the piano trio in twentieth-century music. It is a practical medium but it entails many inherent difficulties, as do all chamber works involving the piano. The pianist must play with strength but with great delicacy as well. The pianist who plays piano chamber music well is a good pianist indeed.

Other trios also appear in abundance; there is a kind of "renaissance" of chamber music. There are, for example, outstanding string trios by Dohnányi, Hindemith, Webern and Schoenberg, to name but a few, and a curious work by Bartók for violin, clarinet and piano—another anomaly.

The String Quartet

Not enough superlatives exist to indicate the great importance of the string quartet. From the Classical Period to the present time the greatest composers have written their finest music for the quartet, and it has remained a favorite kind of *Hausmusik.*

Beethoven

Beethoven inherited from Haydn and Mozart the ready-made framework which was in itself great, even though in some ways it reflected the four-movement plan of the symphony.

Beethoven wrote sixteen quartets and the *Great Fugue,* in addition to arranging the *Sonata,* Op. 14, as a quartet. The quartets all fall into the three convenient periods of his life which are so often pointed out.

FIRST PERIOD:

Six quartets of Op. 18 (F,G,D,c,A,B-flat)

These quartets are all individual, and all are worthy of the master's signature. The most powerful is the Fourth, the *C Minor*—the only one in a minor key, and his favorite minor key. The *F Major* is striking in that the first movement has a persistent rhythm which appears and reappears in many guises—a Beethoven trademark. Traces of this can be found in the other movements if one looks and listens. The *G Major* is actually the third in order of composition, the *F Major* is second and the *D Major* is third. The last three are probably listed in correct order. In some respects the *G Major* is the most like Haydn, except that the third movement is a triple-meter scherzo and the trio is a supercharged minuet; the finale is a gem: the four instruments are nearly equal in prominence. Some writers have "put down" the *D Major,* but it is a proven work of great beauty; its finale contains some unusual scampering counterpoint.

The *C Minor Quartet* displays a new world of sound. True, Mozart and Haydn explored it, but Beethoven came there to live, with only a few return trips or a few glances back. This work almost qualifies for Second Period in its handling of various musical devices. In some ways it presages the great *C Minor Violin Sonata,* Op. 30, No. 2. The second movement is like a fughetta, and is notated in C major. It has so many points of imitation and is so canonic that one does not realize that it is really in sonata-allegro form! Beethoven even disguised the recapitulation; note the differences:

Figure 12-8

Figure 12-9

The second theme is canonic too and returns in the right key! Here, then is a scherzo in sonata-form. (There are some minuets by Mozart in sonata-form.) Beethoven follows the scherzo with a minuet which reminds one of the Haydnesque heavy third-beat Croatian quartets. The trio, however, has an almost Mendelssohnian flavor, and contains the curious notation that the quartet is to *da capo* faster, leading into the furious finale—in which, by the way, all repeats must be taken.

The *Fifth Quartet* displays what is either a curious quirk or a coincidence: when Beethoven writes in A major, he often uses $\frac{6}{8}$ time (see the *Sonata*, Op. 12, No. 2, the finale of the *Sonata*, Op. 47 and the *Seventh Symphony*, among other works). Most fascinating in this quartet is the set of variations in the third movement on a beautiful simple, innocent-sounding little song. The variations are noteworthy for their contrast. The finale is characterized by a three-note figure in staccato eighth notes which acts as a motto.

The Sixth is in many ways the most curious work. It has a very optimistic beginning. The third movement contains great rhythmic variety. The finale begins with a melancholy theme, which in a way anticipates his later quartets; this soon gives way to a chattering conclusion.

SECOND PERIOD:

"Rasumovsky" Quartets, Op. 59 (F,e,C)
"Harp" Quartet, Op. 74
"Serioso" Quartet, Op. 95

The literature on Beethoven's quartets makes up a sizable library, and it continues to grow. One is faced with great problems when trying to describe them. Knowing the historical background is of some importance, since Beethoven was a deeply personal composer and there were some unusual circumstances surrounding these compositions. In the Rasumovsky Quartets, for example, he uses a Russian theme (in honor of the Russian Ambassador to Austria, Andrei Rasumovsky). This theme is also used by at least three nationalistic Russian composers: Mussorgsky in *Boris*, Arensky in a string quartet and Rimsky-Korsakov in *The Czar's Bride*. Here is Beethoven's use in Op. 59, No. 2:

Beethoven: *Quartet in E Minor*, Op. 59, No. 2

Figure 12-10

The Op. 59, No. 1, has a widely-spaced first theme, first announced
in the cello and then answered in the violin:

Figure 12-11

Some have criticized Beethoven for starting with a tonic $\frac{6}{4}$, but it is
one which is more seen than heard. Beethoven often uses effective ar-
ticulated arpeggios which are not necessarily sustained in the other instrumental parts. The development section is very important, from which
the reprise simply emerges. This sonata-allegro is quite the opposite from
those of Schubert or even Haydn and Mozart, since the development is
so extensive and so important to the work.

The second movement is a scherzo, but it is a *serious* joke, amazing in
its harmony and counterpoint. (The Schuppanzigh[9] quartet thought it
was another Mozartian "Musical Joke" with "wrong" notes in the wrong
places.) Its harmony and its modulations do not surprise us, but *we* are
not listening in 1804-1806—the world had heard nothing like it before.
The adagio really provides no rest, although it is expansive. The violin
figurations remind one of the adagio from the *Ninth Symphony*.

The finale grows from the adagio, and its principal theme is a jaunty
one. The finale is a sonata-allegro, strong and brilliant but less important
sounding than the other movements; yet it is so right to end this, the
largest great quartet written up to that time.

The other quartets of Op. 59 are equally good. A noteworthy feature
of *No. 2* is the phrase modulation to the key of the Neapolitan near the
very beginning. This quartet contains some very imaginative harmony.
The student is urged to study the score to discover Beethoven's use of
many devices discussed in Chapter VII, such as the equality of the four
parts—the epitome of fine quartet writing. Note this excerpt from the
beginning of the development in the first movement:

BEETHOVEN: *Quartet*, Op. 59, No. 2;
First Movement

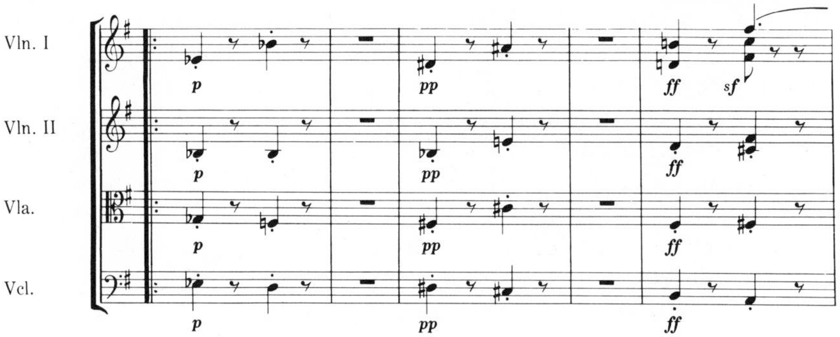

Vln. I
Vln. II
Vla.
Vcl.
p
pp
ff
sf

Figure 12-12

Why did Beethoven not write the second violin part enharmonically? The note is clearly an A-sharp, since the new key will be B minor. The allegretto contains some unusual and famous syncopations.

The *Third Quartet* uses another of Beethoven's non-tonic beginnings; the tonic of C major is not really stated until the allegro, and even then the theme is unsettled. The last movement of this quartet is its crowning glory, and in a sense ends the whole set (I would not object to an all-Rasumovsky concert!). It is a romantic fugue, in that it can branch off into what Demuth likes to call "chopstick chords"; there are also plenty of homophonic passages. But Beethoven knows well what he is doing: these "chopsticks" are actually thematic germs; if the student looks and listens well, he will discover that the movement is a sonata-allegro. (It is surprising that d'Indy[10] thought so poorly of this movement, when it utilizes so many of d'Indy's own principles!)

The "Harp" Quartet gets its nickname from the pizzicato notes used in the development of the first movement:

BEETHOVEN: *Quartet*, Op. 74 ("Harp")

Vln. I
Vln. II
Vla.
Vcl.
pizz.
arco
pizz.

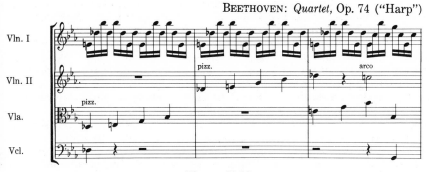

Figure 12-13

This is one of the few quartets which has a slow introduction before the sonata-allegro. Beethoven wrote great slow introductions, which get farther and farther away from the French overture with its stately dotted rhythms. This quartet begins with a tonic chord which is immediately destroyed; somehow, though, Beethoven does not run off to the subdominant. The sonata-allegro of the first movement begins with the dialogue kind of contrapuntal texture which will someday become the complete Beethoven quartet texture. The two middle movements provide great contrast, and are the best parts of the quartet. The finale employs a set of building variations which are effective enough, although Beethoven wrote both better variations and better finales.

The Op. 95 is grim business. Perhaps the nickname "Serioso" comes from the opening of the scherzo. The finale is an "agitated" movement which builds in tempo. The coda is often played as if it were Mendelssohn, but it is far too serious a passage for that.

THIRD PERIOD:

As original as the Middle-Period quartets are, they are quite classical compared to the late quartets, which to this day are subjects of awe to most musicians. The qualities which make them great lie not only in the little details which can be pointed out; there is an inner greatness which is difficult to pinpoint. Perhaps it is best merely to say that they represent lofty ambitions which are fulfilled.

Of the vast literature on the late quartets, Homer Ulrich probably sums them up best:

It is almost impossible to describe the last Beethoven quartets. Music is a matter of moods, of emotional states; to such states must be attached labels which are in common use. Quartets of the first and second period have been gloomy or joyful, pensive or abandoned, light-hearted or somber. But those are all personal, subjective labels. Here, in the works from Opus 127 onward, such labels are no longer adequate. There is no poignancy or sentiment in these quartets, nor even gayety or charm. Rather is there the spiritualized equivalent of those moods. The subjective, merely human emotions have been transformed into their objective, almost disembodied counterparts. Great strength becomes inexorable force; charm becomes austere beauty; extreme joy becomes divine abandon. Beethoven's last quartets become understandable, become one's own, only when one can go beyond everyday emotional experiences and ascend to the world in which he dwelt during his last six years of life. Sensuous beauty has no place in that world, nor has adherence to external forms. Everything in the quartets is flowing, plastic, newly formed; rigid concepts of harmony, form, or melody do not apply. To the extent that one can accept such fluidity, the works reveal themselves as the most divinely inspired music in the literature; by ordinary standards they are cold and unintelligible. Beethoven makes great demands upon his listeners in these quartets. One can meet them only with an open mind receptive to spiritual truths. It is not Beethoven who is being judged here, but we.[11]

One could cite writer after writer who expresses similar awe at these quartets. String players are especially enthusiastic about the late quartets, and audiences who have been fortunate enough to hear great performances by groups such as the late Budapest Quartet are also lavish in their praise. These works have no equal, and probably never will—the great quartets by Bartók and Schoenberg notwithstanding.

The opus numbers of Beethoven's late quartets do not reflect the time of writing:

Composition
Dates

E-flat, Op. 127	1824
A Minor, Op. 132	1825
B-flat, Op. 130	1825

(These three listed above are called the "Galitzin" Quartets, for a prince who commissioned them.)

Composition
Dates

Grosse Fuge, Op. 133	1825
C-sharp Minor, Op. 131	1826
F Major, Op. 135	1826

The first movement of the *E-flat Quartet* is sectional, with abrupt changes in tempo. Beethoven needs big sounds, so he resorts to healthy multiple stopping for each statement of the opening motto (marked "Maestoso"):

BEETHOVEN: *Quartet in E-Flat*, Op. 127;
First Movement

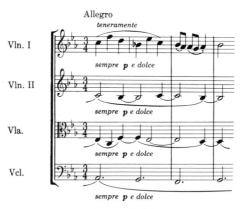

Figure 12-14

BEETHOVEN: Op. 127

Figure 12-15

Figure 12-16

Figure 12-17

Notice that in each case the ensuing music is basically the same theme, but that it is set differently each time: sustained carpet dolce the first time, weaving counterpoint legato the second and detached the third. The second movement is a remarkable set of "character" variations; one is reminded of the *Ninth Symphony* adagio, which was occupying Beethoven's attention at about the same time. The third movement features a study in rhythms, while the finale is a bit Brahmsian. This quartet, as do many of Beethoven's quartets, works with motive structuring in a manner that later composers emulated—but not always with Beethoven's great musical meaning.

The Opp. 132, 130, 133 and 135 are almost as well-unified among themselves as are the operas of the *Ring*, since they share common *Urkeim* or *Grundgestalt* material. (Just which one is *Ur* . . . would be difficult to determine.) He worked on several compositions at a time and sometimes an idea would leak here and there, but this was of peripheral importance. In the case of these quartets it is essential material which is shared. (It is certain that Beethoven did not intend these works to be a cycle, but they could well be called *Die Kunst der Streichquartet!*) Beethoven was seriously ill in 1825, and his recovery was a deep religious experience for him.

Op. 132 begins with an important motive in the cello, answered in the first violin:

Figure 12-18

Note how this same motive is used in Op. 133:

Figure 12-19

On the first page of Op. 132 the treble part in the cello is to be taken down an octave—a custom which persisted until as late as Dvořák. (There is a beastly passage for the cellos in his *Carnaval Overture*, written an octave too high; some modern editions have changed the notation to fit current custom.) This cello theme is important in Beethoven's work, and is perhaps a compression of the *Urkeim* (with interversion). There are clever textures in this movement, from all four instruments moving in the same note values to highly differentiated counterpoints. Each movement of this quartet is based on the germ motive in one way or another.

The third movement is a beautiful, expansive prayer in the Lydian mode, the only clue to a possible programmatic connotation in the late quartets. The patient's illness and new strength are duly noted. Unlike other Beethoven slow movements which are hymnic (except for the *Ninth*), this one has clearly established sections (like the adagio of the *Ninth*) and there is a contrasting section which gives way to the first idea (varied), which again gives way to the second idea (also varied), which again returns to the prayer of the beginning. This is a very similar form to the adagio of the *Ninth*, and it can be shown that the contrasting material is actually a far-out variation of the prayer, which is itself a variation of the *Urkeim-Grundgestalt*! The march is in a triumphant A major after the F cadence which ends the slow movement (remember that the untransposed Lydian has an ambitus of F to F with a B natural). The effect of the A major is another of Beethoven's mediant relationships. This march, however, is really a transition to the finale, and there is a certain fatalistic quality about it. When listening to this quartet, it should be heard both with and without the score (as all music should be by musicians).

These quartets are still based on classical traditions; Beethoven has only obscured the forms. In the B-flat, Op. 130, there are abrupt changes in mood and tempo in the first movement. The second movement, a presto, is highly compressed, and is not really a scherzo—note that there are abrupt changes here also. The slow movement is remarkable; the world had never before seen or heard textures like this in a string quartet:

BEETHOVEN: *Quartet*, Op. 130;
First Movement

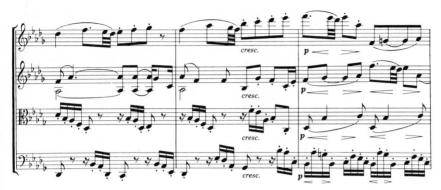

Figure 12-20

The fourth movement is a German dance; while it may serve as a relaxation, it is not meant as a let-down. The fifth movement is a famous cavatina, a form borrowed from opera by several instrumental composers. Beethoven even resorts to German directions (as he sometimes does in his late works) and says "beklemmt" in the first violin part. (This word means "tense," or "anxious.")

The finale looks and sounds like the Beethoven of earlier quartets, but it is based on subtle workings of the germ motive. It is a substitute for the *Grosse Fuge,* which is the original finale. Many authorities agree with d'Indy in asserting that this great quartet is better ended with the fugue; the tacked-on finale is fine music, but the *Grosse Fuge* has no equal. It is so taxing to play and so difficult to "sound" that quartets approach it with fear and trembling. Weingartner made a version for string orchestra which is powerful, but the piece becomes a bit "gritty" with that many violins trying to execute such difficult passages.

In the *Grosse Fuge*[12] fugue spills out of its banks, as it were, and becomes a much bigger matter than it had ever been before. It is actually a double—or rather multiple—fugue, yet it is based on two subjects: one is the motto we have been discussing, and the other is possibly a variation of it. Comment should be made about the notation as eighth notes tied to eighth notes rather than as quarter notes. There are two possibilities: 1) it can be syncopated, or 2) an eighth note tied to another eighth note is somewhat longer in duration than a quarter note, since it involves the release of an eighth note rather than of a quarter note. There are some who would argue the last point, but I first heard this explanation from my violin teacher: the late, great Imre Waldbaner.

Figure 12-21

There is a certain tension-building feature of this music which is amazing; the trills near the end are quite fantastic. In going over this fugue, the student should trace the use of the germ motive; note how old fugue form is followed and hòw it is expanded or even abandoned. There is perhaps some precedence for this in the *Jupiter* finale of Mozart.

The *C-sharp Minor*, Op. 131, begins with a slow fugue, the subject of which is derived from the germ motive. This music is cast in an unbroken cycle of seven movements which are greatly contrasted, but which are also tightly knit. In the fifth movement there is the only spot I know of where Beethoven uses *sul ponticello* (the performers play near the bridges of their instruments, which gives the music an eerie quality). He also uses the same remarks as in the *Ninth Symphony* (*Ritmo di tre Battuta*) to indicate a three-bar phrase.

The last quartet is in many respects the most beautiful—especially the marvelous and touching beauty of this passage:

Figure 12-22

This is a high point of perfection, even for a Beethoven! The finale has caused much comment by many writers and musicians:

BEETHOVEN: *Quartet in F*, Op. 135;
Finale

DER SCHWER GEFASSTE ENTSCHLUS
THE DIFFICULT RESOLUTION

Figure 12-23

What did Beethoven mean? One can see immediately the melodic use of mottos, and it is obvious that the second motto is the inversion of the first and the third is a transposition of the second. The title of this finale (see below) means something like, "the hard-won decision." The motto means, "Must it be?" answered by, "It must be!" Perhaps d'Indy[13] is right when he asserts that the whole finale is a big joke. Looking further in Thayer, we find the following:

ORIGIN OF "ES MUSS SEIN!"

Out of this joke in the late fall of the year grew the finale of the last of the last five quartets, that in F major, Op. 135, to which Beethoven gave the superscription: "The difficult resolution" *(Der schwergefasste Entschluss)*. The story, almost universally current and still repeated, that the phrases: *Muss es sein? Es muss sein*, and *Der schwergefasste Entschluss* had their origin in a scene frequently repeated when Beethoven's housekeeper came to him of a Saturday for the weekly house-money, was spread by Schindler, who was familiar in a way with the Dembscher incident but assigned it to the Quartet in E-flat. Holz was an actor in the scene and is the better witness, being confirmed, more-over, by the Conversation Book. Schindler probably took his clue from a page in the Conversation Book used in December, 1826, in which Beethoven writes the phrases "Must it be?" and "It must be," and Schindler, after a conversation in which Schuppanzigh takes part, concludes with: "It must be. The old woman

BEETHOVEN: CANON ON "ES MUSS SEIN"

Es muss sein! Es muss sein! ja, ja, ja, ja
It must be! It must be! yes, yes, yes, yes

Es muss sein! ja, ja, ja, ja, Es muss sein! ja, ja, ja, ja
It must be! yes, yes, yes, yes, It must be! yes, yes, yes, yes,

He-raus mit dem Beu-tel! He-raus! He-raus: Es muss sein!
Come down with the rhi-no! Come down! Come down! It must be!

Ja, ja, ja, ja, ja, ja, ja, ja, ja, ja, Es muss sein!
Yes, yes, yes, yes, yes, yes, yes, yes, yes, yes, It must be!

Figure 12-24

is again in need of her weekly money." The joke played a part in the conversations with Beethoven for some time.

Other performances of the Quartet were planned, but it does not appear that any took place. Schuppanzigh was indisposed to venture upon a repetition, but Böhm and Mayseder were eager to play it. The latter with his companions gave quartet parties at the house of Dembscher, an agent of the Austrian War Department, and wanted to produce the Quartet there. But Dembscher had neglected to subscribe for Schuppanzigh's concert and had said that he would have it played at his house, since it was easy for him to get manuscripts from Beethoven for that purpose. He applied to Beethoven for the Quartet, but the latter refused to let him have it, and Holz, as he related to Beethoven, told Dembscher in the presence of other persons that Beethoven would not let him have any more music because he had not attended Schuppanzigh's concert. Dembscher stammered in confusion and begged Holz to find some means to restore him to Beethoven's good graces. Holz said that the first step should be to send Schuppanzigh 50 florins, the price of the subscription. Dembscher laughingly asked, "Must it be? *(Muss es sein?)*. When Holz related the incident to Beethoven he too laughed and instantly wrote down a canon on the words: "It must be! Yes, yes, yes, it must be. Out with the purse!"[14]

Other Composers

The quartets of Schubert are not as good as Beethoven's, but not many quartets are as good as Schubert's! His quartets have been mentioned many times in the course of this book, especially movements based on such songs as "Der Tod und das Mädchen" and the *A Minor Quartet* with its theme from *Rosamunde*. The *G Major Quartet* has also been mentioned for its unusual triad color in the recapitulation, compared to the exposition. Also important is the single quartet movement D. 703 (another *Unfinished!*). Here are the Schubert quartets, listed according to the Deutsch numbering:

	Composition Dates
D. 18, in "mixed keys" (starts in C minor, ends in B-flat major	1812
D. 32, in C (unfinished)	1812
D. 36, in B-flat	1812-1813
D. 46, in C	1813
D. 68, in B-flat (two movements are lost)	1813
D. 74, in D	1813
D. 87, in E-flat	1813
D. 94, in D	1814
D. 112, in B-flat	1814
D. 173, in G Minor	1815
D. 353, in E	1816
D. 703, in C Minor (unfinished, the famous *Quartettsatz*)	1820
D. 804, in A Minor	1824
D. 810, in D Minor (*Death and the Maiden*)	1826
D. 887, in G	1826

The early quartets are much more than a youthful exercise. They were played by family and friends, but they transcend mere *Hausmusik*. They are Schubert as only he could compose, although there are some influences of Haydn and Mozart and then later of Beethoven. One finds a great variety of texture and an amazing contrapuntal skill. Schubert early realizes the necessity of a four-way dialogue, although the first violin most often carries the load in virtuoso writing.

The last five quartets rank among the very finest ever penned. The *E Major* is unusual in its choice of key, and shows greater use of harmonic coloring. It also exploits the "orchestration" aspects of quartet writing: chord voicing, voice-leading, alternations of instrument(s) and a convenient lie for the brilliant passages. The *C Minor* is very serious indeed: a tragic movement with no real resolution. The *A Minor* is almost understated: a gentle sadness, and very lyrical throughout. The *D Minor*, however, returns to the dark moods of the *C Minor* and is one of music's great masterpieces. Unlike the *A Minor*, it has moments of stark drama and driving rhythms, ending with an almost morbid tarantella. The *G Major* is in a class by itself. Had Schubert lived the normal life-span he might have gone further in the directions indicated by this great quartet. Specific devices he employs include: massive quasi-orchestral tremolos, alternation of major and minor (especially the relationships between G major-minor in the first movement), and change of keys to expand the classical key relationships in sonata-allegro form. The last quartets of Schubert require performing artists of the first caliber, and are a far cry from "music for friends." Schubert made a great impact (albeit belated) on composers such as Bruckner later in the century. Had he been better-known sooner the history of music would have been quite different.

The quartets of Mendelssohn are unjustly neglected. There are six, as well as a "suite" (an andante, scherzo, capriccio and fugue).

The Op. 12 (1828) is a lyrical, singing quartet containing a pathos rarely found in Mendelssohn. There are also some uses of the cyclic principle. The Op. 13 (1828) uses a motto "Is it true?" from a song which itself quotes Beethoven's "Farewell" Sonata. These works prove that young Felix knew his Beethoven well, for there are some relationships with the last quartets of Beethoven: not only in style, but in treatment as well. The fugue in the second movement of the Op. 13 is a good example. The three quartets of Op. 44 are reminders of the *Violin Concerto*, which is a greater work. Perhaps the best of the three is the D Major (Mendelssohn's favorite). It should not be assumed that all of Mendelssohn's fast movements are inspired by fairyland, even though many of them are. He knew well how to write fine polyphony for a quartet, and his best passages are contrapuntal ones. The third movement of the *E-flat* is a beautiful slow movement, the most difficult type of movement for Mendelssohn to write. As with all Mendelssohn, the parts always "sound" and are well-conceived for the instruments.

With Schumann it is the opposite case so many times, except when he is writing either piano music or songs. He wrote three quartets, dedicated them to his friend Mendelssohn, and wrote them all in six months' time. These are beautiful works, great works—but one only wishes Schumann had taken some violin lessons! Be that as it may, they are worth the effort to perform. As with much Schumann, these works display his "Florestan-Eusebius" nature. The great piano quintet was also written in 1842, as were the piano quartet and the *Fantasy*, Op. 88—here is another instance of Schumann concentrating on one type of music, hence 1842 is called his "chamber music year."

The quartets of Brahms show similar faults, but with adequate rehearsal they can be made to "sound." Brahms approached the string quartet with trepidation, having written (by his own admission) at least twenty before he kept any. Tovey and others have pointed out that Brahms had difficulty limiting his massive sound world to the more transparent medium of the string quartet; he found the quintet, the sextet and piano chamber music to be much more congenial. Be that as it may, the Brahms quartets are among the best written in the later half of the century.

The quartet of Grieg shows similar problems (such as too much heavy multiple stopping). Grieg was known as a miniaturist, so he overcompensated in the quartet by trying to write something larger. The Franck quartet is a great work, as are most of Dvořák's and the Smetana *E Minor*. Tchaikovsky wrote well technically, but his quartets are not his best inspirations. The Brahms string quartets are not without performances, but they need to be better-known, since they have a great content which is well-worth discovering through rehearsals. These works are *Hausmusik* only for very advanced players.

There are three Brahms quartets: two in Op. 51 and the Op. 67. The opening theme of the First Quartet displays two important points: Brahms, with some imagination, could still find music in the old "Mannheim rocket" through the use of non-harmonic tones; secondly, he made effective use of the pathetique downward-moving large interval.

These quartets are valuable to study for Brahms's devotion to and expansions of classical sonata-allegro and other important homophonic forms. The Second Quartet shows Brahms's propensity for unusual rhythms. The entire first movement is constructed on the principle of simultaneous hemiola. The finale is especially strong in its rhythm. Hemiola also figures in the Op. 67.

The three quartets of Reger are more than contrapuntal mazes, and should be played. The First Quartet has a fine scherzo and a powerful double fugue, and the Second an unusual first movement called "bizarro," but the best and the most exciting is the Third, which is an early example of continuous variation on the first theme.

In France the three supreme masterpieces are the quartets of Franck, Debussy and Ravel, although the other men in the Franck group also wrote well—there is a beautiful quartet by Fauré which was written in the 1920's.

The Franck is not played as often as are the Debussy and Ravel, primarily due to its length. (This work was discussed somewhat earlier in this book.) The Franck was written in 1889 and is his last great chamber work. This work is a masterpiece in cyclic form, and repeated hearings and studies of the score reveal relationships which were not apparent before. The Debussy was written in 1893 and is not really impressionistic; it belongs more to the school of Franck in its approach to cyclic treatment, and it also has some Russian flavor. There is also some very expressive and effective orchestration; this helps the work, since it incorporates delicate string writing. The Ravel does the same thing.

Written in 1902-1903, it is monothematic; its cyclic feature is a whole theme, not just a germ. The Ravel quartet is especially colorful in its orchestration.

The best nationalistic quartets are those of Dvořák; these are eight in number, and each one has its own special charm. In this country the "American" Quartet is the best-known, and in many respects it *is* one of the best. It is a fine example of Dvořák's mastery of harmony and counterpoint used in the difficult medium of the quartet. His modulations are imaginative and his melodies have a flavor so characteristic of Dvořák's American period. Dvořák's own life is often reflected in his music, and his quartets are among the most intimate. The *D Minor* displays its deep sorrow (D minor is so often associated with death!). All of these works have more than a touch of Slavonic melos, and the dance movements are not far removed from his *Slavonic Dances*. The *E-flat* is frankly Slavonic and has a merry polka, while the *C Major* illustrates his respect for classical tradition.

Aside from the quartets of Tchaikovsky and Borodin, the quartets of Taneyev and Glazunov should be mentioned. Glazunov wrote some of the best character pieces for string quartet—called *Novelettes*—in addition to six "regular" quartets, which are really marvelous music and do not deserve the neglect they suffer. He often employs the cyclic principle and makes frequent use of unusual textures. Taneyev's chamber music is admirable in its construction and in its great content. If his quartets were played in this country, they would probably be very popular among musicians (they are not too far removed from the *early* Bartók quartets).

Elgar wrote some chamber music of importance which is admired in England, and would be elsewhere if heard enough. Elgar's music almost always has a noble quality about it—at times it is truly noble, and at others only stuffy. He wrote much music that is dull; but when he is at his best, he is very good indeed. His best music falls somewhere between Brahms and Franck. The quintet (1918) is a romantic Franckian cyclic work with a lovely slow movement; for once, his string writing is far better than his piano writing. The quartet (also 1918) is a good work. The last movement uses a form which is employed often enough in romantic music to be pointed out as a major form. The form in question is the "Bogen," or "arch." This form of writing involves reversing the order of themes in the recapitulation: ABCDCBA. The violin sonata also has merit.

American chamber music should have developed faster than it did, considering the excellent music of the Moravians written in Pennsylvania and North Carolina in the eighteenth century. The nineteenth century produced no major works until its very end. Important are the quartets of Ives, Loeffler and Griffes, but the "Boston group" produced some which show good workmanship. Those of Foote and Chadwick are noteworthy, but especially so are those of Daniel Gregory Mason, who wrote well about the music of his time and used folk materials in his quartets: *Folk Song Fantasy* (Fanny Blair) and the quartet based on Negro spirituals. This latter work is possibly one of the most far-reaching results of Dvořák's stay here. The twentieth century has produced some very important American chamber music.

There are some quartets written for other combinations of instruments, but these have not remained in the repertoire. Many of the works (from solo pieces on up) were written by men who were primarily virtuosi of their instruments. Some fantastic solo and chamber literature for instruments such as flute, oboe, clarinet and bassoon was performed in salons and is still studied by performers today, but they are seldom programmed at concerts. The best quartets are the piano quartets, and those by the best composers are quite numerous.

Beethoven's Op. 16 is a quartet for piano and winds which he also arranged for strings.

Schubert's piano quartet is called *Klavier-Konzert*, and is an *Adagio and Rondo Concertante* (D. 487) for the standard violin, viola, cello and piano. It perhaps sets a style for many composers of piano chamber music who looked upon the piano as a concerto instrument. The Schubert work is quite demanding.

Schumann is more "at home" with the piano, hence his piano quartet and quintet are better written than his string quartets. They were both written in the same year (1843) and have some common features, but they are in no way alike. The quartet, Op. 47, suffers from some bad "orchestration," especially in some of its string writing and some unnecessary doubling. To be effective the work needs careful rehearsing; it does not reveal its charms as readily as the quintet does, even when being read by professionals (it is a common vehicle for symphony musicians on a busman's holiday, when they can corner a good pianist).

The greatest master of this medium is, far and away, Brahms. There are three of them, and the first two are masterpieces. There is a quality of true German folk song in Brahms's tonic-dominant harmonies; when Brahms *departs* from this usage, it is therefore arresting. The early *G Minor*, Op. 25, has some Brahmsian chromaticism, parallel thirds and sixths and a very large sonata-allegro for a first movement. This work displays Brahms's ability in his development sections. The *A Major*, Op. 26, is noteworthy for the use of large intervals in its themes; it becomes a habit, almost to the point of cliché, for Brahms to use a theme which moves through the triad.

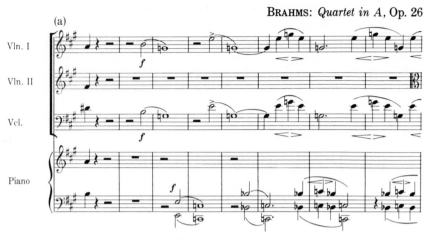

Figure 12-25a

Here is the same device used in his *First Symphony*:

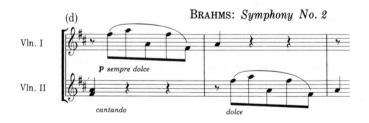

BRAHMS: *Symphony No. 1*

Figure 12-25b, c, d, e

The *C Minor Quartet*, Op. 60, gave Brahms some trouble; it was even written originally in C-sharp minor. Brahms himself did not think highly of this work.

Composers, again, lavished their best efforts on quintets involving strings, piano and strings or clarinets and strings. Beethoven's Op. 29 is not a great work, but Schubert's two-cello quintet (D. 956) is a masterpiece—not the least bit "bottom heavy," as one might expect. C major is a happy choice of key for richness, since the two cellos and the viola have open C strings and they all resonate on the dominant, open G. The trio of the scherzo displays a strange sadness. (This was his last chamber work.)

Schubert's *Trout Quintet* (D. 667) is a mixture of coffeehouse music and serious chamber music.

Mendelssohn wrote two string quintets, each using two violas. These are typical Mendelssohn; one is quite early, the other quite late. They use little padding and are very well written. The Second is perhaps more profound, while the lyrical portions of the First are akin to the *Songs Without Words.*

Schumann is given credit by most authorities for having discovered the piano quintet, and his Op. 44 is still the supreme masterpiece of that instrumentation. One often hears this work performed by a pianist who thinks he is playing the Schumann *Piano Concerto*; however, this is a work for *five* important musicians, and it is one which has the greatest respect of all who know it. Space does not permit much discussion beyond the comments made elsewhere in this book.

The work opens with a passage which uses an important set of themes in the string parts. From the first two bars it can be shown that the whole work evolves from the string motives.

SCHUMANN: *Quintet in E-Flat*, Op. 44;
First Movement

Figure 12-26

The first violin plays a striking line which diminishes the intervals, and the intervals themselves are separated by a semitone (seventh, semitone, sixth, semitone; the viola, for instance, plays a fifth, then a whole tone,

and the violin a fourth). This usage is too regular to be overlooked.
Schumann builds well with this device. Note the second theme:

Figure 12-27

The "sigh" in the first violin is not worn-out to this day. The march
expresses great sorrow but also shows great skill in melodic ornamentation.

Figure 12-28

SCHUMANN: *Quintet*, Op. 44;
Fourth Movement

Figure 12-29

The scherzo uses two trios, as do many other Schumann works (so did Mozart's *Serenade*, K. 361, and his *Clarinet Quintet*, K. 481). Note how the trio theme draws from the second theme of the first movement. The finale is a great *tour de force* for both composer and players; it has to be one of the contrapuntal masterpieces in the entire literature, and it comes from the pen of one of the most ardent romanticists. Its subjects are drawn from the germ motives presented earlier.

Another good work is the Franck *Quintet*, which also uses the cyclic idea; one hears it at the outset, in a very dramatic opening. The consequent of this theme is more typically Franckian than the antecedent, and the composer seizes upon this to form the theme at the allegro. You will notice that many Franck themes employ this same type of intervallic expansion. This quintet, as with most Franck, is very emotional and is as ardently romantic as any work one might cite. There is the danger of the pianist drowning out the quartet, and of the strings overplaying their instruments. Franck makes great demands on the players, especially musical demands. The musicians ought to understand Franck's use of cyclic form and the erotic nature of the music. Even Liszt was "alarmed" at the intense nature of the music. Here is the opening:

FRANCK: *Quintet in F Minor*;
First Movement

FRANCK: *Sonata for Violin and Piano*;
Third Movement

FRANCK: *Symphony in D Minor*;
First Movement.

Figure 12-30a, b, c

This quintet is a very big work, and the players are always exhausted when the performance is over. It is emotionally and physically taxing. The premiere was played by Saint-Saëns; Demuth tells of the insult to Franck:

Saint-Saëns was persuaded to play the piano part. Franck was so delighted with the performance that immediately afterwards he went up to Saint-Saëns to thank him, saying that he would like to dedicate the work to him and handing over the original MS as a present. Then followed a shocking display of bad manners. Saint-Saëns made an ugly face, tossed the MS on to the piano, turned on his heel and strode away. Either Franck did not see this, or else he had a finely developed sense of dignity. Years afterwards the MS was picked up in a pile of waste paper by an employee of Pleyel, the piano manufacturer.[15]

Brahms's quintets for strings alone use two violas. They are rich and full in their writing. Brahms is happy to have the extra instrument for his use; unlike the earlier sextets, these works display the full command of his technique as a composer. In Op. 88 there is an almost endless theme in the first movement. There is a brilliant fugue in the finale. The Op. 111 has a fantastic beginning—no *Hausmusik* this! The great musical and technical difficulty of the first movement has prevented this work from being better-known. The other movements require less virtuosity but are beautiful and profound.

The Brahms *Clarinet Quintet* is one of his best works. Its tonality requires an A clarinet. Here is the beginning:

BRAHMS: *Quintet for Clarinet and Strings,* Op. 115;
First Movement

Figure 12-31

The second movement represents a remarkable bit of clarinet writing. The entire work should be studied by every clarinetist and every string player. The *Clarinet Quintet* of Reger is also a good work in much the same style.

The *Piano Quintet* of Brahms occupies a special place in his life. Op. 34 was written in several different versions before the one which is now played; it is considered the apex of Brahms's early period. The work is well unified by an *Urkeim* which is heard at the outset. The reader is referred to Grout's *A History of Western Music* (p. 528) for an informative discussion of this piece.

Dvořák also wrote significant quintets such as the *E-flat,* written in America and perhaps the only work which really was influenced by Indian music. (I have long been fond of the *A Major Piano Quintet.*)

The century produced many sextets (Brahms), septets (Beethoven), octets (Mendelssohn), nonets (Spohr) and other works for various ensembles. These pieces reflect the principles which have already been pointed out. It is surprising that so much great chamber music came in a century in which composers and audiences were so interested in *big* works. It is a pity that the chamber music is not as well-known as the orchestral literature.

The best chamber music is very special—it *requires* a great composer, a great performer *and* a great listener. A great composer is necessary, since chamber music allows no orchestral "dressing" to cover the dross. Good performers are required who can play passages of great technical difficulty and then play passages which are all but self-effacing; they must be good soloists *and* good accompanists. A good listener is necessary, since chamber music requires close attention to its development. Chamber music "paints" in fine strokes!

Notes

1. These sonatas have much in common with the old trio sonatas, but they also are true duos in an equal-partner sense.

2. WoO 32 is the identification supplied by Kinsky in his *Beethoven Verzeichnis.* It means *Werk ohne Opuszahl* (work without opus number).

3. *Isomelos* means a series of pitches repeated over and over again, not necessarily in the same rhythm or repeated immediately.

4. The *Hymnus* has been performed at musicians' funerals. It was performed at the funeral of the great conductor Nikisch.

5. Peter Yates, *Twentieth Century Music* (New York: Pantheon Books, 1967), pp. 252-270.

6. Eric Salzman, *Twentieth-Century Music: An Introduction* (Englewood Cliffs, N.J.: Prentice-Hall, Inc., 1967), pp. 143-148.

7. William W. Austin, *Music in the Twentieth Century* (New York: W. W. Norton & Company, Inc., 1966), pp. 57-61.

8. Peter Hansen, *An Introduction to Twentieth Century Music,* 2nd Ed. (Boston: Allyn and Bacon, Inc., 1967), pp. 81-88.

9. Ignaz Schuppanzigh (1776-1830) was a close friend of Beethoven and the leader of what was probably the very first great quartet. He also led the Razumovsky quartet from 1808. The backbone of their repertoire was the quartet literature of Beethoven.

10. See his article on Beethoven in Walter Cobbett's *Cyclopedic Survey of Chamber Music*, 2nd Ed. (London: Oxford University Press, 1963).

11. Homer Ulrich, *Chamber Music* (New York: Columbia University Press, 1948), pp. 272-273.

12. The *Grosse Fuge*, Op. 133, was originally a part of Op. 130; but it was felt to be too long and too difficult, so another finale was written for that work.

13. See the article previously cited from Cobbett.

14. Alexander Thayer, *The Life of Ludwig van Beethoven*, Vol. III (New York: The Beethoven Association, 1921), pp. 224-225.

15. Norman Demuth, *César Franck* (London: Dennis Dobson, Ltd., 1949), p. 36.

CHAPTER XIII

VOCAL MUSIC

The Solo Song

MAN'S EARLIEST SELF-MADE MUSIC was probably song. It is not far-fetched to assume that as man developed speech he developed more expressive ways of saying certain things through his voice quality, inflection and tempo. (See Curt Sachs's *Rise of Music in the Ancient World.*) There were two main types of songs (and there still are): *pathogenic* (or passion-engendered) songs, and *logogenic* (or logic-engendered) songs. Most songs actually combine these two extremes, but one finds that the romanticists wrote some of their most passionate music in their songs. The art song comes into its own during the nineteenth century, and it is a major contribution of the period.

Important songs were written by men who were famous in other fields of composition: such men as Schubert, Beethoven, Schumann, Mendelssohn and Brahms. Important works were also written by composers who were known primarily for their songs: such men as Robert Franz, Carl Loewe, Duparc and Jensen. The art of song was already highly developed, and in most instances the songs in the nineteenth century reflect the other developments in music such as melody, harmony, emotional appeal and phrasing. The principal contribution, however, is probably the importance of the piano as the accompanying instrument, although the orchestral song by no means languished.

370

The wedding of poetry and music is apparently a vital product of romanticism: the poem provides the poetic idea (the "program," if you will), while the advances made in piano construction, piano playing and writing make possible remarkable—even astonishing—settings of poetry. Since many poems are short, the composer's formal problems are reduced to a minimum: he can launch a marvelous flight of fantasy without worrying about getting to the *next* fantastic place (a common difficulty in much program music). The poet was perhaps "ahead" of the musician at the beginning of the century, and was capable of providing the composer with moods, structures and subject matter which was congruent with the subjective aspects of musical composition. One idiom actually influenced the other; hence, there were many "weddings" of words and music which were real "love matches."

Poetry, of course, is one of the most important art forms known to man. The very best poetry does not need music; it has a music of its own, and music can only be an intrusion. Nevertheless, great poetry inspires the best creativity in men, and composers are especially responsive. Knowing full well that a great poem doesn't really need music, they still set it to music. Many poems are best-known through their musical settings. Many poems would probably not be known at all otherwise, since composers often have set some rather mediocre poetry. (Maybe these lesser poems needed musical settings to enrich them!) It is not fair to judge a composer's taste in poetry by the poetry he sets to music, but it is fair to judge the suitability of the text for his musical setting. Great songs have been set to great poems, bad songs to great poems, great songs to bad poems and bad songs to bad poems. A song illustrates ideally how the whole *can* be greater than the sum of all its parts; however, while we can find great songs set to bad poetry, we *never* can find a song in which a great text will compensate for a bad musical setting.

One must look to the German-speaking part of the world to find an almost unbroken line of excellence in vocal music from before J. S. Bach to the present. The German Lied, however, although preponderant, is only one kind of important art song. Developments in France led to a very special kind of vocal art which is found nowhere else. The art song in England is quite different from the English-language art song written in America during the nineteenth century. The English composer inherited the native-born tradition of Purcell and the natural simplicity of Arne, to say nothing of the delights of the catches and glees *and* madrigals. These forms all became stilted somehow in the nineteenth century by English composers who tried to wear the wig of Handel, to create in Haydn's style or to water-down Mendelssohn. In America many composers wrote German Lieder, even if the poetry was English. Ives used almost every musical style and wrote some of the finest songs in any tongue (including a setting of Heine's "Ich grolle nicht"); others were impressed by the French and wrote French songs in English—but these songs often need the sounds which one can get only with French vowels.

Italy was so absorbed in opera that this form drowned out most of the attempts to write intimate art songs, although the songs which one can find are indeed gems. After all, vocal art was cultivated and nourished in Italy as nowhere else in the world, and for many years the Italian vocal style exerted great influence on composers all over the world, as far away as Russia, even in the eighteenth century. Russian art songs used a variety of languages, and some great works came from the hands and hearts of men such as Mussorgsky. Scandinavian composers found a somewhat different type of expression and contributed many fine pieces. No Western country escaped the vocal art form; after all, it is one of the most practical performance idioms and it succeeds perhaps more than any other form in touching the sensibilities of the musician and the common man. Cheap songs were written by the ream and died by the ream; but there has been more in common between the great song and the common man than, say, between the great piano sonata and the common man—there was the text to reckon with, and much poetry set by the romantic composer said things which the common man felt but did not have the words to express. Thus we see that poetry is indeed enhanced by music.

Liszt, in this example, applies the overdone principle of major keys for happy moods and minor keys for sad moods, but the unsophisticated listener gets the message. This message is not necessarily true in another context, and this is one facet of musical understanding which requires sophistication: *context*.

The context of a song *must* include the words. The understanding of an art song is largely missed if one does not understand the words, whether it be from bad diction, lack of understanding of a foreign language *or* lack of understanding of the poem. The uninitiated listener interprets happy moods for major keys and sad moods for minor keys, and he can tap his toes, but he completely misses the real message of the song. *If* the language is understood, then he understands the idea of the song; he may even notice that different vowels have different "colors" and—at the most subtle plane—he may realize that the deepest inner musical meanings of the song are lost if the text is translated. For example, the German ö does not exist in English and requires a different vocal color when it is sung; this is an important factor in the complete understanding of the song. Or, a composer may deliberately use subtle counterpoint to set off the words. The music is one thing,

LISZT: *Freudvoll and Leidvoll* ("Joyful and Griefful")

Revised by Eugen d'Albert

Eng. words by John Bernhoff

Figure 13-1

the poetry another, and the song is a summation of the two. Changing word order when translating often ruins the composer's text-painting.

Although Mozart and Haydn both wrote important songs, Beethoven's Lieder are some of the earliest examples of romantic Lieder. In these we often find Beethoven at his most simple and intimate level—one often missed by those who know only his large works. Some of his simple songs come from later in his career than their content would lead one to believe.

Beethoven's cycle *An die ferne Geliebte*, Op. 98 (1816), is considered to be the very first song cycle, only on the technicality that the word "Liederkreis" appears in the subtitle. In 1803 Beethoven wrote the beautiful set of *Gellert Lieder*, which in some respects is more like the later song cycles than *An die ferne Geliebte*. The latter is continuous in sequence, although still written in a way which would allow singing an excerpt if desired. Needless to say, the cycle should be sung as a whole. Some of Beethoven's most striking modulations are to be found here, such as at the end of the first song and the start of the second.

Here is the song "Vom Tode" from the *Gellert* cycle (1803), which shows the romantic flavor of the words and music. Notice how the harmony sets the mood, especially through the open triads in measures 19 and 20.

BEETHOVEN: *Gellert-Lieder*; *Vom Tode*

Figure 13-2

Some of Beethoven's other songs are characterized by an operatic flavor (such as *Adelaide*), some by simplicity ("Gretels Warnung"), some by humor ("Song of the Flea" from *Faust*) or by rather fussy settings (his Italian songs). "Mit einem gemalten Band" might be the source for the hymn tune of the *Ninth Symphony*—even if by accident. It is fascinating to compare settings of the same poem made by different composers or by the same composer. Beethoven, for example, wrote four different settings of Goethe's "Nur wer die Sehnsucht kennt," and they are indeed different one from the other.

Schubert wrote hundreds of songs, and I seriously doubt if more than a very few people know more than a dozen or so. Sad to relate, some of the best-known of these are among his least important works; other well-known songs, however, are among his very finest. While there is always a great deal of study of the Schubert songs, even Schubert authorities admit that *really knowing* all of them would be a large task! (*Cf.*

Einstein's *Schubert*, p. 94.) A persusal of the index of Schubert's complete songs in a work such as Einstein's short but great biography (pp.
331-334) give one some indication of their relative importance in Einstein's mind. Some songs are not mentioned by him at all, some are
mentioned in passing just once, others a few times; "Das Wandern,"
for example, is not only mentioned several times, but it and the rest
of the cycle *Die schöne Müllerin* are discussed for several pages.

The great variety of Schubert's songs makes it difficult to discuss or
classify them. It would be logical to start with his song cycles, since
they are often performed *in toto*, and since his individual songs are
among the most famous of his output. Another category would be
chronological, but this does not teach us much about the songs other
than their expected growth, which can be observed with more ease and
accuracy by considering all his types of works. The system used in
Grove's is probably the best: classification by over-all approach or form
of the song. There are four groups of Schubert songs: 1) the simple
strophic song; 2) the modified-strophic song; 3) the *durchkomponiert*
song (through-composed); and 4) the sectional song, such as an operatic
scena. These forms are discussed in this book in the chapter on form—
except for the fourth type, which is not regular in form and has a
variety of tempi. One of Schubert's earliest songs is the "Dom" ("Cathedral Scene") from Goethe's *Faust* (D. 126). This work, written in 1814,
is amazing in its anticipation of Wagner. A much better-known song is
the second one of the fourteen songs published as the cycle *Schwanenge-
sang*: "Kreigers Ahnung." This song illustrates Schubert's use of sectional form, in its use of differing moods and musical patterns. The tempi
in this song (and in most Schubert songs) are indicated in German—not
in Italian, as are his instrumental works. Other German composers had
used German, but Schubert did so probably because he knew that these
songs were different from anything yet done and would be grossly misunderstood on internal grounds.

There are some who would downgrade Schubert's strophic songs
because they are simple, often folklike, and not as free or as subtle as
his through-composed songs. An examination of his strophic songs reveals that many of them are simple, while others are more complex.
There are several such pieces in the cycle *Die Schöne Müllerin*. The
very first song, "Das Wandern," is a real delight, the kind of song which
one might sing while on a hike. There are five strophes; a good singer
and pianist will do each one differently, even though the printed notes
are exactly the same—it is enough, though, that the words of each
strophe are different, since that makes for different music! Poetry is
also music, so there are different colors for different vowels. The internal
form of this piece is a common German song form: the bar form AAB.

Other songs in this cycle which are strophic are No. 7, "Ungeduld"; No. 8, "Morgengruss"; No. 9, "Des Müllers Blumen"; No. 10, "Thränenregen" and four others. In each song the musical treatment and the internal form are different.

More arresting, however, are the modified-strophic songs in which Schubert repeats music in the stanzas with some kind of modification. Needless to say, these instances are many in number and show Schubert's great technical gift for variation and his extraordinary ability to fit the right music to the sense of the poetry at various levels (the general emotion, the psychological state, the atmosphere, and the moving or static qualities). Perhaps the best-known song of all these is "Die Forelle."

The through-composed songs also defy further classification, other than those which maintain a particular song form for one stanza and a different one for the next. The composer was usually more subtle than this, however, and wrote his songs "straight out." They are often unified through their accompaniment patterns, key relationships or melodic or harmonic motives. One of these is "Die junge Nonne." The song is unified by two devices similar to those used in "Der Erlkönig." The tremolo in the right hand and the dramatic countermelody in the left, which recur in varied form, in many ways actually control the whole song. There is some melodic repetition but each time the accompaniment is different. This song comes late in Schubert's life, and the atmosphere of the poem is beautifully set, down to the last details: the storm, the grave and the little bell ringing through the storm. Perhaps the best touch of all is the change in mode to the major.

Other through-composed compositions are to be found in the non-strophic songs of *Die schöne Müllerin*, although it is sometimes difficult to tell where the line should be drawn between the modified-strophic form and the through-composed form, especially when melodic material is repeated. The most significant works of art frequently defy classification.

Schubert's other great cycle is *Die Winterreise*, twenty-four songs to verses by Müller. These songs are of greater variety and complexity than those of *Die schöne Müllerin*. The scope of expression is astonishing. The last song, "Der Leiermann," is one of Schubert's most modern; its harmonies are truly amazing.

There is no sense in comparing Schubert and Schumann, and in wondering who is greater than whom. Schumann had the advantage of knowing Schubert's music and that of many others of the time. (Obviously, Schubert could hardly have known Schumann.)

Mendelssohn wrote many Lieder at about the same time Schumann wrote his; but, pleasant as they are, they do not represent his best efforts, as do the oratorios or other choral works of Mendelssohn.

Schumann was a major composer of Lieder and, unlike Schubert, biographical details strongly influenced his song writing. Schubert understood poetry naturally (as did Schumann), but Schumann was also a *litterateur*, coming from a literary family.[1] Schumann was also a fine pianist, and his piano parts are even more involved than those of Schubert.

Schumann's marriage in 1840 unleashed what has been called a "torrent of song." Of some importance is the cycle *Liederkreis*,[2] Op. 24 (not to be confused with the better-known Op. 39), based on poetry by Heine, a poet for whom Schumann had a great affinity. This *Liederkreis* cycle contains nine songs. Of even greater importance is the cycle *Myrthen*, which contains several famous songs but is seldom sung in totality, perhaps due to its length. A variety of poets are represented in this composition, including German translations from English poets such as Byron. The first song, "Widmung," has been discussed in the chapter on harmony.

The most famous cycle, called *Liederkreis*, Op. 39, consists of twelve songs set to poems of Joseph Eichendorff. These songs show a remarkable variety, especially in their texture. Note the end of No. 6, compared to the beginning of No. 7.

One of the most remarkable works in all Schumann is the cycle *Frauenliebe und Leben*. Many writers have pointed out that the poet Adelbert Chamisso gave Schumann some insipid verses to set. This may be true, but it only adds to Schumann's stature, since the cycle as a complete work of art is a masterpiece. The cycle should be sung complete and often is, but the second song, "Er, der Herrlichste von allen," is justly popular as a single offering. Schumann unified this cycle in many ways, the most obvious of which is the lengthy coda of the last song (which also recalls the first song, asserts Chopin, and is not far removed from Schumann's own piano concerto).

Most Schumann authorities, singers and others who know Schumann's songs agree that the apogee is the cycle *Dichterliebe*, Op. 48, set to poems of his most commonly-used poet, Heine. It begins with a remarkable dissonance. Note that the vocal line uses many pitches, six in the first phrase. There is an arresting change in texture from the first to the second song, and again from the second to the third. Note also that each song is very short: hardly a page or two at the most. The fifth has a curious texture. Of prime importance is the sonority achieved by the relationship of the eight notes in both hands—only a pianist could have written this.

Note that the vocal line is enriched by doubling in the piano in the seventh bar. It is significant that the words here mean "a song from my beloved." Number 6 is still another German song about the Rhine

SCHUMANN: *Dichterliebe*, Op. 48; "Ich will meine Seele tauchen"

Figure 13-3

(often a source of inspiration); its mood is not too far removed from parts of the *Rhenish Symphony*. Number 7 is another very well-known song.

From the eighth song to the end the songs become more complex and display many of Schumann's trademarks. One such trademark is the long piano postludes, which are absolutely necessary for the form and expression of these songs. This is especially seen in No. 9, "Das ist ein Flöten and Geigen" ("That Is a Flute and a Violin"):

SCHUMANN: *Dichterliebe*, Op. 48; "Das ist ein Flöten und Geigen"

Figure 13-4

The tenth song employs typical Schumann piano figuration and syncopation. From the thirteenth song through the fifteenth there is again a change in texture to reflect the idea of nightmarish dreams, and in the last two songs a great variety of textures within the same song. The cycle ends with an involved piano postlude.

The most popular Schumann song is probably "The Two Grenadiers," a real rouser which somehow does not pale through the years. It is a good example of a song which is between the modified-strophic style and the through-composed style—it even resembles a free rondo. Schumann himself published sets of *Romanzen und Balladen,* and this is the first song of the second set, Op. 49 (1840). The grenadiers are certainly subject matter for a ballad, and the *style* is ballad. This term was used so loosely by both French and German songwriters that one could expect almost any form, although through-composed and modified-strophic forms are often found. In the modified-strophic approach the composer would insert music which was episodic (like a rondo) but almost always of importance in projecting the poem. The episode in rondo or in fugue should not be considered of less importance than the recurrent theme. Schumann quotes "La Marseillaise" as the melodic germ of the last section of this song. Although the rising fourth is very common in songs—in all tonal music, for that matter—it is just possible that Schumann got the musical idea for the recurring melody from "La Marseillaise." The opening piano part is handled very much like a refrain or even a ritornello, and throughout the song this part receives development.

Schumann's songs set the German language in an outstanding way; there are never awkward elongations or accents, and extreme ranges almost always contain an open vowel. But Schumann's vocal melodies seldom exploit extreme ranges; he saves these for the pianist. In "Aufträge" (as we also saw in "Das ist ein Flöten und Geigen") there is a demanding piano part:

SCHUMANN: *Aufträge*; Op. 77, No. 5
Words: C. L'Egru
(Original Key A Major)

Figure 13-5

(Imagine the difficulty involved for the pianist, who has to be able to play these songs in various keys!)

The significant piano part becomes a permanent fixture in the art song. While one would expect this from composers such as Liszt, one finds even more demanding piano parts as the years approach our century. This makes a song much more difficult to sing, since often the composer does not double the singer, nor is the singer's pitch always in the chord. A new subtlety arises in harmonic coloring in which important chord tones appear in the vocal line and not in the piano part, or else they appear in the piano part only *after* the voice sings it. Some songs have effective beginnings for the voice alone (such as Schumann's "Röselein, Röselein!").

There were many songs by composers of Lieder which are pleasant enough—like the ballades of Loewe (mentioned in the chapter on form). Robert Franz (1815-1892) was a narrow specialist; he wrote mostly for mezzo-soprano, and mostly in the strophic style. His songs seldom show any depiction, but they do contain some beautiful melodies and harmonies. Peter Cornelius (1824-1874) was closer to Schumann in style, and at times anticipates some of the more gentle songs of Mahler. Cornelius often set his own poetry, as did Wagner (with whom he was associated). Cornelius wrote an opera, *The Barber of Bagdad,* to his own libretto; this work is still successful. His best-known song is probably "Ein Ton."

The next great figure is Brahms, although the songs of Liszt should not be dismissed lightly. Liszt wrote some songs in Italian and French as well as in German, and these show great sensitivity. He thought well of his songs and revised them from time to time. His seventy-some-odd songs rank among his best works and deserve to be heard more than they are. He achieves many novel effects in his harmony and sets every colorful phrase with his literary sensitivity. "Kennst du das Land" is an effective example.

Brahms was more concerned with musical perfection, so his songs do not employ as many programmatic effects as those of other Lieder composers (although he was not immune to the program device). In "Der Schmied" the accompaniment imitates the smith's hammer. "An eine Aeolsharfe" has a beautiful imitation of the "aleatory" music which the wind plays and which has fascinated many composers (Wolf also wrote a famous song to the same Mörike poem).

When a composer is too graphic, the accompaniment can call one's attention away from the subtleties of the poem and—more importantly —from other aspects of the music. The music can have inner qualities, such as those seen in "Liebe kam aus fernen Landen" from the *Magelone* cycle.

The German word "Innigkeit" can apply often to German songs, but it seems especially appropriate to those of Brahms, in spite of the classical traits which are often pointed out in Brahms's music. "Sehr innig," a term seen often in Mahler, is an expression designed to aid the performer. The word is not the same as "Ausdruck," which means simply "expression"—a very wide term, to say the least. "Innig" implies warmth, intimacy, or even "hearty" or "heartfelt."

This same quality is felt in Brahms's early songs, which come from the period of close association with Robert and Clara Schumann. Although they show a decided influence of Schumann, they still have the melodic and harmonic richness which we almost always associate with any of Brahms's music. The beautiful "Liebestreu" of Op. 3, No. 1 has remarkable features.

The typical Brahmsian love of syncopation (eighths against triplets) is immediately evident. The eighths in the left hand not only anticipate the vocal line, they might be a musical suggestion of "faithfulness," which is the meaning of the title. The key is a little extreme: E-flat minor; but it was important to Brahms, since *he conceived the song in that key.* The doubling of voice and piano is very effective when Brahms does it, since he doesn't do it very often. Usually there is a line of poetic importance when doubling occurs; there is seldom a slavish doubling such as one finds in many lesser songs.

A song called, simply, "Lied"—also from Op. 3 (No. 6)—employs fascinating chromatic passing tones and has a lush quality about it. Many songwriters use a rhythmic pattern which permeates the whole song giving it either unity or monotony, or which suggests some type of movement indicated in the poetry. In this song Brahms achieves a marvelous effect to set off the words which speak of strange things: mountain peaks, people, springs, rocks and trees, like a "dream." The sixteenth-note movement stops momentarily, to imply the strangeness.

In Brahms there are many complicated piano parts, but simple songs

BRAHMS: *Sechs Gesänge*, Op. 3, No. 1; "Liebestreu"

Figure 13-6

can be found—such as the "Volkslied" from Op. 7 and the "Sonntag" from Op. 47. It is an oversimplification to state that these works are in the idiom of Robert Franz. The pianistic difficulties are comparable to those in his own keyboard works and require a large technique to play properly. They often involve odd patterns, massive sonorities and Brahms's peculiar liking for the octave and the third.

Brahms wrote some of his loveliest music in the Op. 91, which consists of two songs for contralto and viola obbligato. These songs have real contrast. The second song has an air like a folk song and the tune is an old carol. Folk song style happens quite frequently, even though Brahms's phrase structures are usually more complicated than those of *German* folk songs.

It is difficult to write about Brahms's songs, since one could say much about any number of them; one cannot find a "typical" song among them, and it is difficult to classify them. There are many famous Brahms songs but some of the very best are seldom heard because of their difficulty. We must again be grateful for the many recordings of these songs which are now available.

Brahms's best-known songs are probably the "Immer leise wird mein Schlummer" (this theme is also used in his *B-flat Piano Concerto*), "Sapphische Ode," Vergebliches Ständchen" and the famous lullaby "Wiegenlied," which is the fourth song in a set of five published as Op. 49.

There are two cycles by Brahms which must be mentioned. The first is long and extensive, in reality a "cycle of cycles": *Magelone*, with words by Ludwig Tieck (1773-1853), an important voice in romantic German literature. The cycle is Brahms's Op. 33 and it consists of fifteen songs written between 1861 and 1868. These songs are rich in variety and lush harmony—almost too sweet, some say. Some of the songs are very long—such as the very first one, which employs a persistent rhythm which perhaps suggests the gait of a horse. Also long is the third song, which has a fascinating, widely-spaced texture. The pianistic agility required for the next-to-last song is considerable.

Magelone is a long cycle to hear at one sitting, but real Brahmsians can take it. It forms nearly a whole program; again, the recording seems to be a wonderful solution. (People often say that the romantic composer must have had some subconscious notion that there would eventually be recordings of their works; otherwise, they wouldn't have been so optimistic in lavishing such musical forces and extreme lengths on their compositions. Interestingly enough, one of the anti-romantic reactions of our century is brevity.)

The other cycle is the deeply religious *Vier ernste Gesänge*, based on texts from the Bible. These represent Brahms's penultimate work. It seems significant that Brahms, in the third song, sets "O Tod, wie bitter bist du" and then returns to Christian optimism (as he often did) in the fourth. Here he sets the thirteenth chapter of First Corinthians, which begins, "Though I speak with the tongues of men and of angels and have not love . . ." and ends, ". . . thus abide Faith, Hope and Love, but the greatest of these is Love."

Hugo Wolf was in the Wagnerian camp, but his songs are far more important than his operas. His songs tend to group according to poets, since he grouped them in that manner. In 1889 he published his songs set to the poems of Eduard Mörike, all written in 1888 (sometimes several in one day). These, as a group, display Wolf's wide scope from a folklike mood to one resembling symphonic construction. Wolf (like Schumann) set some Eichendorff texts, and a collection was published in 1889. Most of the Eichendorff songs were also written in 1888; but, as a whole, they do not impress listeners as much as the *Goethe-Lieder*, also written in 1888 but published in 1890. Perhaps Wolf felt the great awe for Goethe that many did, since he set some of his finest songs to Goethe's words. Also of great worth are his *Spanish* and *Italian Song-books*. Wolf's music is very beautiful in its own way, but it must also be considered as a transition from the earlier Lieder to the later—there are many anticipations of twentieth-century techniques. (See Chapter VI.)

Wolf's expert handling of subtle details in setting the German language has often been pointed out. (See Steven's *A History of Song*, pp.

BRAHMS: *Vier ernste Gesänge*, Op. 121, No. 3; "Wenn ich mit Menschen"

Figure 13-7

253-257, article by Philip Radcliffe.) Wolf's creative period came to an
end at the same time as Brahms's death (1897), but his songs are more
advanced in harmony—as his interest in Wagner might imply. His
output of songs was considerable and their great variety is astounding,
as is the growth from his earlier songs to his later ones. He learned
much from Schubert and Schumann, and composers since Wolf have

learned much from him. His piano writing is just as distinguished as his vocal: from the massive "Prometheus" to the very simple "Gleich und Gleich." Some of his songs seem to reach out for the sounds of the orchestra (he orchestrated twenty-three of them). (See p. 149.) "Kennst du das Land" is especially moving, and it is rewarding to compare the many different settings of Goethe's great poem from *Wilhelm Meister.*

Mahler, the same age as Wolf, was another transition composer who looked well to the future. His best-known songs are cycles which were orchestrated and today receive enough performances to be repertoire pieces. To his own poetry he wrote *Lieder eines fahrenden Gesellen* (Songs of a Wayfarer) (1883), which are beautiful examples of how delicate Mahler could be. *Kindertotenlieder* are heart-breaking songs to tortured lines by Rückert, songs which struck close to home on the death of his own small children. *Das Lied von der Erde* (1908) alternates tenor and contralto soloists, and is actually a "symphony with voices." The poetry used here is a translation by Bethge from *Die chinesische Flöte,* and his music is some of the most delicate and yet most powerful, showing great contrast. Also very important are his songs of *Des Knaben Wunderhorn,* which are very good examples of a highly sophisticated composer using folk material not only for art songs but for symphonic purposes. Mahler is important also as a transition from the Wagnerian era to the twentieth century and to composers such as Schoenberg and his group. Mahler was active with the Schoenbergians, but had to admit that he was perplexed by the direction their music had taken.

There were other Lieder composers of the same period. One of the most outstanding was Richard Strauss, who was perhaps the culmination of the conservative Lieder composers. The Lieder of Strauss are not exploratory in harmony as is, for example, his opera *Elektra.* The songs of Berg are far more advanced, as are those of Reger. Strauss and Reger represent the very end of rich harmony—no more richness is possible without going in the direction of post-tertian harmony. Even the songs of Hindemith belong to the breakthrough rather than to the old tradition. The old tradition should not be regarded as complete *fin-de-siècle* decadence. The songs of Strauss, at their best rank with the very greatest German art songs. He wrote 153 songs, set to a great variety of poetry; perhaps his best ones are very late works: the *Vier letzte Lieder,* which are orchestral songs. Strauss is reported to have been very spontaneous in song composition, since he was so very sensitive to poetry. Most of his songs have a remarkable atmosphere and some have fantastic piano parts; note this passage in "Frühlingsfeier," Op. 56, No. 5:

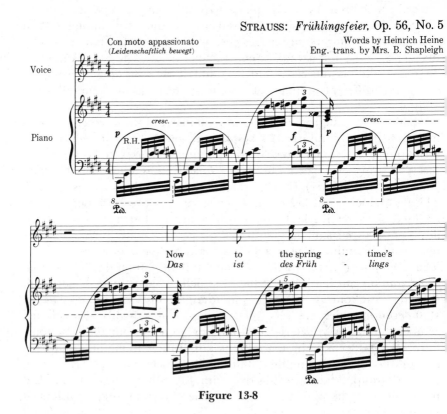

STRAUSS: *Frühlingsfeier,* Op. 56, No. 5

Con moto appassionato
(Leidenschaftlich bewegt)

Words by Heinrich Heine
Eng. trans. by Mrs. B. Shapleigh

Figure 13-8

Far more simple is the justly-famous "Allerseelen," Op. 10, No. 8.

Other composers of the end of the Romantic Period are Hans Pfitzner (1869-1949) and Joseph Marx (b. 1882), whose songs are not really very original even though many are very beautiful—if by now a bit old-fashioned. The old vein of gold had run out; it was up to Schoenberg and others to find a new ore for the development of twentieth-century music.

In the Scandinavian countries there were many beautiful songs written, many of them in a simple, popular vein, and sung internationally by the great Jenny Lind, who made Swedish composers such as Ahlstrom and Lindblad known as far away as the United States. The most important pieces, however, probably come from Norway in the songs of Halfdan Kjerulf (1815-1868), who, like Grieg, was trained in Leipzig. Also like Grieg and many other Scandinavians, Kjerulf set German words in addition to his native tongue. Grieg's songs are among his best works: running from the well-known "Ich liebe dich" (which has been translated into almost every language) to the extremely fascinating "There

Cried a Bird" (where sounds are exploited for their own sake). Grieg wrote a cycle called *Haugtussa* and arranged for string orchestra two other well-known songs, "Heart-Wounds" and "The Last Spring." In Grieg there is almost always harmonic interest; he is at his best in short works (such as songs), where he does not need to develop the music.

The songs of Carl Nielsen are not numerous, but are important in his development as a vital twentieth-century link to the Romantic Period. His songs are not as well-known as they should be. Nielsen and other Danish composers benefited from the influence of Gade, who had made German music very well-known. Sibelius's songs are not as important as his symphonies, but they show a side of him which many do not know. The song "Black Roses" is very well-known. Sibelius's piano writing is not as facile as that of some other composers; he apparently is more at home with the orchestra.

The art song in Russia was developing along important lines, reflecting musical activity in other areas (particularly opera). Glinka is considered the first song composer of lasting importance, but Dargomyzhsky is one of the first to show any originality. He wrote songs resembling the French *romance*, and in the French language (as did other Russians). The newer ideas of realism were exemplified in the use of the ballade form. The Russian-language songs pose some difficulties for performers, but there are numerous translations. (If one is not to sing in Russian, then it is ridiculous to sing in a language other than that which is understood by the audience.) The best Russian songs come from Mussorgsky, although other members of "The Five" and Tchaikovsky wrote some fine pieces. The cycles of Mussorgsky—*The Nursery, Sunless* and *Songs and Dances of Death*—are all outstanding, and are among the finest narrative, realistic songs ever written. The realism is not merely superficial (in text-painting) but portrays very deeply how a man feels at a given moment—a common trait in Russian art and literature of this period.

The French influence—both in language and in use of the *romance* form—has already been mentioned. The *romance* can be traced back to the Troubadours, and was important in the early nineteenth century. The *romance* involved other national styles and influences: German influences in such matters as text-painting, and Italian influences in simple accompaniments and tunefulness. After the early part of the century traces of the *romance* idea could be seen in such devices as dance rhythms and quasi-folk idioms. Another important term is *mélodie*, which became the French equivalent of the German *Lied*.

Berlioz wrote both *romances* and *mélodies*. His best songs are the orchestral *Les Nuits d'Été* (originally accompanied by piano). These songs show that Berlioz had a fine ear for delicacy and could capture moods other than battles and storms.

Gounod wrote some important songs which were admired by Ravel and which are sometimes still sung. Félicien David was important at one time and is credited with bringing a Schubertian influence to the French *romance*. Bizet and Délibes also wrote some fine songs; the songs of Massenet were numerous, and exerted a profound influence on his pupils at the Conservatory.

Almost all French composers of reputation tried the art song—Franck, Saint-Saëns, Chabrier *et al.*—but the best are those by Fauré, Duparc and Debussy, leading to some very unusual songs by twentieth-century composers. Fauré's "Après un Rêve" is an example of simplicity itself— but what beauty it has! More complicated are "Nell" and "Rencontre." "Soir" shows a remarkable use of chromaticism and text-painting when changing texture.

There is more variety of texture in Debussy and Duparc, and in each a remarkable feeling for just the right touch of color (as in Debussy's "Mandoline"). "La Chevelure" is remarkable for its harmony and declamation.

The songs of d'Indy are fascinating: such as the "Lied Maritime," with its varied settings of the melody which is sung at the very beginning. D'Indy would frequently change the harmonization of the accompaniment and keep the same pitches in the melody, in both his instrumental works and his songs.

Duparc's few songs are only twelve in number but contain a great variety of musical style; the piano parts are especially striking. A great loss to music was probably effected by Duparc's severe self-criticism which caused him to destroy some scores, notably a cello sonata. Aside from the songs, there are only two short orchestral pieces and some little pieces for piano. His songs stand unique in music history: they are highly original, deeply moving and stand very high as great examples of French art.

The late-nineteenth–century French songs are very colorful harmonically, as are the other French works. The French approach to harmony and chromaticism differs from that of the Germans and the others. French composers cultivated a kind of harmony which did not depend so much upon the dominant function. One can find in the songs of Chausson, for example, root movements by major seconds or by thirds to color the harmony—here is a sample from "Le Charme":

Figure 13-9

This already shows the parallel movement of chords which is so important in impressionistic music.

Italy (as might be expected) did produce some beautiful songs, although its energies were concentrated on opera. The songs that did appear often reflected the influence of opera. Around 1880 a new generation of composers was born, which again increased the scope of Italian composition. One outstanding result has been the discovery of early Italian music and the application of compositional ideas from other countries (impressionism from France and serial techniques from German-speaking countries). One of the most prominent is Respighi (1879-1936), whose songs are not numerous but significant (such as "Il tramonto" for voice and string quartet). The songs of Casella and Pizzetti were written mostly in the twentieth century.

England and the United States produced entirely different kinds of songs in the English language. Both countries were strongly influenced by German music and—late in the century—by French impressionism. In the United States local color was provided in songs from the musical theater (such as in minstrel shows) and from revival meetings (especially at the frontier). Each of these idioms found their way into American music—especially seen in the songs of Ives, which were written from

Plate XV

Photograph of Charles Ives, American composer (1874-1954) *(Courtesy The Bettmann Archive, N.Y.).*

1888 on and which also show other influences and anticipations of twentieth-century techniques. His 114 songs were not published until 1922. Ives's songs are inspired by hymns, war songs and nature, and pay close attention to a great variety of subject matter. He was not completely immune to the German romantics, but he could be anti-romantic—as in "The Cage," set to his own text and written in 1906. Ives frequently writes in such a way that no two performances will come out exactly the same way—foretastes of *aleatory* music.

The songs of MacDowell (1861-1908) are among the best out-and-out romantic songs by American composers. Loeffler (1861-1935) and Griffes (1884-1920) are almost French in style. Foote (1853-1937), Parker (1863-1919), Paine (1839-1906), Chadwick (1854-1931) and many others are German-influenced, as have been many American composers who figure prominently later. These men and others established music schools as lasting and responsible parts of colleges and universities, and were responsible for the training of many musicians.

There were many salon songs and many banal trifles composed, which —sorry to say—are still sung. Perhaps the best-known is Nevin's (1862-1901) "The Rosary," which has had amazing longevity. This kind of song still is written and has a certain following, since the genteel tradition is still to be found.

The American composers of the twentieth century have distinguished themselves in the field of art song—composers who are as disparate as Barber and Babbit (see Gilbert Chase's *America's Music*). Perhaps a word should be said about the once-popular pseudo-Indian songs; these might have produced some major works, but the real talents (such as Ives) were not too interested in them. Cadman (1881-1946) will suffice as a reminder—his "The Land of the Sky-Blue Water" has as little to do with Indians as parallel fifths! Far more significant—but still frustrating—are the works printed by the Wa-Wan Press, founded by Arthur Farwell to accept the challenge for indigenous music laid down by Dvořák. Chase points out that the thirty-seven composers involved were not in any way a "school" but were individuals. Some of the best Indian music is to be found in their compositions, in addition to folk songs from other ethnic groups.

Dvořák himself had written some significant art songs, but there never was any extensive history of Czech solo songs. His earliest songs, called *Cypresses*, are a set of eighteen inspired by his love for an actress whose sister he later married. He revised these songs, and they are available in the revised version. His earlier versions, however, were often used as source material for other works. With Dvořák and Smetana there is a language problem, since few singers in the English-speaking part of the world sing Czech and the German texts are not always well-versified. Other than "Songs My Mother Taught Me" from the *Gypsy Songs* of 1880, the best-known are probably the late *Biblical Songs*, written in the United States in 1894. These are quite remarkable. Dvořák also wrote twenty-five vocal duets which are settings of Moravian folk songs.

Smetana's best songs occur in his operas.

Janáček is an important composer who used Czech folk materials. *The Diary of One Who Vanished* is a cycle which uses tenor, contralto and female trio. It dates from 1916 to 1919 and is considered one of his masterpieces. Earlier he had made significant collections of folk songs, which permeate his entire output. The best-known works for voice, however, are his operas.

In England the folk song was also an important idiom, as were the eternal influences of Handel, Haydn, Mendelssohn, Brahms and the natural simplicity of songs by men such as Arne. The United States had the likes of Stephen Foster, who wrote very simple songs of such basic beauty that one thinks they are folk songs. Sir Henry Bishop's "Home Sweet Home" is often thought to be a Stephen Foster composition. There are many other similar songs written all during the century. "Home Sweet Home" is, in fact, from an opera: *Clari* (1823), although Bishop had used the tune earlier. Bishop also wrote more serious things, such as songs for Shakespearean plays. Of a rather large group of lesser English composers who excelled in the "Victorian ballade," I shall single

out only Henry Russell, since he was one of the most prominent of the
lot and was very popular in the United States. He played on the frustrated emotions of Victorian audiences with such "masterpieces" as
"Woodman, Spare that Tree" or "A Life on the Ocean Wave." "The
Old Arm Chair" can be seen in the Marocco and Gleason Anthology.[3]
These musical examples of utter, utter bathos represent a curious kind
of double standard, since they were ostensibly "concert music" and yet
were as low-down in style as the music of any pub (and not nearly as
authentic). Sir Arthur Sullivan, who would much rather have written
"important" works, is probably the best at this sort of writing—his
operettas are so *bad* that they are *good*.

With the arrival on the scene of Hubert Parry (1848-1918) and Charles
Villiers Stanford (1852-1924), an infusion of new blood helped the
quality of the English song—transfusions from Brahms especially. The
three best English composers come a little later, however, in Frederick
Delius (1862-1934), Sir Edward Elgar (1857-1934) and Ralph Vaughan
Williams (1872-1958), all of whom (as so many composers we have discussed) belong in both centuries. Delius did not spend too much time
in his native England, having lived in the United States (on a citrus
plantation in Florida) and in Germany and Norway. His music shows
influences from each country; in the Norwegian songs (dedicated to
Grieg's wife), we can see German coloristic harmony and a kind of
harmonic "oozing" which can be very lovely but which can cloy. His
melodies often resemble English folk songs.

Elgar's music contains much to admire, but not especially his solo
songs. They tend to be too Victorian, and they lack the touch of the
great master that we observe in his masterpiece *The Dream of Gerontius*.

Ralph Vaughan Williams, on the other hand, left a wealth of good
vocal music. The cycle *On Wenlock Edge* (1909), with words from
A. E. Housman's *A Shropshire Lad*, contains some remarkable songs
when performed either with piano or—better still—in their original
setting for tenor, string quartet and piano. His songs from the nineteenth century are few in number. By 1911 he had made some folk song
collections which influenced much of his later writing, especially in
matters of melody and harmony. He also wrote some distinguished songs
based on great English poets such as Rossetti, Stevenson, George Herbert,
Bunyan, and the American Walt Whitman—and, of course, Shakespeare.
Vaughan Williams also wrote some outstanding hymns.

Solo song, then, was an important development in the nineteenth
century, and each major country contributed literally hundreds and
thousands of songs. The best are very high examples of musical art
and the worst are terrible ones. As the century moved on, songs with
accompaniment other than piano came into being, such as songs for

voice and string quartet. The orchestral song cycle became important, and—as we shall see—there were also good non-operatic uses of the solo voice in the choral works of the period.

Choral Music

During the nineteenth century the social functions of choral music underwent great changes. There was less and less importance attached to the use of choir and/or orchestra in churches, and attention was turned elsewhere. Many churches, especially the large ones, still had important music, but this music was no longer in the mainstream of musical development. Many works were used from the magnificent backlog which had accumulated, while other church music consisted of sentimental trifles. The fantastic public successes of the great oratorios was in part responsible for the shift of attention to large works for chorus and orchestra. Audiences were much impressed by size, length and number of performers. The works which were supreme classics, and which inspired many imitations, were Handel's *Messiah*, Haydn's *Creation*, Mendelssohn's *Elijah* and the large works of J. S. Bach. Other works by these masters were also performed and emulated. What was once strictly "church music" had now become popular concert music.

Beethoven's *Ninth Symphony* was, of course, impressive; in addition he had written the *Missa Solemnis*, which had exerted great influence. Berlioz's *Romeo and Juliet Symphony*, Liszt's *Faust* and *Dante Symphonies*, and later the Mahler symphonies which use chorus are among the very best of post-Beethoven choral symphonies.

But there was also room for more intimate part songs: some for use in church, others for amateur choral societies and others just for fun (the *Liedertafeln*[4]). The great market for the school chorus did not as yet exist in great profusion. There were "singing schools," however, and almost every town had "clubs" or similar groups which still sang catches and glees—people's tongues often became "loosened" by various cereal-malt beverages. There was such a popular demand for simple music of this kind that Young[5] even contends that the careers of promising composers were severely hampered—and perhaps even ruined—by their trying to keep up with the public demand for this kind of music. Composers did not dare to depart too much from what these amateurs could really sing; the music must not be too difficult or too "modern." Many of the pieces they wrote still survive as Protestant hymns or college *alma mater* songs (some people even think they are folk songs).

This is not to say that there are not some small choral works of great beauty and originality. There are some lovely choruses by such composers as Schubert, Mendelssohn, Loewe and Brahms. There are also some choral works of great originality—even if a bit crude—by William Billings, the amazing American tanner who was a great musical enthusiast. Although he lived from 1746 to 1800, his "Fuguing tunes" exerted great influence on much later music, including that of the twentieth century; his works are still performed with great effect. Perhaps the best-known pieces by Billings are "When Jesus Wept" and "Chester." One of them, "Jargon," is an early American Musical Joke. Billings was also a prominent promoter of singing classes and societies.

This kind of choral music is a rich field for further study. Some of it has been reissued from time-to-time and some has been recorded. So many of these works are of such beauty that it is well worth searching through the chaff to find the few grains of real wheat.

Beethoven's Choral Music

Beethoven is often held to be unskilled and too unvocal as a choral composer; he actually wrote some quite conventional music for church choir use and for his oratorio *Christ on the Mount of Olives*. (The *Ninth Symphony* has been discussed elsewhere in this book—the *Ninth* should not be considered as "normal" Beethoven.)

The great *Missa Solemnis*, Op. 123, owes much to the past; it is very late Beethoven. This is such an overpowering work that the earlier *Mass in C*, Op. 86, a work of rare beauty, is often overlooked or forgotten. The *Mass in C* was written in 1807 and the first performance left everyone bewildered, since it was not the formula-ridden sort of mass the singers were used to performing. It contains some of Beethoven's best choral writing and is particularly notable for its use of rhythm to set off important phrases and ideas in the text.

The *Missa Solemnis* comes from the period of the *Ninth Symphony*, and it is true that the chorus parts are very demanding vocally. The role of the orchestra is at least as important as that of the chorus—at times more important, even when the chorus is singing. One such instance is the beautiful violin solo in the "Benedictus" in which the violin plays a lovely line, first with two flutes and then with two clarinets. This mass represents some of Beethoven's best fugal writing and some of his most overpowering ideas. To him it was a great work, and he lavished great care over it. The first performance was to have been for the enthronement of the Archduke Rudolph in 1820, but Beethoven was so painstaking that he didn't finish the work until two years later. It was at this time that Beethoven began to have some of his greatest difficulty with people such as landlords, who thought that the man had

BEETHOVEN: *Missa Solemnis*;
Benedictus

Andante molto cantabile e non troppo mosso

Figure 13-10

completely lost his mind. On the score he writes: "From the heart—
may it speak to the heart." Wienandt sums up the matter so well when
he states: "The *Missa Solemnis* is Beethoven's towering achievement,
not in spite of the fact that it transcends liturgical limitations and
denominational identification, but because it does so."[6]

Schubert, Schumann and Mendelssohn

Schubert's best choral efforts are not as well-known as they should be.
There are four masses dating from his youth which are free from almost

any vocal complication, and which are ideal for practical performance in schools and churches. The two masses from his adult life are a different matter. The *Mass in A-flat* is one of his greatest works, combining unusual color contrasts of key (A-flat is a most unusual key for a mass) with his love of the mediant relationship (either enharmonic or not). The "Gloria," for example, is in E, after the "Kyrie" in A-flat. Schubert could also write a good fugue (as at the end of the "Gloria"). It was not too common for Schubert to revise (he had so little time!), but the *Mass in A-flat* he revised in many details. One should not forget that Schubert was a great master of harmony; this mass is a good example.

Schubert's last mass, the *Mass in E-flat*, again shows his contrapuntal skill. Einstein and others point out the use of thematic material from Bach's *Well-tempered Clavier* and from his own song "Der Doppelgänger." Schubert's fugal writing should be emphasized, since there is an unfounded popular notion that he never had any skill at this. Some Schubertians feel that the *Mass in E-flat* is Schubert's best, perhaps even his greatest work. It is an important landmark in the history of the mass, in that the handling of the soloists, chorus and orchestra takes on a new relationship, with the chorus all-important. His harmony is handled so smoothly that the average listener does not even realize that anything worthy of note has happened!

Many of Schubert's choral works (which are very singable by school choirs) are difficult to obtain, but can be perused by consulting his complete works. The *Song of Miriam*, one of his better-known works, is for chorus and piano; it contains some interesting text-painting suggestive of the Egyptians drowning in the Red Sea.

Schumann's choral writing is as romantic as his solo song writing. The part songs of Op. 59 or Op. 67 are about such romantic things as forests, dreams and hedge roses, and are among the very best of the intimate songs designed for choral societies. (It must be remembered that Schumann, in Dresden and Düsseldorf, had a *Chorverein* at his disposal.) It is a shame that his *Scenes from Goethe's Faust* were never completed, since some of his finest orchestral music is to be found therein (so many composers have found the subject matter to be a compositional catalyst). Part III is especially profound; it sets the same text as Liszt (*Faust Symphony*) and Mahler (*Eighth Symphony*)—to name just two other composers who used that text.

Shumann also wrote an oratorio *Paradise and the Peri*—which should be performed instead of some works that are! This is a secular work, and this fact is significant because there are practically no Schumann sacred works. There are two masses, one of which is a requiem, but their performances are very rare. Schumann apparently is not at his best either in sacred or dramatic works (most composers wrote a lot of church music), although the above pieces contain passages of great beauty.

Byron's *Manfred* has inspired several composers, notably Schumann and Tchaikovsky. Schumann's music is designed to accompany a reading or a play production, and consists of fifteen numbers arranged in three acts using both chorus and narrator. Most writers agree that this work contains some fine music, including some of Schumann's most imaginative orchestral and choral writing. (Here is perhaps another instance in which the poetry doesn't need music.) Manfred is a character who (like Faust) sells his soul to the devil and (like Orpheus) goes into the underworld in search of his beloved.

The *Manfred* Overture is by far one of Schumann's best orchestral works, and it is a standard repertoire piece. Performances of the complete *Manfred* music are rare, probably since a narrator is needed and recitation with music presents special problems.

Perhaps now is the time for some of Schumann's highly chromatic male choruses to be performed, since there are choral groups today who could do them justice. The student would do well to consult Gerald Abraham's *Schumann, a Symposium* for articles by John Horton and Abraham on Schumann's choral and dramatic works. See also Young's *The Choral Tradition* (pp. 220-227) for an interesting discussion of "Faust" in Mendelssohn, Schumann and Berlioz.

Mendelssohn fared much better with choral composition, since he had solved the technical problems of handling choral and orchestral forces. It is almost a curse for one work to be as popular as *Elijah*, since other worthy works are neglected. Mendelssohn's choral works cover a wider range than most of his other music, even those of the "oratorio" class (*St. Paul, Hymn of Praise* and the great unfinished torso *Christus*). Theodore M. Finney has written an entertaining and informative article entitled "The Oratorio and Cantata Market,"[7] in which he discusses in some detail the rather strange public taste for works such as *Elijah*. The popularity of *Elijah* is understandable, since it has all of the ingredients of a great work of art which appeal to almost all tastes. What is even stranger is the popularity of other works by lesser composers of the period. (In the musical wastelands of some of the operas there was at least a stage spectacle to look at!) These works are now somewhat out of fashion, but recordings may cause some of them to come back into vogue. Young's chapter on this period is called "Mediocrity in Spate."[8]

Mendelssohn's other religious works reflect his interest in different religious groups. There are Latin motets, German Protestant cantatas which use chorales and an Anglican *Te Deum*. There is evidence that he had thought of writing a psalm setting for use in a liberal synagogue, but if the work survives no one knows which of the Psalms it is. It has often been pointed out that Mendelssohn's church music is too much like concert music to be good church music and too much like church music to be good concert music. This is a clever saying, and it is often said about church music by composers who have distinguished themselves in concert music. What should church music be anyway? Should one enjoy church? I believe that any music *honestly* written for a religious purpose is fit for use in church.

Mendelssohn also wrote a number of *Liedertafeln* part songs, and many of these are delightful romantic miniatures. Some of the best allude to nature: such as "There Fell a Frost" from Op. 41, or "The First Day of Spring" from Op. 48.

In the realm of the fantastic there are the lovely fairyland choruses from the complete music for *A Midsummer Night's Dream* and the secular cantata *Die erste Walpurgisnacht*, which some feel to be one of Mendelssohn's most significant works. It was highly admired by Berlioz.

Berlioz and Liszt

Berlioz's most outstanding works in this category are the *Requiem*, the *Damnation of Faust* and *L'Enfance du Christ*. These works are of considerable contrast among themselves—first of all from the subject matter, which has varying degrees of religiosity from the mass to a dramatic oratorio about the infancy of Christ (especially the flight into Egypt), to Berlioz's version of the *Faust* legend with its own religious overtones.

In the *Requiem* Berlioz could not help being himself; he makes the most of the text, which he set for a chorus of hundreds, fifty violins, twenty violas, twenty cellos, eighteen basses, four flutes, two oboes, two English horns, eight bassoons, four clarinets, twelve horns, four cornets, twelve trumpets, sixteen trombones, six ophicleides (now played by tubas), sixteen tympani, two bass drums, four gongs and ten cymbals (five pairs)! The brasses are subdivided into four groups and are used, as one might imagine, mostly for the "Tuba mirum" section of the *Dies irae*. This means that there are actually *five* instrumental groups and *six* musical groups, counting the chorus (if you can hear them). The world had seen spectacular works before. St. Mark's in Venice had been a famous place for polychoral effects, and even Spohr had used more than one orchestra. It is true, of course, that one soon reaches a point beyond which he cannot get more sound—if that is really what Berlioz was after (surely he knew much of the sound would be lost in outdoor performance). The amazing fact is that there is so much delicacy in the *Requiem*; it contains moments of exquisite tenderness.

Do not judge this work by recordings only; one needs to hear a live performance, or—better yet—be *in* one to get the great feeling for space and immensity which Berlioz achieves. With highly-developed modern instruments not quite so many are needed, but the "living presence" of the various choirs is quite amazing.

The Damnation of Faust contains some of Berlioz's best music and at one time enjoyed a great popularity. It, too, is a work which suffers, since it is between opera and oratorio. While being true to Goethe in several essentials, it adds some special Berlioz touches, such as the ride to Hell with Mephisto in which the forest gradually becomes an unholy place (it rains blood). Also non-Goethean is the Hungarian setting Berlioz used for the first scene, to make possible the Rákóczi march.

L'Enfance du Christ is a rare attempt to capture the spirit of older French music; Berlioz perpetrated a hoax by presenting part of the work at first as music by one Pierre Ducré. It is a rare bit of delicate music, but after adding some other scenes the "true Berlioz" came forth. As it stands today it could very well be Berlioz's masterpiece for many reasons: it is delicate and restrained, graphic and dramatic, highly expressive of the plot situations and presents some of Berlioz's best musical ideas with remarkable consistency.

Liszt, in addition to his choral symphonies, wrote two oratorios: *St. Elizabeth* (with remarkable parallels to Wagner's *Tannhäuser*) and *Christus*, written over a long time-span and (like Rubinstein's opera on the same subject) a very long work. Both oratorios attempt the idiom of the then *avant-garde* (Wagnerian), but they are not as successful as his choral symphonies. Liszt also wrote masses and smaller choral works which receive only rare performances today. The masses are known as the *Gran* and the *Hungarian Coronation*. Liszt came into conflict with conservative church authorities, since he insisted on using "modern" elements of harmonic coloring and orchestration in these works. The *Via Crucis* is a musical representation of the fourteen stations of the cross, and is noteworthy for its bold harmonic structure.

Cherubini and Verdi

One of the great French choral composers had been Marc-Antoine Charpentier (1634-1704), but after his death the art of choral composition languished long, except for the magnificent opera choruses of Gluck (and sometimes Meyerbeer) and some of the other operas performed in Paris in the eighteenth and nineteenth centuries. Charpentier had studied in Italy with the great Carissimi, and it took another Italian— Cherubini—to bring back to France a sober kind of choral writing.

Berlioz was in a class by himself and influenced other musicians, but not the politically powerful French ones—one of which Cherubini became. There had been some high-quality choral music written by one of the few men at the Conservatory who understood Berlioz—Jean François Lesueur (1760-1837)—but no deep impression had remained. In a Catholic country one would have expected more ceremonial music for the church, but compositional talents were turned toward the theater. Cherubini was the kind of universal musician needed in France at the time, and the importance of this dour genius was considerable.

Verdi wrote some magnificent choruses in his operas, but his *Manzoni Requiem* remains his supreme choral masterpiece.

Verdi (1813-1901) lived almost all of his life in Italy and was very much involved in the musical life of the important Italian musical centers. Cherubini (1760-1842) belonged to another world, but the difference in life-span is only part of the explanation. He was a true musical cosmopolitan, having worked and/or studied in Italy until 1784 when he went to London, staying there until 1786 when he went to Paris; he remained there until his death but for a visit to Vienna in 1805-1806, where he became acquainted with Beethoven. Beethoven's considerable respect for Cherubini actually influenced his own development, and in a sense might have been indirectly responsible for the unsuccessful aspects of *Fidelio* as musical theater. Cherubini's remarks about Beethoven and *Fidelio* are well-known, and are cited in the chapter on orchestral music (Cherubini complained that he did not know what key Beethoven thought he was in at the beginning of *Leonore No. 3*). Unfortunately, we have very little else of Cherubini's comments on Beethoven. It should be pointed out that the "rescue opera" aspects of *Fidelio* were undoubtedly influenced by Cherubini's *Deux Journées*—the two composers even shared the same librettist: Bouilly.

Cherubini was a bitter man, almost to the point of suggesting mental illness. Some of his trouble at the Conservatory in Paris (which he directed from 1822) probably stemmed from this bitterness and from his dry, often pedantic personality, which became even worse when aggravated by people like Berlioz.

Verdi's life is an object lesson. He was a *great* man who was a great *man*. Verdi's life was full of personal tragedy and disappointment, but also great triumphs. His only bitterness was engendered by a thoughtless audience which treated him badly at the premiere of *Un Giorno di regno*, a comic opera which he had to write while mourning the death of his young daughter, son and wife—all within two months' time! Perhaps one reason for Verdi's greatness is his understanding of the human heart, his empathy for his own characters or his own unselfishness, as evidenced by the establishment of *Casa Verdi*, a home for old or disabled musicians who could not afford homes of their own. Verdi had, from the very beginning, made wise investments in real estate; he even became something of a "gentleman farmer" in his late years.

This is not to say that there is no humanity in Cherubini. It is simply to say that in Verdi's music the humanity shows, while in Cherubini's, as A. Maczewsky states in *Grove's*:

Cherubini's pure idealism resisted the faintest concession to beauty of sound as such and subjugated the whole apparatus of musical representation to the idea; the serious, not to say dry, character of his melody, his epic calmness— never overpowered by circumstances, and even in the most passionate moments never exceeding the bounds of artistic moderation. . . .[9]

In short, Cherubini tends to be more "classical" while Verdi epitomizes the romantic, while never really forgetting classicism.

The *Requiem* of each man is beautiful music; I personally am very fond of both. Composers often write some of their best and most striking music for the requiem mass (Mozart-Sussmayr, Berlioz and Fauré) or for requiem-like works. The Brahms *German Requiem* is based on the German Bible, while Britten's *War Requiem* uses both the Latin Liturgy and poetry by Wilfred Owen.

There is a very old joke which declares that the *Requiem* is the best opera Verdi ever wrote! True, it is operatic in style, but the text is dramatic; Verdi is being honest and, like the juggler of Notre Dame, is offering his best gifts to God.

Cherubini wrote a greater variety of works, and was a universal composer. His church works are among his best and often display his great command of counterpoint. His *Requiem in C Minor* contains some theatrical moments, such as the surprising, melodramatic but awe-inspiring stroke of the tam-tam—reminding one of Mahler's *Symphony No. 2!*

The most obvious differences are not the years which separate the Verdi and Cherubini works, although, of course, that is important too. The Cherubini uses no soloists, while the Verdi uses four; hence, Verdi can employ vocal fireworks for the soloists, as well as the various textures of duo, trio and quartet, or any of these combinations with choral and/or orchestral background.

The orchestra in the Cherubini begins alone, with a mournful line which beautifully works up to a higher and higher member of the dominant dissonance until a complete dominant minor ninth is sounded (bars 5 and 6). In the orchestra the dominant minor ninth of C minor is especially expressive (as we also see often in Beethoven). Note that the soprano line is a sequence of a melodic fragment consisting of three notes ascending scalewise, the sequence occurring a third higher, thus using all the possible pitches of the bottom pentachord of the key. The second orchestral interlude runs only one bar, but is a quasi-inversion of the opening motive. This statement is tonic, while the opening was dominant. The second entrance of the chorus is on the chord of the minor dominant, which modulates temporarily to the relative major. The soprano line follows the same melodic outline of the three descending notes, sequenced as before. The next little interlude modulates to the key of the submediant, A-flat—a nice suggestion of "perpetual light." Cherubini did not always indulge in such trifles, so it may be only a coincidence. Note that again the motive of the three descending notes is sequenced one more time.

Looking back over each choral entrance, it is very apparent that Cherubini has placed each one on a different member of tonic harmony (first on the third, then on the fifth, then on the root). The root, however, is part of the submediant harmony at this point—or he has modulated to A-flat, depending on your point of view. A composer can obviously emphasize a particular region of tonality, as Cherubini does here; there is a full phrase in A-flat, and A-flat as tonic has been affirmed *three* times. (See the setting of the text "et lux perpetua.") There is no trouble in getting back to C minor: with no change of bass, the A-flat chord now becomes submediant, then it becomes the leading-tone diminished seventh chord, which passes smoothly to a German-type augmented sixth, tonic $^6_4$, dominant and then string unison again, but on the dominant this time (the tonic is not actually stated in root position).

At this point many requiem masses now state the second important musical idea. It is quite common for composers to set the next section in contrapuntal style, which both of those composers do.

Verdi begins his *Introit* with a simple line in the celli which outlines the tonic triad downward and then continues through the interval of a fourth scalewise down to the dominant. This is immediately repeated two octaves higher and harmonized as simply as possible; only the men of the chorus sing this first entrance—an open fifth—answered a full bar later by the women, also voiced rather low. In the ninth measure note that the motion is not meant just to keep something moving, but is the consequent of the theme first heard (in parallel block chords). The lowest line (cello and bass) is another one of those common contrary-motion lines and the first entrance of the full chorus is a mere dominant —to be sung as softly as possible, but how expressive it is!

In the next five bars there are several matters of importance: the first violins actually have the main theme, while the four soprani sing the famed "sighing" motive; here their notes are actually 9-8 suspensions. In the first three bars each resolution is preceded by a striking quasi-dominant (not major-minor seventh chords, but root movement always up a fourth; however, the chords of resolution are only a step apart, making a very arresting and expressive bass line). Here again is the chain of downward-moving suspensions we meet so often in tonal music.

Cherubini does something similar in the middle part of the next section, "Te decet"—some very colorful harmony indeed for Cherubini:

CHERUBINI: *Requiem in C Minor;*
Te Decet

Figure 13-11

The difference here is that Cherubini intensifies the inverted pedal B-flat by changing the harmonic function of the B-flat from the third of a G-minor triad, then the seventh of a C minor-minor seventh, the fifth of an E-flat major-major seventh chord, then the fifth of a diminished seventh chord in root position, which finally resolves to an F-major chord, only to undergo still more chromaticism. There is some parallelism here (downward movement of suspensions). Verdi stays in key, and uses chromaticism mostly for chromatic cambiatas or other non-harmonic tones, while Cherubini emphasizes different aspects of the key, providing what some would call "transient modulation." He makes a phrase modulation to possibly F-flat at the beginning of the "Te decet," ending the period on a semi-cadence in G minor, from which point the chromatic passage in question begins.

This section cadences on B-flat, leading to another cadence at the end of the section on A-flat minor. The very next chord is A-flat major, so we see that Cherubini was *not* immune to text-painting. The textual meaning of the "Te decet" is that God is praised in Sion (normal writing), our vows shall be performed in Jerusalem (chromatic), hear our prayer (chromatic) and all flesh shall come to God (the refreshing cross-relation of A-flat minor and A-flat major). This all cadences on the relative major, E-flat; this feels like the true tonality of the entire division leading to the *Kyrie*; the original key, C minor, recurs at the beginning of the *Kyrie*, along with thematic material from the beginning of the *Introit*. Cherubini thereby gives us the suggestion of a large ternery form. The middle section employs the right key relationship for minor, as well as contrasts in texture and melodic line (although it still uses the descending scale line, which seems to be of some importance in unifying the work). Note the beginning of the *Graduale*, the consequent phrases in the *Dies irae*, the important accompaniment figure in the "Recordare," the beginning of the *Offertorium* and one of the subjects of the magnificent double fugue which forms the "Quam olim Abrahae." This middle section of "Te decet" is followed by an unmistakable restatement of the string melody which begins the *Requiem*. (The student would profit from comparing the vocal score, pp. 1 and 2, to the quasi-recapitulation, pp. 5-11.)

Since the text closes with a reprise of "Requiem," many composers use this to advantage by employing the textual reprise for a musical reprise. Cherubini goes beyond this; on page 6 his music recalls page 4 —but how different is the effect! The vocal line on page 7 for "et lux perpetua" is not only beautiful, but it combines: 1) a dominant pedal; 2) a lovely chromatic statement of the downward-moving scale line; and 3) a beautiful short canon in the epidiapente—which itself as a line uses the downward notes with some looping back (compare this theme with the beginning of the *Graduale*). There is a slight family resemblance to some Verdi themes and to the music of other Italians—which makes Cherubini at this point somewhat more Italianate than he usually is.

One more comparison should be made before leaving these two works. Note the marvelous fugue writing in the entire Verdi work, especially in the *Sanctus*. Cherubini's mastery of fugue is also well-known; his *C Minor* contains an excellent fugue in the "Quam olim Abrahae." The student would do well to continue the comparison. The handling of the "Dies irae" in each case in especially noteworthy. The *Pie Jesu* of the Cherubini contains some striking chromaticism, and the *Agnus Dei* was admired by no less than Berlioz. The ending is very unusual: the chorus sings just one pitch on a very effective tonic pedal. The Picardy cadence at the end is effective, since the minor subdominant is used; if the rhythm were wrong, one would modulate to F minor.

Cherubini also wrote a fine *Requiem in D Minor*. It must be remembered that Verdi wrote his *Libera me* section originally for a composite *Requiem* for Rossini, and then apparently built the entire *Manzoni Requiem* around it. Both composers also wrote other significant choral music for their operas and for their church works.

Other Late-Nineteenth–Century Masters

Puccini wrote some church music. He did not succeed (as did Verdi) when out of the opera theater, however. The Puccini mass was published with the title *Messe di Gloria*; Puccini had called it simply *Messa a 4 voci* (1880). According to Carner,[10] it contains traces of Verdi, Bellini and Gounod. It is not only a fascinating example of the youthful Puccini, but it shows him as a remarkable composer of counterpoint and some passages presage the master to come.

Although earlier in time than Puccini, it should be mentioned that Rossini also wrote sacred music which allowed the infusion of opera styles. The best-known work is his *Stabat Mater*, but near the end of his life he wrote a mass (called *Petite Messe Solennelle*) which shows some countrapuntal skill. This mass was first performed in 1864. Important masses were written by Bruckner, who also set the *Te Deum* and *Psalm 150* and many shorter sacred works for various combinations of performers. Bruckner's masses are five in number, and some of them are among his best music and among the best church music of his time. One can be sure that Bruckner believed very strongly in the truth of the words he set. There are so many purely musical beauties in these works that they are fairly often performed in concerts. He handled voices very well and was a master at counterpoint, having studied with the great Sechter.[11] The best three masses are considered the *D Minor*, the *E Minor* and the *F Minor*. The *E Minor* is especially striking in its use of only wind instruments and in its contrapuntal skill. The Bruckner masses are intended to be liturgical, since the lines intoned by the priest are not set. He departs from this format, however, in the *F Minor*.

Reger wrote some beautiful chorale cantatas which revived to a certain extent the form used by Bach. These works do not have the great contrapuntal complexity of many of his other works. His many other choral works, both sacred and secular, are skillfully written and deserve to be done more often.

The most important music of the German late nineteenth century comes from the pen of Brahms. As Wienandt[12] points out, the masses of Bruckner seem to be the end of an era. (Had Brahms been Catholic mass composition might have been different.)

Brahms

Brahms—as we have found in every genre but opera—wrote some of the most significant music in each category. In the standard choral repertoire are the *Alto Rhapsody, Ein Deutsches Requiem* and *Schicksalslied,* which represent some of the greatest musical achievements of the time. Brahms was able to reach sublime heights with the force of music itself. He seldom indulged in orchestral extravaganzas, and yet his orchestral concept is authentic. It is no wonder that the term "classical" is so often applied to his work. These works are well-known to most concertgoers, since they involve the orchestra and often appear both in recordings and on concerts. The *Requiem* is often done at festivals or at the last symphony concert of the season. Its effect is one of great hope and optimism, in spite of its subject matter. Less well-known are his many other choral works, which use a variety of accompaniments or are unaccompanied. For example, Op. 17 consists of four different part songs for female voices accompanied by two horns and harp; there are several motets, many canons and a number of large works for chorus and orchestra which would be popular if they were better-known. *Nänie* (set to words by Schiller) is especially admired by those who know the work well. It is scored for chorus and orchestra, and contains one of Brahms's rare uses of the harp in the orchestra (the *Requiem* also has a harp part). The *Liebeslieder Waltzes* (actually covering two opus numbers: 52, called simply *Liebeslieder,* and Op. 65, called *Neue Liebeslieder*) are unusual, in that solo voices are used in different ways for each waltz and the accompaniment is for four-handed piano (also used by Schumann, Spohr and others). These waltzes are a delight and are often performed in schools, since the instrumentation is so practical. The last choral work is the *Gesang der Parzen* for six-part chorus and orchestra. The text is by Goethe: from his *Iphigenie in Tauris*. Brahms's treatment—as was always the case with a classical subject—could not help but bring to the work an ideal of Christian optimism.

It must be pointed out that *Ein Deutsches Requiem*, Op. 45, occupied Brahms from before 1857 until 1868. Some of the smaller works for chorus and orchestra (such as *Schicksalslied*) were not studies for the *Requiem*, nor was it inspired entirely by the death of his mother. The first parts of the *Requiem* are probably in memory of Schumann (Schumann died in 1856, and Brahms's mother in 1865). The last section was added after the first performance of the work in 1868, and this fifth movement Brahms expressly meant as a memorial to his mother. The *Requiem*, then—like the *First Symphony*—took a long time to write, and the work is almost perfect. If one reacts at all to music "mit Innigkeit," he cannot help but be drawn to this great masterpiece. "How Lovely Is Thy Dwelling Place" is often done as a single piece on choral concerts or as an anthem in church. There is no question but that this work established Brahms as a composer of first rank in the minds of many of his contemporaries; the first complete performance in 1869 was a phenomenal success.

The work begins in the utmost of gloom; however, as Brahms recalls the great promises of the Christian faith the music becomes more and more optimistic and brightly-colored. Brahms handles his scoring very well by using no violins in the first movement and by using rising tonalities throughout. One could write a book on almost any facet of this work: the use of an old Lutheran chorale tune, the fugal writing, the uses of soloists, the orchestration—which is so uniquely Brahmsian, the harmony, the subtle setting of the words and phrases themselves (which, by the way, sound so much better in German) and the implied optimism of a rising melodic line in practically every theme. The fugal writing is magnificent; the two complete fugues draw from Bach and Handel and yet are *Brahms's* fugues, with Brahms's own original touches, especially in the polyphonic relationships of chorus to orchestra.

As might be expected, a work this successful was imitated by all but Brahms himself, who went on to find still different choral expressions in his other works. Brahms retained a unique style, however, that distinguishes his works from those of others. It appears to be intangible—when others try the same sort of thing it becomes trite. In *Schicksalslied*, for example, we recognize the composer of *Ein Deutsches Requiem*, even though the work has a different message.

The student will find many discussions of *Ein Deutsches Requiem* in the literature. Two of the best are Wienandt's *Choral Music of the Church*[13] (pp. 369-371) and Young's *The Choral Tradition*[14] (pp. 239-246).

Some sections of the *Schicksalslied* must be pointed out. First, the very beginning features a beautifully-arched and long melody in the violins:

BRAHMS: *Schicksalslied.* Op. 54;
First Movement
(Winds Omitted)

Figure 13-12

Note Brahms's propensity for thickness in middle-register scoring. This passage *can* be played beautifully if the players do as Brahms directs: *piano sempre* while the melody is *piano espressivo*.

The first entrance of the chorus is significantly a dark-sounding alto line, but the text (referring to "pathways of light") is illuminated by beautiful woodwind writing which follows the style used in the *Requiem*:

BRAHMS: *Schicksalslied,* Op. 54;
First Movement
(Orchestra Omitted)

Figure 13-13

On page five of the score the student should compare the lines of the chorus with those of the strings, to see where there is doubling and where there is not. Page 26 of the score shows Brahms indulging in a bit of onomatopoeia. A lesser composer would have used more common harmonic devices (such as a diminished seventh), and yet Brahms's tonality is still very clear.

There was some precedence for Brahms's *Ein Deutsches Requiem* in the *Deutsche Trauermesse* (also called *Deutsches Requiem*, D. 621) by Schubert; this was written in 1818 and is a small piece, but is a heartfelt ten-movement German approximation of the liturgy. It is in four voices and is accompanied by organ. There are, of course, many other German masses, but this one is of special interest because a major composer is involved. There were many German-language masses, and substitutes for the mass, dating from the time of Luther (16th century). Brahms's text, as pointed out, draws from the Bible and not from the mass.

Dvořák was Catholic and had played the organ in church, but his choral music was intended mainly for the concert hall. Three of his sacred works are the *Stabat Mater* of 1877, the *Mass in D* and the *Requiem* of 1890. The *Stabat Mater* is his own *Kindertotenlieder*, and the circumstances surrounding it are indeed heartbreaking. He began writing it shortly after the death of an infant daughter, and sketched it out only to interrupt it for more urgent works. While working on the *Symphonic Variations* his eleven-month-old daughter (just learning to walk) drank a poison and died on August 13, 1877. Then his three-and-one-half-year-old son died of smallpox on Dvořák's birthday (September 8). This series of deaths left the Dvořáks childless, although other children were born later. This work is criticized for its unskillful use of the voice and for not-too-effective word and phrase repetition.

After some smaller works, during which Dvořák gains practical experience in word-setting, his next major choral work is *The Spectre's Bride*, which was a huge success in England (following the great success there of the *Stabat Mater*). *The Spectre's Bride* contains much striking and lush harmony which seemed to astonish and delight audiences in its time; but the piece is not often done today, nor is *St. Ludmila* (also written for England). This work contains some very beautiful music and does not deserve its lack of attention. There are some themes used in the manner of *Leitmotivs* and there are some excellent and exciting fugues. The *Mass in D*, his next choral work, is quite conventional and not too important. The *Requiem* was a follow-up to the big success of *The Spectre's Bride*. According to Clapham,[15] he had considered Cardinal Newman's great *Dream of Gerontius* (set so well by Elgar for the Birmingham festival of 1900). Dvořák, however, set the *Requiem* instead. This work is unified by what has been called a "grief motif":

F G-flat E F. Dvořák also wrote a *Te Deum, The American Flag* and the *Festival Song*; of these the *Te Deum* is the most important. Dvořák's part songs are beautiful, folksy and impressive in their imaginative handling of male voices.

Smetana's most important vocal music is found in his operas.

Janáček's choral writing for male voices is considerable, and some of it is dedicated to Dvořák. Important are the ballades to poems of Petr Bezruč. These are songs of anguish at the lot of poor men: miners. There is something powerful and elemental about this music; the third song in the set, "Seventy Thousand," is very complicated and was considered impossible to sing. There are also significant female choruses, cantatas and an impressive list of sacred music. A detailed discussion of this important composer belongs in a book on twentieth-century music.

In Russia there was a tradition of choral folk polyphony, as Melgunov[16] discusses. The Russian church had a long history of significant choral music of unique power and beauty. (It must be remembered that the organ and other instruments are hardly ever found in the Russian church.) The outstanding examples of Russian choral writing have to be the magnificent choruses in Mussorgsky's *Boris Godunov*. These choruses represent different aspects of the Russian people.

Many Russian operas make important use of the chorus. Charles Hamm's excellent book on opera[17] points out the uses of chorus in opera as follows: as scenery, as sound, as narrator and commentator, and as protagonist. One can find all of these uses in Russian operas, especially in the operas of Mussorgsky. He also wrote *The Defeat of the Sennacherib* and *Joshua*, which are not as effective as the rousing *Russian Folk Songs* for unaccompanied male chorus. Rimsky-Korsakov wrote some cantatas which, according to Seaman,[18] anticipated modern Russian oratorios. They contain brilliant uses of the orchestra but not of the chorus. When without the orchestra, however, Rimsky-Korsakov could write effectively for the chorus. Op. 19 consists of *Russian Folk Songs* arranged and composed for various kinds of choruses. Tchaikovsky wrote several choral works, but his best music lies elsewhere. He did write some colorful church music, such as the *Vesper Hymns*. Many school children have sung his "Legend." Rachmaninoff's works for chorus are outstanding, especially the choral symphony called *The Bells* (based on Poe). Scriabin wrote a choral symphony using the chorus in the last movement of a six-movement work based on his own poem. Taneev (or Taneyev) wrote several choruses to good texts, but the music does not seem to rise to the quality of the texts.

In France a newer movement—in addition to the sounds of Berlioz and the safe-and-sane choral mastery of Cherubini—was heard in the choral music of Gounod and Franck and (a little later) Fauré. As stated earlier, there was not much choral mastery in France after Marc-Antoine Charpentier, and there were little or no *Liedertafeln*, catches or glees, although there were some lovely carols and some highly-developed choral singing in some centers. There was also some use of the chorus in operas; those of Gluck and Meyerbeer involved many mob scenes. Gounod's best-known choral work is the *St. Cecilia Mass*, which is quite saccharine and sequence-ridden. A list of his choral and church works is quite impressive. There are over 100 works, ranging from rather small hymns to complete masses and oratorios, the most famous of which is *The Redemption*. These works are all a little too much for our taste today. The use of more lively counterpoint would have helped, but counterpoint alone does not save soporiferous music.

Franck fares somewhat better with *Les Béatitudes, Ruth, The Tower of Babel* and *Mass for Three Voices*. The masterpiece of the time is the *Requiem* of Fauré, written in 1885 in memory of his father. This work is a masterpiece of Gallic restraint. There are no shouted howls of anguish at the Day of Judgment, but rather a calm serenity, and yet it is so beautiful. Note that Fauré uses a very small orchestra; there are no violins, except with the solo in the *Sanctus*.

In England choral activity was probably the most plentiful, if not the greatest. One can only wonder at the great popularity of oratorios as entertainment music, when so many of these works seem to us today to be so lacking in any first-rate music. Wienandt calls it "a bleak period," and it is idle to list here the works which now dwell on library shelves waiting to be old enough for dissertation material. William Sterndale Bennett (1816-1875) is of some note since he was a student of Mendelssohn (in the "disciple" sense) and was praised by no less than Schumann. There were works by Parry, Stanford, Sullivan, Stainer and Mackenzie which were popular enough for their composers to be knighted. Sir John Stainer's (1840-1901) *The Crucifixion* is still very popular, especially its setting of John 3:16 (which Luther called the "pocket Gospel"). *The Crucifixion* contains some chorales with many verses for the choir to sing—along with the congregation, as was the case with the older Lutheran chorale cantatas.

Elgar wrote much choral music, but his masterpiece is *The Dream of Gerontius*, one of the great works of this period. The effect of this music is overpowering. It is a very grateful setting of a text which has a remarkable atmosphere about it. Elgar skillfully combines the orchestra, choirs and the soloist (who represents Gerontius). The English did not at first realize the importance of this work, but its German performances gave him the fame he deserved for a work which is fascinating harmonically, is replete with vital counterpoint and is mystical in a very original way. His own Catholic upbringing gave him a feeling for the text, which is set with remarkable faithfulness. Here is the beginning, which is chromatic in its shifting harmonies:

Figure 13-14

From *The Dream of Gerontius,* by Edward Elgar (permission granted by Belwin Music Publishers, New York).

The use of augmented sixth chords is remarkable throughout the work, as is the use of *Leitmotiv.* Part II is the most mystic section. Here is the novel text and music for the passage: "I hear a singing . . . know not whether I hear or touch or taste the tones":

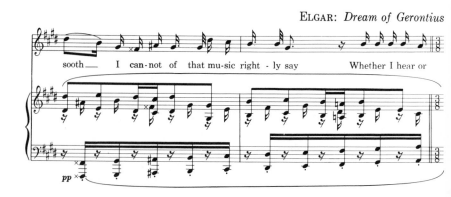

Figure 13-15

From *The Dream of Gerontius,* by Edward Elgar (permission granted by Belwin Music Publishers, New York).

Here is a remarkable bit of counterpoint:

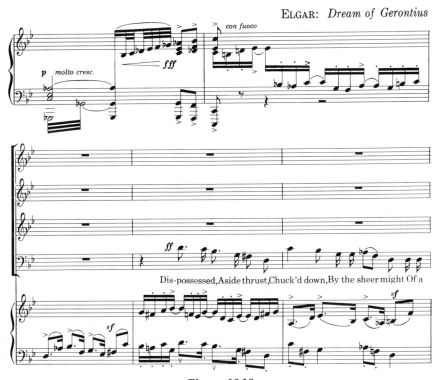

Figure 13-16

From *The Dream of Gerontius,* by Edward Elgar (permission granted by Belwin Music Publishers, New York).

This is a double fugue. While the work is not without its performing difficulties, it is surprising that the Birmingham premiere of *Gerontius* was such a failure. (The chorus would rather have sung something like *Elijah Revisited* by Sir Felix Mendelssohn.) Here in Elgar was something new and different, and it was in the mainstream of an important movement.

The stage was set in England for the choral works of men such as Holst and Vaughan Williams. Britten's *War Requiem* and Walton's *Belshazzar's Feast* must also be mentioned, since they too have profited from the change in direction indicated by *The Dream of Gerontius*.

In England there were also dozens and dozens of sacred and secular part songs at any taste level. The anthem and the hymn were important in the Anglican church and also in English-founded Protestant churches such as the Methodist church.

In America much the same situation existed with Handel and Haydn oratorio societies. Americans tried to vie with the BIG three and lost. Dozens of long choral scores of varying quality lie either dead or dormant. Perhaps the best is Parker's *Hora Novissima* (1893). There are choral works by Ives which are now attracting attention. His *Psalm 67*, with its remarkable use of two different simultaneous signatures, is effective, and the *Harvest Home Chorales* are among the very best America has offered.

Although Schoenberg belongs to the twentieth century and to both the German-speaking world and the United States, it is fitting to end this section by mentioning two of his great works. *Gurrelieder*, a gigantic oratorio-like work for soloists, chorus and orchestra (in the Wagner tradition, but more like Elgar), has an atmosphere of its own. Especially good are the "Song of Tove" and some of the large choruses and the masterful treatment of the orchestra. Also of importance is the *Friede auf Erden*, a remarkable choral work which tells of the first Christmas night. It is very difficult to sing, and Schoenberg, knowing this, suggests that an instrumentation of winds double the chorus. These are both romantic works; and now that there are good recordings, we can expect other groups all over the world to begin performing them more often.

Choral music was not always in the forefront in the nineteenth century. Beethoven's *Ninth* was an important breakthrough for the use of chorus with orchestra. The chorus became another choir of the orchestra, and this led to many new ideas. The French composers of the early twentieth century even give to the chorus textless sounds which then become an adjunct of orchestral color.

Opera

The literature on opera is voluminous. One can find many volumes dealing with such facets as the history of opera, the famous opera houses, opera plots, opera libretti and discourses on opera as vital theater.

Italian Opera

The place to begin is Italy, where opera itself began. At the turn of the century opera was still classical. Plots and story situations were often more romantic than the music to set them. Opera was all too formula-prone. Audiences were not interested in opera as drama, but as a kind of game played according to certain rules. As the century progressed, an element of realism entered opera. The character of consequence in the tragedy became a common person, who didn't need to have anything but red blood and a good high C. By century's end it became quite apparent that the great figure had been Verdi, and that his successor was Puccini.

There were many times when Verdi was accused of not being able to write a melody (see Slonimsky's *A Lexicon of Musical Invective*) and when Puccini was said to have sacrificed melody in favor of the orchestra. For most people sensitive to today's standard repertoire, Verdi and Puccini are considered among the most tuneful.

The history of Italian music has been glorious. It is a real tribute to Italy that most of our musical terms are in the Italian language. Italy exported many fine musicians who manned orchestras and opera houses throughout the world. In the Renaissance and the Baroque Italian music was at the forefront. For some strange reason Italy, in the late eighteenth century and throughout most of the nineteenth, all but abandoned other forms of music and concentrated on opera. There were no great Italian composers of abstract music in the entire nineteenth century—unless one stretches a point and cites Cherubini. Whatever instrumental music was written tended to be of an entertainment kind, designed to compete with opera. There were some great performers, especially violinists and singers. The most outstanding violinist-composer was Paganini (1782-1840), who was a great composer of violin music which still figures in the violinist's repertoire. Unlike Chopin, however, his works did not provide a musical substance to match the great strides which were being made in violin technique (Paganini was a fantastic virtuoso). He did exert a powerful influence on composers such as Berlioz, Schumann and Liszt, and this influence proved to be of lasting value.

One of the earliest Italian opera composers in our period of study is Rossini (1792-1868), who for a variety of reasons wrote little significant music after 1830. His best-known opera is *The Barber of Seville* (1816), which is a classic masterpiece of Italian comic opera. This work abounds in sparkling melodies usually containing simple motival devices which are elaborated upon. Rossini tended to write out his own coloratura passages, and frowned upon the too-prevalent practice of singers embellishing to suit themselves. Rossini often would take an eight-bar period and repeat it, either louder or ascending scalewise—the "Rossini crescendo," it was called. This device was used often in his overtures and in his set numbers. In *William Tell* there is much beautiful music, and much of it is entrusted to Arnold, the tenor. Early in the opera there is a beautiful line sung by Arnold in a duet with Tell, which reflects his own torn affections and conflicts. The dramatic situation demands that he be torn apart emotionally for love of Matilda, his father and his country; each man expresses his own feelings, but Tell comments also on Arnold's feelings. The entire role of Arnold is a sample of tenor writing which, when sung by a great tenor, is thrilling indeed (note the high tessitura).

William Tell is a French romantic opera with plenty of Italian flavor. Rossini was the director of the Italian Theater in Paris, and after that remained in Paris. The subject matter of *Tell* was popular; this could have been a great "protest" opera, but in that capacity it never quite succeeded. Rossini wrote some of his best melodies for this work; the overture seems to be a permanent fixture—at least for "pops" concerts— but the whole work deserves to be revived now and again.

In the second act Matilda gets her chance to star in a recitative and aria (romanze)—the famous "Sombre foret"—which somehow looks back rather strangely to Haydn's *Creation*. The vocal line in her recitative is quite dry, perhaps purposely to contrast with the expressive orchestral writing. When the aria begins, however, there is a beautiful setting of a lovely young girl, deeply in love, noticing the stillness of the forest and everything around her; the music of the short orchestral interlude is especially lovely.

The student would profit from studying the entire score of *William Tell.* Not only is the vocal writing exceptionally brilliant, but also the orchestral writing—aside from the famous overture! Rossini is often a strange mixture of classic and romantic.

If Rossini looks back to Haydn, he seems to look forward to Franz Liszt in this music:

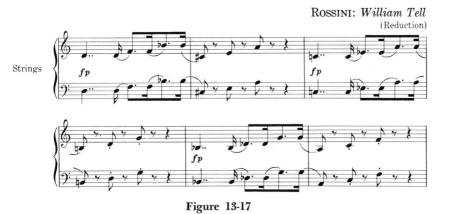

Figure 13-17

Does this not remind *us* of the "Faust" theme of the *Faust Symphony?*

Figure 13-18

Liszt builds his theme on triads other than the augmented:

Trpt.

Trb.

Figure 13-19

I, for one, would like to hear and see this opera revived more often; it was worked on most carefully by Rossini and contains some very fine music. The role of *Otello* in Verdi's opera is often discussed for the difficulty of the tenor's first entrance, but the first bars sung by Arnold in *Tell* are just as taxing.

Donizetti (1797-1848) was a very important international figure in his day; his works were done in New Orleans soon after their premieres in Italy, for example. He provided sure-fire musical theater, brilliance —in other words, entertainment music. Some of his operas still hold the stage, even though they are "dated." Everything of value is in the voice parts, and best performances depend upon brilliant singers. For these singers he left a remarkable number of beautiful arias and ensembles, which, however, do not always really fit the dramatic situations inherent in the words (the dramatic situation involving the famous sextet from *Lucia* is highly un*verismo*, to say the least!).

It must be remembered that opera was performed with different ground rules in those days; perhaps we will be criticized in the future for desiring better coordination between drama and music. Most of us today do not look upon opera as primarily a vehicle for the vocal instrument; in that regard, we are heirs of Wagner and others who maintained that all elements were important.

Donizetti is still mainly a classical composer, romantic as his libretti are. His orchestral treatment is more rudimentary than that of some of the eighteenth-century composers, Mozart especially. Donizetti's harmonies do little to enhance the beauty of the melody; a Donizetti melody must be beautiful for itself alone.

Melodic beauty is a major characteristic for Bellini (1801-1835), who is more in tune with romanticism than Donizetti. His harmony and orchestration enhance the melodic writing much more than that of Donizetti. Bellini—another tragic case of a great talent dying young—has had a considerable comeback in the past several years, due to recordings and to revivals by singers who once again can "conquer" his vocalism. *Norma* never did disappear from the repertoire, but seems to be as popular as ever.

Note that almost all of the Italian opera composers use flourishes or ornaments at the ends of phrases. It was at these spots that so many singers added even more.

Verdi (1813-1901) is the greatest opera composer of all. One can find several melody types in Verdi, but even more important is the development of a style that is uniquely his and yet is very Italian. Verdi follows the sense of the text lines and uses melody and all the other musical resources to characterize. In *La Forza del destino* there is a figure:

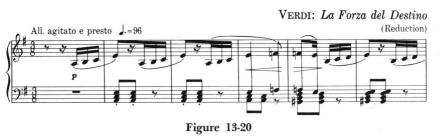

Figure 13-20

which often appears in the opera. This kind of theme can serve either as the principal theme or as a countermelody. It is the basis of the overture and is important in one of the most prominent arias: "Pace, pace, mio Dio." After the entrance of the soprano voice in this aria, there occurs a melodic formula which Verdi (and the other Italians) use almost too much: the appogiatura after a turn:

Figure 13-21

In his later operas Verdi makes better use of this device, and his harmony becomes richer. This music from the love duet at the end of the first act in *Otello* is an example of how sensuous this type of motive writing had become:

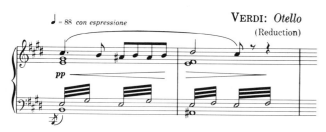

Figure 13-22

A melody of a strikingly different character is to be found in Iago's "Credo":

Figure 13-23

Few opera characters have been so well-pegged by music.

With Verdi one could go on and on. The student should study "Eri tu" from *Un Ballo in maschera* for a marvelous change of mood: while the words set it, the mood is even more deeply reflected in the music. The theme of the "Agnus Dei" in the *Requiem* is unusual, in that two lady singers are asked to sing in octaves. When there are two fine musicians singing these parts, the effect is one of unforgettable beauty; too often, however, the two singers are thinking too much about themselves and not enough about either the Lamb of God or Verdi.

One last word: the role of Violetta in *La Traviata* is astonishing, since she must sing three entirely "different" roles: a different one in each act as the drama unfolds. The "Addio del passato" is especially beautiful; here is the point where human emotions truly transcend any textbook rules—an excellent example of romanticism.

In a sense, the mantle of Verdi fell to Puccini (1858-1924), but a real student of opera could never mistake one for the other. Puccini is easy to imitate—there have been many who have done so—but only Puccini was able to impart the high level of musical theater which has caused his music to be a vital part of the permanent repertoire. By the time

Plate XVI

Title page of piano score of Giacomo Puccini's opera *Madame Butterfly (Courtesy The Bettmann Archive, N.Y.)*.

of Puccini Italian opera had overcome many of the old clichés, and there developed a unique approach to harmony which affected his melodic writing. He and some of the other Italians used a rudimentary kind of musical motive associated with characters, actions or fate; however, they never used them to permeate the entire texture, as did the Germans. Puccini was an important figure at the very end of the development of what is known as *verismo*: opera which seeks to portray reality; musical practice had thereby changed considerably from earlier in the century. Orchestration meant more, and more chromaticism was used. In Puccini and in late Verdi opera becomes more continuous, but not in exactly the same sense as in Wagner and his followers. In earlier opera there had been a sharp distinction between recitative and aria, which musically called for separate treatment: comparatively free in the recitative but regular in the aria.

Arias were constructed, by and large, in regular, closed poetic forms which dictated a similar treatment in the music. Most Italian music, and especially opera music, is characterized by "closed" melody with regularity of phrase structure most of the time. The composer, for dramatic reasons, would disrupt this regularity for shock value or for some other striking purpose. While much German music is also constructed in a closed way, Wagner and others "opened" the phrase through the freer interplay of motives and by the avoiding of cadences. The more-expected periodicity in Italian opera was certainly a contributing factor to its continued popularity, while the lack of an easily-discerned melodic and harmonic phrase in German opera was one reason why the public (and some musicians) were puzzled even after several hearings.

The *verismo* movement can be seen in the works of Pietro Mascagni (1863-1945), whose late date of death does not place him in any sense as a "modern" composer. In 1899 his *Cavalleria Rusticana* won a prize and has remained his best-known work, although *L'Amico Fritz* (1891) and *Iris* (1898) have merit and are occasionally done. *Cavalleria* is a short work, and is almost always done as a twin bill with Ruggiero Leoncavallo's (1858-1919) *I Pagliacci* (1892). Leoncavallo never again found the same touch. He was the same age as Puccini; there was some bad blood between the two men, since they both wrote a *La Bohème*. Puccini's, of course, is a permanent fixture, while Leoncavallo's is only a curiosity. His *Zaza* (1900) enjoyed some popularity, due to Geraldine Farrar's brilliant playing and singing of the title role; the opera was set to the play by Berton and Simon, the lead of which was Mrs. Leslie Carter's most famous role. Both composers wrote many other works which have not held the stage.

Verismo starts a little earlier in Amilcare Ponchielli's (1834-1886) *La Gioconda*, with a libretto by none other than Boito under the name of Tobia Gorrio. The plot is very complicated, with a curious sort of "eternal pentagon" which leads to five cases of frustrated passion, since everyone is in love with the wrong person. The musical style is not all as "bloody" as one might think, but the aria "Suicidio!" is quite realistic when well-sung. The plot source is *Angelo* by Victor Hugo.

It is easy to theorize that opera had to turn to realism to react to the incongruous tales portrayed on the stage, but instead the writing and acting were mainly a reaction to Wagnerism. Verdi was continuing the same line as older Italian opera composers, but was doing it better than it had ever been done. Verdi was able to delve more deeply into the inner aspects of his characters in a way that few composers have ever done. Grout[19] points out that there was no brighter star which burned out faster than *verismo* opera—it literally eats up its own material too fast. In opera there needs to be *time*, for musical action and there needs to be an understanding of the basic premise: that people do not really sing in real-life situations. (In the heat of verbal or physical battle there is no time for da capo arias! One does sing when in pain, however.[20])

Time, however, can be a factor in another way too: an opera can be too long. This is a fault in Boito's *Mefistofele*. Boito occupies a unique spot in musical history, since he was a poet who also composed rather than being a composer who also wrote his own libretti. Wagner wrote his own texts, and he was quite a master of the German language. Wagner, however, only wrote for himself. Boito, in addition to his own operas (*Mefistofele* and *Nerone*), had the good fortune to become acquainted with Verdi at a time in Verdi's career when he needed unusually good libretti. The libretti supplied by Boito for Verdi's two Shakespearean operas—*Otello* and *Falstaff*—are among the finest ever penned. The student would benefit much from comparing Boito's version of both works with Shakespeare's—keeping in mind that *Falstaff* is based on *The Merry Wives of Windsor*, which is considered a faulty play (not all genuine Shakespeare). (There have been many papers written on *that* subject.)

Musically, Boito's operas have much to admire and the setting of *Mefistofele* is quite faithful to Goethe. It exists in two versions, and the second one is amazing in its improvement over the first. Boito had learned much from the study of the great operatic masters of the past and present, and was able to recast his works with skill. Brockway[21] points out Huneker's apt statement that the younger Italian composers profited too, by actually raiding Boito's works.

In summary, here is a list of what one might call the standard fare of Italian opera:

ROSSINI (1792-1868)
The Barber of Seville (1816)
Cinderella (1817)
William Tell (1829)

Tell is now performed the least. *Cinderella* is better-known by its Italian title: *La Cenerentola*. There is no magic in this story, as there is in the folk tale known by all English-speaking people. The opera is witty, and is full of brilliant vocalism.

DONIZETTI (1797-1848)
The Elixir of Love (1832)
Lucia di Lammermoor (1835)
The Daughter of the Regiment (1840; French libretto)
Don Pasquale (1843)

Donizetti's operas came at the best time for opera, in that premieres were frequent and were important events. True, there were a few "reruns," but a classical repertoire did not exist in the same sense as today. People came mainly to see and hear a *new* work. As was pointed out above, opera was like a game with strict rules, and the stars were the vocally athletic singers. This kind of opera waned for a time, but it is enjoying a comeback with the rise (or re-rise) of a new kind of vocal virtuoso: one who can sing and also look believable in the part.

The Elixir of Love is a beautifully balanced comedy-love story which has soaring melodies and a fine libretto by Romani. One of its most beautiful arias is "Una furtiva lagrima." *Lucia* is based on a novel by Sir Walter Scott. The sextet in Act II is debatable in its dramatic effect, but it is amazing music. The "Mad Scene" is one of many of the period, and it takes a rare artist to perform it and maintain the dramatic situation. (It must have been considered a symptom of madness if one sang coloraturas!)

The Daughter of the Regiment was written for performance in Paris and was one of the last great Italian comic operas, along with *Don Pasquale*. Although written in French, Paris did not particularly like the work; but it has somehow remained on the boards, probably because of its ingratiating melodies. In *Don Pasquale* there is a comic patter-duet that is one of the best of its type.

BELLINI (1801-1835)
La Sonnambula (1831)
Norma (1831)
I Puritani (1835)

Bellini was one of the greatest composers of the nineteenth-century *bel canto cantilena*. Unlike Donizetti, Bellini was somewhat of an explorer in matters harmonic. In *I Puritani* he dispenses with the harpsichord for the recitatives, which proves to be very worthwhile musically (this also requires less reheasal time since accompanied recitative is the most difficult kind of opera music to perform). Bellini's vocal writing is well-balanced in all parts. A famous example is the duet from Act II between Norma and Adalgisa.

VERDI (1813-1901)
Rigoletto (1851)
Il Trovatore (1853)
La Traviata (1853)
Simon Boccanegra (1857; revised, 1881)
Un Ballo in maschera (1859)
La Forza del destino (1862)
Don Carlos (1867)
Aida (1871)
Otello (1887)
Falstaff (1893)

This is some accomplishment! He wrote many other operas, but those listed are the ones which hold the stage year after year with that strange combination of music and theater which is so powerful when the performance is as it should be. There was a great deal of political intrigue during his career, and at times out-and-out censorship. His name became a cry for a single, united Italy under one king—"Viva Verdi" meant "Viva Vittorio Emmanuele Re D'Italia." (This may have helped, for Italy was united in 1861.)

With Verdi opera became less of a "game" and more true theater, where one could be entertained and enlightened at the same time. Under his hands the orchestra became an important part of the score. The old set pieces melted away, but in a manner quite different from that of Wagner. His harmonies became more and more chromatic, but never Wagnerian. His command of the voice changed from a sheer vocal showcase to a touchstone for man's innermost passions. His technique began to include more and more vital counterpoint which contributed much to the total effect of the music.

PUCCINI (1858-1924)
Manon Lescaut (1893)
La Bohème (1896)
Tosca (1900)
Madame Butterfly (1904)
Il Trittico (a group of three unrelated one-act operas: *Il Tabarro, Suor Angelica* and *Gianni Schicchi*), *Turandot* and *The Girl of the Golden West* belong to the twentieth century

There is no mistaking a Puccini passage; there is a certain turn of the phrase, and a harmony which can be imitated but is never "echt" unless the master himself writes it. He was in a sense a strange artist, as Mosco Carner points out in his excellent study of Puccini.[22] He was certainly a specialist, even more so than Verdi. In Puccini there is a kind of melodic formula for pathétique effects: for one thing, the falling large interval, as in *Manon Lescaut*:

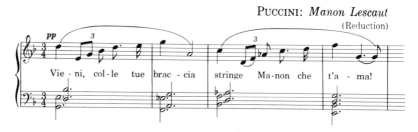

Figure 13-24

There are definite *Leitmotiv*, such as these chords used to portray Scarpia in *Tosca*:

Figure 13-25

Madame Butterfly is actually based on some Japanese music Puccini took from a book *Sammlung von Japanischen Volksliedern* by Isawa Shuji and others.[23]

Puccini's harmony is drawn from a variety of sources: from Debussy as well as Wagner or Strauss. His orchestration is a little thick with violins at times, but in *Gianni Schicchi* and *Turandot* remarkable orchestrations occur.

The Girl of the Golden West (1910) is an Italian-American Western, and somehow its Japanese exoticism does not fit; but then, to Puccini California was as exotic as Japan. It contains much beautiful music, once you get past the shock of American cowboys and miners singing in beautiful Italian!

Plate XVII

Giacomo Puccini in his newly-acquired automobile. Photograph
made in 1902 *(Courtesy The Bettmann Archive, N.Y.)*.

German Opera

BEETHOVEN (1770-1827)
Fidelio (1805; 1814)

Fidelio is really an old-fashioned "rescue" opera in which someone is
unjustly imprisoned; the story-line hinges on whether or not he will be
freed. Many stories are based on a similar plot device (accomplishing
some purpose or goal, such as a trip, an escape, a murder or the blowing
up of a bridge). In this opera Beethoven was definitely influenced by
Cherubini's *Les deux Journées,* even to the extent of using the same
librettist. *Fidelio* is technically a *Singspiel*: it contains spoken dialogue,
and it begins as if it is to be a comic opera. It is difficult to maintain
pace in a work such as this, since the dialogue is of one standard and
the music of another. *Fidelio* gave Beethoven almost as much trouble
as his nephew (see Forbes's *Thayer's Life of Beethoven,* pp. 374 *f*). There
are many numbers of great musical beauty, such as Leonore's aria
"Abscheulicher wo eilst du hin," the tenor aria "Gott, welch' dunkel
hier" or the male chorus "O welche Lust."

WEBER (1786-1826)
Der Freischütz (1821)

The first real romantic opera of any importance in the German language is *Der Freischütz. Fidelio* is romantic in many ways, but is still

basically a classical opera. The overture to *Der Freischütz* is based on themes from the opera. Noteworthy in the opera itself is the "Wolf Glen Scene," which is one of the first (and best) examples of vivid musical portrayal. Perhaps the most challenging role is that of Agathe. The choral writing is also wonderful: a real *Chorverein* kind of music (similar to the *Liedertafeln*). The vigorous "Hunting Chorus" is especially fine.

Some "minor" works which are sometimes performed are Nicolai's (1810-1849) *The Merry Wives of Windsor*, which can be compared in some ways to Verdi's *Falstaff*; Lortzing's (1801-1851) *Zar und Zimmermann*; Marschner's (1795-1861) *Der Vampyr* and *Hans Heiling*; and Johann Strauss's (1825-1899) *Die Fledermaus*.

WAGNER (1813-1883)	Performance Dates
The Flying Dutchman	1843
Tannhäuser	1845; 1861
Lohengrin	1850
Tristan und Isolde	1865
Die Meistersinger von Nürnberg	1868
Der Ring des Nibelungen	
Das Rheingold	1869
Die Walküre	1870
Siegfried	1876
Die Götterdämmerung	1876
Parsifal	1882

Here is an impressive list! One might also mention *Rienzi* (1842), since it is sometimes performed. Space does not permit a thorough discussion, although Wagner is one of the most fascinating figures in the whole art of music. Many authorities have made intensive and extensive studies of Wagner, such as Ernest Newman, Aylmer Buesst and Robert Donington, just to mention three English-speaking writers. After *The Flying Dutchman* Wagner refined his techniques of the *Leitmotiv*, which was in itself a great contribution to music. His treatment of the orchestra and the voice, his use of harmony, counterpoint and development, and his insistence upon the union of all the arts was such that it actually not only altered the course of musical history but in a way dictated it. Ardent Wagnerians worshipped and employed Wagner's theories (which *were* supported by great music!), while anti-Wagnerians were so negatively influenced that they developed new musical approaches which became an *avoidance* of Wagner. Others became reactionary in their classicism, and tried to cling to older principles.. The animosity toward Wagner was really quite heated. Wagnerism was almost a religion, and the "temple" was built at Bayreuth. Even Debussy was sometimes an anti-Wagnerian, and said some unkind words about *Parsifal*. Still, he admitted:

The above remarks only apply to the poet whom we are accustomed to admire in Wagner and have nothing to do with the musical beauty of the opera, which is supreme. It is incomparable and bewildering, splendid and strong. *Parsifal* is one of the loveliest monuments of sound ever raised to the serene glory of music.[24]

I shall spare the reader the parade of devastating criticism which, if he wishes, he can read in Slonimsky's *Lexicon of Musical Invective*, pp. 222-248. It is amazing to recall that during World War II there were people who declared we should shun Wagner's music because Hitler liked it! In 1855 the London *Musical World* called him a communist (Slonimsky, p. 226). Hanslick's quarrel with Wagner has not been given fair treatment; now that there are good editions of Hanslick's writings available, the student should read for himself. Henry Pleasants asserts:

Hanslick's quarrel was not with Wagner alone. He rejected Berlioz and Liszt just as consistently, and later Richard Strauss and Anton Bruckner. Wagner was simply the most gifted, and the most influential, of the prophets of the 'music of the future' and, therefore, the most dangerous. If one were required to define the basis of Hanslick's objections to this school, one might cite: (1) the introduction of foreign elements (prose, poetry, colour for graphic purpose), and (2) transcendentalism. He was against programme music because he felt that music lost rather than gained by being pegged to a specific plot or idea, and his fundamental objection to Wagner was directed against the subordination of melodic development to the elucidation of the text.[25]

There are two moral concepts which appear in one way or another in many Wagner works: redemption through love and the Christian ideal vs. the pagan (as in *Lohengrin* and *Tannhäuser*).

A notable feature of *The Flying Dutchman* is the use of the sea as a backdrop. In *Tannhäuser* the Paris version of 1861 is the best-known version; this contains the "Venusberg music," which was added after Wagner had written *Tristan*. This work clearly portrays redemption through love (as does *Dutchman*), as well as the Christian concept vs. the pagan. A curious use of the chorus occurs in the call of Venus's handmaidens. *Tannhäuser* succeeds in presenting two kinds of musical characterizations: Venus and Elizabeth. *Lohengrin* has been criticized for its lack of rhythmic variety and praised for its angelic "Grail" music. *Tristan und Isolde* is thought by many to be Wagner's masterpiece; it doesn't really deal with much but sexual love, and it contains some of the most sensuous music ever written. The famous prelude is quoted elsewhere. This motive—the "Motive of the Glance of Love"—uses a descending minor seventh, which has been pointed out again and again as a special interval used by Wagner and other romantic composers.

Die Meistersinger was supposed to be a return to the simple comic opera idea of the past. It is comic, but more, it is anything but simple.

Figure 13-26

Motives are again highly developed, as in *Tristan*, but in *Meistersinger* there is a slight return to the old idea of set orchestral pieces. The introduction to Act III is a remarkable character sketch of Hans Sachs. The opera also is filled with vivid symbolism: the character Beckmesser, a pedant, was originally called "Hans Lick" as an attack on the critic Hanslick.

Some have pointed out that Wagner's approach to musical form is not the mishmash that some people would have us believe. A. Lorenz[26] is discussed in Gerald Abraham's *A Hundred Years of Music*,[27] in the admirable chapter "Wagner and the Music Drama" (pp. 77-136 should be required reading for all music students). Lorenz's theory is that Wagner used mainly bar forms and Bogen forms. Bar form is represented as AAB, where, of course, A can be further subdivided into any form, and B likewise. A-phrases are called *Stollen*, and B-phrases *Abgesang*. Bogen, or arch form at its most simple, is represented as ABA, but it can be expanded to ABCBA or ABCDCBA; again, the microform of each is variable. Wagner's reprise sections are not necessarily exact repetitions. There is much evidence to support Lorenz's theory. The opera *Meistersinger* has been pointed out to be a huge bar form, in which Act I is Stollen A, Act II is Stollen A' and Act III is B Abgesang. This is not to say that these breakdowns are exact, but there is an amazing correspondence of number for number in Acts I and II; however, the playing time of Act III does not double that of either of the other acts.

Form in Wagner has not been studied to the extent that harmony and polyphony have, since harmony was one of the first elements which was severely criticized and was therefore either condemned or praised, according to how it did or did not kill tonality or concord (as in the music of Palestrina, St. Caecilia, Fux, Rameau and others). Many of the earlier essays tried very hard to show that Wagner was merely extending Beethoven; and there developed some far-fetched theories of modulation, altered chords and borrowed chords which encountered varying degrees of success. Now that several decades or more have elapsed since "music of the future" originated, one can appreciate it as music of the past; listening to it is a much easier job for us who have heard so much more recent music, which makes Wagner sound a little quaint and almost old-fashioned. The problem, it seems to me, is the question of cadence and the meaning of cadence and its relation to tertian harmony. (Is Wagner's harmony always tertian? If tertian, are the cadences triadic?) We must recognize the fact that the points of repose are *relative* and that the pillars might still have tonal roots, but they also have sevenths and ninths which are not resolved in the traditional sense. Wagner did what must be correct, since it *sounds* correct. Can you imagine the *Ring* or *Tristan* with the orchestration and harmony of Mozart's *Così fan tutte*? It is true that Mozart used harmonies which "sound" Wagnerian, but he always returned to his own style (even in the *Adagio*, K. 611)!

The point is that Wagner is "contemporary" *all* or most of the time, especially in *Tristan*, the *Ring* and much of *Parsifal*. He himself called it the "music of the future," so why analyse it with the tools of music of the *past*? Can one really analyse Rameau's *Castor et Pollux* and any mature work of Wagner in the same way with the same symbols? Alan Walker offers some suggestions about the analysis of music which are food for thought.[28] An overlooked factor is the motives! People have been so busy trying to find the "Tarnhelm" or any other of Wagner's *Leitmotiv* that they have often overlooked his symphonic development. A very important book is Donington's *Wagner's Ring and Its Symbols*—indeed a welcome addition to the Wagner literature. Donington points out the problem:

How many musical motives are there in the *Ring*? That all depends on what we call a motive. At one extreme, the motives dwindle into mere fragments of figuration; at the other extreme, they pass into passages of development or even tunes; but neither dividing line can be sharply drawn, and no attempt has been made to do so here. Most but not all of the following examples are motives on any showing. Not all of them have been included for the same reason, but they are all illustrations of my text, at the points indicated in the text by numbers.

There is no motive in the *Ring* which cannot be traced either directly or indirectly to the simple arpeggio figure (it is scarcely yet a motive) with which *Rhinegold* opens. Some of the remoter motives have undergone many transmutations before reaching their extreme forms; but similarities can be noticed, I believe in every case, which lead from one motive to another until the extremes are reached. Some similarities have always been familiar; some others are so conspicuous that the wonder is they have not yet become familiar; some again are not conspicuous at all, and might fairly be doubted were it not that the entire fabric of the *Ring* shows such clear signs of holding together. A merely casual and undetermined motive is almost inconceivable in such a context.[29]

While he is discussing the *Ring*, it follows that one could and should do the same sort of analysis of other mature works. The book, however, is much more than tune-detecting in the *Ring*; as Donington says, "This book is an approach to Wagner by way of his symbols."[30] Musical symbolism is, of course, only one kind of symbolism, and that kind is precisely what Hanslick found objectionable. In Donington, pp. 278-307, there is a remarkable appendix which shows the gradual growth of the entire *Ring* cycle from the motive of the "Rhine."

I cannot speak for Donington, but it seems that Beethoven's *Ninth Symphony*—a work of which Wagner had much to say—has a comparable growth from the cryptic opening through the entire first movement. Reti all but affirms that,[31] and a good case can be developed for the Beethoven being a great precedent for Wagner—in almost the same sense as the Wagnerian growth from the *Urkeim* of the "Depths of the Rhine as undifferentiated nature," as Donington calls it. We have observed, in other chapters, that a composer of formal variations would often let variation II grow from variation I, III, from II and I, and so on. There are also possibilities, of course, that variation XXXVIII could use something from any of the others not hitherto used, thus allowing for an almost infinite variety of possibilities.

This is not to say that Wagner has turned his back on tonal harmony or its implications. The devices of two contrasting kinds of music serve his purpose in *Tannhäuser, Lohengrin* and *Parsifal* (diatonic music for the Christian or innocent or forthright concepts, and chromatic music for pagan concepts, devious plots or circumstances with uncertain outcomes).

Meistersinger is somewhat unusual, in that Wagner achieves even more violent contrast between diatonic and chromatic usage; the chromatic here refers to the "right" side of the story, while the diatonic is associated both with the Mastersingers (good) and Beckmesser (bad). The overture shows this well: the diatonic march of the Mastersingers vs. the chromaticism of the "Prize Song," not only in the melodies but in the countermelodies as well.

The Wagner literature is huge: over 10,000 books and articles. I would like to call the student's attention to one more informative source: Jacobs's and Sadie's *Great Operas in Synopsis*.[32] Although alluding to Buesst, the authors approach the *Leitmotiv* according to what is being represented (a thing, a person or inner relationships).

HUMPERDINCK (1854-1921)
Hansel and Gretel (1893)

See Chapter VI.

R. STRAUSS (1864-1949)
Salome (1905)

Elektra (1909)
Der Rosenkavalier (1911)
Ariadne auf Naxos (1912; 1916)

These operas belong to both the Romantic Period and to the "Period of Sound," the "Post-tertian Period"—or whatever future writers will choose to call it when they can no longer say "contemporary" or "modern" and mean any music from Debussy on. Strauss, in his operas and tone poems—unlike his songs—looks forward and in a sense writes "music of the future."

Salome had a bad press from the very beginning (see Slonimsky, *Music Since 1900*[33] for some scathing press notices). "The Dance of the Seven Veils" was the main cause, but the music was unintelligible to many listeners, including some who were just beginning to be able to endure Wagner and Brahms. The scene of Salome kissing the trunkless head of John the Baptist was hard for some others to stomach. Like Wagner, Strauss makes the most of musical coloring to show the contrast between John the Baptist (and what he stands for) and the garish court of Herod. The opera is well-unified musically and dramatically. Since the playing time is about one and one-half hours, sometimes a small work of less intensity shares the bill. This work requires artists of the utmost virtuosity, down to the last man in the orchestra. The singer who portrays Salome must obviously make the famous dance compelling, or the whole performance will be a farce. Opera singers at the time of the premiere were not known for attractive figures, hence stand-ins were sometimes used. This opera is pungent, but it has something to say without preaching; one masterful part of this work is the characterization and strength of John the Baptist.

Elektra in a way is even more pungent, and is perhaps Strauss's most advanced work. The playing time is about the same as that of *Salome*, but I doubt if anyone has ever seriously entertained the idea of performing the two as a twin bill! *Elektra* was one of three operas on which Strauss collaborated with Hugo von Hofmannsthal, and all three are fairly well-entrenched in the repertoire (*Rosenkavalier* and *Ariadne* are the other two). Its basis is mainly Sophocles and it is a tale of violence and horror; it stands out as a masterpiece of psychological drama, and Strauss was able to find just the right music to depict its horror. There are those who shake their heads and wonder how Strauss could have written this and *Rosenkavalier*, but it is a real tribute to his genius that he could write two masterpieces of such contrasting character. (The differences between *Salome* and *Elektra* alone are astounding enough!)

The work begins with the Agamemnon theme. When Elektra makes her first entrance, the orchestra "screams" the motive of her hate for her father's murderers. (Note how the Agamemnon motive resembles the Salome theme. There are many other musical characterizations which are masterful. This is not music for those who expect "Moonlight and Roses," although there *is* much tenderness in the score—which, as we have pointed out before, makes the horror still more vivid.

Der Rosenkavalier can only be described as "delicious" music. It has a rather complicated plot, but by and large is a delightful comedy with broadly-drawn characters (Baron Ochs) and also some finely-drawn ones (the Marschallin). The orchestration sparkles, is warm and is just perfect. But, like Wagner, Strauss attempted to write a classical comedy that ended up as a great romantic comedy. The hero is a "trousers" role: that is, a soprano sings the part of a young man (Octavian), just as was done in many roles in the eighteenth century (roles such as Despina in *Così fan Tutte*—she portrays a male notary in the last act—and Cherubino in *The Marriage of Figaro*). The *Rosenkavalier* waltzes would have warmed the heart of Johann Strauss (who was not related to Richard in any way).

Ariadne was originally intended as an opera within a play, to be performed during Moliere's *Le Bourgeois Gentilhomme,* for which Strauss had also written other music. In the revised version the plot situation is updated but it is still an opera within an opera; Monsieur Jourdain is replaced by the Major-domo, who speaks for his master, a contemporary, newly-rich Viennese. There is much beauty and humor in this work, although it is very small in orchestration and concept compared to the other Strauss masterpieces.

The other operas of Strauss (such as *Arabella, Capriccio* and *Die Frau ohne Schatten*) are occasionally revived, with mixed reactions.

French Opera

Romantic French operas have not been very durable in the repertoire, but were very important when new and were vital to the audiences who enjoyed them, from New Orleans east. The so-called "War of the Buffons" in 1752 all but put an end to French Baroque opera as the new concept of comic opera came into being. A newer kind of serious opera was developing which resulted in what became known as "grand opera": not only opera which was "all sung," but which was full of spectacle, and often based on history (and all very, very serious). The French had outside help from Gluck, Cherubini, Rossini and Meyerbeer. Remember that Paris was one of the showplaces of the world, but that other capitals were also visited from time to time by artists from foreign countries. There was much interchange of ideas, and most composers knew well what was going on elsewhere.

The above-named composers vied with French composers, who in the main were Grétry (1742-1813), Méhul (1763-1817), Bóieldieu (1775-1834), Auber (1782-1871), Halévy (1799-1862), Félicien David (1810-1876) and some others. Of these Auber still lives on through performances of his overtures here and there (they are real "barn burners"). Halévy's opera *La Juive* is replete with beautiful music and is sometimes played today, albeit with many cuts. David was an important influence; he traveled through the Orient and brought back to France a striking kind of orientalism. His once-very-popular symphonic ode, *Le Désert*, and *Lalla-Roukh* (1862) held the boards until the 1890's. His exotic flavoring was used in many works by other composers.

Gluck and his operas belong to the eighteenth century, but they exerted an enormous influence on Berlioz and others who were to build grand opera in France. Cherubini has been mentioned many times but needs to be again, since his "French" operas were important both for themselves and for their influences. *Medea* has been revived in recent years, and was known by both Beethoven and Berlioz and was admired by Brahms. The score still packs power today; the orchestral writing is superb, and the experience of hearing the right singer in the title role is an unforgettable one.

Berlioz was never a success in his lifetime as a theater composer, but our times are giving him a hearing. The orchestral portions of his operas are, of course, superb and they were perplexing to orchestras which first tried to play them. His vocal writing is also skillful, and he shows great ability to move about from scenes of intimacy to scenes of great grandeur—this he does without resorting to mere pianissimos in the former and noise in the latter. Most authorities agree that his masterpiece is *Les Troyens* (not performed until after the composer's death in 1890, and then in Karlsruhe). Donald Grout pays it two supreme compliments when he calls it the "Latin counterpart of Wagner's Teutonic *Ring*; its strange fate is paralleled by nothing in the history of music unless it be the century-long neglect of Bach's *Passion According to St. Matthew.*"[34]

Gounod's *Faust* (1859), as we have said, is *too* popular, but it is a remarkable work nevertheless. It is always sure-fire with audiences and will remain in the repertoire for a long time. His *Romeo and Juliet* (1867) was once equally as popular and deserves to be revived more often. The stage helps the music of Gounod. His handling of the orchestra is good and colorful, yet it is comfortable for the singers.

Offenbach (1819-1880) wrote a whole host of operettas which are now performed only occasionally. His masterpiece is the serious opera *The Tales of Hoffmann*, which, however, he did not finish. It was finished by a French composer who was born in America: Ernest Guiraud (1837-1892), who wrote eight operas of his own, wrote the orchestral recitatives for Bizet's *Carmen* (very good ones, too!) and finished Offenbach's masterpiece. *Hoffmann* abounds in fine, if not profound music, which wears well with imaginative stagings. The "Barcarolle" is overplayed, and is not even original in this work (it is from his failure *Sprites of the Rhine*). The "Doll Song" and the "Diamond Aria" are two famous numbers which are sure-fire hits if sung well at all. Guiraud should have touched up the orchestration more than he did; it is rather thin compared to Gounod. An unusual feature is the fact that between the Prologue and the Epilogue are three acts which tell three entirely different stories; these are bound together only through the fact that the heroines are Hoffmann's three former loves—in reality, three different aspects of Stella, his current love.

Delibes (1836-1891) is remembered today for the opera *Lakmé* and the ballets *Coppélia* and *Sylvia*. *Lakmé* is a "vehicle opera" for a coloratura capable of singing the celebrated "Bell Song." It has an exotic atmosphere which was once admired. Thomas (1811-1896) is remembered for *Mignon*, with its story based on Goethe's *Wilhelm Meister*, and for a setting of *Hamlet*. *Mignon* is another "vehicle opera," built around the leading female role of Mignon. There are some great moments in this opera, and it is one of the few with a happy ending.

Bizet's *Carmen* is almost a "perfect" opera, although its premiere at the Comique was a fiasco. People had thought of the Opéra Comique as a "family" theater, and the sight of girls smoking in 1875 was almost more than the family audience could bear (it was more than some of the girls could bear, too!). Bizet was born in 1838 and died in 1875. He never knew what a success *Carmen* was to become and still is. It is probably one of the best introductions to opera for the uninitiated, yet it still has much to say to the opera veteran and can be exciting for professional musicians when performed with a good cast and adequate staging. The opera abounds in rich effects of orchestra, chorus, ensemble and dance—there is never a dull moment. The pace of the action is so fast that Micaela's prayer is a welcome change from what has transpired earlier. There are clever changes of scene, along with fascinating little happenings, such as little boys playing soldier, the spookiness of the smugglers' den and the noise and excitement of the bullring—a brilliant counterpoint to the tragedy of Carmen and Don José being played before our eyes.

Saint-Saëns's best work may well be the opera *Samson and Delilah* (1877), which is a mixture of opera and oratorio but contains much stimulating music.

The date 1871 is important because of the formulation of the Société Nationale de Musique. One good result of the Franco-Prussian War was that French artists turned away from concentrating on opera to showing greater interest in other kinds of music: a *French* music. Grout[35] characterizes the generation before (1840-1870) as one which adored Meyerbeer, neglected Berlioz and was crazy about Offenbach. The two big opera houses in Paris changed their policies to a certain extent; the Comique, in addition to its usual fare, began to include "avant-garde" works while the larger Paris Opéra did mostly the large, conventional works. *Samson* is a work of this time (although it was first performed under Liszt in Weimar), as were Bizet's *Carmen* and Delibes' *Lakmé*, to mention operas known to American audiences. There were many other important works and composers which deserve to be better-known. French music from about 1870 on is very striking and musically important. Ernest Reyer (1823-1909) championed the works of Wagner and Berlioz. He is best-known for his *Sigurd*, which is almost Wagnerian; his earlier works are exotic in oriental coloring. Reyer's Wagnerism is not as prominent as that displayed by such composers as Chabrier, Franck, d'Indy, Chausson and a few others.

Massenet has been mentioned earlier but must be again, since he was an old-fashioned opera composer who used the latest innovations in his music. He was old-fashioned in that he gave the public what it wanted in popular opera subjects and simple yet effective melody; yet, he was up-to-date in his use of such devices as a kind of *Leitmotiv* and an expressive chromaticism which does not strain tonality in the slightest. *Werther* and *Manon* are his best works.

Debussy's *Pelléas et Mélisande* is a "new world": a world ostensibly anti-romantic, but perhaps more romantic than any other; anti-Wagnerian, but perhaps closer to Wagner's music drama ideal than any of Wagner's works. It is fragmentary, yet unified; understated, but somehow even more intense by implication. There is much sound basis in the theory that Debussy was influenced by Mussorgsky's *Boris*. *Pelléas* is a remarkable example of words set to music, and one of the few cases in history in which the play has been used almost intact (there is no librettist, only Maeterlinck's play).[36] Debussy explored sound for its own sake, yet produced one of the most original operas ever penned.

The rather strange affinities between French and Russian music are often mentioned. Perhaps one explanation would be that the Russians represent an Eastern anti-Italo–Germanic style and the French a western one. French, as the official court and diplomatic language, strongly influenced Russian high society.

Russian Opera

Russian opera, as we have seen, starts with Glinka. Glinka's harmony and melodic writing employs whole-tone effects and occasionally uses $\frac{5}{4}$ and changing meter, which is characteristic of later Russians. Dargomyzhsky's *Russalka* (1856) and *The Stone Guest* (1872) are outstanding examples of an increasing realism, the breakdown of set numbers and the use of the whole-tone scale (see Ex. 119 in Grout's *Short History of Opera*). *The Stone Guest* is a setting of the Don Juan legend based on a play by Pushkin; it was finished by Cui. It has been pointed out from time to time that the nineteenth century—especially the romantic movement—was paradoxical. One of the most amazing instances is this highly personal (yet nationalistic) music which was completed by someone else!

Wagner's influence in Russia was considerable, both positively and negatively. This is seen in the use of *Leitmotiv*, chromatic harmony and conscious avoidance of obvious "Wagnerisms." The very versatile Alexander Serov[37] tried to combine Wagnerian techniques with Russian subjects, but his efforts were apparently ineffectual. He was quite vocal in his opposition to the "Mighty Five"—as was Anton Rubinstein, who was highly-trained and academic.

Tchaikovsky wrote some cosmopolitan operas and in a sense—with the outstanding exception of Mussorgsky—proves that a vital mixing of elements, even eclecticism, can be productive. Tchaikovsky was certainly a Russian, but he was influenced by German symphonism, by an almost Italianate sense of good melody, and by a French use of ballet and brilliant orchestration. Of his ten operas the best seem to be *Eugen Onegin* (1879) and *The Queen of Spades (Pique Dame)* (1890). Both operas display his best and worst features: beautiful melodies well-harmonized, but formal designs which do not allow for free declamation as do the operas of Mussorgsky. On the positive side, Tchaikovsky's vocal settings illustrate many of the melodic principles discussed in Chapter II.

Most of the "Mighty Five" wrote operas, and other Russian musicians seem to have made a hobby of finishing or "improving" them. Borodin's *Prince Igor* was completed by both Rimsky-Korsakov and Glazunov. The latter is supposed to have copied the overture from memory, having heard the composer play it "many times" at the piano. (One can only wonder how much of it is Borodin and how much is Glazunov!) It is based on themes from the opera. The best-known music is the colorful "Dances of the Polovetsian Maidens" in Act II, but there are also other fine spectacle scenes.

One of the supreme operatic masterpieces is Mussorgsky's *Boris Godunov* (1874), which has been "improved" by so many people! Rimsky-Korsakov's version was one such tampering, even though there were certain practical details in which Rimsky was absolutely right. He could not understand, however, the basic crudity which is so effective in this work of raw human passions on a grand scale, and in the mind and conscience of one man: Boris. Mussorgsky himself wrote the libretto, which is loosely based on Pushkin's drama and on history. Boris actually did reign from 1598 until 1605, a mad yet somehow pitiable, monstrous man whose characterization by the composer is absolutely superb. The protagonist is the Russian people themselves, represented by the choruses. Boris is a Russian Macbeth without a Lady Macbeth.

Rimsky's misunderstandings were mainly these: he took what he thought were crudities from the harmony and thereby "corrected" them (such devices as parallel fifths, dissonances and chords used for their own color—features greatly admired by Debussy); he changed the order of scenes—especially near the end, where the scene of the wailing simpleton should come *after* the death of Boris, not as *melodramatic action* but as *meaningful symbolism*; and he "polished" the orchestration, by adding color and spectacle to the "Coronation Scene"—which Mussorgsky intended to be more stark and forced. Mussorgsky's orchestration is almost pointillistic and is quite modern in its effect; Rimsky's is colorful, but employs the same colors through each phrase. Shostakovitch also wrote a version, and there are several others. It is certainly true that much of the popularity of this work is due in no small measure to Rimsky's colorful scoring; his version of the "Coronation Scene" is one of the best spectacle scenes in all opera. Strong arguments have been posed by all the various factions involved in the controversy over *Boris*. Some say we should leave well enough alone and do the Rimsky, which is what everyone knows and expects. Others come right out and say there is no more justification for doing Rimsky's version.[38]

Some authors have pointed out the thematic development of *Boris* as an important aspect of the score. It can be shown that the very opening is indeed an *Urkeim* and that the work steadily grows from it. People are having great fun these days looking for germ motives, and these motives are often of extreme importance. Composers *do* work through conscious or unconscious motive structuring. Perhaps true artistic inspiration comes from the optimum orientation of nerves and muscles, rather than from a "guiding angel."

Boris contains some remarkable music. The very opening—which is so *Russian*—is, again, the germ for the entire work. Keep this opening theme before you as you look at the others; a study such as Donington's could be made for this work too.[39]

Here is a paragraph from Leonard's excellent book on Russian music:

Mussorgsky's use of a *Leitmotiv* scheme in *Boris Godunov* is further proof of his willingness to experiment with what was then a radically new idea. It is also a refutation of the notion that he was technically ignorant. Recurring themes in *Boris Godunov* are not employed as persistently or as openly as in the Wagnerian method; some seem only vaguely touched upon, or they are deeply embedded in the texture of the music, as in Debussy's *Pelléas et Mélisande*; nevertheless, they germinate the entire score. Calvocoressi notes that in the first scene of the opera "all the music is derived from the melody with

Plate XVIII

Feodor Chaliapin (1873-1938), Russian opera singer and leading
basso of the Metropolitan, shown in costume in Mussorgsky's *Boris
Godunov (Courtesy The Bettmann Archive, N.Y.).*

which the Prelude opens, all the patterns of this melody being used in turn
for structural (not symbolic or allusive) purposes with extraordinary thoroughness and appositeness."[40]

There are numerous *Boris* studies, and Calvocoressi's books are excellent sources of early thought in these matters.

Note how the first choral appeal draws from the opening theme. The
"Coronation Scene" is justly famous for its harmony and for the themes
based on it. The "Song of Varlaam" is one of the most famous drinking
songs in all opera.

Here is a famous bit of "psychological music," that depicting Boris's
tortured conscience (in the famous "Clock Scene"):

MUSSORGSKY: Boris Godunov;
Third Act
(Reduction)

Figure 13-27

The third act is often criticized, since it was added for the second Mussorgsky version; this act introduces the love element. The "Revolutionary Scene"—which should close the opera—contains many quotable lines.

Here, indeed, is a supreme masterpiece, important in every aspect— no wonder it is admired by so many! One more comment should be added. The language of *Boris* is Russian; but if translated, there is absolutely no excuse for any language to be used other than that of the country where the opera is being produced. I have heard *Boris* effectively done in French (at the Paris Opéra) and in English, and I have suffered through performances where Boris sang in Russian and the rest of the cast in bad Italian. If a work *must* be translated, it should be sung in the language understood by the audience! The rather lame excuse that the singers know it only in Italian, French or Swahili is no longer valid nowadays.

Mussorgsky wrote other operas—notably *Khovanshtchina*—also finished by Rimsky and others, and also filled with beautiful music.

Rimsky-Korsakov's own operas are thirteen in number and contain much beautiful music. According to Emil Cooper,[41] they are far more representative of his work than the compositions most often played. One can find tantalizing samples by thumbing through the musical examples in his *Principles of Orchestration*, which contains 152 pages of text and 336 pages of examples. The book as a whole teaches one to orchestrate as Rimsky-Korsakov did (which wasn't too bad!)—romantic, exotic, almost impressionistic and often close to early twentieth-century works. (Remember that Stravinsky was one of his pupils; the influence is obvious in works as late as the symphonic poem version of *The Nightingale*.) I will cite just a few passages from Rimsky-Korsakov's operas, and urge the student to find others equally effective. This passage reminds one of the *Ring*, but the melody is quite Russian. The outlining of the harmony is striking, in the "Nocturne" from *Pan Voyevoda*:

Figure 13-28

May Night contains this passage which shows his subtlety in harmonic and melodic writing; note the solo cello doubling the first violins and the voice.

The English horn part is somewhat unusual, in that it is a harmonic part, whereas English horns usually have melodic parts. The doubling with cello is especially colorful, so the pedal point is more than harmonic here. The clarinet has a striking dissonance: the concert A♯ against the A natural in the bassoons. Also colorful is the widespread viola part. Although the part-writing is very much a clear tonality, the parts are laid out in a very colorful way.

Allegretto quasi andantino

RIMSKY-KORSAKOV: *The May Night*

Nos chants vont charmer le jeune hom - me, nos ri-res font fuir le vieil-

Figure 13-29

The student can learn much by studying Rimsky's other compositions.

Rimsky's best-known opera in this country is *The Golden Cockerel* (1909), his last opera and in many respects his best work. It is a fairy tale, and he supplies two kinds of music for it: chromatic for the unreal portions, and diatonic (tonal or modal) for real-life portions. The role of the Astrologer (a tenor) is vocally demanding, calling for an E above high C. Rimsky uses leading motives, but only in an identifying sense. The very opening is colorful: the Golden Cockerel is portrayed by a muted trumpet (how apt!), and the Queen by a cello.

Rimsky's great pupil, Stravinsky, carried on a great stage tradition which surpassed the national school, but for *Boris*.

The Bohemian masters have been mentioned elsewhere in this book. Smetana's *The Bartered Bride* still wears well. The role of Kezal, the broker, is the meaty role in this opera. Vashek is a stutterer, while the sextet is a fine, expressive ensemble. Marie's aria after the sextet is also beautiful. At the change of key there is a strange anticipation of *Till Eulenspiegel.* Before leaving *The Bartered Bride* it should be pointed out that the choruses and dances are important.

Dvořák's operas are still prominent in Czech theaters, and would be elsewhere if they were better-known. Dvořák had a practical knowledge of opera. He had been principal violist at the Provisional Theater in Prague, which had opened in 1862 for the performance of Czech theater, operas and plays. While there Dvořák played many works, including Smetana's *Brandenburgers in Bohemia, The Bartered Bride* and *Dalibor.* He had also played (in 1863) in concert under Wagner, in which a healthy cross-section of his musical works was presented: the *Faust Overture,* music from *Meistersinger, Tristan* and a short excerpt from the *Ring.* Needless to say, this concert made a profound impression on Dvořák (remember, he had been able to work with Wagner in rehearsal). The Wagner influence can be seen in many ways in most of Dvořák's mature music, but he was able to make the music uniquely his own. Some of Dvořák's operas were written in German, and others in Czech. The early operas contain much music to admire, but they show that Dvořák was a fine musician with a dramatic sense not yet developed. He chose bad libretti; as Clapham asserts simply, "The words are poor"[42]— another case of fine compositions suffering from bad libretti. One striking aspect of his third opera, *The Stubborn Lovers* (a one-act comedy), is his attempt to make the music monothematic. This work is seldom performed, however.

His fifth opera, *Dimitri,* is noteworthy in that it is based on the character of the false Dimitri (who figures so prominently in *Boris*). It was successfully performed in 1882 and was admired by Hanslick. *The Jacobin,* Dvořák's sixth, was a successful work; Clapham feels it is one of his best.[43]

There are three more operas of Dvořák, coming from his last period. *The Devil and Kate* is a fine comic opera; especially fascinating is the "hell theme," which is used in various ways. Some of the sketches for this opera were written in America.

Rusalka is Dvořák's most famous opera, and in Dvořák's homeland it is almost as popular as *The Bartered Bride,* (One should not confuse this with Dargomyzhsky's work of the same name. It is yet another musical picture of the underwater world of Undine.)

His last opera, *Armida,* is hardly known; the premiere was not a success. It seems to some to be a re-hash of Wagner, but it might better be thought of as a farewell to this kind of opera (now that it was 1904).

The sad truth is that there are far more operas in libraries than on the boards of theaters. The future, however, promises occasional revivals of some forgotten works, especially in university opera workshops where musical merit is paramount, not the satisfying of a fickle public.

The operas of Janáček are exciting more and more opera-goers; this composer is in many ways the heir of Dvořák and has to be called the "Czech Bartók" (his works really belong to the twentieth century). In England and the United States, opera activity in the nineteenth century was but scattered here and there. Gilbert and Sullivan operettas are in a class by themselves, and *The Bohemian Girl* by Balfe once enjoyed a vogue. The great period of English opera (other than the masques and the works of Purcell) begins in the early twentieth century, with the works of Vaughan Williams, Britten and some others. In the United States, Bristow, Fry and a few others tried to develop an opera style based on American subjects. There is still an untapped resource of American literature which could well inspire some great operatic compositions. There have already been some outstanding operas written in the twentieth century, ranging from Menotti's works to Sessions's *Montezuma* and Schuller's *The Visitation*—and, of course, Gershwin's *Porgy and Bess*. It is only fair that Victor Herbert's works and those of others be at least mentioned. More serious works are of some importance, but the student can study Chase's *America's Music*[44] for further details.

Opera did much, by its very nature, to help the downfall of tonality by changing from a highly formalized entertainment for the wealthy to an expression of the feelings of people, where *real* passion filled the stage. To depict this passion, music became concerned with new ideas of beauty—even beauty as the defeat of ugliness or as submission to it. Since tonality had much to do with form and order in earlier periods, it follows that the new exploitation of passion required a new type of music. Wagner, Mussorgsky, Verdi, Debussy and a host of others, rather than being chastised for tearing down a magnificent old edifice, should instead be admired as the planners and architects of a new one which the twentieth-century "builders" enriched: a new "music of the future" which, one day, will be called "classical."

Notes

1. Schumann's father, August, was something of a genius himself. A writer and a successful novelist, he had a great interest in the world's literature. Robert was reared in a home which loved good books.
2. The word *Liederkreis* means song cycle.
3. *Music in America, An Anthology*, compiled by W. Thomas Marocco and Harold Gleason (New York: W. W. Norton & Company, Inc., 1964).
4. So-called because the singers often sat about a table as they sang.
5. Percy Young, *The Choral Tradition* (London: Hutchinson and Co., 1962), Chap. 6.
6. Elwyn Wienandt, *Choral Music of the Church* (New York: The Free Press, 1965), p. 229.

7. Arthur Jacobs, ed., *Choral Music* (Harmondsworth: Penguin Books, Ltd., 1963), Chap. 12.

8. Young, *op. cit.*

9. A. Maczewsky, "Cherubini," *Grove's Dictionary of Music and Musicians*, 5th Ed., ed. Eric Blom (New York: St. Martin's Press, Inc., 1966), Vol. II, p. 200.

10. Mosco Carner, *Puccini* (London: Gerald Duckworth & Co., Ltd., 1958), p. 283.

11. Simon Sechter (1788-1867) was to have taught Schubert, but his death in 1828 prevented it. Bruckner was one of his last pupils.

12. Wienandt, *op. cit.*

13. Wienandt, *ibid.*, pp. 369-371.

14. Young, *op. cit.*, pp. 239-246.

15. John Clapham, *Antonin Dvořák* (New York: St. Martin's Press, Inc., 1966), pp. 254-255.

16. Julius Melgunov (1846-1893) developed an accurate method of taking down folk songs. He published several treatises on the subject.

17. Charles Hamm, *Opera* (Boston: Allyn and Bacon, Inc., 1966), Chap. 5.

18. Gerald Seaman, "Slavonic Nationalism from Dvořák to the Soviets," in *Choral Music*, ed. Arthur Jacobs (Harmondsworth: Penguin Books, Ltd., 1963), p. 295.

19. Donald Grout, *A Short History of Opera* (New York: Columbia University Press, 1947), p. 437.

20. There are some theories about man's first music being a direct response to pain, elation or some other emotion. This applies to prehistoric man and to the crying of a baby, as well as sing-song cursing by an adult who is hurt or frustrated.

21. Wallace Brockway and Herbert Weinstock, *The Opera* (New York: Simon and Schuster, 1941), p. 390.

22. Carner, *op. cit.*, Chap. 21.

23. See Carner's *Puccini*, pp. 366-368, for a good discussion.

24. Claude Debussy, *Monsieur Croche, the Dilettante Hater*, anon. trans. (London: Noel Douglas, 1927), pp. 110-111.

25. Eduard Hanslick, *Music Criticisms 1846-99*, ed. and trans. Henry Pleasants (Baltimore: Penguin Books, Inc., 1950), p. 13.

26. A very important work on Wagner is Lorenz's *Das Geheimnis der Form bei Richard Wagner*, which is in four parts and discusses all of his late music dramas.

27. Gerald Abraham, *A Hundred Years of Music*, 3d Ed. (Chicago: Aldine Publishing Co., 1964), pp. 77-136.

28. Alan Walker, *A Study in Musical Analysis* (New York: The Free Press of Glencoe, 1962).

29. Robert Donington, *Wagner's Ring and Its Symbols* (London: Faber and Faber, 1963), p. 275.

30. Donington, *ibid.*, p. 15.

31. Rudolph Reti, *The Thematic Process in Music* (New York: The Macmillan Co., 1951), pp. 1-30.

32. Arthur Jacobs and Stanly Sadie, *Great Operas in Synopsis* (New York: Thomas Y. Crowell, 1966).

33. Nicholas Slonimsky, *Music Since 1900*, 3d Ed. (New York: Coleman-Ross, 1949).

34. Grout, *op. cit.*, p. 319.

35. Grout, *ibid.*, p. 411.
36. Edward Lockspeiser, *Debussy* (New York: Pellegrini and Cudaby, Inc., 1951), pp. 208-228.
37. Alexander Serov (1820-1871) was an outstanding critic, and in the 1860's was the idol of the Russian public for his *Judith* and *Rogneda*. He was an ardent Wagnerian but an outspoken critic of the national school.
38. Jacobs and Sadie, *op. cit.*, p. 259.
39. See M. D. Calvocoressi, *Mussorgsky* (New York: E. P. Dutton & Co., Inc., 1946).
40. Richard Leonard, *A History of Russian Music* (New York: The Macmillan Co., 1957), p. 108.
41. This was in a conversation with the author during the 1950s. Cooper was a famous Russian conductor and composer who conducted many performances of the Rimsky-Korsakov operas, including the premiere of *The Golden Cockerel*.
42. Clapham, *op. cit.*, p. 271.
43. Clapham, *ibid.*, p. 281.
44. Gilbert Chase, *America's Music* (New York: McGraw-Hill Book Company, Inc., 1955), Chap. 30.

CHAPTER XIV

ORCHESTRAL MUSIC

Poematic Symphonism

THE EXTRAMUSICAL ASPECTS OF romantic music are evidenced most spectacularly in the remarkable orchestral works bearing a "program." Romanticists were so struck by storytelling and by fanciful titles that they even published older works with ridiculous titles.[1]

Some very important music, of course, *did* have an extramusical basis and the composers believed in it. The mistake some people make is in trying to force *all* music to tell a story. As Apel states:

It is generally agreed that music is basically an art in its own right and of its own substance: that its fundamental purpose is to work with its own material, and that too great a reliance on outside program is likely to weaken rather than to enhance the artistic merit of a composition. As a matter of fact, one cannot help feeling that a good deal of the interest which composers have taken in program music is but the avowal of a lack of truly musical imagination and constructive ideas, a lack for which they hoped to make up by an interesting program. In the final analysis, there are two types of program music: that which is good music regardless of the program; and that which is poor music even with a good program.[2]

Some music, however, must serve a storytelling function: music such as opera, ballet, incidental music or songs. This function has been very useful in the advancement of music. Some of the most vital ideas in the history of orchestration have developed in this way. The *stile concitato*

448

(agitated style) of the early Baroque—as exemplified in the *Combattimento di Tancredi e Clorinda* (1624) of Claudio Monteverdi (1567-1643) —is a good example, for it shows the first use by a great composer of bowed tremolo in the strings to suggest agitation. This novel idea was destined to become one of the most threadbare in the history of theatrical music—especially when used with the diminished seventh chord!

Many vital musical ideas, exciting and new at their inception, have been ruined (at least temporarily) by overuse in movies, television or the stage. What is even worse, of course, is the hideous distortion of great, "singable" themes by tin-pan alley.

But even before the orchestra became a significant musical reality, composers were composing "appropriate" music for particular texts and often introduced what were then novel harmonic and/or rhythmic devices. While one would expect this in secular music (especially entertainment music), one can find striking passages in masses and motets as well. As Ferguson states (although discussing Liszt):

. . . the association of theme with poetic idea not only adds to the vividness of expression, but also suggests many novel forms of transformation which would not have occurred to polyphonic writers or to homophonic composers who were chiefly concerned with formal construction for its own sake."[3]

It follows that *all* musical dimensions can be thus transformed—and indeed they have, as history shows.

The rise of opera was also the rise of coloristic orchestration in the scores of imaginative composers who, with deft touches of instrumentation, could greatly enhance the atmosphere of a scene. Many of these devices were so successful they became permanent fixtures in orchestral technique. While the Baroque and Classical Periods contributed many of these devices, the Romantic Period all but exploded with them, since this type of composing was so congruent with the popular thinking about all music. These devices were often grafted onto abstract orchestral works simply as colorful adjuncts.

The Baroque style of musical depiction was unique in many ways. The *stile rappresentive* of the early Baroque attempted it in almost every musical way: melody, harmony, rhythm, even orchestration. The great masters of the high Baroque carried this concept on through the use of musical figures temporarily assigned certain specific meanings, only to be used again with different meanings: such as Bach did in the *St. Matthew Passion* and Handel in *Israel in Egypt*. These are literal, almost naive depictions. *The Creation* of Haydn shows the use of this concept as well, such as the "Representation of Chaos" and the depiction of various animals.

The nineteenth century, then, is not unique in the attempt to tell stories in instrumental music; the unique element is the *way* it is done.

While some composers later try to disclaim any motivation by extra-musical stimuli, one wonders why—in Berlioz's case especially—so many symphonic works *have titles* and rather specific programs and yet employ many passages that are merely sound effects. Why should a composer apologize or feel self-conscious about storytelling music? (Was he attaching a program only to make the work more approachable by the public?) There was a relatively unsophisticated *new* audience of the rapidly-growing middle class who needed a story (or at least a title) upon which to depend when there was no text present.

The twentieth century has witnessed a decided reaction against story-telling music—by composers and critics alike—but we would be doing the nineteenth century a real disservice and would be misunderstanding the century if we were to ignore the propensity for extramusical ramifications in music.

Beethoven

Beethoven's stature as a composer is so great that it is really pointless to argue whether he is classical or romantic. Like many great men, he is both. His career indicates that he was the *right* man at the *right* time in history. We must begin our discussion of poematic symphonism with Beethoven, for reasons that are very apparent after careful study of his music, the background of his commissions, his ideals, his dramatic interests and the sum total of his musical development.

The non-symphony works of great importance which have programmatic content are:

Overtures:
Coriolan, Op. 62 (for Collin's play)
Four for the opera *Fidelio* (the *Fidelio* Overture and *Leonore* Nos. 1, 2 and 3)
The Consecration of the House, Op. 124 (1822) (for Meisl's play)
Stage Music:
Incidental music for Goethe's *Egmont*, Op. 84 (Overture and nine other numbers)
Ballet *The Creatures of Prometheus*, Op. 43 (Overture and sixteen numbers)
(Of lesser importance are the scores for *The Ruins of Athens* (play by Kotzebue), Op. 113, and the same author's *King Stephen*, Op. 117)

There are also works for chorus and orchestra (other than the great *Missa Solemnis* and the oratorio *Christ on the Mount of Olives*), but these are rarely performed. Of special interest, however, is the instrumentation of some of them: the *Elegiac Song*, Op. 118, is for four voices and string quartet; *Song of Fellowship*, Op. 122, is for two solo voices, chorus and wind instruments; and—rarest scoring of all—the *Fantasia in C Minor,* Op. 80, for piano solo, chorus and orchestra.

Concert arias by Beethoven's time are a common type of composition. Only two will be mentioned here: the early (1796) aria "Ah, Perfido," Op. 65, which is quite delightful; and the *Calm Sea and Prosperous Voyage,* Op. 112, for four voices and orchestra (also set by Mendelssohn).

The overture had, by Beethoven's time, become a piece of music not for just "opening the door," but a "preview": a passing parade of hit tunes, or a synopsis of the play or opera. Beethoven's great overtures are excellent examples of the latter type; when played in concert, they are without a doubt prototypes of later symphonic tone poems, and hence must be included in a discussion of poematic symphonism.

The overture to the ballet *Die Geschöpfe des Prometheus,* Op. 43 (*The Creatures of Prometheus*) and one of its dances (the theme being used later in his *Piano Variations,* Op. 35, and also in his *Eroica Symphony*) are all that are usually performed today from the sixteen numbers which Beethoven wrote. Perhaps too much has been said about Beethoven himself being the Prometheus of music, stealing fire from the gods and giving it to man, but there is a kernel of truth in it. The overture has a somewhat unusual beginning, presenting almost the same chord progression which begins Beethoven's *First Symphony*: a dominant seventh chord in the third inversion with the seventh in the bass, and a tonic root which resolves to a first inversion of the subdominant, altered to an Italian sixth which in turn resolves to a powerful dominant with a fermata:

BEETHOVEN: *Prometheus Overture*
(Winds Omitted)

Figure 14-1

Non-tonic beginnings were to become frequent in the nineteenth century, but in 1801 they were still a novelty.

The work shows many romantic and classical characteristics intermixed, as do most of Beethoven's earlier works (remember that the opus number is misleading: it should be numbered in the early twenties to show the correct chronology). The romantic traits are the non-tonic beginning, the imaginative use of solo instruments in the ballet and the interesting use of non-strict sonata-form in the overture. However, the composition does not yet reveal Beethoven the Titan.

The overture to Collin's drama *Coriolan is* Titanic—indeed, more Promethean than *Prometheus*. One must remember that this *Coriolan* is not Shakespeare, even though Wagner thought that it was!

Beethoven did not write any incidental music as such, but this overture must go down in history as one of the first great psychological musical works, as dramatic as any ever penned—a high standard indeed as one of the prototypes of the yet-to-come symphonic tone poems. In musical worth it has seldom been equaled, even by Beethoven himself. The tonality of C minor must have had special meaning for Beethoven, as G minor did for Mozart.

The essential ingredient of the main theme also figures in the transition to the second theme, which is as softly feminine as the first theme is masculine and heroic. Second themes in the nineteenth century tend to be in greater contrast to the first than they did in the eighteenth century, and in this overture there is a possible programmatic reason. The tonality of the second theme is, as expected, in the relative major: E-flat.

This work was important to Beethoven's career, especially his much-desired career as a *dramatic* composer. In spite of everything, *Fidelio* had not been the success for which Beethoven had hoped.

The *Egmont* music is at least as important, especially the overture. The complete music consists of ten numbers, including the overture and the concluding "Victory Symphony," which is based on the conclusion of the overture. Goethe's great play is an early piece, having been completed in 1775. Beethoven knew the work well and the basic poetic idea—struggle against tyranny and the triumph of freedom—was one which Beethoven used or contemplated again and again. He had wanted to make a musical setting of Schiller's *William Tell* (which also deals with tyranny), but the administration of the Court Theater ordered the *Egmont* music. Some claim that this might have been skullduggery on their part, since they thought the Goethe work contained less inherent drama. They did posterity a great favor, however, since Beethoven's *Egmont* is perhaps even more beloved than *Coriolan*, if that is possible. Beethoven, of course, did not mind and was enthusiastic, forgetting *Tell*.

The *Egmont* Overture is somewhat unusual in its form, even for Beethoven. The second subject is powerful and masculine. The development is short. The slow introduction is more than just an introduction— it is a beautiful study of an oppressed people, while the coda depicts liberation. The quasi-sonata–allegro in between tells how the liberation was brought about.

The other overtures are less important musically, except for the *Consecration of the House (Die Weihe des Hauses)*, Op. 124, which is an example of abstract music. Of the lesser overtures, the *Ruins of Athens*, Op. 113, is by far the best, but it falls far beneath great masterpieces such as *Egmont* or *Coriolan*. As stated above, Beethoven could write his share of music which somehow lacked "the great spark." In the case of his theatrical music it could well have been the nobility of the conflict in the stage piece in question; where Beethoven could identify, there was his heart.

Beethoven's programmatic works are actually more advanced in many details than are the dozens of similar works by other composers which followed. There is little straight sound effect; as with *Egmont*, one can supply a program even though it is not sure that the composer intended it except in a general way. Only one Beethoven work is so literal: the so-called "Battle Symphony" (*Wellington's Victory* or the *Battle of Victoria*), Op. 91. This work was a sensation at its premiere December 8, 1813. The great victory of the English forces under Wellington over Napoleon and his troops at Victoria, Spain, was won on June 21, 1813, an event which caused great celebration in Vienna. Thayer[4] and Misch[5] have much to say about the historical background of the work; the student would do well to consult such research in order to see an example of the ultimate fate of much music which is hailed as great at first, only to fade as its novelty wears off. One should put the "Battle Symphony" in its proper perspective, however. It is a mistake to compare it to the symphonies since, for once, Beethoven frankly is writing for the immediate public—and he succeeds!

Johann Nepomuk Maelzel (1772-1838), better-known as the inventor of the metronome, had shown the Viennese public the Panharmonicon (a mechanical orchestra which consisted of a trumpet, clarinet, viola and cello and which was capable of many percussion effects and great dynamic contrast) and had asked Beethoven to write a piece for him in return for some kind of hearing aid. Maelzel did supply him with four different ones, but apparently with little success. While the Panharmonicon did not make a lasting contribution to music as did the metronome, the basic principle of "stored," mechanically reproduced music lives on today in recorded music. The history of this concept is a fascinating one, and it is significant that men of Beethoven's importance should have been so interested in it. Works of Handel, Haydn, Cherubini and Moscheles (see Misch) were already "on the barrel" when Beethoven was approached for a contribution. Beethoven needed money, and Maelzel was shrewd enough to suggest the popular defeat of Napoleon as a fit musical subject, not only for a Vienna performance, but for a projected trip to London.

The student should attempt at least one hearing of this work, for it is not without good passages! As Misch points out, Beethoven succeeded brilliantly in his plan to write a work of sensational popular appeal, and even today it never fails to get a rousing cheer if performed in the right atmosphere (perhaps Shea Stadium or the Astrodome). At the first performance there was such a festive atmosphere, as Misch points out:

The Battle of Victoria was performed for the first time at a charity concert for the benefit of Austrian and Bavarian war invalids—that noteworthy concert of December 8, 1813, which also marked the first performance of the Seventh Symphony. If the symphony in A received an enthusiastic reception even then, the Battle Symphony, as Maelzel had foreseen, proved a sensation. The participation musicians under Beethoven's personal direction were, as we know, all the local and visiting artists of distinction, from Salieri (the Court Conductor "who did not consider it beneath him to beat time for the drums and cannonades") to young Meyerbeer, who with Hummel served the "heavy guns"! From the chamber virtuosi Schuppenzigh (Beethoven's favorite violinist) and Spohr, to the traveling double-bass virtuoso Dragonetti. The success was so brilliant that after two "repeat performances," on December 12 and January 2, Beethoven was able to give two more during the course of the next three months. The *Battle Symphony* which (as he put it) "completely bowled over the Viennese" carried him to the pinnacle of popularity.

But voices gradually began to be heard that condemned the work as mediocre, some even going so far as to call it "unworthy of a Beethoven." And this verdict has become so firmly in the consciousness of later generations that the work can be characterized as a forgotten or, more exactly, suppressed work.[6]

Even a Beethoven should have occasional fun, and this is exactly what he must have had in arranging the work for a live orchestra. He even indicated in the score (with signs which look like cannon muzzles—showing which cannons are French, and which ones are English) exactly at what point the artillery should be fired.

The four overtures to *Fidelio* are certainly among the great curiosities in all music history. They figure on many symphony programs—especially the *Leonore No. 3*, which is one of the greatest orchestral essays in the literature. Beethoven did indulge in some programmatic effects: for one, the trumpet call announcing the arrival of the "good guys." The overture which was first performed at the premiere of the opera is now identified as *Leonore No. 2* (1805). For a performance at Prague in May, 1807 (which did not come off), Beethoven wrote the *Leonore No. 1*; the *Fidelio* Overture was not performed until 1814, but now it almost always serves as the overture to the opera itself. The *Leonore*

Plate XIX

Beethoven's studio. Lithograph *(Courtesy The Bettmann Archive, N.Y.)*.

No. 3 is now played as an introduction to the second act, or else as an interlude between the scenes of that act. It was composed for the production of 1806.

The numbering of the *Leonore* overtures seems strange when one realizes that *Leonore No. 2* was played at the premiere of the opera. The opera was a failure, and a year later (in 1806) the overture was reworked as *No. 3*. The 1814 performance brought out what is now known as the *Fidelio* Overture. *No. 1* will probably never be settled to everyone's satisfaction. It was discovered after Beethoven's death and carries a very late opus number (138). Internal evidence leads one to believe that it was probably composed first, hence the numbering as number one. The first *Leonore* overture is a pleasant enough piece, but it is not the great masterpiece that either two or three is, nor is it the effective curtain-raiser that the *Fidelio* Overture is. *No. 1* is episodic and somewhat disjointed. The very beginning uses almost the same melody as one used in the violin concerto; but this could be merely an accident. Florestan's aria theme from the second act is also used— as it is in the other *Leonore* overtures—but it somehow just doesn't work.

The second and third overtures are quite similar, but the differences are also of importance. It is a personal opinion as to which one is better, since both are great works. Both begin with a huge concert G followed by a descending line. *No. 2* seems to make a false start. *No. 3* has always seemed to give the impression of passing from the sunshine into poor Florestan's deep dungeon. The scale is not too clear in its tonality, and its ending on F-sharp and the use of F-sharp as the dominant of B minor is somewhat remote from C major. The deceptive cadence between bars nine and ten is arresting too. We first hear the G-major chord as the submediant of B minor, even though it is the dominant of what will eventually be the tonic key of the work. The G chord becomes a dominant minor ninth, however, and one thinks that we might now have a cadence in C, but A-flat is entered as a deceptive resolution.

BEETHOVEN: *Leonore No. 3*

Figure 14-2

Florestan's aria theme is now stated in a lovely passage for bassoons and horns. Note that Beethoven is using horns in two different keys (E-flat and C), so he has more pitches—and, therefore, more tonalities—at his disposal.

The foregoing shows romantic tendencies, and the use of Florestan's aria at this point is indeed programmatic, since he is the one who is in the dungeon! In *No. 2* the clarinets and horns support the theme; but in *No. 3* the strings help, giving a richer sound. The trombones replace the horns at this point in *No. 3*, but do not serve the same function at all. The whole passage has in reality been reorchestrated, and it is a good early example of romantic harmony. Note how Beethoven modulates from A-flat to the dominant of E minor through an augmented sixth chord (bar 18 in *No. 3*). The B-major chord introduces a curious dialogue between the flute and violins, which in turn accompanies a murky fragment of the scale theme which began the overture. In *No. 2* more is made of this passage and of the ensuing rush of 32nd notes, which are detaché and played once in *No. 3* but are legato and played twice in *No. 2*. The introduction is prolonged a little more in *No. 2*, but ends quite abruptly in *No. 3*. It is now left to the student to make further comparisons since, after all, Beethoven looked upon *No. 3* as an improvement of *No. 2*. One can gain some insight into a composer's "second thoughts," as it were. Note especially differences in orchestration, form, harmony, key relationship and development. The entrance of the famous trumpet call occurs earlier in *No. 2* than in *No. 3*, which is important, since it occurs at the right moment in the story.

Both *2* and *3* are splendid examples of dramatic sonata-allegro form, and both show how flexible the form really is. Many writers have expressed various opinions about the use of either one as the overture for the opera; most of them are convinced that they are too dramatic in view of the rather light nature of the opening scene—and I certainly concur. The *Fidelio* Overture is just about right: it is short, brilliant, with some power, but a much better curtain-raiser for the opera. It is really anti-climatic for the trumpet call to be heard long before it occurs in the opera—or afterwards either, for that matter. Most lovers of *Fidelio* (and there are many) do not worry about such matters now, since they know how the story ends and heartily endorse the playing of *No. 3* as an interlude or as an isolated concert piece.

Beethoven's mature orchestral works set a great standard for the century to follow. Since he was such a profound figure, it follows that more than one kind of music could develop, each composer thinking that he was either following in Beethoven's footsteps or else going beyond. Some noted his classical traits, but others were reassured that a pursuit of program music, chromatic harmony and colorful orchestration was a logical path for music to take.

The latter group was led by Berlioz-Liszt-Wagner; but there were other influences as well, especially from the more imaginative opera composers. Since some of their operas survive today only through performances of the overtures, they will be discussed here.

Lesser Composers

Carl Maria von Weber (1786-1826) has been called the founder of the German romantic school of opera. He is best-known for quite frequent performances on symphony programs of the overtures to the operas *Der Freischütz* (1820), *Euryanthe* (1823) and *Oberon* (1826). All three are brilliant, tuneful and important historically for their approach to orchestration, which was certainly influenced by the subject matter and atmosphere of the plot and setting. As Newman points out apropos *Der Freischütz*:

> The overture is one of the world's masterpieces of its genre. It was a striking novelty for its time. With rare exceptions, such as Mozart's use of the music of the Supper Scene for the andante introduction to the overture to *Don Giovanni*, composers until then had not drawn upon the themes of the opera. Weber began a new genre with the overture to *Der Freischütz*, without which, in all probability, we should never have had such overtures as those to *Tannhäuser* and *The Mastersingers*.
>
> Further, Weber was not only a born musical dramatist but a very original and skilful orchestral colourist; and the overture to *Der Freischütz* has a depth and brilliance and variety of tone to which there was nothing to compare in any previous operatic overture.[7]

Der Freischütz deals with common people, magic, romance, horror— the overture is a capsule version of the opera in programmatic content and uses themes from the opera. The most striking part is the use of music from the Wolf Glen scene: a marvelous bit of atmospheric writing which points the way to the likes of Berlioz. The form is still an applied sonata-allegro, with bobtailed recapitulation. *Euryanthe* is a brilliant curtain-raiser; in the middle there occurs a novel bit of orchestration for divided strings, which must have been stunning at the premiere[8] and is still effective today. The overture also uses a fugato. The story is an old French romance which has been told and retold many times, in Boccaccio and in Shakespeare *(Cymbeline)*. *Oberon*, the most famous overture of the three, has a wonderful fairyland atmosphere, using for a closing subject the theme from one of the big arias: "Ocean, thou mighty monster." As with the others, the *Oberon* Overture is somewhat awkward in form, but is more successful than the countless potpourris of "hit tunes from the show" on the one hand and the only-too-correct textbook forms of others. Weber was the originator—a real breakthrough —of coloristic orchestrations, as Ulrich declares:

> The instrumental color of Weber's overtures, however, represents a new element in orchestral writing. His use of extreme instrumental ranges, his imagination in devising new combinations, his subtlety in contrasting dynamics and unusual instrumental effects—these and many more factors contribute to the new sound of his music. The interest in orchestration as an art may be said to have begun in Weber's time; principles revealed in his works were employed and expanded by Berlioz, Wagner, and a long line of orchestral masters who succeeded them. The end result was the huge, colorful, modern orchestra and the flexible, imaginative orchestration which called that orchestra into being; but credit for the original stimulus undoubtedly belongs to Weber.[9]

Brief mention should be made of some naive programmatic music by composers such as Karl Ditters von Dittersdorf (1739-1799), who wrote several symphonies based on works of Ovid; Haydn's far more successful prelude to *The Creation*; the opera overtures of Cherubini (1760-1842)— especially *Medea* (1797), which influenced Beethoven, and the lofty programmatic symphonies of Spohr (1792-1859), which are but historical curiosities today. They are performed and/or recorded occasionally, but rarely do they make the impression upon *us* that the works of Weber or Rossini do.

Rossini (1792-1868) occupies a special place in the programming of symphony orchestras today. Many of his overtures receive brilliant performances each season, and *William Tell* is one of the best-known of all pieces of music. *William Tell* (1829) has had its "ins and outs" on the operatic stage, but the overture somehow has the right mixture of melodrama and contrast to live on. In 1829 the world had not yet heard the works which we have heard (in great abundance) since. The use of divided celli at the premiere must have been as stunning for the audience as it was terrifying for the cellists, since such a device *was* rare in those days. The over-all form resembles a symphonic suite: the first section depicts an Alpine sunrise; the second, one of the best storms in all music (a nice one, though); the third part, the abatement of the storm (a typical pastoral: "after the storm is over, here come the cows"); and the finale, a wild gallop (well-known to millions of American children as the "Lone Ranger" music). The work as a whole really deserves a better fate, but perhaps the overture being loved by so many people is not such a bad fate, after all!

The other overtures which are still performed to any extent are *The Barber of Seville* (also used by Rossini for other operas), *Semiramide*, *La Scala di seta*, *The Thieving Magpie* and *La Cenerentola (Cinderella)*. All of these are tuneful and contain programmatic elements. Rossini had a habit of building up to a climax by repeating a strain of music with added orchestration and crescendo, and used it so much that such a device is called the "Rossini crescendo."

Berlioz

In the *New College Encyclopedia of Music* there is this arresting statement:

An eccentric and sometimes unbalanced personality, whose music, romantic in spirit, ranges from vivid imagination to utter banality. His originality showed itself particularly in his handling of the orchestra.[10]

Jacques Barzun's study,[11] however, shows an entirely different opinion and is highly recommended to the student for its valuable treatment of Berlioz and his contemporaries.

The orchestra is used in almost every Berlioz work, and with the same kind of richness one finds in symphonies. The *Requiem*, for example, is not "churchy" at all, but treats the holy text of the mass as a colorful text—which, of course, it is. Other composers had written Requiems, but with Berlioz there is no setting apart, no separate "sacred style." Others to follow did the same thing: Verdi's *Manzoni Requiem* is as operatic as an opera, and often more dramatic than many operas. Berlioz's use of the orchestra to portray extramusical ideas was most original, and he was a good enough composer that, by and large, the music stands on its own merit (albeit often episodic). Most composers in the Classical Period wrote for almost every kind of musical production; there was not too much specialization. Haydn, Mozart, Beethoven and many others were masters of "the whole art." Berlioz—and, as we shall see, many others of the nineteenth century—did not even try to master everything. Berlioz wrote no significant keyboard music, and Chopin no orchestral masterpieces (the concerti a possible exception). Mahler and Bruckner are remembered mostly for their symphonies, and Wagner for his music dramas. Mendelssohn is a notable exception to this rule.

The most important orchestral works of Berlioz are these:

SYMPHONIES
Symphonie fantastique (1830)
Harold in Italy (1834), symphony with concerto-like viola solo.
Romeo and Juliet (1839), dramatic symphony for contralto, baritone, chorus and orchestra.
OVERTURES (non-opera)

Francs-Juges (1826)
Waverley (1828)
Rob Roy (1833)
Roman Carnival (1844) (originally the introduction to Act II of *Benvenuto Cellini*)
Corsair (1850-1851)
OTHER WORKS (important historically, but not often performed)
Lélio (1831-1832), a sequel to the *Symphonie fantastique*
Funeral and Triumphal Symphony (1840)

Overtures and excerpts from his operas and other works often appear on symphony programs. With Berlioz the orchestra is all-important; no work of his fails to display remarkable growth in his ability to handle the instruments in the most subtle manner. He did not always grow in other musical matters, however, but there is far more to praise than to deprecate. Since these other works are of such importance in the development of orchestral music, they will be mentioned and discussed here.

OPERAS
Benvenuto Cellini (1838)
Damnation of Faust (1846) (actually a secular oratorio, but sometimes staged)
Les Troyens (1855)
Beatrice and Benedict (1862)
OTHER IMPORTANT WORKS (involving the orchestra)
Requiem (1837)
Summer Nights, song cycle with orchestra (1843)
Te Deum (1849)
Childhood of Christ (1854)

The career of Berlioz had many unusual features—he certainly was an *individual!* He was at first trained in the profession of his father—medicine, but did not complete the course, since the call of music was too strong. His knowledge of the dissecting room, however, probably gave him plenty of ideas about the atmosphere of the wierd and the grotesque which can be found in many of his works. He was one of the first major composers who did not really play any instrument well, although he eventually became a virtuoso conductor and expected virtuoso performances from his players. He disliked formal training and was almost always at odds with Cherubini at the Conservatory, but learned much from Lesueur. Berlioz authored the first good text on orchestration, which has been used in many formal classes. He was never properly appreciated in France until long after his death, but he scored huge successes in Germany and later in Russia. He was also successful as a critic and as a man of letters about music. His literary works remain primary sources of eye-witness reports on the state of music in his time. He was really "the right man at the right time," despite the great difficulties he encountered; his talent grew in the fertile romantic atmosphere of Paris in the 1830's. One of the most moving accounts of his place in his time was written by Richard Anthony Leonard—written so well that I must quote it at some length:

No age or place ever produced a denser concentration of individualists, each intent upon the free proliferation of his own ego, than Paris during the years 1830-40—the bright morning of the romantic era. The city swarmed with wild men of genius, with exotic personalities as brilliantly coloured as so many tropical birds. Romanticism had come of age and 1830 formally celebrated its adulthood. In that year the stupid Bourbonism of Charles X met its end in revolution; in another quarter the riots over the production of Victor Hugo's *Hernani* signalled the victory of the new romantic drama over a dogmatic classicism. In that year Berlioz, 'mad Hector of the flaming locks,' composed the *Fantastic Symphony*, a musical landmark that he said was a testimonial to his unrequited (and later all too completely requited) passion for an Irish actress. Hugo was beginning his long career as dramatist, novelist, and poet; Balzac was toiling away his anchorite existence in an attic, already started on the stupendous task of the *Comédie Humaine*. Gautier was there, brilliant stylist and passionate romantic; Dumas, the French Scheherazade; Sainte-Beuve, the greatest critical mind of the nineteenth century; George Sand, the woman who dressed like a man, smoked cigars, and performed man's work of writing novels; the German, Heinrich Heine, a poet 'who dipped his pen in honey and gall, who sneered and wept in the same couplet,' and Mérimée, Stendhal, Lamartine, Musset, and Chateaubriand. Delacroix was there, a man of bold imagination, intellect, and courage, whose work became a lasting ornament to French painting; and Delaroche, Vernet, Corot, Ingres, Ary Scheffer, Rousseau. The roll call of musicians was no less impressive. Besides Berlioz and Chopin there was Liszt, then in the zenith of his flaming youth ('the wild, lightning-flashing, volcanic, heaven-storming Liszt,' Heine called him), conquering the piano and women with the same Jovian ease; Rossini, the strangest of geniuses, who abandoned success when he was thirty-seven at the height of his career and lived to be seventy-six; Meyerbeer, the man who made opera 'grand,' *i.e.* added the elements of spectacle, pageantry, and bombast to the fundamentals of music and drama; Thalberg and Kalkbrenner, the rivals of Liszt as piano-taming virtuosi; Auber, Herold, and a score of other men, once lions but now mere small type in music's footnotes.

The time was one of excess and extravagance. To be an apostle of romanticism it seems that one had first to be odd. A strain of morbidity also ran through the minds of half of these romantics. They were filled with obsessions, illnesses of the flesh and of the spirit—and they gloried in them. Dumas wrote that 'it was the fashion to suffer from the lungs; everyone was consumptive, poets especially; it was good form to spit blood after every emotion in any way sensational, and to die before reaching thirty'. It was also the fashion to weep, faint, or otherwise carry on during theatrical performances. When Lesueur, an operatic composer and Berlioz's teacher, first heard Beethoven's Fifth Symphony he was left so emotionally disorganized that when he started to put on his hat he could not find his head. When Alfred de Musset listened to lines by Racine he would take his head in his hands and blanch with emotion. This same young poet admitted that, after his affair with George Sand had ended with her in the arms of the Italian Dr. Pagello, he spent four months shut up in his room in incessant tears.

It was the day of the grand passion and the *idée fixe*. Men's minds seemed to be conditioned less according to rational patterns than in imitation of some literary figure—the more morbid the better. If one did not fancy oneself a Werther with suicidal melancholia, one might be a Faust in the throes of a soul struggle, or a Manfred hiding in his bosom some nameless sin of sins. Lord Byron himself had been one of the most popular literary figures in Europe; he had personified Werther, Don Juan, and Manfred all rolled into one; he was poet, adventurer, cynical sensualist, and possibly murderer. His very death was a piece of romantic idealism—an Englishman dying for the cause of Greek freedom.

If anyone could be said to personify that age—to typify (paradoxically) an era that was all untyped individualists—that man was surely Hector Berlioz.[12]

Berlioz's affairs with women in real life were almost as fantastic as those in his stories. Berlioz had seen Harriet Smithson play Juliet in Paris and fell madly in love with her, vowing that he would win her and write for her the symphony which would be his greatest work. He did marry her (much to the sorrow of them both) and did write the *Fantastic Symphony*, which is certainly Berlioz's most popular work; however, it should by no means be used as a final judgment of Berlioz, since he was a young man in his twenties when it was written. His later works show greater maturity in most aspects, and perhaps they exaggerate his weaknesses at the same time.

Berlioz himself often wrote either the program or the libretto of his own works; this is what he says about the *Fantastic*:

A young musician of morbid sensibility and ardent imagination poisons himself with opium in a fit of amorous despair. The narcotic dose, too weak to result in death, plunges him into a heavy sleep accompanied by the strangest visions, during which his sensations, sentiments, and recollections are translated in his sick brain into musical thoughts and images. The beloved woman has become for him a melody, like a fixed idea which he finds and hears everywhere.

PART I. DREAMS, PASSIONS

He first recalls that uneasiness of soul, that *vague des passions*, those moments of causeless melancholy and joy, which he experienced before seeing her whom he loves; then the volcanic passion with which she suddenly inspired him, his moments of delirious anguish, of jealous fury, his returns to loving tenderness, and his religious consolations.

PART II. A BALL

He sees his beloved at a ball, in the midst of the tumult of a brilliant fete.

PART III. SCENE IN THE FIELDS

One summer evening in the country he hears two shepherds playing a *Ranz-des-vaches* in alternate dialogue; this pastoral duet, the scene around him, the light rustling of the trees swayed by the breeze, some hope he has recently conceived, all combine to restore an unwonted calm to his heart and to impart a more cheerful coloring to his thoughts; but *she* appears once more, his heart stops beating, he is agitated with painful presentiments; if she were to betray him! . . . One of the shepherds resumes his artless melody, the other no longer answers him. The sun sets . . . the sound of distant thunder . . . solitude . . . silence.

PART IV. MARCH TO THE SCAFFOLD

He dreams that he has killed his beloved, that he is condemned to death, and led to execution. The procession advances to the tones of a march which is now somber and wild, now brilliant and solemn, in which the dull sound of the tread of heavy feet follows without transition upon the most resounding of outbursts. At the end the *idée fixe* reappears for an instant, like a last love-thought, interrupted by the fatal stroke.

PART V. WALPURGIS NIGHT'S DREAM

He sees himself at the witches' Sabbath, in the midst of a frightful group of ghosts, magicians, and monsters of all sorts, who have come together for his obsequies. He hears strange noises, groans, ringing laughter, shrieks to which other shrieks seem to reply. The *beloved melody* again reappears, but it has lost its noble and timid character; it has become an ignoble, trivial and grotesque dance-tune; it is *she* who comes to the witches' Sabbath . . . . Howlings of joy at her arrival . . . she takes part in the diabolic orgy. . . . Funeral knells, burlesque parody on the *Dies irae*. Witches' dance. The witches' dance and the *Dies irae* together.[13]

In the *Fantastic Symphony* the *idée fixe* is replete with possibilities *other* than those pointed out in almost every music appreciation text.

At the very beginning, the chromatic melodic movement in the oboe and the clarinet occurs at bar 36 of the "source melody." The first entrance of the first violin occurs at bars 16 and 17 of the source melody and the melody continues in much the same way, but the effect is so different through Berlioz's mastery of orchestration, some counterpoint and a smoother texture. A little searching by the student will reveal that the entire slow introduction is derived in the same way.

At this point we should mention that Berlioz has constructed what we might even call a "source set" of melodic ideas, and he takes full advantage of every "parameter": every aspect of music which can be varied. We have been looking at the pitch-melodic parameter, and further looking shows the remarkable fact that Berlioz can write themes which are diatonic stepwise, chromatic, angular through common triads (compare bars 1, 2, 9 and 10 of the source set), more freely angular (bars 32-35) or combinations of the above (bars 36-40).

Any long melody can be made to do exactly this—study the very long and beautiful theme which begins the *Seventh Symphony* of Bruckner. There must be additional means of identification with the source set, and Berlioz provides this through another parameter: the rhythm. The *total* content of bar 2 is of great importance. Notice how Berlioz takes the first interval and inverts it to obtain the agitated movement in the cello and bass. Later on, as the theme gets more involved, the interval expands, but the rhythm remains. Both ideas are used—the interval and the rhythm—at these agitated spots. Notice the contrabass part. Later on there is a beautiful development of this, coupled with the idea of the broken triad and as accompaniment in a middle voice.

The development section begins with a good working-out of this first melodic idea—broken triad which at first includes the passionate rising semitone, D to E-flat, answered by the descending semitone, D-flat to C, and then sequenced. Berlioz now compresses these ideas; on page 22 of the full score, second system, one sees the broken triad as the accompaniment, with expressive semitones either up or down and with the two eighth notes legato.

Any symphony of this period could contain a development section beginning this way—it is just what we mean by the term "symphonic." It takes on added meaning here, in view of the program which Berlioz himself provides. The romanticism is more subjective in this work, and would be romantic, program or no. Berlioz uses the theme of the *idée fixe* in another work: the sequel piece *Lélio*, which does not succeed at all. The important point is that Berlioz has written convincing music which is unified technically; if the Baroque composer could use a figure which depicted a hill at one point and the flight of the soul at another, what is so wrong about Berlioz using a tune which had had other connotations? This music attains importance through its treatment of musical elements. One should never assume that there is ever an absolute meaning for a given scrap of music; the context and the totality—the *Gestalt* —are the important factors.

It is almost amusing to peruse the literature on the *Fantastic Symphony*; no two writers agree on the importance of this or that. Some claim that the finale is unintelligible without the program, while others declare it is actually a revival of an old Baroque form: the fantasy and fugue! It is true that there is, for the first time, a generous intrusion of the composer's private life into his music. There is great difference of opinion as to how much of the symphony actually came into being through Berlioz's love for Harriet Smithson, the Irish-English Shakespearean actress. (The program certainly would lead one to believe that there is a wish to kill her! We know from many sources that the married life of the two was anything but "As You Like It"! Some have said that *Lélio* is not the success it should be due to the souring of their marriage, but in truth the marriage failed much earlier.)

There are also literary sources for the *Fantastic*: among them, de Quincey's *Confessions of an Opium Eater* and some concepts from *Faust* and *Manfred*.

The second movement, "Un bal," must be contrasting; yet, it still can be shown to derive from the source set, and in other ways besides the obvious statement on page 70 of the full score. Some say that this waltz tune does not deserve to be part of the symphony, while others contend that it is the most delightful part. For those of us who have known this symphony all of our lives, the movement belongs simply because *it has always been there!* It has a form of its own, however, and is unified technically and cyclically with the rest of the work.

The other movements also have a life of their own, and yet show this same unity. It is not difficult to derive the waltz tune from the main theme of the "Scène aux champs," nor is it difficult to derive that from the source set. Notice the two eighth notes on page 102 in the score. Compare page 113 to page 71, and one can see the unity of the two rapid notes, which as a unit form a *Leitmotiv.*

Mention should also be made of Berlioz's use of the famed *Dies irae* in the finale. The *Dies irae* figure:

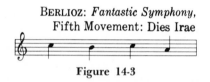

BERLIOZ: *Fantastic Symphony,*
Fifth Movement: Dies Irae

Figure 14-3

has been used in works almost from the very beginning of musical history, since it is a natural figuration, especially in contrapuntal music. As the century progressed, other composers used at least the first four notes to suggest death. Berlioz uses much more of the theme, applying his own rhythm, and then supercharges the theme at the end of each phrase. This grows and grows until the "Ronde du Sabbat," which is actually a good romantic version of a double fugue. There are homophonic episodes, which are based thematically on the outlines of the subjects and which are coloristic. A few bars later, after fascinating outlines which maintain the rhythm of one of the subjects but not the pitches, Berlioz reintroduces the *Dies irae* in the celli.

Next follows a striking compression of the theme in the violas, in reality a second subject for the fugue. Things really quiet down, then comes a typical Berlioz build-up; at the climax the *Dies irae* is blasted out by the winds while the strings continue the fugal material.

This is a good example of the kind of counterpoint used quite often by the romantic composer. In a way this passage is the "glorification" of the *Dies irae.* Here is one time when the doubling *is* for power. The string writing does continue the fugue, but there are comparable passages in Berlioz where the strings would have a freely-composed excitement.

Figure 14-4

A remarkable transformation of the theme for the "Hexentanz" shows some of Berlioz's best writing; it is exciting music, brilliantly orchestrated (notice the *col legno* in the strings: the players tap the strings with the wooden parts of their bows, giving an unforgettable sound), and Berlioz displays his skill as a writer of good counterpoint (Cherubini would not have approved)—counterpoint which does not appear in instruction manuals. The next passage is a remarkable bit of woodwind writing: rare for its time, but used often since:

BERLIOZ: *Fantastic Symphony*, Fifth Movement

Figure 14-5

The *Fantastic Symphony* is periodically laid to rest by various detractors; but, to paraphrase a classical comment from Mark Twain: "Reports of its death are greatly exaggerated!" The *Fantastic* has itself become a classic.

Harold in Italy has not fared so well. It is a work which contains great beauty and exciting, brilliant orchestral writing. Its failure to hold a commanding position in the repertoire was first suspected by Paganini, for whom the work was written. The great virtuoso has been blamed by some for not playing it, although it is not really a viola concerto. The premiere took place in 1834, with Urhan as soloist, and the reception was cordial. Paganini knew that Berlioz was disappointed and performed a very dramatic, almost theatrical, act in compensation. On

December 16, 1838, when Berlioz was at a low point in his career, he conducted a moving performance of the *Fantastic* and *Harold in Italy* which was received with sensational enthusiasm by the audience. Paganini came to the stage and bowed as if in fealty to Maestro Berlioz, and a few days later sent him the large sum of 20,000 francs. This magnificent gesture probably saved Berlioz's career.

Harold, then, is too soloistic to be a symphony but not soloistic enough to be a real concerto. There are some fine recordings of the work, however. (Problems of many kinds are solved by recording!) In passing, it should be pointed out that there is in reality a strange three-way split among the listeners of serious music today: 1) the live audience at concerts; 2) the record collector; and 3) the FM or AM radio listener. While it is true that many people belong to all three groups, it is also true that many music lovers who know many works have never been to a real concert! The excitement of the live human performance shared by you and the rest of the audience is something which can never be captured on records.

Berlioz's symphony *Harold in Italy* shows the impact of Lord Byron on fellow romantics. Byron's *Childe Harold's Pilgrimage* is its literary basis, and the student should read Byron's masterpiece after he has heard the symphony as music. The music is organized along lines similar to the *Fantastic*. There is an *idée fixe* which depicts Harold, and his personality is associated with the solo viola throughout the work. The symphony abounds in lovely orchestral effects which anticipate many works to come later.

There are practical performance difficulties with *Romeo and Juliet*, as there always are when a chorus and soloists are needed.

The dramatic symphony *Romeo and Juliet* (as Berlioz called it) is dedicated to Paganini, and uses a text by Emile Deschamps. It was written during 1839, was revised and published in 1847, with further revision and publication in 1857. Berlioz's work was Op. 17 and bears the complete French title: *Roméo et Juliette Symphonie dramatique avec Choeurs, Solos de Chant et Prologue en récitatif choral, composée d'après la Tragédie de Shakespeare.* The first performance was at the Paris Conservatoire on November 24, 1839, with Berlioz himself conducting. It is probable that this work (and many others of Berlioz as well) would not exist if it were not for Beethoven's *Ninth Symphony.* The Berlioz work resembles a large cantata more than a symphony, but contains the remarkable thematic unity and development that one would expect in a symphony, and a non-operatic, orchestral treatment of the more dramatic moments. It is significant that Romeo and Juliet themselves are *not* characters with solo parts, but are depicted by the orchestra. (Interest in Shakespearean subjects was quite frequent in Berlioz.) The work is extremely important in the repertoire, and would certainly be performed with greater frequency if smaller forces were called for.

The complete outline of the work is as follows:

The work begins with a tumultuous fugue, which is probably overlooked by those who would point out the paucity of counterpoint in romantic music! The most arresting part, however, is the very beginning. When all the voices have entered, contrapuntal interest almost ceases and the texture becomes quite homophonic, with suggestions of the subject here and there.

Here is the beginning, indeed tumultuous:

BERLIOZ: *Romeo and Juliet,*
First Movement

Figure 14-6

Next follows the famous recitative "Intervention of the Prince," calling for horns in E, E-flat, G and F; two trumpets in D, a cornet in A and one in E-flat; three tenor trombones; and the ophicleide (a forerunner of the tuba), now played by tuba. This is a good example of the great orchestral imagination of Berlioz. No other composer before had ever dreamed of such writing, but *afterward* the likes of Wagner and Liszt knew good composing when they heard it. It is no exaggeration to assert that Berlioz's *Romeo and Juliet* changed the course of music history. Wagner's correspondence with Berlioz and others gives Berlioz credit for causing a kind of breakthrough in Wagner's own musical thinking, as a result of hearing *Romeo and Juliet.*

Next comes the "Prologue," sung by contralto solo and divided chorus, which voices the exposition of the drama. It is a choral recitative of strange effect. Many have thought it odd that Berlioz did not make Romeo a tenor and Juliet a soprano—but Berlioz did not believe in typecasting! He felt that it was enough for the audience to be told what it needed to know by the chorus, and then for the orchestra to investigate the mental states of the principals.

The prologue is followed by the "Strophes" for contralto solo, which describe the joys of the lovers. Next is the "Scherzetto" for tenor and chorus, which sets Mercutio's *Queen Mab* speech.

The second part is completely orchestral and is frequently heard as a separate number on symphony concerts. It is a remarkable bit of orchestral writing, with three main divisions: Romeo's solitude and sadness, the ball and the party at the Capulets. Study the first page of the full score. The student should notice the size of the orchestra and Berlioz's concern over the harp part. This movement is a good example of Berlioz's use of chromatic melody and harmony, and is an excellent study in the art of orchestration.

Part III is the Love Scene, greatly armired by Wagner and a model for *Tristan und Isolde.* The chorus again tells the audience what is transpiring, but it is the orchestra which creates the real atmosphere and projects the emotions of young love: a beautiful night, a moment one wishes could last forever.

Part IV begins with the famous "Queen Mab" Scherzo, which is often programmed as an excerpt. Here is one of the rare indications of the horn crooked in A-flat alto: the *high* crook. This means that there must have been a crook in A-flat *bassus,* and Berlioz feared that the third horn might play an octave too low. There must be two tympani players: the first uses normal tuning (tonic and dominant), but the second tunes in D-flat and A. There are two antique cymbals or crotales, in B-flat and F, and there are two solo harps. There is a little Mendelssohn influence in this movement, but Mendelssohn's "fairylands" are within the framework of the classical orchestra, while Berlioz's "fairyland" is romantic; there are pastel tints, bright flashes and diaphanous opulence. But this section is also a masterpiece as pure music. The development of the motives which are important in the whole work and the developments within this movement alone are worthy of emulation, as indeed they have been by many composers since. Berlioz influenced composers in ways other than sheer orchestral noise. A study of American scores of the Romantic Period will show striking similarities—works such as

Chadwick's *Symphonic Sketches.* There are even traces of Berlioz in the scherzo of Tchaikovsky's *Pathétique Symphony,* in the "Waterfall" portion of the *Manfred Symphony* and in much of *The Nutcracker.* Barzun's title of his great study is so apt: *Berlioz and the Romantic Century.*

Berlioz is Shakespearean in his juxtaposition of moods. Berlioz follows the "Queen Mab" with "Juliet's Funeral March," which is intensified in its sorrow through its contrast to the delights of the scherzo. Shakespeare does not use this same kind of contrast, since Mercutio's Queen Mab speech occurs in Act I. Perhaps Berlioz took the idea from *Hamlet*: Hamlet and the Gravedigger vs. the death of Ophelia. (This is not the first time that composers have altered the order of the plot to suit their own purposes.) Notice that Berlioz explains the exact relationship which must exist between the chorus and the orchestra; the chorus represents the Capulets. Musically the section is strangely fascinating. The orchestra plays a moving, expressive fugue while the chorus sings on one pitch, in the manner of a psalm tone. When the chorus finally moves to a contrapuntal texture, the effect is most impressive.

The next section is "Romeo at the Tomb of the Capulets," and is remarkable for its sudden shifts of mood and the strange complex of emotions. The tragedy in the story, of course, is that Romeo does not know that Juliet has taken a magic potion and is not really dead. He returns to the tomb of the Capulets, kills his rival, Paris, and then drinks poison. Friar Lawrence arrives, Juliet awakens and, seeing that Romeo is dead, stabs herself with his dagger. This is all very stimulating to Berlioz's sense of drama, and he rises to the occasion. Some feel that Berlioz should have ended at this point and that the finale is an anticlimax, but Berlioz himself attached great importance to the character of Friar Lawrence and to the reconciliation of the two families. As Berlioz often does, he employs the finale to resolve the music of the whole work. There are reminiscences of the earlier movements, but more subtle than in his other symphonies. The aria of Friar Lawrence is very beautiful, with orchestral colors setting each mood of the text.

The last section is the "Oath," and it employs a triple chorus: the first is a Shakespearean chorus and the other two represent the two feuding families. These massive forces are handled with greater skill by Berlioz than they are by some conductors. It is essential that clarity rule —it is so easy to end up in a shouting contest.

There are few works in the entire repertoire which remotely resemble *Romeo and Juliet.* The gigantic symphonies of Mahler owe much to Berlioz, but they are more tightly-knit. If Berlioz does not succeed completely, it is because the kind of work he tried to write does not really exist: something between opera and oratorio on the one hand and a large symphony on the other. Mahler composes wholly within the framework of the symphony and does not let opera intrude. Berlioz's *Damnation of Faust* is more successful as a totality, since it frankly moves toward opera and is sometimes staged as one. *Romeo and Juliet*, despite its impossibilities, is full of beautiful music and is vital historically. Many composers other than Wagner admitted that the work pointed the way to new possibilities in music.

Liszt

Few literary figures have captured the imaginations of so many composers as Faust, the man who dared to sell his soul to the devil in exchange for ultimate answers to life. The most important setting is the great play by Goethe; but Lessing, Lenau and Marlowe also created important literary versions, as did others. Faust actually did live: a mysterious professor of black magic who was apparently a great master of magic and human psychology, since many wild tales began to be told about his great powers. He was especially adept in bringing back to earth the shades of great historical figures such as Aristotle, Helen of Troy and others. The times (the first half of the fifteenth century) were such that the common folk actually believed in all kinds of magic, both good and bad. When the historical Faust met with a violent death shrouded by curious circumstances and great mystery, it was natural for all kinds of stories to circulate, including the one which has come down to posterity. Dr. Faust had sold his soul to the devil, and the devil had come to claim his part of the bargain. The clergy saw in this a chance to moralize, and the first literary works were sermons which held Faust up as a wicked, anti-Christ kind of character.

From these folk plays emerged, some of which were played by puppets and others at live folk theaters in village squares. Goethe saw some of these performances, and a real impression was made on him. Goethe mentions this in *Dichtung und Wahrheit* (Werke: XXVII, 320). It is thought that these plays were also influenced by performances of Marlowe's *Faustus* early in the seventeenth century. Goethe was also influenced by Lessing's famous seventeenth *Literaturbrief* (published in 1759). In this "letter" Lessing states a brilliant case for the excellence of English drama, especially Shakespeare, as opposed to the current vogue of emulating the very correct, but not very vital, French theater of the period. As an example of how an English drama might be written in German, Lessing composed a scene from *Faust*, inadvertently changing the course of literary and music history.

Faust is best-known through the opera by Gounod, which is only superficially based on Goethe. Boito's *Mefistofele* is well-known in Europe and is much more true to Goethe. Other stage works, ballets, symphonic works, songs and literary pieces draw from Goethe and from other sources as well. Liszt's *Mephisto Waltz* is from Lenau, but his *Faust Symphony* is directly from Goethe. The subject matter is still of great interest to composers: Busoni, Reutter and the present writer have written Faust music. The theme is a basic one: man's striving to know and to understand. The pact with the devil is fascinating, but it is mainly a *modus operandi* in Goethe; the other aspects of the story are also superficial to the "message" of Goethe. The "eternal woman" as exemplified by Gretchen is an important point (virtue unassayed is not really virtue). The Gounod opera notwithstanding, in the end Faust is saved through the prayers of Gretchen—certainly a basic Christian teaching: forgiveness even for monstrous wrong. Through the famulus named Wagner, Goethe also shows the great contrast between dead scholarship and the wisdom which comes from living the full life. (The scene of the "Easter Walk" is one such passage.)

The treatment by Franz Liszt is a bit puzzling, since at once we see Liszt at his best and at his worst. In the passages of the *Faust Symphony* we can see and hear the imagination of a great musical colorist translating, as it were, Goethe's words into music, rather than setting them. The transformations of the themes are masterly and do impart a musical unity; the work is well worth serious study. The orchestration is one of the most effective in the literature. The harmonies are strange and unsettled where the play demands them, and are normal and stable by contrast when a return is made to the "real world." The themes associated with Faust are outstanding and illustrate many of the important aspects of melodic writing in the nineteenth century (these aspects are discussed in the chapter on melody). As a general rule Faust's themes are distorted and placed out of focus in the sections of the work showing the influence of Mephistopheles, while Margaret's (Gretchen) themes show that she was not influenced by the minion of the devil. These themes are among the worst ever penned by Liszt, although one must admit they do portray the kind of girl she was before she got mixed up with Faust!

The "Gretchen" movement is almost salvaged by Liszt, however, since his treatment is indeed masterful—Liszt does show how he interprets the character of the girl. While it is a great compliment to "das ewige Weibliche" ("the eternal woman"), it does not do justice to the real Gretchen created by Goethe. True, *before* Gretchen meets Faust she is a paragon of virtue. In Faust (helped, of course, by Mephistopheles) she has her ideal man and does all that he wants. After all, her meetings with Faust were not just of the innocent "boy-meets-girl" type—she has a child by Faust. To keep her date with Faust she gives her mother a sleeping potion (lent to her by Faust) which she doubles in strength, just to make sure it works. And make sure she does: the mother never awakens. Gretchen drowns the child . . . and none of this is the influence of the Evil One!(?) The point Goethe seems to be making is that—even in the face of all this—the love of God *is* infinite, and she *is* saved. Faust is also saved, since she prays for his forgiveness (to the "Mater Gloriosa") and her prayer is answered—again showing that *she* really represents the essence of the whole question: Christ himself, on the cross, said, "Father, forgive them; for they know not what they do!"

Liszt, of course, was writing a symphony, not a sermon; but he seems to have overlooked a major point, and could have handled the Gretchen themes in a better way. His handling of the Faust themes in the "Mephistopheles" movement is masterful, so one wonders all the more how he might have developed the Gretchen material.

Another weakness of the work, it seems to me, is a weakness in Liszt himself: too much literal repetition. Even though he is writing a symphony, one wishes that the recapitulations were not so literal and that he sequenced less and repeated less *within* passages themselves.

The over-all organization is like that of a large symphony, in that the first movement is a gigantic sonata, the second a lyrical song and the third a brilliant scherzo; even though more than mere symphonic diversion, it does end the piece properly. The addition of the tenor solo and the male chorus seems necessary for the proper conclusion; the element which is missing in the "Gretchen" treatment now appears to have been supplied, at least in part.

The first movement ("Faust") begins with a vivid picture of Faust in his study (imagine an alchemist's laboratory, with skulls, foul-smelling concoctions and animals in various stages of dissection), where he is attempting a translation of the Gospel according to St. John. Liszt sets the scene visually and psychologically with this theme:

LISZT: *Faust Symphony,*
First Movement

Figure 14-7

The augmented triad by nature is unsettled in tonality, and thus makes for an imaginative setting of the subject matter. This part of the theme could be called the striving, yearning, insatiable desire to *know* which drives all great men. The answering phrase in the woodwinds is Faust the man, very capable of loving Gretchen and even Helen of Troy. Liszt seems to maintain these themes as "fixed ideas" (remember that the work is dedicated to Berlioz). The love music, for example,

Figure 14-8

is transformed into the fugato subject in the third movement. The whole symphony, and the *Dante Symphony* as well, show at once the originality of Liszt and his connection with both Berlioz and Wagner. There is always the question of the musicality of these works without their programs; but they are, after all, settings of literary works, were obviously inspired by them and would not exist without them.

Beethoven's Program Symphonies

The Beethoven symphonies are among the first great ones to indicate any programmatic tendencies, and they are landmarks. The third, sixth and ninth symphonies have rather special extramusical aspects important to Beethoven himself. Since the third is more important in its abstract context, it will be discussed later. The *Sixth*, in F major, Op. 68, is aptly called "Pastoral" and uses subtitles created by Beethoven himself. It is often cited as a romantic precedent by a classical composer. Beethoven, in his own comments on the work, implies that bucolic feelings are of greater importance than any direct imitation of nature. This attention to "feelings" aroused by something as specific as nature is a very common feature of nineteenth-century composition, especially in regard to works and composers in which it would seem to be in bad taste to imitate nature—even though the composer had done so! Beethoven's own subtitles give one at once the general mood of the scene. These are:

First Movement: "Cheerful impressions awakened by arrival in the country"
Second Movement: "Scene by the brook"
Third Movement: "Merry gathering of country folk"

Fourth Movement: "Thunderstorm; tempest"
Fifth Movement: "Shepherd's song; glad and grateful feelings after the storm"

Beethoven was by no means the first composer to use subtitles. In Vivaldi's *The Seasons* there are indications *within* the movements of such things as bird songs and rain. Beethoven was known to be a great lover of nature, but seldom indulged in "landscapes" in his music. *His* "storms" were those of the human soul. There is little conflict in the *Pastoral*, even in development sections where he usually allows the great stormy battles of the soul to be waged. Beethoven was at peace in the country. (Great men must face many trying hours with lesser men who fail to understand them.) The great conflicts, in most of Beethoven's music, are sheer *musical* conflicts and need no nice stories, although Beethoven's own life provided plenty of them. He had the amazing ability to work on several pieces at once, pieces which are as different from each other as the fifth and sixth symphonies (which he wrote almost simultaneously) and which he could resume work on years later with no great discontinuity. These great works needed time; those done in haste (such as the *Choral Fantasia*, Op. 80, also written in 1808, the year of the fifth and sixth symphonies) almost always lack the great Beethoven inner strength, are episodic, hackneyed and not worthy of Beethoven's signature.

The *Pastoral* is set in what has been called the "Lydian" key of F major (so-called, no doubt, from the fact that the Lydian, or fifth, mode includes an untransposed ambitus of F to F). The Lydian mode was often considered the "pastoral" mode and did not always employ the raised fourth degree (the B was flatted frequently in practical usage). (The real Greek Lydian, by the way, became our descending major scale.) Many who "see colors" when they hear music point out that F major is in truth a "verdant" key: a good "chlorophyll green." Beethoven's own "Spring" *Sonata*, Op. 24, for violin and piano is also in F major, which might be a coincidence. The "Spring" *Symphony*, Op. 38, of Schumann is in B-flat major—of which F is dominant. Not all pastoral or bucolic pieces are in F, nor are all "green" pieces in F—but many *are*. This is only an interesting coincidence; the important factor is the unusual lack of conflict, regardless of key. The storm involves some conflict, of course (one feels that the crops got a good watering), but the techniques used for musical portrayal are the same as those used in operas—diminished sevenths, tremolos and what-have-you. The suggestion of a fugato at the beginning was seldom used for operatic storms, but is an example of programmatic counterpoint which possibly exerted an influence on later composers. Berlioz begins *Romeo and Juliet* with a fugue, Liszt uses the device quite often in dramatic spots (compare *Prometheus* and the *Faust Symphony*) and even Tchaikovsky uses it in the finale of his *Manfred Symphony*. One wishes that Beethoven had carried his fugato farther in the *Pastoral*—it seems to promise more than it gives (as is often the case in nineteenth-century fugati). The delightful quasi-fugato in the "Victory Symphony" section of his *Battle Symphony*, Op. 91, is even more disappointing, since it peters out into "musical sawdust." The storm fugato in the *Pastoral* gives one at least a refreshing shower of rain!

Another touch of literalness is the musical imitation of birdcalls in the "Brook" movement; composers often used this device, but were seldom successful with it (Janequin's *Le Chant des oiseaux* is one of the best). Beethoven's second movement is especially engaging for the flute soloist, and is good for a few laughs when the cuckoo imitation is called for. Beethoven actually creates a very strange atmosphere in the final section of the "Brook" movement; this atmosphere is much more meaningful if one forgets the birds and listens to the music. Even more successful is the humor of the village band and of the bassoonist, who apparently has but three notes he can play.

The instrumentation is, of course, masterful; the use of tympani only in the storm sequence is a case in point—the effectiveness of percussion is inversely proportional to the frequency with which it is used. Nor is the "imitation" of the birds the only woodwind role, as Tovey points out:

The real cuckoo, nightingale, and quail happen to be the musical birds whose themes are exactly what Beethoven wants for a break in the rhythm at a point of repose in the coda of his slow movement. . . . Not a bar of the "Pastoral" Symphony would be otherwise if its "programme had never been thought of."[14]

Thayer, after pointing out that the *Pastoral* is, after all, only one of many attempts to portray nature in music, makes one of the most salient observations ever made about Beethoven:

It was never so much the ambition of Beethoven to invent new forms of musical works, as to surpass his contemporaries in the use of those already existing.[15]

The autograph of the score is in the Beethoven-Haus in Bonn. According to Forbes the word "pastoral" was first used on a violin part at the first performance:

Sinfonia Pastorella
Pastoral-Sinfonie
    oder
Erinnerung an das Landleben
Mehr Ausdruck der Empfindung als Mahlerei

The last line is, of course, the key to the whole work: "more the expression of feeling than painting."

Anton Schindler (1794-1864), who has been called "Beethoven's Boswell" by many, mentions many "incidents" in the life of the master which have been seriously doubted. Some of these references lead one to believe that Schindler was much closer to Beethoven than he actually was. Schindler was probably a bother, even though he was actually Beethoven's secretary for years and even cared for him in his final illness. The Schindler biography has probably been responsible for more wrong information than any other. Thayer and others are constantly correcting him in some details, even in matters as diverse as the geographical layout around Heiligenstadt or the musical shape of the call of the yellowhammer. What has often been written up by Schindler about Beethoven is probably nothing more than his own personal impression of him (see Forbes's *Thayer's Life of Beethoven*, pp. 437-438).[16] Many of Schindler's ideas are at odds with Beethoven's musical practice, as is readily apparent in Beethoven's best works. When Ferdinand Ries (1784-1838) or other Beethoven pupils express either the same or similar ideas as Schindler, then we can more readily believe them! There seems to have been some ridicule of musical "painting," even though there was much of it done (Beethoven seems to have done plenty of *both*).

Beethoven's great grasp of symphonic technique *is* in evidence in the *Pastoral*, in spite of whatever one might say about the subjective aspects of the work. The first four bars present the germinal pitch and rhythm motives which obviously permeate the first movement, and can be shown to be a source for the others as well:

BEETHOVEN: *Symphony No. 6* ("Pastoral");
FIRST THEME   First Movement

Figure 14-9

The rhythm of the second bar is one of Beethoven's motto patterns. The development section and other passages show this device so well.

Notice also the striking counter-rhythm of the first violins against the celli and basses. This device is used through much of the development section.

The "Brook" movement makes only passing reference to the initial motto, but the middle part of the scherzo (actually quasi-trio) uses it and adds something more.

FIRST MOVEMENT, DEVELOPMENT (MOTTO RHYTHM)

Figure 14-10

THIRD MOVEMENT,
FOURTH THEME (MOTTO RHYTHM)

Figure 14-11

The use of the motto in the "Storm" might be subconscious,

FOURTH MOVEMENT (MOTTO RHYTHM)

Figure 14-12

as might be this use of it in the "Shepherd's Song":

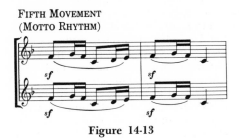

FIFTH MOVEMENT
(MOTTO RHYTHM)

Figure 14-13

The melodic outline of the first four notes is also of great importance. It is used as a bridge:

BRIDGE PASSAGE (MOTTO)

Figure 14-14

In the coda it is used this way:

CODA

Fls.

Figure 14-15

I fail to see why writers on Beethoven have so little to say about the *Pastoral*. When they do comment, it is usually not in flattering terms. The "weaknesses" which are pointed out are to me the charming features of the work. Even Schauffler seems to be sorry that he wrote it! After a brief history of program music he states:

Almost word for word, he (Beethoven) used the program of "The Musical Portrait of Nature," a "grand symphony," published in 1783 by Justin Knecht. We know that this program had been familiar to Beethoven for a quarter of a century, because it had been advertised on the cover of the three piano sonatas which he published as a lad of twelve.

The Master studied such crude old descriptive music as Knecht's. He reflected deeply about it and decided that it was on the wrong track. It attempted the

impossible. It set out to convert a cart horse into Pegasus; but it succeeded
only in making an ass of the creature. It tried to make music do unmusical
things. Beethoven's Sketch Books of this period are filled with random reflec-
tions on the problem of program music:

Sinfonia caracteristica, or a recollection of country life.

The hearers should be allowed to discover the situations.

People will not require titles to recognize the general intention to be
more a matter of feeling than of painting in sounds.

Pastoral symphony: no picture, but something in which the emotions are
expressed which are aroused in men by the pleasure of the country.

All painting in instrumental music, if pushed too far, is a failure.

These, then, were his principles. If he had stuck steadfastly to them we might
have had, in the Sixth symphony, a somewhat less original, less epoch-making
work. But it would probably have been a better piece of music. We should
have missed an influence which has fathered many of the most interesting and
suggestive tone-poems of the last century and more, but which has, on the
other hand, misled many a talent into bypaths; and has on the whole exercised
a constantly constricting, if not degenerating, effect on the art. For program
music is dramatic music. And dramatic music, as the composer Henri Duparc
justly observed, "is an inferior species, which does not allow the artist to
express himself directly, to reveal freely the beautiful soul."[17]

Much of what Schauffler says is true, but the quote from Duparc
merely substitutes one kind of program music for the other, does it not?

The whole matter was perhaps best summed up by Beethoven himself,
when he pointed out (see the quote above) that any true lover of nature
would understand the piece. To downgrade the *Pastoral* on the grounds
of its programmatic nature would then require one to do the same with
the *Ninth*, which in some ways is even more literal! For that matter, one
would thereby have to downgrade all vocal music other than the "truly
great music," since it tries to express the ideas of poetry. Why have music
if it is not poetic? Can't the poem be *silent*? If, as Keats said, "Heard
melodies are sweet, unheard melodies are sweeter,"[18] then one could as
well say the same for unvoiced poetry—a symphonic "poem of nature,"
one which the present author finds to be most charming.

Tovey's comment quoted above needs restating now in its full context:

Beethoven's Theory of Expression.—On the other hand, when superior persons
object to the childishness of the birds and the thunderstorms in Beethoven's
"Pastoral" Symphony, it is they who are childish in supposing that realism is
in question at all. The real cuckoo, nightingale, and quail happen to be musical
birds whose themes are exactly what Beethoven wants for a break in the rhythm
at a point of repose in the coda of his slow movement. Similar final digressions
can be seen in slow movements with no programme at all, e.g., in the Violin
Sonata, op. 24, the Pianoforte Sonata in D minor, op. 31, no. 2, and the String
Quintet in C major, op. 29. Not a bar of the "Pastoral" Symphony would be
otherwise if its "programme" had never been thought of. The "merry meeting

of country folk" is a subject that lends itself admirably to Beethoven's form of scherzo (q.v.); and the thunderstorm, which interrupts the last repetition of this scherzo and forms a tremendous introduction to the peaceful finale, is as musical as other unique features in Beethoven's pure art-forms.

Beethoven is recorded to have said that he always composed according to a "picture" he had in his mind; and he sometimes gave his friends an explanation, jocular or evasive, of some particular composition. But the word *Bild* is much more indefinite than "picture"; and Beethoven's dull Boswell, Schindler, often exasperated him into defending himself by saying the first nonsense that would serve to stop foolish questions. Composers who have much to express cannot spare time for translating it into other terms than those of their own art. The "Eroica" Symphony, though inspired by Beethoven's short-lived belief in Napoleon as the liberator of mankind, is not programme music at all. The funeral march represents heroic death and a mourning world, but not the obsequies of a biographical subject; and when critics tell us that the finale is "an inappropriate concession to sonata form," they merely show themselves unmusical without thereby becoming literary. The profound and subtle Sonata *Les Adieux, l'Absence, et le Retour* is true programme music. It represents Beethoven's feelings on parting from the Archduke Rudolph when the royal family left Vienna shortly before its bombardment. It deals only with the parting, the absence, and the rejoining of the two men. Nothing is heard of war, and the sentiment is as deep as it is manly. Beethoven's private sketch-books record that the work is "written from the heart," no courtly formula, even if this was shown to the Archduke. Ingenuity is misplaced in tracing external details. (The end of the first movement of *Les Adieux* has been compared to the departure of a coach.) The real emotional basis is universal and musical.

Beethoven summed up the whole theory of great programme music in his note to the "Pastoral" Symphony; "rather the expression of feelings than sound-painting."[19]

The presence of extramusical ideas in the *Pastoral* has prevented perhaps the same proliferation of writings that exist about Beethoven's other symphonies. These writings, by and large, are aimed at the non-musician and frequently supply programs—often ridiculous ones! The student should re-study the entire score of the *Pastoral* AS AN ABSTRACT SYMPHONY; he will discover that, as usual, Beethoven's programmatic treatments take place within the framework of classical forms which, even in strict application, allow expansion and some use of personal option. This is one of the most important reasons why the so-called "standard" forms *are* standard—they are actually very flexible in the hands of a master. Beethoven's insertion of the "storm" is actually an introduction to the last movement. He often wrote "bridge" passages from penultimate movements, even in three-movement works.

A great master has sense enough to learn from another great master. The introduction to the finale of Brahms's *First Symphony* is also a kind of "storm," but not a meteorological one. Another master, Berlioz, has this to say:

FIRST MOVEMENT
(Cheerful impressions awakened by arrival in the country:
Allegro ma non troppo, F major, 2-4)
This astonishing landscape seems as if it were the joint work of Poussin and Michaelangelo. The composer of *Fidelio* and of the *Eroica* wishes in this symphony to depict the tranquility of the country and the peaceful life of shepherds. The herdsmen begin to appear in the fields, moving about with their usual nonchalant gait; their pipes are heard afar and near. Ravishing phrases caress one's ears deliciously, like perfumed morning breezes. Flocks of chattering birds fly overhead; and now and then the atmosphere seems laden with vapors; heavy clouds flit across the face of the sun, then suddenly disappear, and its rays flood the fields and woods with torrents of dazzling splendor. These are the images evoked in my mind by hearing this movement; and I fancy that, in spite of the vagueness of instrumental expression, many hearers will receive the same impressions.

SECOND MOVEMENT
(Scene by the Brook: Andante molto moto, B-flat major,
12-8)
Next is a movement devoted to contemplation. Beethoven, without doubt, created this admirable adagio (sic) while reclining on the grass, his eyes uplifted, ears intent, fascinated by the thousand varying hues of light and sound, looking at and listening at the same time to the scintillating ripple of the brook that breaks its waves over the pebbles of its shores. How delicious this music is![20]

With the *Ninth Symphony* we approach a "magnum opus" really unique in the history of mankind. Performances today almost always have an air of great festivity; they often occur at the last concert of a season. It can be an expensive piece to perform, since it calls for four vocal soloists as well as a chorus and, of course, the orchestra. Few works have been so honored, and no work deserves it more. Few of these performances, however, are completely satisfactory; and this is not always the fault of the performers. The choral sections employ an excessively high tessitura and seem to require yelling more than singing, which obscures the counterpoint in the orchestra—any resemblance to a text is often just a coincidence! No other vocal music of Beethoven makes any such demands—nor does any other avowed masterpiece of the past, for that matter. Many reasons have been given for the difficulties of this work, but none seem to be quite satisfactory. Some say that, after all, Beethoven was deaf and could not possibly have "heard" the work in his mind at the pitches indicated, and therefore the work should be transposed down to be more singable. Although it is true that we tune to a higher concert pitch today (A440) and that the human voice has probably changed but little in this respect, transposing would be unthinkable for the orchestra. It must remain in D; no other pitch will do. Singers like to transpose the key of a song up or down to suit their voices on a particular day, but they do so with little or no regard for what this does to the sound of the piano. Key *does* make a difference on the piano, mainly in the different relationships between black and white keys (the actual finger patterns). Some keys are more brilliant for *this* reason, and some songs employ piano parts which are at least as important as the vocal lines. (After all, more pianists than singers have probably written songs!) Similar shifting of keys to accommodate singers occurs in operas in which the orchestration is not too significant. Recitatives often use different endings, modulating to alternate keys for the arias which follow. This, of course, requires printing of the parts in two or three keys, and instrumentalists sometimes feel as if their parts are a kind of "labyrinth" (personal experience!).

Practical considerations must not stand in the way of art—this is *precisely* why the original key must be maintained! The actual key sound in the orchestra *is* different from key to key; and in operas where the orchestral part is of great importance, there has never been widespread transposition to fit the vagaries of singers. In the case of the *Ninth* transposition would be criminal anyway, since the preservation of the tonal arch in Beethoven is of utmost importance. No, one must put up with what Beethoven has left. He is supposed to have replied to a complaining violinist who found a certain passage difficult to play, "When genius speaks, what do I care for your damn fiddle!" (Perhaps he could say the same to singers!) The fact remains that, when the vocal portions of the *Ninth* are performed well, the effect is stunning and the beautiful setting of the words is enhanced.

One could write reams of interpretive literature on the first three movements, and he could be both right and wrong. The last movement leaves no doubt, since it contains a text; it seems impossible to pay *no* attention to the text when writing or performing vocal music, no matter when the music was written. The finale not only sets the words, but is the logical denouement of the entire symphony—a magnificent unity of every aspect of musical structure, as well as a great spiritual unity.

At the beginning of the *Ninth*, a great door is opened—how to begin a symphony! So many works *since* then start with a cryptic tremolo, but no composer had ever thought of it before. The opening statements let us know we are in for a long work, but we do not lose interest; Beethoven's additive technique unfolds with suppressed excitement, as if one is hunting for something. This is a sort of "still-waters-run-deep" kind of movement, almost requiring the great rush of the scherzo in the second movement—a fugal scherzo actually in sonata-form. The adagio is again leisurely in pace; there are variations on two themes of haunting beauty, especially the D-major "song" so beautifully played by the second violins and violas (the second of the two themes which are varied).

The opening chord of the finale is a real jar when it occurs. There should be very little (if any) pause between the last two movements (the singers should be on stage during the instrumental movements—it won't hurt them to hear the orchestra!). Beethoven's programmatic idea is obviously to create discord: *unpleasant* discord.[21] The celli and basses now enter, trying to find "joy," but the stridency will not cease. Again there is a recitative by the celli and basses, giving way to the mystic music which opened the symphony, but changed here: the third of the dominant triad is in the bass, while the open triad (root and fifth) hang in space in the high woodwinds. Again the recitative occurs, and again it gives way, but now to a suggestion of the scherzo. Still again comes the recitative, giving way now to the beginning of the adagio, and yet again giving way in the woodwinds (in an almost "Brahmsian" scoring) to a "preview" of the great hymn tune, only to give way for one last time to the recitative. The various recitative fragments are all related in design, all suggesting the "Ode to Joy" but always searching. While one can interpret this in many ways (such as a reminder that true joy is not really found in the earlier movements), the fact remains that this is *almost* the first half of an exposition for a gigantic sonata, the second theme being the hymn tune which begins in bar 92.

True joy is finally found, in one of the greatest tunes ever penned! But how simple it is! Using the additive principle similar to that employed in the first movement, but less subtly, Beethoven proceeds with several strophes of the hymn, each time adding a voice or two; each verse is really a variation, in which the variable element is not the theme but the accompaniment. One also gets the impression of a gigantic canon: at bar 140 the celli and violi continue the theme which the basses announced at bar 116. The new voice at bar 140 is a *new* bass line. At bar 164 the full orchestra "sings" the tune in great glory, running headlong in a burst of brilliance, when suddenly—the music hesitates, as if something had been forgotten. Another short burst occurs, and then—a real shocker: a complete D-minor scale harmonized as one chord! This is probably the first *intentional* discord of this magnitude.

Notice that this is the same music which began the movement, but it is now greatly intensified. The baritone soloist now utters words to the pitches of the recitative:

> "O Freunde, nicht diese Töne!"
> (O friends, not these sounds!)

And so music history was made. The human voice had been heard in a symphony for the first time at the hands of a great composer.

Thirty-one years earlier Beethoven had become acquainted with Schiller's great *Ode to Joy* and had planned to make some sort of musical setting for it, turning to it time and time again, but not as a part of the

Ninth until his work on it had already begun. It is apparent that Bee-thoven had a Tenth in mind, and *that* piece was to receive the choral treatment. Even after Beethoven had made the decision to use the *Ode* for the *Ninth*, he was not completely convinced and expressed some doubts in 1823, as Graf describes so well:

But Beethoven had to wrestle for a long time with the idea of giving the symphony a choral finale. As late as June or July of 1823 he was considering an instrumental finale, and in the fall of the same year he reverted to the passionate theme that he had decided upon for the finale:

BEETHOVEN
(Reduction)
FINALE: REJECTED INSTRUMENTAL THEME-SYMPHONY NO. 9

Figure 14-16

Had Beethoven carried out this plan, the Ninth Symphony would have had a dismal, stormy, passionate ending like the String Quartet in A minor, opus 132, which, three years later, received the same music for its final movement.

From the sketch books of the Ninth Symphony from the years 1822 and 1823 one can see quite plainly how the idea of the hymn of joy thrusts itself out of the subconscious, is repressed and pushes itself through. On pages from June or July of 1823 a note is to be found: "Maybe the chorus of Freude Schoener after all."

The joyful melody assumed various shapes. Even after Beethoven had found the present melody, he sketched an entirely different melody in 3/8 time during the last months of 1822:

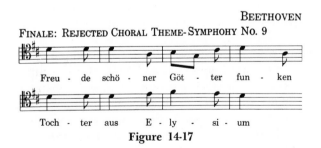

BEETHOVEN
FINALE: REJECTED CHORAL THEME-SYMPHOHY NO. 9

Freu - de schö - ner Göt - ter fun - ken

Toch - ter aus E - ly - si - um

Figure 14-17

It was finally the accumulated strength of the unconscious that helped the melody of joy to emerge. Here, in the subconscious, the old plans of a choral arrangement of the joy melody—from the years 1793, 1798, 1805, 1808 and 1812—had been thrown together and had finally achieved such strength that they raised the dome of the great choral finale to the summit.[22]

Beethoven's doubts seem to have little foundation for us today, but we have never imagined the finale in any other way as he did. Could he have had some intuition about the great impact this work was to make? After all, some had grumbled about the use of trombones in the *Fifth*, and Rossini was challenged to a duel for having used two snare drums in *The Thieving Magpie*. Calling for such forces in the *Ninth* (the orchestra was larger also) could have brought forth reactions from the *status quo* keepers; but apparently it didn't, since all reports from the premiere echoed great enthusiasm for Beethoven and the symphony. Since that time all kinds of symphonic works using the human voice have been written. Wagner was even moved to declare that the symphony or art music form of the future *must* include the voice. Apparently he was not too impressed by the *other* late works of the master, such as the last quartets or the piano sonatas.

The musical history of the *Ninth* is fascinating and is well-chronicled in his own notebooks, as well as in the better biographical studies of Beethoven. Elliot Forbes's *Thayer's Life of Beethoven* is one of the best such works, and should be studied by the student (see pp. 886-on). Musical sketches of themes actually used appear as early as 1815, but the most fruitful work began in 1822. Of great import are the comments made by Beethoven and his attempts to compose a text which would serve to introduce Schiller's poetry. One set of these sketches shows how concerned he was with the thematic connections of the movements, since the sung portions emerge from the adagio theme as well as the hymn tune itself.

But, back to the music. Beethoven continues a more or less modified strophic treatment of the hymn tune—which, by the way, Schauffler has traced back to an old church tune (see his *Beethoven, the Man Who Freed Music*, p. 401—at the point where it is taken up by the chorus alternating with the soloists. The variables again occur in the treatment of the accompaniment. The use of contrapuntal detail in solo woodwinds is often overlooked in this passage, but here is a beautiful example of great attention paid to detail by a truly great composer. There are no automatic "noodles and boomp chinks" here, and the tune is one that would have been set in stock patterns by a lesser man. The oboe in bar 241 anticipates the march, with a special use of theme and rhythm throughout the entire variation. Against this jerky line is a legato theme played by the clarinet, a theme derived from the hymn tune itself and at times doubled at the tenth. In bar 245 these two instruments trade parts in double counterpoint at the octave. At the *tutti* (bar 257) both voices become involved in the orchestral mass. At bar 269 Beethoven drops the jerky line and introduces an inverted-arch legato line which begins as a doubler for the baritone solo, but this line is imitated two bars later in flute and bassoon two octaves apart; this version is ingeniously figurated and is really a quasi-doubling of the theme. At letter E this gives way to a figure in celli answered by flute and bassoon, which Brahms must have known when writing his *Second Symphony*. After the *tutti* codetta the soli present an ornate version of the hymn tune, against which Beethoven now adds some trills. Adding orchestration to orchestration, Beethoven works up to the first great climax of the choral part, which ends with a pregnant mediant relationship.

The student is urged to study the rest of the movement and discover for himself how Beethoven has set Schiller's great text. Notice Beethoven's use of fugal devices, text-painting and sheer sound coming from his inner ear and innermost self. Small wonder that the *Ninth* was the fountainhead of musical thought of the nineteenth century.

Liszt and Tone Poems

The twelve tone poems of Liszt are very uneven in quality but all twelve are of the utmost importance in the history of orchestral music, since they establish a new form—or rather, provide the means for a composer to "through-compose" an orchestral work as he would "through-compose" a song. As one might imagine, there were many authorities who thought that this was not a good idea; they held that music is best when it expresses only *itself*. That is true but for one thing—what about vocal music? Certainly the text and mood of the poem have *something* to do with the music, or there would be no need for using poetry—it would be better for the singer to sing neutral vowels or make some other kind of sound. The basic tool of Liszt and others to come was the "program" of the poem, which was not sung. The concert overture employed the same concept, but in a pre-set form. The Lisztians were in effect trying to show that, in music, it is possible for form and matter to be the same thing: that music should not be a preconceived notion of any sort other than whatever sounds the composer wants to employ to tell his tale. More important, the possibility of free-form music *without* a program became a reality: a form which was valid for but one musical work—the one in question.

This all sounds wonderful (except for people who have to teach form and analysis). In actual practice the result was most often a huge ABA, a lopsided variegated rondo or multi-variations, as themes were repeated and varied. A vital form *sui generis* is difficult to write, but it has been done. One of the best forms is the process of continuous variation, such as Wagner employed in the *Ring*. Ideally this form involves a scheme something like this: $a_1a_2a_3a_4 \ldots a_n$, in which the nature of "a" is changed and varied or developed, such that somewhere along the line there is actually $b_1b_2b_3 \ldots b_n$, which in turn is like c_1, and so on. There is nothing to prevent a return of "a" material which would not be equivalent to any of the already stated "a's." Needless to say, such formal plans (and many others) do not depend on key or on any other formal device which the composer himself does not invent. This is true artistic freedom, but it is successful only under the inspiration of a mature artist who is a master of his art and craft.

The descriptive works of Liszt are the two symphonies (*Faust* after Goethe and *Dante* after the poet); the scenes from Lenau's *Faust*; a short work, "From the Cradle to the Grave"; and the twelve symphonic tone poems. These are:

1. *Ce qu'on entend sur la Montagne* (What one hears on the mountain), from a poem by Victor Hugo (1848, 1856)

This displays some original touches in orchestration, such as the beginning roll on the bass drum and later the lovely violin solo in the B major section. It draws on Berlioz, repeats itself too much and its bombastic passages are replete with clichés of the times. The best parts are the delicate effects, which are quite good. Thematic transformation is there but is not yet fully developed.

There are those who maintain that motive structuring is of no value unless one can hear it. The better one listens the more he hears! It must be remembered that a lot of the worst music in the world is tonal and employs keys, regular phrases and regular forms. *The more vulgar music is, the more "regular" it is!* The converse is certainly *not true.* The world's best music is that in which form and content unite and are appropriate to each other. The best tone poems of Liszt almost accomplish their aims.

2. *Tasso,* from Goethe (1849) (an epilogue was added later)

The opening string unison and the pyramid chord in the winds are devices which other composers liked, notably Tchaikovsky. This work contains an important solo for the bass clarinet, with a footnote in the score to the effect that *three* muted celli can be used if the orchestra doesn't have a bass clarinet (that instrument was not common in 1849). Liszt writes for the bass clarinet in the French manner: he transposes down a major ninth and uses treble clef. Also of importance is the note on page 36 of the score, where Liszt indicates a dual nature of expression for the orchestra: the strings "sentimentally graceful" yet "cantando espressivo," and the winds "lightly and flutteringly." The winds will be unheard if the strings emote too much. The ending is very loud, calling to mind the end of Berlioz's overture to *Benvenuto Cellini*.

3. *Les Préludes*, after a poem by Lamertine (Life is a prelude to the unknown song of death) (1854)

Liszt did not attach a permanent meaning to this music, especially to the motives themselves. Liszt had used some of this music in earlier works. *Les Préludes* is still very popular and can still generate great enthusiasm. The advance in the composer's knowledge of harmony and his surer grasp of soloistic orchestration are very apparent. The work is marred by marziale sections which seem a little too melodramatic. The famous "storm" section is still effective and has influenced much music since its composition. Writers of film music have known this music a bit too well. The unresolved diminished sevenths are famous. Liszt might have "raided" the finale of Berlioz's *Fantastic Symphony* for this passage.

4. *Orpheus*, from the legend (1854)

This piece has even been used as an overture at performances of Gluck's opera—this makes about as much sense as eating a roast turkey dinner as an appetizer for a roast beef dinner! Both works do justice to the Orpheus legend, but each is altogether unique in style. Since Orpheus is the subject matter, much attention is attached to the harp writing (Liszt calls for two harps). The orchestra also does some of Liszt's best "orchestral singing." The woodwind solos are very well scored, both soloistically and in combination with other wind instruments. There is also a lovely violin solo, which is unusual in that the concertmaster is given the same role as a solo wind player: he not only acts as a soloist but also engages in subtle doublings with other solo instruments. The violin solo follows solos by the English horn and the oboe. At a climactic point all the violins join in octaves—an effect often used for expression of pathos, but meaningless if done all the time. When the solo line resumes it enters into a fascinating relationship with the oboe, then with the flute, while the important motive of the falling fifth occurs in the English horn. At one of the most expressive points in the score the oboe doubles the violin in unison and then continues in a solo role, finally joined by other winds. The next period of the theme is played by the solo cello, in a similar capacity. Perhaps the programmatic connotation is that the violin and high woodwinds represent Euridice, and the cello and its doublers represent Orpheus; Liszt does not tell us.

This lengthy description illustrates an important point about the subtlety of orchestral doublings used to obtain an artful mixture of timbres. The student is urged to hear this passage while watching the score, to observe how different the sound is in each case.

One short excerpt must be quoted, since it illustrates yet another principle:

Figure 14-18

Remember that the English horn transposes down a fifth and the A clarinet up a minor third, which means that both instruments are doubling the cello! The English horn, however, plays only the descending interval: in this work most often a sixth. Remember also that the nineteenth-century composer often uses a large interval downward to depict pathos.

5. *Prometheus,* after Herder (1850, 1855)

This piece also has merit and contains some remarkable orchestration. It contains a rather good fugato which, however, passes into bombast at the very point at which Liszt should have looked further into the possibilities of his theme—not necessarily to write a good fugue, but to do some vital developing. (Liszt often repeats where he might better have developed.) *Prometheus* also suffers from forced modulations through use of recitatives which conveniently end in "the right key" for the next part.

6. *Mazeppa,* after Victor Hugo (more satisfactory in its original form as a piano etude)
7. *Festklänge* (a noisy "festival")
8. *Heldenklage*

This piece is a kind of threnody, replete with devices and themes which remind one of the slow sections of the *Hungarian Rhapsodies,* but it has some nobility.

9. *Hungaria* (1848, 1856)

This contains some striking passages, and is a better work than many Liszt pieces which are played more often (such as his *Second Rhapsody*). It is rhapsodic, but is not really an Hungarian rhapsody. Instead of a brilliant friska there occurs another one of Liszt's "tasteless" marches.

10. *Hamlet,* after Shakespeare (1858)

The opening of this work is quite amazing, and the piece, as a whole, almost succeeds. In the pensive passages (which recall Berlioz's treatment of Shakespearean subjects) the composer is at his best, but there are bars and bars of "noise." In short, Liszt is once again at his best when he does not employ the full forces of the orchestra at once. He is at his best and most progressive when he does not have to worry about the brasses and their chromatic limitations of that period.

11. *Hunnenschlacht* (1857) (suffers from the same problems)
12. *Die Ideale,* after Schiller (contains great moments; each section in the score is prefaced by a section of the poem)

With these works the lines were clearly drawn between classical tradition and "music of the future." Much of the controversy, however, was just "talk." There are passages of surprising conservatism in Berlioz and Liszt, and there are surprising progressive passages in Mendelssohn and Brahms. Most of the composers on both sides of the controversy had some strict theoretical training and were very familiar with at least the basic theories of the theoretical treatises, if not with their exact texts. The student must not get the idea that the romanticist was an anarchist —how could he "go out-of-bounds" unless he knew what the "bounds" were?

The symphonic poems of Liszt prompted other composers to write similar works. Some of these are still played and some surpass those of Liszt.

The well-known cycle of tone poems by Smetana is important, since it fuses nationalism and the programmatic "school" in a manner quite different from the Russian one. The title of the cycle is *My Homeland.* Its six sections are not all of equal importance. The most popular is *The Moldau,* the depiction of a river in Bohemia. The "Five" produced several very popular tone poems, which are fading somewhat in popularity today. Rimsky's *Scheherazade* and *Capriccio espagnol* are still colorful, but figure mostly on "pops" concerts. Mussorgsky's *Night on Bald Mountain* is much more significant, as is Rimsky's *Russian Easter Overture.* Rimsky's exotic *Antar* deserves more hearings than it gets, but it lives mainly on its brilliant orchestration.

Tchaikovsky's works of this type are very uneven in quality. *1812* is passé, while *Romeo and Juliet* is still effective; *Hamlet* and *Francesca da Rimini* are somewhat less successful, but the latter contains passages of real power and beauty and the orchestration is masterful. Tchaikovsky greatly admired the classical composers and, unlike Liszt, developed a form for his programmatic works. Each work was to have a slow and doleful introduction, and then an adaptation of sonata-allegro; each was to be like the older opera overture, except that the sections were to be longer.

The "love" theme from *Romeo and Juliet* is one of his most famous melodies, and it shows the effective use of a single woodwind with a string section—the violas in this case. The woodwind is not meant to help the violas at all; it possesses an entirely different color.

An unjustly neglected work which has been mentioned from time to time is the *Manfred Symphony.* This is one of Tchaikovsky's most stimulating symphonies, if not his very best. The orchestration is very original and the harmonies, especially in the last movement, are most effective.

Many nationalistic works employ a certain cliché type of style. One of the best of these is *Symphonie espagnole,* by the French composer Lalo. It is really a violin concerto, and is still esteemed by violin virtuosi. His *Cello Concerto* is also performed, and in some respects is an even better work. His overture to a moderately successful opera *Le Roi d'Ys* possesses some musical value, and would be a welcome relief at concerts from yet another performance of, say, Tchaikovsky's *Capriccio italien* or *Marche slav.*

The "ultimate" works of this type are probably the programmatic symphonies and symphonic poems of Richard Strauss—works which figure prominently in twentieth-century music and point to the end of romanticism. Strauss's technical skill with the orchestra was prodigious, surpassing that of almost everyone. His compositions are based on a variety of subjects and are different in approach from similar works by Liszt. Strauss expresses not the sentiments of a situation, but rather the situation itself. When *Don Juan* makes love the music is more than merely sensuous; the dying man in *Death and Transfiguration* is actually "seen," and there is empathy with him. *Also sprach Zarathustra* is a vivid philosophical dissertation, translating Nietzsche into an orchestra of "supermen"; in *Don Quixote* we actually "hear" the sheep. *Ein Heldenleben,* a veritable symphony, is either a tasteless bit of bravado or one of the most moving of musical autobiographies—the listener must decide for himself; The *Domestic Symphony* is most literal, and so is the *Alpine Symphony.* As to the Strauss orchestral works, it is largely a question of personal taste. The best might well be *Till Eulenspiegel* —at least, audiences still like it. They are all very difficult to play, although most orchestras today do not consider them as insurmountable as did the orchestras which first played them. Strauss made the orchestra play higher, lower, faster, and slower, softer and louder—more so than anyone before and few since.

In the twentieth century the concept of the symphonic poem has continued as a rather convenient way to write a short piece for orchestra. The literary influence becomes less and less important; a composer suggests an abstract program, using a title such as "Essay" or "Statements." Another rather common source of inspiration is a great event such as the death of a great man or a war, but these occurrences are—unfortunately—always with us.

The orchestra became one of the most important musical organizations during the nineteenth century, and orchestral music well reflects the most important tendencies of the times.

Abstract Symphonism

One of the greatest achievements of the Classical Period was the symphonic idea, the four-movement structure (or three) so well exemplified by the symphonies of Haydn and Mozart. The nineteenth-century abstract symphony begins with Beethoven and Schubert, continues with Mendelssohn, Schumann and Cherubini, culminates with Brahms, Bruckner, Dvořák, Tchaikovsky and Franck, and bridges to the twentieth with Mahler. It is still one of the major musical forms, and in audience interest one of the most popular.

Beethoven

The symphonies of Beethoven are like the plays of a Goethe or a Shakespeare: they set a standard and will forever be great summits of art—time seems to erode but little of their grandeur. Some oft-played symphonies written later in the century have not worn so well. It is often pointed out that the odd-numbered Beethoven symphonies—excepting the first—are especially powerful and epic, while the even-numbered ones are more gentle—"valleys between the peaks," as it were.

If one divides Beethoven's work into three basic periods (the early, quasi-Haydn-Mozart; the second, pure Beethoven; and the third, the period of the late quartets and piano sonatas—highly original, introspective music of a rarefied atmosphere), then the symphonies would align themselves with the first in the first period, the second a real transition work from the first to the second period, symphonies three to seven in the middle period, eight a transition to the last period and the ninth in the late period.

Here are Beethoven's symphonies, with their premiere dates:

> I: C Major, Op. 21 (1800)
> II: D Major, Op. 36 (1803)
> III: E-flat Major, Op. 55 ("Eroica") (1805)
> IV: B-flat Major, Op. 60 (1807)
> V: C Minor, Op. 67 (1808)
> VI: F Major, Op. 68 ("Pastoral") (1808)
> VII: A Major, Op. 92 (1813)
> VIII: F Major, Op. 93 (1814)
> IX: D Minor, Op. 125 ("Choral") (1824)

The *First Symphony* is not without some surprises. It begins with the "wrong" chord (the dominant seventh of the subdominant), in a manner as striking as that used in the overture to *Prometheus*. These non-tonic beginnings, which can be found in many compositions of the period, almost always occur in introductory material. When the main theme is announced, the supremacy of the tonic is really established. The symphonies of Beethoven are especially noteworthy in this regard, since Beethoven finds ways to affirm the tonic and yet not employ the tonic triad with its "skyrocket" cliché; even when there is a suggestion of the rocket, there is a fascinating quirk which sets it apart.

Look at and listen to the principal themes of the first movements of all nine symphonies for comparison. Were there ever such individual themes? It is impossible to pick out one which is "typical." The only "typical" thing which Beethoven does is to use the theme as a building block for a great symphonic edifice. The sketchbooks are of great value, since they reveal Beethoven's marvelous polishing of his material. We must remember, however, that what we do *not* see (as with any composer) are the changes made mentally. With Beethoven the inspiration is not the theme itself but the way the theme has been chiseled into shape—almost like the work of a sculptor. We see his genius in finding the right combination and the right sequence, rather than a "full-blown Minerva." With Beethoven it is not always a simple question of melody and accompaniment, nor is it a simple one of foreground, middle ground and background. Rather, it is a fusion of elements, a rapid change of interest area, almost pointillistic, at least fragmentized, but a perfect whole in its integrated summation. This all seems very complicated, but a study of the exposition of the first movement of his very first symphony will show this characteristic. No other composer prior to Beethoven tossed melodic fragments about as he does.

Beethoven did not invent this idea of thematic fragmentation. It can be found in earlier music; Haydn's *Sinphonia Concertante in B-flat* for solo violin, oboe, bassoon and cello with orchestra uses a similar design in the first movement.

The second movement of Beethoven's *First Symphony* brings to mind the second movement of Mozart's *G Minor Symphony* in treatment, but the content is very different. The third movement is a minuet gone mad, and we discover *almost* the first scherzo used in a symphony. The finale is a merry romp. Leading an orchestra into it is a bit of a conducting problem, and this often appears as part of a conducting class's final examination.

The *Second Symphony* uses a lovely slow introduction which suggests some premonitions of the *Ninth*. The slow movement is one of Beethoven's loveliest, and the third is a genuine scherzo with a real sense of humor. The finale is quite wild.

The *Eroica* is in a class by itself, and is possibly the greatest symphony in existence. Some works are more perfect and some may even be more beautiful, but this has to be the greatest. It is the largest symphony the world had seen up to that time; indeed, the sonata-allegro first movement is still one of the largest, *successful* examples in the history of that basic form. Each part of the form is itself large, but each is built from smaller motives. The entire symphony is built on an

Urkeim, and Beethoven builds his themes in a remarkable way from this germ. The exact form, or the original form, of the motive for the *Eroica* is difficult to determine, and it is probably not important to know it. We have no way of knowing how much of this unity is subconscious and how much is purposeful, other than what we can deduce from the notebook discovered and described by Nottebohm *(Ein Skizzenbuch von Beethoven aus den Jahre 1803)*. So much fuss has been made about the title page and the erasure of "Bonaparte" which Beethoven made after realizing that Napoleon was a tyrant! The year 1804—the year of the *Eroica* ("Heroic")—is the year of a breakthrough in the symphony; Beethoven himself had claimed that it was "a new road."

The *Eroica* is without a slow introduction; the "heroic" theme is announced immediately in the celli, with a remarkable answer in the violins. It is just possible that the most basic statement of the *Grundgestalt* is the *Prometheus* theme used in the finale. Was not Napoleon a Prometheus in Beethoven's mind? Was not Beethoven *himself* a Prometheus? (Prometheus, it must be remembered, was the titan who stole fire from heaven and gave it to man. I need not dwell on the meaning of the parable.)

The second theme of the first movement in a sense emerges from the first theme, the real end of which is difficult to determine—the bridge passage is so coordinated that it is a vital part of the music. It seems clear that this music is derived from the little chromatic twist at the end of the cello theme at the very beginning. The development is fantastic in its drive, its good sense and its counterpoint, which is the essence of the music. This is not a fugue *per se*, but the section is fugal. It is characterized by fragments tossed about, but contains no holes; it even introduces a "new" theme! This theme, however, is a development of the second subject and is a remarkable contrast to the widely-spaced principal theme which, after all, is a "Mannheim rocket" with a chromatic twist at the end. The canonic entrances over a "walking bass" remind us of that fact. The bass could be explained as an octave displacement of the principal theme and a new rhythm. The reprise is preceded by a surprise:

BEETHOVEN: *Symphony No. 3* ("Eroica")

Figure 14-19

Such writing was unheard of in Beethoven's time, and has even been "corrected." Sir George Grove even asserted: "At that time all the rules of harmony were against it; it was absolutely wrong—as wrong as stealing or lying—and yet how perfectly right and proper it is in its place!" The recapitulation is not "normal" either. There are new relationships and some amazing modulations for a "classical" symphony. After the famous horn entrance the violins' trill ascends from E-flat to F major for a lovely statement of the heroic theme; Beethoven once again uses the mediant relationship, and then comes the famous statement in D-flat! There are other surprises, but when the recapitulation is over there is still more to go! The coda is no less than 140 bars long, but it is no ordinary coda; it is another development section which is replete with amazing contrapuntal combinations.

Lorenz has discovered that the development itself contains a form which is in itself a complete symphony. Others have written volumes about this magnificent movement, and only Beethoven has the answer— if there is one. A great work of art is capable of many interpretations and mis-interpretations, which do not kill it. The movement is so beautifully integrated that almost any theory of microform can be advanced. Perhaps the greatest technical feature is Beethoven's great ability to keep the music moving; there is real continuity of counterpoint, with no padding—each note is vital. The sonata-form which is there is only "the visible part of the iceberg"; the *real* form lies beneath, supporting the whole structure. Franck's comments about cyclic form seem to apply to this piece. Leopold Mozart's comments to Wolfgang about "filo" are germane as Einstein asserts:

The mystery of mysteries in Mozart's instrumental works, however, is the unity of the individual movements—what Leopold called *il filo*, the "thread," the succession and connection of the ideas. This connection is less obvious than with most of the other great composers—for example with Beethoven, who employs contrast much more than Mozart does, and whose movements and successions of movements much more frequently grow out of a single germinal motive. Beethoven and his predecessor Haydn—both in a certain sense revolutionaries—had much more need than Mozart to give their works a perceptible, demonstrable unity; their work had to carry with it its own clear justification.[23]

The "Funeral March" gave Beethoven great labor pains, as his sketches show, but even at its crudest the "filo" of the heroic is clear. The movement is set in the relative minor. (How great is this movement!) The figure of the "Grim Reaper" is all too apparent, but somehow there is hope: at the end of the movement the specter slowly vanishes. This movement contains features of rondo and sonata-form, and it approximates free variation. Rondo, because there is a refrain with different material in between each statement; sonata, because there is a polarity of themes and development; free variation, because each theme presented is varied. A high point is the fugato.

With the completion of the first two movements, we arrive at the end of the first part of this symphony. The scherzo and finale belong to a different world; and yet, could it be that the first movement depicts MAN and his struggle on earth, the second his death and the last two a sort of Elysian Fields? This is, of course, too simple an explanation. The scherzo is the very first true symphonic scherzo, and the finale has no counterpart in the symphonic literature. It is amazing in its fresh approach to the variation form; Beethoven wrote veritable "character" variations, and when he wished to dispense with the form he did so. One would have expected a larger orchestra for a symphony such as this, but it still employs the classical orchestra—the "bigness" is in the musical ideas.

The *Fourth Symphony* is in many ways a tour-de-force for the orchestra. I have never been able to understand why conductors have not programmed this symphony more often, since it is no less a symphony than the others. The slow introduction to the first movement is remarkable. The slow arpeggios presage the cutting "Mannheim rocket," which is the principal theme of the first movement. This movement, like the *Eroica*, employs some strong syncopations. Beethoven happily discovers that the first theme can subsequently be used as an accompaniment. The second movement is a lovely adagio which is unified by one of Beethoven's "knocking" rhythms. No composer ever showed greater variety in a third movement than Beethoven. The finale is a glorious "mad rush," with some exposed solos for wind players.

The *Fifth Symphony* hardly needs discussion. The *Urkeim,* however, seems to be not the descending third, but rather "three notes up, three notes down." The entire symphony falls into place thematically. The most intriguing fact is that at least two other great symphonies are built on the same musical figure: Schubert's "Great" *C Major* and Sibelius's *Second*.

The *Seventh* was called by Wagner "The apotheosis of the dance." And dance it does. It uses an important slow introduction, like no other music in existence. The sonata begins with a characteristic rhythm which permeates the entire work.

The second movement is not called "Funeral March," but it almost is one. A funeral atmosphere, however, would ruin its impact. I have heard it played much too fast and also much too slow—the fugato should be tense, not stiff, and with a moving tempo (but not like a Mendelssohn scherzo).

The scherzo is once again an amazing movement. It is unlike any other Beethoven scherzo, and yet it is the very essence of the Beethoven scherzo. The rhythms and peculiar harmonic treatment are important in the make-up of this movement. The trio provides a remarkable contrast, and the very end (which suggests yet another statement of the trio) is a stroke of genius. The finale is like steel—almost machine-like in its grinding movement; yet it is all so human, like Beethoven's own drive.

The *Eighth* has been called Beethoven's "small" symphony, yet I do not find it so. It is overpowered when it stands between the *Seventh* and the *Ninth*, but is so tall when it stands by itself.

The overture *The Consecration of the House*, Op. 124, is an expansion of the Handel overture. It is purely abstract music, written for the opening of the Josephstadt Theater in Vienna in 1822. The fugal writing is among Beethoven's best. Its form is that of a gigantic sonata, and its course is intensified by a series of gradually faster tempi.

Beethoven's orchestral mastery carries over into his concerti, which continue the great form Mozart developed. There are five piano concerti, one violin concerto and a triple concerto. There is an early piano concerto in E-flat (WoO 4), which is somewhat "Mannheimisch" but for the parallel octaves at the beginning:

BEETHOVEN: *Concerto in E-Flat* (WoO4)

Figure 14-20

This device is, of course, intentional. This concerto is sometimes dubbed "Concerto No. 1/2."

Another interesting fragment is a *Violin Concerto in C Major* (WoO 5), which was finished by Hellmesberger. There is also a *Rondo in B-flat* (WoO 6) which is sometimes played. These works are all very early in Beethoven's career. The two "Romanze" (Opp. 40 and 50) for violin and orchestra are middle-period works and are quite beautiful, but there are other works of a similar nature by lesser composers which are actually better.

Beethoven's concerti for piano are these:

I: C Major, Op. 15 (1797) (actually the third)
II: B-flat, Op. 19 (1795) (actually the second)
III: C Minor, Op. 37 (1800) (actually the fourth)
IV: G Major, Op. 58 (1805)
V: E-flat, Op. 73 ("Emperor") (1809)
(An arrangement of the *Violin Concerto* for piano is inept.)

Although the *C Major* is a vigorous and exciting work, the first great concerto is the *C Minor*, which is beautiful, inspired music and important in structure. The opening *tutti* is one of the best in the literature, presenting a theme which sounds in many guises and dynamics. In taking it apart one sees how Beethoven derived three important shapes from it:

BEETHOVEN: *Concerto No. 3*, Op. 37

Figure 14-21

Note that Beethoven uses: 1) a triad, 2) a scale line and 3) a "knocking" motto. The entrance of the solo piano presents the theme in a new light. The theme sequences well to the dominant minor ninth (see the very beginning). The second theme is in the relative major, a lovely sequence which, however, derives somewhat from the first theme. The antecedent turns about the triad and the consequent uses the scale. The rhythm is found only in the short "pick-up" notes inside the theme.

The slow movement is in E major, which comes as something of a shock. It is one of the most highly developed slow movements in the entire literature. It could perhaps be construed as the "enharmonic key of the relative major's Neapolitan," but such an explanation would be grasping at a thin straw. There are enharmonic points of contact, however: G-sharp–A-flat and D-sharp–E-flat. Also important is the fact that B is the dominant of E and the leading tone of C minor. The start of the rondo shows this procedure, and its coda shows it a semitone higher. This rondo is one of Beethoven's best.

The *Fourth Piano Concerto* begins with the solo, but the double exposition idea is still maintained. Notice, however, the use of the lower mediant relationship in the entrance of the orchestra:

Figure 14-22

This *tutti* contains some of Beethoven's best orchestral writing. The entire concerto is a remarkable balance of piano and orchestra in sound and in musical importance, yet it is one of the "big" concerti in the standard repertoire and perhaps is the most often performed of all the Beethoven piano concerti. The slow movement is a marvelous conversation between a man and a woman—perhaps they are lovers. Liszt, however, claims that it is Orpheus taming the wild beasts. The finale is both brilliant and important.

The *Emperor* is a "first," in that it starts with a cadenza (his others all require an added one). It is "big" music in every respect. The slow movement is in a remote key, like the *C Minor*—a key which he used briefly in the first movement. The key's enharmonic points of contact are more critical near the end of the movement, since the rondo is an *attacca*. B major is enharmonically the lower mediant relationship; hence, the relationship Eb, B, Eb of keys shows the application of a principle often found in Beethoven's progressions. The rondo is one of the best in the literature, in which there is striking contrast between diatonic and chromatic melody and a great feeling of grandeur. (Many composers have "raided" this movement!)

The *Violin Concerto*, Op. 61—at the risk of indulging in meaningless superlatives—is the best ever written. It can be learned technically without too much difficulty by a good advanced student, but its musical content is so profound that it requires years of study. Its Mozartean simplicity belies its great difficulty, but the piece is nothing like Mozart. The first movement is a very long sonata-allegro which is unified by two main elements: 1) the four notes tapped by the tympani at the beginning, and 2) the simple, diatonic themes which comprise the dual themes of the sonata-form. This requires the key contrast to be of considerable importance. The very beginning exposes the drum beats and the lovely opening theme. Note that the entrance of the violins is on D-sharp for the tapping notes! This D-sharp has caused no end of discussion. In early sketches the note appears as E-flat, which shows that Beethoven in his first inspiration thinks of the *sound* and writes the "correct" notation after he has had second thoughts. Notice that the second theme emphasizes a different part of the major scale; it contains two important melodic leaps and uses the tapping motive.

The entrance of the soloist is treacherous, as is a parallel passage later in C major (octaves sound great on solo violin when well-executed, but are very difficult to play well).

Much could be said about this concerto: factors such as the relationships of soloist and orchestra, the truly symphonic significance of the orchestral parts, the key relationships and the great expansion of sonata-form. The slow movement is a simple theme and variations, and the finale an *attacca* which contains one of Beethoven's most catchy tunes. The rondo is a sonata-rondo which contains some of Beethoven's most successful "side themes."

The *Triple Concerto*, Op. 56, is a much-maligned work. Criticism of it is unjust and causes one to wonder how well the detractor knows the work—is he merely repeating an opinion he read in a book? Is *that* opinion one which the original author saw in yet another book? To know this work is to love it. It is something like *Fidelio*, in that it is loved for itself as it is, and not for what it might have been. There had been many attempts, after the Baroque Period, to write pieces for more than one soloist, but this is one of the most successful ones. It is a particularly demanding work, since each soloist must be taken into consideration. Beethoven is very clever in using the soloists as a piano trio and in writing for each as a soloist in his own right or in the three possible duo combinations.

Beethoven's concerti are among the very best. The nineteenth century and its virtuosity produced many concerti, but for sheer musical value the world had to wait for those of Brahms. Beethoven expanded Mozart's concerto concept by elongating the first movements, making changes in the long opening *tutti* expositions (long introductions make some in the audience nervous: they wonder why the "expensive soloist" isn't playing!), writing his own cadenzas, inserting cadenzas at the beginnings and using techniques and features of his other music: such as advanced harmony, arresting inner parts, remote key relationships, personal expression and *Urkeim* techniques.

Schubert

Sir Donald Tovey (1875-1940) was an English composer and conductor of well-made but not great music. He knew about musical greatness, however, and was a musical scholar of the first rank. Our generation is just now beginning to read his works again, and we are astonished at how much he really has to say. He wrote the articles on music for the *Encyclopedia Britannica* and many other essays. Every musician should read the introduction to his six-volume set of analytical essays. This introduction is a short course in itself, touching upon the most important facts and philosophies, and shows an over-all grasp of music which is so difficult to present in the classroom. His essays in Volume I cover important symphonies, and his essays on those of Schubert are especially good. Also vital for a more mature understanding of Schubert is the essay "Tonality in Schubert," which appears in his *The Main Stream of Music* (pp. 134-159).

The Schubert symphonies occupy a unique place in history, since they are the first such works which a composer did not ever hear played. They went mostly unnoticed by his contemporaries. The individual differences among these works are more striking than those in many earlier symphonies.

There are actually eight Schubert symphonies; an arrangement of the *C Major Piano Duo* was written in the hope that it would turn out to be the lost "Gastein" Symphony (Joachim made the orchestration). While one can hear any of these works from time to time, only the *B-flat,* the *Great C Major* and the *Unfinished* are permanent repertory fixtures. The *B-flat* is the *Fifth,* D. 485, and is sometimes called the "Symphony without trumpets and drums." It is justly popular for its remarkable lyrical themes, its brilliance and its structure. The opening shows its mood and reveals how Schubert fills in long notes in the theme by employing echoes of the theme.

This symphony was heard by Schubert in a performance at Hatwig's in the autumn of 1816. The only other symphony which he probably heard in actual performance was the earlier D Major, heard at the Seminary in 1813. Schubert's orchestration is quite marvelous, considering how little of his own orchestral music was heard by him. He had studied other scores and had learned well from them! Here is the beginning of the *Fifth Symphony*:

SCHUBERT: *Symphony No. 5*, in B♭

Figure 14-23

The recapitulation is notated in the "wrong" key, the key of the subdominant. This is not ignorance on Schubert's part; it actually enhances the work, and he is not alone in using this kind of reprise. Perhaps this is one successful attempt to lend subdominant key balance to sonata-form.

The slow movement is one of Schubert's most beautiful "songs," while the minuet is in the relative minor and is "folksy." The finale is a fine classical romp.

A beautiful but seldom-played symphony is the *C Minor*, called the *Tragic*, D. 417. It is quite advanced for Schubert and its nickname is very appropriate, although *Pathétique* could also qualify. The slow introduction is chromatic, canonic and most expressive. The allegro could well serve as opera music. The second theme contains striking chromaticisms, and the minuet's theme is almost a twelve-tone row:

SCHUBERT: *Symphony No. 4,* in C Minor ("Tragic");
Third Movement

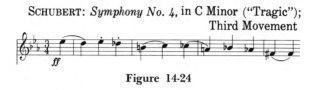

Figure 14-24

The finale is surprising in its quietness. This work is one of the best of its age. It entails some very difficult string writing, but should be played instead of the *Unfinished* on occasions.

The *Great C Major,* D. 944, is actually Schubert's last. It debunks the popular notion that death prevented him from completing the *Unfinished.* The *Unfinished* is D. 759 and was actually begun as early as 1822. The sketches for the scherzo show a remarkable beginning but no continuation. To us the two completed movements are well-balanced and form a complete symphony. It is probably more beautiful than anyone realizes, since it has been overplayed at the expense of other delightful symphonies such as the "Little" *C Major,* D. 589, or one of the others. (Overexposure can jade our senses to music, just as underexposure leaves us truly ignorant.)

The *Great C Major* is not admired by some musicians for reasons of its inordinate length. It is a work which I personally have known from childhood, but to which I do not feel overexposed at all. It is a splendid example of cyclic form, although Schubert himself may not have realized it. The best aspects of music are those growing from the composer's intuition, expanded and developed by study, experience and living. This symphony contains perhaps the most beautiful slow introduction in all music. The sonata-allegro is important for its themes (always true in Schubert) and for the working-out of the themes in all its movements, not just in the first. The use of the trombone is a novelty for its time.

The symphonies of Schubert occupy a special place in history, since—like those of Beethoven—they represent the end of classicism and the beginnings of romanticism.

The *Rosamunde* Overture often appears on concert programs. It is a work of great beauty and of somewhat rare tonality in places.

Mendelssohn

The orchestral works of Mendelssohn are among his best. They are beautifully scored and are laborious in but a few places. The works which we hear and play today are but a fraction of his total output; although they are a cross-section, one wonders if they are a representative cross-section. One needs only to compare the best-known symphonies: the *Italian*, the *Scotch* and the *Reformation*. How different they are from each other and from the works of his contemporaries! The overtures are just as individual, and the two piano concerti and the violin concerto are in three different worlds. Werner[24] classes the *Hymn of Praise* as a "symphony-cantata." The last section is an extensive cantata, and is much longer than the first three completely instrumental movements. It is often performed as a cantata, omitting the first movements. The music cycles around some germ cells (on the line "All that has life and breath, sing to the Lord").

This work (often called by the German title, *Lobgesang*) is sometimes called the second symphony, but in order of composition is actually the fourth. Perhaps a word should be said about why these mix-ups occur. Numbering of compositions is confusing to everyone, and is often most confusing to the composer himself. A composer sometimes works on more than one piece at a time. Often one particular symphony is performed or published, while another one written earlier remains unplayed. Those that are played earlier are often given the earlier number. This is why the use of itemized catalogues such as the Koechel-Einstein for Mozart or the Deutsch for Schubert is so important: the assigned numbers truly reflect the chronology and are much more accurate than opus numbers or any other numbers. Nicknames are also helpful, but they can give a false impression of the music: a fancy title might lead to expectations on the part of the listener which are not fulfilled. Many people have claimed that the *Italian Symphony* has nothing at all to do with Italy, or that the *Scotch Symphony* has nothing to do with Scotland. One thus sees the danger in using a title for music, and can see why many of the best works use only generic titles—such as *Symphony in D Minor*. It is a shame that the symphonies of Mendelssohn and Schumann, the concerti of Beethoven and the symphonies of Haydn—among others—have to be so confusing in their numberings. The important thing for the student to know, obviously, is not the correct numbering but the music itself.

The *Scotch Symphony* is, by Mendelssohn's own admission, music suggested by "Auld Reekie," the land of mists, haggis, heather, highland and lowlands, a spooky Loch Ness—a beautiful land of much lore. Mendelssohn captures this atmosphere in the music, and not simply in bagpipe imitations. There are more subtle devices than that. The theme of the sonata-allegro in the first movement has the flavor of a Scotch dance. The first three movements are somber, with only a few passages of brilliance. The finale is quite impressive.

The *Italian Symphony*, as a whole, is not as good as the *Scotch*, but its high points surpass those of the *Scotch*. The first part of the third movement doesn't seem to belong to the rest of the symphony. The opening of the symphony has already been quoted, and also part of the beautiful "Pilgrim's March"—which Berlioz must have known when he wrote his *Harold in Italy*. The finale is brilliant, and it more than makes up for the letdown of the third movement. The trio of the third movement is a delight, however—although Mendelssohn had to go to fairlyland, not Italy, to get the inspiration for it.

The *Reformation Symphony* is the most uneven, but its great moments outweigh its technical difficulties. It seems to display some strange premonitions of Mahler.

Of the overtures the best are *Fingal's Cave* and the *Midsummer Night's Dream*. The latter was written when Mendelssohn was sixteen, but the form we know is a mature rewrite. The piece is a huge sonata-allegro which is frankly programmatic—even to the braying of Bottom after he has been "translated" into a donkey. A visit to Fingal's cave was an experience which Mendelssohn never forgot, and his overture does not let us forget. This is for all practical purposes a true prototype of the symphonic poem; but it is, as Beethoven said of his *Pastoral*, "more feeling than painting."

The two piano concerti sound old-fashioned to us today, but the violin concerto is almost as good as Beethoven's. The work abounds in lovely themes: heroic themes, angelic themes and fairyland themes. There are a few points which should be made: 1) the soloist enters immediately; 2) the formal structure is highly telescoped in two different ways: a) the movements are connected, and b) the internal form of each movement is so smooth that one passes from one part of the form to the next with ease; 3) the cadenza is by Mendelssohn (helped by Ferdinand David, his concertmaster at the Gewandhaus in Leipzig, who probably helped in some other technical details even though Mendelssohn could play the violin), and it occurs just before the recapitulation.

The second theme of the first movement can cause the soloist some anxiety if his open G string is not exactly in tune.

Schumann

We have commented here and there on Schumann's unhappy experiences in orchestration. It is a mystery why some works were rather well-scored: the *Manfred* and *Genoveva* overtures, the piano and cello concerti. The symphonies have been retouched by various conductors, among them Mahler. They contain honest, earthly music, but they are not often brilliant. Tovey declared "Schumann's dreams do not come from opium."[25] Tovey, in the same essay, ventures the theory that the doubling (which is overdone) is notated partly to make the conducting of them easier, since Schumann himself had to conduct them. If this be true, it certainly has made rehearsing more difficult, since many passages sound well only if rehearsed and played just so.

The *B-Flat Symphony* begins with a motto:

Figure 14-25

Does one need to be told that this is a *Spring* symphony? The beginning of the *Rhenish Symphony* is also very striking:

SCHUMANN: *Symphony No. 3,* in E♭ ("Rhenish")
(Wind Parts Omitted)

Figure 14-26

The *D Minor* also has a nickname: *Romantic*, which could apply to any of them. Only the *C Major Symphony* has no nickname. The *D Minor* really works out this motto:

SCHUMANN: *Symphony No. 4* ("Romantic");
First Movement

Figure 14-27

The symphonies of Schumann do not contain one weak movement! Each work is a masterpiece, albeit sometimes a little plodding when classical forms are followed. The basic musical ideas and their working-out are highly original. Since they are performed season after season, they are important in the repertoire and are there because of their important content.

The *Piano Concerto* is a duo—not a "duel"—between the orchestra and the piano. The opening is striking:

Allegro affettuoso   SCHUMANN: *Piano Concerto*

Figure 14-28

Grieg also thought this was a good way to open a concerto! There is also a curious resemblance in Grieg (in his cello sonata, in his string quartet and in one of his songs).

There is a peculiar family resemblance in the three-note-up-and-three-note-down figures used in these three concerti (by Schumann, Grieg and MacDowell):

SCHUMANN: *Piano Concerto*

Figure 14-29

GRIEG: *Piano Concerto*

Figure 14-30

MACDOWELL: *Piano Concerto*

Figure 14-31

This same device is also found in the finale of the Dvořák *New World,*

DVORAK: *New World Symphony,* Finale

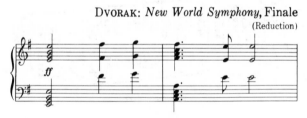

Figure 14-32

and again in his *Cello Concerto*:

DVORAK: *Cello Concerto,* Op. 104

Figure 14-33

These are probably coincidences, except in the case of Schumann and Grieg. Note this C major statement in the Schumann *Piano Concerto,* which shows how the theme works in major:

SCHUMANN: *Piano Concerto*

Figure 14-34

The first movement was first performed by Clara as a *Phantasie* for piano and orchestra, and it was so successful she prevailed upon him to add the other movements, which are anything but "tacked on." They are integral parts of the work, and the whole piece is one of the best written in cyclic form. The *Urkeim* is three notes down and four notes up, as seen in the first orchestral *tutti* in the concerto. The second movement is based on the same figure. Note well the cello part! The gorgeous theme in the cello is a spread-out tonic triad with added sixth. The second and third movements are connected. The first theme of a sonata-allegro is vigorously announced by the soloist, and is also based on the germ. The finale contains one of the trickiest rhythmic devices in the literature up to that time; it is the second subject of the form:

SCHUMANN: *Piano Concerto*
(Reduction)

Figure 14-35

The cadenza in the first movement was written by Schumann himself, in order to prevent the horrid graftings on his work which he undoubtedly had heard done to Mozart and Beethoven.

The *Cello Concerto* is also a great work, but the orchestral part is not as important; one would hardly miss it but for a *tutti* here and there.

In his role as a conductor and as a concertgoer he undoubtedly noticed that the orchestra is a "cello-killer" unless the cello stays on the A string. Schumann solves this problem by "holding back" in the orchestra while the cello is playing. This work is based on the same germ as that of the *Piano Concerto*, which shows that a germ is not dictatorial but is truly germinal.

This concerto is often dismissed as a late Schumann piece of a mentally-ill man. Nonetheless, the slow movement is as fine as any he ever wrote.

The *Violin Concerto* was "discovered" in 1937. It contains moments of great beauty, and deserves more performances than it receives. There are excellent recordings available. There are also some short works for piano and orchestra, and for violin and orchestra, as well as the curious *Concertstück* for four solo horns.

Brahms

The orchestral music of Brahms is not only considerable, it is some of the best ever written and it lives for its content. As mentioned earlier, with Brahms there is never any orchestral coloration *per se*. It is sometimes difficult to pinpoint the exact dates of Brahms's compositions. Here are the publication dates from the *Thematic Catalogue*:

Serenade in D Major, Op. 11 (1860)
Piano Concerto No. 1 in D Minor, Op. 15 (1861)
Serenade for Small Orchestra, Op. 16 (1875)
Variations on a Theme by Haydn, Op. 56a (1874)
First Symphony in C Minor, Op. 68 (1877)
Second Symphony in D Major, Op. 73 (1878)
Violin Concerto in D Major, Op. 77 (1879)
Academic Festival Overture, Op. 80 (1881)
Tragic Overture, Op. 81 (1881)
Piano Concerto No. 2 in B-flat, Op. 83 (1882)
Third Symphony in F Major, Op. 90 (1884)
Fourth Symphony in E Minor, Op. 98 (1886)
Double Concerto for Violin, Cello and Orchestra, Op. 102 (1888)

The two serenades are early, but are delightful. The second has an unusually youthful exuberance and displays the sure hand of a young master (it contains an arresting viola part, but employs no violins).

The two piano concerti differ greatly from each other, and the differences are not all in the years that separate them. The *D Minor Concerto* was planned originally to take other forms. It was Brahms's first major orchestral work, and it reflects the personal tragedy which was happening to Schumann, especially the bad year of 1854. It is no accident that the work is cast in the somber key of D minor. The opening is more tragic than his own *Tragic Overture* (also in D minor). The second subject contains plenty of Brahms's sixths, but is a lovely bit of music which only Brahms could write. The slow movement uses a scale-line melody which gives way to an angular subject. The rondo is among the most stormy in the repertoire.

The *Second Piano Concerto* has a beautiful beginning. Notice the dialogue between the horn and the soloist; the horn theme is a classical example of a question-answer, antecedent-consequent phrase. This music was sketched somewhat and then laid aside for work on the *Violin Concerto*, then taken up again in 1881. Composers do some of their best work without pen and paper—perhaps their *only* compositional work. The act of putting music on paper is a necessary evil, but some touching-up and recasting must still be done after it is on paper. The first movement is difficult music to perform but not difficult to hear, since it falls so well on the ear. It is calm, not tortured like the *D Minor*. (If Schumann were the composer, one would say that the *D Minor* is "Florestan" and the *B-flat* is "Eusebius," with a little "Raro.") While one can find elements of sonata-form, he rather notices an unfolding— a constant development, as is so often the case in Brahms. It is symphonic movement, and it is a concerto. The pianist has a part which makes this one of the "big" concerti, but at the same time one is reminded of the ensemble sonatas, the piano trios and quartets. One important aspect which sets apart the concerti of Brahms and Schumann from all the others is this approach to the role of the soloist.

The first movement is so fascinating that one could point out many features. The exposition is not really done away with simply because the soloist enters so soon and even has a bit of a cadenza:

BRAHMS: *Piano Concerto*, Op. 83

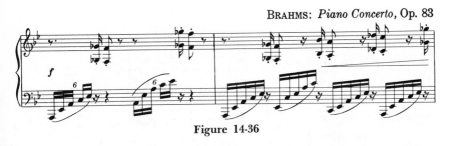

Figure 14-36

The real orchestral *tutti* starts afterwards, as in Beethoven's *Emperor*. This movement abounds in lovely themes which are real melodies: either thematic structurally, as in the sonata, or derived from other material. With sonata-forms as large as those used in the late nineteenth century by Reger, Bruckner, Brahms, Tchaikovsky and others, composers solved the problem of length in part by presenting a family of themes which are distinguishable by tonality and character.

The second movement is one of the few concerto scherzi in the literature. Scherzo, here, does not mean "joke." This movement is one of Brahms's most passionate (observe that the key is D minor). The form satisfies the requirements of both sonata and scherzo-trio.

Figure 14-37

Later in the movement the change of key to D major is tremendous in its effect.

The third movement is like a song; in fact, it is very much like his song "Immer leise wird mein Schlummer."

BRAHMS: *Piano Concerto*, Op. 83

Figure 14-38

Notice that the solo cello carries the melody at the beginning. This movement is one of the most unusual in the literature, and is as close as Brahms ever gets to a misty impressionism.

The finale is amazing. It is full of light and grace, and maybe even "Gemütlichkeit." It is rondo-like, and one of the episodes contains one of Brahms's most beautiful melodies:

BRAHMS: *Piano Concerto*, Op. 83

Figure 14-39

The *Violin Concerto in D Major,* Op. 77, was actually Brahms's second concerto—the first being, of course, the *D Minor Piano Concerto.* In time it lies between the two great piano concerti, and in temperament it does also. It is lyrical, firey, brilliant—all of the adjectives one can apply to the violin and to the orchestra and to violin and orchestra. The violin fights for its very life in this work; in truth, there is certainly the competition, the striving of one element against the other, which one finds in the meaning of the word from which "concerto" derives: *concertare.* The opening *tutti* is a marvelous series of themes which are truly a "family" of themes; as Tovey suggests, these are very long themes with different "parts." The opening is a slow "Mannheim rocket" with added sixth. The entrance of the soloist is a thrilling moment:

Figure 14-40

The soloist's statement of the main theme high on the E string is a marvel, as are the eighth notes in the violas. Note that the viola figure consists of the germ idea of the first theme: a triad with an added note:

Figure 14-41

The entrance of the soloist is a developed version of this motive, which is basic to the construction of the whole work. The violin's statement of the second subject is one of Brahms's great melodic inspirations. The development is worthy of years of study, just to see how a master composes and scores it.

The slow movement was criticized for using so much woodwind! The opening is one of the most outstanding woodwind passages in the repertoire. The violin enters later, with an expanded version of the oboe theme. The movement continues in Brahms's singular "Entwickelung" technique, the unfolding coming (like a blossom from the bud) little by little. But Brahms knows when to stop the process; lesser composers bring on an "explosion" or show us "wilted petals." In a very real sense, the form of the slow movement is one long song spun out by continuous variation of the motives—which are basically triads with added notes.

The finale is a Brahms version of Hungarian music. It is a protracted Hungarian dance, but it incorporates many devices of counterpoint and compositional technique. The built-in cadenza which Brahms wrote is quite effective. This work was written for Joachim, and its Hungarian flavor may well have been a compliment to his native country.

The cadenza in the first movement has been a real performance problem; Tovey even wrote one, a very good one. Since Joachim is so tied in with this work, it seems right that only his should be played. An educated audience is always held in suspense, wondering which cadenza will be played.

The Brahms *Violin Concerto* was held to be impossible to play by the first ones who tried it, but Brahms was proven right; his techniques are now mastered by the very best students in their most advanced studies. As a violin concerto it is surpassed only by the Beethoven, and there are many musicians who think that it surpasses them all in musical importance. It is idle to make such comparisons; mention of it here only indicates to the student how important this work is. It is important as music *per se*, which is where many concerti fail as "vehicles"—in innate musicality. Another such work is the famous *Concerto in G Minor* by Max Bruch (1838-1920), as well as his lesser-known *Concerto in D Minor* and his *Scottish Fantasy*. The G Minor even shows some thematic resemblance (in its finale) to the greater Brahms concerto.

The Bruch *Concerto in G Minor* is in a rather condensed form, and bears rather strange titles for each movement: Prelude, Adagio and Finale. The best movement is probably the second. Bruch's version of *Kol Nidrei* for cello and orchestra has given many the impression that he was a Jewish composer, which he was not; but it is true that there is the quality of Jewish lament in much of his music. He wrote many Christian works such as masses, and some cantatas on subjects such as Easter. These works were once in vogue, but only the *G Minor Violin Concerto*—with its Brahms melos but without Brahms's great technique and taste—is still an important fixture in violinists' programs.

Brahms's last concerto suffers in some places from what one might call lapses, but on the whole it is a great work; its weaknesses recede into the background when the work is well played, as the classic recording by Heifetz and Feuermann with Ormandy conducting will testify. It was written in 1887. The very opening divides the responsibility of the three participants: violinist, cellist and orchestra. The two quarters against the triplet are typical of Brahms's love of syncopation. The composer does his poorest writing in some of the *tutti*—which sound more like Walküre swooping over some battlefield. The best writing is that for violin against orchestra, cello against orchestra or for violin and cello together, which can be made to resemble a string quartet:

Figure 14-42

The second movement is one of the best ever penned:

Figure 14-43

The octave leap in this melody is very important and very expressive. Notice that the intervals in the first three eighths are in the same relationship as the theme which begins the first movement. The finale has been cited elsewhere in this book for its use of a melody which does not really end in the usual sense. The entire movement is a Brahms "ode to joy," especially after the change to A major.

The Brahms concerti for strings employ unusually rich orchestration, and require truly great artists to play them. Hearing such works only on recordings does not give one a true picture (for *any* kind of solo work), since the solo parts are so prominently engineered. Not that recordings are wrong; nevertheless, the first "live" performance of a concerto or an opera might be very surprising for one who has previously known only recordings.

The four symphonies of Brahms also represent high points in symphonic history. It took Brahms a long time to produce his first symphony; he had already written many accompaniments for choral works, as well as the *First Piano Concerto* and the *Haydn Variations*. Before discussing the symphonies, let us look at the shorter works for orchestra, since they are important in Brahms's development and also in the history of orchestral music. Aside from the serenades, *all* of Brahms's orchestral works are constantly played—which makes them obviously vital to the standard repertoire.

The *Haydn Variations* represents Brahms's first mature attempt at orchestral composition. True, the *D Minor Concerto* was earlier, and it is mature, but the use of solo piano was helpful in that work. The *Haydn* theme is stimulating in its phrase structure, in that it comprises five bars. Brahms retains Haydn's own instrumentation for the theme. These are character variations, and some are double period. Variation IV contains some effortless difficult counterpoint. In this variation there is actually invertible counterpoint at the ninth, which theory books tell us is impossible. There are also many other contrapuntal tricks. The final variation is a revival of the old Baroque ground bass—note: *revival*, not imitation.

The two contrasting overtures are very mature and rank among the best works in that form. The *Academic Festival*, as observed earlier, uses German student songs in a way which makes them Brahms's own—from a "beer and skittles" tune,

BRAHMS: *Academic Festival Overture*, Op. 80;
"Was kommt dort von der Höh"

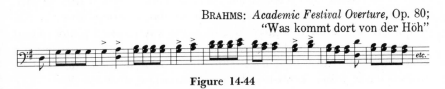

Figure 14-44

to the stately "Wir hatten gebaut ein stattliches Haus,"

Op 80, "Wir hatten gebaut ein stattliches Haus"

Figure 14-45

and from the "Melodie des Landesvaters"

Op. 80, "Melodie des Landesvaters"

Figure 14-46

to "Gaudeamus igitur."

Op. 80, "Gaudeamus igitur"

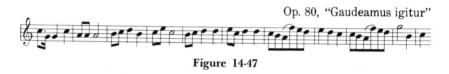

Figure 14-47

The overture was in a sense his doctoral dissertation for a Ph.D. *honoris causa* from the University of Breslau (1879). The reaction of the university dignitaries upon hearing these tunes was not one of good humor, since the citation had named Brahms *artis musicae severioris in Germania nunc princeps* (now the leader in Germany in music which is severe). We can well imagine a scene today, if a stuffy faculty were to offer a "serious" composer an honorary doctorate and for the occasion ask him to write a major work for orchestra. In this country suppose the composer were to start with the "Beer Barrel Polka," continue with a few bars of the "Whiffenpoof Song" and "On Wisconsin," ending with "I'm a Ramblin' Wreck from Georgia Tech." As a matter of fact, Ives's use of well-known tunes elicits a similar reaction. Brahms was severely criticized for this piece, but in a real way it *was* a philosophical dissertation. He respected tradition but not convention, freedom but not anarchy. These tunes used by Brahms have by now been ennobled by Brahms's use; this is probably the most important doctoral dissertation in music ever written!

The *Tragic* is in another world. Some have said that the composer had *Faust* in mind, others *Lear*; Brahms himself never did say. The overture begins with a "stab" and emotionally never lets go. The essence of noble tragedy pervades this work, yet it is very personal and human.

Figure 14-48

The key of D minor serves once again for stark, almost wild writing:

Figure 14-49

The second theme affords welcome relief in a beautiful melody:

Figure 14-50

This work, and many others of Brahms, employs rhythm almost to a fault but it is always apt to my ears. It is almost always written to be played against strict moving rhythms, so that there is an effect of cross-rhythm. (One wonders how Brahms would have used the rhythms of jazz if he had known what they were!) Brahms's rhythms are among his finest compositional techniques. Here is an example from the *Tragic Overture*:

BRAHMS: *Tragic Overture*

Figure 14-51

Those who like Brahms call it a point of style; those who don't call it a cliché.

The Brahms symphonies are in C minor, D, F and E minor—which happens to be the whole-note subject which is so cryptic in the Mozart *Jupiter* finale (the notes C D F E). This is probably mere coincidence, but. . . .

The *First Symphony* is characterized by broad themes, incisive rhythms and a very subtle use of the germ motive technique. The binding motive is the rising chromatic line which one hears in the strings at the very beginning, answered by the dipping sixteenth notes, which in their wideness answers well the compressed nature of the chromatic line. The slow introduction is one of the most impressive in the literature; it causes the allegro, when it occurs, to be that much more brilliant. Space does not permit the further analysis of this fabulous movement, which is a masterpiece of form, counterpoint and symphonic inspiration. The modulations and distant-key relationships used by Brahms in this and in many other works makes one wonder why he was so insistent about using the natural horn, which he obviously thought was superior to the valved horn (available but never used). The natural horn, when well-played, was a very beautiful instrument, and Brahms did not want to part with it.

The key relationship is quite remote in the second movement, exactly the same as that used in the Beethoven *Third Piano Concerto*: C minor to E major. This is one of the most beautiful movements in all Brahms, and perhaps in all music.

The third movement is like one of his piano intermezzos, and is the kind of movement Brahms prefers rather than a jolly scherzo. The consequent of the first theme is an inversion of the antecedent:

BRAHMS: *Symphony No. 1,*
Third Movement
(Reduction)

Figure 14-52

Brahms uses this same device in the *Fourth Symphony*, but on a smaller scale:

BRAHMS: *Symphony No. 4*

Figure 14-53

The finale has a very dramatic introduction, after which comes one of Brahms's most famous themes. This is the first theme of a great sonata-form where, in spite of the greatness of the themes, the handling is of the utmost importance. This movement, like the first, is part of the serious business of writing a symphony. The middle movements are more lovely and the outer movements are more impressive because of the contrasts among them.

The *Second Symphony* is more obvious in its use of a germ:

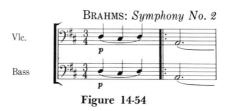

Figure 14-54

Brahms tosses this figure around in obvious ways, as Beethoven does in his *Fifth*. Near the end of the movement occurs this marvelous counterpoint:

Figure 14-55

Now the motive is in the bass and the violins have a variant of the horn melody heard at the beginning. The key relationships in the filling-out of the sonata-form are indeed fascinating, as are the compositional devices. Brahms learned well from Marxsen and Schumann, and from his study of Beethoven and Bach.

The slow movement is most original in its basic music and in its orchestral touches. Here is one instance in which one can comment on the orchestral imagination of Brahms. One theme follows another in great profusion, but careful study will reveal that the germ of the very beginning of the first movement is again in evidence, but now very subtly. Notice the characteristics of the motive, the intervals of a second and a fourth:

BRAHMS: *Symphony No. 2*
(Reduction)

Figure 14-56

The first two bars present two themes which are quasi-inversions of each other and which are virtually inseparable throughout the movement.

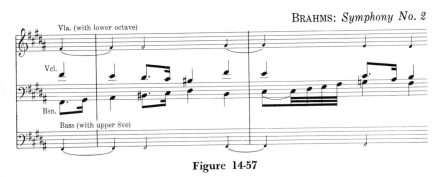

BRAHMS: *Symphony No. 2*

Figure 14-57

The third movement once again presents the *Urkeim*, but this time in more obvious ways:

BRAHMS: *Symphony No. 2*

Figure 14-58

The oboe tune is obviously a developed inversion of:

BRAHMS: *Symphony No. 1,*
Third Movement

Figure 14-59

The strings supercharge this theme:

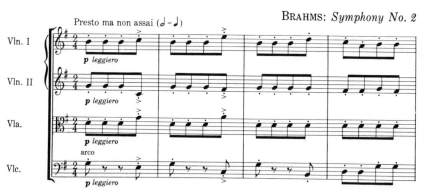

Figure 14-60

The return to $\frac{3}{4}$ reharmonizes the theme.

Figure 14-61

The finale employs another development of the *Urkeim*, which turns into one of Brahms's most brilliant symphonic finales.

The *Third Symphony* has been discussed in an earlier chapter. (See pages 86-89.)

The *Fourth Symphony* is one of Brahms's most unusual works. This theme begins the work:

Figure 14-62

If we remove the octave displacements, we see that the melody consists of a string of thirds which is a complete statement of the notes of the E minor scale. Notice also the intervals actually used in the melody: 3 6 3 6 8 3 8 3 8—a most striking symmetry. Brahms again spins out very long themes which contain smaller subdivisions, set off by changes in the instrument(s) on the principal melody being heard at the time. With such a prolixity of themes a lesser composer would have ended up with only a "tapeworm," but Brahms can build as skillfully as any composer. Who knows exactly where the theme ends and the bridge begins when the bridge is an important theme itself? The development leaves no doubt where it begins, however; the main theme returns for the serious business of being developed. The entire development utilizes the implied arpeggio from the main theme, among much else. The recapitulation is anything but literal. The very end of the movement is serious: a plagal cadence.

The special structure of the theme of the second movement has been pointed out. As in the *Violin Concerto*, the opening of this movement is all woodwinds, with important thematic comments in the strings, pizzicato. The first arco entrance of the strings is even more poignant after the long use of pizzicato. This movement contains much contrast and is one of the most important second movements of the Romantic Period. The melodies are not pretty at all; even calling them beautiful takes away some of their greatness.

The third movement is a brilliant one and is a kind of sonata-form. The brilliance is very much in place, in view of the serious nature of the other three movements. This is not to say that there is any flippancy intended—there is too much substance for that. The use of the triangle (rare in Brahms) is arresting. He also used the triangle in the *Haydn Variations*, but in a different role.

The finale has caused much ink to be shed. Usually a musical analyst decides if it is a passacaglia or a chaconne, and then goes on with a bar-by-bar description. I will obviate the difficulty by asserting that it is really both, and let it go at that. There is both a chord progression and a ground bass. The important line occurs in the flutes, oboes and trombones at the beginning:

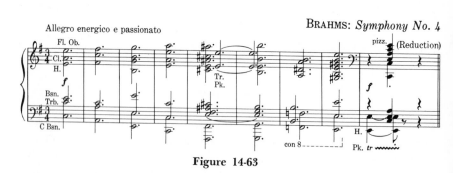

Figure 14-63

While this passage traverses eight bars, there is still the problem of tempo for the composer to face. He must somehow keep the musical pace going between each variation, and Brahms does this admirably. The very first variation, however, shows a miscalculation by Brahms. The theme in the violins is the actual variation, and we never hear it. This brings up a moot point: did Brahms consider the chord progression more important than the theme, or did he "underscore" the theme? An oboe playing staccato would have brought it out well, but the passage should be performed exactly as Brahms left it. The conductor can require the first violins to play more and the others less. Space permits pointing out only a few high points. In general Brahms solves the problem of the eight-bar period very well. At the $\frac{3}{2}$ the flute solo is very beautiful. The low register at the end is sometimes obscured by over-zealous strings and horns (why two?) and by underzealous flute-players. Most of the time, however, this passage is well-played; it is a high point in music, like a famous speech in a great play. The brass writing in the very next two variations is also outstanding. The ending, although tragic, is very effective. This is one of the symphonies in which the music is resolved but the content isn't. The answer is found in eternity.

It is not really right to call Brahms a classic-romantic or a romantic-classic, since he is both. There are many progressive tendencies evident in these symphonies, yet they are so classical von Bülow was moved to call the first, "Beethoven's Tenth." Brahms was not a product of his time; the time, at least in part, was a product of him.

Reger, Bruckner and even Mahler, in addition to Berg, Webern and Schoenberg, would have written entirely different music without the influence of Brahms.

Other Abstract Symphonists

Bruckner (1824-1896) wrote eleven symphonies but only nine of them bear numbers. It is only natural that he would be compared to his German-speaking near-contemporaries, especially Mahler and Brahms, but Bruckner himself was in great awe of Wagner and was influenced by him. As sides were chosen in the journalistic wars, Bruckner was enlisted on the side of the Wagnerians and seemed to be quite bewildered by the uproar. He remained the "Rustic Genius," as one biographer[26] called him, with a childlike but not naive faith in God— ". . . it is always a coming to terms with God," as Einstein puts it.[27] For some reason, Bruckner and Mahler are usually mentioned in the same breath. There is a fine organization known as the Mahler-Bruckner Society. Both composers wrote long, involved symphonies. They knew and respected each other. Usually a Mahlerite is also a Brucknerite, and one does not lose a taste for Bruckner as he might for a composer such as Tchaikovsky.

Bruckner represents a striking fusion of the two mainstreams of nineteenth-century music: the orchestral techniques of the Wagner group, but the abstract qualities of the Brahms group. Attempts have been made to give Bruckner orchestral works programs; even Bruckner himself attempted this, but the results were far from satisfactory. One can understand, however, why such attempts are made, since his scores are colorful, epic and visionary. One is surprised to learn that he was a shy, retiring little man who was much more at home in the schoolroom as a schoolmaster than as a major composer. Bruckner was Roman Catholic and served for many years as church organist at St. Florian's and Linz (he is buried beneath the organ at St. Florian's). Mahler, on the other hand, was a brilliant conductor—very much a man of the world. Wolff makes an arresting observation:[28] Mahler was Jewish by birth, became a Roman

Catholic in 1897 but, as he said, "I am a thrice homeless man."[29] (See pages 140-149 for more discussion of Mahler and Bruckner.)

The best nationalistic symphonies were written by Dvořák and Tchaikovsky. Dvořák was the better composer but Tchaikovsky is the more popular at the present time. I say Dvořák is better, since his works display more profound content, a better technique, less padding and a more secure grasp of form. The last three symphonies of Tchaikovsky are masterpieces, however, and the first three are worth playing now and again. Tchaikovsky's best symphony as a whole is the *Fourth*, which is well-known and uses the cyclic principle on two levels: the obvious and the very subtle. It can be shown that the famous tune about "the birch tree" used in the finale generates the entire work. The *Fifth* is as well-coordinated, but it suffers from lack of vital connective tissue in a way that the *Fourth* doesn't. I feel, however, that the high points of the *Fourth* are not as high as those of the *Fifth*. The third movement of the *Fifth* is a waltz—a very fine concert waltz, which is unusual in a symphony. The finale can become a bit tiring to a cultured listener. The *Sixth*, or *Pathétique*, is also well-unified melodically and displays better form than the *Fifth*. The composition problem in the *Sixth* results from some unusual formalizing on Tchaikovsky's part, when the "elfin-scherzo" turns into a horrifying march. If the march is performed only as a brilliant orchestral piece (which it certainly *is*), then the symphony is a failure, for the finale is a letdown. If, however, there is a fatalistic interpretation of the march—an inexorable movement to a conclusion one cannot change—then the finale occurs as sweet relief, but a relief full of great sadness. These symphonies are now a bit "threadbare" in the souls of the performers who must play them season after season. They are difficult to play well today, since they are so well-known. Many interpretations of a work are possible—but not all at the same time!

Tchaikovsky's first three symphonies would be welcome changes from so many performances of the last three. The *Third*, or *Polish Symphony*, is very tuneful and brilliantly orchestrated; curiously, it contains five movements. The additional movement in this case is the second, something akin a Brahms intermezzo. The finale contains some wonderful ideas (it is a polonaise), but it seems to ramble, as many Tchaikovsky finales do.

The Russian repertoire starts with the overtures of Glinka which, as we have said, are only tinged with a Russian flavor. The "Mighty Five" produced much orchestral music which is popular. Some of this is from opera, but there are a number of orchestral works which can stand alone. The *Second Symphony* of Borodin is performed often enough to be

standard fare. Its opening motto was used by Ravel and other "Apaches"
as a kind of greeting:

Figure 14-64

The scherzo bears the unusual meter signature of $\frac{1}{1}$. The rhythms and
modal flavors of this symphony make it very Russian-sounding indeed!
   The Balakirev *First Symphony* is greatly admired by many musicians.
Islamey, or possibly *Tamara,* however, are the best-known works by the
composer who was one of the leaders of the nationalistic ferment in
Russia at the time. The symphony is generated from one motive but
manages to include many nationalistic elements. Most of the orchestral
music of the "Five" was programmatic and, technically, the best of it
was written by Rimsky-Korsakov, although Mussorgsky's *Night on Bald
Mountain* might well be the best work. One can gain a better idea of
Tchaikovsky's true worth by comparing his music to comparable works
by other Russians of his time. The Rimsky-Korsakov *Piano Concerto* is
quite dull, and only the Glazunov *Violin Concerto* outshines Tchaikovsky's. The Tschaikovsky *Violin Concerto* is a great work, but it contains many weak passages; its rambling finale is always cut some in
performance. Some of the transitions in the first movement ought to be
cut, especially in the *tutti* before the second theme. The cadenza in the
first movement (a good one) is Tchaikovsky's own. The Glazunov concerto is in one long movement and does not need cutting. It presents
no formal problems and there are no passages in which the audience
is completely bored.
   The Glazunov symphonies should be played more often, although
none of them are too "individual"; but any one of them, especially the
Fifth, is quite attractive in the context of romantic Russian symphonies
by second-rank composers. The *Fifth* was written in 1897 and contains
a delightful scherzo. Glazunov was one of the many Russians who knew
how to orchestrate brilliantly. It is too bad that some of the Germans
who had better musical ideas could not have had a better sense of the
orchestra as an expressive instrument coloristically, and that some of the
Russians could not have employed better musical substance.
   The symphonies of Sibelius are somewhat Russian-sounding, the *First*
especially, but they show many German influences which stem from his
years in Germany. There is a stark, bleak "landscape" quality about

them which is so characteristic of his music. His *Violin Concerto* and his *Fourth Symphony* will probably outlive many of his other works.

The symphonies of Dvořák seem to be of more musical importance than any of the late nineteenth century except those of Brahms, Mahler, Bruckner and possibly the Franck. The numbering of the Dvořák symphonies is highly confusing. The last five symphonies are actually numbered from one to five under the old system of numbering, which completely omits the first four. These first four symphonies show us some of the Dvořák characteristics to come: the change from major to minor and back, the use of Bohemian dance rhythms, daring modulations and good orchestration—but they ramble. The composer has not yet learned the value of the *Leitmotiv*, even though he is under the spell of Wagner and uses music which resembles Wagnerian motives. The *Third Symphony* is the more concise.

The true *Seventh Symphony*, the *D Minor*, is Dvořák's earliest one which is played with any frequency in this country. It dates from 1885 and is a masterpiece of orchestral writing. There are few weak spots and many great ones. In spite of the key and the lack of a program, there seems to be much "forest" atmosphere in this work—perhaps a somewhat spooky forest, where Weber's "Wolf Glen" might be! The most striking movement is the scherzo, which is really a furiant; notice the hemiola:

Figure 14-65

The *Eighth Symphony*, perhaps known better in this country as the *Fourth, in G Major*, is also a beautiful symphony to those who like Slavonic symphonies. There are some "labored" spots in the finale, but the work is so well-written that its great moments overshadow the others. The use of cyclic form is apparent.

The *New World Symphony* is the only Dvořák piece some people know. In spite of much overplaying and some silly arranging of the theme from the second movement, the work lives on. The use of pentatonic melodies, an arresting use of the *Urkeim* technique, brilliant orchestration and a steady high level of excellence make this an important work of its time. Dvořák was very interested in America and had even read American literature in Czech translations before visiting this country. He was often homesick, however, especially while in New York, and was happiest when he spent the summers in Spillville, Iowa, among Czech immigrants. The opening of the second movement is often quoted, since it is not only a beginning but also a good modulation. The composer must change the tonality from E to D-flat, and how well he does it!

Figure 14-66

The root progression through a diminished fifth between the first two chords is accomplished through masterful voice-leading. Here is certainly an application of what one might call "the whole house of music," since it clearly shows that all keys are related in some way to all other keys; this is possible only through equal temperament, which makes possible such fascinating enharmonic progressions as the mediant relationship of the D-flat chord moving to the A chord. The finale contains some of Dvořák's most stormy and yet most delicate writing.

Just as Brahms was given an honorary degree and complied with the *Academic Festival,* so was Dvořák honored by the University of Prague. He complied with the *Carnival Overture,* which he had intended as part of a cycle of overtures. He was influenced somewhat, of course, by the extramusical idea of the Carnival: a pre-Lenten revelry, and a subject often set to music. An additional programmatic element was added by Dvořák, when he commented that the carnival was being watched by a lonely wanderer who does not belong to the gaiety. It is a very colorful piece and has opened many symphony concerts.

There are three mature Dvořák concerti. The *Piano Concerto in G Minor* (1876) is an early work which pianists complain is not pianistic.

I have heard it played very well indeed. The piano writing is not as effective as the string writing in his string concerti, since he was not a keyboard virtuoso (even though he played the piano quite well for a viola player). The *Violin Concerto* is much better and contains some of Dvořák's most beautiful moments. The slow movement uses the mediant relationship: the first movement is in A minor and the second in F major, while the finale is in A major. The finale contains some very catchy rhythms. This concerto has had its ups and down in public appeal. It is at least as good a work as the Tchaikovsky and almost as difficult, only in a different way. The Dvořák is difficult in a string-player's way, while the Tchaikovsky is difficult because the composer does not play the instrument and hence does not really know how to write for it effectively.

The Dvořák *Cello Concerto* is one of the best for that instrument, and it is good Dvořák. The orchestration is very heavy, considering the nature of the solo instrument. The work contains some extremely difficult passages which are effective, beautiful melodies, and it is one of his "American" works. The second theme of the first movement reminds one of "Deep River." This concerto also employs the *Urkeim* of three notes and the principle of quasi-inversion for the consequent of the phrase.

The concerti and symphonic music of Elgar are a welcome relief, after all the English oratorios and symphonic music which are well-made but rather trivial in musical substance. The important music of Elgar includes the *Enigma Variations* (1899) and the two concerti: one for cello and one for violin. The *Enigma* was but one of many works which Elgar wrote for the orchestra; his two symphonies and his tone poem *Falstaff* are of sufficient merit to warrant far more hearings than they receive. The *Enigma Variations* each are musical "pictures" of someone he knew. Each variation but XIII is prefaced by initials, so the "enigma" can be solved by anyone who knew Elgar's immediate circle of friends. The theme itself is like a variation, so perhaps the true "enigma" is what the real theme is!

The *Violin Concerto* has been discussed elsewhere; suffice it to say here that it could not have been written if Elgar himself had not been a rather good violinist and if he had not had the Brahms work before him. An unusual feature is not only an accompanied cadenza, but the only use in a famous work of *pizzacato tremolando*, in which the string-players in the orchestra play repeated notes by brushing their fingers very rapidly over the strings; each man plays inaudibly, but eighteen violinists doing this produces a lovely quivering. The *Cello Concerto* is very different from the *Violin Concerto*. Elgar's orchestration is by nature very rich and full but not thick. The orchestral style of the *Cello*

Concerto is much more lean and sparse. In a sense the parent of this concerto is the Schumann *Cello Concerto*, except that the Elgar displays a more efficient use of the orchestra. It is said that Elgar favored the *Cello Concerto* over any of his other orchestral works. Considering the paucity of great cello concerti, one wonders why cellists do not program this work more and the Saint-Saëns *A Minor* less—beautiful as it is. *Falstaff* is a major English work. Elgar does well with the oft-told tale of Sir John. It is frank program music, but, like *The Dream of Gerontius*, it is a beautiful bit of musical characterization and yet an effective orchestral piece. The form is Shakespeare's and there are as many characters in it as there are themes. Some of these themes are variations or developments of others.

The symphonic music of Vaughan Williams and Delius belongs to the twentieth century.

French symphonic music owes much to Liszt and Wagner, and also to Cherubini. This composer helped, not only with his symphonies— which are very beautiful (notably the *D Major*)—but also because he was a source of the great classical tradition in letter (if not always in spirit). Berlioz was another strong influence. The French composer, by mid-century, had quite a variety of musical styles to choose from! Influences also came from classrooms and from the chamber music studios of men such as Reicha and Lesueur. The music of Saint-Saëns has been frequently mentioned in this book.

The Franck *Symphony* has been mentioned elsewhere, but it is of prime importance in French music. The philosophies and techniques which produced it are also evident in Franck's other orchestral works, which are uneven in quality. *Le Chasseur maudit* (The Accursed Huntsman) is one of the few works of Franck which bears any evidence of the influence of Berlioz in an orchestral sense. It employs a wild orchestration, as the title would imply, but the work is better enjoyed if one doesn't know the story. The music repeats itself literally a little too much. More successful is the cycle of tone poems called *Psyché*, which in its delicate moments anticipates impressionism. Its melodies are among the best of the French school.

D'Indy, Chausson and other Franck pupils produced important works. The *Istar* variations of d'Indy carry on the orchestral variation form as a complete work; in our time the variation becomes an important form of composition for composers such as Schoenberg, Webern, Elliot Carter and Dallapiccola, who have written great works in that form. There is a curious mixture of oriental exoticism and musical construction which permeates *Istar*. Chausson's *Poème for Violin and Orchestra* is an important short work; this piece is often performed by a guest soloist with another short work such as Ravel's *Tzigane*. Other composers, such as Dohnányi and Rachmaninoff, have combined the idea of orchestral variations with that of a short work for soloist and orchestra. The Franck *Symphonic Variations* must be a prototype for excellence, although the Chopin *Variations on "Là ci darem"* (from *Don Giovanni*, and also used by Beethoven for variations) is another important work. These works all feature prominent parts for the piano. The d'Indy *Symphony on a French Mountain Air* is somewhat different in concept, although the piano part is by no means "child's play." The piano parts of *Petrouchka* and other contemporary works are quite complicated. The piano is used frequently in our century, and it is now being used in more orchestral works, with special attention being paid to its own color. Many of the effects for the piano with orchestra used by d'Indy have been adopted by other composers.

American composers produced some concerti and symphonies; these, however, are not of great significance until the symphonies of Ives, which are all very romantic works. Only his *Fourth Symphony* displays the techniques which have made him so famous as a pioneer. The romantic glow of his first three symphonies was not realized until recent performances and recordings made it apparent. The works of Ives are hard to date, and it is difficult to tell if they are complete. The date given for the *First Symphony* is 1896; the *Second*, 1897; the *Third*, 1911; and the *Fourth*, 1910-1916. Interspersed in his entire creative life are extraordinary works for groups of instruments of sizes which could be called orchestral. This man may have been an amateur (he earned a living selling insurance) but, like the "Mighty Five," he was a great musical genius.

The symphonies of Carl Nielsen also bridge the centuries; like Janáček, Nielsen is just beginning to become known in this country. Although somewhat older, the music of Reger is also important. We have discussed Reger from time to time and his characteristics have been listed. One of his most fascinating works is the *Serenade* for orchestra, which is a rather light (for Reger) and diverting piece, although very long. It employs a double-string section: half muted, the other half not; this effect is lovely for awhile, but the novelty wears off. The occasional uses of this device, as in his *Variations on a Theme by Mozart*, are far more successful. The four tone poems on pictures by Boecklin are also imaginative. The third one is a setting of *The Isle of the Dead*, which was also the source of a very good orchestral piece by Rachmaninoff. The picture itself is not as evocative as the music of either composer, and the Rachmaninoff is a more important work.

Many other orchestral works were written, played or not, and now reside in libraries. As Adam Carse has stated so often in his books on

Plate XX

The Island of the Dead, painting by Arnold Boecklin which inspired orchestral works by Reger and Rachmaninoff *(Courtesy The Bettmann Archive, N.Y.).*

the orchestra, we have to put up with a lot of dross and do not have sense enough to know which works are really great and which ones are not. Those works which were immediately well-received were sociologically important for the people who enjoyed them. Some works have always received a cool reception, and probably always will. The symphony orchestra as a major performing ensemble reached a certain height at the turn of the century, and it still enjoys great popularity among all musical people. Concepts from the "Colossal Romantic" have changed much, but much remains and many works are played today in ways composers could only have imagined. What would a Berlioz have done with the Philadelphia or any other of today's great orchestras? We should be better musicians than we are, since it is so easy for us to learn what is happening elsewhere. The student during the Romantic Period had to go to *live* concerts to hear music and *he had to study the scores.* These are still among the best ways to learn about music. The best thing of all is to play the music yourself and to really study what you are rehearsing. After this comes the phonograph: that remarkable invention which took so much "coolie labor" from music study that in many cases work has become too easy. The best formula is still the "summation of perspiration and inspiration." One can never gain the second until he has experienced the first.

Notes

1. Most of the famous nicknames for eighteenth-century music came about in this way. Even *The Well-tempered Clavier* was not spared.

2. Willi Apel, *The Harvard Dictionary of Music* (Cambridge: Harvard University Press, 1947), p. 605.

3. Donald N. Ferguson, *A History of Musical Thought* (New York: Appleton-Century-Crofts, 1959), p. 438.

4. Consult Elliot Forbes, *Thayer's Life of Beethoven* (Princeton, N.J.: Princeton University Press, 1964).

5. Ludwig Misch, *Beethoven Studies* (Norman: University of Oklahoma Press, 1953).

6. *Ibid.*, pp. 155-156.

7. Ernest Newman, *Stories of the Great Operas and Their Composers* (Philadelphia: The Blakiston Company, 1930), p. 525.

8. During this time the curtain opens to reveal a tableau.

9. Homer Ulrich, *Symphonic Music* (New York: Columbia University Press, 1952), p. 163.

10. J. A. Westrup and F. Ll. Harrison, *The New College Encyclopedia of Music* (New York: W. W. Norton & Company, Inc., 1960) , p. 68.

11. Jacques Barzun, *Berlioz and the Romantic Century* (Boston: Little, Brown and Company, 1950), p. 379.

12. Richard Anthony Leonard, *The Stream of Music* (London: Hutchinson & Co., 1961), pp. 160-161. Copyright 1943, by Richard Anthony Leonard. Reprinted by permission of Doubleday & Company, Inc.

13. This can be found in many sources. One source is Ferguson's *Masterworks of the Orchestral Repertoire* (Minneapolis: University of Minnesota Press, 1954).

14. Sir Donald Tovey, "Program Music," *Forms of Music: Musical Articles from the Encyclopedia Britannica* (London: Oxford University Press, 1944), p. 168.

15. Forbes, *op. cit.*, Vol. I, p. 436.

16. In all fairness it must be pointed out that much of the Schindler biography was written from memory, and he may have forgotten the exact information. See the MacArdle edition: Anton Schindler, *Beethoven as I Knew Him*, trans. Constance S. Jolly and ed. Donald W. MacArdle (Chapel Hill: The University of North Carolina Press, 1966).

17. Robert Haven Schauffler, *Beethoven, the Man Who Freed Music* (New York: Tudor Publishing Company, 1946), pp. 253-254; quoted by permission.

18. This is from "Ode on a Grecian Urn."

19. Tovey, *op. cit.*, pp. 168-169.

20. Quoted in the booklet accompanying the record album *Beethoven's Nine Symphonies*, Arturo Toscanini, conductor (RCA Victor LM-6901). This booklet is drawn from Lawrence Gilman's *Orchestral Music: An Armchair Guide*, ed. Edward Cushing (London: Oxford University Press, 1951), pp. 45-47.

21. Mozart's *Ein musikalischer Spass*, K. 522 *(A Musical Joke)* contains some strident discords, but the intent is by no means as serious as Beethoven's in the *Ninth*.

22. Max Graf, *From Beethoven to Shostakovitch* (New York: Philosophical Library, 1947), pp. 236-237.

23. Alfred Einstein, *Mozart*, trans. Arthur Mendel and Nathan Broder (New York: Oxford University Press, 1962), p. 140.

24. Reprinted with permission of The Macmillan Company from Eric Werner, *Mendelssohn*, trans. D. Newlin. Copyright © by The Free Press of Glencoe, a Division of The Macmillan Company, 1963, p. 352.

25. Sir Donald Tovey, *Essays in Musical Analysis*, Vol. II (London: Oxford University Press, 1936), p. 48.

26. Werner Wolff, *Anton Bruckner: Rustic Genius* (New York: E. P. Dutton, 1942).

27. Alfred Einstein, *Music in the Romantic Era* (New York: W. W. Norton & Company, Inc., 1947) , p. 156.

28. Wolff, *op. cit.*, p. 151.

29. H. F. Redlich, *Bruckner and Mahler* (New York: Farrar, Straus and Cudahy, 1955), p. 110.

CONCLUSIONS

1. Romanticism was not the sole accomplishment of the nineteenth century. Throughout most of the century romanticism was a progressive tendency which was advanced by composers and performers in opposition to an "establishment" of school classicism not only by lesser composers, but also by important critics, theorists and some great and near-great composers. Later in the century even the "establishment" began to teach the "rules" of romanticism.

2. Neither romanticism nor classicism *per se* is either good or bad; it is the intrinsic value of a work of art which is relatively good or bad —and this value is subject to change; there is really no absolute—one needs only to study the reactions of various generations to Bach, Mozart and countless others.

3. The nineteenth century was only a *part* of the romantic period, which began at least as early as 1789 and lasted at least until 1925.

4. Romanticism is almost always present in Western music, since one aspect of romanticism is the "going out-of-bounds" to find beauty. A larger number of composers turned to this style after 1800, in part due to the new sociological import of "music for the masses"—can the man

542

in the street really identify with music intended for the nobility and an educated audience? The composer in many instances looked upon himself as the spokesman for the masses, even though they did not always cater to them but preferred to write unproblematic music— music not too different from that of the immediate past.

5. There were many journalistic polemics, with Rellstab, Fink, Dwight and others on the side of the "establishment," and Berlioz, Schumann, Liszt and their followers in favor of new music and romanticism. The great Hanslick actually fell in between. He appreciated the beauties of Wagner's music but disapproved of its underlying philosophy (that music could express something other than itself).

6. Romanticism was the prime force which overthrew the tonal system of traditional keys. The world's greatest (and worst) music is written in the standard key system, a system which was discovered by our Western civilization. No other culture can claim it, but other cultures have copied it and in some instances have added something vital (Japan, for instance).

7. Well-tempered tuning and equal temperament were great forces in uniting all the keys into one massive structure, a device soon used by composers in all forms of composition—not only in keyboard writing (one can find complete chromaticism used earlier in string writing). Heinrich Bach (1615-1692), in his cantata *Ich danke dir, Gott*, uses all twelve tones in a dominant function within the framework of one tonality. (See Karl Geiringer's *Music of the Bach Family*, pp. 13-22, for the full score.) This facet of musical evolution begins with J. S. Bach, the first truly great composer to use it.

Peter Yates, in his important book *Twentieth Century Music* (pp. 22-23), asserts that Bach laid the foundations of the chromatic "new" music of the nineteenth century. He goes on to state that there is a direct line through Mozart, Beethoven, Chopin and the rest; this facet of music contributed mightily to the ultimate downfall of common-practice harmony by the end of the century. Yates's view is also shared by many other writers on music.

8. The out-and-out romantics can be surprisingly classical, and the classicists can be surprisingly romantic (consider any work of Berlioz *sans program* and the sheer sound of composers such as Cherubini).

9. Sheer sound becomes of utmost importance. Many of the best composers realize that music is sound and not just signs on paper. Composers pursue sonorities and the flow thereof, rather than age-old harmonies and harmonic progressions employing figured bass.

10. Aggregate sounds other than mere triads are considered stable entities, especially if the chord is voiced as if overtones of the lowest tone serve as a fundamental. Instability results from violating this prin-

ciple, and using strong dissonance in the classical sense, parallelism, pungent orchestration or odd rhythms.

11. Composers discover ethnic music and use modes and rhythms foreign to the textbook. The great music of the past is also discovered and becomes a strong influence.

12. Theorists approach music pragmatically and write prose descriptions for use by all music students, not just for speculation. The influential harmony texts are those by Riemann (1849-1919), Jadassohn (1831-1902), Prout (1835-1909) and others; outstanding counterpoint manuals are those by Cherubini, Fux, Marpurg and Kirnberger (among others), while the best fugue texts are those by men such as Gedalge, Higgs and Reicha. There is, however, an apparent dichotomy between "school" harmony, counterpoint and fugue, and the actual practice of the best composers.

13. Melody becomes more chromatic and more angular, and is no longer judged by its "singability"—a true instrumental technique develops. Melodies are, of course, important *per se*, but the fate of melodies and their orientation of genes, chromosomes and cells is equally—if not more—important. Themes in the same work are related through the *Urkeim* principle. Related and similar (but not congruent) terms are: *germ motive, generating cell, cycle, Leitmotiv, idée fixe, Grundgestalt* and others mentioned throughout this book.

14. Sheer sound and new uses of harmony inspire composers to write treatises on the art of orchestration. Those of Berlioz, Widor and Rimsky-Korsakov are among the most important. Orchestral advances are also made through the new esthetic of program music, the new "virtuoso" technique, the mechanical improvements in instruments and the development of a new concept of the conductor—who now directs the whole orchestra and concentrates on the sheer sound of the ensemble, and does not merely "beat time" (either by beating a large stick on the floor, by bobbing and weaving from a clattering keyboard where he plays a figured bass or—even worse—by trying to conduct while playing the first violin part). It becomes apparent that the conductor's psychological gestures are more important than his gyrations as a "human metronome."

15. The rate of change in music increases throughout the century, so that a "common practice" is difficult (if not impossible and misleading) to delineate. Since romanticism by its very nature is (whether Brahmsian or Wagnerian) a subjective facet, it follows that there are personal styles which *do* conform to general principles but are very difficult to classify in every single aspect. For example, a composer may be programmatic or not, but not always; he may be nationalistic or not, but not always. There is a "Dvořák" style, a "Tchaikovsky" style or a

"Brahms" style, but each of these is individual. There are similarities, but the differences are more significant.

16. All aspects of music are eventually affected by the inroads of romanticism—quietly in some types (church music) and obstreperously in others (orchestral music).

17. The century is unified only in its departure from past practice, in its cultivation of individual differences, in the increasing importance it places upon subjectivity and in its increased use of equal temperament. All of these developments are brought about by inclination and rapid communication.

18. Music, then, begins to act as the recorder of the passion and philosophy of an age as never before. This book has presented facts, speculations, opinions and—above all—the fascinating paradoxes of the times, from the Fall of the Bastille to World War I.

BIBLIOGRAPHY

General

Abraham, Gerald. *A Hundred Years of Music*. Chicago: Aldine Publishing Company, 1964.

Barzun, Jacques. *Classic, Romantic, Modern*. Garden City, N.Y.: Doubleday & Company, Inc., 1961.

Brandt, William E. *The Way of Music*, 2nd Ed. Boston: Allyn and Bacon, Inc., 1968.

Crocker, Richard L. *A History of Musical Style*. New York: McGraw-Hill, Inc., 1966.

Grout, Donald Jay. *A History of Western Music*. New York: W. W. Norton & Company, Inc., 1960.

Grove, Sir George. *Grove's Dictionary of Music and Muscians*, ed. Eric Blom. New York: St. Martin's Press, Inc., 1966.

Lang, Paul Henry. *Music in Western Civilization*. New York: W. W. Norton & Company, Inc., 1941.

Leonard, Richard Anthony. *The Stream of Music*. London: Hutchinson & Co., 1961.

Longyear, Rey M. *Nineteenth-Century Romanticism in Music.* Englewood Cliffs, N.J.: Prentice-Hall, Inc., 1969.

Mellers, W., Harman, A. and Milner, A. *Man and His Music.* New York: Oxford University Press, Inc., 1961.

Smoldon, William L. *A History of Music.* London: Herbert Jenkins, 1965.

Strunk, Oliver. *Source Readings in Music History: The Romantic Era* (Vol. V). New York: W. W. Norton & Company, Inc., 1965.

Tovey, Donald. *Essays in Musical Analysis* (Vols. 1-5). London: Oxford University Press, 1946.

————. *Forms of Music: Musical Articles from the Encyclopedia Britannica.* London: Oxford University Press, 1943.

————. *The Main Stream of Music, and Other Essays.* New York: Oxford University Press, Inc., 1949.

Ulrich, Homer and Pisk, Paula. *A History of Music and Musical Style.* New York: Burlingame, Harcourt, Brace & World, Inc., 1963.

Biography and Autobiography

Forbes, Elliott. *Thayer's Life of Beethoven* (Vols. I and II). Princeton, N.J.: Princeton University Press, 1964.

MacArdle, Donald, ed., and trans. Jolly, Constance. *Schindler—Beethoven as I Knew Him.* Chapel Hill: The University of North Carolina Press, 1966.

Barzun, Jacques. *Berlioz and the Romantic Century* (Vols. I and II). Boston: Little, Brown & Co., 1949.

Geiringer, Karl. *Brahms, His Life and Work.* New York: Oxford University Press, Inc., 1947.

Weinstock, Herbert. *Chopin.* New York: Alfred A. Knopf, Inc., 1949.

Clapham, John. *Antonín Dvořák, Musician and Craftsman.* New York: St. Martin's Press, Inc., 1966.

Demuth, Norman. *César Franck.* London: Dennis Dobson, Ltd., 1949.

Searle, Humphrey. *The Music of Franz Liszt.* London: Dent, 1954.

Sitwell, S. *Liszt.* New York: Philosophical Library, Inc., 1956.

Cardus, Neville. *Gustav Mahler: His Mind and His Music.* New York: St. Martin's Press, Inc., 1965.

Werner, Eric, and trans. Newlin, D. *Mendelssohn.* London: Collier-Macmillan, 1963.

Calvocoressi, M. D. *Modest Mussorgsky, His Life and Works.* Fairlawn, N.J.: Essential Books, Inc., 1956.

Carner, Mosco. *Puccini.* London: Duckworth & Co., Ltd., 1958.

Brown, Maurice. *Schubert.* New York: St. Martin's Press, Inc., 1958.

Deutsch, Otto. *The Schubert Reader.* New York: W. W. Norton & Company, Inc., 1947.

Einstein, Alfred. *Schubert.* New York: Oxford University Press, Inc., 1951.

Pleasants, Henry, trans. and ed. *The Musical World of Robert Schumann* (A Selection from Schumann's Own Writings). New York: St. Martin's Press, Inc., 1965.

Del Mar, Norman. *Richard Strauss, A Critical Commentary on his Life and Works.* London: Barrie and Rockliff, 1962.

Weinstock, H. *Tchaikowsky.* New York: Alfred A. Knopf, Inc., 1946.

Toye, F. *Giuseppe Verdi: His Life and Works.* New York: Alfred A. Knopf, Inc., 1946.

Barzun, Jacques. *Darwin, Marx, Wagner.* Garden City, N.Y.: Doubleday & Company, Inc., 1958.

Donington, Robert. *Wagner's Ring and Its Symbols.* London: Faber & Faber, 1963.

Newman, E. *The Life of Richard Wagner.* New York: Alfred A. Knopf, Inc., 1933-1946.

Chamber Music

Cobbett, Walter. *Cobbett's Cyclopedic Survey of Chamber Music,* New Ed. (2nd). London: Oxford University Press, 1963.

Dunhill, Thomas F. *Chamber Music.* London: Macmillan, 1938.

Mason, Daniel Gregory. *The Chamber Music of Brahms.* New York: The Macmillan Co., 1933.

Robertson, Alec., ed. *Chamber Music.* Baltimore: Penguin Books, Inc., 1965.

Ulrich, Homer. *Chamber Music.* New York: Columbia University Press, 1966.

Keyboard Music

Apel, Willi. *Masters of the Keyboard.* Cambridge: Harvard University Press, 1947.

Cockshoot, John. *The Fugue in Beethoven's Piano Music.* London: Routledge & Kegan Paul, 1959.

Dale, Kathleen. *Nineteenth Century Piano Music.* London: Oxford University Press, 1954.

Demuth, Norman. *French Piano Music.* London: Museum Press Limited, 1959.

Kirby, F. E. *A Short History of Keyboard Music.* New York: Free Press of Glencoe, Inc., 1966.

Orchestra Music

Bamberger, Carl, ed. *The Conductor's Art.* New York: McGraw-Hill, Inc., 1965.

Carse, Adam. *The History of Orchestration.* New York: Dover Publications, Inc., 1964.

Hill, Ralph. *The Concerto.* Baltimore: Penguin Books, Inc., 1952.

Hill, Ralph, ed. *The Symphony.* Baltimore: Penguin Books, Inc., 1949.

McKay, George F. *Creative Orchestration,* 2nd Ed. Boston: Allyn and Bacon, Inc., 1969.

Piston, Walter. *Orchestration.* New York: W. W. Norton & Company, Inc., 1955.

Ulrich, Homer. *Symphonic Music.* New York: Columbia University Press, 1952.

Veinus, Abraham. *The Concerto.* New York: Dover Publications, Inc., 1964.

Songs, Choral Music and Opera

Capell, Richard. *Schubert's Songs*, 2nd Ed., Rev. New York: Basic Books, Inc., 1957.
Stevens, Denis, ed. *A History of Song*. New York: W. W. Norton & Company, Inc., 1960.
Jacobs, Arthur, ed. *Choral Music*. Baltimore: Penguin Books, Inc., 1963.
Young, Percy M. *The Choral Tradition*. London: Hutchinson, 1962.
Dent, Edward J. *Opera*. Harmondsworth, England: Penguin Books, 1949.
Fellner, Rudolph. *Opera Themes and Plots*. New York: Simon and Schuster, Inc., 1958.
Grout, Donald Jay. *A Short History of Opera*. New York: Columbia University Press, 1947.
Hamm, Charles. *Opera*. Boston: Allyn and Bacon, Inc., 1966.
Jacobs, Arthur and Sadie, S. *Great Operas in Synopsis*. New York: Thomas Y. Crowell Company, 1966.

Theory

Gedalge, André. *Treatise on the Fugue*. Norman: University of Oklahoma Press, 1965.
Goldman, Richard F. *Harmony in Western Music*. New York: W. W. Norton & Company, Inc., 1965.
Green, Douglas M. *Form in Tonal Music*. New York: Holt, Rinehart & Winston, Inc., 1965.
Horsley, Imogene. *Fugue: History and Practice*. New York: Free Press of Glencoe, Inc., 1966.
Lloyd, Ll. S. and Boyle, Hugh. *Intervals, Scales, and Temperaments*. London: Macdonald, 1963.
Reti, Rudolph. *The Thematic Process in Music*. New York: The Macmillan Co., 1951.
Sessions, Roger. *Harmonic Practice*. New York: Harcourt, Brace & World, Inc., 1951.
Shirlaw, Matthew. *The Theory of Harmony*. New York: H. W. Gray & Co.
Szabolcsi, Bence. *A History of Melody*. New York: St. Martin's Press, Inc., 1965.
Tischler, Hans. *Practical Harmony*. Boston: Allyn and Bacon, Inc., 1964.
Tyndall, Robert E. *Musical Form*. Boston: Allyn and Bacon, Inc., 1964.

INDEX

HIGHSMITH 45-220